Lecture Notes in Computer Science 5923

Commenced Publication in 1973
Founding and Former Series Editors:
Gerhard Goos, Juris Hartmanis, and Jan van Leeuwen

W0235297

Tarek Abdelzaher   Michel Raynal
Nicola Santoro (Eds.)

Principles of Distributed Systems

13th International Conference, OPODIS 2009
Nîmes, France, December 15-18, 2009
Proceedings

 Springer

Volume Editors

Tarek Abdelzaher
University of Illinois at Urbana Champaign
Department of Computer Science
Urbana, IL 61801, USA
E-mail: zaher@cs.uiuc.edu

Michel Raynal
Université de Rennes1
IRISA
Campus de Beaulieu
Avenue du Général Leclerc
35042 Rennes Cedex, France
E-mail: raynal@irisa.fr

Nicola Santoro
Carleton University
School of Computer Science
1125 Colonel By Drive
Ottawa K1S 5B6, Canada
E-mail: santoro@scs.carleton.ca

Library of Congress Control Number: 2009939927

CR Subject Classification (1998): C.2.4, C.1.4, C.2.1, D.1.3, D.4.2, E.1, H.2.4

LNCS Sublibrary: SL 1 – Theoretical Computer Science and General Issues

ISSN   0302-9743
ISBN-10   3-642-10876-8 Springer Berlin Heidelberg New York
ISBN-13   978-3-642-10876-1 Springer Berlin Heidelberg New York

springer.com

© Springer-Verlag Berlin Heidelberg 2009
Printed in Germany

Typesetting: Camera-ready by author, data conversion by Scientific Publishing Services, Chennai, India
Printed on acid-free paper   SPIN: 12808168   06/3180   5 4 3 2 1 0

Preface

OPODIS, the International Conference on Principles of Distributed Systems, is an annual forum for presentation of state-of-the-art knowledge on principles of distributed computing systems, including theory, design, analysis, implementation and application of distributed systems, among researchers from around the world. The 13th edition of OPODIS was held during December 15–18, in Nimes, France.

There were 71 submissions, and this volume contains the 23 regular contributions and the 4 brief annoucements selected by the Progam Committee. All submitted papers were read and evaluated by three to five PC members assisted by external reviewers. The final decision regarding every paper was taken after long discussions through EasyChair.

This year the Best Paper Award was shared by two papers: "On the Computational Power of Shared Objects" by Gadi Taubenfeld and "Transactional Scheduling for Read-Dominated Workloads" by Hagit Attiya and Alessia Milani. The Best Student Paper Award was given to the paper "Decentralized Polling with Respectable Participants" co-authored Kevin Huguenin and Maxime Monod and their advisors.

The conference also featured two very interesting invited talks by Anne-Marie Kermarrec and Maurice Herlihy. Anne-Marie's talk was on "Navigating Web 2.0 with Gossple" and Maurice's talk was on "Transactional Memory Today: A Status Report."

OPODIS has now found its place among the international conferences related to principles of distributed computing and distributed systems. We hope that this 13th edition will contribute to the growth and the development of the conference and continue to increase its visibility.

Finally we would like to thank Nicola Santoro, Conference General Chair, Hacène Fouchal, Steering Committee Chair, and Bernard Thibault for their constant help.

October 2009

Tarek Abdelzaher
Michel Raynal

Organization

General Chair

Nicola Santoro   Carleton University, Canada

Program Committee Co-chairs

Tarek Abdelzaher   University of Illinois at Urbana Champaign, USA

Michel Raynal   IRISA Rennes, France

Program Committee

Tarek Abdelzaher	University of Illinois at Urbana Champaign, USA (Co-chair)
Marcos Aguilera	Microsoft, USA
James Anderson	University of North-Carolina, USA
Jean Arlat	LAAS, Toulouse, France
Hagit Attiya	Technion, Israel
Theodore P. Baker	Florida State University, USA
Roberto Baldoni	University of Roma1, Italy
Gregor v. Bochmann	University of Ottawa, Canada
Wei-ge Chen	Microsoft, Beijing, China
UmaMaheswari Devi	IBM Research Laboratory, India
Stefan Dobrev	Slovak Academy of Science, Slovakia
Antonio Fernández	University Rey Juan Carlos, Spain
Christof Fetzer	Dresden University, Germany
Vijay K. Garg	University of Texas at Austin/IBM, USA
Cyril Gavoille	University of Bordeaux, France
M. Gonzalez Harbour	University of Cantabria, Spain
Joel Goossens	U.L.B, Belgium
Fabiola Greve	U.F. Bahia, Brazil
Rachid Guerraoui	EPFL, Switzerland
Hervé Guyennet	University of Franche-Comté, France
Ralf Klasing	CNRS, Bordeaux, France
Xenofon Koutsoukos	Venderbilt University, USA
Danny Krizanc	Wesleyan University, USA
Chenyang Lu	Washington University, USA
Marina Papatriantafilou	Chalmers University of Technology, Sweden
Andrzej Pelc	University of Quebec, Canada
Michel Raynal	IRISA Rennes, France (Co-chair)

Binoy Ravindran	Virginia Tech, USA
Luis Rodrigues	INESC-ID/IST, Portugal
Pierre Sens	University Pierre et Marie Curie, France
Paul Spirakis	Patras University, Greece
Gadi Taubenfeld	Interdisiplinary Center, Israel
Eduardo Tovar	ISEP-IPP, Portugal
Sebastien Tixeuil	University Pierre et Marie Curie, France
Maarten Van Steen	Amsterdam University, The Netherlands
Marko Vukolic	IBM, Zurich, Switzerland
Kamin Whitehouse	University of Vivgirid, USA
Masafumi Yamashita	Kyushu University, Japan

Web and Publicity Chair

Thibault Bernard	University of Reims Champagne-Ardenne, France

Organizing Committee

Martine Couderc	University of Nîmes, France
Alain Findeli	University of Nîmes, France
Mostafa Hatimi	University of Nîmes, France
Dominique Lassarre	University of Nîmes, France
Thiery Spriet	University of Avignon, France

Steering Committee

Tarek Abdelzaher	University of Illinois at Urbana Champaign, USA
Alain Bui	University of Versailles St. Q. en Y., France
Marc Bui	EPHE, France
Hacene Fouchal	University of Antilles-Guyane, France (*Chair*)
Roberto Gomez	ITESM-CEM, Mexico
Michel Raynal	IRISA Rennes, France
Nicola Santoro	Carleton University, Canada
Sebastien Tixeuil	University of Pierre et Marie Curie, France
Philippas Tsigas	Chalmers University of Technology, Sweden

External Referees

Isaac Amundson	Bharath Balasubramanian
Bjorn Andersson	Diogo Becker
Luciana Arantes	Xiaohui Bei
Shah Asaduzzaman	Bjoern Brandenburg
Roberto Beraldi	Andrey Brito
Jaiganesh Balasubramanian	Yann Busnel

Daniel Cederman
Ioannis Chatzigiannakis
Octav Chipara
Stephan Creutz
Shantanu Das
Jyotirmoy Deshmukh
UmaMaheswari Devi
Jos Mara Drake
Lcia Drummond
Philippe Duchon
Aida Ehyaei
Glenn Elliott
Robert Elsasser
Emeka Eyisi
Luis Lino Ferreira
Chien-Liang Fok
Hossein Fotouhi
Leszek Gasieniec
Gilles Geeraerts
Giorgos Georgiadis
Sascha Grau
Jos Carlos Palencia Gutirrez
Greg Hackmann
Kai Han
David Hay
Phuong Ha Hoai
Michel Hurfin
Bijoy Jose
Manish Kushwaha
Shouwen Lai
Heath LeBlanc
Joao Leitao
Hennadiy Leontyev
Giorgia Lodi
Adnan Mian

Othon Michail
Alessia Milani
Neeraj Mittal
Jose Mocito
Alfredo Navarra
Nicolas Nisse
Martin Nowack
Vinit Ogale
Stephen Olivier
Filipe Pacheco
Guanhong Pei
Lucia Draque Penso
Shashi Prabh
Guido Proietti
Ying Qiao
Leonardo Querzoni
Tomasz Radzik
Carlos Ribeiro
Torvald Riegel
Mario Aldea Rivas
Mariusz Rokicki
Paulo Romano
Kunihiko Sadakane
Abusayeed Saifullah
Roopsha Samanta
Andre Schmitt
Christopher Thraves
Corentin Travers
Maryam Vahabi
Stefan Weigert
Jialin Zhang
Bo Zhang
Yuanfang Zhang
Dakai Zhu

Table of Contents

Wireless and Social Networks

Synchronization

Storage Systems

Distributed Agreement

Distributed Algorithms

Transactional Memory Today: A Status Report

Maurice Herlihy

Computer Science Department
Brown University
Providence (RI), USA

Abstract. The term "Transactional Memory" was coined back in 1993, but even today, there is a vigorous debate about its merits. This debate sometimes generates more heat than light: terms are not always well-defined and criteria for making judgments are not always clear.

In this talk, I will try to impose some order on the conversation. TM itself can encompass hardware, software, speculative lock elision, and other mechanisms. The benefits sought encompass simpler implementations of highly-concurrent data structures, better software engineering for concurrent platforms, enhanced performance, and reduced power consumption. We will look at various terms in this cross-product and evaluate how we are doing. So far.

T. Abdelzaher, M. Raynal, and N. Santoro (Eds.): OPODIS 2009, LNCS 5923, p. 1, 2009.

Navigating the Web 2.0 with GOSSPLE*

Anne-Marie Kermarrec

INRIA, Rennes Bretagne-Atlantique, France
Anne-Marie.Kermarrec@inria.fr

Abstract. Social networks and collaborative tagging systems have taken off at an unexpected scale and speed (Facebook, YouTube, Flickr, Last.fm, Delicious, etc). Web content is now generated by you, me, our friends and millions of others. This represents a revolution in usage and a great opportunity to leverage collaborative knowledge to enhance the user's Internet experience. The GOSSPLE project aims at precisely achieving this: automatically capturing affinities between users that are potentially unknown yet share similar interests, or exhibiting similar behaviors on the Web. This can fully personalizes the Web 2.0 experience process, increasing the ability of a user to find relevant content, get relevant recommandation, etc. This personalization calls for decentralization. (1) Centralized servers might dissuade users from generating new content for they expose their privacy and represent a single point of attack. (2) The amount of information to store grows exponentially with the size of the system and centralized systems cannot sustain storing a growing amount of data at a user granularity. We believe that the salvation can only come from a fully decentralized user centric approach where every participant is entrusted to harvest the Web with information relevant to her own activity. This poses a number of scientific challenges: How to discover similar users, how to build and manage a network of similar users, how to define the relevant metrics for such personalization, how to preserve privacy when needed, how to deal with free-riders and misheavior and how to manage efficiently a growing amount of data.

* This work is supported by the ERC Starting Grant GOSSPLE number 204742.

T. Abdelzaher, M. Raynal, and N. Santoro (Eds.): OPODIS 2009, LNCS 5923, p. 2, 2009.

Transactional Scheduling for Read-Dominated Workloads*

Hagit Attiya and Alessia Milani**

Department of Computer Science, Technion, Haifa 32000, Israel
{hagit,alessia}@cs.technion.ac.il

Abstract. The transactional approach to contention management guarantees atomicity by aborting transactions that may violate consistency. A major challenge in this approach is to schedule transactions in a manner that reduces the total time to perform all transactions (the *makespan*), since transactions are often aborted and restarted. The performance of a transactional scheduler can be evaluated by the ratio between its makespan and the makespan of an optimal, clairvoyant scheduler that knows the list of resource accesses that will be performed by each transaction, as well as its release time and duration.

This paper studies transactional scheduling in the context of read-dominated workloads; these common workloads include *read-only* transactions, i.e., those that only observe data, and *late-write* transactions, i.e., those that update only towards the end of the transaction.

We present the BIMODAL transactional scheduler, which is especially tailored to accommodate read-only transactions, without punishing transactions that write most of their duration, called early-write transactions. It is evaluated by comparison with an optimal clairvoyant scheduler; we prove that BIMODAL achieves the best competitive ratio achievable by a non-clairvoyant schedule for workloads consisting of early-write and read-only transactions.

We also show that late-write transactions significantly deteriorate the competitive ratio of any non-clairvoyant scheduler, assuming it takes a conservative approach to conflicts.

1 Introduction

A promising approach to programming concurrent applications is provided by *transactional synchronization*: a *transaction* aggregates a sequence of resource accesses that should be executed atomically by a single thread. A transaction ends either by *committing*, in which case, all of its updates take effect, or by *aborting*, in which case, no update is effective. When aborted, a transaction is later *restarted* from its beginning.

Most existing transactional memory implementations (e.g. [3, 13]), guarantee consistency by making sure that whenever there is a conflict, i.e. two transactions access a same resource and at least one writes into it, one of the transactions involved is aborted.

---

* This research is partially supported by the *Israel Science Foundation* (grant number 953/06).
** On leave from Sapienza, Universitá di Roma; supported in part by a fellowship from the Lady Davis Foundation and by a grant Progetto FIRB Italia- Israele RBIN047MH9.

T. Abdelzaher, M. Raynal, and N. Santoro (Eds.): OPODIS 2009, LNCS 5923, pp. 3–17, 2009.

We call this approach *conservative*. Taking a non-conservative approach, and ensuring progress while accurately avoiding consistency violation, seems to require complex data structures, e.g., as used in [16].

A major challenge is guaranteeing *progress* through a *transactional scheduler*, by choosing which transaction to delay or abort and when to restart the aborted transaction, so as to ensure that work eventually gets done, and all transactions commit.[1] This goal can also be stated quantitatively as minimizing the *makespan*—the total time needed to complete a finite set of transactions. Clearly, the makespan depends on the *workload*—the set of transactions and their characteristics, for example, their arrival times, duration, and (perhaps most importantly) the resources they read or modify.

The *competitive* approach for evaluating a transactional scheduler A calculates the *ratio* between the makespan provided by A and by an optimal, clairvoyant scheduler, for each workload separately, and then finds the maximal ratio [2, 8, 10]. It has been shown that the best competitive ratio achieved by simple transactional schedulers is $\Theta(s)$, where s is the number of resources [2]. These prior studies assumed *write-dominated* workloads, in which transactions need exclusive access to resources for most of their duration.

In transactional memory, however, the workloads are often *read-dominated* [12]: most of their duration, transactions do not need exclusive access to resources. This includes *read-only* transactions that only observe data and do not modify it, as well as *late-write* transactions, e.g., locating an item by searching a list and then inserting or deleting.

We extend the result in [2] by proving that every deterministic scheduler is $\Omega(s)$-competitive on read-dominated workloads, where s is the number of resources. Then, we prove that any non-clairvoyant scheduler which is conservative and thus too "coarse", is $\Omega(m)$ competitive for some workload containing late-write transactions, where m is the number of cores. (These results appear in Section 3.) This means that, for some workloads, these schedulers utilize at most one core, while an optimal, clairvoyant scheduler exploits the maximal parallelism on all m cores. This can be easily shown to be a tight bound, since at each time, a reasonable scheduler makes progress on at least one transaction.

Contemporary transactional schedulers, like CAR-STM [4], Adaptive Transaction Scheduling [20], and Steal-On-Abort [1], are conservative, thus they do not perform well under read-dominated workloads. These transactional schedulers have been proposed to avoid repeated conflicts and reduce wasted work, without deteriorating throughput. Using somewhat different mechanisms, these schedulers avoid repeated aborts by *serializing* transactions after a conflict happens. Thus, they all end up serializing more than necessary in read-dominated workload, but also in what we call *bimodal* workload, i.e., a workload containing only early-write and read-only transactions. Actually, we show that there is a *bimodal* workload, for which these schedulers are at best $\Omega(m)$-competitive (Section 4).

These counter-examples motivate our BIMODAL scheduler, which has an $O(s)$ competitive ratio on bimodal workloads with equi-length transactions. BIMODAL alternates

---

[1] It is typically assumed that a transaction running solo, without conflicting accesses, commits with a correct result [13].

between *writing epochs* in which it gives priority to writing transactions, and *reading epochs* in which it prioritizes transactions that have issued only reads so far. Due to the known lower bound [2], no algorithm can do better than $O(s)$ for bimodal traffic. BIMODAL also works when the workload is not bimodal, but being conservative it can only be trivially bound to have $O(m)$ competitive makespan when the workload contains late-write transactions.

Contention managers [13,19] were suggested as a mechanism for resolving conflicts and improving the performance of transactional memories. Several papers have recently suggested that having more control on the scheduling of transactions can reduce the amount of work wasted by aborted transactions, e.g., [1,4,14,20]. These schedulers use different mechanisms, in the user space or in the operating system level, but they all end up serializing more than necessary, in read-dominated workloads.

Very recently, Dragojevic et al. [6] have also investigated transactional scheduling. They have taken a complementary approach that tries to predict the accesses of transactions, based on past behavior, together with a heuristic mechanism for serializing transactions that may conflict. They also present counter-examples to CAR-STM [4] and ATS [20], although they do not explicitly detail which accesses are used to generate the conflicts that cause transactions to abort; in particular, they do not distinguish between access types, and the portion of the transaction that requires exclusive access.

Early work on non-clairvoyant scheduling (starting with [15]) dealt with multiprocessing environments and did not address the issue of concurrency control. Moreover, they mostly assume that a preempted transaction resumes execution from the same point, and not restarted. For a more detailed discussion, see [2,6].

2 Preliminaries

2.1 Model

We consider a system of m identical *cores* with a finite set of shared data items $\{i_1, \ldots, i_s\}$. The system has to execute a *workload*, which is a finite partially-ordered set of transactions $\Gamma = \{T_1, T_2, \ldots\}$; the partial order among transactions is induced by their arrival times. Each transaction is a sequence of operations on the shared data items; for simplicity, we assume the operations are *read* and *write*. A transaction that only reads data items is called *read-only*; otherwise, it is a *writing* transaction.

A transaction T is *pending* after its first operation, and before T completes either by a *commit* or an *abort* operation. When a transaction aborts, it is restarted from its very beginning and can possibly access a different set of data items. Generally, a transaction may accesses different data items if it executes at different times. For example, a transaction inserting an item at the head of a linked list, may access different memory locations when accessing the item at the head of the list at different times.

The sequence of operations in a transaction must be atomic: if any of the operations takes place, they all do, and that if they do, they appear to other threads to do so atomically, as one indivisible operation, in the order specified by the transaction. Formally, this is captured by a classical consistency condition like *serializability* [17] or the stronger *opacity* condition [11].

Two overlapping transactions T_1 and T_2 have a *conflict* if T_1 reads a data item X and T_2 executes a write access to X while T_1 is still pending, or T_1 executed a write access to X and T_2 accesses X while T_1 is still pending. Note that a conflict does not mean that serializability is violated. For example, two overlapping transactions $[read(X), write(Y)]$ and $[write(X), read(Z)]$ can be serialized, despite having a conflict on X. We discuss this issue further in Section 3.

2.2   Transactional Schedulers and Measures

The set of data items accessed by a transaction, i.e., its data set, is not known when the transaction starts, except for the first data item that is accessed. At each point, the scheduler must decide what to do, knowing only the data item currently requested and if the access wishes to modify the data item or just read it.

Each core is associated with a list of transactions (possibly the same for all cores) available to be executed. Transactions are placed in the cores' list according to a strategy, called *insertion policy*. Once a core is not executing a transaction, it selects, according to a *selection policy*, a transaction in the list and starts to execute it. The selection policy determines when an aborted transaction is restarted, in an attempt to avoid repeated conflicts. A scheduler is defined by its insertion and selection policies.

Definition 1 (Makespan). *Given scheduler A and a workload Γ, makespan$_A(\Gamma)$ is the time A needs to complete all the transactions in Γ.*

Definition 2 (Competitive ratio). *The* competitive ratio *of a scheduler A for a workload Γ, is $\frac{\text{makespan}_A(\Gamma)}{\text{makespan}_{Opt}(\Gamma)}$, where* OPT *is the optimal, clairvoyant scheduler that has access to all the characteristics of the workload.*
The competitive ratio *of A is the maximum, over all workloads Γ, of the competitive ratio of A on Γ.*

We concentrate on "reasonable" schedulers, i.e., ones that utilize at least one core at each time unit for "productive" work: a scheduler is *effective* if in every time unit, some transaction invocation that eventually commits executes a unit of work (if there are any pending transactions).

We associate a real number $\tau_i > 0$ with each transaction T_i, which is the execution time of T_i when it runs uninterrupted to completion.

Theorem 1. *Every effective scheduler A is $O(m)$-competitive.*

Proof. The proof immediately follows from the fact that for any workload Γ, at each time unit some transaction makes progress, since A is effective. Thus, all transactions complete no later than time $\sum_{T_i \in \Gamma} \tau_i$ (as if they are executed serially). The claim follows since the best possible makespan for Γ, when all cores are continuously utilized, is $\frac{1}{m} \sum_{T_i \in \Gamma} \tau_i$. □

We say that transaction T_i is *early-write* if the time from its first write access until its completion, denoted ω_i, is at least half of its duration (any other constant can be used, in fact). Formally, $2\omega_i > \tau_i$.

We pick a small constant $\alpha > 0$ and say that a transaction T_i is *late-write* if $\omega_i \leq \alpha \tau_i$, i.e., the transaction needs exclusive access to resources during at most an α-fraction of its duration. For a *read-only* transaction, $\omega_i = 0$.

A workload Γ is *bimodal* if it contains only early-write and read-only transactions; said otherwise, if a transaction writes, then it does so early in its execution.

3   Lower Bounds

We start by proving a lower bound of $\Omega(s)$ on the competitiveness achievable by any scheduler, where s is the number of shared data items, for *late-write workloads*, including only late-write transactions. This complements the lower bound proved in [2], for workloads that include only early-write transactions.

We use R_h, W_h to denote (respectively) a read and a write access to data item i_h.

Theorem 2. *There is a late-write workload Γ, such that every deterministic scheduler A is $\Omega(s)$-competitive on Γ.*

Proof. To prove our result we first consider the scheduler A to be *work-conserving*, i.e., it always runs a maximal set of non conflicting transactions [2], and then show how to remove this assumption.

Assume that s is even and let $q = \frac{s}{2}$. The proof uses an execution of $q^2 = \frac{s^2}{4}$ equal-length transactions, described in Table 1. Since transactions have all the same duration, we normalize it to 1.

The data items $\{i_1, \ldots, i_s\}$ are divided into two disjoint sets, $D_1 = \{i_1, \ldots, i_q\}$ and $D_2 = \{i_{q+1}, i_{q+2}, \ldots, i_{2q}\}$. Each transaction reads q data items in D_1 and reads and writes to one data item in D_2. For every $i_j \in D_2$, q transactions read and write to i_j (the ones in row $j - q$ in Table 1).

All transactions are released and available at time $t_0 = 0$. The scheduler A knows only the first data item requested and if it is accessed for read or write. The data item to be read and then written is decided by an adversary during the execution of the algorithm in a way that forces many transactions to abort. Since the first access of all transactions is a read and A is work conserving, A executes all q^2 transactions.

Let time t_1 be the time at which all q^2 transactions have executed their read access to the data item they will then write, but none of them has already attempt to write. It is

Table 1. The set of transactions used in the proof of Theorem 2

	1	2	$\cdots$	q
1	$[R_1, \ldots, R_q, R_{q+1}, W_{q+1}]$	$[R_1, \ldots, R_q, R_{q+1}, W_{q+1}]$	$\cdots$	$[R_1, \ldots, R_q, R_{q+1}, W_{q+1}]$
2	$[R_1, \ldots, R_q, R_{q+2}, W_{q+2}]$	$[R_1, \ldots, R_q, R_{q+2}, W_{q+2}]$	$\cdots$	$[R_1, \ldots, R_q, R_{q+2}, W_{q+2}]$
$\vdots$	$\vdots$	$\vdots$	$\vdots$	$\vdots$
i	$[R_1, \ldots, R_q, R_{q+i}, W_{q+i}]$	$[R_1, \ldots, R_q, R_{q+i}, W_{q+i}]$	$\cdots$	$[R_1, \ldots, R_q, R_{q+i}, W_{q+i}]$
$\vdots$	$\vdots$	$\vdots$	$\vdots$	$\vdots$
q	$[R_1, \ldots, R_q, R_{2q}, W_{2q}]$	$[R_1, \ldots, R_q, R_{2q}, W_{2q}]$	$\cdots$	$[R_1, \ldots, R_q, R_{2q}, W_{2q}]$

simple to see that transactions can be scheduled for this to happen. Then, at some point after t_1 all transactions attempt to write but only q of such transactions can commit (the transactions in a single column of Table 1). Otherwise, serializability is violated. All other transactions abort.

When restarted, all of them write to the same data item i_1, i.e., $[R_1,\ldots,R_q,R_{q+1},W_1]$. This implies that after the first q transactions commit (any set in a column), having run in parallel, the remaining $q^2 - q$ transactions end up being executed serially (i.e., even though they are run in parallel only one of them can commit at each time). So, the makespan of the on-line algorithm is $1 + q^2 - q$.

On the other hand, an optimal scheduler OPT executes the workload as follows: at each time τ_i with $i \in \{0,\ldots,q-1\}$, OPT will execute the set of transactions depicted in column $i+1$ in Table 1. Thus, OPT achieves makespan q. Therefore, the competitive ratio of any work-conserving algorithm is $\frac{1+q^2-q}{q} = \Omega(s)$.

As in [2] to remove the initial assumption that the scheduler is work conserving, we modify the requirement of data items in the following way: if a transaction belonging to Γ is executed after time q then it requests to write into i_1 as done in the above proof when a transaction is restarted. Otherwise, it requests the data items as in Table 1. Thus the online scheduler will end up serializing all transactions executed after time q.

On the other hand, the optimal offline scheduler is not affected by the above change in data items requirement since it executes all transactions by time q. The claim follows.   □

Next, we prove that when the scheduler is too "coarse" and enforces consistency by aborting one conflicting transaction whenever there is a conflict, even if this conflict does not violate serializability, the makespan it guarantees is even less competitive. We remark that all prior competitive results [2, 8, 10] also assume that the scheduler is conservative. Formally,

Definition 3. *A scheduler A is* conservative *if it aborts at least one transaction in every conflict.*

Note that prominent transactional memory implementations (e.g., [3, 13]) are conservative.

Theorem 3. *There is a late-write workload Γ, with $\alpha < \frac{1}{m}$, such that every deterministic conservative scheduler A has $\Omega(m)$-competitive makespan on Γ.*

Proof. Consider a workload Γ with m late-write transactions, all available at time $t = 0$. Each transaction $T \in \Gamma$ first reads items $\{i_1, i_2, \ldots i_{s-1}\}$, and then modifies item i_s, i.e., $T_i = [R_1, \ldots, R_{s-1}, W_s]$, for every $i \in \{1, \ldots, m\}$. All transactions have the same duration d, and they do not modify their data set when running at different times.

The scheduler A will immediately execute all transactions. At time $d - \epsilon$ all transactions will attempt to write into i_s. Since A is conservative, only one of them commits, while the remaining $m - 1$ transactions abort. Aborted transactions will be restarted later, and each transaction will write into i_1 instead of i_s. Thus, all the remaining transactions have to be executed serially in order not to violate serializability. Since A executes all transactions in a serial manner, makespan$_A(\Gamma)=\sum_{i=1}^{m} d_i = md$.

	1	$1+\epsilon$	$1+2\epsilon$		$d-\epsilon$	d	$d+\epsilon$		$d+(m-1)\epsilon$
$T_1{:}R_1$		R_2	R_3	$\circ\,\circ\,\circ$	W_s	commit			
$T_2{:}$		R_1	R_2	R_3	R_{s-1}	W_s	commit		
$T_3{:}$			R_1	R_2	R_{s-1}	W_s	commit		
$\vdots$									
$T_m{:}$					R_1	$\circ\,\circ\,\circ$	R_{s-1}	W_s	commit

Fig. 1. The execution used in the proof of Theorem 3

On the other hand, the optimal scheduler OPT has complete information on the set of transactions, and in particular, OPT knows that at time $d-\epsilon$, each transaction attempts to write to i_s. Thus, OPT delays the execution of the transactions so that conflicts do not happen: at time $t_0 = 0$, only transaction T_1 is executed; for every $i \in \{2, \ldots, m\}$, T_i starts at time $t + (i-1)\epsilon$, where $\epsilon = \alpha d$. (See Figure 1.)

Thus, makespan$_{Opt}(\Gamma){=}d + (m-1)\epsilon$, and the competitive ratio is $\frac{md}{d+(m-1)d\alpha} > \frac{m}{1+\alpha\cdot m} \geq \frac{m}{2}$. $\qquad\qquad\square$

In fact, the makespan is not competitive even relative to a clairvoyant *online* scheduler [6], which does not know the workload in advance, but has complete information on a transaction once it arrives, in particular, the set of resources it accesses.

As formally proved in [6], knowing at release time, the data items a transaction will access, for transactions which do not change their data sets during the execution, facilitates the transactional scheduler execution and greatly improves performance.

4 Dealing with Read-Only Transactions: Motivating Example

Several recent transactional schedulers [1, 4, 14, 20] attempt to reduce the overhead of transactional memory, by serializing conflicting transactions. Unfortunately, these schedulers are conservative and so, they are $\Omega(m)$-competitive. Moreover, they do not distinguish between read and write accesses and do not provide special treatment to read-only transactions, causing them not to work well also with bimodal workloads.

There are bimodal workloads of m transactions (m is the number of cores) for which both CAR-STM and ATS have a competitive ratio (relative an optimal offline scheduler) that is at least $\Omega(m)$. This is because both CAR-STM and ATS do not ensure the so-called *list scheduler property* [7], i.e., no thread is waiting to execute if the resource it needs are available, and may cause a transaction to wait although the resources it needs are available. In fact, to reduce the wasted work due to repeated conflicts, these schedulers may serialize also read-only transactions.

Steal-on-Abort (SoA) [1], in contrast, allows free cores to take transactions from the queue of another busy core; thus, it ensures the list scheduler property, trying to execute as many transactions concurrently as possible. However, in an overloaded system, with more than m transactions, SoA may create a situation in which a starved writing transaction can starve read-only transactions. This yields bimodal workloads in which the makespan of Steal-on-Abort is $\Omega(m)$ competitive, as we show below. (Steal-on-abort [1], as well as the other transactional schedulers [4, 14, 20], are effective, and hence they are $O(m)$-competitive, by Theorem 1.)

The Steal-On-Abort (SoA) scheduler: Application threads submit transactions to a transactional threads pool. Each transactional thread has a work queue where available transactions wait to be executed. When new transactions are available they are distributed among the transactional threads' queues in round robin.

When two running transactions T and T' conflict, the contention manager policy decides which to commit. The aborted transaction, say T', is then "stolen" by the transactional thread executing T and is enqueued in a designated *steal queue*. Once the conflicting transaction commits, the stolen transaction is taken from the steal queue and inserted to the work queue. There are two possible insertion policies: T' is enqueued either in the top or in the tail of the queue. Transactions in a queue are executed serially, unless they are moved to other queues. This can happen either because a new conflict happen or because some transactional thread becomes idle and steals transactions from the work queue of another transactional thread (chosen uniformly at random) or from the steal queue if all work queues are empty.

SoA suggests four strategies for moving aborted transactions: *steal-tail*, *steal-head*, *steal-keep* and *steal-block*. Here we describe a worst case scenario for the steal-tail strategy, which inserts the transactions aborted because of a conflict with a transaction T, at the tail of the work queue of the transactional thread that executed T, when T completes. Similar scenarios can be shown for the other strategies.

The *SoA* scheduler does not specify any policy to manage conflicts. In [1], the *SoA* scheduler is evaluated empirically with three contention management policies: the simple *Aggressive* and *Timestamp* contention managers, and the more sophisticated *Polka* contention manager.[2] Yet none of these policies outperform the others, and the optimal one depends on the workload. This result is corroborated by an empirical study that has shown that no contention manager is universally optimal, and performs best in all reasonable circumstances [9] .

Moreover, while several contention management policies have been proposed in the literature [10, 19], none of them, except *Greedy* [10], has nontrivial provable properties.

Thus, we consider the *SoA* scheduler with a contention management policy based on timestamps, like Greedy [10] or Timestamp [19]. These policies do not require costly data structures, like the *Polka* policy. Our choice also provides a fair comparison with *CAR-STM*, which embeds a contention manager based on timestamps.

Theorem 4. *Steal-on-Abort with steal-tail has $\Omega(m)$-competitive makespan for some bimodal workload.*

Proof. We consider a workload Γ with $n = 2m - 1$ unit-length transactions, two writing transactions and $2m - 3$ read-only transactions, depicted in Table 2. At time

---

[2] In the *Aggressive* contention manager, a conflicting transaction always aborts the competing transaction. In the *Timestamp* contention manager, each transaction is associated with the system time when it starts and the newer transaction is aborted, in case of a conflict. The *Polka* contention manager increases the priority of a transaction whenever the transaction successfully acquires a data item; when two transactions are in conflict, the attacking transaction makes a number of attempts equal to the difference among priorities of the transactions before aborting the competing transaction, with a exponential backoff between attempts [19].

$t_1 = 0$, a writing transaction $U_1=[R_1,W_1]$ is available and at time $t_1 + \epsilon$, when the writing transaction is executing its first access, $m-1$ read-only transactions $[R_2,R_1,R_3]$ become available. Let S_1 denote this set of read-only transactions.

All the transactions are immediately executed. But in their second access, all the read-only transactions conflict with the writing transaction U_1. All the read-only transactions are aborted, because U_1 have a greater priority than these latter, and they are inserted in the work queue of the transactional thread where U_1 was in execution.

At time t_2, immediately before U_1 completes, $m-1$ other transactions become available: a writing transaction $U_2=[R_1,W_4,W_3]$ and a set of $m-2$ read-only transactions $[R_1,R_4]$, denoted S_2. Each of these transactions is placed in one of the idle transactional threads, as depicted in Table 2.

Immediately after time t_2, U_2, all the transactions in S_2 and one read-only transaction in S_1 are running. In their second access all the read-only transactions in S_2 conflict with the writing transaction U_2. We consider U_2 to discover the conflict and to abort all the read-only transaction in S_2. Actually, if U_2 arrives immediately before the read-only transactions, it has a bigger priority.

The aborted read-only transactions are then moved to the queue of the worker thread which is currently executing U_2. Then, U_2 conflicts with the third access of the read-only transaction in S_1. Thus, U_2 is aborted and it is moved to the tail of the corresponding work queue. We assume the time between cascading aborts is negligible.

In the following we repeat the above scenario, until all transactions commit. In particular, for every $i \in \{3,\ldots m\}$, we have that immediately before time t_i, there are $m-i+1$ read-only transactions $[R_2,R_1,R_3]$ and the writing transaction U_2 in the work queue of thread 1 and $m-2$ read-only transactions $[R_1,R_4]$ in the work queue of thread $i-1$. All the remaining threads have no transaction in their work queues. Then, at time t_i, the worker thread i takes the writing transaction from the work queue of thread 1 and the other free worker threads take a read-only transaction $[R_1,R_4]$ from the work queue of thread $i-1$. Thus, at each time t_i, $i \in \{3,\ldots m\}$, the writing transaction U_2, one read-only transaction $[R_2,R_1,R_3]$ and $m-2$ read-only transactions $[R_1,R_4]$ are executed, but only the read-only transaction in S_1 commits.

Finally, at time t_m U_2 commits, and ,hence, all read-only transactions in S_2 commit at time t_{m+1}.

Note that, in the scenario we built, the way each thread steals the transactions from the work queues of other threads is governed by a uniformly random distribution as requested by the Steal on Abort work-steal strategy.

Thus, makespan$_{SoA}(\Gamma)=m+2$. On the other hand, the makespan of an optimal offline algorithm is less than 4, because all read-only transactions can be executed in 2 time units, and hence, the competitive ratio is at least $\frac{m+2}{4}$.   □

In the following section, we present a conservative scheduler, called BIMODAL, which is $O(s)$-competitive for bimodal workloads. BIMODAL embeds a simple contention management policy utilizing timestamps.

Table 2. Steal-On-Abort with steal-tail strategy: illustration for Theorem 4. Each table entry (i,j) shows at the top the transaction executed by thread j at time t_i, and at the bottom, the status of the main queue of thread j immediately before time t_{i+1}. $<(k)[R_i, W_j]; [R_h, R_l] >$ denotes a work dequeue with k transactions $[R_i, W_j]$ and one read-only transaction $[R_h, R_l]$, in this order, from head to tail. If there is no transaction in such a dequeue, the bottom line is empty.

time	thread 1	thread 2	...	thread $i-1$	thread i	...	thread $m-1$	thread m
t_1	$[R_1,W_1]$							
$t_1 + \epsilon$	$[R_1,W_1]$ $<(m-1)[R_2,R_1,R_3]>$	$[R_2,R_1,R_3]$	...	$[R_2,R_1,R_3]$	$[R_2,R_1,R_3]$	...	$[R_2,R_1,R_3]$	$[R_2,R_1,R_3]$
t_2	$[R_2,R_1,R_3]$ $<(m-2)[R_2,R_1,R_3];$ $[R_3,W_4,W_3] >$	$[R_3,W_4,W_3]$ $<(m-2)[R_1,R_4]>$	...	$[R_1,R_4]$	$[R_1,R_4]$	...	$[R_1,R_4]$	$[R_1,R_4]$
...	...	...	...	...	...	...	...	...
t_{i-1}	$[R_2,R_1,R_3]$ $<(m-i+1)[R_1,R_4];$ $[R_3,W_4,W_3] >$	$[R_3,W_4,W_3]$	...	$[R_1,R_4]$ $<(m-2)[R_1,R_4]>$	$[R_1,R_4]$	...	$[R_1,R_4]$	$[R_1,R_4]$
t_i	$[R_2,R_1,R_3]$ $<(m-i)[R_2,R_1,R_3];$ $[R_3,W_4,W_3] >$	$[R_1,R_4]$	...	$[R_1,R_4]$	$[R_3,W_4,W_3]$ $<(m-2)[R_1,R_4]>$	...	$[R_1,R_4]$	$[R_1,R_4]$
...	...	...	...	...	...	...	...	...
t_{m-1}	$[R_2,R_1,R_3]$ $<[R_3,W_4,W_3]>$	$[R_1,R_4]$	...	$[R_1,R_4]$	$[R_1,R_4]$	...	$[R_3,W_4,W_3]$ $<(m-2)[R_1,R_4]>$	$[R_1,R_4]$
t_m	-	$[R_1,R_4]$	...	$[R_1,R_4]$	$[R_1,R_4]$	...	$[R_1,R_4]$	$[R_3,W_4,W_3]$
t_{m+1}	-	$[R_1,R_4]$	...	$[R_1,R_4]$	$[R_1,R_4]$	...	$[R_1,R_4]$	-

5 The BIMODAL Scheduler

The BIMODAL scheduler architecture is similar to CAR-STM [4]: each core is associated with a work dequeue (double-ended queue), where a *transactional dispatcher* enqueues arriving transactions. BIMODAL also maintains a fifo queue, called RO-queue, shared by all cores to enqueue transactions which abort before executing their first writing operation and that are predicted to be read-only transactions.

Transactions are executed as they are available unless the system is overloaded. BIMODAL requires visible reads in order for a conflict to be detected as soon as possible.

Once two transactions conflict, one of them is aborted and BIMODAL prohibits them from executing concurrently again and possibly repeating the conflict. In particular, if the aborted transaction is a writing transaction, BIMODAL moves it to the work dequeue of the conflicting transaction; otherwise, it is enqueued in the RO-queue.

Specifically, the contention manager, embedded in BIMODAL, decides which transaction to abort in a conflict, according to two levels of priority:

1. In a conflict between two writing transactions, the contention manager aborts the newer transaction. Towards this goal, a transaction is assigned a timestamp when it starts, which it retains even when it aborts, as in the greedy contention manager [10].
2. To handle a conflict between a writing transaction and a read-only transaction, BIMODAL alternates between periods in which it privileges the execution of writing transactions, called *writing epochs*, and periods in which it privileges the execution of read-only transactions, called *reading epochs*.

Below, we detail the algorithm and we provide its competitive analysis.

5.1 Detailed Description of the BIMODAL Scheduler

Transactions are assigned in round-robin to the work dequeues of the cores (inserted at their tail), starting from cores whose work dequeue is empty; initially, all work dequeues are empty.

At each time, the system is in a given epoch associated with a pair $(mode, ID)$, where $mode \in \{Reading, Writing\}$ is the type of epoch and ID is a monotonically increasing integer that uniquely identifies the epoch. A shared variable ξ stores the pair corresponding to the current epoch and it is initially set to $(Writing, 0)$.

When in a writing epoch i, the system moves to a reading epoch $i + 1$, i.e., $\xi = (Reading, i + 1)$, if there are m transactions in the RO-queue or every work dequeue is empty. Analogously, if during a reading epoch $i+1$, m transactions have been dequeued from the RO-queue or this queue is empty, the system enters writing epoch $i + 2$, and so on. A process in the system, called ξ-*manager*, is responsible to managing epoch evolution and updating the shared variable ξ. The ξ-manager checks if the above conditions are verified and sets the variable ξ in a single atomic operation (e.g., using a Read-Modify-Write primitive).

A transaction T that starts in the i-th epoch, is associated with epoch i up to the time it either commits or aborts. An aborted transaction may be associated to a new epoch when restarted. Moreover, it may happen that while a transaction T, associated with epoch i, is running, the system transitions to an epoch $j > i$. When this happens, we say that epochs *overlap*. To manage conflicts between transactions associated with different epochs, we give higher priority to the transaction in the earlier epoch. Specifically, if a core executes a transaction T belonging to the current epoch i while some core is still executing a transaction T' in epoch $i - 1$, and T and T' have a conflict, T is aborted and immediately restarted.

Writing epochs. The algorithm starts in a *writing epoch*. During a writing epoch, each core selects a transaction from its work dequeue (if it is not empty) and executes it. During this epoch:

1. A read-only transaction that conflicts with a writing transaction is aborted and en-queued in the RO-queue. We may have a *false positive*, i.e., a writing transaction T, wrongly considered to be a read-only transaction and enqueued in the RO-queue, because it has a conflict before invoking its first writing access.
2. If there is a conflict between two writing transactions T_1 and T_2, and T_2 has lower priority than T_1, then T_2 is inserted at the head of the work dequeue of T_1. (As in the *permanent serializing* contention manager of CAR-STM.)

Reading epochs. A *reading epoch* starts when the RO-queue contains m transactions, or the work dequeues of all cores are empty. The latter option ensures that no transaction in the RO-queue is indefinitely, waiting to be executed.

During a reading epoch, each core takes a transaction from the RO-queue and ex-ecutes it. The reading epoch ends when m transactions have been dequeued from the RO-queue or this latter is empty. Conflicts may occur during a reading epoch, due to false positives or because epochs overlap. If there is a conflict between a read-only trans-action and a false positive, the writing transaction is aborted. If the conflict is between two writing transactions (two false positives), then one aborts, and the other transaction simply continues its execution; as in a writing epoch, the decisions are based on their priority. Once aborted, a false positive is enqueued in the head of the work dequeue of the core where it executed.

5.2 Analysis of the BIMODAL Scheduler

We first bound (from below) the makespan that can be achieved by an optimal conser-vative scheduler.

Theorem 5. *For every workload Γ, the makespan of Γ under an optimal, conservative offline scheduler* OPT *satisfies* $makespan_{Opt}(\Gamma) \geq \max\{\frac{\sum \omega_i}{s}, \frac{\sum \tau_i}{m}\}$.

Proof. There are m cores, and hence, the optimal scheduler cannot execute more than m transactions in each time unit; therefore, $makespan_{Opt}(\Gamma) \geq \frac{\sum \tau_i}{m}$.

For each transaction T_i in Γ with $\omega_i \neq 0$, let X_{f_i} be the first item T_i modifies.

Any two transactions T_i and T_j whose first write access is to the same item, i.e., that have $X_{f_i} = X_{f_j}$, have to execute the part after their write serially.

Thus, at most s transactions with $\omega_i \neq 0$ proceed at each time, implying that makespan $Opt(\Gamma) \geq \frac{\sum \omega_i}{s}$. $\qquad\square$

We analyze BIMODAL assuming all transactions have the same duration.

A key observation is that if a false positive is enqueued in the RO-queue and executed during a *reading epoch* because it is falsely considered to be a read-only transaction, either it completes successfully without encountering conflicts or it is aborted and treated as a writing transaction once restarted.

Theorem 6. BIMODAL *is $O(s)$-competitive for bimodal workloads, in which for every writing transaction T_i, $2\omega_i \geq \tau_i$.*

Proof. Consider the scheduling of a bimodal workload Γ under BIMODAL. Let t_k be the starting time of the last reading epoch after all the work deques of cores are empty, and such that some transactions arrive after t_k.

At time t_k, no transactions are available in the work queues of any core, and hence, no matter what the optimal scheduler OPT does, its makespan is at least t_k.

Let Γ_k be the set of transactions that arrive after time t_k, and let $n_k = |\Gamma_k|$. Since at time t_k, OPT does not schedule any transaction, it will schedule new transactions to execute as they arrive. On the other hand, BIMODAL may delay the execution of new available transactions because the cores are executing the transactions in the RO-queue (if any). Since RO-queue has less than m transactions, this will take at most τ time units, where τ is the duration of a transaction (the same for all transactions).

By Theorem 5,

$$\text{Makespan}_{Opt}(\Gamma_k) \geq \frac{1}{2}\left(\frac{\sum_{i=1}^{n_k} \omega_i}{s} + \frac{\sum_{i=1}^{n_k} \tau_i}{m}\right),$$

and therefore,

$$\text{Makespan}_{Opt}(\Gamma) \geq t_k + \frac{1}{2}\left(\frac{\sum_{i=1}^{n_k} \omega_i}{s} + \frac{\sum_{i=1}^{n_k} \tau_i}{m}\right).$$

On the other hand, we have that

$$\text{Makespan}_{Bimodal}(\Gamma) \leq t_k + \tau + \sum_{i=1}^{n_k} 4\omega_i + \frac{1}{m}\sum_{i=1}^{n_k} \tau_i.$$

The penultimate term holds because $2\omega_i \geq \tau_i$, for every writing transaction $T_i \in \Gamma_k$, and taking into account the impact of false positives during reading epochs. In fact, a writing transaction T may conflict only once during a reading epoch, because when restarted T will be treated as a writing transaction. This is just as if T is executed during a writing epoch with its duration doubled, to account for the time spent for the execution of the read-only transaction that aborted T (if there is one). The last term holds since all transactions have the same duration.

Therefore, the competitive ratio is

$$\frac{\text{Makespan}_{Bimodal}(\Gamma)}{\text{Makespan}_{Opt}(\Gamma)} \leq \frac{t_k + \tau + \sum_{i=1}^{n_k} 4\omega_i + \frac{1}{m}\sum_{i=1}^{n_k} \tau_i}{t_k + \frac{1}{2}\left(\frac{\sum_{i=1}^{n_k} \omega_i}{s} + \frac{\sum_{i=1}^{n_k} \tau_i}{m}\right)},$$

which can be shown to be in $O(s)$.

Note that if t_k does not exist, we can take t_k to be the time immediately before the first transaction in Γ is available, and repeat the reasoning with $t_k = 0$ and $\Gamma_k = \Gamma$. □

6 Discussion

We have studied the competitive ratio achieved by non-clairvoyant transactional schedulers on read-dominated workloads. The BIMODAL transactional scheduler, presented in this paper, allows to achieve maximum parallelism on read-only transactions, without harming early-write transactions. On the other hand, we proved that the long reading periods of late-write transactions cannot be overlapped to exploit parallelism, and must be serialized if the writes at the end of the transactions are in conflict.

This last result assumes that the scheduler is conservative, namely, it aborts at least one transaction involved in a conflict. This is the approach advocated in [13] as it reduces the cost of tracking conflicts and dependencies. It is interesting to investigate, whether less conservative schedulers can reduce the makespan and what is the cost of improving parallelism. Keidar and Perelman [18] prove that contention managers that abort a transaction only when it is necessary to ensure correctness have local computation that is NP-complete; however, it is not clear whether being less accurate in ensuring consistency can be done more efficiently.

Our study should be completed by considering other performance measures, e.g., the average response time of transactions.

The contention manager embedded in SwissTM [5] is also bimodal, distinguishing between *short* and *long* transactions, and it would be interesting to see whether our analysis techniques can be applied to it.

Finally, while we have theoretically analyzed the behavior of BIMODAL, it is important to see how it compares, through simulation, with prior transactional schedulers, e.g., [1, 4, 14, 20].

Acknowledgements. We would like to thank Adi Suissa for many helpful discussions and comments, Richard M. Yoo for discussing ATS, and the referees for their suggestions.

References

1. Ansari, M., Lujn, M., Kotselidis, C., Jarvis, K., Kirkham, C.C., Watson, I.: Steal-on-abort: Improving transactional memory performance through dynamic transaction reordering. In: HiPEAC 2009, pp. 4–18 (2009)
2. Attiya, H., Epstein, L., Shachnai, H., Tamir, T.: Transactional contention management as a non-clairvoyant scheduling problem. In: PODC 2006, pp. 308–315 (2006)
3. Dice, D., Shalev, O., Shavit, N.: Transactional locking ii. In: Dolev, S. (ed.) DISC 2006. LNCS, vol. 4167, pp. 194–208. Springer, Heidelberg (2006)
4. Dolev, S., Hendler, D., Suissa, A.: CAR-STM: scheduling-based collision avoidance and resolution for software transactional memory. In: PODC 2008, pp. 125–134 (2008)
5. Dragojevic, A., Guerraoui, R., Kapalka, M.: Stretching transactional memory. In: PLDI, pp. 155–165 (2009)
6. Dragojevic, A., Guerraoui, R., Singh, A.V., Singh, V.: Preventing versus curing: Avoiding conflicts in transactional memories. In: PODC 2009, pp. 7–16 (2009)
7. Garey, M.R., Graham, R.L.: Bound for multiprocessor scheduling with resource constraints. SIAM Journal Computing 4, 187–200 (1975)

8. Guerraoui, R., Herlihy, M., Kapałka, M., Pochon, B.: Robust contention management in software transactional memory. In: OOPSLA 2005 Workshop on Synchronization and Concurrency in Object-Oriented Languages, SCOOL 2005 (October 2005)
9. Guerraoui, R., Herlihy, M., Pochon, B.: Polymorphic contention management. In: Fraigniaud, P. (ed.) DISC 2005. LNCS, vol. 3724, pp. 303–323. Springer, Heidelberg (2005)
10. Guerraoui, R., Herlihy, M., Pochon, B.: Toward a theory of transactional contention managers. In: PODC 2005, pp. 258–264 (2005)
11. Guerraoui, R., Kapalka, M.: On the correctness of transactional memory. In: PPoPP 2008, pp. 175–184 (2008)
12. Guerraoui, R., Kapalka, M., Vitek, J.: Stmbench7: a benchmark for software transactional memory. In: EuroSys 2007, pp. 315–324 (2007)
13. Herlihy, M., Luchangco, V., Moir, M., Scherer III, W.N.: Software transactional memory for dynamic-sized data structures. In: PODC 2003, pp. 92–101 (2003)
14. Maldonado, W., Marlier, P., Felber, P., Lawall, J., Muller, G.: Transaction activation: Scheduling support for transactional memory. Technical Report 6807, INRIA (January 2009)
15. Motwani, R., Phillips, S., Torng, E.: Non-clairvoyant scheduling. Theor. Comput. Sci. 130(1), 17–47 (1994)
16. Napper, J., Alvisi, L.: Lock-free serializable transactions. Technical Report TR-05-04, The University of Texas at Austin (2005)
17. Papadimitriou, C.H.: The serializability of concurrent database updates. J. ACM 26(4), 631–653 (1979)
18. Perelman, D., Keidar, I.: On avoiding spare aborts in transactional memory. In: SPAA 2009, pp. 59–68 (2009)
19. Scherer III, W.N., Scott, M.L.: Advanced contention management for dynamic software transactional memory. In: PODC 2005, pp. 240–248 (2005)
20. Yoo, R.M., Lee, H.-H.S.: Adaptive transaction scheduling for transactional memory systems. In: SPAA 2008, pp. 169–178 (2008)

Performance Evaluation of Work Stealing for Streaming Applications*

Jonatha Anselmi and Bruno Gaujal

INRIA and LIG Laboratory
MontBonnot Saint-Martin, 38330, FR
{jonatha.anselmi,bruno.gaujal}@imag.fr

Abstract. This paper studies the performance of parallel stream computations on a multiprocessor architecture using a work-stealing strategy.
Incoming tasks are split in a number of jobs allocated to the processors
and whenever a processor becomes idle, it steals a fraction (typically
half) of the jobs from a busy processor. We propose a new model for the
performance analysis of such parallel stream computations. This model
takes into account both the algorithmic behavior of work-stealing as well
as the hardware constraints of the architecture (synchronizations and bus
contentions). Then, we show that this model can be solved using a recursive formula. We further show that this recursive analytical approach
is more efficient than the classic global balance technique. However, our
method remains computationally impractical when tasks split in many
jobs or when many processors are considered. Therefore, bounds are proposed to efficiently solve very large models in an approximate manner.
Experimental results show that these bounds are tight and robust so that
they immediately find applications in optimization studies. An example
is provided for the optimization of energy consumption with performance
constraints. In addition, our framework is flexible and we show how it
adapts to deal with several stealing strategies.

Keywords: Work Stealing, Performance Evaluation, Markov Model.

1 Introduction

Modern embedded systems perform on-the-fly real-time applications, (e.g., com-
press, cipher or filter video streams) whose computational complexity requires
using multiprocessor architectures (in terms of FLOPS as well as energy consumption). This paper is concerned with such systems where stream computations are processed by a multiprocessor architecture using a work-stealing
scheduling algorithm. We take our inspiration from an experimental board developed by ST Microlectronics (Traviata) over the STM8010 chip. The chip is
composed of three almost identical ST231 processors communicating via a multi-
com network. This board is used as an experimental platform for portable video

---

* This work is supported by the Conseil Régional Rhône-Alpes, Global competitiveness
cluster Minalogic contract SCEPTRE.

T. Abdelzaher, M. Raynal, and N. Santoro (Eds.): OPODIS 2009, LNCS 5923, pp. 18–32, 2009.

processing devices of the near future [1]. What we call a stream computation here can be modeled as a sequence of independent *tasks* characterized by their arrival times and their sizes that may vary, e.g., a video stream under Mpeg coding. As for the system architecture, it is modeled by a multiprocessor system interconnected by a very fast communication network, typically a fast bus. The system functions according to the work-stealing principle specified in Section 2.

Generally speaking, work stealing is a scheduling policy where idle resources steal jobs from busy resources; see [16,5,9,3] for an exhaustive overview of related work. The work stealing paradigm has been implemented in several parallel programming environment such as Cilk [11] and Kaapi [14,2]. The success of the work-stealing paradigm is due to the fact that it has many interesting features. First, this scheduling policy is very easy to implement and does not require many information on the system to work efficiently, because it is only based on the current state of each processor (idle or not). Second, it is asymptotically optimal in terms of worst-case complexity [6]. Finally, it is processor oblivious since it automatically adapts on-line to the number and the size of jobs in the system as well as to the changing speeds of processors [8].

Many variants of work stealing have been developed. In the following, we will consider a special case of the work-stealing principle introduced above: at each steal, half of the remaining work is stolen from the busiest processor. Let n_r be the number of unit jobs initially assigned to processor $1 \leq r \leq R$, with speed μ_r. It should be clear that after R steals the maximum backlog is cut by at least half so that the total number of steals is upper bounded by $R \log_2(\max_r n_r)$ and if γ is the time needed for one steal, then by summing, the completion time C satisfies: $\frac{\sum_r n_r}{\sum_r \mu_r} \leq C \leq \frac{\sum_r n_r + \gamma R \log(\max_r n_r)}{\sum_r \mu_r}$. In [5] similar bounds holding with high probability are provided for a more general case where the victim is chosen at random. However, to the best of our knowledge, very few performance evaluations of work-stealing have been proposed in the literature that take into account higher moments of the completion time that are needed to estimate mean performance measures such as waiting time. Also, few studies use accurate stochastic models taking into account hardware constraints such as exclusive communications among processors (bus contentions) as well as software features (stealing jobs from the busiest processor). In [7] the generic work-stealing principle is proven to be stable when the input rate is smaller than the processing rate but no quantitative formulas of its performance are given. Scheduling policies where idle processors steal from busy processors are analyzed in [17]. However, the latter approach does not take into account the synchronizations and assumes that all processors are independent, unlike what is done here.

In this paper, we propose a two-level model for a streaming system evolving in a changing environment. At the task level, the system is reduced to a simple queueing system (M/G/1 queue) so that the Pollaczek–Khintchine formula, e.g., [10], can be used to assess the mean performance of the system provided that the mean and the second moment of the (task) service time distribution can be computed. At the job level, the system is modeled as a continuous time Markov chain whose transitions correspond to job services or steals. This is used to compute the first two moments of the service time distribution useful for the task level model. We show that this approach drastically reduces the computational requirements of the classic global balance technique, e.g., [10]. However, it remains computationally impractical when tasks split in many jobs and when many processors are considered. Therefore, we propose efficient bounds aimed at quickly obtaining the model solution in an approximate manner. With respect to mean waiting times, experimental results show that the proposed bounds are very tight and robust capturing very well the dynamics of the work-stealing paradigm above. The analytical simplicity of the proposed bounds lets us devise a convex optimization model determining the optimal number of processors and processing speeds which minimize energy consumption while satisfying a performance constraint on the mean waiting time. We also show how our framework adapts to different stealing strategies aimed at balancing the load among processors. The goodness of these strategies turns out to strongly depend on the structure of communication costs so that their impact is non-trivial to predict without our model. Due to space limitations, we refer to [4] for proofs, details and additional experimental results.

2 Model of Work Stealing over a Multi-processor Architecture

To assess the performance of the systems introduced above, one must take into account both the algorithmic features of work-stealing and the hardware constraints of the architecture. The system presented in Figure 1 fits rather well the Traviata multiprocessor dsp system developed by ST Microelectronics for streaming video codec [1] where tasks are images and jobs are local processing algorithms to be performed on each pixel (or group of pixels) of the image.

We now introduce a queueing model for the system displayed in Figure 1, to capture the performance dynamics of the real-world problem introduced above. It is composed of R service units (or processors) and each service unit r has a local buffer. If not otherwise specified, indices r and s will implicitly range in set $\{1, \ldots, R\}$ indexing the R processors. We assume that *tasks* arrive from an external source according to a Poisson process with rate λ. When a task enters the system, it splits into $N_k \cdot R$ independent *jobs*, $N_k \in \mathbb{Z}^+$, with probability p_k, $k = 1, \ldots, K$, and, for simplicity, these jobs are equally distributed among all processors, that is N_k jobs per processor (any initial unbalanced allocation can also be taken into account with minimal changes in the following results). This split models the fact that tasks can have different sizes or jobs can be encoded in different ways. When all jobs of task $i - 1$ have been processed, all jobs of task i (if present in the input buffer) are equally distributed among all processors in turn. Service discipline of jobs is FCFS and their service time in processor r is exponential with rate μ_r^{-1}. During the execution of task i, if processor r becomes idle, then it attempts to steal $\lfloor n_{\max}/2 \rfloor$ jobs from the queue of the processor with the largest number of jobs, i.e., $n_{\max}$. When a processor steals jobs from the queue of another processor, it uses the communication bus

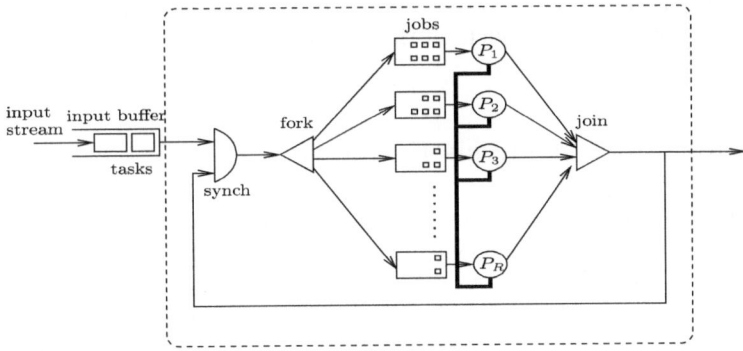

Fig. 1. The fork-join nodes are coupled: the join has to wait for all jobs to be treated before sending a signal back and releasing one pending task. The synch node ensures that tasks are treated in sequence, i.e., no processor starts executing a job of a given task if there exists a job of its previous task which is still handled by some processor. The thick lines represent the interconnection network that is used to steal in a mutual exclusive manner. The global system can be seen as one $M/G/1$ queue when the dotted area is seen as one processor for tasks.

in an exclusive manner (no concurrent steal can take place simultaneously). This further incurs a *communication cost* which depends on the number of jobs to transfer (exponential with rate γ_i when $\lfloor i/2 \rfloor$ jobs are stolen)). This is interpreted as the time required to transfer jobs between the processor queues. We assume that the time needed by a processor to probe the local queues of the other processors is negligible. This is because multiprocessor embedded systems are usually composed of a limited number of processors.

Let $\mathbf{n}(t) = (n_1(t), \dots, n_R(t))$ be the vector denoting the number of jobs in each internal buffer at time t.

Assumption 1. *In* $\mathbf{n}(t)$, *if more than one processor can steal jobs from the queue of processor* r, *i.e.,* $\| \{s : n_s = 0\} \| > 1$, *then only processor* $\min\{s : n_s = 0 \wedge s > r\}$ *is allowed to perform the steal from* r *if it exists. Otherwise the jobs are stolen by* $\min\{s : n_s = 0 \wedge s < r\}$.

On the other hand, when processor r can steal jobs from more than one processor, we also make the following assumption stating which processor is stolen.

Assumption 2. *In* $\mathbf{n}(t)$, *if* $\| \{s : n_s = \max_r n_r\} \| > 1$, *then jobs can be stolen only from the queue of processor* $\min\{s : n_s = \max_r n_r\}$.

Under the foregoing assumptions and assuming that $K = 1$,

$$\{(m(t), \mathbf{n}(t)) : m(t) \geq 0, \ \mathbf{n}(t) \geq \mathbf{0}\}_{t \in \mathbb{R}^+} \tag{1}$$

is the continuous-time Markov chain describing the number of tasks waiting for service at time t in the system (i.e., m), and the number of jobs associated to each processor, (i.e., $\mathbf{n}$), in the proposed model. The goal of our study is to provide efficient analysis for (1) to compute the value of (stationary) performance indices, i.e., when $t \to \infty$, such as the mean task waiting time and the mean number of tasks in the system.

3   Performance Analysis Framework

Let us observe that the exact solution of the proposed model can be obtained by applying classic global balance equations, e.g., [10], of the underlying Markov chain (1). However, this requires a truncation of the Markov chain state space and the solution of a prohibitively large linear system. This motivates us to investigate alternative approaches for obtaining the exact model solution.

The key point of our approach consists in computing the first two moments of the service time distribution of each task in order to define a M/G/1 queue and obtain performance indices estimates by exploiting standard formulas. This approach provides an alternative analytical framework able to characterize the exact solution of the proposed work-stealing model without applying standard (computationally impractical) methods for continuous-time Markov chains.

3.1   Exact Analysis

Let us first consider an example with two processors, assuming that tasks always split in 10 jobs. We show in Figure 2 the continuous-time Markov chain whose hitting time from initial state $(5,5)$ to absorbing state $(0,0)$ represents the service time of one incoming task.

Stealing of jobs only happens on the states at the boundary of the diagram. Considering the general case $R \geq 2$ and job allocation $\mathbf{n} \in \{1, \dots, N_{\max}\}^R$ such that exists $s : n_s = 0$, according to Assumptions 1 and 2 we note that a steal removes half of the jobs from the queue of processor $s' = \min\{r : n_r = \max_s n_s\}$

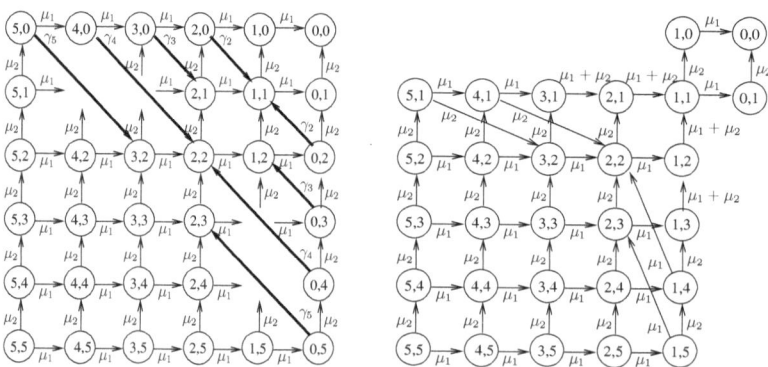

Fig. 2. The reducible Markov chains of task service time with $K = 1$, $N_K = 5$, $\gamma_n < \infty$ (on the left) and $\gamma_n \to \infty$ (on the right, studied in Section 4). States (n_1, n_2) indicate the number of jobs in each processor.

and can be performed only by processor $r' = \min\{s : n_s = 0 \land s > s'\}$ if it exists and otherwise by $r' = \min\{s : n_s = 0 \land s < s'\}$. Therefore, from state $\mathbf{n}$ of the service time state diagram, a stealing action moves to state

$$\mathbf{n}^* = \mathbf{n} + \lfloor 0.5 \max_s n_s \rfloor \mathbf{e}_{r'} - \lfloor 0.5 \max_s n_s \rfloor \mathbf{e}_{\min\{r:n_r=\max_s n_s\}} \qquad (2)$$

where r' is the processor that steals from s' and $\mathbf{e}_r$ is the unit vector in direction r. The transition rates of the generalization of the Markov chain depicted in Figure 2 (on the left) are summarized in Table 1.

Table 1. Transition rates of the Markov chain characterizing the task service time distribution (on the left); $\mathbf{e}_r$ is the unit vector in direction r

Condition on state $\mathbf{n}$	State transition	Rate
1) $n_r \geq 1, \forall r$	$\forall r : \qquad \mathbf{n} \mapsto \mathbf{n} - \mathbf{e}_r$	μ_r
2) $\exists r : n_r = 0 \land \exists s : n_s > 1$	$\mathbf{n} \mapsto \mathbf{n}^*$	$\gamma_{\max_t n_t}$
	$\forall t : n_t > 0 : \mathbf{n} \mapsto \mathbf{n} - \mathbf{e}_t$	μ_t
3) $n_r \leq 1, \forall r \land \exists s : n_s = 0$	$\forall r : n_r = 1 \quad \mathbf{n} \mapsto \mathbf{n} - \mathbf{e}_r$	μ_r

Let $\mathcal{T}_\mathbf{n}$ denote the random variable of the task service time in job allocation $\mathbf{n}$, i.e., when n_r jobs are assigned to processor r, $\forall r$, $T_\mathbf{n} := \mathbb{E}[\mathcal{T}_\mathbf{n}]$ and $V_\mathbf{n} := \mathbb{E}[\mathcal{T}_\mathbf{n}^2]$. The (Markovian) representation of the task service time above can be used to derive recursive formulas for the first two moments of $\mathcal{T}_\mathbf{n}$. The following theorems provide recursive formulas for $T_\mathbf{n}$ and $V_\mathbf{n}$ where we denote

$$\mu = \sum_r \mu_r, \quad \mu_{0,\mathbf{n}} = \gamma_{\max_s n_s} + \sum_{s:n_s>0} \mu_s. \qquad (3)$$

Theorem 1. *For all job allocations $\mathbf{n}$, the following relations hold true*

$$T_\mathbf{n} = \begin{cases} \dfrac{1}{\mu} + \sum_{r=1}^{R} \dfrac{\mu_r}{\mu} T_{\mathbf{n}-\mathbf{e}_r}, & \text{if } n_r > 1 \\[3ex] \dfrac{1}{\mu_{0,\mathbf{n}}} + \dfrac{\gamma_{\max_s n_s}}{\mu_{0,\mathbf{n}}} T_{\mathbf{n}^*} + \sum_{r:n_r>0} \dfrac{\mu_r}{\mu_{0,\mathbf{n}}} T_{\mathbf{n}-\mathbf{e}_r}, & \text{if } \exists r, s : n_r = 0 \land n_s > 1 \\[3ex] \dfrac{1}{\sum\limits_{s:n_s=1} \mu_s} + \sum_{r:n_r=1} \dfrac{\mu_r}{\sum\limits_{s:n_s=1} \mu_s} T_{\mathbf{n}-\mathbf{e}_r}, & \text{if } n_r \leq 1, \forall r \end{cases}$$

$$(4)$$

and

$$
V_{\mathbf{n}} =
\begin{cases}
\dfrac{2}{\mu^2} + \sum_{r=1}^{R} \dfrac{\mu_r}{\mu}\left(V_{\mathbf{n}-\mathbf{e}_r} + 2\dfrac{T_{\mathbf{n}-\mathbf{e}_r}}{\mu}\right), & \text{if } n_r > 1, \forall r \\[2ex]
\dfrac{2}{\mu_{0,\mathbf{n}}^2} + \dfrac{\gamma_{\max_s n_s}}{\mu_{0,\mathbf{n}}}\left(V_{\mathbf{n}^*} + 2\dfrac{T_{\mathbf{n}^*}}{\mu_{0,\mathbf{n}}}\right) + \sum_{r:n_r>0} \dfrac{\mu_r}{\mu_{0,\mathbf{n}}}\left(V_{\mathbf{n}-\mathbf{e}_r} + \dfrac{2T_{\mathbf{n}-\mathbf{e}_r}}{\mu_{0,\mathbf{n}}}\right), \\[1ex]
\qquad \text{if } \exists r, s : n_r = 0 \wedge n_s > 1 \\[2ex]
\dfrac{2}{\left(\sum\limits_{s:n_s=1}\mu_s\right)^2} + \sum_{r:n_r=1} \dfrac{\mu_r}{\sum\limits_{s:n_s=1}\mu_s}\left(V_{\mathbf{n}-\mathbf{e}_r} + \dfrac{2T_{\mathbf{n}-\mathbf{e}_r}}{\sum\limits_{s:n_s=1}\mu_s}\right), & \text{if } n_r \leq 1, \forall r,
\end{cases}
\tag{5}
$$

where $\mathbf{n}^*$ *is given by* (2).

Proof. The above formulas are obtained by applying standard one-step analysis and taking into account the transition rates in Figure 1 of the Markov chain characterizing the task service time distribution.

For more details on the interpretation of the formula above see [4].

We now explicit performance indices formulas of the proposed work-stealing model which are expressed in terms of the results of Theorem 1. Since tasks split into different numbers of jobs, namely $N_k R$ with probability p_k, the mean service time of incoming tasks T is simply obtained by averaging over all possible splits. Assuming, for simplicity, that jobs are equally distributed among processors, we obtain

$$
\begin{aligned}
T &= \mathbb{E}[\textstyle\sum_{k=1}^{K} p_k T_{\mathbf{N}_k}] = \sum_{k=1}^{K} p_k T_{\mathbf{N}_k}. \\
V &= \mathbb{E}[(\textstyle\sum_{k=1}^{K} p_k T_{\mathbf{N}_k})^2] = \sum_{k=1}^{K} p_k^2 V_{\mathbf{N}_k} + \sum_{i,j=1,i\neq j}^{K} p_i p_j T_{\mathbf{N}_i} T_{\mathbf{N}_j}.
\end{aligned}
\tag{6}
$$

Notice that these formulae can be easily extended to the case where jobs do not evenly split among the processors. The mean waiting time W is then given by Pollaczek–Khintchine formula, e.g., [10], yielding

$$
W = 0.5\lambda V/(1 - \lambda T),
\tag{7}
$$

the mean response time is $W + T$, and the mean number of tasks in the system follows by Little's law [10].

3.2 Computational Complexity and Comparison with Global Balance

In this section, we analyze the computational cost of our approach in terms of model input parameters and make a comparison with a classic technique. It is clear that the critical issue is the computation of T and V by means of (6). Let $N_{\max} = \max_{k=1,\dots,K} N_k$. Since $T_{N_{\max},\dots,N_{\max}}$ requires the computation of $T_{N_k,\dots,N_k}$, for all k, the direct computation of T through (6) has the complexity of computing $T_{N_{\max},\ldots,N_{\max}}$. Assuming that one can iterate over set $\Omega(i) := \{\mathbf{n} : \sum_r n_r = i, 0 \leq n_r \leq N_{\max}\}$ in $O(\|\ \Omega(i)\ \|)$ steps (by means, e.g., of recursive calls), the computational requirements of the proposed analysis become $O(RN_{\max}^R)$ for time, and $O(N_{\max}^{R-1})$ for space. The former follows from the fact that we need to (diagonally) span each possible job allocation and for each of them perform $O(R)$ elementary operations, and the latter follows from the fact that we need to store the value of each state reached by a steal. Once T is known, V is obtained at the same computational cost.

The classic global balance technique (see, e.g., [10]) can also be applied to our model to obtain the exact (stationary) solution. Let $(m, \mathbf{n})$ be a state of the proposed work-stealing model as in (1) where $m \geq 0$ and $0 \leq n_r \leq N_{\max} = \max_{k=1,\ldots,K} N_k$. To make global balance feasible and perform the comparison, we consider a state space truncation of process (1) which limits to M the number of tasks in the system. For a given λ, it is known that such truncation yields nearly exact results if M is sufficiently large (note that M should be much larger than $RN_{\max}$). The resulting complexity is given by the computational requirement of the solution of a linear system composed of $O(MN_{\max}^R)$ equations, which is orders of magnitude worse than our approach.

4   Bounding Analysis

Even though the analytical framework introduced in previous section has computational complexity much lower than the one of standard global balance, it remains computationally impractical when tasks split in many jobs or when systems with many processors are considered. We now propose an approximation of the task service time distribution which provides efficient bounds on both T and V, and, as a consequence, on the mean task waiting time W. These bounds are obtained by assuming that the communication delay for transferring jobs among the processors tends to zero, i.e., $\gamma_i \to \infty$, $\forall i$. This assumption is motivated by the fact that the communication delay is often much smaller than the service time of each job (multiprocessor systems are usually interconnected by very fast buses). In the following, all variables related to the case where $\gamma_i = \infty$ will be denoted with the superindex L. Consider the two-processor case and, thus, the state diagram of Figure 2 (on the left). With respect to state $(n_1, 0)$, we observe that if $\gamma_{n_1} \to \infty$, then with probability 1 the next state becomes $(\lceil n_1/2 \rceil, \lfloor n_1/2 \rfloor)$ and the sojourn time in state $(n_1, 0)$ tends to zero so that these states become vanishing states. Figure 2 (on the right) depicts the resulting Markov chain.

Theorem 2. *Under the foregoing assumptions, for all* $\mathbf{n}$, *$T_{\mathbf{n}}^L \leq_{st} T_{\mathbf{n}}$. This implies* $T_{\mathbf{n}}^L \leq T_{\mathbf{n}}$ *and* $V_{\mathbf{n}}^L \leq V_{\mathbf{n}}$.

We refer to [4] for the proof, involving a coupling argument.

In the transition matrix of this new Markov chain, we observe that the sojourn times of each state (n_1, n_2) such that $n_1, n_2 \geq 1$ are i.i.d. random variables exponentially distributed with mean $1/\mu$. Since any path from initial state (N, N) to absorbing state $(1, 1)$ involves $2N - 2$ steps, we conclude that the distribution of the time needed to reach state $(1, 1)$ from (N, N) is Erlang with rate parameter μ and $2N - 2$ phases. Including the sojourn times of states $(1, 1)$, $(1, 0)$ and $(0, 1)$, the task service time distribution becomes $T^L_{N,N} =_{db}$ Erlang$(\mu, 2N-2)+\max\{X_1, X_2\}$, where X_r denotes an exponential random variable with mean μ_r^{-1}. It is easy to see that this observation holds even in the more general case where $R \geq 2$ and tasks can split in different numbers of jobs. The resulting task service time distribution becomes (when $\gamma_i \to \infty$)

$$T^L =_{db} \sum_{k=1}^{K} p_k T^L_{\mathbf{N}_k} =_{db} \sum_{k=1}^{K} p_k \left(\text{Erlang}(\mu, N_k R - R) + \max_{r=1,\dots,R}\{X_r\} \right). \quad (8)$$

Therefore, as shown in (6),

$$T^L = T_1 + \sum_{k=1}^{K} p_k \frac{N_k R - R}{\mu}, \quad V^L = \sum_{k=1}^{K} p_k^2 V^L_{\mathbf{N}_k} + \sum_{\substack{i,j=1 \\ i \neq j}}^{K} p_i p_j T^L_{\mathbf{N}_i} T^L_{\mathbf{N}_j}, \quad (9)$$

$$\text{where} \quad V^L_{\mathbf{N}_k} = \mathbb{E}[(T^L_{\mathbf{N}_k})^2] = \frac{N_k R - R + (N_k R - R)^2}{\mu^2} + V_1 + 2\frac{N_k R - R}{\mu} T_1 \quad (10)$$

$k = 1, \dots, K$, are lower bounds on the first two moments of T by means of Theorem 2. In turn, the mean waiting W straightforwardly becomes a lower bound by means of (7).

In (9), the computational complexity of T^L and V^L is then dominated by the computation of T_1 (note that V_1 is obtained at the same computational cost as T_1). By means of Formula (4), this is given by $O(R2^R + K)$ for time and $O(R+K)$ for space. Therefore, the computational complexity of the proposed bounds becomes independent of $N_{\max}$. Even though our bounding analysis has a complexity which is exponential in the number of processors, we observe that multiprocessor embedded systems are usually composed of a limited number of processors. In our context, this makes our bounds efficient.

Homogeneous Processors In many cases of practical interest, multiprocessor systems are composed of identical processors. In our model, this implies $\mu_1 = \dots = \mu_R$. In this particular case, we observe that very efficient expressions can be derived for T_1 and V_1. Noting that T_1 is the maximum of R i.i.d. exponential random variables, it is a well-known result of extreme-value statistics, e.g., [12], that $T_1 = \mu_1^{-1} \sum_{r=1}^{R} r^{-1}$ and $V_1 = \mu_1^{-2} \sum_{r=1}^{R} r^{-2} + T_1^2$, which are computationally much more efficient than Formulae (4) and (5).

5   Numerical Results

In this section, we numerically assess the accuracy of our approach. Numerical results are presented relative to three different sets of experiments. First, we

Table 2. Parameters used in the validation of the proposed bound

	Interval		Value
No. of processors (R)	$\{2,3,4\}$	Distr. of task splits (p_k)	$1/K$
Proc. service rates (μ_r)	$[0.1, 10]$	No. of jobs for type-k task (N_k)	$k \cdot 20$
Task splits (K)	$\{2, \ldots, 10\}$	Communication delay (γ_i^{-1})	$\lfloor \frac{i}{2} \rfloor / (10\frac{\mu}{R})$

perform a validation of the proposed bounds on a wide test-bed of randomly generated models to assess the general quality of the percentage relative errors. In this setting, we distinguish between the homogeneous and heterogeneous case. Then, we show asymptotic performances of our bounds when $N_{\max}$ is large.

To assess the general accuracy of the proposed bound with respect to the exact model solution, we consider a test bed of $3,000$ randomly-generated models, and for each test we compute

$$100\% \cdot (W_{exact} - W_{bound})/W_{exact}, \tag{11}$$

i.e., the percentage relative error on mean waiting time. Instead of considering the errors of T_{bound} and V_{bound}, we directly consider the error (11) because it is much less robust than the formers by means of (7). Exact model solutions have been obtained through the analysis presented in Section 3. The input parameters used to validate the proposed bounds are shown in Table 2. Since real-world embedded systems are composed of a limited number of processors, in our tests we consider $R \leq 4$. We did not consider tests with a larger size of $\max_{k=1,\ldots,K} N_k$ because of the computational requirements needed to obtain the exact solution and the consequent cost of computing robust results for the large number of test cases. The communication delay γ_i^{-1} is assumed to be linear in the number of task to transfer and we also assume that the time needed to transfer one job is ten times lower than the mean service time of that job. We now perform a parametric analysis by varying the mean task arrival rate λ such that the mean system utilization, i.e., $U = \lambda T$ (see, e.g., [15]), range between 0.1 (light-load) and 0.9 (heavy-load). We first conduct a numerical analysis assuming that the processors are homogeneous. In Figure 3 (on the left) we illustrate the quality of the error (11) by means of the Matlab *boxplot* command, where each box is referred to an average of 3,000 models. In this figure, our bounds provide very accurate results with an average error less than 2%. As the system utilization U increases, a slight loss of accuracy occurs due to the analytical expression of Formula (7) which makes the mean waiting time W very sensitive to small errors on T as U grows to unity. However, in the worst-case where $U = 0.9$, our bound provides again a very small average error, i.e., 3.4%. Also, our bounds are robust because the variance of the waiting-time errors is very small.

We now focus on the quality of error (11) within the same setting above but in the heterogeneous case, i.e., assuming that all processors are identical but one, which is faster than the other ones. We assume that the *speed-up* of the fastest processor, i.e., the ratio between its mean service rate and the one of

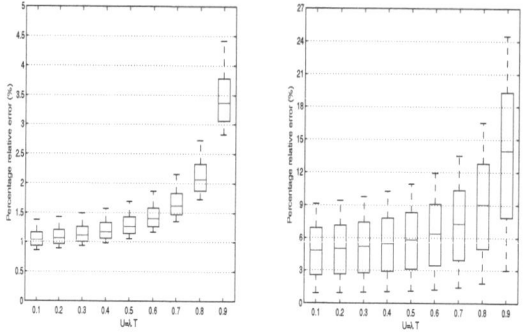
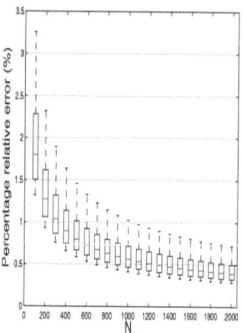

Fig. 3. Boxplot of errors (11) in the cases of homogeneous (on the left) and heterogeneous (on the right) processors

Fig. 4. Boxplot of errors (11) when tasks split in a large number of jobs

the other processors, is a random variable uniformly distributed in range $(1, 2]$ (in real-world embedded systems, the typical speed ratio is below 1.5). Figure 3 (on the right) displays the error (11), where each box refers to the average over 3,000 models. Again, our bounds are accurate even though there is a slight loss of accuracy with respect to previous cases. This because the fastest processor performs more steals than in the homogeneous case so that the overall communication delay becomes less negligible. However, the average error remains small and it assesses to 7%. The fact that the error (11) is increasing in U finds the same explanation discussed above for the homogeneous case.

We now assume that tasks split in a very large number of jobs (see Section 2). Due to the expensive computational effort of calculating the exact model solution, we limit such analysis to two-processor systems, i.e., $R = 2$. Within the input parameters shown in Table 2, we perform a parametric analysis by increasing the mean number of jobs per task. We consider homogeneous processors and assume $K = 1$, which means that tasks always split in $N := RN_1$ jobs, where N_1 varies from 100 to 2,000 with step 100, i.e., a task can split in 4,000 jobs at most. To better stress the accuracy of the bounds, we consider the worst case where the input arrival rate λ is such that $U = \lambda T$ ranges in $[0.7, 0.9]$ (see Figure 3). In Figure 4 we show the quality of error (11) with the Matlab boxplot command, where each box is referred to 1,000 models. Our bounds yield nearly exact results when tasks split in a large number of jobs and the average error decreases as N_1 increases. When $N_1 \geq 400$, the average error becomes lower than 1%. Within the large number of test cases, we note that the proposed bounds are also robust.

6   Optimal Number of Processors

In this section, we show how the proposed analysis can be applied in the context of optimization. Here, the objective is to minimize infrastructural costs (energy consumption), determined by both the speed and the number of processors, while satisfying constraints on waiting times. We assume that the task arrival rate λ is given and that the mean waiting time of tasks must not exceed , $\overline{W}$ units of time. Our optimization model applies at *run-time*, and must be re-executed whenever λ (or $\overline{W}$) changes to determine the new optimal number of active processors and their speed. The latters can be adjusted by means of *frequency scaling* threads. We also assume the case of homogeneous processors because it often happens in practice. Therefore, the optimization is obtained by solving the following mathematical program

$$\min Rc(\mu_1), \quad \text{subject to: } W(\mu_1, R) \leq \overline{W}, \ \mu_1 \in \mathbb{R}^+, \ R \in \mathbb{N}, \qquad (12)$$

where $c(\mu_1)$ is the *cost* of using a single processor having processing speed μ_1. If the cost corresponds to the instantaneous power consumption, then for each processor, the cost can be approximated by $c(\mu_1) = A\mu_1^{\alpha}$, where A is a constant and $\alpha \geq 1$, typically $2 \leq \alpha \leq 3$ for most circuit models (see e.g., [13]). The solution of (12) provides the optimal speed and number of processors w.r.t. energy use, in order to satisfy the performance requirement. Since operating speeds of processors can be controlled by power management threads, in our model these are assumed to be positive real numbers. Since the exact solution of (12) is computationally difficult we exploit the bounds shown in previous sections to obtain an approximate solution in closed form. In this homogeneous case, our bounds are very tight (see Section 5) so that the following does not really depend on work stealing but rather on some form of an ideal parallelism. Noting that with a fixed R, say $\overline{R}$, both $c(\mu_1)$ and $W(\mu_1, \overline{R})$ are convex and, respectively, monotonically increasing and decreasing in μ_1, the structure of program (12) ensures that the optimum is achieved when $W(\mu_1, \overline{R}) = \overline{W}$. Adopting formulas (9), this yields a polynomial with degree two and with only one positive root:

$$\mu_1^*(\overline{R}) = \frac{1}{2\overline{R}} \left(\lambda T(1) + \sqrt{(\lambda T(1))^2 + 2\lambda V(1)/\overline{W}} \right) \qquad (13)$$

where $T(1)$ and $V(1)$ are given by (9) with $R = \overline{R}$ and $\mu_r = 1/\overline{R}$, $\forall r$. For R fixed, Equation (13) explicits the dependence between $\overline{W}$ and the optimal processing rate: as $\overline{W}$ decreases (being positive), μ_1 must increase with the power of a square root. This immediately shows the benefit of work-stealing with respect to, for instance, a "no-steal" policy, which makes μ_1 increases linearly as $\overline{W}$ decreases. Also note that the optimal speed of the processor does not depend on the parameter α so that it is insensitive to the exact model of energy consumption (we only use the fact that this energy use is convex in the processor speed).

To determine the global optimum of (12), we iterate (13) over R. Within parameters of practical interest, in Figure 5 we plot the values of $Rc(\mu_1^*(R))/c(\mu_1^*(1))$ and $\mu_1^*(R)/\mu_1^*(1)$, by varying R only from 1 to 6 (we remark that R is small in the context of embedded systems). These functions represent, respectively, the benefit, in terms of costs, of adopting R processors operating with the work-stealing algorithm with respect to the optimal single-processor configuration, and how much the rate of service of each processor varies (as R varies) to guarantee the waiting time requirement in (12). We consider two scenarios: on the left (on the right), we

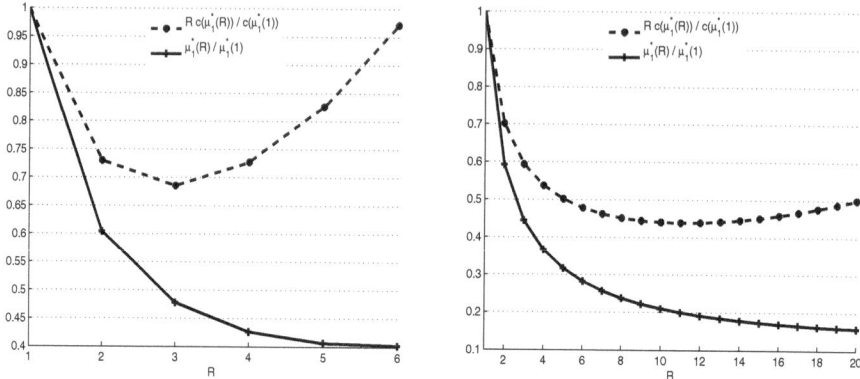

Fig. 5. Cost benefits of the work-stealing algorithm with respect to the optimal single-processor configuration when $\lambda = 1$ jobs per unit of time, $W = 1$, $K = 1$ (on the left) and $K = 10$ (on the right), each task generates $N_k = 100k$ jobs with probability $1/K$, and the cost parameter is $\alpha = 2$

assume that tasks split in a relatively small (large) number of jobs. In any case, we impose $\overline{W} = \lambda^{-1} = 1$ time unit because embedded systems are usually aimed to perform on-the-fly real-time operations. Within these parameters, Little's law [10] ensures that the mean number of waiting tasks is one. In the figures, we see that work-stealing yields a remarkable improvement in terms of costs even when $R = 2$, for which a cost reduction of nearly 30% is achieved in both cases. This is obtained with two (identical) processors having speeds reduced of a factor of nearly 1.7. In the first scenario, we observe that the optimum is achieved with $R = 3$ processors. For $R > 3$, the R term in the objective function becomes non-negligible. In the second scenario, a much higher number of processors is needed to make the objective function increase because tasks generate a much larger workload. In fact, to guarantee the waiting time constraint, in this case processors must have a much higher service rate than the corresponding ones of the previous case, and this impacts significantly on the term μ_1^α of the objective function. In this case, the optimum is achieved with $R = 12$ processors, and even when $R = 2$, work stealing yields a non-negligible cost reduction.

7   Adapting the Fraction of Jobs to Steal

In previous sections, we analyzed the performance of the work-stealing algorithm which steals half of the jobs from some processor queue. However, other stealing functions can be considered, and the proposed framework lets us evaluate their impact by slightly adapting the formulas in Theorem 1. We now numerically show that some gains can be obtained by adapting the amount of jobs stolen.

Considering job allocation **n** and assuming that processor s is the most loaded one, one could consider the following stealing functions which balance the mean

Table 3. Evaluation of the stealing strategies L and G with respect to the *classic* one

	Linear		Logarithmic		Constant	
	Err_i^1	Err_i^2	Err_i^1	Err_i^2	Err_i^1	Err_i^2
$i = L$	10.30%	10.37%	-3.64%	-3.53%	-3.4%	-3.43%
$i = G$	-8.80%	-8.94%	7.14%	7.11%	11.2%	11.46%

load among processors: i) *Adaptive Local (L)*: an idle processor (say r) steals $\alpha(\mathbf{n}) = n_s \cdot \mu_r / (\mu_r + \mu_s)$ jobs from s, and ii) *Adaptive Global (G)*: an idle processor (say r) steals $\alpha(\mathbf{n}) = n_s \cdot \mu_r / \mu$ jobs from s. The concept behind L is to steal the weighted fraction of jobs which balances the mean load between the processor which steals and the one which is stolen. In this manner, after a steal different processors tend to finish the execution of their jobs at nearly the same time with no further steals, and, thus, the overall communication cost is essentially reduced. Similarly, the policy G steals the weighted fraction of jobs which balances the mean global mean load between all processors. We now numerically evaluate the two strategies above within three different scenarios. We first assume that stealing costs are linear in the number of jobs to transfer. Secondly, we consider the case where the jobs to steal (in the FIFO queue of some processor) have consecutive memory addresses, so that a logarithmic (in $\alpha(\mathbf{n})$) amount of data can be transferred, i.e., the memory address of the initial job and the number of jobs to transfer. Finally, we consider the ideal case where the stealing cost is a constant. In the linear case, we have $\gamma_{\alpha(\mathbf{n})}^{-1} = \alpha(\mathbf{n}) / \left(10 \frac{\mu}{R}\right)$ (see Section 5), in the logarithmic case, $\gamma_{\alpha(\mathbf{n})}^{-1} = \log_2(\alpha(\mathbf{n})) / \left(10 \frac{\mu}{R}\right)$, and, in the constant case $\gamma_{\alpha(\mathbf{n})}^{-1} = 1$. Within the parameters of Table 2 and the settings above, in Table 3 we show the percentage relative errors $\mathrm{Err}_i^1 = 100 \cdot (C_i - C_{1/2})/C_{1/2}$ and $\mathrm{Err}_i^2 = 100 \cdot (U_i - U_{1/2})/U_{1/2}$, averaged over 2,000 random models, where C_x and U_x are respectively the first and second moment of the total time spent for stealing where $x \in \{L, G, 1/2\}$ refers to the stealing strategy. In the linear case, strategy G is better (on average) than both L and the strategy stealing halves of jobs (i.e. $i = 1/2$) yielding a 8.8% reduction in both moments of communication cost. However, this is not true in the other cases, where L turns out to be the best. Hence, the goodness of one policy strongly depends on the structure of communication costs and the impact of adopting a different strategy is not immediate to understand without our analytical framework, which is well-suited to evaluate new strategies. In any case, we notice that $C_{1/2}$ and $U_{1/2}$ tend to be between the corresponding values for the strategies L and G. The impact of the results in Table 3 on waiting times is negligible because the communication cost of stealing one job is small if compared to its execution time (see [4]).

8   Conclusions

In this paper, we analyzed the performance of parallel stream computations on a multiprocessor architecture implementing the work-stealing principle. Our work can be extended in several directions. Firstly, we leave as future work the development of new analyses in some limiting regime, e.g., when both N and R grow to infinity, secondly, the analysis of the task service time distribution when *state-dependent* service rates are considered, and, finally, the modeling of task service times when jobs have dependencies.

Acknowledgements. The authors are grateful to Jean-Louis Roch for fruitful discussions on work stealing.

References

1. Description of traviata architecture (2008),
   http://www.stlinux.com/drupal/hw/boards/mb426
2. kaapi software (MOAIS, INRIA project-team) (2008),
   http://gforge.inria.fr/projects/kaapi
3. Acar, U.A., Blelloch, G.E., Blumofe, R.D.: The data locality of work stealing. In: SPAA 2000: Proc. of the twelfth annual ACM symposium on Parallel algorithms and architectures, pp. 1–12. ACM, New York (2000)
4. Anselmi, J., Gaujal, B.: Performance analysis of work stealing for streaming systems and optimizations. Technical Report 6988, INRIA (2009)
5. Arora, N.S., Blumofe, R.D., Plaxton, C.G.: Thread scheduling for multiprogrammed multiprocessors. Theory Comput. Syst. 34(2), 115–144 (2001)
6. Bender, M.A., Rabib, M.O.: Online scheduling of parallel programs on heterogeneous systems with applications to cilk. Theory of Computing Systems 35, 289–304 (2002); Special issue on SPA00
7. Berenbrink, P., Friedetzky, T., Goldberg, L.A.: The natural work-stealing algorithm is stable. In: Proc. of the 42nd FOCS, pp. 178–187. IEEE, Los Alamitos (2001)
8. Bernard, J., Roch, J.-L., Traore, D.: Processor-oblivious parallel stream computations. In: 16th Euromicro International Conference on Parallel, Distributed and network-based Processing, Toulouse, France (February 2008)
9. Blumofe, R.D., Leiserson, C.E.: Scheduling multithreaded computations by work stealing. Journal of the ACM 46(5), 720–748 (1999)
10. Bolch, G., Greiner, S., de Meer, H., Trivedi, K.S.: Queueing Networks and Markov Chains. Wiley-Int., Chichester (2005)
11. Frigo, M., Leiserson, C.E., Randall, K.H.: The implementation of the cilk-5 multithreaded language. In: PLDI 1998: Proc. of SIGPLAN 1998 conf. on Progr. lang. design and implementation, pp. 212–223. ACM, New York (1998)
12. Gumbel, E.J.: Statistics of extremes. Columbia University Press, New York (1958)
13. Rabaey, J., Pedram, M.: Low Power Design Methodologies. Kluwer Academic Publishers, Dordrecht (1996)
14. Jafar, S., Gautier, T., Krings, A., Roch, J.-L.: A checkpoint/recovery model for heterogeneous dataflow computations using work-stealing. In: Proc. European Conf. Parallel Processing (EuroPar 2005), pp. 675–684 (2005)
15. Lazowska, E.D., Zahorjan, J., Graham, G.S., Sevcik, K.C.: Quantitative system performance. Prentice-Hall, Upper Saddle River (1984)
16. Neill, D., Wierman, A.: On the benefits of work stealing in shared-memory multiprocessors, http://www.cs.cmu.edu/~acw/15740/paper.pdf
17. Squillante, M.S., Nelson, R.D.: Analysis of task migration in shared-memory multiprocessor scheduling. SIGMETRICS Perf. Eval. Rev. 19(1), 143–155 (1991)

Not All Fair Probabilistic Schedulers Are Equivalent*

Ioannis Chatzigiannakis[1], Shlomi Dolev[2], Sándor P. Fekete[3],
Othon Michail[1], and Paul G. Spirakis[1]

[1] Research Academic Computer Technology Institute (RACTI), and Computer
Engineering and Informatics Department (CEID), University of Patras, 26500,
Patras, Greece
[2] Department of Computer Science, Ben-Gurion University of the Negev, Israel 84105
[3] Department of Computer Science, Braunschweig University of Technology,
Braunschweig, Germany
{ichatz,michailo,spirakis}@cti.gr, dolev@cs.bgu.ac.il, s.fekete@tu-bs.de

Abstract. We propose a novel, generic definition of *probabilistic schedulers* for population protocols. We then identify the *consistent* probabilistic schedulers, and prove that any consistent scheduler that assigns a non-zero probability to any transition $i \rightarrow j$, where i and j are configurations satisfying $i \neq j$, is fair with probability 1. This is a new theoretical framework that aims to simplify proving specific probabilistic schedulers fair. In this paper we propose two new schedulers, the *State Scheduler* and the *Transition Function Scheduler*. Both possess the significant capability of being *protocol-aware*, i.e. they can assign transition probabilities based on information concerning the underlying protocol. By using our framework we prove that the proposed schedulers, and also the *Random Scheduler* that was defined by Angluin et al. [2], are all fair with probability 1. Finally, we define and study *equivalence* between schedulers w.r.t. *performance* and *correctness* and prove that there exist fair probabilistic schedulers that are not equivalent w.r.t. to performance and others that are not equivalent w.r.t. correctness.

Keywords: population protocol, probabilistic scheduler, fair scheduler, fairness, communicating automata, sensor network.

1 Introduction

Recently, Angluin et al. [2,3] introduced the notion of a computation by a *Population Protocol* to model distributed systems in which individual agents are extremely limited and can be represented as finite-state machines. In their model, complex behavior of the system as a whole emerges from the rules governing pairwise interaction of the agents. The computation is carried out by a collection of agents, each of which receives a piece of the input. These agents move

---

* This work has been partially supported by the ICT Programme of the European Union under contract number ICT-2008-215270 (FRONTS).

T. Abdelzaher, M. Raynal, and N. Santoro (Eds.): OPODIS 2009, LNCS 5923, pp. 33–47, 2009.
© Springer-Verlag Berlin Heidelberg 2009

around and information can be exchanged between two agents whenever they come into contact with (or sufficiently close to) each other. The goal is to ensure that every agent can eventually output the value that is to be computed.

An execution of a protocol proceeds from the initial configuration by interactions between pairs of agents. In a real distributed execution, interactions could take place simultaneously, but, when writing down an execution, simultaneous interactions can be ordered arbitrarily. Angluin et al. think of the order in which pairs of agents come into contact and interact as being chosen by an adversary. From a particular system configuration, the adversary decides which of the possible different interactions will be selected; essentially, it decides the computation sequence (i.e. schedule of interactions). So, the designer's goal is to make protocols work correctly under any schedule the adversary may choose.

In such models there may exist diverging (infinite) schedules of interactions such that during their execution some *event becomes possible infinitely often* but it has not an infinite number of occurrences. If the adversary selects such a sequence, it will lead the system to unfair situations, where although an event is realizable infinitely often, it never occurs because conflicts are resolved in a non equitable manner. To deal with these issues, a **fairness** restriction is imposed on the adversarial scheduler: the scheduler is not allowed to avoid a possible step forever. The fairness constraint allows the scheduler to behave arbitrarily for an arbitrarily long period of time, but does require that it behave nicely eventually. Therefore correctness is a property that can be satisfied eventually.

Fairness relative to a set of states is important since most of the "interesting" system properties express reachability relations of some set of states [16]. In other words, fairness becomes crucial when a property is to be proven in formal systems based on non-deterministic models. In this work we try to apprehend the concept of fairness in the *basic population protocol model*. To do so, we focus on the class of *probabilistic schedulers* proposed in [2,3], in which the scheduler selects randomly the next pair to interact. We define two new adversaries that are bound by the fairness constraint of [2]. The "reasonable" scheduling policies that they introduce lead to significantly different performance characterizations for some protocols well studied in the relevant literature. We show that the current notion of fairness gives rise to many difficulties in studying not only performance but also protocol correctness.

In the area initiated by the proposal of the *Population Protocol* (PP) model [2] much work has been devoted to the, now, well-known fact that the set of computable predicates of the basic (complete interaction graph) PP model and most of its variants is exactly equal or closely related to the set of *semilinear predicates*. Moreover, in [2,3], the *Probabilistic Population Protocol* model was proposed, in which the scheduler selects randomly and uniformly the next pair to interact. More recent work has concentrated on performance, supported by this random scheduling assumption. Additionally, several extensions of the basic model have been proposed in order to more accurately reflect the requirements of practical systems. In [1], Angluin et al. studied what properties of restricted communication graphs are stably computable, gave protocols for some of them, and proposed a model extension with *stabilizing inputs*. In [11] the *Mediated Population Protocol* (MPP) model was proposed that extends the PP model with communication links that are able to store states. The MPP model was proved to be computationally stronger than the PP model and it was observed that it is especially capable of deciding graph properties, concerning the communication graph on which the protocol runs. In [9] the decidable graph properties by MPPs where studied for the first time and it was proven that connectivity cannot be decided by the new model. Unfortunatelly, the class of decidable graph languages by MPPs remains open. Finally, some works incorporated agent failures and gave to the agents slightly increased memory capacity. For the interested reader, [7] and [12] constitute nice introductions to the subject.

In Section 2 we provide a brief introduction to the PP model. In Section 3.1 we give a novel generic definition of *probabilistic schedulers*. We then study separately those that are *consistent*, i.e. those that never change the one-step transition probabilities between configurations, and state and prove a theorem that constitutes a useful tool for proving that a specific probabilistic scheduler is fair. In 3.2 we present the *protocol-oblivious Random Scheduler* as was proposed in [2] and define two new schedulers that are *protocol-aware*, namely the *State Scheduler* and *Transition Function Scheduler*. We then use our tool and prove that all these schedulers are fair with probability 1. In Section 3.3 we define *time equivalence* and *computational equivalence* of two probabilistic fair schedulers w.r.t. some population protocol $\mathcal{A}$. In Section 4 we study the performance of the OR Protocol (based on an example of [7]) when faced with our schedulers. This makes it evident that the fairness condition alone, as has been defined by Angluin et al. in [2], is not sufficient to guarantee the construction of protocols that perform well under all kinds of allowed schedulers. It seems that a protocol may perform optimally under some fair scheduler but at the same time reach its worst-case performance under some other, also provably fair, scheduler. In other words, we show that there exists a protocol for which two fair probabilistic schedulers are not time equivalent. Thus, either some stronger definition of fairness needs to be proposed or there needs to be some other way to formally exclude protocol-aware schedulers and other (yet unknown) types of schedulers that can be adjusted to lead to divergent performance scenarios. In Section 5 we show that, due to the weakness characterizing the selected notion of fairness, not only performance but also protocol correctness depends greatly on the underlying scheduler. To do so, we consider the Majority Protocol that was proven correct with high probability in [6] (if certain rational assumptions are satisfied), and study its behavior under the Transition Function Scheduler. We show that the Majority Protocol has a great probability of failure if the underlying scheduler is assumed to be the protocol-aware Transition Function Scheduler, which in turn implies that the Transition Function Scheduler is not computationally equivalent to the Random Scheduler w.r.t. the Majority Protocol. Finally, in Section 6 we discuss some promising future research directions.

2   Population Protocols

A *population protocol* (PP) is a 6-tuple (X, Y, Q, I, O, δ), where X, Y, and Q are all finite sets, and X is the *input alphabet*, Y is the *output alphabet*, Q is the set of *states*, $I : X \rightarrow Q$ is the *input function*, $O : Q \rightarrow Y$ is the *output function*, and $\delta : Q \times Q \rightarrow Q \times Q$ is the *transition function*. If $\delta(a, b) = (a', b')$, we call $(a, b) \rightarrow (a', b')$ a *transition* and we define $\delta_1(a, b) = a'$ and $\delta_2(a, b) = b'$.

A population protocol $\mathcal{A} = (X, Y, Q, I, O, \delta)$ runs on a *communication graph* (also known as *interaction graph*) $G = (V, E)$ (G is here assumed to be directed and without multiple edges or self-loops). From now on we will use the letter n to denote the cardinality of V (size of the population). Initially, all agents (i.e. the elements of V) receive a global start signal, sense their environment and each one receives an input symbol from X. After receiving their input symbol, all agents apply the input function to it and go to their initial state (e.g. all agents that received $\sigma \in X$ begin with initial state $I(\sigma) \in Q$). An adversary scheduler selects in each step a directed pair of agents $(u, v) \in E$, where $u, v \in V$ and $u \neq v$, to interact. Assume that the scheduler selects the pair (u, v), that the current states of u and v are $a, b \in Q$, respectively, and that $\delta(a, b) = (a', b')$. Agent u plays the role of the *initiator* in the interaction (u, v) and v that of the *responder*. When interacting, u and v apply the transition function to their directed pair of states, and, as a result, u goes to a' and v to b' (both update their states according to δ, and specifically, the initiator applies δ_1 while the responder δ_2).

A *configuration* is a snapshot of the population states. Formally, a configuration is a mapping $C : V \rightarrow Q$ specifying the state of each agent in the population. C_0 is the initial configuration (for simplicity we assume that all agents apply the input function at the same time) and, for all $u \in V$, $C_0(u) = I(x(u))$, where $x(u)$ is the input symbol sensed by agent u. Let C and C' be configurations, and let u, v be distinct agents. We say that C goes to C' via encounter $e = (u, v)$, denoted $C \overset{e}{\rightarrow} C'$, if $C'(u) = \delta_1(C(u), C(v))$, $C'(v) = \delta_2(C(u), C(v))$, and $C'(w) = C(w)$ for all $w \in V - \{u, v\}$, that is, C' is the result of the interaction of the pair (u, v) under configuration C and is the same as C except for the fact that the states of u, v have been updated according to δ_1 and δ_2, respectively. We say that C can go to C' in one step, denoted $C \rightarrow C'$, if $C \overset{e}{\rightarrow} C'$ for some encounter $e \in E$. We write $C \overset{*}{\rightarrow} C'$ if there is a sequence of configurations $C = C_0, C_1, \ldots, C_t = C'$, such that $C_i \rightarrow C_{i+1}$ for all i, $0 \leq i < t$, in which case we say that C' is *reachable* from C.

3   Schedulers

3.1   Fair Probabilistic Schedulers

As defined in [3], the *transition graph* $T(\mathcal{A}, G)$ of a protocol $\mathcal{A}$ running on a communication graph G (or just T when no confusion arises) is a directed graph whose nodes are all possible configurations and whose edges are all possible one-step transitions between those configurations.

Definition 1. *A probabilistic scheduler, w.r.t. a transition graph $T(\mathcal{A}, G)$, defines for each configuration $C \in V(T)$ an infinite sequence of probability distributions of the form $(d_1^C, d_2^C, \ldots)$, over the set $\Gamma^+(C) = \{C' \mid C \to C'\}$ (the possibly closed out-neighbourhood of C), where $d_t^C : \Gamma^+(C) \to [0,1]$ and such that $\sum_{C' \in \Gamma^+(C)} d_t^C(C') = 1$ holds, for all t and C.*

The initial configuration C_0 depends only on the values sensed by the population and, in particular, it is formed by their images under the input function. So, for the time being, we can assume that C_0 is selected in a deterministic manner. Let C_t denote the configuration selected by the scheduler at step t (the configuration of the system after t selections of the scheduler and applications of the transition function). Assume that it is the lth time that C_t is encountered during the execution so far; then a probabilistic scheduler selects C_{t+1} randomly, according to the distribution $d_l^{C_t}$. In other words, d_l^C denotes the probability distribution over $\Gamma^+(C)$ when C is encountered for the lth time.

Definition 2. *We call a probabilistic scheduler consistent, w.r.t. a transition graph $T(\mathcal{A}, G)$, if for all configurations $C \in V(T)$, it holds that $d^C = d_1^C = d_2^C = \ldots$, which, in words, means that any time the scheduler encounters configuration C it chooses the next configuration with the same probability distribution d^C over $\Gamma^+(C)$, and this holds for all C (each with its own distribution).*

From now on, and when no confusion arises, we shall use the letters i and j not only to denote configuration indices but also to denote configurations themselves. Note that a consistent probabilistic scheduler for $T(\mathcal{A}, G)$ is simply a labeling $P : E(T) \to [0,1]$ on the arcs of T, such that for any $i \in V(T)$, $\sum_{j \in \Gamma^+(i)} P(i,j) = 1$. So, any time a consistent scheduler encounters a configuration i, it selects the next configuration j according to the probability distribution defined by the labels of the arcs leaving from i. Note that in the latter case, if we remove from T all $e \in E(T)$ where $P(e) = 0$ then the resulting graph D is the underlying graph of a finite Markov chain where the state space is $\mathcal{C} = Q^V$ (all possible configurations) and for all $i, j \in \mathcal{C}$, if $i \to j$ then $\mathbb{P}_{ij} = P(i,j)$, i.e. equal to the label of arc (i,j), otherwise $\mathbb{P}_{ij} = 0$.

A strongly connected component of a directed graph is *final* iff no arc leads from a node in the component to a node outside. A *configuration* is final iff it belongs to a final strongly connected component of the transition graph.

An *execution* is a finite or infinite sequence of configurations $C_0, C_1, C_2, \ldots$, where C_0 is an initial configuration and $C_i \to C_{i+1}$, for all $i \geq 0$. An infinite execution is *fair* if for every possible transition $C \to C'$, if C occurs infinitely often in the execution then C' also occurs infinitely often. A *computation* is an infinite fair execution.

Let y_C, where $y_C(u) = O(C(u))$ for all $u \in V$, denote the output (assignment) of configuration C. We say that a computation of a population protocol $\mathcal{A}$ *stabilizes* to output y_C if it contains a configuration C such that for all C' reachable from C we have that $y_{C'} = y_C$.

Theorem 1. *Let $\Xi = C_0, C_1, \ldots$ be an infinite execution of $\mathcal{A}$ on G, $\mathcal{F}_\Xi$ be the set of configurations that occur infinitely often in Ξ, and $T_{\mathcal{F}_\Xi}$ be the subgraph of*

$T(\mathcal{A}, G)$ induced by $\mathcal{F}_\Xi$. Ξ is a computation (i.e. it is additionally fair) iff $T_{\mathcal{F}_\Xi}$ is a final strongly connected component of $T(\mathcal{A}, G)$.

Proof. The "only if" part was proven in [3]. We prove here the "if" part. Assume that $T_{\mathcal{F}_\Xi}$ is a final strongly connected component of $T(\mathcal{A}, G)$ and that Ξ is not fair (i.e. that the statement of the "if" part does not hold). Then there exists some configuration $C \in \mathcal{F}_\Xi$ (i.e. appearing infinitely often) and a $C' \notin \mathcal{F}_\Xi$ such that $C \to C'$. But this contradicts the fact that $T_{\mathcal{F}_\Xi}$ is final.   □

We now keep the preceding definitions of Ξ, $T(\mathcal{A}, G)$, $\mathcal{F}_\Xi$, $T_{\mathcal{F}_\Xi}$, but additionally assume a consistent scheduler.

Theorem 2. *If for all $i \in \mathcal{F}_\Xi$ and all configurations j s.t. $i \to j$ it holds that $\mathbb{P}_{ij} > 0$, then Ξ is a computation with probability 1.*

Proof. Because i is persistent and all its successor configurations j may occur in one step from i with non-zero probability it follows that those j are also persistent with probability 1, i.e. they also occur infinitely often in Ξ, thus Ξ is a computation with probability 1, by definition.   □

Definition 3. *A scheduler S is fair if for any protocol $\mathcal{A}$, any communication graph G, and any infinite execution Ξ of $\mathcal{A}$ on G caused by S, Ξ is also a computation (i.e. additionally fair).*

Intuitively a scheduler is fair if it always leads to computations.

Theorem 3. *Any consistent scheduler, for which it holds that $\mathbb{P}_{ij} > 0$, for any protocol $\mathcal{A}$, any communication graph G, and all configurations $i, j \in V(T(\mathcal{A}, G))$ where $i \to j$ and $i \neq j$, is fair with probability 1.*

Proof. First of all, note that the underlying Markov chain graph of such a scheduler is the transition graph without possibly some self-loops. Assume that the statement does not hold. Then the probability that a specific infinite execution Ξ of some protocol $\mathcal{A}$ on some graph G caused by the scheduler is not a computation is non-zero. This means that a Ξ may occur, for which there exists some configuration $i \in \mathcal{F}_\Xi$ and $j \notin \mathcal{F}_\Xi$ such that $i \to j$. Now there are two cases:

1. $i = j$. In this case the contradiction is trivial, because it follows that $i \in \mathcal{F}_\Xi$ while at the same time $i \notin \mathcal{F}_\Xi$.
2. $i \neq j$. However, by assumption $\mathbb{P}_{ij} > 0$, and because i is persistent j must also be with probability 1.   □

3.2   Proposed Schedulers

In [2] a probabilistic scheduler that selects the next ordered pair to interact at random, independently and uniformly from all ordered pairs corresponding to arcs of the communication graph (i.e. elements of E) was defined. Here we call this scheduler Random Scheduler, and define two new probabilistic schedulers, namely the State Scheduler and the Transition Function Scheduler.

The **Random Scheduler**. To generate C_{i+1} the Random Scheduler selects an ordered pair $(u, v) \in E$ at random, independently and uniformly (each with probability $1/|E|$), and applies the transition function to $(C_i(u), C_i(v))$.

The **State Scheduler**. Consider a population protocol for k-mutual exclusion, in which only k agents are in state 1 and the rest of the population is in state 0. When an agent that holds a token interacts with another agent, it passes the token. Now consider an execution where $n \gg k$ and we use the Random Scheduler. In the case in which the communication graph is complete, the probability of selecting a pair with states $(1, 0)$ is much smaller than selecting a pair with states $(0, 0)$, meaning that the scheduler may initiate a large number of interactions that do not help the protocol in making progress. The *State Scheduler* instead of selecting a pair of processes independently and uniformly it selects a pair based on the states of the processes. It first selects a pair of *states* and in the sequel it selects one process from each state. Thus it allows the "meaningful" transitions to be selected more often and may avoid selecting a large number of interactions that delay the protocol's progress.

More formally, an ordered pair of states (q, q') is said to be an *interaction candidate* under configuration C if $\exists (u, v) \in E$ such that $C(u) = q$ and $C(v) = q'$. Then a configuration C_{i+1} is generated from C_i as follows: (i) by drawing an order pair (q, q') of states at random, independently and uniformly from all ordered pairs of states that are interaction candidates under C_i, (ii) drawing an ordered pair (u, v) such that $C_i(u) = q$ and $C_i(v) = q'$ from all such pairs at random, independently and uniformly, (iii) applying the transition function δ to $(C_i(u), C_i(v))$ and updating the states of u and v accordingly to obtain C_{i+1}.

The **Transition Function Scheduler**. Continuing the same argument, we define one more scheduler that assumes knowledge of the protocol executed. It examines the transition function δ and selects pairs of agents based on the defined transitions. In the case in which function δ defines transitions that do not change the state, neither of the initiator nor of the responder agent (e.g., $(\alpha, \beta) \to (\alpha, \beta)$), these transitions are ignored by the scheduler. This scheduler guarantees that all interactions will lead to a state change of either the initiator or the responder or both.

More formally, suppose $\to$ is a binary relation over Q^2 which is the relation analogue of the corresponding transition function δ. The reflexive reduction of $\to$, denoted by $\overset{.}{\to}$, is simply $\to$ without members related to themselves by $\to$. A configuration C_{i+1} is generated from C_i as follows: (i) by drawing a pair $((q_1, q_2), (q_1', q_2'))$ at random, independently and uniformly from all such pairs belonging to $\overset{.}{\to}$ for which (q_1, q_2) is an interaction candidate under C_i, (ii) drawing an ordered pair (u, v) such that $C_i(u) = q_1$ and $C_i(v) = q_2$ from all such pairs at random, independently and uniformly, (iii) applying the transition function δ to $(C_i(u), C_i(v))$ and updating the states of u and v accordingly to obtain C_{i+1} (if in step (i) there exists no such interaction candidate, then the

Transition Function Scheduler becomes a Random Scheduler, and remains in the same configuration for an infinite number of steps).

Given the above schedulers we can classify any scheduler for population protocols based on whether it assumes any knowledge on the actual protocol executed or not.

Definition 4. *We call a scheduler* protocol-oblivious *(or* agnostic*) if it constructs the interaction pattern without any knowledge on the protocol executed and* protocol-aware *if it takes into account information concerning the underlying protocol.*

Based on this classification, the Random Scheduler is a protocol-oblivious scheduler while the State and Transition Function Schedulers are protocol-aware.

Theorem 4. *The Random Scheduler, State Scheduler, and Transition Function Scheduler are all fair with probability 1.*

Proof. Let $T(\mathcal{A}, G)$ be any transition graph.

- *Random Scheduler.* Let i be any configuration in $V(T)$. Any time i is encountered, any j for which $i \rightarrow j$ is selected with probability $\mathbb{P}_{ij} = |K_{ij}|/|E|$, where $K_{ij} = \{e \mid e \in E(G) \text{ and } i \xrightarrow{e} j\}$, which is independent of the number of times i has been encountered. Thus the Random Scheduler is consistent. Moreover, $|K_{ij}| > 0$, because from definition of $i \rightarrow j$ we have that $\exists e \in E$ (E is used instead of $E(G)$) such that $i \xrightarrow{e} j$. Thus $\mathbb{P}_{ij} > 0$ and Theorem 3 applies implying that the Random Scheduler is fair with probability 1.
- *State Scheduler.* Let i, j be distinct configurations in $V(T)$ such that $i \rightarrow j$. When the State Scheduler has chosen i to select the next configuration of the execution, it performs two experiments. First it selects a pair of states (q, q') from all interaction candidates. Then it selects an arc e from all $(u, v) \in E$ such that $i(u) = q$ and $i(v) = q'$. Let K_{ij} again denote the set of arcs (i.e. interactions) that convert i to j. Let also $M_{ij} = \{(q, q') \mid \exists (u, v) \in K_{ij}$ such that $i(u) = q$ and $i(v) = q'\}$ and IC_i denote the set of all interaction candidates under i (note that $M_{ij} \subseteq IC_i$). Now $1/|IC_i|$ is the probability that a specific interaction candidate is selected by the scheduler. Let $K_{ij}^{(q,q')} = \{(u, v) \mid (u, v) \in K_{ij}$ and $i(u) = q, i(v) = q'\}$ (the subset of K_{ij} containing all arcs (u, v) that convert i to j and where the state of u is q and the state of v is q') and $E_i^{(q,q')} = \{(u, v) \mid (u, v) \in E$ and $i(u) = q, i(v) = q'\}$. Now given a chosen interaction candidate $(q, q') \in M_{ij}$ the probability that j is selected is equal to $|K_{ij}^{(q,q')}|/|E_i^{(q,q')}|$. Thus we have

$$\mathbb{P}_{ij} = \sum_{(q,q') \in M_{ij}} \frac{|K_{ij}^{(q,q')}|}{|IC_i||E_i^{(q,q')}|}.$$

$|K_{ij}^{(q,q')}|$, $|IC_i|$ and $|E_i^{(q,q')}|$ for all $(q, q') \in M_{ij}$ only depend on the specific configurations i and j and are always the same w.r.t. different times at which

i is encountered by the scheduler. Thus the State Scheduler is consistent. Moreover, since $(i \to j) \Rightarrow \exists e = (u, v) \in E$ such that $i \xrightarrow{e} j$. Let q and q' be the states of u and v under i, respectively. It follows that $(q, q') \in M_{ij}$ and that $|M_{ij}| > 0$. Finally, note that $e \in K_{ij}^{(q,q')}$, because $e \in K_{ij}$, $i(u) = q$, and $i(v) = q'$. Thus $\mathbb{P}_{ij} > 0$, Theorem 3 applies and as a consequence the State Scheduler is fair with probability 1.

- *Transition Function Scheduler.* In the case in which $i \neq j$, $\mathbb{P}_{ij}$ is defined as in the State Scheduler, by simply replacing the phrase "interaction candidate" with "interaction candidate that constitutes the lhs of some rule in the reflexive reduction of δ". So also this scheduler is consistent and fair with probability 1. Note that when $i = j$ and i has at least one out-neighbor in T different from i, then $\mathbb{P}_{ij} = 0$, since this scheduler does not select transitions that leave the states of the participating agents unaffected. Moreover, if i has a unique out-going arc (in T) pointing to itself, then the scheduler selects i for an infinite number of steps with probability 1 (in this case becomes a Random Scheduler). In both cases no problem arises, because for Theorem 3 to apply we only require $\mathbb{P}_{ij} > 0$ for all $i \neq j$ such that $i \to j$. $\square$

3.3   Equivalence between Schedulers

Definition 5. *Two fair probabilistic schedulers S_1 and S_2 are called* time equivalent *w.r.t. a protocol $\mathcal{A}$ iff all computations of $\mathcal{A}$ under S_1 and S_2 beginning from the same initial configuration take asymptotically the same expected time (number of steps) to convergence.*

Definition 6. *Two fair probabilistic schedulers S_1 and S_2 are called* computationally equivalent *w.r.t. a protocol $\mathcal{A}$ iff for all computations of $\mathcal{A}$ under S_1 and S_2 beginning from the same initial configuration, w.h.p., $\mathcal{A}$ stabilizes to the same output assignment (the output assignment of a configuration C is $y_C : V \to Y$ defined as $y_C(u) = O(C(u))$ for all $u \in V$).*

4   Not All Fair Probabilistic Schedulers Are Time Equivalent

We use a simple protocol, called the *OR Protocol* or the *One-Way Epidemic Protocol*, based on an example of [7], in which each agent with input 0 simply outputs 1 as soon as it interacts with some agent in state 1. We, also, assume that the underlying communication graph is complete. Formally, we have $Q = X = Y = \{0, 1\}$ and the transitions defined by δ are the following:

$$
\begin{array}{ll}
(0,0) \to (0,0) & (1,0) \to (1,1) \\
(0,1) \to (1,1) & (1,1) \to (1,1)
\end{array}
$$

Essentially, if all agents have input 0, no agent will ever be in state 1. If some agent has input 1, given a fair scheduler, we expect that the number of agents with state 1 will increase and will eventually reach n. In both cases, due to fairness, all agents will eventually stabilize to the correct output value, though an important fundamental questions is "how fast is stability reached?" and "how do different schedulers affect the performance of the protocol?".

In [4], Angluin et al. characterized the behavior of the OR Protocol in complete communication graphs as a *one-way epidemic*. They showed that the number of interactions for the epidemic to finish in the case of the Random Scheduler is $\Theta(n \log n)$ w.h.p., by exploiting the well-known coupon collector problem.

Theorem 5. *The State Scheduler and the Transition Function Scheduler are time equivalent w.r.t. the One-Way Epidemic Protocol.*

Proof. Both schedulers require only $\mathcal{O}(n)$ interactions. In particular, the Transition Function Scheduler can choose only between transitions $(1,0) \rightarrow (1,1)$ and $(0,1) \rightarrow (1,1)$ that both increase the number of agents in state 1 by one. If initially at least one agent is in state 1, then in each step one agent goes from state 0 to state 1 (no new agents in state 0 emerge) and because the agents are n, in at most $n-1$ steps all agents will be in state 1 and stability will have been reached. In the case of the State Scheduler, assume the worst-case scenario in which initially only one agent is in state 1. Because the graph is complete, the interaction candidates are in the first step $(0,0)$, $(0,1)$, and $(1,0)$. So, initially, there is a $2/3$ probability to select a transition that gives birth to a new 1. When this happens, in an expected number of 1.5 steps, all four left-hand sides of the rules of δ will be interaction candidates (until the step in which only one 0 remains, when again the probability of progress becomes $2/3$). In all other possible configurations the probability to progress is $1/2$, thus progress is always made with at least probability $1/2$, which in turn implies that on average at most $2(n-1)$ (i.e. again $\mathcal{O}(n)$) steps are expected until stability is reached. $\square$

The above discussion indicates that the performance of a population protocol clearly depends on the scheduler's functionality. In fact, it seems here that the additional knowledge, concerning the transition function, allowed to the State Scheduler and the Transition Function Scheduler provides us with interaction patterns that always lead to optimal computations. However, we can show that the same knowledge may also allow the definition of fair schedulers that lead the protocols to worst-case scenarios. To do so we slightly modify the State Scheduler to obtain a new scheduler, called the *Modified Scheduler*. Let us consider the case in which the scheduler is *weakly protocol-aware* in the sense that it can only partition the rules of the transition function to classes (possibly with elements sharing some common property and assign some probability to each class.

Definition 7. *The Modified Scheduler selects from the class of the identity rules (rules that leave both the state of the initiator and that of the responder unaffected) with probability $1 - \varepsilon$ and from all the remaining rules with probability ε, where $0 < \varepsilon < 1$. Those probabilities are then evenly divided into the corresponding class members. All other components of the Modified Scheduler's definition remain the same as in the case of the State Scheduler.*

Theorem 6. *The Modified Scheduler can lead the One-Way Epidemic Protocol to arbitrarily bad performance.*

Proof. First of all, note that the Modified Scheduler is fair with probability 1, because the transition probabilities may have been modified but still remain nonzero for non-loop arcs of T and independent of the number of steps. Consider now the situation in which $n - 2$ nodes are initially in state 0 and the remaining 2 are in state 1. Because $n - 2$ 0s have to be converted to 1s, it follows that the probability that the computation stabilizes in less than $n - 2$ steps is 0. Let the random variable D denote the number of steps until the computation stabilizes (all agents become 1). We have already shown that $\mathbb{P}[D = i] = 0$ for $i < n - 2$. Note that $\mathbb{P}[D = i]$ equals $\mathbb{P}$[the last remaining 0 becomes 1 in step i]. Let also N_i denote the number of non-identity rules that have appeared in i steps. For the computation to stabilize in i steps, exactly $n - 3$ non-identity rules must have been chosen in the first $i - 1$ steps ($n - 3$ 0s converted to 1s and one 0 remaining) and also a non-identity rule in the last step (the last 0 is converted to a 1). Note that N_i is a binomial random variable having parameters (i, ε). Then for all $i \geq n - 2$

$$\mathbb{P}[D = i] = \mathbb{P}[N_{i-1} = n - 3] \cdot \mathbb{P}[\text{non-identity rule appears in step } i]$$

$$= \left[\binom{i-1}{n-3} \varepsilon^{n-3} (1-\varepsilon)^{i-1-(n-3)} \right] \cdot \varepsilon$$

$$= \binom{i-1}{n-3} \varepsilon^{n-2} (1-\varepsilon)^{i-n+2}$$

and the expectation of D is

$$\mathbb{E}[D] = \frac{(n-2)}{\varepsilon}.$$

The calculation of the above result can be found in the technical report at http://fronts.cti.gr/aigaion/?TR=93.

Obviously, $\mathbb{E}[D]$ can become arbitrarily large, by decreasing ε (that is, the probability that a non-identity rule is selected) and the theorem follows. For example, if we set $\varepsilon = (n - 2)/2^n$, given that $n > 2$, then the expected number of steps to convergence is exponential in the size of the population. □

Thus, it is evident that the fairness condition, as has been defined by Angluin et al. in [2], is not sufficient to guarantee the construction of protocols that perform well under all kinds of allowed schedulers. It seems that a protocol may perform optimally under some fair scheduler but at the same time reach its worst-case performance under some other, also provably fair, scheduler. Obviously, either some stronger definition of fairness needs to be proposed, that, for example, would characterize the Modified Scheduler as unfair in the case in which ε is far away from $1/2$, possibly because it always seems to prefer some class of rules from others, or maybe protocol-aware schedulers and other kinds of yet unknown schedulers that can be adjusted to lead to divergent performance scenarios, should somehow be formally prohibited.

Theorem 7. *There exists at least one protocol w.r.t. which some fair probabilistic schedulers are not time equivalent.*

Proof. Follows by comparing the expected running time of the One-Way Epidemic Protocol under the State and Transition Function Schedulers to its expected running time under the Random and Modified Schedulers (the latter expected times are from [4] and Theorem 6). □

5   Not All Fair Probabilistic Schedulers Are Computationally Equivalent

Now we are about to show that, due to the weakness characterizing the selected notion of fairness, not only performance but also protocol correctness depends greatly on the underlying scheduler. Assume that each agent initially votes for one of some election candidates x and y or chooses to vote blank, denoted by b. If x is the majority vote, then we want every agent to eventually output x, otherwise y (we assume here that the state of an agent is also its output). Now let us consider the following one-way protocol that was proposed in [6].

$$(x, b) \rightarrow (x, x) \qquad (x, y) \rightarrow (x, b)$$
$$(y, b) \rightarrow (y, y) \qquad (y, x) \rightarrow (y, b)$$

In words, when an x meets a b it convinces it to vote x, when a y meets a b it convinces it to vote y, an x switches a y to the blank-undecidable state, and a y does the same to an x. Given an initial configuration of xs, ys and blanks that contains at least one non-blank, the goal is for the agents to reach consensus on one of the values x or y. Additionally, the value chosen should be the majority non-blank initial value, provided it exceeds the minority by a sufficient margin. In [6] it was proven that if the above protocol runs under the Random Scheduler on any complete graph with n nodes then with high probability consensus is reached in $\mathcal{O}(n \log n)$ interactions and the value chosen is the majority provided that its initial margin is $\omega(\sqrt{n \log n})$.

It seems that this is not the case when the underlying scheduler is the Transition Function Scheduler. Intuitively, the Transition Function Scheduler does not take into great account the advantage of xs. Let $N_x(t)$, $N_y(t)$, and $N_b(t)$ denote the number of xs, ys, and bs before step $t+1$, respectively. Note that when all xs, ys and bs appear in the population then the probability of $N_x(t+1) = N_x(t)+1$ is $1/4$ and the same holds for $N_y(t + 1) = N_y(t) + 1$. But when the Random Scheduler is assumed, then the greater the number of xs, the more the arcs leading from xs to bs, thus the greater the probability of $N_x(t+1) = N_x(t)+1$.

Lemma 1. *The Majority Protocol errs under the Transition Function Scheduler with constant probability, when $x = \Theta(y)$ in the initial configuration (x and y are used instead of N_x and N_y, respectively).*

Proof. The probability of the minority to win is equal to the probability that the symmetric walk (N_x, N_y) beginning from the initial point (x_0, y_0) will meet

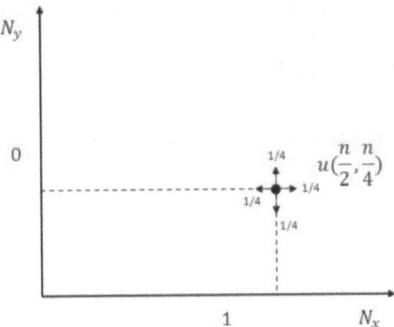

Fig. 1. The two-dimensional symmetric random walk. We show that the probability that the particle will reach the N_y axis before reaching the N_x axis is constant.

the N_y axis before meeting the N_x axis. The particle moves to each of its 4 neighboring points with probability 1/4 (see Figure 1, where 0 and 1 are the probabilities that we assign to the boundaries that constitute the collection of points for which the system stabilizes to a winning vote). The only exception is when the number of bs becomes equal to zero. But in this case the xs decrease by one with probability 1/2, the same holds for the ys and with probability 1 a b appears again and the walk returns to its initial symmetric distribution (to simplify the argument we ignore those states, because they do not strongly affect the probability that we want to compute). To the best of our knowledge, this kind of symmetric random walk in two dimensions has only been studied in [15], a paper cited by Feller [13], and is closely related to the Dirichlet problem. For any interior point (x, y), if $u(x, y)$ denotes the probability that the minority wins (the walk meets the N_y axis before meeting the N_x axis), then

$$u(x, y) = \frac{1}{4}(u(x + 1, y) + u(x, y + 1) + u(x - 1, y) + u(x, y - 1)), \quad (1)$$

and we are interested in the value of $u(x, y)$ when $x = \Theta(y)$, that is the initial number of xs and the initial number of ys are of the same order (e.g. $x = n/2$ and $y = n/4$). The homogeneous solution of (1) is $u(x, y) = \frac{x+y}{2n}$ and the general (with the boundary conditions into account) is $\frac{x+y}{2n} + f(x, y)$, where $f(x, y)$ is a particular non-homogeneous solution. When $x, y = \Theta(n)$ the $u(x, y)$ behaves as the homogeneous, thus $u(n/2, n/4)$ is equal to 3/8, which is constant. $\square$

Theorem 8. *There exists at least one protocol w.r.t. which two fair probabilistic schedulers are not computationally equivalent.*

Proof. The Random Scheduler is not computationally equivalent to the Transition Function Scheduler w.r.t. the Majority Protocol, because there exists some initial margin in the case in which the majority is x, which is $\omega(\sqrt{n \log n})$ and also the initial number of xs and the initial number of ys are of the same order. For example, in the case in which $x = 3n/4 - k$ (where $k \ll n$) and $y = n/4$, x and y are of the same order and $x - y \simeq n/2 = \omega(\sqrt{n \log n})$ for sufficiently large n. But given an initial configuration satisfying the above dynamics, under the Random Scheduler the protocol w.h.p. stabilizes to a majority winning configuration, while under the Transition Function Scheduler from Lemma 1 there is a constant probability that the protocol will stabilize to a minority winning configuration. Thus, it does not hold that w.h.p. those schedulers make the protocol stabilize to the same output assignment (see again Definition 6).   □

6   Future Research Directions

In the area initiated by the proposal of the Population Protocol (PP) model [2] many unresolved problems remain. The PP model makes absolutely minimal assumptions about the underlying system. The agents follow a completely unpredictable movement, they cannot store unique identifiers, and even a single Byzantine failure can lead to global failure of the system. How can we readjust (relax) those assumptions to more accurately reflect practical sensor network systems? For example in [14], Guerraoui and Ruppert assumed that the agents are equipped with read-only IDs (from the industry) and that they are also capable of storing a constant number of other agents' IDs. In this manner they obtained a very strong model, which they call the *Community Protocol* model, that can solve any decision problem in $NSPACE(n \log n)$ (and is additionally robust to Byzantine failures of a constant number of agents). In [11] they allowed the communication links to store states from a set of cardinality that is independent of the population size, to obtain the *Mediated Population Protocol* model that is also stronger than the PP model. In the case of wireless communication is there some architecture to reasonably implement the proposed model without using a global storage (for more information about the global storage idea the reader is referred to http://fronts.cti.gr/aigaion/?TR=65, i.e. the corresponding technical report of [11])? In the latter model either an exact characterization of the class of solvable problems has to be found or at least some impossibility results should appear to provide a first insight of what the model is incapable of computing (a first attempt can be found in [9], and in [11] it was proven that all stably computable predicates belong to $NSPACE(m)$, where m denotes the number of edges of the communication graph). Finally, how can someone verify safely and quickly, in a distributed or centralized way, that a specific protocol meets its design objectives? This crucial problem remains open and has to be solved if our protocols are to be run in real critical application scenarios.

Acknowledgements. We wish to thank an anonymous reviewer who made very useful comments to a previous version of this work.

References

1. Angluin, D., Aspnes, J., Chan, M., Fischer, M.J., Jiang, H., Peralta, R.: Stably computable properties of network graphs. In: Proc. Distributed Computing in Sensor Systems: 1st IEEE International Conference, pp. 63–74 (2005)

2. Angluin, D., Aspnes, J., Diamadi, Z., Fischer, M.J., Peralta, R.: Computation in networks of passively mobile finite-state sensors. In: 23rd Annual ACM Symposium on Principles of Distributed Computing (PODC), pp. 290–299. ACM, New York (2004)
3. Angluin, D., Aspnes, J., Diamadi, Z., Fischer, M.J., Peralta, R.: Computation in networks of passively mobile finite-state sensors. Distributed Computing 18(4), 235–253 (2006)
4. Angluin, D., Aspnes, J., Eisenstat, D.: Fast computation by population protocols with a leader. Distributed Computing 21(3), 183–199 (2008)
5. Angluin, D., Aspnes, J., Eisenstat, D.: Stably computable predicates are semilinear. In: Proc. 25th Annual ACM Symposium on Principles of Distributed Computing, pp. 292–299 (2006)
6. Angluin, D., Aspnes, J., Eisenstat, D.: A simple population protocol for fast robust approximate majority. In: Pelc, A. (ed.) DISC 2007. LNCS, vol. 4731, pp. 20–32. Springer, Heidelberg (2007)
7. Aspnes, J., Ruppert, E.: An introduction to population protocols. Bulletin of the European Association for Theoretical Computer Science 93, 98–117 (2007); Columns: Distributed Computing. Mavronicolas, M. (ed.)
8. Chatzigiannakis, I., Spirakis, P.G.: The dynamics of probabilistic population protocols. In: Taubenfeld, G. (ed.) DISC 2008. LNCS, vol. 5218, pp. 498–499. Springer, Heidelberg (2008)
9. Chatzigiannakis, I., Michail, O., Spirakis, P.G.: Decidable Graph Languages by Mediated Population Protocols. In: 23nd International Symposium on Distributed Computing (DISC), Elche, Spain (September 2009); Also FRONTS Technical Report FRONTS-TR-2009-16, http://fronts.cti.gr/aigaion/?TR=80
10. Chatzigiannakis, I., Michail, O., Spirakis, P.G.: Experimental verification and performance study of extremely large sized population protocols. FRONTS Technical Report FRONTS-TR-2009-3 (January 2009), http://fronts.cti.gr/aigaion/?TR=61
11. Chatzigiannakis, I., Michail, O., Spirakis, P.G.: Mediated Population Protocols. In: 36th International Colloquium on Automata, Languages and Programming (ICALP), Rhodes, Greece, pp. 363–374 (2009)
12. Chatzigiannakis, I., Michail, O., Spirakis, P.G.: Recent Advances in Population Protocols. In: 34th International Symposium on Mathematical Foundations of Computer Science (MFCS), Novy Smokovec, High Tatras, Slovakia, August 24-28 (2009)
13. Feller, W.: An Introduction to Probability Theory and Its Applications, 3rd edn., vol. 1. Wiley, Chichester (1968)
14. Guerraoui, R., Ruppert, E.: Names Trump Malice: Tiny Mobile Agents Can Tolerate Byzantine Failures. In: 36th International Colloquium on Automata, Languages and Programming (ICALP), Rhodes, Greece, pp. 484–495 (2009)
15. McCrea, W.H., Whipple, F.J.W.: Random Paths in Two and Three Dimensions. Proc. Roy. Soc. Edinburgh 60, 281–298 (1940)
16. Queille, J.P., Sifakis, J.: Fairness and Related Properties in Transition Systems - A temporal Logic to Deal with Fairness. Acta Informatica 19, 195–220 (1983)

Brief Announcement:
Relay: A Cache-Coherence Protocol for Distributed Transactional Memory

Bo Zhang and Binoy Ravindran

ECE Department, Virginia Tech
Blacksburg VA 24061, USA
{alexzbzb,binoy}@vt.edu

Abstract. Distributed transactional memory promises to alleviate difficulties with lock-based (distributed) synchronization and object performance bottlenecks in distributed systems. The design of the cache-coherence protocol is critical to the performance of distributed transactional memory systems. We evaluate the performance of a cache-coherence protocol by measuring its worst-case competitive ratio — i.e., the ratio of its makespan to the makespan of the optimal cache-coherence protocol. We establish the upper bound of the competitive ratio and show that it is determined by the worst-case number of abortions, maximum locating stretch, and maximum moving stretch of the protocol — the first such result. We present the Relay protocol, a novel cache-coherence protocol, which optimizes these values, and evaluate its performance. We show that Relay's competitive ratio is significantly improved by a factor of $O(N_i)$ for N_i transactions requesting the same object when compared against past distributed queuing protocols.

1   Introduction

Conventional synchronization methods based on locks and condition variables are inherently error-prone. Transactional memory (TM) [4,5,8] is an alternative synchronization model (for shared in-memory data objects) that promises to alleviate the difficulties with lock-based synchronization. In this paper, we focus on distributed transactional memory. We are motivated by the difficulties of lock-based synchronization that plague distributed control-flow programming models such as RPCs. For example, distributed deadlocks (e.g., due to RPCs that become remotely blocked on each other) and livelocks are unavoidable for such solutions. Furthermore, in the RPC model, an object can become a "hot spot," and thus a performance bottleneck. In the data-flow distributed TM model of [6] (that we also consider), such bottlenecks can be reduced by exploiting locality: move the object to nodes. Distributed (data-flow) TM can therefore alleviate these difficulties, where distributed transactional conflicts and object inconsistencies are resolved through distributed contention managers and cache-coherence protocols, respectively.

T. Abdelzaher, M. Raynal, and N. Santoro (Eds.): OPODIS 2009, LNCS 5923, pp. 48–53, 2009.
© Springer-Verlag Berlin Heidelberg 2009

We are interested in the design of a cache-coherence protocol to minimize its worst-case competitive ratio, which is the ratio of its makespan (the last completion time for a given set of transactions) to the makespan of an optimal cache-coherence protocol. We first establish the upper bound of the competitive ratio and show that it is determined by the worst-case number of abortions, maximum locating stretch, and maximum moving stretch of the protocol. The design of a cache-coherence protocol should therefore minimize these values.

We present a novel cache-coherence protocol, called the Relay protocol, which works on a network spanning tree. Hence, its maximum locating stretch and maximum moving stretch are determined by the maximum stretch of the underlying spanning tree. The Relay protocol efficiently reduces the worst-case number of total abortions to $O(N_i)$. As a result, we show that the protocol has a better worst-case competitive ratio than the arrow protocol by a factor of $O(N_i)$.

Thus, the paper's contribution is twofold. First, we identify the three factors that critically affect the performance of a cache-coherence protocol. Second, we present the Relay protocol, illustrate how these factors are optimized in its design, and show that its worst-case competitive ratio is better than that of the arrow protocol by a factor of $O(N_i)$. To the best of our knowledge, these are the first such results.

The rest of the paper is organized as follows. We present our system model and formulate our problem in Section 2. We analyze the general case of the competitive ratio and establish its upper bound in Section 3. Section 4 presents the Relay protocol. The paper concludes in Section 5.

2   System Model and Problem Description

Network Model. Let $G = (V, E, d)$ be a weighted connected graph, where $|V| = n$ and d is a function that maps E to the set of positive real numbers. Specifically, we use $d(u, v)$ to denote the communication cost of the edge $e(u, v)$. For two nodes u and v in V, let $d_G(u, v)$ denote the *distance* between them in G, i.e., the length of a shortest path between u and v.

We assume that the proposed Relay protocol runs on a *fixed*-rooted spanning tree of G. Given a spanning tree T of G, we define the distance in T between a pair of two nodes, u and v, to be the sum of the lengths of the edges on the unique path in T between u and v. Now, we define the *stretch* of u and v in T with respect to G as: $\text{str}_{T,G}(u, v) = \frac{d_T(u,v)}{d_G(u,v)}$. When there is no ambiguity, we omit G, for convenience, i.e., we say $\text{str}_T(u, v)$. We define the *normalized diameter* of G as: $D = \max_{u,v,x,y \in V}\{\frac{d_G(u,v)}{d_G(x,y)}\}$.

Transaction Model. We are given a set of $m \geq 1$ transactions $T_1, \ldots, T_m$ and a set of $s \geq 1$ objects $R_1, \ldots, R_s$. Since each transaction is invoked on an individual node, we use v_{T_i} to denote the node that invokes the transaction T_i, and $V_T = \{v_{T_1}, \ldots, v_{T_m}\}$. We use $T_i \prec T_j$ to represent that transaction T_i is issued a higher priority than T_j by the contention manager.

Each transaction is a sequence of actions, each of which is an access to a single object. Each transaction T_j requires the use of $R_i(T_j)$ units of object R_i for one of its actions. If T_j updates R_i, i.e., a write operation, then $R_i(T_j) = 1$. If it reads

R_i without updating, then $R_i(T_j) = \frac{1}{n}$, i.e., the object can be read by all nodes in the network simultaneously. When $R_i(T_j) + R_i(T_k) > 1$, T_j and T_k conflict at R_i. We use $v_{R_i}^0$ to denote the node that holds R_i at the start of the system, and $v_{R_i}^j$ to denote the jth node that fetches R_i. We denote the set of nodes that requires the use of the same object R_i as $V_T^{R_i} := \{v_{T_j} | R_i(T_j) \geq 0, j = 1, \ldots, m\}$. The duration of transaction T_j running locally (without taking into account the time for fetching objects) is denoted by τ_i.

We consider Herlihy and Sun's data-flow model [6] to support the transactional memory API in a distributed system. A *contention manager* module is responsible for mediating between conflicting accesses to avoid deadlocks and livelocks. We assume a fixed contention manager A, which satisfies the *work conserving* [1] and *pending commit* [3] properties, e.g, the Greedy manager [1]. A distributed transactional memory system uses a *distributed cache-coherence protocol* to locate and move the cached copy of the object in the network.

Problem Statement. We evaluate the performance of a distributed transactional memory system by measuring its *makespan*. Given a set of transactions accessing a set of objects under a contention manager A and a cache-coherence protocol C, makespan(A, C) denotes the duration that the given set of transactions are successfully executed under the contention manager A and cache-coherence protocol C. We use makespan(A, OPT) to denote the makespan of the optimal cache-coherence protocol with respect to A. We evaluate the performance of a cache-coherence protocol C with respect to A by measuring its *competitive ratio*: $\text{CR}(A, C) = \frac{\text{makespan}(A,C)}{\text{makespan}(A,\text{OPT})}$. When there is no ambiguity on the contention manager used, for convenience, we drop it from the notations— i.e., we simply write makespan(C), makespan(OPT), and CR(C). Our goal is to design a cache-coherence protocol C to minimize its competitive ratio.

3   Competitive Ratio Analysis

We first analyze the makespan of the optimal cache-coherence protocol makespan(OPT). Let the makespan of a set of transactions which require accesses to an object R_i, be denoted as makespan$_i$. It is composed of three parts: (a) Traveling Makespan (makespan$_i^d$): the total communication cost for R_i to travel in the network; (b) Execution Makespan (makespan$_i^\tau$): the duration of transactions' executions involving R_i, including all successful and aborted executions; and (c) Waiting Makespan (makespan$_i^w$): the time that R_i waits for a transaction request.

Generally, a cache-coherence protocol performs two functions: 1) locating the up-to-date copy of the object and 2) moving it in the network to meet transactions' requests, denoted by $\delta^C(u, v)$ and $\zeta^C(u, v)$, respectively.

For the set of nodes $V_T^{R_i}$ that invoke transactions with requests for object R_i, we build a *complete* graph $G_i = (V_i, E_i, d_i)$, where $V_i = \{V_T^{R_i} \bigcup v_{R_i}^0\}$ and $d_i(u, v) = d_G(u, v)$. We use $H(G_i, v_{R_i}^0, v_{T_j})$ to denote the cost of the *minimum-cost Hamiltonian path* that visits each node from $v_{R_i}^0$ to v_{T_j} exactly once. Now, we can directly prove the following theorem:

Theorem 1. $makespan_i^d(\text{OPT}) \geq \min_{v_{T_j} \in V_T^{R_i}} H(G_i, v_{R_i}^0, v_{T_j})$, $makespan_i^\tau(\text{OPT}) \geq$
$\sum_{v_{T_j} \in V_T^{R_i}} \tau_j$, $makespan_i^w(\text{OPT}) \geq \sum_{v_{T_j} \in V_T^{R_i}} \min_{v_{T_k} \in \{V_T^{R_i} \cup v_{R_i}^0\}} d_G(v_{T_k}, v_{T_j})$

Let $\lambda_C^*(j)$ denote T_j's worst-case number of abortions under cache-coherence protocol C and $\lambda_C(j) = \lambda_C^*(j) + 1$. Let Λ_C^* denote the worst-case number of total transactions' abortions under C and $\Lambda_C = \Lambda_C^* + N_i$. Generally, we have the following theorem for a cache-coherence protocol C:

Theorem 2. $CR_i^d(C) \leq \dfrac{\Lambda_C \cdot \max_{v_{T_j} \in V_T^{R_i}} \{\max_{v_{T_k} \in \{V_T^{R_i} \cup v_{R_i}^0\}} \zeta^C(v_{T_j}, v_{T_k})\}}{\sum_{v_{T_j} \in V_T^{R_i}} \{\min_{v_{T_k} \in \{V_T^{R_i} \cup v_{R_i}^0\}} dist_G(v_{T_j}, v_{T_k})\}}$,

$CR_i^\tau(C) \leq \max_{v_{T_j} \in V_T^{R_i}} \lambda_C(j)$, $CR_i^w(C) \leq \dfrac{\Lambda_C \cdot \max_{v_{T_j} \in V_T^{R_i}} \{\max_{v_{T_k} \in \{V_T^{R_i} \cup v_{R_i}^0\}} \delta^C(v_{T_j}, v_{T_k})\}}{\sum_{v_{T_j} \in V_T^{R_i}} \{\min_{v_{T_k} \in \{V_T^{R_i} \cup v_{R_i}^0\}} d_G(v_{T_j}, v_{T_k})\}}$

We define the *locating stretch* and *moving* stretch of u and v under cache-coherence protocol C as: $str_C^\delta(u, v) = \frac{\delta^C(u,v)}{d_G(u,v)}$ and $str_C^\zeta(u, v) = \frac{\zeta^C(u,v)}{d_G(u,v)}$. Let the *maximum locating stretch* and *maximum moving stretch* with respect to C be denoted, respectively, as: $\text{Str}_C^\delta = \max_{u,v \in V}\{\frac{\delta^C(u,v)}{d_G(u,v)}\}$ and $\text{Str}_C^\zeta = \max_{u,v \in V}\{\frac{\zeta^C(u,v)}{d_G(u,v)}\}$. Let $N_i = |V_T^{R_i}|$, i.e, N_i represents the number of transactions that request access to object R_i. Now we have the following theorem:

Theorem 3. $CR_i(C) \leq \max\{\max_{v_{T_j} \in V_T^{R_i}} \lambda_C(j), \frac{\Lambda_C}{N_i} \cdot \max\{\text{Str}_C^\zeta, \text{Str}_C^\delta\} \cdot D\}$

4   The Relay Protocol

Motivated by the arrow protocol of Raymond [2,7], which has an $O(N_i^2)$ worst-case queue length for N_i transactions requesting the same object, we design a novel cache-coherence protocol, called the Relay protocol, based on a fixed spanning tree T on G. The Relay protocol inherits the advantages of the Arrow protocol and significantly reduces the number of transaction abortions by a factor of $O(N_i)$.

The protocol is initialized in the same way as the Arrow protocol. The node where the object resides is selected to be the tail of the queue. Each node $v \in V$ maintains a pointer $p(v)$ and is initialized so that following the pointers from any node leads to the tail. After the initialization, the protocol works as follows. To request the object, a transaction T_p invoked by node v sends a find message to node $p(v)$. Note that $p(v)$ is not modified when a find message is forwarded. If a node w between v and the tail of the queue receives a find message, it simply forwards the find message to $p(v)$. At the end, the find message will be forwarded to the tail of the queue without changing any pointers.

The find message from v keeps a *path vector* $r(v)$ to record the path it travels. Each node receiving the find message from v appends its ID to $r(v)$. When the find message arrives at the tail of the queue, the vector $r(v)$ records the path from v to the tail. Suppose the tail of the queue x receives a find message from node v. Now, there are two possible cases: a) if the transaction T_x on x has

committed, then the object will be moved to p; and b) if the transaction T_x has
not committed, the contention manager will compare the priorities of T_x and T_p.
We discuss this scenario case by case.

- Case 1: If $T_p \prec T_x$, then T_x is aborted and the object will be moved to p. Node
  p stores a field $next(p) = T_x$ after receiving the object.
- Case 2: If $T_x \prec T_p$, then T_p will be postponed to let T_x commit. Node x
  stores a field $next(x) = T_p$. Node x may receive multiple find messages since
  the pointers are not changed before the object is moved. Suppose it receives
  another find message from node u. If $T_u \prec T_x$, then it falls into Case 1. If
  $T_x \prec T_u$, then the contention manager compares the priorities of $next(x)$ (in
  this case it is T_p) and T_u. If $T_p \prec T_u$, then the find message from u is forwarded
  to p. If $T_u \prec T_p$, then u sets $next(x)$ to T_u and forwards the find message from
  p to u.

The key idea of the Relay protocol is the way it updates the pointers and path
vectors to make those operations feasible. When the object is available at node
x, it will be moved to $next(x)$ via the path from x to $next(x)$ of the spanning
tree T. The problem is, how does x learn that path so that the object can be
correctly moved? Note that the Relay protocol uses path vectors to record the
path. Suppose that x moves an object to v. The Relay protocol keeps a *route
vector* **route** at x which records the path from v to x by copying the path vector
$r(v)$ after the find message from v arrives. Hence, node x is able to move the
object by following the reverse path saved in **route**.

The pointers are updated when the object is moved. Suppose that node x
moves the object to node v, node x sends a *move* message with the object
to $move(x).$**route**$[max]$. Meanwhile, node x sets $p(x)$ to $move(x).$**route**$[max]$.
Suppose a node u receives a move message from one of its neighbors. It updates
$move(x).$**route** by removing $move(x).$**route**$[max]$ and sends the object to the
new $move(x).$**route**$[max]$, setting $p(u) = move(x).$**route**$[max]$. Finally, when
the object arrives at v, $p(v)$ is set to v and all pointers are updated. Such
operations guarantee that at any time, there exists only one sink in the network,
and, from any node, following the direction of its pointer leads to the sink.

Performance Analysis. We now focus on the performance of the Relay protocol, which we measure through its competitive ratio. We can directly derive
the following relationships from the protocol description: $\text{Str}^{\delta}_{Relay} = \text{Str}^{\zeta}_{Relay} =$
$str(T)$, since the object is located and moved via a unique path on T. To illus-
trate the advantage of the Relay protocol on reducing the number of abortions,
we have the following theorem:

Theorem 4. $A_{Relay} \leq 2N_i - 1$

Proof. We first order the set of transactions in the priority order such that
$\{T_1 \prec T_2 \prec \ldots \prec T_{N_i}\}$. Suppose a transaction T_v is aborted by another transaction. In this case, T_v is restarted immediately and a find message is sent to
its predecessor on the queue. Finally, a node w keeps a variable $next(w) = v$. In
other words, for each time that a node is aborted, a successor link $next$ between
two nodes is established. Now, assume the next abortion occurs and a succes-
sor link $next(w') = v'$ is established. If $T_w \prec \{T_{w'} \text{ or } T_{v'}\} \prec T_v$, we say that

these two links are *joint*; otherwise we say that they are *disjoint*. We can prove that, if $next(w)$ and $next(w')$ are joint, at least one transaction in $\{T_w, \ldots, T_v\}$ has committed. Hence, there are only two outcomes for an abortion: at least one transaction's commit or a successor link disjoint to other successor links established. Hence, we just need at most $N_i - 1$ abortions to let N_i transactions commit or establish a chain of links among all transactions (since they are disjoint). For the latter case, no more abortion will occur since the object is moved following that chain. The theorem follows.

5   Concluding Remarks

We conclude that the worst-case performance of a cache-coherence protocol is determined by its worst-case number of abortions, maximum locating stretch, and maximum moving stretch. Compared with the traditional distributed queuing problem, the design of a cache-coherence protocol must take into account the contention between two transactions because transaction abortions increase the length of the queue. Motivated by a distributed queuing protocol with excellent performance, the Arrow protocol, we show that its worst-case number of total abortions is $O(N_i^2)$ for N_i transactions requesting the same object. Based on this protocol, we design the Relay protocol which reduces the worst-case number of total abortions to $O(N_i)$. As a result, the Relay protocol yields a better competitive ratio.

Acknowledgment

This work was supported by the US National Science Foundation CCF (Software and Hardware Foundations) grant 0915895.

References

1. Attiya, H., Epstein, L., Shachnai, H., Tamir, T.: Transactional contention management as a non-clairvoyant scheduling problem. In: PODC 2006, pp. 308–315 (2006)
2. Demmer, M.J., Herlihy, M.P.: The Arrow Distributed Directory Protocol. In: Kutten, S. (ed.) DISC 1998. LNCS, vol. 1499, pp. 119–133. Springer, Heidelberg (1998)
3. Guerraoui, R., Herlihy, M., Pochon, B.: Toward a theory of transactional contention managers. In: PODC 2005, pp. 258–264 (2005)
4. Hammond, L., Wong, V., Chen, M., Hertzberg, B., Carlstrom, B.D., Davis, J.D., Prabhu, M.K., Wijaya, H., Kozyrakis, C., Olukotun, K.: Transactional Memory Coherence and Consistency. In: ISCA 2004, pp. 102–113 (2004)
5. Herlihy, M., Luchangco, V., Moir, M.: Obstruction-free Synchronization: Double-ended Queues as an Example. In: ICDCS 2003, pp. 522–529 (2003)
6. Herlihy, M., Sun, Y.: Distributed Transactional Memory for Metric-space Networks. Distributed Computing 20(3), 195–208 (2007)
7. Raymond, K.: A tree-based algorithm for distributed mutual exclusion. ACM Trans. Comput. Syst. 7(1), 61–77 (1989)
8. Shavit, N., Touitou, D.: Software Transactional Memory. In: PODC 1995, pp. 204–213 (1995)

Byzantine Convergence in Robot Networks: The Price of Asynchrony

Zohir Bouzid, Maria Gradinariu Potop-Butucaru, and Sébastien Tixeuil

Université Pierre et Marie Curie - Paris 6, LIP6-CNRS 7606, France
FirstName.LastName@lip6.fr

Abstract. We study the convergence problem in fully asynchronous, uni-dimensional robot networks that are prone to Byzantine (*i.e.* malicious) failures. In these settings, oblivious anonymous robots with arbitrary initial positions are required to eventually converge to an *a priori* unknown position despite a subset of them exhibiting Byzantine behavior. Our contribution is twofold. We propose a deterministic algorithm that solves the problem in the most generic settings: fully asynchronous robots that operate in the non-atomic CORDA model. Our algorithm provides convergence in $5f+1$-sized networks where f is the upper bound on the number of Byzantine robots. Additionally, we prove that $5f + 1$ is a lower bound whenever robot scheduling is fully asynchronous. This constrasts with previous results in partially synchronous robot networks, where $3f + 1$ robots are necessary and sufficient.

Keywords: Robot networks, Byzantine tolerance, Asynchronous systems, Convergence.

1 Introduction

The use of cooperative swarms of weak inexpensive robots for achieving complex tasks such as exploration or tracking in dangerous environments is a promising option for reducing both human and material costs. Robot networks recently became a challenging research area for distributed systems since most of the problems to be solved in this context (*e.g.* coordination, agreement, resource allocation or leader election) form the core of distributed computing. However, the classical distributed computing solutions do not translate well due to fundamentally different execution models.

In order to capture the essence of distributed coordination in robot networks, two main computational models are proposed in the literature: the ATOM [1] and CORDA [2] models. The main difference between the two models comes from the granularity for executing a *Look-Compute-Move* cycle. In such a cycle, the Look phase consists in taking a snapshot of the other robots positions using its visibility sensors. In the Compute phase a robot computes a target destination based on its previous observation. The Move phase simply consists in moving toward the computed destination using motion actuators. In the ATOM model, the whole cycle is atomic while in the CORDA model, the cycle is executed in a

T. Abdelzaher, M. Raynal, and N. Santoro (Eds.): OPODIS 2009, LNCS 5923, pp. 54–70, 2009.

continuous manner. That is, in the ATOM model, robots executing concurrently always remain in the same phase while in CORDA it is possible that *e.g.* a robot executes its Look phase while another robot performs its Move phase, or that a robot executes its Compute phase while its view (obtained during the Look phase) is already outdated. Of course, executions that may appear in the CORDA model are a strict superset of those that may appear in the ATOM model, so a protocol that performs in the CORDA model also works in the ATOM model, but the converse is not true. Similarly, impossibility results for the ATOM model still hold in the CORDA model. Complementary to the granularity of robots action is the amount of *asynchrony* in the system, that is modeled by the scheduler: *(i)* a *fully synchronous* scheduler operates all robots in a lock-step manner forever, while *(ii)* a k-bounded scheduler preserves a ratio of k between the most often activated robot and the least often activated robot, finally *(iii)* a *fully asynchronous* scheduler only guarantees that every robot is activated infinitely often in an infinite execution. The robots that we consider have weak capacities: they are *anonymous* (they execute the same protocol and have no mean to distinguish themselves from the others), *oblivious* (they have no memory that is persistent between two cycles), and have no compass whatsoever (they are unable to agree on a common direction or orientation).

Convergence is a fundamental agreement primitive in robot networks and is used in the implementation of a broad class of services (*e.g.* the construction of common coordinate systems or specific geometrical patterns). Given a set of oblivious robots with arbitrary initial locations and no agreement on a global coordinate system, *convergence* requires that all robots asymptotically approach the same, but unknown beforehand, location. Convergence looks similar to distributed approximate agreement since both problems require nodes to agree on a common object (that is instantiated to be a position in space for the case of convergence, or a value in the case of distributed agreement).

Related works. Since the pioneering work of Suzuki and Yamashita [1], gathering[1] and convergence have been addressed in *fault-free* systems for a broad class of settings. Prencipe [3] studied the problem of gathering in both ATOM and CORDA models, and showed that the problem is intractable without additional assumptions such as being able to detect the multiplicity of a location (*i.e.*, knowing if there is more than one robot in a given location).

The case of *fault-prone* robot networks was recently tackled by several academic studies. The faults that have been investigated fall in two categories: *crash* faults (*i.e.* a faulty robots stop executing its cycle forever) and *Byzantine* faults (*i.e.* a faulty robot may exhibit arbitrary behavior and movement). Of course, the Byzantine fault model encompasses the crash fault model, and is thus harder to address. *Deterministic* fault-tolerant gathering is addressed in [4] where the authors study a gathering protocol that tolerates one crash, and an algorithm for the ATOM model with fully synchronous scheduling that tolerates up to f Byzantine faults, when the number of robots is (strictly) greater than

---

[1] Gathering requires robots to actually *reach* a single point within finite time regardless of their initial positions.

$3f$. In [5] the authors study the feasibility of *probabilistic* gathering in crash-prone and Byzantine-prone environments. *Deterministic* fault-tolerant convergence was first addressed in [6, 7], where algorithms based on convergence to the center of gravity of the system are presented. Those algorithms work in the ATOM [6] and CORDA [7] models with a fully asynchronous scheduler and tolerate up to f $(n > f)$ crash faults, where n is the number of robots in the system. Most related to this paper are [8, 9], where the authors studied convergence in Byzantine-prone environments when robots move in a uni-dimensional space. In more details, [8] showed that convergence is impossible if robots are not endowed with strong multiplicity detectors which are able to detect the exact number of robots that may simultaneously share the same location. The same paper defines the class of *cautious* algorithms which guarantee that correct robots always move inside the range of positions held by correct robots, and proved that any cautious convergence algorithm that can tolerate f Byzantine robots requires the presence of at least $2f + 1$ robots in fully-synchronous ATOM networks and $3f + 1$ robots in k-bounded (and thus also in fully asynchronous) ATOM networks. The lower bound for the ATOM model naturally extends to the CORDA model, and [9] provides a matching upper bound in the k-bounded CORDA model.

Interestingly enough, all previously known deterministic Byzantine tolerant robot protocols assume either the more restrictive ATOM model [5], or the constrained fully synchronous [4] or k-bounded [8, 9] schedulers, thus the question of the existence of such protocols in a fully asynchronous CORDA model remains open.

Our contribution. We present the first study of Byzantine resilient robot protocols that considers the most general execution model: the CORDA model together with the fully asynchronous scheduler. We concentrate on the convergence problem and prove that the fully asynchronous scheduler implies a lower bound of $5f + 1$ for the number n of robots for the class of cautious protocols (this bound holds for both ATOM and CORDA models). We also exhibit a deterministic protocol that matches this lower bound (that is, provided that $n \geq 5f + 1$, our protocol is deterministic and assumes the CORDA model with fully asynchronous scheduling). Table 1 summarizes the characteristics of our protocol with respect to previous work on Byzantine tolerant robot convergence (better characteristics for a protocol are depicted in boldface).

Table 1. Byzantine resilience bounds for deterministic convergence

Reference	Computation Model	Scheduler	Bounds
[4]	ATOM	fully synchronous	$n > 3f$
[8]	ATOM	fully synchronous	$n > 2f$
	ATOM	k-bounded	$n > 3f$
	CORDA	k-bounded	$n > 4f$
[9]	**CORDA**	k-bounded	$n > 3f$
This paper	CORDA	**fully asynchronous**	$n > 5f$

Outline. The remaining of the paper is organized as follows: Section 2 presents our model and robot network assumptions. This section also presents the formal specification of the convergence problem. Section 3 presents the Byzantine resilience lower bound proof. Section 4 describes our protocol and its complexity, while concluding remarks are presented in Section 5.

2   Model and Problem Definition

Most of the notions presented in this section are borrowed from [1, 2, 4]. We consider a network that consists of a finite set of robots arbitrarily deployed in a uni-dimensional space. The robots are devices with sensing, computing and moving capabilities. They can observe (sense) the positions of other robots in the space and based on these observations, they perform some local computations that can drive them to other locations.

In the context of this paper, the robots are *anonymous*, in the sense that they cannot be distinguished using their appearance, and they do not have any kind of identifiers that can be used during the computation. In addition, there is no direct mean of communication between them. Hence, the only way for robots to acquire information is by observing their positions. Robots have *unlimited visibility*, *i.e.* they are able to sense the entire set of robots. Robots are also equipped with a strong multiplicity sensor that provides robots with the ability to detect the exact number of robots that may simultaneously occupy the same location. We assume that the robots cannot remember any previous observation nor computation performed in any previous step. Such robots are said to be *oblivious* (or *memoryless*).

A *protocol* is a collection of n *programs*, one operating on each robot. The program of a robot consists in executing *Look-Compute-Move cycles* infinitely many times. That is, the robot first observes its environment (Look phase). An observation returns a snapshot of the positions of all robots within the visibility range. In our case, this observation returns a snapshot (also called *configuration* hereafter) of the positions of *all* robots denoted with $P(t) = \{P_1(t), ..., P_n(t)\}$. The positions of correct robots are referred as $U(t) = \{U_1(t), ..., U_m(t)\}$ where m denotes the number of correct robots. Note that $U(t) \subseteq P(t)$. The observed positions are *relative* to the observing robot, that is, they use the coordinate system of the observing robot. We denote by $P^i(t) = \{P_1^i(t), ..., P_n^i(t)\}$ the configuration $P(t)$ given in terms of the coordinate system of robot i ($U^i(t)$ is defined similarly). Based on its observation, a robot then decides — according to its program — to move or to stay idle (Compute phase). When a robot decides a move, it moves to its destination during the Move phase. An *execution* $e = (c_0, \ldots, c_t, \ldots)$ of the system is an infinite sequence of configurations, where c_0 is the initial configuration[2] of the system, and every transition $c_i \rightarrow c_{i+1}$ is associated to the execution of a subset of the previously defined actions.

---

[2] Unless stated otherwise, we make no specific assumption regarding the respective positions of robots in initial configurations.

A *scheduler* is a predicate on computations, that is, a scheduler defines a set of *admissible* computations, such that every computation in this set satisfies the scheduler predicate. A *scheduler* can be seen as an entity that is external to the system and selects robots for execution. As more power is given to the scheduler for robot scheduling, more different executions are possible and more difficult it becomes to design robot algorithms. In the remaining of the paper, we consider that the scheduler is *fully asynchronous*, that is, in any infinite execution, every robot is activated infinitely often, but there is no bound for the ration between the most activated robot and the least activated one.

We now review the main differences between the ATOM [1] and CORDA [2] models. In the ATOM model, whenever a robot is activated by the scheduler, it performs a *full* computation cycle. Thus, the execution of the system can be viewed as an infinite sequence of rounds. In a round one or more robots are activated by the scheduler and perform a computation cycle. The *fully-synchronous ATOM* model refers to the fact that the scheduler activates all robots in each round, while the regular *ATOM* model enables the scheduler to activate only a subset of the robots. In the CORDA model, robots may be interrupted by the scheduler after performing only a portion of a computation cycle. In particular, phases (Look, Compute, Move) of different robots may be interleaved. For example, a robot a may perform a Look phase, then a robot b performs a Look-Compute-Move complete cycle, then a computes and moves based on its previous observation (that does not correspond to the current configuration anymore). As a result, the set of executions that are possible in the CORDA model are a strict superset of those that are possible in the ATOM model. So, an impossibility result that holds in the ATOM model also holds in the CORDA model, while an algorithm that performs in the CORDA model is also correct in the ATOM model. Note that the converse is not necessarily true.

The faults we address in this paper are *Byzantine* faults. A Byzantine (or malicious) robot may behave in arbitrary and unforeseeable way. In each cycle, the scheduler determines the course of action of faulty robots and the maximal distance to which each non-faulty robot will move in this cycle. However, a robot i is guaranteed to be able to move a distance of at least δ_i towards its destination before it can be stopped by the scheduler.

Our convergence algorithm performs operations on multisets. A multiset or a bag S is a generalization of a set where an element can have more than one occurrence. The number of occurrences of an element a is referred as its *multiplicity*. The total number of elements of a multiset, including their repeated occurrences, is referred as the *cardinality* and is denoted by $|S|$. $\min(S)$(resp. $\max(S)$) is the smallest (resp. largest) element of S. If S is nonempty, $range(S)$ denotes the set $[\min(S), \max(S)]$ and $diam(S)$ (diameter of S) denotes $\max(S) - \min(S)$.

Given an initial configuration of n autonomous mobile robots (m of which are correct such that $m \geq n - f$), the *point convergence problem* requires that all correct robots asymptotically approach the exact same, but unknown beforehand, location. In other words, for every $\epsilon > 0$, there is a time t_ϵ from which all correct robots are within distance of at most ϵ of each other.

Definition 1 (Point Convergence Problem). *A system of oblivious robots satisfies the Byzantine convergence specification if and only if* $\forall \epsilon > 0, \exists t_\epsilon$ *such that* $\forall t > t_\epsilon$, $\forall i, j \leq m$, $distance(U_i(t), U_j(t)) < \epsilon$, *where* $U_i(t)$ *and* $U_j(t)$ *are the positions of any two* correct *robots i and j at time t in the same cartesian coordinate system, and where* $distance(a, b)$ *denote the Euclidian distance between two positions.*

Definition 1 requires the convergence property only from the *correct* robots. Note that it is impossible to obtain the convergence for all robots since Byzantine robots may exhibit arbitrary behavior and never join the position of correct robots.

3 Impossibility for $n \leq 5f$ and a Fully Asynchronous Scheduler

In this section we prove the fact that, when the number of robots in the network does not exceed $5f$ (with f of those robots possibly being Byzantine), the problem of Byzantine resilient convergence is impossible to solve under a fully asynchronous scheduler. The result is proved for the weaker ATOM model, and thus extends to the CORDA model.

Our proof is based on a particular initial setting from which we prove that no cautious convergence algorithm is possible if the activation of robots is handled by a fully asynchronous scheduler. Consider a network N of n robots placed on a line segment $[A, B]$, f of which may be Byzantine with $n \leq 5f$. We consider that robots are ordered from left to right. This order is only given for ease of presentation of the proof and is unknown to robots that cannot use it in their algorithms. It was proved in [9] that the problem is impossible to solve when $n \leq 3f$, we thus consider here the case when $3f < n \leq 5f$ only. The initial placement of the m correct robots (with $m \geq n - f$) is illustrated in Figure 1: f robots are at location A, another f correct robots are at location B and the remaining $m - 2f$ ones are located at some intermediate location between A and B. The impossibility proof depends on the ability of the adversary to move these $m - 2f$ robots along $[A, B]$, so their position is denoted by a variable X, with X belonging to interval (A, B). In the following, these three groups of robots located at A, B and X will be referred as $SetA$, $SetB$ and $SetX$ respectively. The positions of the Byzantine robots are determined by the adversary.

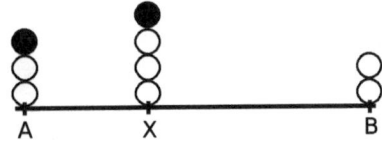

Fig. 1. Robot Network N (Configuration C_1) for $(n = 9, f = 2)$

We show by contradiction that in these conditions, no cautious convergence algorithm is possible. Assume that there exists a cautious convergence algorithm P that is correct when the robots are activated by a fully asynchronous scheduler, then we show that in this setting, any cautious algorithm P satisfies properties that can by used by the adversary to prevent convergence of P, which is a contradiction.

The properties satisfied by all cautious protocols are captured in the following two basic facts:

- **Fact 1:** If all *Byzantine* robots are inside $[A, X]$ (resp. $[X, B]$) then when a robot of $SetA$ (resp. $SetB$) is activated, its calculated destination point is necessarily inside $[A, X]$ (resp. $[X, B]$). This fact is proved by Lemma 1.
- **Fact 2:** The adversary is able to move the robots of $SetX$ as close as desired to location A (resp. B). This is proved by Lemmas 2, 3 and 4.

Based on this, the adversary first moves the robots of $SetX$ very close to A (using Fact 2) and then activates the robots of $SetA$ that remain in the neighborhood of A (due to Fact 1). Afterward, it moves the intermediate robots of $SetX$ very close to B (using Fact 2) and activates the robots of $SetB$ which also remain in the neighborhood of B (due to Fact 1). By repeating these actions indefinitely, the adversary ensures that every robot is activated infinitely often in the execution yet prevents convergence at the same time since robots at A and B remain always arbitrarily close to their initial positions and never converge.

In the following, we prove $Fact1$ and $Fact2$ by a sequence of lemmas, and then give a formal presentation of the algorithm used by the adversary to prevent any cautious protocol from achieving convergence.

Lemma 1. *In the robot network N, $\forall X \in (A, B)$, if $|SetB| = f$ (resp.$|SetA| = f$) and if all Byzantine robots are inside $[A, X]$ (resp. $[X, B]$) then when robots of SetA (resp. SetB) are activated, their destination points computed by any cautious algorithm are necessarily inside $[A, X]$ (resp. $[X, B]$).*

Proof: We prove the lemma only for the case when all Byzantine robots are inside $[A, X]$, and we denote the corresponding configuration by C_1 (see Figure 1). The case where all Byzantine robots are inside $[X, B]$ is symmetric.

Let C_2 (see Figure 2) be a similar configuration of n robots where the distribution of positions is isomorphic to that of C_1, but where the correct and Byzantine robots are located differently: all robots at B are Byzantine (there

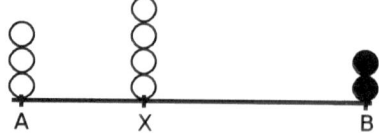

Fig. 2. Illustration of Lemma 1, configuration C_2

are f such robots), and all robots inside $[A, X]$ are correct. Since the robot convergence algorithm is cautious, the diameter of correct robots in C_2 must never increase, and then all their calculated destination points must lay inside $[A, X]$. Since C_1 and C_2 are indistinguishable to individual robots of $SetA$, the Look and Compute phases give the same result in the two cases, which proves our lemma.   □

To prove $Fact2$, we use the robot network N described above (see Figure 1). We prove only the capability of the adversary to move the intermediate robots at X as close as wanted to B, the other case being symmetric. $Fact2$ implies that if the number of robots in the network is lower or equal to $5f$ then it always exists a judicious placement of the Byzantine robots that permits the adversary to make the intermediate robots in X move in the direction of B up to a location that is as close as desired to B. We divide the analysis in two cases depending on the parity of $(n - f)$.

Case 1: $(n - f)$ **is even.** To push the robots of $SetX$ as close to A or B as wanted, the adversary uses algorithm $GoToBorder1$ ($G2B1$) described as Algorithm 1. Informally, the algorithm divides Byzantine robots between position X and the target border to which the adversary wants to push the robots of $SetX$ (e.g. B in what follows). The aim of the adversary is to maintain the same number of robots in X and B (this is possible because $n - f$ is even). We prove that in this case, any cautious convergence algorithm makes the robots of $SetX$ move towards B. However, the distance traveled by them may be too small to bring them sufficiently close to B. Since the scheduler is fully asynchronous, it is authorized to activate the robots of $SetX$ as often as necessary to bring them close to B, as long as it does so for a finite number of times.

Algorithm 1. GoToBorder1 ($G2B1$)

Input: $Border$: the border towards which robots of $SetX$ move (equal to A or B).
Input: d: a distance.

Actions:
while $distance(X, Border) > d$ **do**
    Place $(n - 3f)/2$ Byzantine robots at $Border$.
    Place $(5f - n)/2$ Byzantine robots at X.
    Activate simultaneously all robots of $SetX$ and make them move to their computed destination D.
    $X \leftarrow D$
end while

Lemma 2. *Let* $3f < n \le 5f$ *with* $(n - f)$ *even. If robots run a cautious convergence algorithm then algorithm* $G2B1(Border, d)$ *terminates for any* $d < distance(A, B)$ *and any* $Border \in \{A, B\}$.

Proof: We prove the Lemma by contradiction. We assume that the algorithm does not terminate for a given input distance d_0, and we prove that this leads

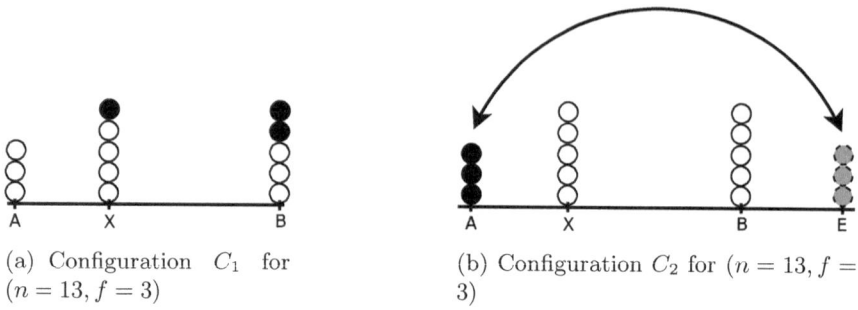

(a) Configuration C_1 for $(n = 13, f = 3)$

(b) Configuration C_2 for $(n = 13, f = 3)$

Fig. 3. Illustration of lemma 2 (Fact2, $(n - f)$ even)

to a contradiction. We consider only the case where $Border = B$, the other case being symmetric. The non-termination of the algorithm implies that there exists some distance $d_1 \leq d_0$ such that robots at X and B always remain distant by at least d_1 from each other, even if robots at X are activated indefinitely.

Note that the placement of Byzantine robots in $G2B1$ implies that initially, and for $n \leq 5f$, the number of robots located at X and B is the same and is equal to $(n - f)/2$ as illustrated in Figure 3.(a). We denote by C_1 the resulting configuration. We now construct a configuration C_2 (see Figure 3.(b)) that is isomorphic to C_1 but with a different distribution of Byzantine and correct robots: correct robots are divided equally between X and B, $(n - f)/2$ correct robots at X and $(n - f)/2$ others at B. By hypothesis, these robots are supposed to converge to a single point (located between X and B as the convergence point is computed by a cautious algorithm).

The placement of Byzantine robots and the choice of activated robots at each cycle is divided into two parts. During even cycles, Byzantine robots are placed at point A and robots located at X are activated. During odd cycles, the scheduler constructs a strictly symmetrical configuration by moving Byzantine robots from A to a point E with $E > B$ and $distance(B, E) = distance(A, X)$. In this case, the scheduler activates robots at B.

In these conditions, activating robots at X ensures that they always remain at a distance of at least d_1 from those located at B (as in configuration C_1). Indeed, configurations C_1 and C_2 are equivalent and completely indistinguishable to individual robots which must behave similarily in both cases (as the algorithm is deterministic). And by symmetry, the activation of robots at B during odd cycles also ensures that minimum distance of d_1 between the two groups of robots. Hence, robots at X and B remain separated by a distance of at least d_1 forever even if activated indefinitely, which prevents the convergence of the algorithm and leads to a contradiction. This proves our Lemma.   □

Case 2: $(n - f)$ **is odd.** To prove Lemma 2, we relied on the symmetry induced by the placement of Byzantine robots. This symmetry is possible only because $(n - f)$ is even. Indeed, having the same number of robots in B and X implies that convergence responsibility is delegated to both robots at X and at B (there is no asymmetry to exploit to get one of these two groups to play a role that would be different from the other group. Robots of $SetX$ and $SetB$ have thus no other choice but to move toward each other when they are activated. The distance traveled at each activation must be large enough to ensure the eventual convergence of the algorithm.

However, the situation is quite different when $(n - f)$ is odd. Indeed, the number of robots is necessarily different in X and B, which means that one of the two points has a greater multiplicity than the other. Then in this case there is no guarantee that a cautious convergence algorithm will order the robots of $SetX$ to move toward B when they are activated (the protocol could delegate the convergence responsibility to robots of $SetB$). Nevertheless, we observe that whatever the cautious algorithm is, if it does not move the robots that are located at the greatest point of multiplicity, it must do so for those at the smallest one (and *vice versa*), otherwise no convergence is ever possible. The convergence is thus either under the responsibility of robots at the larger point of multiplicity or those at the smaller one (or both).

This observation is exploited by Algorithm $GoToBorder2$ $(G2B2)$ that is presented as Algorithm 2, that tries the two possible cases to ensure its proper functioning when confronted to any cautious algorithm. The algorithm forms the larger point of multiplicity at B at one cycle, and the next cycle at X. Thus, point X will be the larger point of multiplicity one time, and the smallest one the next time. This implies that the robots of $SetX$ must move towards B at least once every two cycles. So by repeatedly alternating between the two configurations where robots of $SetX$ are successively the set of larger and smaller multiplicity, the adversary ensures that they end up moving towards B. The fully asynchrony of the scheduler ensures that they are activated as many times as it takes to move them as close to B as wanted, provided that the algorithm terminates.

Algorithm 2. GoToBorder2 (G2B2)

Input: *Border*: the border towards which the robots of $SetX$ move (equal to A or B).

Input: d: a distance.

Actions:
Place $(n - 3f + 1)/2$ Byzantine robots at *Border*.
Place $(5f - n - 1)/2$ Byzantine robots at X.
while $distance(X, Border) > d$ **do**
    Activate simultaneously all robots at X and make them move to their computed destination D.
    $X \leftarrow D$.
    Move a Byzantine robot from *Border* to X.
    Activate simultaneously all robots at X and make them move to their computed destination D.
    $X \leftarrow D$
    Move a Byzantine robot from X to *Border*.
end while

Lemma 3. *Let $3f < n \le 5f$ with $(n - f)$ odd. If robots run a cautious convergence algorithm then algorithm $G2B2(Border, d)$ terminates for any $d < distance(A, B)$ and any $Border \in \{A, B\}$.*

Proof: We consider in our proof only the case when $Border = B$ since the other case is symmetric. The placement of Byzantine robots in $G2B2$ is such that the multiplicity of X exceeds that of B by 1 during even cycles, and lowers it by 1 during odd cycles. We denote by C_0 the initial configuration (in which the multiplicity of X is less than of B by 1 as illustrated in Figure 4.(a)).

We assume for the purpose of contradiction that $G2B2$ does not terminate for some input distance d_0. This means that robots of $SetX$ and $SetB$ remain always distant from each others by a distance at least equal to d_1 with d_1 being some distance $\le d_0$. The resulting execution in this case is denoted by $E_0 = \{C_0, C_1, C_2, C_3, ...\}$. A configuration C_{i+1} is obtained from C_i by activating robots at X, letting them execute their Move phases, and moving one Byzantine robot from X to B or *vice versa*.

We construct a configuration C'_0 equivalent to C_0 but where correct robots are divided between X and B with $\lfloor(n - f)/2\rfloor$ robots at X and $\lceil(n - f)/2\rceil$ robots at B (see Figure 4.(b)). By definition, these robots must converge to a point between X and B since they are endowed with a cautious convergence algorithm. Byzantine robots are at A. Since C'_0 and C_0 are equivalent, the activation of robots at X and the displacement of Byzantine robots to the right of B will produce a configuration C'_1 that is equivalent to C_1 by symmetry.

This time, activated robots are those at B. By moving them to their calculated destination points and by moving Byzantine robots again to the left of X the scheduler can form a configuration C'_2 which is equivalent to C_2.

This process can be repeated: during odd cycles, Byzantine robots are at the left of X and robots at X are activated. During even cycles, the situation is symmetrical: Byzantine robots are to the right of B and robots at B are activated. The obtained execution $E'_0 = \{C'_0, C'_1, C'_2, C'_3, ...\}$ is equivalent to E_0, and robots at X and B remain separated by a distance at least equal to d_1 forever even if they are activated indefinitely. This prevents the convergence of

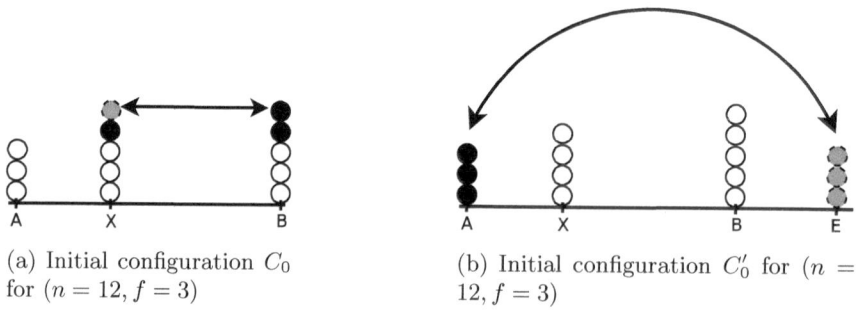

(a) Initial configuration C_0 for $(n = 12, f = 3)$

(b) Initial configuration C'_0 for $(n = 12, f = 3)$

Fig. 4. Illustration of lemma 3 (Fact2, $(n - f)$ odd)

the convergence protocol while ensuring fairness of activations, which contradicts the assumptions and proves our Lemma.   □

We are now ready to prove $Fact2$.

Lemma 4. *For $3f < n \leq 5f$, $\forall d < distance(A, B)$, if the robots run a cautious convergence algorithm, the fully distributed scheduler is able to move the robots of $SetX$ into a position $\geq B - d$ or $\leq A + d$.*

Proof: The proof follows directly from Lemmas 2 and 3.   □

The Split function. The purpose of Algorithms $G2B1$ and $G2B2$ is to push the intermediate robots of $SetX$ as close as the adversary wants to the extremities of the network. For ease of the description, we assume the following that the adversary wants to push them towards the extremity B. These two routines are then used by the adversary to prevent the convergence of the algorithm. For the algorithm of the adversary to work, it is necessary to keep the robots of $SetA$, $SetB$ and $SetX$ separated from each other and to avoid for example that the robots of $SetX$ merge with those of $SetB$ and form a single point of multiplicity. Yet, functions $G2B1$ and $G2B2$ cannot prevent such a situation to appear because the destinations are computed by the convergence algorithm which can order the robots to move exactly towards B. If the distance to travel is too small ($distance(X, B) \leq \delta_i$ for all $i \in SetX$), then the adversary can not stop the robots of $SetX$ before they arrive at B. To recover from this situation and separate the robots that have merged, we define a new function $Split(Set, Border)$ which separates the robots of Set from those located at $Border$. For example, $Split(SetX, B)$ separates the robots of $SetX$ from those of $SetB$ by directing them towards A. Lemma 5 is used to prove that function $Split$ performs as planned. Let N be a network of n robots divided between two positions A and B. let p and q be the number of robots at A and B respectively such that $|p - q| \leq f$. These robots are endowed with a cautious convergence algorithm that tolerates the presence of up to f Byzantine robots. Lemma 5 proves that if a robot in A or B is activated, it cannot remain in its position and moves toward the robots located in the other point.

Lemma 5. *Let N be a network of n robots divided between two positions A and B, and let p and q be the number of robots at A and B respectively such that $|p - q| \leq f$, then if a robot at A (resp. B) is activated, its destination computed by any cautious convergence algorithm lays inside $(A, B]$ (resp. $[A, B)$).*

Proof: Let C_1 be the initial configuration, and consider the computed destination by an activated robot located at A (the case of a robot located at B is symmetric). Since the algorithm is cautious, this destination point is necessarily located inside $[A, B]$. For the lemma to be correct, it suffices then to prove that this destination is different from A. In other words, we must prove that the robot moves towards B upon its activation. So assume for the sake of contradiction that it is not the case, that is, the computed destination is A and let us separate the analysis into three cases depending on the relationship between p and q:

- **Case 1** ($p > q$): Let C_2 be a configuration isomorphic to C_1 with the following placement of robots: At A there are f Byzantine robots and $p - f$ correct ones, and at B are located q correct robots. Since Configurations C_1 and C_2 are indistinguishable to individual robots, the destinations computed in the two cases are the same. So when the robots at A are activated, they do not move. The next cycle, the adversary moves $p - q$ Byzantine robots from A to B to obtain a configuration C_3 symmetric to C_2 with respect to individual robots. This time, the adversary activates the robots at B which do not move neither since robots cannot distinguish between C_2 and C_3. Then, the adversary brings back the $p - q$ Byzantine robots to A to get again the configuration C_2 and then activates the robots at A. The process repeats, and by placing these $p - q$ Byzantine robots in one cycle at A and the next cycle at B, the adversary prevents the convergence of the algorithm. This is a contradiction.
- **Case 2** ($p < q$): We can reach a contradiction by using an argument similar to Case 1.
- **Case 3** ($p = q$): If the activated robots at A do not move upon their activation, it is also the case at B since the configuration is symmetric. This prevents the convergence of the algorithm and leads also to a contradiction.

□

We now present Function $Split(Set, Border)$ that is presented as Algorithm 3. We first define $Max\delta$ as $max\{\delta_i/i$ is a correct robot$\}$ such that δ_i is the minimum distance that can be traveled by a robot i before it may be stopped by the adversary. This means that if a group of robots ($SetX$ in our case) are distant from their destination by more than $Max\delta$, the adversary is able to stop them all before they reach their destination. Notice now that in the setting of network N described in Figure 1, $SetA$ and $SetB$ contain each exactly f correct robots. If robots of $SetX$ merge with those of $SetB$ for example, they form a set of $n - 2f$ correct robots colocated in the same multiplicity point. By placing all the Byzantine robots at A, this location contains a set of $2f$ robots. The difference between the two sets of robots in A and B is lower or equal to f (because $3f < n \leq 5f$). Then if we activate the robots of $SetX$ (which are located at B), they will move towards A according to Lemma 5. By stopping these robots once they all travelled a distance equal to $Max\delta$ or reached their destination before, we ensure that the three sets $SetA$, $SetX$ and $SetB$ are disjoint, because the initial distance between A and B is $> Max\delta$.

The fully asynchronous scheduler algorithm

Theorem 1. *In the ATOM model, the problem of Byzantine resilient convergence is impossible to solve with a cautious algorithm under a fully asynchronous scheduler in unidimensional robot networks when $n \leq 5f$.*

Proof: We prove that for network N, there can be no cautious convergence algorithm for $n \leq 5f$ if the robots are activated by a fully asynchronous scheduler. It was shown in [9] that convergence of robots is impossible in unidimensional networks in the presence of Byzantine failures when $n \leq 3f$. The algorithm of the

---

Algorithm 3. Function Split(Set, Border)

Require: $distance(A, B) > Max\delta$

Variables:
Input: $Border$: is equal to A or to B.
Input: Set: the set of robots to move away from $Border$.
$OppositeBorder$: is equal to B if the input $Border$ is equal to A, and vice versa.

Actions:
Place all Byzantine robots in $OppositeBorder$.
Activate the robots of Set, and stop them at a point $Max\delta$ away from $Border$.

Algorithm 4. Adversary Algorithm

Require: $distance(A, B) > Max\delta$

Definitions:
d_0: any distance that is strictly smaller than $distance(A, B)/4$, let $d_0 \leftarrow distance(A, B)/10$.
$G2B(Border, d)$: equal to $G2B1(Border, d)$ if $n - f$ is even and equal to $G2B2(Border, d)$ if $n - f$ is odd

Actions:
while true **do**
   $G2B(A, d_0)$.
   Activate the robots at A.
   if the robots of SetX are at A, then $Split(SetX, A)$.
   $G2B(B, d_0)$.
   Activate the robots at B.
   if the robots of $SetX$ are at B, then $Split(SetX, B)$.
   $d_0 \leftarrow d_0/2$
end while

---

adversary for the case when $3f < n \leq 5f$ is given as Algorithm 4 and it can prevent any cautious algorithm to converge. Indeed, if the initial distance between robots at A and B is equal to d, then these robots will always remain distant from each other by a distance at least equal to $d - 2\sum_{k\geq0}(d_0/2^k) = 6d/10$. The proof of algorithm 4 follows directly from Lemmas 1, 4 and 5. □

4   Deterministic Asynchronous Convergence

In this section, we propose a deterministic convergence algorithm and prove its correctness in CORDA model under a fully asynchronous scheduler when there are at least $5f + 1$ robots, f of which may be Byzantine.

Algorithm Description. The idea of our algorithm is based on three mechanisms: (1) a trimming function for the computation of destinations, (2) location dependency and (3) an election procedure. The purpose of the trimming function is to ignore the most extreme positions in the network when computing the destination. Robots move hence towards the center of the remaining positions. Consequently, the effect of Byzantine robots is canceled since they cannot drag the correct robots away from the range of correct positions.

Location dependency affects the computation of the trimming function such that the returned result depends on the position of the calling robot. This leads to interesting properties on the relation between the position of a robot and its destination that are critical to convergence. The election procedure instructs to move only the robots located at the two extremes of the network. Thus, by the combined effect of these three mechanisms, as the algorithm progresses, the extreme robots come together towards the middle of the range of correct positions which ensures the eventual convergence of the algorithm.

The algorithm uses three functions as follows. The trimming function $trim^i_{2f}()$ removes among the $2f$ largest positions of the multiset given in parameter *only* those that are greater than the position of the calling robot i. Similarly, it removes among the $2f$ smallest positions only those that are smaller than the position of the calling robot. It is clear that the output of $trim^i_{2f}()$ depends on the position of the calling robot. Formally, let $minindex_i$ be the index of the minimum position between $P_i(t)$ and $P_{2f+1}(t)$ (if $P_i(t) < P_{2f+1}(t)$ then $minindex_i$ is equal to i, otherwise it is equal to $2f+1$). Similarly, let $maxindex_i$ be the index of the maximum position between $P_i(t)$ and $P_{n-2f}(t)$ (if $P_i(t) > P_{n-2f}(t)$ then $maxindex_i$ is equal to i, otherwise it is equal to $n-2f$). $trim^i_{2f}(P(t))$ is the multiset consisting of positions $\{P_{minindex_i}(t), P_{minindex_i+1}(t), \ldots, P_{maxindex_i}(t)\}$.

The function $center()$ simply returns the median point of the input range. The two functions are illustrated in Figure 5).

The election function returns true if the calling robot is allowed to move. Only the robots that are located at the extremes of the networks are allowed to move, that is those whose position is either $\leq P_{f+1}(t)$ or $\geq P_{n-f}(t)$.

By definition, convergence aims at asymptotically decreasing the range of possible positions for the correct robots. The shrinking property captures this property. An algorithm is shrinking if there exists a constant factor $\alpha \in (0, 1)$ such that starting in any configuration the range of correct robots eventually decreases by a multiplicative α factor. Note that to deal with the asynchrony of the model, the diameter calculation takes into account both the positions and destinations of correct robots.

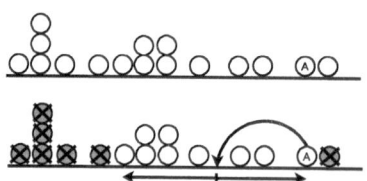

Fig. 5. Illustration of functions $trim^i_{2f}$ and $center$ for robots A in a system of ($n = 16, f = 3$) robots

---

Algorithm 5. Convergence Algorithm under a fully asynchronous Scheduler

---

Functions:

$trim^i_{2f}(P(t))$: removes up to $2f$ largest positions that are larger than $P_i(t)$ and up to $2f$ smallest positions that are smaller than $P_i(t)$ from the multiset $P(t)$ given in parameter.

$center()$: returns the point that is in the middle of the range of points given in parameter.

$elected() \equiv ((P_i(t) \leq P_{f+1}(t))$ or $(P_i(t) \geq P_{n-f}(t)))$. This function returns true if the calling robot is allowed to move.

Actions:

if $elected()$ move towards $center(trim^i_{2f}(P(t)))$

Definition 2 (Shrinking Algorithm). *An algorithm is* shrinking *if and only if* $\exists \alpha \in (0,1)$ *such that* $\forall t, \exists t' > t$, *such that* $diam(U(t') \cup D(t')) < \alpha * diam(U(t) \cup D(t))$, *where* $U(t)$ *and* $D(t)$ *are respectively the the multisets of positions and destinations of correct robots.*

A natural way to solve convergence is to never let the algorithm increase the diameter of correct robot positions. In this case the algorithm is called *cautious*. This notion was first introduced in [10]. A cautious algorithm is particularly appealing in the context of Byzantine failures since it always instructs a correct robot to move inside the range of the positions held by the correct robots regardless of the locations of Byzantine ones. The following definition introduced first in [8] customizes the definition of cautious algorithm proposed in [10] to robot networks.

Definition 3 (Cautious Algorithm). *Let* $D_i(t)$ *be the last destination calculated by the robot* i *before time* t *and let* $U^i(t)$ *the positions of the correct robots as seen by robot* i *before time* t. [3] *An algorithm is* cautious *if it meets the following conditions: (i)* ***cautiousness:*** $\forall t$, $D_i(t) \in range(U^i(t))$ *for each robot* i, *and (ii)* ***non-triviality:*** $\forall t$, *if* $diameter(U(t)) \neq 0$ *then* $\exists t' > t$ *and a robot* i *such that* $D_i(t') \neq U_i(t')$ *(at least one correct robot changes its position whenever convergence is not achieved).*

Theorem 2. *[8] Any algorithm that is both cautious and shrinking solves the convergence problem in faulty robots networks.*

In order to prove the correctness of Algorithm 5 in the CORDA model under a fully asynchronous scheduler, we prove first that it is cautious then we show that it satisfies the specification of a shrinking algorithm. Convergence then follows from Theorem 2. The proof is omitted due to space limitations; please refer to [11] for details.

---

[3] If the last calculation was executed at time $t' \leq t$ then $D_i(t) = D_i(t')$.

5 Concluding Remarks

Our work closes the study of the convergence problem for unidimensional robot networks. We studied the convergence problem under the most generic settings: asynchronous robots under unbounded adversaries and Byzantine fault model. We proved that in these settings the Byzantine resilience lower bound is $5f + 1$ and we propose and prove correct the first deterministic convergence algorithm that meets this lower bound. We currently investigate the extension of the current work to the multi-dimensional spaces.

References

[1] Suzuki, I., Yamashita, M.: Distributed anonymous mobile robots: Formation of geometric patterns. SIAM Journal of Computing 28(4), 1347–1363 (1999)
[2] Prencipe, G.: Corda: Distributed coordination of a set of autonomous mobile robots. In: Proc. 4th European Research Seminar on Advances in Distributed Systems (ERSADS 2001), Bertinoro, Italy, May 2001, pp. 185–190 (2001)
[3] Prencipe, G.: On the feasibility of gathering by autonomous mobile robots. In: Pelc, A., Raynal, M. (eds.) SIROCCO 2005. LNCS, vol. 3499, pp. 246–261. Springer, Heidelberg (2005)
[4] Agmon, N., Peleg, D.: Fault-tolerant gathering algorithms for autonomous mobile robots. In: Symposium on Discrete Algorithms: Proceedings of the fifteenth annual ACM-SIAM symposium on Discrete algorithms, vol. 11(14), pp. 1070–1078 (2004)
[5] Defago, X., Gradinariu, M., Messika, S., Parvedy, P.: Fault-tolerant and self-stabilizing mobile robots gathering. In: Dolev, S. (ed.) DISC 2006. LNCS, vol. 4167, pp. 46–60. Springer, Heidelberg (2006)
[6] Cohen, R., Peleg, D.: Robot convergence via center-of-gravity algorithms. In: Kralovic, R., Sýkora, O. (eds.) SIROCCO 2004. LNCS, vol. 3104, pp. 79–88. Springer, Heidelberg (2004)
[7] Cohen, R., Peleg, D.: Convergence properties of the gravitational algorithm in asynchronous robot systems. SIAM Journal on Computing 34(6), 1516–1528 (2005)
[8] Bouzid, Z., Potop-Butucaru, M.G., Tixeuil, S.: Byzantine-resilient convergence in oblivious robot networks. In: International Conference on Distributed Systems and Networks (ICDCN 2009), January 2009, pp. 275–280 (2009)
[9] Bouzid, Z., Potop-Butucaru, M.G., Tixeuil, S.: Optimal byzantine resilient convergence in asynchronous robot networks. In: Guerraoui, R., Petit, F. (eds.) SSS 2009. LNCS, vol. 5873, pp. 165–179. Springer, Heidelberg (2009)
[10] Dolev, D., Lynch, N., Pinter, S., Stark, E., Weihl, W.: Reaching approximate agreement in the presence of faults. Journal of the ACM (JACM) 33(3), 499–516 (1986)
[11] Bouzid, Z., Potop-Butucaru, M.G., Tixeuil, S.: Byzantine convergence in robots networks: The price of asynchrony. CoRR abs/0908.0390 (2009)

Deaf, Dumb, and Chatting Asynchronous Robots

Enabling Distributed Computation and Fault-Tolerance among Stigmergic Robots*

Yoann Dieudonné[1], Shlomi Dolev[2], Franck Petit[3], and Michael Segal[4]

[1] MIS, Université of Picardie Jules Verne, France
[2] Department of Computer Science, Ben-Gurion University of the Negev, Israel
[3] LiP6/CNRS/INRIA-REGAL, Université Pierre et Marie Curie - Paris 6, France
[4] Communication Systems Engineering Dept, Ben-Gurion University of the Negev, Israel

Abstract. We investigate avenues for the exchange of information (explicit communication) among deaf and dumb mobile robots scattered in the plane. We introduce the use of movement-signals (analogously to flight signals and bees waggle) as a mean to transfer messages, enabling the use of distributed algorithms among robots. We propose one-to-one deterministic movement protocols that implement explicit communication among asynchronous robots. We first show how the movements of robots can provide implicit acknowledgment in asynchronous systems. We use this result to design one-to-one communication among a pair of robots. Then, we propose two one-to-one communication protocols for any system of $n \geq 2$ robots. The former works for robots equipped with observable IDs that agree on a common direction (sense of direction). The latter enables one-to-one communication assuming robots devoid of any observable IDs or sense of direction. All three protocols (for either two or any number of robots) assume that no robot remains inactive forever. However, they cannot avoid that the robots move either away or closer of each others, by the way requiring robots with an infinite visibility. In this paper, we also present how to overcome these two disadvantages.

These protocols enable the use of distributing algorithms based on message exchanges among swarms of Stigmergic robots. They also allow robots to be equipped with the means of communication to tolerate faults in their communication devices.

Keywords: Explicit Communication, Mobile Robot Networks, Stigmergy.

1 Introduction

Although research in achieving coordination among teams (or swarms) of mobile robots is challenging, it has great scientific and practical implications. Swarms of mobile robots are currently being utilized and are expected to be employed even more in the future, in various critical situations. Swarms foster the ability to measure properties, collect information, and act in any given (sometimes dangerous) physical

---

* The work of Shlomi Dolev and Michael Segal has been partially supported by US Air Force grant.

T. Abdelzaher, M. Raynal, and N. Santoro (Eds.): OPODIS 2009, LNCS 5923, pp. 71–85, 2009.
© Springer-Verlag Berlin Heidelberg 2009

environment. Numerous potential applications exist for such multi-robot systems: environmental monitoring, large-scale construction, risky area surrounding or surveillance, and the exploration of awkward environments, to name only a few.

In any given environment, the ability of a swarm of robots to succeed in accomplishing the assigned task depends greatly on the capabilities that the robots possess, that is, their moving capacities and sensory organs. Existing technologies allow the consideration of robots equipped with sensory devices for vision (camera, radar, sonar, laser, etc.) and means of communication (wireless devices). Furthermore, means of communication are required to enable classical distributed algorithms and to achieve the completion of several tasks, such as information relay, surveillance, or intelligence activities.

An interesting question is *"What happens if the means of communication are lost or do not exist?"* In this case, the robots can observe the location of other robots but cannot communicate with them. Such robots are called *deaf and dumb*. There are numerous realistic scenarios where there are no means for communication among robots. Such scenarios are easily deciphered, *e.g.,*

- Wireless devices are faulty,
- Robots evolve in zones with blocked wireless communication (hostile environments where communication is scrambled or forbidden), or
- Physical constraints prevent placing wireless devices on robots.

The latter may arise when no space is available on the robots or the robots themselves are too small with respect to the size of the wireless device. Such is the case with swarms of nano-robots.

The question of solving distributed tasks with swarms of deaf and dumb robots is not a novel one. This question has been extensively posed in different fields of computed science such as artificial intelligence [18], control theory [15,20,6], and recently in the distributed computing field [24,21]. Some of these approaches are inspired by biological studies of animal behavior, mainly the behavior of social insects [3]. Indeed, these social systems present an intelligent collective behavior, despite being composed of simple individuals with extremely limited capabilities. Solutions to problems "naturally" emerge from the self-organization and indirect communication of these individuals. The capacity to communicate using such *indirect communication* (or, *implicit* communication) is referred to as *stigmergy* in the biological literature [17]. There are numerous examples of such indirect communication in nature, for instance ants and termites communicating using pheromones, or bees communicating by performing waggle dances to find the shortest paths between their nests and food sources. The question of whether the waggle of bees is a language or not is even an issue [27]. Bee waggle dances has been an inspiration source in recent researches in various areas related to the distributed systems, *e.g., swarm intelligence* [11] and *communication technologies* [26,25].

However, stigmergy leads to the completion of only one given task at a time. Communication is not considered as a task in and of itself. In other words, the stigmergic phenomenon provides indirect communication; guidance for a specific assignment. Even if stigmergy sometimes allows insects to modify their physical environment, —this phenomenon is sometime referred to as *sematectonic stigmergy* [12]— stigmergy never provides a communication task alone. Stigmergy does not allow tasks such as chatting, intelligence activities, or the sending of information unrelated to a specific task.

In this paper, we investigate avenues for the exchange of information among deaf and dumb mobile robots scattered in the plane. In the sequel, we refer to this task as *explicit communication*—sometimes, also referred to as *direct* communication [18]. Explicit communication enables the use of distributed algorithms among robots. We study the possibility of solving this problem deterministically so that robots communicate only by moving.

Contribution. We introduce the use of movement-signals (analogously to flight signals and bee waggles) as a mean to transfer messages between deaf and dumb robots. We propose one-to-one deterministic protocols that implement explicit communication among asynchronous robots.

In asynchronous settings, each computation step may contain some robots that remain inactive. So, a number of robot movements can go unnoticed and, thus, some messages can be lost as well. As a consequence, each message is required to be acknowledged by the addressees. We first demonstrate how robot movements can provide implicit acknowledgment in asynchronous settings. We straightforwardly use this result in the design of asynchronous one-to-one communication among a pair of robots.

Next, we propose two one-to-one communication protocols that fits the general case of asynchronous systems of $n \geq 2$ robots. The former protocol assumes robots equipped with observable IDs that agree on a common direction (sense of direction). The latter is a routing protocol enabling one-to-one communication among robots that agree on a common handedness (*chirality*) only, *i.e.*, they are *anonymous* and *disoriented*—devoid of any observable IDs and have no sense of direction. Since one-to-one communication must include a technique allowing any robot to send messages to a specific robot, our protocol builds a naming system based on the positions of the robots that allows them to address one another.

All three protocols, either for two or n robots, are presented in the *semi-synchronous model* [24], imposing a certain amount of synchrony among the active robots, *i.e.*, at each time instant, the robots which are activated, observe, compute, and move in one atomic step. However, no other assumption is made on the relative frequency of robot activations with respect to each other, except that each robot is activated infinitely often (uniform fair activation). This lack of synchronization among the robots prevents the robots either to move away of or to get closer to each other infinitely often. As a consequence, the robots are required to have an *infinite visibility*. Visibility capability of the robots is an important issue [1,14]. In this paper, we also show how to overcome these drawbacks by introducing relaxed form of synchrony. By relaxed, we mean that the robots are not required to be strictly synchronous. A bound $k \geq 1$ is assumed on the maximum activation drift among the robots, *i.e.*, no robot can be activated more than k times between two consecutive activations of any other robot.

Note that our protocols can be easily adapted to efficiently implement one-to-many or one-to-all explicit communication. Also, in the context of robots (explicitly) interacting by means of communication (*e.g.*, wireless), since our protocols allow robots to explicitly communicate even if their communication devices are faulty, in a very real sense, our solution can serve as a communication backup, *i.e.*, it provides *fault-tolerance* by allowing the robots to communicate without means of communication (wireless devices).

Related Work. The issue of handling swarms of robots using deterministic distributed algorithms was first studied in [24]. Beyond supplying formal correctness proofs, the main motivation is to understand the relationship between the capabilities of robots and the solvability of given tasks. For instance, *"Assuming that the robots agree on a common direction (having a compass), which tasks are they able to deterministically achieve?"*, or *"What are the minimal conditions to elect a leader deterministically?"* As a matter of fact, the motivation turns out to be the study of the minimum level of ability that the robots are required to have to accomplish basic cooperative tasks in a deterministic way. Examples of such tasks are specific problems, such as *pattern formation, line formation, gathering, spreading,* and *circle formation*—refer for instance to [24,13,7,21,4,14,22,8,5] for these problems,— or more "classical" problems in the field of distributed systems, such as *leader election* [21,13,9]. To the best of our knowledge, no previous work addresses the problem of enabling explicit communication in swarms of robots.

Roadmap. In the next section (Section 2), we describe the model and the problem considered in this paper. In Section 3, we show how robot movements can provide implicit acknowledgment in asynchronous settings. In the same section, we propose a straightforward communication protocol for two asynchronous robots. Section 4 is devoted to one-to-one communication for any number of robots. The motion containment is discussed in Section 5. Finally, we make some concluding remarks in Section 6.

2   Preliminaries

In this section, we first define the distributed system considered in this paper. We then state the problem to be solved.

Model. We adopt the model introduced in [24], below referred to as *Semi-Synchronous Model (SSM).* The distributed system considered in this paper consists of n mobile *robots* (*agents* or *sensors*). Any robot can observe, compute, and move with infinite decimal precision. The robots are equipped with sensors enabling them to instantaneously detect (to take a snapshot) of the position of the other robots in the plane in their own Cartesian coordinate system. Viewed as points in the Euclidean plane, the robots are mobile and autonomous. There is no kind of explicit communication medium between robots.

Each robot r has its own local x-y Cartesian coordinate system with its own unit measure. Given an x-y Cartesian coordinate system, *handedness* is the way in which the orientation of the y axis (respectively, the x axis) is inferred according to the orientation of the x axis (resp., the y axis). The robots are assumed to have the ability of *chirality*, *i.e.*, the n robots share the same handedness. We consider *non-oblivious* robots, *i.e.*, every robot can remember its previous observations, computations, or motions made in any step.

We assume that the system is either *identified* or *anonymous*. In the former case, each robot r is assumed to have a visible (or observable) identifier denoted id_r such that, for every pair r, r' of distinct robots, $id_r \neq id_{r'}$. In the latter, no robot is assumed to have a visible identifier. In this paper, we will also discuss whether the robots agree on the orientation of their y-axis or not. In the former case, the robots are said to have the *sense of direction*. (Note that since the robots have the ability of chirality, when the robots have the sense of direction, they also agree on their x-axis).

Time is represented as an infinite sequence of time instants $t_0, t_1, \ldots, t_j, \ldots$ Let $P(t_j)$ be the set of the positions in the plane occupied by the n robots at time t_j ($j \geq 0$). For every t_j, $P(t_j)$ is called the *configuration* of the distributed system in t_j. $P(t_j)$ expressed in the local coordinate system of any robot r_i is called a *view*. At each time instant t_j ($j \geq 0$), each robot r_i is either *active* or *inactive*. The former means that, during the computation step (t_j, t_{j+1}), using a given algorithm, r_i computes in its local coordinate system a new position $p_i(t_{j+1})$ depending only on the system configuration at t_j, and moves towards $p_i(t_{j+1})$. In the latter case (inactive), r_i does not perform any local computation and remains at the same position.

The concurrent activation of robots is modeled by the interleaving model in which the robot activations are driven by a *fair distributed scheduler*, i.e., at every instant, a non-empty subset of robots can be activated (distributed scheduler), and every robot is activated infinitively often (fairness).

In every single activation, the distance traveled by any robot r is bounded by σ_r. So, if the destination point computed by r is farther than σ_r, then r moves toward a point of at most σ_r. The value of σ_r may differ for different robots.

Problem. *Indirect* communication is the result of the observations of other robots. Using indirect communication, we aim to implement *Direct* communication that is a purely communicative act, with the sole purpose of transmitting messages [18]. In this paper, we consider directed communication that aims at a particular receiver. Such communication is said to be *one-to-one*, specified as follows: ($Emission$) If a robot r wants to send a message m to a robot r', then r eventually sends m to r'; ($Receipt$) Every robot eventually receives every message which is meant for it.

Note that the above specification induces that r is able to address r'. This implies that any protocol solving the above specification has to develop (1) A *routing* mechanism and (2) A *naming* mechanism, in the context of anonymous robots.

The specification also induces that the robots are able to communicate explicit messages. Hence, any one-to-one communication protocol in our model should be able (3) to code explicit messages with implicit communication, *i.e.*, with (non-ambiguous) movements.

3   Enabling Acknowledgment

Devoid of any mean of communication, the robots implicitly communicate by observing the position of the other robots in the plane, and by executing a part of their program accordingly. So, in our model, every letter of any message needs to be coded by a non-ambiguous movements. In a synchronous system where every robot is active at each time instant, every movement made by any robot would be seen by all the robots of the system. So, in such settings, there would be no concern with the receipt of each letter. Therefore, no acknowledgment would be required.

By contrast, in an asynchronous system, only fairness is assumed, *i.e.*, in each computation steps, some robots can remain inactive. So, some robot movements can go unnoticed, and as a consequence, some letters (by the way, some messages) can be lost as well. Therefore, a synchronization mechanism is required, ensuring acknowledgment of each message sent.

In the next subsection (Subsection 3.1), we first establish general results to implement such a synchronization mechanism. Next, in Subsection 3.2, we show that these results provide a straightforward solution working with two robots.

3.1 Implicit Acknowledgment

Let us first focus on both *Emission* and *Receipt* properties. We first state the following results:

Lemma 1. *Let r and r' be two robots. Assume that r always moves in the same direction each time it becomes active. If r observes that the position of r' has changed twice, then r' must have observed that the position of r has changed at least once.*

Proof. By contradiction, assume that at time t_i, r notes that the position of r' has changed twice and r' has not observed that the position of r has changed at least once. Without loss of generality, we assume that t_i is the first time for which r notes that the position of r' has changed twice. So at time t_i, r knows three distinct positions of r' and $t_i \geq 2$. Let p_j be the last (or the third) position of r' that r has observed, and t_j the first time instant for which p_j is occupied by r'. Obviously, $t_j < t_i$. Now we have two cases to consider :

- *Case 1 : $t_j = t_i - 1$.* The fact that r knows three distinct positions of r' implies that r is become active and has moved at least twice between $t = 0$ and $t = t_i - 1$ and, thus at least once between $t = 0$ and $t = t_i - 2$. Consequently, at time $t_j = t_i - 1$, r' would have noted that r's position has changed at least once. Contradiction.
- *Case 2 : $t_j \leq t_i - 2$.* We have two cases to consider :
  - *Case a :* r' moves at least once between $t_j + 1$ and $t_i - 1$. In this case, r notes that the position of r' has changed twice before time t_i : which contradicts the fact that t_i is the first time for which r notes that the position of r' has changed twice.
  - *Case b :* r' does not move between $t_j + 1$ and $t_i - 1$. As mentioned above, the fact that r knows three distinct positions of r' implies that r has become active and has moved at least twice between $t = 0$ and $t = t_i - 1$. However, r' does not move between $t_j + 1$ and $t_i - 1$. Hence, r has moved at least twice between $t = 0$ and $t = t_j$ and, thus at least once between $t = 0$ and $t = t_j - 1$. Therefore, at time t_j r' would have noted that r's position has changed at least once. A contradiction.

□

As a consequence of Lemma 1, r' knows the line over which r has moved, *i.e.*, the line and the direction passing through the first two distinct positions of r that r' has observed. This remark leads to the following corollary:

Corollary 1. *Let r and r' be two robots. Assume that r always moves in the same direction on line l as soon as it becomes active. If r observes that the position of r' has changed twice, then r' knows the line l and the direction towards which r moved.*

Note that in [24], the authors made a similar observation in the design of a protocol that solves the gathering problem with two non-oblivious robots. In the next subsection, we show how the above results provide a straightforward protocol for two robots, Protocol $\mathtt{Async_2}$.

3.2   One-to-One Communication with Two Asynchronous Robots

Both robots follow the same scheme. Each time a robot, say r, becomes active, it moves in the opposite direction of the other robot, r'. Let us call this direction $North_r$. Robot r behaves like this while it has nothing to send to r'. As soon as r observes that the position of r' has changed twice, by Corollary 1, r is guaranteed that r' knows the line H and the direction that r has moved. Let us call the line H the *horizon line*. Note that since the two robots follow the same behavior, H is common to both of them, and their respective Norths are oriented in the opposite direction.

From this moment on, r can start to send messages to r'. When r wants to send a bit "0" ("1", respectively) to r', r moves along a line perpendicular to on East side (West side, resp.) of H with respect to $North_r$. It then moves in the same direction each time it becomes active until it observes that the position of r' has changed twice. From this moment on, from Lemma 1, r knows that r' has seen it on its East side. Then, r comes back to H. Once r is located at H, it starts to move again towards the $North_r$ direction until it observes that r' has moved twice. This way, if Robot r wants to communicate another bit (following the same scheme), it is allowed to move on its East or West side again. So, the new bit and the previous bit are well distinguished by Robot r' even if they have the same value. An example of our scheme is shown in Figure 1.

Note that the lack of synchrony (*i.e.*, asynchronism) does not prevent the robots to move infinitely often, even having no message to send, as well as it does not allow to predict the travelled distance on each segment. This issues are addressed in Section 5. By Lemma 1, Protocol $\mathtt{Async_2}$ ensures the *Receipt* property provided the following condition: r observed that the position of r' changed twice before any direction change. We now show that Protocol $\mathtt{Async_2}$ ensures this condition.

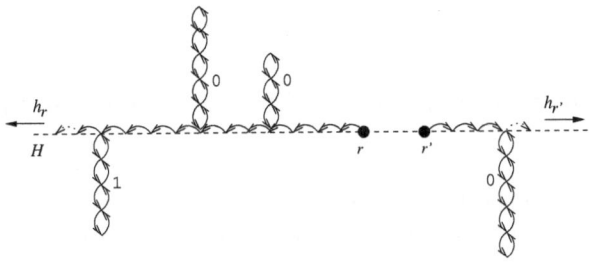

Fig. 1. Asynchronous communication for 2 robots. Robot r sends "001...", Robot r' sends "0...".

Remark 1. If any robot becomes active, it then moves.

Lemma 2. *Let r and r' be two robots. In every execution of Protocol* Async_2, r *observes that the position of r' changes infinitely often.*

Proof. Assume by contradiction that there exists some executions of Protocol Async_2 such that, eventually, r observes that the position of r' remains unchanged. Consider the suffix of such an execution where r observes that the position of r' remains unchanged. Assume that r' is eventually motionless. By fairness and Remark 1, this case is impossible. So, r' moves infinitely often. Thus, each time that r observes r', r' is at the same position. There are two cases to consider:

1. Robot r' eventually sends no bits. In that case, by executing Protocol Async_2, r' moves infinitely often in the same direction on H. This contradicts that each time r observes r', r' is in the same position.
2. Robot r' sends bits infinitely often. Since r' is at the same position each time r observes it, r' goes in a direction and comes back at the same position infinitely often. From Protocol Async_2, a robot can change its direction only when it observed that the position of the other robot changed twice. Since r' changes its direction infinitely often, r' observed that the position of r changed twice infinitely often. So, from Lemma 1, while moving in the same direction, each time r' observes that the position of r changed twice, r observes that the position of r' has changed at least once. A contradiction. □

Lemmas 1 and 2 prove that Protocol Async_2 ensures the *Receipt* property. Furthermore, Lemma 2 guarantees that no robot is starved sending a bit (*i.e.*, it can change its direction infinitely often). So, Property *Emission* is guaranteed by Protocol Async_2. This leads to the following theorem:

Theorem 1. *Protocol* Async_2 *implements one-to-one explicit communication for two robots.*

Note that if each robot r knows the maximum distance $\sigma_{r'}$ that the other robot r' can cover in one step, then, the protocol can easily be adapted to reduce the number of moves made by the robots to send bytes (instead of "bits"). In that case, the total distance $2\sigma_{r'}$ made by r' on its right and its left can be divided by the number of possible bytes sent by the robots. Then, r' moves on its right or on its left of a distance corresponding proportionally to the byte to be sent.

4   One-to-One Communication with Any Number of Asynchronous Robots

In this section, we adapt the previous results in the design of two protocols working with any number of asynchronous robots. In Subsection 4.1, we present our main routing scheme with Protocol Async_n^I. It works with the strongest assumptions, *i.e.*, robots equipped with observable IDs and sense of direction. In Subsection 4.2,

Protocol $\texttt{Async}_n^A$ provides one-to-one routing for anonymous robots devoid of any sense of direction. In the sequel, we omit the upperscript (either I or A) to refer to any of the two protocols ($\texttt{Async}_n^I$ or $\texttt{Async}_n^A$).

4.1 Routing with Identified Robots Having Sense of Direction

First, each robot being *a priori* surrounded by several robots, our method requires the inclusion of a mechanism for avoiding collisions. Next, it must include a technique allowing any robot to send messages to a specific robot. In order to deal with collision avoidance, we use the following concept, *Voronoi diagram*, in the design of our method.

Definition 1 (Voronoi diagram). *[2] The Voronoi diagram of a set of points $P = \{p_1, p_2, \cdots, p_n\}$ is a subdivision of the plane into n cells, one for each point in P. The cells have the property that a point q belongs to the Voronoi cell of point p_i iff for any other point $p_j \in P$, $dist(q, p_i) < dist(q, p_j)$ where $dist(p, q)$ is the Euclidean distance between p and q. In particular, the strict inequality means that points located on the boundary of the Voronoi diagram do not belong to any Voronoi cell.*

We assume that the robots know $P(t_0)$, *i.e.*, either the positions of the robots are known by every robot in t_0 or all the robots are awake in t_0. Note that given $P(t_0)$, the Voronoi diagram can be computed in $O(n \log n)$ time [2]. Using $P(t_0)$, when a robot wakes for the time (possibly after t_0), it computes the two following preprocessing steps:

1. Each robot computes the Voronoi Diagram, each Voronoi cell being centered on a robot position—refer to Case (a) in Figure 2, the plain line. Every robot is allowed to move within its Voronoi cell only, ensuring collision avoidance.
2. For each associated Voronoi cell c_r of robot r, each robot r computes the corresponding *granular* g_r, the largest disc of radius R_r centered on r and enclosed in c_r—Case (a) in Figure 2, the dotted lines. Notice that the radii of different disks might vary. Each granular is sliced into $2n$ slices, *i.e.*, the angle between two adjacent diameters is equal to $\frac{\pi}{n}$. Each diameter is labeled from 0 to $n-1$, the diameter labeled by 0 being aligned to the North, the other numbered in a natural order, progressing the clockwise direction—Case (b) in Figure 2.

Since the robots share a common handedness (chirality), they all agree on the same clockwise direction. Having a common sense of direction, they all agree on the same granular and diameter numbering.

In the sequel, we assume that no robot transmits bits to itself—otherwise, an extra slice would be necessary. For every robot r, let us refer to the diameter labelled with r's ID as κ. In our method, κ plays the role of the horizon line H as for the case with two robots. That is, each robot moves on κ to indicate that it has no bit to transmit.

We now informally describe Protocol $\texttt{Async}_n^I$ for every robot r. The general scheme is as follows: While r has no bit to send, r keeps moving on κ in both directions. When r wants to send a bit to a particular robot r', then after it comes back at $P(t_0)$ (the center of its granular g_r), then r moves on the diameter labelled with r' in either the Northern/Eastern/North-Eastern or the Southern/Western/South-Western direction with

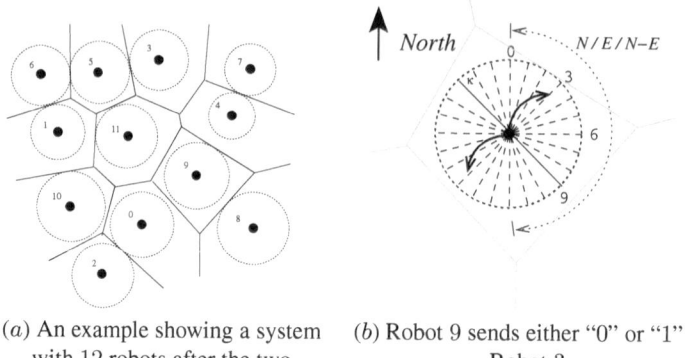

(a) An example showing a system   (b) Robot 9 sends either "0" or "1" to
    with 12 robots after the two   Robot 3.
    preprocessing phases.

Fig. 2. One-to-one communication with n identified robots with the sense of direction

respect to H_r and the bit r wants to send to r', either 0 or 1—refer to Case (b) in Figure 2.

As for the case with two robots only, our scheme needs to deal with the asynchronism. That is, by sending either no bit (by moving on κ) or a bit to a particular r' (by moving on the respective diameter of r'), r must make sure that all the robots observed its movements before it changes its direction. With respect to Lemma 1, r must move in the same direction until it observes that the position of every robot has changed twice. In order to satisfy this constraint, each time r leaves $P(t_0)$ toward the border of g_r in a particular direction, it first move at a distance d_1 from the border of its granular g_r equal to $R_r - min(\sigma_r, \frac{R_r}{x})$, R_r being equal to the radius of g_r and x being a positive real greater than or equal to 2. Next, for each of its k-th movement in the same direction, r moves a distance equal to $min(\sigma_r, \frac{d_{k-1}}{x})$, where d_{k-1} is the remaining distance to cover from the current position of r to the border of g_r in that direction.

By applying the same reasoning as in Subsection 3.2 for every pair of robots, we can claim:

Theorem 2. *Protocol* $\mathtt{Async}_n^I$ *implements one-to-one explicit communication for any number $n \geq 1$ of identified robots having the sense of direction.*

4.2   Routing with Anonymous Robots Having No Sense of Direction

With robots devoid of observable IDs, it may seem difficult to send a message to a specific robot. However, it is shown in [13] that if the robots have sense of direction and chirality, then they can agree on a total order over the robots. This is simply obtained as follows: Each robot r labels every observed robot with its local $x - y$ coordinate in the local coordinate system of r. Even if the robots do not agree on their metric system, by sharing the same x- and y-axes, they agree on the same order.

By contrast, with the lack of sense of direction, due to the symmetry of some configurations, the robots may be unable to deterministically agree on a common labeling for the cohort.

We now describe our method, Protocol $\mathtt{Async}_n^A$ in the design of a relative naming (w.r.t. each robot) allowing the implementation of one-to-one communication for anonymous robots with no common sense of direction. We refer to Figure 3 to explain our scheme.

Our method starts (at t_0) with the two preprocessing steps described above. At the end we have the Voronoi Diagram and the sliced granulars—to avoid useless overload in the figure, the latter is omitted in Figure 3, Case (a). Then, still at time t_0, each robot r computes the *smallest enclosing circle*, denoted by SEC, of the robot positions. Note that SEC is unique and can be computed in linear time [19]. Since the robots have the ability of chirality, they can agree on a common clockwise direction of SEC.

Next, r considers the *"horizon line"*, denoted by H_r, as the line passing through itself and 0, the center of SEC. Given H_r, r considers each radius of SEC passing through a robot. The robots are numbered in increasing order following the radii in the clockwise direction starting from H_r. When several robots are located on the same radius, they are numbered in increasing order starting from 0. Note that this means that r is not necessary labeled by 0 if some robots are located between itself and 0 on its radius. The robots being devoid of any sense of direction, they cannot agree on a common North. So, North is given relatively to each robot by its position with respect to 0. In other words, there exists a "North" relatively to each robot. An example of this preprocessing phase is shown in Case (a) of Figure 3 for a given robot r.

The method to send messages to a given robot is similar to the previous case. Every robot r slices its granular according to H_r into $n+1$ slices. The diameter corresponding to H_r being labeled by 0 and so on in the clockwise direction—refer to Case (b) in Figure 3. Consider that the extra slice, corresponding to H_r (the diameter being on radius of SEC passing through r) is not assigned to a particular robot. Let us call this slice κ. Again, κ plays the role of the horizon line H on which every robot moves on to indicate that it has no bit to transmit. The sending of a bit is made following the same scheme as above, the Northern being given by the direction of H_r and the Eastern following the clockwise direction. Each robot addresses bits according to its relative

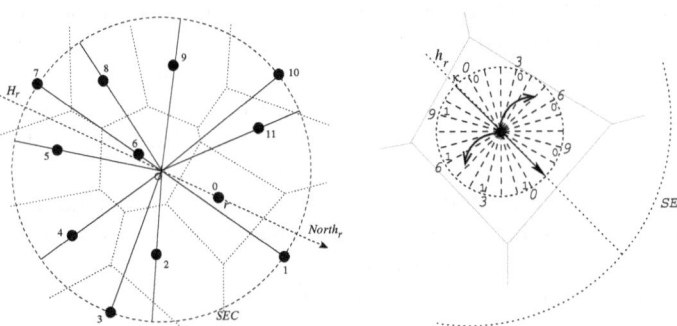

(a) An example showing how the relative naming is built w.r.t. r.

(b) An example showing how the granular is sliced with respect to r.

Fig. 3. One-to-one communication with n anonymous robots having no sense of direction

labeling. By construction, the labeling is specific to each robot. However, every robot, r, is able to compute the labeling with respect to each robot of the system. Therefore, by observing each movement made by any robot r', r is able to know to whom a bit is addressed, and in particular, when it is addressed to itself. Every robot is able to compute the message address, by being able to compute the relative naming of all the robots.

Theorem 3. *Protocol* $\texttt{Async}_n^A$ *implements one-to-one explicit communication for any number* $n \geq 1$ *of anonymous robots having no sense of direction.*

5   Motion Containment and Limited Visibility

The above schemes have the drawback of either making the robots moving away from each other infinitely often (Protocol $\texttt{Async}_2$) or requiring that the robots are able to move (and to observe) an infinitesimally small distance (both Protocols $\texttt{Async}_n$). Note that this is due to the extreme weakness of the system considered in this paper. Indeed, the only assumption made on the concurrent activation of robots is uniform fairness, that is no assumption models the "*interleaving*" of activations of each robot with respect to the other.

Definition 2 (Interleaving Degree). *Let* $k > 0$ *be the interleaving degree such that, for every pair of distinct robots* r *and* r', *for every suffix of computation in which* r *is activated* k *times,* r' *is activated at least once.*

Note that if $k = 1$, then the system is (fully) *synchronous, i.e.,* every robot is activated at each time instant. Assuming that $k > 1$, there is a certain amount of asynchrony ensuring that every k moves of any robot r, every robot r' ($\neq r$) observed at least one move made by r. The following lemma is straightforward:

Lemma 3. *Let* r *and* r' *be two robots. Assuming an interleaving degree of* $k \geq 1$, *every* k *moves of* r, *then* r' *have observed that the position of* r *has changed at least once.*

Lemma 3 plays the same role as Lemma 1. So, assuming an interleaving degree of $k \geq 1$, for any pair of robots r and r', every $2k$ activations of a robot r, r sees r' moving at least twice and r' see r moving at least once.

We directly use this result to modify Protocol $\texttt{Async}_2$ as follows: Instead of moving infinitely often in the opposite direction of r' on H, r comes back on its initial position after each bit sent—or byte sent if r knows $\sigma_{r'}$, refer to Subsection 3.2. This ensures that each robot r does not move farther than a distance d_r equal to $k\sigma_r$.

Note that by making this modification, both robots are no longer required to have an infinite visibility. If each robot knows k and $\sigma_{r'}$, then the visibility of r can be bounded by $k(\sigma_r + \sigma_{r'}) + \delta$, δ is equal to the distance between the initial positions of both r and r'. Otherwise, the visibility can be finite but cannot be bounded.

Similarly, if for every robot r', each robot r is able to observe that r' moved a distance equal or less than $d_{r'} = min(\sigma_{r'}, \frac{R_{r'}}{k})$, then Protocol $\texttt{Async}_n$ works assuming that each robot r moves a distance equal to d_r. As for the case with two robots, the visibility of the robots is no longer required to be infinite, and can be bounded to the radius of the smallest enclosing circle.

Note that this latter bound can be reduced in the case when the robots have observable IDs. Indeed, Protocol Async_n^I assumes that the observable IDs of the robots maps $1 \ldots n$. So, combined with a "classical" algorithm to maintain a routing table [23], the same scheme can be easily used to implement one-to-one communication among robots with a visibility limited to its neighbors only, provided that (i) every robot knows n, and (ii) no robot movement breaks the graph of observability [14]. Each robot adds the ID of the addressee and (directly) communicates with its neighbors using our protocol. The message is then routed towards its destination using any "classical" routing algorithm.

6   Concluding Remarks, Extensions, and Open Problems

In this work we proposed (deterministic) movement protocols that implement explicit communication, and therefore allow the application of (existing) distributed algorithms; distributing algorithms that use message exchanges. Movements-signals are introduced as a means to transfer messages between deaf and dumb robots. The movement protocols can serve as a backup to other means of (e.g., wireless) communication. Several protocols and enhancements have been proposed that implement one-to-one communication in various asynchronous environments. Note that our solutions allow every robot to read each message sent by any robot r to any robot r'. This provides fault-tolerance by redundancy, any robot being able to send any message again. This also enables one-to-many or one-to-all communication. For instance, one-to-all communication can be implemented in Protocol Async_n by adding an extra slice labelled by $n + 1$ intended to communicate a message to every robot.

We call the ability of a communication protocol to be *silent* when a robot eventually moves if it has some message to transmit. Note that this desirable property would help to save energy resources of the robots. The proposed asynchronous protocols are not silent (Remark 1). The question of whether the design of silent asynchronous algorithms is possible or not remains open.

A related issue concerns the distance (eventually) covered by the robots. In this paper, we provided a solution to overcome this problem by introducing a certain amount of synchrony among the robots, the interleaving degree. As a matter of fact, we believe that the lack of interleaving degree implies an impossibility for communication by a finite number of moves. Intuitively, the fact that an asynchronous robot that sequentially observes another robot at the same place, cannot determine whether the robot moved and returned to the same position or did not move at all.

Computations with an *infinite decimal precision* is different and, in a way, weaker assumption than infinitely small movements. Indeed, one can assume infinite decimal precision with the "reasonable" assumption of finite movements, *i.e.*, with a *minimal* and *maximal* distance covered in one atomic step, or even step over a grid. In this paper, we assumed a maximal covered distance (σ_r), but not a minimal covered distance. This would be the case by assuming that the plane is either a grid or a hexagonal pavement [16]. For instance, with such assumption, the robots could be prone to make computation errors due to round off, and, therefore, face a situation where robots are not able to identify all of possible $2n$ directions obtained by slices inside of disks and are limited to recognize only a certain number of directions. This case could be solved by avoiding the use of $2n$ slices of granular by transmitting the index of the robot to whom the message intended following the message itself. For this we would need only $k+1, 1 \leq k < 2n$ segments (or $2k+1$ slices). In particular, we would use one segment for message transmission (as in the case of two robots); using the other k segments the robot who wants to transmit a message allows to transmit the index of the robot to whom the message is designated. Definitely, such index can be represented by $\frac{\log n}{\log k} = \log_k n$ symbols. Notice, this strategy would slow down the algorithm and increase the number of steps required to transmit a message. More precisely, the number of steps required in this method to identify the designated robot is $\log_k n$. For example, by taking $O(\log n)$ slices instead of $O(n)$, the number of steps to transmit a message would increase by $O(\frac{\log n}{\log \log n})$.

In the continuation of the above discussion, an other important feature in the field of mobile robots is the weakness/strength of the model. For instance, in this paper, we used the semi-synchronous model (SSM). It would be interesting to relax synchrony among the robots in order to reach solutions for a fully asynchronous model (*e.g.,* CORDA [21]).

Finally, *Stabilization* [10] would be a very desirable property to enable. It seems that, in our case, stabilization could be achieved assuming an interleaving degree equal to 1 (*i.e.,* synchronous settings) by carefully adapting Protocol Async_n, say by assuming a global clock (using GPS input) returning to the initial location and (re)computing the prepossessing phase every round timestamp. The self-stabilization property assuming no interleaving degree (*i.e.,* the asynchronous case) requires further study.

References

1. Ando, H., Oasa, Y., Suzuki, I., Yamashita, M.: A distributed memoryless point convergence algorithm for mobile robots with limited visibility. IEEE Transaction on Robotics and Automation 15(5), 818–828 (1999)
2. Aurenhammer, F.: Voronoi diagrams- a survey of a fundamental geometric data structure. ACM Comput. Surv. 23(3), 345–405 (1991)
3. Beckers, R., Holland, O.E., Deneubourg, J.L.: From local actions to global tasks: Stigmergy and collective robotics. In: Artificial Life, 4th Int. Worksh. on the Synth. and Simul. of Living Sys., vol. 4, pp. 173–202 (1994)
4. Cieliebak, M., Flocchini, P., Prencipe, G., Santoro, N.: Solving the robots gathering problem. In: Baeten, J.C.M., Lenstra, J.K., Parrow, J., Woeginger, G.J. (eds.) ICALP 2003. LNCS, vol. 2719, pp. 1181–1196. Springer, Heidelberg (2003)
5. Cohen, R., Peleg, D.: Local spreading algorithms for autonomous robot systems. Theor. Comput. Sci. 399(1-2), 71–82 (2008)
6. Kube, C.R.: Task modelling in collective robotics. Auton. Robots 4(1), 53–72 (1997)
7. Defago, X., Konagaya, A.: Circle formation for oblivious anonymous mobile robots with no common sense of orientation. In: 2nd ACM International Annual Workshop on Principles of Mobile Computing (POMC 2002), pp. 97–104 (2002)
8. Dieudonné, Y., Labbani-Igbida, O., Petit, F.: Circle formation of weak mobile robots. ACM Transactions on Autonomous and Adaptive Systems 3(4) (2008)
9. Dieudonné, Y., Petit, F.: Deterministic leader election in anonymous sensor networks without common coodinated system. In: Tovar, E., Tsigas, P., Fouchal, H. (eds.) OPODIS 2007. LNCS, vol. 4878, pp. 132–142. Springer, Heidelberg (2007)

10. Dolev, S.: Self-Stabilization. MIT Press, Cambridge (2000)
11. Engelbrecht, A.P.: Fundamentals of Computational Swarm Intelligence. John Wiley & Sons, Chichester (2006)
12. Wilson, E.O.: Sociobiology. Belknap Press of Harward University Press (1975)
13. Flocchini, P., Prencipe, G., Santoro, N., Widmayer, P.: Hard tasks for weak robots: The role of common knowledge in pattern formation by autonomous mobile robots. In: Aggarwal, A.K., Pandu Rangan, C. (eds.) ISAAC 1999. LNCS, vol. 1741, pp. 93–102. Springer, Heidelberg (1999)
14. Flocchini, P., Prencipe, G., Santoro, N., Widmayer, P.: Gathering of asynchronous robots with limited visibility. Theor. Comput. Sci. 337(1-3), 147–168 (2005)
15. Fukuda, T., Nakagawa, S.: Approach to the dynamically reconfigurable robotic sytem. Journal of Intelligent and Robotic System 1, 55–72 (1988)
16. Gordon, N., Wagner, I.A., Brucks, A.M.: Discrete bee dance algorithms for pattern formation on a grid. In: IAT 2003: Proceedings of the IEEE/WIC International Conference on Intelligent Agent Technology, pp. 545–549. IEEE Computer Society, Los Alamitos (2003)
17. Grassé, P.-P.: La reconstruction du nid et les coordinations inter-individuelles chez bellicositermes natalensis et cubitermes sp. la theorie de la stigmergie: Essai dinterpretation des termites constructeurs. Insectes Sociaux 6, 41–83 (1959)
18. Matarić, M.J.: Issues and approaches in the design of collective autonomous agents. Robotics and Autonomous Systems 16(2-4), 321–331 (1995)
19. Megiddo, N.: Linear-time algorithms for linear programming in R^3 and related problems. SIAM Journal on Computing 12(4), 759–776 (1983)
20. Noreils, F.R.: An architecture for cooperative and autonomous mobile robots. In: IEEE International Conference on Robotics and Automation, pp. 2703–2710 (1992)
21. Prencipe, G.: Distributed Coordination of a Set of Autonomous Mobile Robots. PhD thesis, Dipartimento di Informatica, University of Pisa (2002)
22. Prencipe, G., Santoro, N.: Distributed algorithms for autonomous mobile robots. In: The 2006 IFIP International Conference on Embedded And Ubiquitous Computing, EUC 2006 (2006)
23. Santoro, N.: Design and Analysis of Distributed Algorithms. John Wiley & Sons, Inc., Chichester (2007)
24. Suzuki, I., Yamashita, M.: Distributed anonymous mobile robots - formation of geometric patterns. SIAM Journal of Computing 28(4), 1347–1363 (1999)
25. Tovey, C.: The honey bee algorithm: A biological inspired approach to internet server optimization. Engineering Enterprise, the Alumni Magazine for ISyE at Georgia Institute of Technology, Spring 13–15 (2004)
26. Wedde, H.F., Farooq, M.: A comprehensive review of nature inspired routing algorithms for fixed telecommunication networks. J. Syst. Archit. 52(8), 461–484 (2006)
27. Wenner, P.H., Wells, A.M.: Anatomy of a Controversy: the Question of a "Language" Among Bees. Columbia University Press, New York (1990)

Synchronization Helps Robots to Detect Black Holes in Directed Graphs*

Adrian Kosowski[1,2], Alfredo Navarra[3], and Cristina M. Pinotti[3]

[1] LaBRI - Université Bordeaux 1 - CNRS,
351 cours de la Libération, 33405 Talence cedex, France
[2] Department of Algorithms and System Modeling, Gdańsk University of Technology,
Narutowicza 11/12, 80233 Gdańsk, Poland
adrian@kaims.pl
[3] Dipartimento di Matematica e Informatica, Università degli Studi di Perugia,
Via Vanvitelli 1, 06123 Perugia, Italy
{navarra,pinotti}@dmi.unipg.it

Abstract. The paper considers a team of robots which has to explore a graph G where some nodes can be harmful. Robots are initially located at the so called *home base* node. The dangerous nodes are the so called *black hole* nodes, and once a robot enters in one of them, it is destroyed. The goal is to find a strategy in order to explore G in such a way that the minimum number of robots is wasted. The exploration ends if there is at least one surviving robot which knows all the edges leading to the black holes. As many variations of the problem have been considered so far, the solution and its measure heavily depend on the initial knowledge and the capabilities of the robots. In this paper, we assume that G is a directed graph, the robots are associated with unique identifiers, they know the number of nodes n of G (or at least an upper bound on n), and they know the number of edges Δ leading to the black holes. Each node is associated with a white board where robots can read and write information in a mutual exclusive way.

A recently posed question [Czyzowicz et al., *Proc. SIROCCO'09*] is whether some number of robots, expressed as a function of parameter Δ only, is sufficient to detect black holes in directed graphs of arbitrarily large order n. We give a positive answer to this question for the synchronous case, i.e., when the robots share a common clock, showing that $O(\Delta \cdot 2^{\Delta})$ robots are sufficient to solve the problem. This bound is nearly tight, since it is known that at least 2^{Δ} robots are required for some instances. Quite surprisingly, we also show that unlike in the case of undirected graphs, for the directed version of the problem, synchronization can sometimes make a difference: for $\Delta = 1$, 2 robots are always sufficient and sometimes required to explore the graph regardless of whether synchronization is present; however, for $\Delta = 2$, in the synchronous case 4 robots are always sufficient, whereas in the asynchronous case at least 5 robots are sometimes required.

---

* This work was done during a research collaboration supported by the Italian CNR Short-Term Mobility Program.

T. Abdelzaher, M. Raynal, and N. Santoro (Eds.): OPODIS 2009, LNCS 5923, pp. 86–98, 2009.

1   Introduction

The subject of exploring an unknown graph by means of mobile entities has been widely considered during the last years. The increasing interest to the problem comes from the variety of applications that it meets. In robotics, it might be very useful to let a robot or a team of robots exploring dangerous or impervious zones. In networking, software agents might automatically discover nodes of a network and perform updates and/or refuse their connections. In this paper we are interested in the exploration of a graph with faulty nodes, i.e. nodes that destroy any entering entity. Such nodes are called *black holes*, and the exploration of a graph in such kind of networks is usually referred as *black hole search*. In what follows, we refer to the mobile entities as robots. According to the assumed initial settings of the network, and the knowledge and the capabilities of the robots, many results have been provided. Pure exploration strategies, without dealing with black holes, has been widely addressed, see for instance [8,11] and references therein. In this case, the requirement is usually to perform the exploration as fast as possible. When black holes are considered, along with the time (or equivalently the number of edge traversals) required for a full exploration, the main goal resides in minimizing the number of robots that may fall into some black hole. A full exploration means that, at the end, all the edges which do not lead to any black hole must be marked as safe edges.

1.1   Related Work

In [2], the exploration subject to black holes has been restricted to tree topology in a synchronous setting. The authors show that 2 robots are enough for computing the full exploration when only one black hole is admitted. They provide a $\frac{5}{3}$-approximation algorithm with respect to the required edge traversals. In [6], the attention is devoted to rings. The authors show that 2 robots are enough in order to detect one black hole and they provide an algorithm which requires $O(n \log n)$ moves, where n is the dimension of the ring. Other restrictions have been considered like the knowledge of a map in [7] where the authors provide a strategy for locating one black hole by means of 2 robots in $O(n + d \log d)$ moves, where n is the size of the network and d its diameter. Also in [10], the map is known and the authors show that the problem of locating one black hole by means of 2 synchronous robots is not polynomial time approximable within any constant factor less than $\frac{388}{389}$, and provide a 6-approximation algorithm. A slightly different problem has been considered in [1] where the network admits many black holes and if a robot gets destroyed into one, then such a black hole disappears but not the underlying node. In [4], one black hole is optimally located by 2 robots in $O(n)$ moves in the case the input graph has size n and its topology is among hypercubes, cube-connected cycles, star graphs, wrapped butterflies, chordal rings, multidimensional meshes or tori of restricted diameter. Most general results can be found in [5] where the asynchronous case is considered in presence of a single black hole without any limitation to the network topology. The authors show that $\Delta + 1$ robots are sufficient and require $\Theta(n)$

steps, with Δ being the maximum degree of the input network and n its size. The variant in which the robot entering the node cannot learn the link by which it has arrived was studied in [9]. For this scenario, a bound of $\frac{\Delta^2+\Delta}{2} + 1$ on the number of required robots was established and shown to be tight for some instances of the problem.

So far, the input graph has been always considered as undirected. The additional property of having directed edges can only increase the difficulty of the problem as once traversed an edge, the robot cannot directly come back in general. The first results concerning directed graphs have been recently published in [3]. The authors have considered a setting where robots are associated with unique identifiers (IDs), they know the number of nodes n of the input directed graph $G = (V, A)$, and they know the number Δ of edges belonging to G leading to the black holes. If $BH \subset V$ is the set of black holes in G, the induced subgraph $G[V \setminus BH]$ is assumed to be strongly connected. Each node $v \in V$ is associated with a so called *white board* which is an available bounded memory (with size polynomial in n) accessible in a mutually exclusive way by the robots located at node v. The obtained results show a general case lower bound on the number of robots required in order to accomplish the black hole search.

Theorem 1 ([3]). *In both the asynchronous and synchronous models, 2^Δ robots are sometimes required to solve the directed black hole search problem, for all $\Delta \geq 1$.*

Moreover, in [3] it is shown that $2\Delta+1$ robots are enough for solving the problem on planar graphs with the planar embedding known by the robots, and 2Δ robots are needed in the worst case.

1.2   Our Results

In this paper, we extend the results on directed graphs by also separately considering the synchronous and the asynchronous cases, i.e. when the robots share or not a common clock. Under the same settings of [3], for the synchronous case we provide a general strategy which requires $O(\Delta \cdot 2^\Delta)$ robots. This answers the main question posed in [3], i.e. whether some number of robots, expressed as a function of parameter Δ only, is sufficient to detect black holes in directed graphs of arbitrarily large order n. We also provide a strategy for $\Delta = 1$ and $\Delta = 2$ which requires 2 and 4 robots, respectively. For the asynchronous case, we show that 2 robots are still sufficient when $\Delta = 1$, but for $\Delta = 2$ at least 5 robots are sometimes required.

1.3   Outline

The paper is organized as follows. In Section 2 we recall the most important assumptions regarding the directed black hole search problem, and introduce some further notation. In Section 3 we state the main positive results of the paper for synchronous robots, proving that $O(\Delta \cdot 2^\Delta)$ robots suffice to explore any graph, and 4 robots suffice when $\Delta = 2$. The results for asynchronous robots for $\Delta = 1$ and $\Delta = 2$ are given in Section 4. Section 5 contains some concluding remarks.

2   The Model

We apply essentially the same scenario as that introduced in [3]. The explored digraph $G = (V, A)$ contains a distinguished node called the *home base* (*hb*) from which all the robots start the exploration, and a distinguished set of black holes $BH \subseteq V \setminus \{hb\}$. All the black holes are sinks of the digraph (i.e., with an out-degree of 0); we remark that from the perspective of this work, setting the number of black holes equal to $|BH| = 1$ does not affect any of the stated results. It is assumed that the induced subgraph $G[V \setminus BH]$ is strongly connected. The set of arcs leading into some black hole, $BA = A \cap ((V \setminus BH) \times BH)$, is known as the set of *black hole arcs*. All robots know two parameters of the graph: its order $n = |V|$, and the total number of black hole arcs, $\Delta = |BA|$. A robot located at a node v has access to its own built-in memory, the white board associated with the node, a global timer counting the steps of the algorithm, and a local labeling of the arcs leaving node v (called an assignment of port numbers), which can be used to select the next arc in the robot's traversal. Note that nodes do not have unique identifiers, although such identifiers can potentially be created by the robots exploring the graph.

For a node v of a directed (multi)graph H, the number of arcs entering v is denoted by $\text{indeg}_H(v)$, and the number of arcs exiting v is denoted by $\text{outdeg}_H(v)$.

3   Upper Bound in the Synchronous Model

Theorem 2. *There exists a strategy for solving all instances of the directed black hole search problem using $O(\Delta \cdot 2^\Delta)$ synchronous robots.*

Proof. The strategy works as follows. The robots are released from *hb* one-by-one, at regular intervals of a time steps (where $a \in \Theta(n^4)$ steps is a value which results from the subsequent formulation of the strategy), in such a way as to guarantee that within a steps, i.e. before the next robot is released, exactly one of the following events will occur:

- The currently active robot successfully completes the entire exploration, returns to *hb*, and terminates the algorithm.
- The currently active robot is destroyed in some black hole.

The procedure is divided into a certain number of phases, and the p-th phase consists of $(\Delta + 2) \cdot S_p$ robot releases, where S_p is a value which will be fixed further on in the analysis.

- In the first part of the p-th phase, S_p *searching robots* are released using a set of rules specified below.

– The second part of the phase consists of Δ iterations. In each iteration, S_p *cycle detection robots* are released which follow along a slight modification of the paths used by the searching robots from the first part of the phase.
– In the third part of the phase, S_p *cycle contraction robots* are released in a similar way as in one iteration of the second part of the phase.

Throughout the algorithm, each node v maintains a label $f(v)$ stored in its white board. Let the subgraph $H_{f(v)}$ of G consist of all nodes $u \in V \setminus BH$ having $f(u) = f(v)$, and all arcs $(u_1, u_2) \in A$ such that $f(u_1) = f(u_2) = f(v)$ and (u_1, u_2) has been visited by at least one robot. The procedure is defined in such a way that initially $f(v)$ is unique for all visited nodes (the definition of $f(v)$ for unvisited nodes is irrelevant), whereas each of the graphs $H_{f(v)}$ is strongly connected; moreover, for each node v, the structure of the graph $H_{f(v)}$ and its embedding in the ports of G is encoded on the white board of v. To avoid confusion, we will sometimes write $f^{(2)}$ and $H^{(2)}$ to denote the value of labels f and graphs H throughout the second part of the phase (the cycle detection robots do not update the labels), and likewise $f^{(3)}$ and $H^{(3)}$ to denote these graphs at the end of the whole phase (after releasing all the cycle contraction robots).

Procedure for the first part of the phase. The procedure for each searching robot r is defined as follows. Directly before and directly after traversing an arc, the robot writes this information on the white boards of the starting node and of the end node of the arc, respectively, together with its unique ID and number of the move in the robot's move sequence. The robot proceeds to make its next move as follows:

1. Let the robot be located at an arbitrary node of some graph H_i. Then, the robot explores all nodes of H_i, identifying all arcs of G which leave or enter these nodes and do not belong to H_i. If there exists an outgoing arc (u_1, v_1) which was used by some robot r' at time t_1, and an incoming arc (v_2, u_2) which was used by the same robot r' at some later time t_2, where $u_1, u_2 \in V(H_i)$ and $v_1, v_2 \notin V(H_i)$, then robot r proceeds to extend component H_i by including in it all the nodes on the route $(v_1, \ldots, v_2)$ used by the robot r' between times t_1 and t_2. (Robot r' was either a previously released robot, or $r' = r$.) More precisely, robot r visits all the nodes of all the graphs $H_{f(v)}$, with $v \in (v_1, \ldots, v_2)$, setting their labels to $f(v) := i$, and updating the stored graphs $H_{f(v)}$ accordingly.
2. When the extension from Step 1 can no longer be applied, the robot performs the next move as follows.
   – If there exists an arc leaving H_i which has never been visited by any robot, then the robot proceeds along this arc.
   – Otherwise, the robot proceeds along the arc leaving H_i which has not been used by any robot for the longest time. (Observe that since the extension from Step 1 can no longer be applied, each arc leaving H_i has been used by each robot at most once, so the robot simply chooses the arc leaving H_i used by the robot which was released the earliest.)

Note that the actions performed in Step 1 will never lead the robot into a black hole, and do not lead it out of the current explored strongly connected component, whereas either of the actions performed in Step 2 can potentially destroy the robot or lead it into a node which does not belong to component H_i.

Procedure for the second and third parts of the phase. Looking at the labels $f^{(2)}$ and graphs $H^{(2)}$, which are defined at the time of the destruction of the last searching robot, observe that each searching robot r can be seen as performing a traversal of some sequence of graphs $(H^{(2)}_{f_1}, \ldots, H^{(2)}_{f_k})$, where a graph $H^{(2)}_{f_i}$ appears in the sequence if at least one of its nodes has been visited by robot r. This implies a natural precedence relation $(\prec)$ between graphs $H^{(2)}_{f_i}$ and $H^{(2)}_{f_j}$, that is, we will write $H^{(2)}_{f_i} \prec H^{(2)}_{f_j}$ if for some searching robot r, graph $H^{(2)}_{f_i}$ appears before graph $H^{(2)}_{f_j}$ in the robot's sequence of visits; see Figure 1 for an illustration.

The goal of the cycle detection robots is to detect cycles of length at most Δ in the graph of relation $\prec$. To do this, we release the robots in such a way that after the l-th of Δ iterations, each node of graph $H^{(2)}_{f_j}$ stores a list of all f_i such that $H^{(2)}_{f_i} \prec^l H^{(2)}_{f_j}$, where $(\prec^l)$ is the l-th power of relation $(\prec)$. This is achieved using a standard approach. With each graph $H^{(2)}_{f_i}$, we associate a precedence set P_{f_i} whose copies are stored in the white boards of all of the nodes of $H^{(2)}_{f_i}$, and initially $P_{f_i} = \emptyset$. In the l-th iteration, for each searching robot r, exactly one cycle detection robot r' will retrace the route of r. Robot r' is defined so as to visit all nodes of all graphs in the same order $(H^{(2)}_{f_1}, \ldots, H^{(2)}_{f_k})$ as robot r,

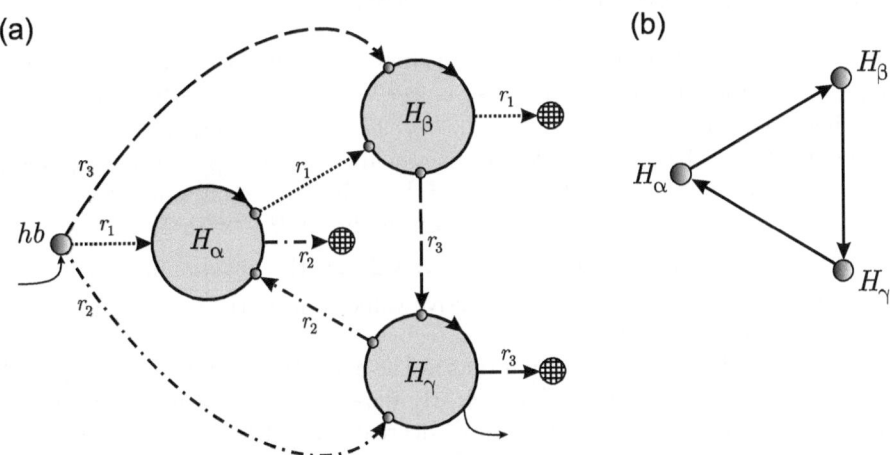

Fig. 1. (a) A schematic representation of the paths followed by three consecutive searching robots r_1, r_2, r_3. The strongly connected components $H_\alpha, H_\beta, H_\gamma$ associated with respective black hole arcs are assumed to remain unchanged during the phase. (b) The corresponding graph of the precedence relation $(\prec)$ on $H_\alpha, H_\beta, H_\gamma$.

with transitions between adjacent graphs $H_{f_i}^{(2)}$ performed using the same arcs as those visited by robot r (this can be achieved since robot r may be assumed to store the information about its next move on the white boards of the nodes it is passing through). Additionally, for each $H_{f_j}^{(2)}$, robot r' now appends to the contents of set P_{f_j} the contents of all sets P_{f_i}, for all $i < j$, and also adds to P_{f_j} the element f_i, for all $i < j$; all the copies of set P_{f_j} stored in the nodes of $H_{f_j}^{(2)}$ are updated accordingly. Clearly, we have $H_{f_i}^{(2)} \prec^l H_{f_j}^{(2)}$ if and only if $f_i \in P_{f_j}$. For easier manipulation of data in the next part of the phase, the precedence sets should store additional information about the ID of the searching robots r inducing the respective precedence relations.

Finally, the goal of the cycle contraction robots is to contract into a single connected component all graphs $H_{f_i}^{(2)}$ forming cycles of length at most Δ in the precedence graph induced by relation ($\prec$). The cycle contraction once again retraces the route of corresponding searching robots from r. Upon detecting a cycle of length Δ in the precedence relation, i.e., $f_i \in P_{f_i}$ for some graph $H_{f_i}^{(2)}$, they follow the arcs of the directed cycle of G which induces this relation (the identifiers of these arcs should be stored in set P_{f_i} as auxiliary information). For all the nodes v of all the graphs $H_{f_i}^{(2)}$ encountered in this cycle, the robots then update their labels, setting the new value $f^{(3)}(v) = f_i$ and constructing the new contracted component $H_{f_i}^{(3)}$ accordingly. These labels and components are then used by the searching robots in the next phase of the algorithm.

Termination condition. The algorithm terminates once the strongly connected component containing hb, $H_{f(hb)}$ has exactly Δ arcs exiting it and no arcs entering it. Any searching robot which is released can of course detect this immediately, and return with this information to hb.

Analysis. To complete the proof, we will show that, when the number of searching robots in the p-th phase is set as $S_p = \lceil 2^\Delta / \sqrt{3}^{p-1} \rceil$, the algorithm will always terminate within Δ phases. Let $\{v_1, \ldots, v_\Delta\}$ be the set of vertices from which it is possible to exit by a black hole arc. At any given time step, consider the set of labels $\{f(v_1), \ldots, f(v_\Delta)\} = \{f_1, f_2, \ldots, f_d\}$, with $1 \le d \le \Delta$, and let δ_i denote the number of black hole arcs exiting from nodes of H_{f_i}, with $\sum_{1 \le i \le d} \delta_i = \Delta$. As in the case of the other parameters, we will use the notation $d^{(2)}$, $d^{(3)}$, $f_i^{(2)}$, $f_i^{(3)}$, and $\delta_i^{(2)}$, $\delta_i^{(3)}$ to denote the respective values during the second part and at the end of the third part of the phase.

First, we will prove by induction that at the end of the p-th phase, $1 \le p < \Delta$, we have $d^{(3)} \le \Delta - p$. The claim is clearly true for $p = 0$; we will show that in each subsequent phase, the value of $d^{(3)}$ decreases by at least 1, or equivalently, that some two components H_{f_i} and H_{f_j} are contracted into each other during each phase. Consider for a moment the situation during the second part of the phase, and define the directed multigraph $(\mathcal{H}, R)$, where the set of nodes is $\mathcal{H} = \{s, H_{f_1}^{(2)}, H_{f_2}^{(2)}, \ldots, H_{f_d}^{(2)}\}$, with s being a special source node, while arcs are defined as follows. For each searching robot r released in the current phase, we add one arc from node $H_{f_i}^{(2)}$ to $H_{f_j}^{(2)}$ if and only if robot r visited at least one node of $H_{f_i}^{(2)}$ before visiting a node of $H_{f_j}^{(2)}$, and did not visit any node of any other graph from $\mathcal{H} \setminus \{H_{f_i}^{(2)}, H_{f_j}^{(2)}\}$ in between these two visits. For each robot r, we also add an arc from the special source node s to the first of the graphs $H_{f_i}^{(2)}$ which the robot visits. Note that $\text{indeg}_{(\mathcal{H},R)}(s) = 0$, and $\text{outdeg}_{(\mathcal{H},R)}(s) = S_p$.

We consider the following cases.

(a) Multigraph $(\mathcal{H}, R)$ contains a directed cycle. Then, since the relation R restricted to nodes from $\mathcal{H} \setminus \{s\}$ is a sub-relation of precedence relation ($\prec$), and $|F| \leq \Delta$, the graph of relation ($\prec$) also contains a cycle of length at most Δ on the connected components from $\mathcal{H}$. Since all such components are contracted into one in the cycle contraction phase, we immediately obtain that the value of $d^{(3)}$ is smaller than that of $d^{(2)}$ for the current phase, hence $d^{(3)}$ decreases with respect to the previous phase.

(b) Multigraph $(\mathcal{H}, R)$ is acyclic, and no contractions are performed ($d^{(2)} = d^{(3)}$); we can then extend R to a linear order, simply writing $f_1 < f_2 < \ldots f_d$; each searching robot of the current phase visits some subsequence of graphs $H_{f_i}^{(2)}$ in ascending orders of labels. For each f_i, consider the set of black hole arcs exiting the component $H_{f_i}^{(2)}$. If at the start of the current phase some of these arcs exited different strongly connected components H_a, H_b (which were contracted into one by some searching robot), then the inductive claim holds, since for the current phase the value of $d^{(2)}$ is less than that of $d^{(3)}$ at the end of the previous phase. Thus, w.l.o.g. we can assume that $H_{f_i}^{(2)}$ is obtained from some component H_{f_i}, which is perhaps enlarged by searching robots, but has the same set of exiting black hole arcs as $H_{f_i}^{(2)}$, throughout the phase. With this assumption, we now proceed to show the following auxiliary lemma.

Lemma 1. *We either have $d = 1$ and $H_{f_1}^{(2)} = G[V \setminus BH]$, or for all i, $1 \leq i \leq d^{(2)}$, the following condition holds:*

$$\text{outdeg}_{(\mathcal{H},R)} H_{f_i}^{(2)} \geq \left\lceil \frac{\text{indeg}_{(\mathcal{H},R)} H_{f_i}^{(2)}}{\delta_i + 1} \right\rceil.$$

Proof. Let i be arbitrarily chosen, and consider an arbitrary sequence of $\delta_i + 1$ robots $r_1, \ldots, r_{\delta_i+1}$ which consecutively went through $H_{f_i}^{(2)}$, ordered by increasing release times. We will show that at least one of the robots did not use a black hole arc to leave $H_{f_i}^{(2)}$. Let $H_{f_i}(r_j)$ denote component H_{f_i} directly after the destruction of robot r_j; recall that we have $H_{f_i}(r_1) \subseteq H_{f_i}(r_2) \subseteq \ldots \subseteq H_{f_i}(r_{\delta_i+1}) \subseteq H_{f_i}^{(2)}$, and each $H_{f_i}(r_j)$ has the same set of black hole arcs as $H_{f_i}^{(2)}$. Suppose now, to the contrary, that each of the robots r_j left $H_{f_i}^{(2)}$ by a black hole arc; this means that each of these robots also left $H_{f_i}(r_j)$ by a black hole arc; moreover, since preference is given to arcs which were not used for a longer time, each of the robots $r_1, \ldots, r_{\delta_i}$ will be destroyed by a different black hole arc. Consider now the robot r_{δ_i+1}. By the strong connectivity property of graph $G[V \setminus BH]$, unless $H_{f_i}(r_{\delta_i+1}) = G[V \setminus BH]$, there exists at least one arc e outgoing from $H_{f_i}(r_{\delta_i+1})$ which is not a black hole arc. This arc could not have been visited by any robot r released between r_1 (inclusive) and r_{δ_i+1} (exclusive). Indeed, r never returns to component $H_{f_i}(r_{\delta_i+1})$ after leaving it by arc e (since otherwise arc e would have been included into $H_{f_i}(r_{\delta_i+1})$ by robot r_{δ_i+1}), and since we have $r \in \{r_1, \dots, r_{\delta_i}\}$ (because r visits $H_{f_i}(r_{\delta_i+1}) \subseteq H_{f_i}^{(2)}$), one of the robots $\{r_1, \dots, r_{\delta_i}\}$ would have not been destroyed by any black hole arc leading out of $H_{f_i}(r_{\delta_i+1})$, a contradiction. Hence, robot r_{δ_i+1} finally leaves component $H_{f_i}(r_{\delta_i+1})$ by an arc which is not a black hole arc, so it must contribute to the out-degree of node $H_{f_i}^{(2)}$ in multigraph $(\mathcal{H}, R)$. Since the sequence of $\delta_i + 1$ consecutive robots going through $H_{f_i}^{(2)}$ was arbitrarily chosen, the claim follows directly.

Now, we make a simple structural claim which relies only on properties of directed acyclic multigraphs.

Lemma 2. *Let M be any directed acyclic multigraph having set of nodes $\{s, v_1, v_2, \dots, v_d\}$, such that $\mathrm{indeg}(s) = 0$, and for all v_i, $1 \le i \le d$, we have:* $\mathrm{outdeg}_M(v_i) \ge \left\lfloor \frac{\mathrm{indeg}_M(v_i)}{\delta_i+1} \right\rfloor$. *Then:* $\mathrm{outdeg}(s) < \prod_{i=1}^d (\delta_i + 1)$.

The proof of the lemma proceeds by induction with respect to d; we omit the details. We also make one more simple arithmetic observation, which we leave without proof.

Lemma 3. *Let $\{\delta_1, \dots, \delta_d\}$ be positive integers such that $\sum_{i=1}^d \delta_i = \Delta$. Then* $\prod_{i=1}^d (\delta_i + 1) \le 2^\Delta / \sqrt{3}^{\,\Delta-d}$.

Now, set the number of searching robots released in the current p-th phase as $S_p = \lceil 2^\Delta / \sqrt{3}^{\,p-1} \rceil$. Since we have that $d \le \Delta - p + 1$ (by the inductive claim from phase $p-1$), we obtain from the preceding lemma: $\mathrm{outdeg}_{(\mathcal{H},R)}(s) = S_p \ge 2^\Delta / \sqrt{3}^{\,\Delta-d} \ge \prod_{i=1}^d (\delta_i + 1)$. This means that the claim of Lemma 2 does not hold, and so the assumption $\mathrm{outdeg}_{(\mathcal{H},R)} H_{f_i}^{(2)} \ge \left\lfloor \frac{\mathrm{indeg}_{(\mathcal{H},R)} H_{f_i}^{(2)}}{\delta_i+1} \right\rfloor$ is violated for some component $H_{f_i}^{(2)}$. From Lemma 1 we thus immediately conclude that $d = 1$ and $H_{f_1}^{(2)} = G[V \setminus BH]$, hence in this case one of the robots successfully solves the black hole search problem.

Finally, we remark that if the algorithm reaches phase Δ, we have $d = 1$, and so only one strongly connected component H_{f_1}. Since the algorithm cannot perform any further contractions, by the same argument, $S_\Delta = \Delta + 1$ searching robots in this phase are sufficient to complete the exploration of the graph.

To finish the proof, observe that the total number of robots used during all the phases of the algorithm is at most: $\sum_{p=1}^\Delta (\Delta+2) S_p = (\Delta+2) \sum_{p=1}^\Delta \lceil 2^\Delta / \sqrt{3}^{\,p-1} \rceil \in O(\Delta \cdot 2^\Delta)$.

Theorem 3. *In the synchronous model, 4 robots are always sufficient and sometimes required to solve the directed black hole search problem with $\Delta = 2$.*

Proof. The lower bound on the number of required robots is a direct consequence of Theorem 1. The upper bound is obtained by a similar strategy as that used in the proof of Theorem 2, simply releasing 4 searching robots r_1, r_2, r_3, r_4 in a single phase (without any cycle detection or cycle contraction robots). Let $\{e_1, e_2\} = BA$ be the two black hole arcs, originating from nodes v_1 and v_2 respectively. Robot r_1 may either successfully solve the black hole search instance, or may be destroyed on one of the black hole arcs, say, e_1. In the latter case, robot r_2 will either successfully solve the instance or be destroyed in the other black hole arc e_2 (recall that robots choose to use unvisited arcs, whenever possible, and the graph is strongly connected). Suppose that robot r_3 is also destroyed in some black hole. Now, taking into account Lemma 2, we observe that at some point during the traversal performed by robot r_4, nodes v_1 and v_2 will necessarily belong to the same strongly connected component H_f ($f(v_1) = f(v_2) = f$). Once robot r_4 has reached this component, it will always exit it by unvisited arcs. Since both arc e_1 and e_2 have already been used (by robots r_1 and r_2, respectively), robot r_4 will never enter a black hole and will proceed to enlarge component H_f, until the whole of the graph has been explored, $H_f = G[V \setminus BH]$, and will thus successfully complete the task.

4   Results for the Asynchronous Model

Theorem 4. *In both the asynchronous and synchronous models, 2 robots are always sufficient and sometimes required to solve the directed black hole search problem with $\Delta = 1$.*

Proof. The lower bound on the number of required robots is a direct consequence of Theorem 1. The upper bound (which we obviously need to show for the asynchronous model, only) is obtained by simultaneously releasing two robots, each of which applies a strategy identical to that used by searching robots in the proof of Theorem 2. It is easy to observe that, throughout the process, each robot is either traversing arcs of an already identified strongly connected subgraph H_f of $G[V \setminus BH]$, or is exiting such a subgraph by some outgoing arc e. Arc e has either never been visited before by any robot, or is the unique arc exiting H_f, which, due to the strong connectivity property of $G[V \setminus BH]$, has to lead to some node of $V \setminus BH$. Thus, a robot may potentially enter a black hole only when using an arc which has been never visited before by any robot. Since $\Delta = 1$, this means that the black hole may destroy at most one robot, since the remaining robot will not traverse the unique black hole arc at any later time. The surviving robot(s) perform a search of the graph, exploring unvisited arcs, until the whole of the strongly connected component $G[V \setminus BH]$ has been discovered and the search is complete.

Theorem 5. *In the asynchronous model, at least 5 robots are sometimes required to solve the directed black hole search problem with $\Delta = 2$.*

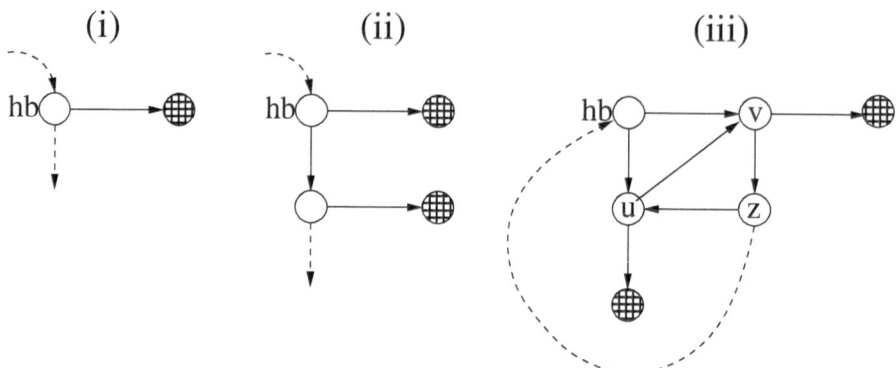

Fig. 2. The three possible ways that an adversary has to defeat any strategy which aims to solve the directed black hole search problem when using less than 5 robots. Dashed arcs will be never traversed because of the adversary.

Proof. The proof considers some possible cases that must be considered by any strategy $\mathcal{A}$ in order to solve the directed black hole search problem with $\Delta = 2$. We first assume that 4 robots are sufficient for solving the problem and then we obtain the claim by showing how an adversary can easily defeat all the robots. As usual, all the 4 robots start from hb which has two outgoing arcs. According to $\mathcal{A}$, there are three possible cases for the first move of each robot (see Figure 2 for a visualization of the corresponding strategies of the adversary): (i) all of them follow one direction; (ii) one goes through one direction and the remaining three to the other; (iii) the four robots are equally distributed among the two directions.

If (i), then the adversary can easily locate one black hole on the reached node, and all the robots get destroyed. If (ii), then the adversary can locate one black hole on the node reached by the majority of the robots, hence destroying three of them. The surviving one reaches a safe node admitting another branching off. One of the two options leads to the black hole, while the other one to hb. As the robot has no further knowledge to distinguish among the two options, the branch it chooses will be set by the adversary as the one leading to the black hole, and again all the robots get destroyed. If (iii), by referring to Figure 2 we have that after the first move, two robots are on node u and two robots are on node v. Note that since from the point of view of the robots located at u (respectively, v), this situation is indistinguishable from that in graph (ii), where all but one of the robots are destroyed; hence, no robot can wait at u (resp. v), since this could lead to an infinite deadlock. Now, the pair of robots on u (resp. v) cannot choose to move along the same arc because they may both be destroyed by the adversary. So, they have to move on distinct arcs. This implies that one robot from u and one from v get destroyed. The snapshot of the network now gives a robot on v and another on z. From v, both outgoing arcs have been already traversed and hence the robot has no further knowledge to distinguish among the two options apart from the IDs of the robots that have been passing through such arcs. However, these IDs can be exchanged by the adversary by swapping the labels of ports exiting v, thus making this information useless. The robot is thus forced either to wait at v, or enters the black hole. The other robot, which is on z, has again two unexplored options, one leading to hb, and the other to u. The adversary forces the robot to reach u, from there it is analogously forced either to wait or to enter the black hole. Thus, all the robots are either destroyed or deadlocked, and the claim holds.

5   Conclusions

In this paper, we have considered the black hole search in directed graphs under both the synchronous and the asynchronous settings. The obtained results reflects the difficulty of the problem on directed graphs as well as the difference between the synchronous and the asynchronous settings. It is worth noting how the behavior of the robots must change even for small values of Δ like 2. This was not the case for undirected graphs. This makes the study of the problem on directed graphs even more intriguing. One major remaining open problem concerns the possibility of bounding the number of required robots in terms of Δ in the asynchronous case.

Many variations of the problem still deserve investigation. Changing the assumptions to the initial knowledge of the robots, for instance, could lead to completely different results.

References

1. Cooper, C., Klasing, R., Radzik, T.: Locating and repairing faults in a network with mobile agents. In: Shvartsman, A.A., Felber, P. (eds.) SIROCCO 2008. LNCS, vol. 5058, pp. 20–32. Springer, Heidelberg (2008)
2. Czyzowicz, J., Kowalski, D.R., Markou, E., Pelc, A.: Searching for a black hole in tree networks. In: Higashino, T. (ed.) OPODIS 2004. LNCS, vol. 3544, pp. 67–80. Springer, Heidelberg (2005)
3. Czyzowicz, J., Dobrev, S., Kralovic, R., Miklik, S., Pardubska, D.: Black Hole Search in Directed Graphs. In: SIROCCO 2009. LNCS, vol. 5869. Springer, Heidelberg (to appear, 2010)
4. Dobrev, S., Flocchini, P., Kralovic, R., Prencipe, G., Ruzicka, P., Santoro, N.: Black hole Search in Common Interconnection Networks. Networks 47(2), 61–71 (2006)
5. Dobrev, S., Flocchini, P., Prencipe, G., Santoro, N.: Finding a black hole in an arbitrary network: optimal mobile agents protocols. In: Proc. of 21st ACM Symposium on Principles of Distributed Computing (PODC), pp. 153–162 (2002)
6. Dobrev, S., Flocchini, P., Prencipe, G., Santoro, N.: Mobile search for a black hole in an anonymous ring. Algorithmica 48(1), 67–90 (2007)
7. Dobrev, S., Flocchini, P., Santoro, N.: Improved bounds for optimal black hole search with a network map. In: Kralovic, R., Sýkora, O. (eds.) SIROCCO 2004. LNCS, vol. 3104, pp. 111–122. Springer, Heidelberg (2004)

8. Gąsieniec, L., Klasing, R., Martin, R.A., Navarra, A., Zhang, X.: Fast periodic graph exploration with constant memory. Journal of Computer and System Sciences (JCSS) 74(5), 802–822 (2008)
9. Glaus, P.: Locating a Black Hole without the Knowledge of Incoming Link. In: Dolev, S. (ed.) ALGOSENSORS 2009. LNCS, vol. 5804, pp. 128–138. Springer, Heidelberg (2009)
10. Klasing, R., Markou, E., Radzik, T., Sarracco, F.: Approximation bounds for Black Hole Search problems. Networks 52(4), 216–226 (2008)
11. Kosowski, A., Navarra, A.: Graph Decomposition for Improving Memoryless Periodic Exploration. In: Královič, R., Niwiński, D. (eds.) MFCS 2009. LNCS, vol. 5734, pp. 501–512. Springer, Heidelberg (2009)

The Fault Detection Problem

Andreas Haeberlen[1] and Petr Kuznetsov[2]

[1] Max Planck Institute for Software Systems (MPI-SWS)
[2] TU Berlin / Deutsche Telekom Laboratories

Abstract. One of the most important challenges in distributed computing is ensuring that services are correct and available despite faults. Recently it has been argued that fault detection can be factored out from computation, and that a generic fault detection service can be a useful abstraction for building distributed systems. However, while fault detection has been extensively studied for crash faults, little is known about detecting more general kinds of faults.

This paper explores the power and the inherent costs of generic fault detection in a distributed system. We propose a formal framework that allows us to partition the set of all faults that can possibly occur in a distributed computation into several *fault classes*. Then we formulate the *fault detection problem* for a given fault class, and we show that this problem can be solved for only two specific fault classes, namely *omission faults* and *commission faults*. Finally, we derive tight lower bounds on the cost of solving the problem for these two classes in asynchronous message-passing systems.

Keywords: Fault classes, fault detection problem, message complexity, lower bounds.

1 Introduction

Handling faults is a key challenge in building reliable distributed systems. There are two main approaches to this problem: *Fault masking* aims to hide the symptoms of a limited number of faults, so that users can be provided with correct service in the presence of faults [14, 4], whereas *fault detection* aims at identifying the faulty components, so that they can be isolated and repaired [7, 10]. These approaches are largely complementary. In this paper, we focus on fault detection.

Fault detection has been extensively studied in the context of "benign" crash faults, where it is assumed that a faulty component simply stops taking steps of its algorithm [6, 5]. However, this assumption does not always hold in practice; in fact, recent studies have shown that general faults (also known as Byzantine faults [15]) can have a considerable impact on practical systems [17]. Thus, it would be useful to apply fault detection to a wider class of faults. So far, very little is known about this topic; there is a paper by Kihlstrom et al. [12] that discusses Byzantine fault detectors for consensus and broadcast protocols, and there are several algorithms for detecting certain types of non-crash faults, such

T. Abdelzaher, M. Raynal, and N. Santoro (Eds.): OPODIS 2009, LNCS 5923, pp. 99–114, 2009.

as PeerReview [10] and SUNDR [16]. However, many open questions remain; for example, we still lack a formal characterization of the types of non-crash faults that can be detected in general, and nothing is known about inherent costs of detection.

This paper is a first step towards a better understanding of general fault detection. We propose a formal model that allows us to formulate the *fault detection problem* for arbitrary faults, including non-crash faults. We introduce the notion of a *fault class* that captures a set of *faults*, i.e., deviations of system components from their expected behavior. Solving the fault detection problem for a fault class F means finding a transformation τ_F that, given any algorithm A, constructs an algorithm $\bar{A}$ (called an *extension* of A) that works exactly like A but does some additional work to identify and expose faulty nodes. Whenever a fault instance from the class F appears, $\bar{A}$ must expose at least one faulty suspect (completeness), it must not expose any correct nodes infinitely long (accuracy), and, optionally, it may ensure that all correct nodes expose the same faulty suspects (agreement).

Though quite weak, our definition of the fault detection problem still allows us to answer two specific questions: Which faults can be detected, and how much extra work from does fault detection require from the extension? To answer the first question, we show that the set of all fault instances can be divided into four non-overlapping classes, and that the fault detection problem can be solved for exactly two of them, which we call *commission faults* and *omission faults*. Intuitively, a commission fault exists when a node sends messages a correct node would not send, whereas an omission fault exists when a node does *not* send messages a correct node *would* send.

To answer the second question, we study the *message complexity* of the fault detection problem, that is, the ratio between the number of messages sent by the most efficient extension and the number of messages sent by the original algorithm. We derive tight lower bounds on the message complexity for commission and omission faults, with and without agreement. Our results show that a) the message complexity for omission faults is higher than that for commission faults, and that b) the message complexity is (optimally) linear in the number of nodes in the system, except when agreement is required for omission faults, in which case it is quadratic in the number of nodes.

In summary, this paper makes the following four contributions: (1) a formal model of a distributed system in which various kinds of faults can be selectively analyzed, (2) a statement of the fault detection problem for arbitrary faults, (3) a complete classification of all possible faults, including a precise characterization of the set of faults for which the fault detection problem can be solved, and (4) tight lower bounds on the message complexity of the fault detection problem. Viewed collectively, our results constitute a first step toward understanding the power and the inherent costs of fault detection in a distributed system.

The rest of this paper is organized as follows: We begin by introducing our system model in Section 2 and then formally state the fault detection problem in Section 3. In Section 4, we present our classification of faults, and we show for which classes the fault detection problem can be solved. In Section 5, we derive tight bounds on the message complexity, and we conclude by discussing related work in Section 6 and future work in Section 7. Omitted proofs can be found in the full version of this paper, which is available as a technical report [9].

2   Preliminaries

2.1   System Model

Let N be a set of *nodes*. Each node has a terminal[1] and a network interface. It can communicate with the other nodes by sending and receiving messages over the network, and it can send outputs to, and receive inputs from, its local terminal. We assume that processing times are negligible; when a node receives an input, it can produce a response immediately.

Each message m has a unique *source* $src(m) \in N$ and a unique *destination* $dest(m) \in N$. We assume that messages are authenticated; that is, each node i can initially create only messages m with $src(m) = i$, although it can delegate this capability to other nodes (e.g., by revealing its key material). Nodes can also forward messages to other nodes and include messages in other messages they send, and we assume that a forwarded or included message can still be authenticated.

A computation unfolds in discrete *events*. An event is a tuple (i, I, O), where $i \in N$ is a node on which the event occurs, I is a set of inputs (terminal inputs or messages) that i receives in the event, and O is a set of outputs (terminal outputs or messages) that i produces in the event. An *execution* e is a sequence of events $(i_1, I_1, O_1), (i_2, I_2, O_2), \ldots$ We write $e|_S$ for the subsequence of e that contains the events with $i_k \in S$; for $i \in N$, we abbreviate $e_{\{i\}}$ as $e|_i$. When a finite execution e is a prefix of another execution e', we write $e \sqsubseteq e'$. Finally, we write $|e|$ to denote the number of unique messages that are sent in e.

A system is modeled as a set of executions. In this paper, we assume that the network is reliable, that is, a) a message is only received if it has previously been sent at least once, and b) a message that is sent is eventually received at least once. Formally, we assume that, for every execution e of the system and every message m:

$$m \in I_k \Rightarrow [i_k = dest(m) \wedge \exists l < k : (i_l = src(m) \wedge m \in O_l)]$$

$$(m \in O_k \wedge src(m) = i_k) \Rightarrow [\exists l : i_l = dest(m) \wedge m \in I_l]$$

An *open execution* is an execution for which only the first condition holds. Thus, an open execution may contain some messages that are sent, but not received. This definition is needed later in the paper; an actual execution of the system is never open. Finally, we introduce the following notation for brevity:

---

[1] Instead of an actual terminal, nodes may have any other local I/O interface that cannot be observed remotely.

- RECV$(i, m) \in e$ iff m is a message with $i = dest(m)$ and $(i, I, O) \in e$ with $m \in I$.

- SEND$(i, m, j) \in e$ iff m is a message with $j = dest(m)$ and $(i, I, O) \in e$ with $m \in O$.

- IN$(i, t) \in e$ if t is a terminal input and $(i, I, O) \in e$ with $t \in I$.

- OUT$(i, t) \in e$ if t is a terminal output and $(i, I, O) \in e$ with $t \in O$.

2.2 Algorithms and Correctness

Each node i is assigned an *algorithm* $A_i = (M_i, TI_i, TO_i, \Sigma_i, \sigma_0^i, \alpha_i)$, where M_i is the set of messages i can send or receive, TI_i is a set of terminal inputs i can receive, TO_i is a set of terminal outputs i can produce, Σ_i is a set of states, $\sigma_0^i \in \Sigma_i$ is the initial state, and $\alpha_i : \Sigma_i \times P(M_i \cup TI_i) \rightarrow \Sigma_i \times P(M_i \cup TO_i)$ maps a set of inputs and the current state to a set of outputs and the new state. Here, $P(X)$ denotes the power set of X. For convenience, we define $\alpha(\sigma, \emptyset) := (\sigma, \emptyset)$ for all $\sigma \in \Sigma_i$.

We make the following four assumptions about any algorithm A_i: a) it only sends messages that can be properly authenticated, b) it never sends the same message twice, c) it discards incoming duplicates and any messages that cannot be authenticated, and d) it never delegates the ability to send messages m with $src(m) = i$, e.g., by revealing or leaking i's key material. Note that assumption b) does not affect generality, since A_i can simply include a nonce with each message it sends. We also assume that it is possible to decide whether A_i, starting from some state σ_x, could receive some set of messages X in any order (plus an arbitrary number of terminal inputs) without sending any messages. This trivially holds if $|\Sigma_i| < \infty$.

We say that a node i is *correct* in execution $e|_i = (i, I_1, O_1), (i, I_2, O_2), \ldots$ with respect to an algorithm A_i iff there is a sequence of states $\sigma_0, \sigma_1, \ldots$ in Σ_i such that $\sigma_0 = \sigma_0^i$ and, for all $k \geq 1$, $\alpha_i(\sigma_{k-1}, I_k) = (\sigma_k, O_k)$. Note that correctness of a node i implies that the node is *live*: if i is in a state σ_{k-1} and receives an input I, then i must produce an output O_k such that $\alpha_i(\sigma_{k-1}, I_k) = (\sigma_k, O_k)$. If i is not correct in $e|_i$ with respect to A_i, we say that i is *faulty* in $e|_i$ with respect to A_i.

A *distributed algorithm* is a tuple $(A_1, \ldots, A_{|N|})$, one algorithm per node, such that $M_i = M_j$ for all i, j. When we say that an execution e is an execution of a distributed algorithm A, this implies that each node i is considered correct or faulty in e with respect to the algorithm A_i it has been assigned. We write $corr(A, e)$ to denote the set of nodes that are correct in e with respect to A.

2.3 Extensions

$(\bar{A}, A, \mu_m, \mu_s, XO)$ is called a *reduction* of an algorithm $\bar{A} = (\bar{M}, \bar{TI}, \bar{TO}, \bar{\Sigma}, \bar{\sigma}_0, \bar{\alpha})$ to an algorithm $A = (M, TI, TO, \Sigma, \sigma_0, \alpha)$ iff μ_m is a total map $\bar{M} \mapsto P(M)$, μ_s is a total map $\bar{\Sigma} \mapsto \Sigma$, and the following conditions hold:

X1 $\bar{TI} = TI$, that is, A accepts the same terminal inputs as $\bar{A}$;

X2 $\bar{TO} = TO \cup XO$ and $TO \cap XO = \emptyset$, that is, A produces the same terminal outputs as $\bar{A}$, except XO;

X3 $\mu_s(\bar{\sigma}_0) = \sigma_0$, that is, the initial state of $\bar{A}$ maps to the initial state of A;

X4 $\forall m \in M \ \exists \bar{m} \in \bar{M} : \mu_m(\bar{m}) = m$, that is, every message of A has at least one counterpart in $\bar{A}$;

X5 $\forall \sigma \in \Sigma \ \exists \bar{\sigma} \in \bar{\Sigma} : \mu_s(\bar{\sigma}) = \sigma$, that is, every state of A has at least one counterpart in $\bar{\Sigma}$;

X6 $\forall \bar{\sigma}_1, \bar{\sigma}_2 \in \bar{\Sigma}, \bar{mi}, \bar{mo} \subseteq \bar{M}, ti \subseteq TI, to \subseteq TO : [\bar{\alpha}(\bar{\sigma}_1, \bar{mi} \cup ti) = (\bar{\sigma}_2, \bar{mo} \cup to)] \Rightarrow [\alpha(\mu_s(\bar{\sigma}_1), \mu_m(\bar{mi}) \cup ti) = (\mu_s(\bar{\sigma}_2), \mu_m(\bar{mo}) \cup (to \setminus XO))]$, that is, there is a homomorphism between $\bar{\alpha}$ and α.

If there exists at least one reduction from an algorithm $\bar{A}$ to an algorithm A, we say that $\bar{A}$ is an *extension* of A. For every reduction $(\bar{A}, A, \mu_m, \mu_s, XO)$ we can construct an *execution mapping* μ_e that maps executions of $\bar{A}$ to (possibly open) executions of A as follows:

1. Start with $e = \emptyset$.
2. For each new event $(i, \bar{I}, \bar{O})$, perform the following steps:
   (a) Compute $I := (\bar{I} \cap TI_i) \cup \mu_m(\bar{I} \cap \bar{M})$ and $O := (\bar{O} \cap TO_i) \cup \mu_m(\bar{O} \cap \bar{M})$.
   (b) Remove from I any $m \in M$ with $dest(m) \neq i$ or $\text{RECV}(i, m) \in e$.
   (c) Remove from O any $m \in M$ with $\text{SEND}(i, m, j) \in e$.
   (d) For each node $j \in N$, compute $O_j := \{m \in O \mid src(m) = j\}$.
   (e) If $I \neq \emptyset$ or $O_i \neq \emptyset$, append (i, I, O_i) to e.
   (f) For each $j \neq i$ with $O_j \neq \emptyset$, append $(j, \emptyset, O_j)$ to e.

A simple example of a reduction is the identity $(A, A, id, id, \emptyset)$. Note that there is a syntactic correspondence between an extension and its original algorithm, not just a semantic one. In other words, the extension not only solves the same problem as the original algorithm (by producing the same terminal outputs as the original), it also solves it in the same way (by sending the same messages in the same order). Recall that our goal is to detect whether or not the nodes in the system are following a given algorithm; we are *not* trying to find a better algorithm. Next, we state a few simple lemmas about extensions.

Lemma 1. *Let $\bar{A}$ and A be two algorithms for which a reduction $(\bar{A}, A, \mu_m, \mu_s, XO)$ exists. Then, if $\bar{e}$ is an execution in which a node i is correct with respect to $\bar{A}$, i is correct in $\mu_e(\bar{e})$ with respect to A.*

Note that, if a node i is correct in $\bar{e}$ with respect to $\bar{A}$, then it must be correct in $\mu_e(\bar{e})$ with respect to A, but the reverse is not true. In other words, it is possible for a node i to be faulty in $\bar{e}$ with respect to $\bar{A}$ but still be correct in $\mu_e(\bar{e})$ with respect to A.

Lemma 2. *Let $\bar{A}$ and A be two algorithms for which a reduction $(\bar{A}, A, \mu_m, \mu_s, XO)$ exists, let $\bar{e}_1$ be an execution of $\bar{A}$, and let $\bar{e}_2$ be a prefix of $\bar{e}_1$. Then $\mu_e(\bar{e}_2)$ is a prefix of $\mu_e(\bar{e}_1)$.*

Lemma 3. *Let $\bar{A}$ and A be two algorithms for which a reduction $(\bar{A}, A, \mu_m, \mu_s, XO)$ exists, and let e be an execution of A. Then there exists an execution $\bar{e}$ of $\bar{A}$ such that a) $\mu_e(\bar{e}) = e$ (modulo duplicate messages sent by faulty nodes in e), and b) a node i is correct in $\bar{e}$ with respect to $\bar{A}$ iff it is correct in e with respect to A.*

2.4 Facts and Evidence

To detect faults, and to identify faulty nodes, the correct nodes must collect information about the current execution. Clearly, no correct node can expect to know the entire execution at any point, since it cannot observe events on other nodes. However, each node can locally observe its inputs and outputs, and each input or output rules out some possible executions that *cannot* be the current execution. For example, if a node i receives a message m, this rules out all executions in which m was never sent. If i manages to rule out all executions in which some set S of nodes is correct, it has established that at least one node $s \in S$ must be faulty. Thus, we can use sets of plausible executions to represent a node's knowledge about the current execution.

Formally, we define a *fact* ζ to be a set of executions, and we say that a node i *knows* a fact ζ at the end of an execution prefix e iff ζ contains all infinite executions e' where $e|_i$ is a prefix of $e'|_i$ (in other words, e' is consistent with all the inputs and outputs i has seen in e). If a node knows two facts ζ_1 and ζ_2, it can combine them into a new fact $\zeta_3 := \zeta_1 \cap \zeta_2$. If the system is running an extension $\bar{A}$ of an algorithm A, we can map any fact $\bar{\zeta}$ about the current execution $\bar{e}$ of $\bar{A}$ to a fact $\zeta := \{\mu_e(x) \mid x \in \bar{\zeta}\}$ about $\mu_e(\bar{e})$.

Different nodes may know different facts. Hence, the nodes may only be able to detect a fault if they exchange information. However, faulty nodes can lie, so a correct node can safely accept a fact from another node only if it receives *evidence* of that fact. Formally, we say that a message m is evidence of a fact ζ iff for any execution $\bar{e}$ of $\bar{A}$ in which any node receives m, $\mu(\bar{e}) \in \zeta$. Intuitively, evidence consists of signed messages. For more details, please see Section 4.

2.5 Fault Instances and Fault Classes

Not all faults can be detected, and some extensions can detect more faults than others. To quantify this, we introduce an abstraction for an individual 'fault'. A *fault instance* ψ is a four-tuple (A, C, S, e), where A is a distributed algorithm, C and S are sets of nodes, and e is an infinite execution, such that a) C and S do not overlap, b) every $c \in C$ is correct in e with respect to A, and c) at least one node $i \in S$ is faulty in e with respect to A. A *fault class* F is a set of fault instances, and the nodes in S are called *suspects*.

Intuitively, the goal is for the correct nodes in C to identify at least one faulty suspect from S. Of course, an ideal solution would simply identify *all* the nodes that are faulty in e with respect to A; however, this is not always possible. Consider the scenario in Figure 1. In this scenario, the nodes in C know that at least one of the nodes in S must be faulty, but they do not know which ones, or how many. Thus, the size of the set S effectively represents the precision with

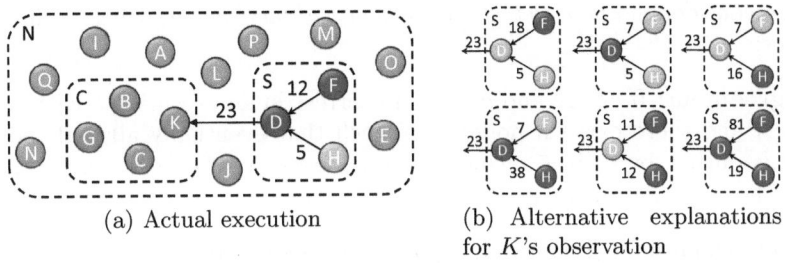

(a) Actual execution   (b) Alternative explanations
for K's observation

Fig. 1. Example scenario. Nodes F and H are supposed to each send a number between 1 and 10 to D, who is supposed to add the numbers and send the result to K. If K receives 23, it knows that at least one of the nodes in $S = \{D, F, H\}$ must be faulty, but it does not know which ones, or how many.

which the fault can be localized. The best case is $|S| = 1$; this indicates that the fault can be traced to exactly one node. The worst case is $S = N \setminus C$; this indicates that the nodes in C know that a fault exists somewhere, but they are unable to localize it.

2.6   Environments

Our formulation of the fault detection problem does not require a bound on the number of faulty nodes. However, if such a bound is known, it is possible to find solutions with a lower message complexity. To formalize this, we use the notion of an *environment*, which is a restriction on the fault patterns that may occur in a system. In this paper, we specifically consider environments E_f, in which the total number of faulty nodes is limited to f. If a system in environment E_f is assigned a distributed algorithm A, the only executions that can occur are those in which at most f nodes are faulty with respect to A.

3   The Fault Detection Problem

Let $\nu := \{\text{FAULTY}(X) \mid X \subseteq N\}$ be a set of *fault notifications*. Then the *fault detection problem* for a fault class F is to find a transformation τ_F that maps any distributed algorithm A to an extension $\bar{A} := \tau_F(A)$ such that $\bar{TO} = TO \cup \nu$ and the following conditions hold:

C1 **Nontriviality:** If $\bar{e}$ is an infinite execution of $\bar{A}$ and $i \in N$ is correct in $\bar{e}$ with respect to $\bar{A}$, then i outputs infinitely many fault notifications in $\bar{e}$.

C2 **Completeness:** If (A, C, S, e) is a fault instance in F, $\bar{e}$ is an infinite execution such that $\mu_e(\bar{e}) = e$, and each node $c \in C$ is correct in $\bar{e}$ with respect to $\bar{A}$, then there exists a correct node $c' \in N$ and a node $j \in S$ such that eventually all fault notifications output by c' contain j.

C3 **Accuracy:** If $\bar{e}$ is an infinite execution of $\bar{A}$ and $c_1, c_2 \in N$ are any two nodes that are correct in $\bar{e}$ with respect to $\bar{A}$, then c_1 outputs infinitely many fault notifications that do not include c_2.

We also consider the *fault detection problem with agreement*, which additionally requires:

C4 **Agreement:** If $c_1 \in N$ and $c_2 \in N$ are correct in an execution $\bar{e}$ with respect to $\bar{A}$ and there exists a node $i \in N$ such that eventually all fault notifications output by c_1 in $\bar{e}$ include some node $i \in N$, then eventually all fault notifications output by c_2 in $\bar{e}$ include i as well.

Note that condition C2 does not require us to detect nodes that are faulty in $\bar{e}$ with respect to $\bar{A}$, but correct in $\mu_e(\bar{e})$ with respect to A. Thus, we avoid the infinite recursion that would result from trying to detect faults in the detector itself. Note also that condition C3 is weaker than the definition of eventual strong accuracy in [6], which requires that correct nodes eventually output only faulty nodes. This change is necessary to make the problem solvable in an asynchronous environment.

4   Which Faults Can Be Detected?

In the rest of this paper, we assume that the only facts for which evidence can exist are a) message transmissions, and b) message receptions. Specifically, a properly authenticated message $\bar{m}$ with $\mu_m(\bar{m}) = m$ and $src(m) = i$ in an execution $\bar{e}$ is evidence of a fact $\{e \mid \text{SEND}(i, m, dest(m)) \in e\}$ about $\mu_e(\bar{e})$, and a properly authenticated message $\bar{m}'$ with $src(\bar{m}') = i$, $m \in \bar{m}'$, and $dest(m) = i$ in an execution $\bar{e}$ is evidence of a fact $\{e \mid \text{RECV}(i, m) \in e\}$ about $\mu_e(\bar{e})$. Note that in some systems it may be possible to construct evidence of additional facts (e.g., when the system has more synchrony or access to more sophisticated cryptographic primitives). In such systems, the following results may not apply.

4.1   Definitions

We define two *fact maps* ϕ^+ and ϕ^- as follows. Let e be an infinite execution or an execution prefix, and let C be a set of nodes. Then $\phi^+(C, e)$ is the intersection[2] of all facts ζ for which at least one node in C can construct evidence in e (note that there is usually no single node that can construct evidence of *all* facts), and $\phi^-(C, e)$ is the intersection of all facts ζ such that, if the complement $\bar{\zeta}$ were a fact in e (i.e., $e \in \zeta$), then at least one node in C could construct evidence of $\bar{\zeta}$ in e, but $\bar{\zeta} \notin \phi^+(C, e)$. For brevity, we write $\phi^{\pm}(C, e)$ to represent both kinds of facts, that is, $\phi^{\pm}(C, e) := \phi^+(C, e) \cap \phi^-(C, e)$.

Intuitively, $\phi^{\pm}$ represents the sum of all knowledge the nodes in C can have in e if they exchange all of their evidence with each other. Since we have restricted the admissible evidence to messages earlier, $\phi^+(C, e)$ effectively represents knowledge about all the messages sent or received in e by the nodes in C, while $\phi^-(C, e)$

---

[2] Recall that facts are combined by forming the intersection. Since facts are sets of plausible executions, an execution that is plausible given two facts ζ_1 and ζ_2 must be a member of $\zeta_1 \cap \zeta_2$.

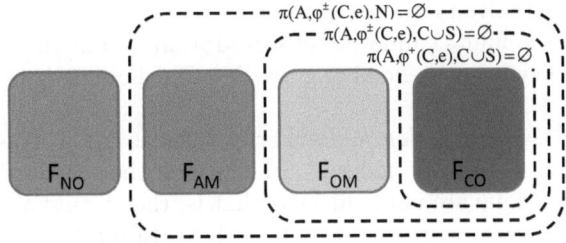

Fig. 2. Classification of all fault instances. The fault detection problem cannot be solved for fault instances in F_{NO} (Theorem 2) or F_{AM} (Theorem 3), but solutions exist for F_{OM} and F_{CO} (Theorem 4).

effectively represents knowledge about all the messages *not* sent or received in e by the nodes in C.

We also define the *plausibility map* π as follows. Let A be a distributed algorithm, Z a set of facts, and C a set of nodes. Then $\pi(A, Z, C)$ represents all infinite executions $e \in Z$ in which each node $c \in C$ is correct in e with respect to A. Intuitively, $\pi(A, Z, C)$ is the set of executions of A that are plausible given the facts in Z, and given that (at least) the nodes in C are correct.

A few simple properties of ϕ and π are: 1) $C_1 \subseteq C_2 \Rightarrow \phi(C_2, e) \subseteq \phi(C_1, e)$, that is, adding evidence from more nodes cannot reduce the overall knowledge; 2) $p_1 \downharpoonright p_2 \Rightarrow \phi(C, p_2) \subseteq \phi(C, p_1)$, that is, knowledge can only increase during an execution; 3) $C_1 \subseteq C_2 \Rightarrow \pi(A, Z, C_2) \subseteq \pi(A, Z, C_1)$, that is, assuming that more nodes are correct can only reduce the number of plausible executions; and 4) $Z_1 \subseteq Z_2 \Rightarrow \pi(A, Z_1, C) \subseteq \pi(A, Z_2, C)$, that is, learning more facts can only reduce the number of plausible executions.

4.2   Fault Classes

We define the following fault classes (see also Figure 2):

$$F_{NO} := \{(A, C, S, e) \mid \pi(A, \phi^{\pm}(C, e), N) \neq \emptyset\}$$
$$F_{AM} := \{(A, C, S, e) \mid \pi(A, \phi^{\pm}(C, e), N) = \emptyset \wedge \pi(A, \phi^{\pm}(C, e), C \cup S) \neq \emptyset\}$$
$$F_{OM} := \{(A, C, S, e) \mid \pi(A, \phi^{\pm}(C, e), C \cup S) = \emptyset \wedge \pi(A, \phi^{+}(C, e), C \cup S) \neq \emptyset\}$$
$$F_{CO} := \{(A, C, S, e) \mid \pi(A, \phi^{+}(C, e), C \cup S) = \emptyset\}$$

F_{NO} is the class of *non-observable faults*. For executions in this class, the nodes in C cannot even be sure that the system contains any faulty nodes, since there exists a correct execution of the entire system that is consistent with everything they see. We will show later in this section that the fault detection problem cannot be solved for faults in this class.

F_{AM} is the class of *ambiguous fault instances*. When a fault instance is in this class, the nodes in C know that a faulty node exists, but they cannot be sure that it is one of the nodes in S. We will show later that the fault detection problem cannot be solved for fault instances in this class. Note that the problem here is not that the faults cannot be observed from C, but that the set S is too small. If S is sufficiently extended (e.g., to $N \setminus C$), these fault instances become solvable.

F_{OM} is the class of *omission faults*. For executions in this class, the nodes in C could infer that one of the nodes in S is faulty if they knew all the facts, but the positive facts alone are not sufficient; that is, they would also have to know that some message was *not* sent or *not* received. Intuitively, this occurs when the nodes in S refuse to send some message they are required to send.

F_{CO} is the class of *commission faults*. For executions in this class, the nodes in C can infer that one of the nodes in S is faulty using only positive facts. Intuitively, this occurs when the nodes in S send some combination of messages they would never send in any correct execution.

Theorem 1. $(F_{NO}, F_{AM}, F_{OM}, F_{CO})$ *is a partition of the set of all fault instances.*

Proof. First, we show that no fault instance can belong to more than one class. Suppose $\psi := (A, C, S, e) \in F_{NO}$; that is, there is a plausible correct execution e' of the entire system. Then ψ can obviously not be in F_{AM}, since $\pi(A, \phi^{\pm}(C, e), N)$ cannot be both empty and non-empty. Since all nodes are correct in e', the nodes in $C \cup S$ in particular are also correct, so $\psi \notin F_{OM}$ (Section 4.1, Property 3), and they are still correct if negative facts are ignored, so $\psi \notin F_{CO}$. Now suppose $\psi \in F_{AM}$. Obviously, ψ cannot be in F_{OM}, since $\pi(A, \phi^{\pm}(C, e), C \cup S)$ cannot be both empty and non-empty. But ψ cannot be in F_{CO} either, since using fewer facts can only increase the number of plausible executions (Section 4.1, Property 1). Finally, observe that ψ cannot be in both F_{OM} and F_{CO}, since $\pi(A, \phi^{+}(C, e), C \cup S)$ cannot be both empty and non-empty.

It remains to be shown that any fault instance belongs to at least one of the four classes. Suppose there is a fault instance $\psi \notin (F_{NO} \cup F_{AM} \cup F_{OM} \cup F_{CO})$. Since ψ is not in F_{NO}, we know that $\pi(A, \phi^{\pm}(C, e), N) = \emptyset$. But if this is true and ψ is not in F_{AM}, it follows that $\pi(A, \phi^{\pm}(C, e), C \cup S) = \emptyset$. Given this and that ψ is not in F_{OM}, we can conclude that $\pi(A, \phi^{+}(C, e), C \cup S) = \emptyset$. But then ψ would be in F_{CO}, which is a contradiction.

Theorem 2. *The fault detection problem cannot be solved for any fault class F with $F \cap F_{NO} \neq \emptyset$.*

Proof sketch. The proof works by showing that, for any fault instance $\psi := (A, C, S, e) \in F_{NO}$, we can construct two executions $\bar{e}_{good}$ and $\bar{e}_{bad}$ of $\bar{A} := \tau(A)$ such that a) all the nodes are correct in $\bar{e}_{good}$, b) the fault occurs in $\bar{e}_{bad}$, and c) the two executions are indistinguishable from the perspective of the nodes in C (that is, $\bar{e}_{good}|_C = \bar{e}_{bad}|_C$). Hence, the nodes in C would have to both expose some node in S (to achieve completeness in $\bar{e}_{bad}$) and *not* expose any node in S (to achieve accuracy in $\bar{e}_{good}$) based on the same information, which is impossible. For the full proof, see [9].   □

Theorem 3. *The fault detection problem cannot be solved for any fault class F with $F \cap F_{AM} \neq \emptyset$.*

Proof sketch. The proof is largely analogous to that of Theorem 2, except that we now construct two executions $\bar{e}_{\in S}$ and $\bar{e}_{\notin S}$ of $\bar{A} := \tau(A)$ such that a) in $\bar{e}_{\in S}$ the faulty node is a member of S, b) in $\bar{e}_{\notin S}$ all the nodes in S are correct, and c) the two executions are indistinguishable from C. For the full proof, see [9]. $\square$

Corollary 1. *If the fault detection problem can be solved for a fault class F, then $F \subseteq F_{OM} \cup F_{CO}$.*

Theorem 4. *There is a solution to the fault detection problem with agreement for the fault class $F_{OM} \cup F_{CO}$.*

For a transformation that solves the fault detection problem for this class, please refer to the proof of Theorem 8 (Section 5.2) that appears in [9].

5 Message Complexity

In this section, we investigate how expensive it is to solve the fault detection problem, that is, how much additional work is required to detect faults. The metric we use is the number of messages that must be sent by correct nodes. (Obviously, the faulty nodes can send arbitrarily many messages). Since the answer clearly depends on the original algorithm and on the actions of the faulty nodes in a given execution, we focus on the following two questions: First, what is the maximum number of messages that may be *necessary* for some algorithm, and second, what is the minimum number of messages that is *sufficient* for any algorithm?

5.1 Definitions

If τ is a solution of the fault detection problem, we say that the *message complexity* $\gamma(\tau)$ of τ is the largest number such that for all k, there exists an algorithm A, an execution e of A, and an execution $\bar{e}$ of $\tau(A)$ such that

$$(\mu_e(\bar{e}) = e) \wedge (|e| \geq k) \wedge \left[\frac{|\{\bar{m} \mid \text{SEND}(i, \bar{m}, j) \in \bar{e} \wedge i \in corr(\tau(A), \bar{e})\}|}{|e|} \geq \gamma(\tau) \right]$$

In other words, the message complexity is the maximum number of messages that must be sent by correct nodes in any $\bar{e}$ *per* message sent in the corresponding $e := \mu_e(\bar{e})$. The message complexity of the fault detection problem as a whole is the minimum message complexity over all solutions.

5.2 Lower and Upper Bounds

In this section, we present a collection of tight lower bounds for solving various instances of the fault detection problem. Omitted proofs can be found in the technical report [9].

First we show that message complexity of the fault detection problem in the environment E_f for both commission and omission faults is optimally linear in f.

Theorem 5. *Any solution τ of the fault detection problem for F_{CO} in the environment E_f has message complexity $\gamma(\tau) \geq f+2$, provided that $f+2 < |N|$.*

Theorem 6. *The message complexity of the fault detection problem with agreement for F_{CO} in the environment E_f is at most $f+2$, provided that $f+2 < |N|$.*

Corollary 2. *The message complexity of the fault detection problem (with or without agreement) for F_{CO} in environment E_f is $f+2$, provided that $f+2 < |N|$.*

Theorem 7. *Any solution τ of the fault detection problem for F_{OM} in the environment E_f has message complexity $\gamma(\tau) \geq 3f+4$, provided that $f+2 < |N|$.*

Theorem 8. *The message complexity of the fault detection problem for F_{OM} in the environment E_f is at most $3f+4$, provided that $f+2 < |N|$.*

Interestingly, if we additionally require agreement, then the optimal message complexity of the fault detection problem with respect to omission faults is quadratic in $|N|$, under the condition that at least half of the nodes may fail. Intuitively, if a majority of N is known to be correct, it should be possible to delegate fault detection to a set ω with $|\omega| = 2f+1$, and to have the remaining nodes follow the majority of ω. This would reduce the message complexity to approximately $|N| \cdot (2f+1)$.

Theorem 9. *Any solution τ of the fault detection problem with agreement for F_{OM} in the environment E_f has message complexity $\gamma(\tau) \geq (|N|-1)^2$, provided that $\frac{|N|-1}{2} < f < |N| - 2$.*

Proof sketch. In contrast to commission faults, there is no self-contained proof of an omission fault; when a node is suspected of having omitted a message m, the suspicion can always turn out to be groundless when m eventually arrives. We show that, under worst-case conditions, such a 'false positive' can occur after every single message. Moreover, since agreement is required, a correct node must not suspect (or stop suspecting) another node unless every other correct node eventually does so as well. Therefore, after each message, the correct nodes may have to ensure that their own evidence is known to all the other correct nodes, which in the absence of a correct majority requires reliable broadcast and thus at least $(|N|-1)^2$ messages. For the full proof, see [9].   □

Theorem 10. *The message complexity of the fault detection problem with agreement for F_{OM} in the environment E_f is at most $(|N|-1)^2$, provided that $f+2 < |N|$.*

5.3   Summary

Table 1 summarizes the results in this section. Our two main results are that a) detecting omission faults has a substantially higher message complexity than

Table 1. Message complexity in environments with up to f faulty nodes

Fault class	Fault detection problem	Fault detection problem with agreement
F_{CO}	$f + 2$ (Corollary 2)	$f + 2$ (Corollary 2)
F_{OM}	$3f + 4$ (Theorems 7 and 8)	$(|N| - 1)^2$ (Theorems 9 and 10)

detecting commission faults, and that b) the message complexity is generally linear in the failure bound f, except when the fault class includes omission faults *and* agreement is required, in which case the message complexity is quadratic in the system size $|N|$.

6 Related Work

There is an impressive amount of work on fault detection in the context of *failure detectors* (starting from the original paper by Chandra and Toueg [6]). However, literature on failure detectors conventionally assumes crash-fault models, and usually studies theoretical bounds on the information about failures that is necessary to solve various distributed computing problems [5], without focusing on the costs of implementing failure detectors.

Faults beyond simple crashes have been extensively studied in the context of arbitrary (Byzantine) fault tolerance (starting from the original paper by Lamport et al. [15]). Byzantine fault-tolerant systems aim to keep faults from becoming "visible" to the system users. One example is Castro and Liskov's Practical Byzantine fault-tolerance (PBFT) [4] that extends Lamport's state-machine replication protocol [14] to the Byzantine failure model. However, BFT systems do not detect and expose faulty nodes.

In the context of *synchronous* Byzantine agreement algorithms, Bar-Noy et al [2] use the terms "fault detections" and "fault masking" in a more restrictive manner than this paper does. In [2], a processor in an agreement protocol is said to be "detected" if all correct processors agree that the processor is faulty. All subsequent actions of this processor are then ignored and thus "masked".

Also with respect to Byzantine agreement algorithms, Bracha [3] describes a protocol in which all messages are broadcast, and in which all nodes track the state of every other node in order to identify messages that could not have been sent by a correct node.

Intrusion detection systems (IDS) can detect a limited class of protocol violations, for example by looking for anomalies [7] or by checking the behavior of the system against a formal specification [13].

A technique that statistically monitors quorum systems and raises an alarm if the failure assumptions are about to be violated was introduced in [1]. However, this technique cannot identify which nodes are faulty.

To the best of our knowledge, Kihlstrom et al. [12] were the first to explicitly focus on Byzantine fault detection. The paper also gives informal definitions of the commission and omission faults. However, the definitions in [12] are specific to consensus and broadcast protocols.

Our notions of facts and evidence in a distributed system are inspired by the epistemic formalism of Halpern and Moses [11].

The results in this paper have important consequences for research on *accountability* in distributed computing. Systems like PeerReview [10] provide accountability by ensuring that faults can eventually be detected and irrefutably linked to a faulty node. Since fault detection is an integral part of accountability, this paper establishes an upper bound on the set of faults for which accountability can be achieved, as well as a lower bound on the worst-case message complexity. Note that practical accountability systems have other functions, such as providing more detailed fault notifications, which we do not model here.

7   Conclusion and Future Work

In reasoning about computing systems, it is very important to find the right language. Somewhat dangerously, intuitive claims sometimes become "folklore" before they are actually stated precisely and proved. For example, exact bounds on the information about crash failures needed for solving agreement, though informally anticipated earlier [14,8], were captured precisely only with the introduction of failure detectors [6], and especially the notion of the weakest failure detector [5].

Similarly, this paper has developed a language for reasoning about fault detection with general fault models (beyond simple crash faults). We have proposed a framework in which generic faults can be precisely defined and classified. Unlike crash faults, generic faults cannot be defined without reference to an algorithm, which is why we have introduced the expected system behavior into the definition. To determine the inherent costs of generic fault detection, we have proposed a weak definition of the fault detection problem, and we have derived exact bounds on the cost of solving it in asynchronous message-passing systems where nodes are able to digitally sign their messages.

The framework we have presented can also be used to study fault detection in other system models. If the model is weakened or strengthened (e.g., by varying the assumptions about the network, the degree of synchrony, or the available cryptographic primitives), the kinds of evidence available to correct nodes can change, as can the set of executions that are plausible given some specific evidence. This change, in turn, affects the ability of correct nodes to detect and isolate faulty nodes. For instance, if bounds on communication and processing times are known, it is possible to establish in finite time that an omission fault has occurred, and the culprits can safely be suspected forever. The model could also be changed by introducing bounds on the message size and/or the set of states Σ. These changes would likely increase the message complexity and reduce the size of the fault classes for which detection is possible.

Our framework can be used to study different variants of the fault detection problem. The (weak) formulation of the problem chosen in this paper was primarily instrumental for establishing impossibilities and complexity lower bounds that capture inherent costs of detection in the asynchronous systems. In other scenarios, however, different formulations may make more sense. For example, accuracy could be strengthened such that eventually no correct node is suspected by any correct node; this would require stronger synchrony assumptions [8, 6]. On the other hand, completeness could be relaxed in such a way that faults must only be detected with high probability. Preliminary evidence suggests that such a definition would substantially reduce the message complexity [10].

In conclusion, we believe that this work is a step toward a better understanding of the costs and limitations of fault detection in distributed systems. We also believe that this work could be used as a basis for extending the spectrum of fault classes with new intermediate classes, ranging between the "benign" crash faults (which have proven to be too restrictive for modern software) and the generic but rather pessimistic Byzantine faults.

References

1. Alvisi, L., Malkhi, D., Pierce, E.T., Reiter, M.K.: Fault detection for Byzantine quorum systems. IEEE Trans. Parallel Distrib. Syst. 12(9), 996–1007 (2001)
2. Bar-Noy, A., Dolev, D., Dwork, C., Strong, H.R.: Shifting gears: changing algorithms on the fly to expedite Byzantine agreement. In: PODC, pp. 42–51 (1987)
3. Bracha, G.: Asynchronous Byzantine agreement protocols. Information and Computation 75(2), 130–143 (1987)
4. Castro, M., Liskov, B.: Practical Byzantine fault tolerance and proactive recovery. ACM Transactions on Computer Systems 20(4), 398–461 (2002)
5. Chandra, T.D., Hadzilacos, V., Toueg, S.: The weakest failure detector for solving consensus. J. ACM 43(4), 685–722 (1996)
6. Chandra, T.D., Toueg, S.: Unreliable failure detectors for reliable distributed systems. J. ACM 43(2), 225–267 (1996)
7. Denning, D.E.: An intrusion-detection model. IEEE Transactions on Software Engineering 13(2), 222–232 (1987)
8. Dolev, D., Dwork, C., Stockmeyer, L.: On the minimal synchronism needed for distributed consensus. J. ACM 34(1), 77–97 (1987)
9. Haeberlen, A., Kuznetsov, P.: The fault detection problem, Technical Report MPI-SWS-2009-005, Max Planck Institute for Software Systems (October 2009)
10. Haeberlen, A., Kuznetsov, P., Druschel, P.: PeerReview: Practical accountability for distributed systems. In: SOSP, October 2007, pp. 175–188 (2007)
11. Halpern, J.Y., Moses, Y.: Knowledge and common knowledge in a distributed environment. J. ACM 37(3), 549–587 (1990)
12. Kihlstrom, K.P., Moser, L.E., Melliar-Smith, P.M.: Byzantine fault detectors for solving consensus. The Computer Journal 46(1), 16–35 (2003)

13. Ko, C., Fink, G., Levitt, K.: Automated detection of vulnerabilities in privileged programs using execution monitoring. In: Proceedings of the 10th Annual Computer Security Application Conference (December 1994)
14. Lamport, L.: The part-time parliament. ACM Trans. Comput. Syst. 16(2), 133–169 (1998)
15. Lamport, L., Shostak, R., Pease, M.: The Byzantine generals problem. ACM Trans. Progr. Lang. Syst. 4(3), 382–401 (1982)
16. Li, J., Krohn, M., Mazières, D., Sasha, D.: Secure untrusted data repository (SUNDR). In: OSDI (December 2004)
17. Vandiver, B., Balakrishnan, H., Liskov, B., Madden, S.: Tolerating Byzantine faults in transaction processing systems using commit barrier scheduling. In: SOSP (October 2007)

The Minimum Information about Failures for Solving Non-local Tasks in Message-Passing Systems*

Carole Delporte-Gallet[1], Hugues Fauconnier[1], and Sam Toueg[2]

[1] LIAFA, University Paris Diderot, France
{cd,hf}@liafa.jussieu.fr
[2] University of Toronto, ON, Canada
sam@cs.toronto.edu

Abstract. This paper defines the basic notions of local and non-local tasks, and determines the minimum information about failures that is necessary to solve any non-local task in message-passing systems. It also introduces a natural weakening of the well-known set agreement task, and show that, in some precise sense, it is the weakest non-local task in message-passing systems.

1 Introduction

In this paper, we investigate the following question: *What is the minimum information about failures that is necessary to solve* any *non-local task in message-passing systems?*

To understand this question, we must first explain what we mean here by "non-local task". Roughly speaking, an (input/output) task is a relation between the input and the output values of processes [2,15,17]. In this paper, we consider *one-shot* tasks where each process has a single input value drawn from a finite number of possible input values, and each process outputs a single value. To classify a task as being local or non-local, we consider its input/output requirement in simple systems with no failures. Intuitively, a task is *local* if, in systems with no failures, every process can compute its output value locally by applying some function on its own input value. A task is *non-local* if it is not local.

To illustrate the concept of task locality, consider the trivial "identity" task which requires that every process simply outputs a copy of its input. Intuitively, this task is local: every process can compute its output locally, without any message exchange. Now consider the binary consensus task. This task is not local, in the sense that at least one process cannot compute its output from its individual input only (this holds even in a system where all processes are correct). So consensus is a non-local task.

To determine the minimum information about failures that is necessary to solve non-local tasks, we use the abstraction of failure detectors [4]. Failure detectors have been used to solve several basic problems of fault-tolerant distributed computing and to capture the minimum information about failures that is necessary to solve these problems

---

* Work partially supported by supported by the ANR verso SHAMAN and the National Science and Engineering Research Council of Canada.

T. Abdelzaher, M. Raynal, and N. Santoro (Eds.): OPODIS 2009, LNCS 5923, pp. 115–128, 2009.

(e.g., consensus [3,4], set agreement [8,19], non-blocking atomic commit [6], mutual exclusion [7], uniform reliable broadcast [1,14], boosting obstruction-freedom to wait-freedom [12], implementing an atomic register in a message-passing system [6], etc.).

In this paper, we show that there is a non-trivial failure detector, denoted $\mathcal{FS}^*$, that is necessary to solve non-local tasks in message-passing systems. By this we mean that $\mathcal{FS}^*$ can be extracted from *any* failure detector that can be used to solve *any* non-local task in such systems. We also show that $\mathcal{FS}^*$ is the strongest failure detector with this property. More precisely, we prove that:

1. NECESSITY: $\mathcal{FS}^*$ is necessary to solve non-local tasks, i.e., if a failure detector $\mathcal{D}$ can be used to solve a non-local task $\mathcal{T}$ then $\mathcal{FS}^*$ is weaker than $\mathcal{D}$,[1] and
2. MAXIMALITY: if a failure detector $\mathcal{D}^*$ is necessary to solve non-local tasks, then $\mathcal{D}^*$ is weaker than $\mathcal{FS}^*$.

So, intuitively, $\mathcal{FS}^*$ is the greatest lower bound of the set of failure detectors that solve non-local tasks, and it captures the minimum information about failures necessary for solving such tasks in message-passing systems.

$\mathcal{FS}^*$ is a very weak failure detector, so one may ask wether it is too weak to solve any interesting problem. We show that this is not the case: $\mathcal{FS}^*$ can be used to solve a natural weakening of the well-known *set agreement* task [5], that we call *weak set agreement (WSA)*. In fact, we prove that $\mathcal{FS}^*$ is the weakest failure detector to solve this task.[2] Our results imply that, in some precise sense, *WSA* is the weakest non-local task for message-passing systems: for *any* non-local task $\mathcal{T}$, if $\mathcal{T}$ is solvable using a failure detector $\mathcal{D}$, then *WSA* is also solvable with $\mathcal{D}$.

Finally, we compare $\mathcal{FS}^*$ to two closely related failure detectors, namely, $\mathcal{L}$ and anti-Ω, which are the weakest failure detectors to solve set agreement in message-passing and shared memory systems, respectively [19,8]. We prove that anti-Ω is strictly weaker than $\mathcal{FS}^*$ and $\mathcal{FS}^*$ is strictly weaker than $\mathcal{L}$, in message-passing systems.

It is worth noting that the failure detector $\mathcal{FS}^*$ and the weak set agreement task *WSA*, introduced here, are both very simple. Intuitively, failure detector $\mathcal{FS}^*$ outputs GREEN or RED at each process such that (1) if *all* processes are correct, then $\mathcal{FS}^*$ outputs GREEN forever at some process, and (2) if *exactly one* process is correct, then there is a time after which $\mathcal{FS}^*$ outputs RED at this process. Weak set agreement is like set agreement, except that the condition that there are at most $n - 1$ distinct decision values is required *only for failure-free runs*.

Roadmap. We informally describe our message-passing model, and define the concept of a local task, in Section 2. We define $\mathcal{FS}^*$ in Section 3 and prove that it is necessary to solve non-local tasks in Section 4. In Section 5, we define weak set agreement task and show that $\mathcal{FS}^*$ is necessary to solve it, and, in Section 6, we prove that $\mathcal{FS}^*$ is also sufficient to solve it. In Section 7, we show that $\mathcal{FS}^*$ is the minimum failure detector for solving non-local tasks. We compare $\mathcal{FS}^*$ to anti-Ω and $\mathcal{L}$ in Section 8, and conclude

---

[1] We say that $\mathcal{D}'$ is weaker than $\mathcal{D}$ if processes can use $\mathcal{D}$ to emulate $\mathcal{D}'$ [3], i.e., if $\mathcal{D}'$ can be extracted from $\mathcal{D}$.

[2] This means that (a) $\mathcal{FS}^*$ can be used to solve *WSA* and (b) $\mathcal{FS}^*$ is weaker than any failure detector that can be used to solve *WSA* [3].

the paper with a brief description of related works in Section 9. Due to space limitations omitted proofs can be found in the full version of this paper [9].

2   Model

Our model is based on the one for unreliable failure detectors described in [3]. We focus here on the main aspects of the model that are necessary to explain our results; details are left to the full version of the paper. Henceforth, we assume the existence of a discrete global clock; the range of this clock's ticks is $\mathbb{N}$.

2.1   Asynchronous Message-Passing Systems

We consider distributed message-passing systems with a set of $n \geq 2$ processes $\Pi = \{1, 2, \ldots, n\}$. Processes execute steps asynchronously and they communicate with each other by sending messages through reliable but asynchronous communication links. Each process has access to a failure detector module that provides some information about failures, as explained below.

2.2   Failures, Failure Patterns and Environments

Processes are subject to *crash failures*, i.e., they may stop taking steps. A *failure pattern* is a function $F : \mathbb{N} \to 2^{\Pi}$, where $F(t)$ is the set of processes that have crashed through time t. Processes never recover from crashes, and so $F(t) \subseteq F(t+1)$. Let $faulty(F) = \bigcup_{t \in \mathbb{N}} F(t)$ be the set of faulty processes in a failure pattern F; and $correct(F) = \Pi - faulty(F)$ be the set of correct processes in F. When the failure pattern F is clear from the context, we say that process p is *correct* if $p \in correct(F)$, and p is *faulty* if $p \in faulty(F)$. The *failure-free failure pattern*, i.e., the pattern where all the processes are correct, is denoted F_{ff}.

An *environment* $\mathcal{E}$ is a non-empty set of failure patterns. Intuitively, an environment describes the number and timing of failures that can occur in the system. We denote by $\mathcal{E}^*$ the set of *all* failure patterns. Intuitively, in a system with environment $\mathcal{E}^*$ each process may crash, and it may do so any time.

2.3   Failure Detectors

Each time a process queries its failure detector module, the response that it gets is a finite binary string from $\{0, 1\}^*$. A *failure detector history* describes the behavior of a failure detector during an execution. Formally, it is a function $H : \Pi \times \mathbb{N} \to \{0, 1\}^*$, where $H(p, t)$ is the value output by the failure detector module of process p at time t.

A *failure detector* $\mathcal{D}$ is a function that maps every failure pattern F to a nonempty set of failure detector histories. $\mathcal{D}(F)$ is the set of all possible failure detector histories that may be output by $\mathcal{D}$ when the failure pattern is F. Typically we specify a failure detector by stating the properties that its histories satisfy. The *trivial failure detector* $\mathcal{D}_{\perp}$ always outputs $\perp$ at all processes, forever: $\forall F \in \mathcal{E}^*, \forall p \in \Pi, \forall t \in \mathbb{N}, \forall H \in \mathcal{D}_{\perp}(F) : H(p, t) = \perp$.

2.4 Message Buffer

A *message buffer*, denoted M, contains all the messages that were sent but not yet received. When a process p attempts to receive a message, it either receives a message $m \in M$ addressed to p or the "empty" message $\perp$.

2.5 Input/Output Variables

To model input/output tasks, we assume that each process p can read an *input variable*, denoted $IN(p)$, and write an *output variable*, denoted $OUT(p)$; both variables are external to p. We assume that $IN(p)$ is initialized to some input value in $\{0, 1\}^*$, and that $IN(p)$ does not change after its initialization. Moreover, we assume that $OUT(p)$ is initialized to the special value $\perp \notin \{0, 1\}^*$ (to denote that it was not yet written by p).

2.6 Algorithms

An *algorithm* $\mathcal{A}$ consists of n deterministic automata, one for each process; the automaton for process p is denoted $\mathcal{A}(p)$. The execution of an algorithm $\mathcal{A}$ proceeds as a sequence of *process steps*. In a step, a process p performs the following actions atomically: (1) receive a single message m from the message buffer M, or the empty message $\perp$; (2) read its input variable $IN(p)$; (3) query its local failure detector module and receive some value d; (4) change its state; (5) may write a value in its output variable $OUT(p)$; and (6) may send messages to other processes.

2.7 Runs of an Algorithm

A *run of algorithm $\mathcal{A}$ using failure detector $\mathcal{D}$ in environment $\mathcal{E}$* is a tuple $R = (F, H, I, S, T)$ where F is a failure pattern in $\mathcal{E}$, H is a failure detector history in $\mathcal{D}(F)$, I is an initial input ($I(p)$ is the initial value of the input variable $IN(p)$, for each p), S is a sequence of steps of $\mathcal{A}$, and T is a list of times in $\mathbb{N}$ ($T[i]$ is the time when step $S[i]$ is taken) such that F, H, I, S, T satisfy some standard validity conditions. Specifying the above conditions formally is straightforward (e.g., see [3]) but tedious. Since this formalization is not necessary to present our results, we omit it from this extended abstract.

Since we focus on algorithms that solve *one-shot* input/output tasks, we restrict our attention to algorithms where each process writes its output variable at most once. That is, henceforth we consider only algorithms $\mathcal{A}$ that satisfy the following condition: For any failure detector $\mathcal{D}$, any environment $\mathcal{E}$, and any run R of $\mathcal{A}$ using $\mathcal{D}$ in $\mathcal{E}$, every process p writes $OUT(p)$ at most once.

2.8 The Input/Output of a Run

Let $R = (F, H, I, S, T)$ be a run of an algorithm $\mathcal{A}$ (using some failure detector $\mathcal{D}$ in an environment $\mathcal{E}$). The processes' input/output behavior in run R is defined as follows. The *input of run R* is I; recall that for each process $p \in \Pi$, $I(p)$ is the initial value of the input variable $IN(p)$ in R. The *output of run R*, denoted O, is the vector of values written by processes in run R; more precisely, for each process $p \in \Pi$, $O(p)$ is the value that p writes in its variable $OUT(p)$ in R, and $O(p) = \perp$ if p never writes $OUT(p)$ in run R. It is also convenient to say that F *is the failure pattern of run* R.

2.9   Input/Output Tasks

We consider *one-shot input/output tasks*, i.e., problems where each process has an input value and writes an output value. To specify a task, we must give the set of possible input values, the set of possible output values, and the input/output behaviors that satisfy the task. For any task T, each process p has a non-empty set $\mathcal{I}_p$ of possible input values, and a set $\mathcal{O}_p$ of possible output values that contains the special value $\perp$ (intuitively, $\perp$ denotes an empty output). Henceforth, $\mathcal{I} = \mathcal{I}_1 \times \mathcal{I}_2 \times \cdots \times \mathcal{I}_n$ and $\mathcal{O} = \mathcal{O}_1 \times \mathcal{O}_2 \times \cdots \times \mathcal{O}_n$; moreover, $I \in \mathcal{I}$ and $O \in \mathcal{O}$ denote vectors of input and output values, respectively: one value for each of the processes $\{1, 2, \ldots, n\}$ of Π.

To specify a task T, we must specify the desired input/output behavior of processes under each possible failure pattern. We can do so by giving a set T_S of tuples of the form (F, I, O): intuitively, $(F, I, O) \in T_S$ if and only if, when the failure pattern is F and the processes input is I, the processes output O is acceptable, i.e., it "satisfies" task T. This definition of a task is a generalization of the ones given in [2,15,17] which are based solely on the input/output requirement in failure-free runs. This generalization allows us to capture tasks where the desired input/output behavior depends on the failure pattern. For example, in the *Atomic Commit* task, if *all* processes vote COMMIT (this is the input), then processes are allowed to output ABORT *if and only if a failure occurs*.

In summary, a task T is specified by giving (1) the sets $\mathcal{I}_p$ and $\mathcal{O}_p$ of possible input and output values of each process $p \in \Pi$, and (2) a set T_S of tuples of the form (F, I, O), where $F \in \mathcal{E}^*$, $I \in \mathcal{I} = \mathcal{I}_1 \times \mathcal{I}_2 \times \cdots \times \mathcal{I}_n$, and $O \in \mathcal{O} = \mathcal{O}_1 \times \mathcal{O}_2 \times \cdots \times \mathcal{O}_n$, such that:

1. (*T is well-defined*) For every possible failure pattern and every possible input, there is at least one output that satisfies T:
   $\forall F \in \mathcal{E}^*, \forall I \in \mathcal{I}, \exists O \in \mathcal{O} : (F, I, O) \in T_S$
2. (*T terminates*) Every correct process outputs some value:
   $\forall (F, I, O) \in T_S, \forall p \in correct(F) : O(p) \neq \perp$

In this paper, we consider only tasks where each process $p \in \Pi$ has a *finite* set of possible inputs $\mathcal{I}_p$.

2.10   Solving an Input/Output Task

Let T be a task defined by some sets $\mathcal{I}_p$ and $\mathcal{O}_p$ (for each process p), and T_S. Let $\mathcal{A}$ be an algorithm, $\mathcal{D}$ a failure detector, and $\mathcal{E}$ an environment. We say that:

- A run $R = (F, H, I, S, T)$ of $\mathcal{A}$ using $\mathcal{D}$ in $\mathcal{E}$ *satisfies* T if and only if either $I \notin \mathcal{I}_1 \times \mathcal{I}_2 \times \cdots \times \mathcal{I}_n$, or $(F, I, O) \in T_S$, where F, I and O are the failure pattern, the input and the output of run R, respectively.
- $\mathcal{A}$ *solves* T *using* $\mathcal{D}$ *in* $\mathcal{E}$ if and only if every run R of $\mathcal{A}$ using $\mathcal{D}$ in $\mathcal{E}$ satisfies T.
- $\mathcal{D}$ *can be used to solve* T *in* $\mathcal{E}$ if and only if there is an algorithm that solves T using $\mathcal{D}$ in $\mathcal{E}$.

2.11   Local versus Non-local Tasks

To classify a task as being local or non-local we consider its input/output requirement in the simple case of systems with no failures. Intuitively, we say that a task $\mathcal{T}$ is local if, in a system with no failures, each process can determine its output value *based only on its input value*.

More precisely, let $\mathcal{T}$ be a task specified by some sets $\mathcal{I}_p$ and $\mathcal{O}_p$ of possible input and output values for each process p, and a set $\mathcal{T}_S$. We say that $\mathcal{T}$ *is local* if and only if there are functions $f_1, f_2, \ldots, f_n$ such that for each possible input $I = (i_1, i_2, \ldots, i_n) \in \mathcal{I}_1 \times \mathcal{I}_2 \times \cdots \times \mathcal{I}_n$ of $\mathcal{T}$, the output $O = (f_1(i_1), f_2(i_2), \ldots, f_n(i_n))$ satisfies the specification of $\mathcal{T}$ when all the processes are correct, i.e., $(F_{ff}, I, O) \in \mathcal{T}_S$. Note that for each process p, the output $f_p(i_p)$ of p depends only on the input i_p of p, and so p can compute its own output locally. We say that $\mathcal{T}$ *is non-local* if and only if $\mathcal{T}$ is not local.

2.12   Comparing Failure Detectors

To compare two failure detectors $\mathcal{D}$ and $\mathcal{D}'$ in some environment $\mathcal{E}$, we use the concept of failure detector transformation. Intuitively, an algorithm transforms $\mathcal{D}$ to $\mathcal{D}'$ if it can use $\mathcal{D}$ to emulate (the failure detector outputs of) $\mathcal{D}'$. Such an algorithm, denoted $\mathcal{T}_{\mathcal{D} \to \mathcal{D}'}$, uses $\mathcal{D}$ to maintain a local variable $out\text{-}\mathcal{D}'_p$ at every process p; $out\text{-}\mathcal{D}'_p$ functions as the output of the emulated failure detector module $\mathcal{D}'_p$ of $\mathcal{D}'$ at p. For each run R of $\mathcal{T}_{\mathcal{D} \to \mathcal{D}'}$, let H_{out} be the history of all the $out\text{-}\mathcal{D}'$ variables in R; i.e., $H_{out}(p, t)$ is the value of $out\text{-}\mathcal{D}'_p$ at time t in R. Algorithm $\mathcal{T}_{\mathcal{D} \to \mathcal{D}'}$ *transforms $\mathcal{D}$ to $\mathcal{D}'$ in environment* $\mathcal{E}$ if and only if for every run R of $\mathcal{T}_{\mathcal{D} \to \mathcal{D}'}$ using $\mathcal{D}$ in $\mathcal{E}$, $H_{out} \in \mathcal{D}'(F)$. We say that:

- $\mathcal{D}'$ *is weaker than* $\mathcal{D}$ in $\mathcal{E}$, if there is an algorithm $\mathcal{T}_{\mathcal{D} \to \mathcal{D}'}$ that transforms $\mathcal{D}$ to $\mathcal{D}'$ in $\mathcal{E}$.
- $\mathcal{D}'$ *is necessary to solve a task* $\mathcal{T}$ in $\mathcal{E}$, if, for every failure detector $\mathcal{D}$ that can be used to solve $\mathcal{T}$ in $\mathcal{E}$, $\mathcal{D}'$ is weaker than $\mathcal{D}$ in $\mathcal{E}$.
- $\mathcal{D}'$ *is necessary to solve non-local tasks in* $\mathcal{E}$ if, for every non-local task $\mathcal{T}$, $\mathcal{D}'$ is necessary to solve $\mathcal{T}$ in $\mathcal{E}$.

3   The $\mathcal{FS}^*$ Failure Detector

The failure detector $\mathcal{FS}^*$ outputs GREEN or RED at each process. If *all* processes are correct, then $\mathcal{FS}^*$ outputs GREEN forever at some process. If *exactly one* process is correct, then there is a time after which $\mathcal{FS}^*$ outputs RED at this process. (Note that since we consider systems with at least $n \geq 2$ processes, these two preconditions are mutually exclusive.) Formally, for every failure pattern $F \in \mathcal{E}^*$:

$$\mathcal{FS}^*(F) = \{H \mid \forall p \in \Pi, \forall t \in \mathbb{N} : H(p, t) = \text{GREEN} \vee H(p, t) = \text{RED}) \wedge$$
$$(|correct(F)| = n \Rightarrow \exists p \in \Pi, \forall t \in \mathbb{N} : H(p, t) = \text{GREEN}) \wedge$$
$$(|correct(F)| = 1 \Rightarrow \exists p \in correct(F), \exists t \in \mathbb{N}, \forall t' \geq t : H(p, t') = \text{RED})\}$$

We observe that $\mathcal{FS}^*$ is non-trivial in the sense that it cannot be implemented "from scratch" in an asynchronous system where each process may crash at any time. Formally, we say that an algorithm implements $\mathcal{FS}^*$ in $\mathcal{E}^*$, if it transforms the trivial failure detector $\mathcal{D}_\perp$ into $\mathcal{FS}^*$ in environment $\mathcal{E}^*$.

Observation 1. *No algorithm implements $\mathcal{FS}^*$ in $\mathcal{E}^*$.*

4 $\mathcal{FS}^*$ Is Necessary to Solve Non-local Tasks

We now show that for every non-local task $\mathcal{T}$, $\mathcal{FS}^*$ is necessary to solve $\mathcal{T}$. We start with the following lemma that relates the ability to solve a task without exchanging messages to the definition of task locality given in Section 2.11.

Lemma 1. *Let $\mathcal{T}$ be any task and $\mathcal{E}$ be any environment that contains the failure-free failure pattern F_{ff}. Suppose that there is an algorithm $\mathcal{A}$, a failure detector $\mathcal{D}$, and a failure detector history $H \in \mathcal{D}(F_{ff})$ such that:*

1. *$\mathcal{A}$ solves $\mathcal{T}$ using $\mathcal{D}$ in $\mathcal{E}$, and*
2. *for every input $I \in \mathcal{I} = \mathcal{I}_1 \times \mathcal{I}_2 \times \cdots \times \mathcal{I}_n$, there is a run $R_I = (F_{ff}, H, I, S, T)$ of $\mathcal{A}$ using $\mathcal{D}$ in $\mathcal{E}$ such that every process outputs a value before receiving any message.*

Then $\mathcal{T}$ is a local task.

Proof. Let $\mathcal{T}$ be any task, and let $\mathcal{I}_p$ and $\mathcal{O}_p$ be the corresponding sets of possible input and output values for each process p, and $\mathcal{T}_S$ be the corresponding set of acceptable (F, I, O) tuples. Let $\mathcal{E}$ be any environment that contains F_{ff}. Suppose that there is an algorithm $\mathcal{A}$, a failure detector $\mathcal{D}$, and a failure detector history $H \in \mathcal{D}(F_{ff})$, that satisfy conditions (1) and (2) of the lemma.

We now show that task $\mathcal{T}$ is local by first defining a function $f_p : \mathcal{I}_p \to \mathcal{O}_p$ for every process $p \in \Pi$, and then showing that these functions give correct outputs. For each process $p \in \Pi$, and every possible input $z \in \mathcal{I}_p$ of p, we start by defining a run R_p^z of $\mathcal{A}$, which in turn defines the value of $f_p(z)$.

Let $I = (i_1, i_2, \ldots, i_n) \in \mathcal{I} = \mathcal{I}_1 \times \mathcal{I}_2 \times \cdots \times \mathcal{I}_n$ be an arbitrary (but fixed) input of task $\mathcal{T}$. To define R_p^z and $f_p(z)$, let $I_p^z \in \mathcal{I}$ be the input of $\mathcal{T}$ that is identical to I except that the input of process p is z; more precisely, $I_p^z(p) = z$ and, for all $q \neq p$, $I_p^z(q) = I(q)$. By our assumptions (1) and (2) on $\mathcal{A}$, $\mathcal{D}$, and $H \in \mathcal{D}(F_{ff})$, there is a run $R_p^z = (F_{ff}, H, I_p^z, S_p^z, T_p^z)$ of $\mathcal{A}$ using $\mathcal{D}$ in $\mathcal{E}$, such that every process outputs a value before receiving any message. We define $f_p(z)$ to be the output of process p in run R_p^z,[3] and t_p^z to be the time when this output occurs in run R_p^z.

To prove that $\mathcal{T}$ is a local task, it now suffices to show that for every input $I = (x_1, x_2, \ldots, x_n) \in \mathcal{I}$, we have $(F_{ff}, I, O) \in \mathcal{T}_S$ where $O = (f_1(x_1), f_2(x_2), \ldots, f_n(x_n))$. To show this, we construct a run $R = (F_{ff}, H, I, S, T)$ of $\mathcal{A}$ such that, in the sequence of steps S and the corresponding times T, each process $p \in \Pi$ takes exactly the same sequence of steps at the same times as in the run $R_p^{x_p} = (F_{ff}, H, I_p^{x_p}, S_p^{x_p},$

---

[3] Note that since $\mathcal{A}$ solves $\mathcal{T}$ using $\mathcal{D}$ in $\mathcal{E}$, the output of p in run R_p^z must be in $\mathcal{O}_p$.

$T_p^{x_p}$) up to time $t_p^{x_p}$.[4] Note that for every process $p \in \Pi$, runs R and $R_p^{x_p}$ are indistinguishable up to time $t_p^{x_p}$; this is because in both runs: (a) process p has the same input, namely x_p, (b) process p receives no messages up to time $t_p^{x_p}$, (c) the failure dectector history H is the same, and (d) process p takes the same sequence of steps, at the same times, up to time $t_p^{x_p}$. Thus, in run R, every process $p \in \Pi$ outputs at time $t_p^{x_p}$ the same value that it outputs in run $R_p^{x_p}$, which is, by definition, $f_p(x_p)$. So the output of run R is $O = (f_1(x_1), f_2(x_2), \ldots, f_n(x_n))$. Since R is a run of $\mathcal{A}$ using $\mathcal{D}$ in $\mathcal{E}$, and $\mathcal{A}$ solves $\mathcal{T}$ using $\mathcal{D}$ in $\mathcal{E}$, we have $(F_{ff}, I, O) \in \mathcal{T}_S$, as we wanted to show.

Theorem 2. *For every environment $\mathcal{E}$, failure detector $\mathcal{FS}^*$ is necessary to solve non-local tasks in $\mathcal{E}$.*

Proof. Let $\mathcal{E}$ be any environment. We must show that for every non-local task $\mathcal{T}$, if a failure detector $\mathcal{D}$ can be used to solve $\mathcal{T}$ in $\mathcal{E}$, then $\mathcal{FS}^*$ is weaker than $\mathcal{D}$ in $\mathcal{E}$, i.e., there is an algorithm that transforms $\mathcal{D}$ to $\mathcal{FS}^*$ in $\mathcal{E}$.

Let $\mathcal{T}$ be any non-local task, $\mathcal{D}$ be any failure detector that can be used to solve $\mathcal{T}$ in $\mathcal{E}$, and $\mathcal{A}$ be any algorithm that solves $\mathcal{T}$ using $\mathcal{D}$ in $\mathcal{E}$. We now describe an algorithm $\mathcal{T}_{\mathcal{D} \to \mathcal{FS}^*}$ that uses $\mathcal{A}$ and $\mathcal{D}$ to transform $\mathcal{D}$ to $\mathcal{FS}^*$ in $\mathcal{E}$. In the following, $\mathcal{I}_p = \{i_p^1, i_p^2, \ldots, i_p^{k_p}\}$ is the set of possible input values of process p in task $\mathcal{T}$ (recall that we consider only tasks with a finite number of inputs).

The transformation algorithm $\mathcal{T}_{\mathcal{D} \to \mathcal{FS}^*}$, shown in Figure 1, emulates the output of $\mathcal{FS}^*$ as follows. Each process $p \in \Pi$ has a local variable $out\text{-}\mathcal{FS}_p^*$ that represents the output of the failure detector module $\mathcal{FS}_p^*$ of $\mathcal{FS}^*$. This variable is initialized to GREEN at every process $p \in \Pi$. In $\mathcal{T}_{\mathcal{D} \to \mathcal{FS}^*}$, every process $p \in \Pi$ concurrently executes several independent instances of the algorithm $\mathcal{A}$ (these executions proceed in a round-robin way to ensure the progress of every execution). More precisely, for each input $i_p \in \mathcal{I}_p$, process p emulates an execution of the local code $\mathcal{A}_p$ of the algorithm $\mathcal{A}$ with input i_p, using the given failure detector $\mathcal{D}$. In each emulated execution, process p faithfully follows the "code" of $\mathcal{A}_p$, except that when a message is received, p discards the message and continues this execution of $\mathcal{A}_p$ *as if no message was actually received*. Note that by doing so, it is possible that in some (or all) of these emulated executions of $\mathcal{A}_p$, process p never outputs a value for task $\mathcal{T}$. If *every* emulated execution of $\mathcal{A}_p$ by process p actually outputs some value, then process p sets its local variable $out\text{-}\mathcal{FS}_p^*$ to RED; thereafter $out\text{-}\mathcal{FS}_p^* = $ RED forever.

CLAIM: *The algorithm in Figure 1 transforms $\mathcal{D}$ to $\mathcal{FS}^*$ in environment $\mathcal{E}$.*

PROOF: Consider an *arbitrary* run R of algorithm $\mathcal{T}_{\mathcal{D} \to \mathcal{FS}^*}$ using $\mathcal{D}$ in $\mathcal{E}$. Let $F \in \mathcal{E}$ be the failure pattern of R and $H \in \mathcal{D}(F)$ be the failure detector history of R. We must show that, in run R, the local variables $out\text{-}\mathcal{FS}_p^*$, which are maintained by $\mathcal{T}_{\mathcal{D} \to \mathcal{FS}^*}$, emulate the output of failure detector $\mathcal{FS}^*$; i.e., their values satisfy the two properties of $\mathcal{FS}^*$ stated in Section 3: (1) if exactly one process is correct in R, say it is process p, then there is a time after which $\mathcal{FS}_p^* = $ RED, and (2) if all processes are correct in R then, at some process q, we have $\mathcal{FS}_q^* = $ GREEN forever. So we only need to consider the following two cases.

---

[4] After time $t_p^{x_p}$, the steps of process p in run R may diverge from those it takes in run $R_p^{x_p}$; in particular, after time $t_p^{x_p}$ in R, p receives all the messages that were previously sent to it in run R, *not* those that were sent in run $R_p^{x_p}$.

CODE FOR PROCESS p

Local Variables:

out-$\mathcal{FS}_p^* = $ GREEN $\qquad\qquad$ { variable that emulates the output of $\mathcal{FS}_p^*$ }

$j = 1$ $\qquad\qquad\qquad\qquad$ { p executes $\mathcal{A}_p$ with input i_p^j for every j, $1 \le j \le k_p$ }

$outputs = 0$ $\qquad\qquad\qquad$ { number of executions of $\mathcal{A}_p$ that output a value so far }

Main Code:

1   **while** $outputs < k_p$ **do** $\qquad$ { continue until all k_p executions of $\mathcal{A}_p$ output a value }

2   emulate the next step of $\mathcal{A}_p$ with input $i_p^j \in \mathcal{I}_p$ using $\mathcal{D}$, except that
         any message received in this step is discarded as if no message was received

3   **if** this step of $\mathcal{A}_p$ outputs a value (for task $\mathcal{T}$)

4   **then** $outputs \leftarrow outputs + 1$

5          $j \leftarrow (j \bmod k_p) + 1$

6   out-$\mathcal{FS}_p^* = $ RED

Fig. 1. Transformation algorithm $\mathcal{T}_{\mathcal{D} \to \mathcal{FS}^*}$

    Case 1: $|correct(F)| = 1$, i.e., there is exactly one correct process in run R. Let p be this correct process and $i_p \in \mathcal{I}_p$ be any input of p. Consider the run of $\mathcal{A}_p$ with input i_p that is emulated by process p in run R of $\mathcal{T}_{\mathcal{D} \to \mathcal{FS}^*}$. To process p, this emulated run is indistinguishable from a run $R' = (F, H, I', S', T')$ of $\mathcal{A}$ using $\mathcal{D}$ in $\mathcal{E}$ such that (1) p's input in $I'(p)$ is i_p, (2) p is the only correct process in R', and (3) all the other processes take no steps before they crash in R' (that's why p never receives any message in this run). Since $\mathcal{A}$ solves $\mathcal{T}$ in $\mathcal{E}$, by the termination requirement of tasks (namely, that each correct process must output a value), p eventually outputs a value in this emulated run of $\mathcal{A}_p$ with input i_p. Thus, each of the k_p runs of $\mathcal{A}_p$ (one run for each possible input $i_p \in \mathcal{I}_p$) that p emulates in run R eventually outputs some value. So eventually p exits the while loop of line 1, it sets its local variable out-$\mathcal{FS}_p^*$ to RED in line 6, and thereafter out-$\mathcal{FS}_p^* = $ RED.

    Case 2: $|correct(F)| = n$, i.e., $F = F_{ff}$ and all processes are correct in run R. We must show that there is some process q such that out-$\mathcal{FS}_q^* = $ GREEN, forever. Suppose, for contradiction, that this does not hold. Then, it must be that every process $p \in \Pi$ eventually reaches line 6 and sets out-$\mathcal{FS}_p^*$ to RED in run R. So, for every process $p \in \Pi$ and every input $i_p \in \mathcal{I}_p$, the execution of $\mathcal{A}_p$ with input i_p that p emulates in run R eventually outputs some value (even though p never receives any message in this emulation). Let t_{out} be the time the last such output occurs (across all processes and all inputs) in run R.

    Consider any input vector $I = (i_1, i_2, \ldots, i_n) \in \mathcal{I} = \mathcal{I}_1 \times \mathcal{I}_2 \times \cdots \times \mathcal{I}_n$ of task $\mathcal{T}$. We now show that there is a run $R_I = (F_{ff}, H, I, S', T')$ of $\mathcal{A}$ using $\mathcal{D}$ in $\mathcal{E}$ such that every process outputs a value before receiving any messages. We construct run $R_I = (F_{ff}, H, I, S', T')$ of $\mathcal{A}$ using, for each process p, the emulated execution of $\mathcal{A}_p$ with input i_p in run R, as follows. In run R_I, for every process $p \in \Pi$: (1) up to time t_{out}, p takes the same steps at the same times as in the emulated execution of $\mathcal{A}_p$ with input i_p in run R (in these steps p does not receive any message and it outputs some value), and (2) after time t_{out}, p continues its execution of $\mathcal{A}_p$ with input i_p, but now p starts receiving every message sent to it by every other process $q \in \Pi$ in its execution of $\mathcal{A}_q$ with input i_q (including messages that were discarded by p in its emulation of $\mathcal{A}_p$ with input i_p in run R). In other words, run $R_I = (F_{ff}, H, I, S', T')$ of $\mathcal{A}$ is built as follows: (1) up to time t_{out}, R_I is the merging of the n independent executions of $\mathcal{A}_1, \mathcal{A}_2, \ldots, \mathcal{A}_n$ with the local inputs $i_1, i_2, \ldots, i_n$, emulated by processes $1, 2, \ldots, n$, respectively, in run R (in these emulated executions no messages are received — it is as if all messages are delayed to after time t_{out} — and every process outputs some value by time t_{out}); and (2) after time t_{out}, in R_I processes $1, 2, \ldots, n$ continue their executions of $\mathcal{A}_1, \mathcal{A}_2, \ldots, \mathcal{A}_n$ with local inputs $i_1, i_2, \ldots, i_n$, respectively, such that they eventually receive every message that are sent to them in these executions, including all those sent before time t_{out}.

Note that $R_I = (F_{ff}, H, I, S', T')$ is a run of $\mathcal{A}$ using $\mathcal{D}$ in $\mathcal{E}$. Moreover, in run R_I every process outputs a value by time t_{out}, before receiving any message. Since I is an *arbitrary* input in $\mathcal{I}$, it is now clear that $\mathcal{A}$, $\mathcal{D}$ and $H \in \mathcal{D}(F_{ff})$ satisfy both conditions (1) and (2) of Lemma 1. Note also that $\mathcal{E}$ includes F_{ff}. So, by Lemma 1, $\mathcal{T}$ is a *local* task — a contradiction. We conclude that there is some process q such that $out\text{-}\mathcal{FS}_q^* = \text{GREEN}$, forever.

Case 1 and Case 2 show that the local variables $out\text{-}\mathcal{FS}^*$ emulate the output of failure detector $\mathcal{FS}^*$ correctly, as we needed to show.

5   Weak Set Agreement

Weak set agreement (WSA) is a weaker version of the well-known *set agreement* task [5]: the condition that there are at most $n - 1$ distinct decision values is required *only for failure-free runs*. More precisely, each process can propose any value in $V = \{1, 2, \ldots, n\}$ and must decide some value such that:

- TERMINATION: Every correct process eventually decides some value.
- VALIDITY: Each decided value was proposed by some process.
- WEAK AGREEMENT: If all processes are correct then there are at most $n-1$ distinct decision values.

It is clear that *WSA* can be formally defined as an input/output task.

Theorem 3. *WSA is a non-local task.*

Corollary 1. *For every environment $\mathcal{E}$, $\mathcal{FS}^*$ is necessary to solve WSA in $\mathcal{E}$.*

Proof. This is an immediate consequence of Theorems 2 and 3.

6   Solving Weak Set Agreement Using $\mathcal{FS}^*$

We now prove that $\mathcal{FS}^*$ can be used to solve the weak set agreement task, and in fact it is the *weakest failure detector* to solve this task; intuitively, this means that $\mathcal{FS}^*$ is

---

CODE FOR PROCESS p:

1   **to propose**(v_p)   { v_p is p's proposal value }

2   **send** v_p **to** every process $q > p$

    { *p decides a value as follows:* }

3   **upon receipt** of a value v **do**

4   **send** v **to all**

5   **decide** v ; **halt**

6   **upon** $\mathcal{FS}_p^* = \text{RED}$ **do**

7   **send** v_p **to all**

8   **decide** v_p ; **halt**

Fig. 2. Using $\mathcal{FS}^*$ to solve WSA in any environment $\mathcal{E}$

---

necessary and sufficient for this task [3]. More precisely: A failure detector $\mathcal{D}$ is the *weakest failure detector to solve a task T in $\mathcal{E}$* iff:[5]

- NECESSITY: $\mathcal{D}$ is necessary to solve T in $\mathcal{E}$, and
- SUFFICIENCY: $\mathcal{D}$ can be used to solve T in $\mathcal{E}$.

The algorithm in Figure 2 solves the weak set agreement task using $\mathcal{FS}^*$. It is identical to the one that solves the set agreement task using $\mathcal{L}$ given in [8]. In this algorithm, lines 3-5 and lines 6-8 are executed atomically.

Theorem 4. *For every environment $\mathcal{E}$, the algorithm in Figure 2 solves WSA using $\mathcal{FS}^*$ in $\mathcal{E}$.*

Corollary 2. *For every environment $\mathcal{E}$, $\mathcal{FS}^*$ is the weakest failure detector to solve WSA in $\mathcal{E}$.*

Proof. This is an immediate consequence of Corollary 1 and Theorem 4.

We conclude that WSA is the weakest non-local task in message-passing systems in the following sense:

Corollary 3. *For every environment $\mathcal{E}$, any non-local task T, and any failure detector $\mathcal{D}$, if $\mathcal{D}$ can be used to solve T in $\mathcal{E}$, then $\mathcal{D}$ can also be used to solve WSA in $\mathcal{E}$.*

Proof (Sketch). Since $\mathcal{D}$ can be used to solve T in $\mathcal{E}$, by Theorem 2, $\mathcal{FS}^*$ is weaker than $\mathcal{D}$ in $\mathcal{E}$. So processes can use $\mathcal{D}$ to emulate $\mathcal{FS}^*$ in $\mathcal{E}$, and then they can use this emulated $\mathcal{FS}^*$ to solve WSA with the algorithm in Figure 2.

---

[5] There may be several distinct failure detectors that are the weakest to solve a task T. It is easy to see, however, that they are all equivalent in the sense that each is weaker than the other. For this reason we speak of *the* weakest, rather than *a* weakest failure detector to solve T.

7 $\mathcal{FS}^*$ Is the Minimum Failure Detector for Non-local Tasks

We now show that $\mathcal{FS}^*$ is the strongest failure detector necessary to solve non-local tasks.

Theorem 5. *Let $\mathcal{E}$ be any environment.*

1. (NECESSITY:) $\mathcal{FS}^*$ *is necessary to solve non-local tasks in $\mathcal{E}$.*
2. (MAXIMALITY:) *Every failure detector $\mathcal{D}$ that is necessary to solve non-local tasks in $\mathcal{E}$ is weaker than $\mathcal{FS}^*$ in $\mathcal{E}$.*

Proof. Part (1) was already shown in Theorem 2. We now prove Part (2). Let $\mathcal{E}$ be any environment. Let $\mathcal{D}$ be any failure detector that is necessary to solve non-local tasks in $\mathcal{E}$, i.e.: (*) for any non-local task $\mathcal{T}$, if a failure detector $\mathcal{D}'$ can be used to solve $\mathcal{T}$ in $\mathcal{E}$ then $\mathcal{D}$ is weaker than $\mathcal{D}'$ in $\mathcal{E}$. We must show that $\mathcal{D}$ is weaker than $\mathcal{FS}^*$ in $\mathcal{E}$. Consider the WSA task. By Theorem 3, WSA is a non-local task. By Theorem 4, $\mathcal{FS}^*$ can be used to solve WSA in $\mathcal{E}$. By "plugging in" $\mathcal{T} = WSA$ and $\mathcal{D}' = \mathcal{FS}^*$ in (*), we get that $\mathcal{D}$ is weaker than $\mathcal{FS}^*$ in $\mathcal{E}$.

8   Comparing $\mathcal{FS}^*$ to anti-Ω and $\mathcal{L}$ In Message-Passing Systems

The following theorem compares $\mathcal{FS}^*$ to two closely related failure detectors, namely, $\mathcal{L}$ and anti-Ω, which are the weakest failure detectors to solve set agreement in message-passing and shared memory systems, respectively. Intuitively, failure detector $\mathcal{L}$ outputs GREEN or RED at each process such that (1) it outputs GREEN forever at some process, and (2) if exactly one process is correct, then there is a time after which $\mathcal{L}$ outputs RED at this process. Anti-Ω outputs a process id at each process such that, if there is a correct process, then there is a correct process c and a time after which anti-Ω never outputs c at any correct process.

Theorem 6. *Anti-Ω is strictly weaker than $\mathcal{FS}^*$ in $\mathcal{E}^*$, and $\mathcal{FS}^*$ is strictly weaker than $\mathcal{L}$ in $\mathcal{E}^*$.*[6]

9   Related Work

Failure detectors have been used to capture the minimum information about failures that is necessary to solve some basic problems in message-passing and shared-memory systems (e.g., [1,3,4,6,7,8,12,14,19]). Recently, failure detectors were also used to investigate the minimum information about failures that is necessary (but not necessarily sufficient) to solve some interesting *sets* of problems.

   In particular, Guerraoui et al. consider the set of wait-free tasks $\mathcal{S}_{\text{wf}}$ that cannot be solved in asynchronous shared-memory systems with failures [11]. They introduce a failure detector denoted Υ and prove that (1) among the set of *"eventually stable failure*

---

[6] We say that $\mathcal{D}$ is strictly weaker than $\mathcal{D}'$ in $\mathcal{E}^*$, if $\mathcal{D}$ is weaker than $\mathcal{D}'$ in $\mathcal{E}^*$ but $\mathcal{D}'$ is not weaker than $\mathcal{D}$ in $\mathcal{E}^*$ (recall that $\mathcal{E}^*$ is the environment where any process can fail at any time).

detectors", Υ is necessary to solve any task in $\mathcal{S}_{wf}$, and (2) Υ is sufficient to solve set agreement. Zielinski generalizes this result in [19]: he introduces the failure detector anti-Ω and proves that (1) anti-Ω is necessary to solve any task in $\mathcal{S}_{wf}$, and (2) anti-Ω is the weakest failure detector to solve set agreement. In contrast to the results in [11,19] which are in shared-memory systems, in [18] Zielinsky considers message-passing systems, and proves that anti-Ω is the weakest failure detector among the set of *eventual* failure detectors that are not implementable in such systems.

Delporte et al. also consider message-passing systems in [8]: they introduce failure detector $\mathcal{L}$ and show that it is the weakest failure detector to solve set agreement in such systems. The failure detector $\mathcal{FS}^*$ introduced here is a simple weakening of $\mathcal{L}$.

Our definition of weak set agreement was obtained by taking a well-known problem, namely set agreement, and weakening one of its property *in the case of failures*. This method of weakening a task was already proposed in the early 80's to obtain weaker versions of some classical problems such as consensus and reliable broadcast [10,13]. For example, the validity property of consensus (which requires that any decision value must be a proposed value) can be weakened to "if there are no failures, then the validity property must hold" (this property is called *weak unanimity* in [10]). The specification of such tasks can be captured by our definition of a task because it includes the failure pattern (to the best of our knowledge, such definition of a task first appeared in [16]). This is a generalization of the definitions of a task given in [2,15,17] which are based solely on the input/output requirement in *failure-free runs*.

Acknowledgement

We are grateful to Marcos K. Aguilera for valuable discussions on this work.

References

1. Aguilera, M.K., Toueg, S., Deianov, B.: Revisiting the weakest failure detector for uniform reliable broadcast. In: Jayanti, P. (ed.) DISC 1999. LNCS, vol. 1693, pp. 13–33. Springer, Heidelberg (1999)
2. Biran, O., Moran, S., Zaks, S.: A combinatorial characterization of the distributed 1-solvable tasks. J. Algorithms 11(3), 420–440 (1990)
3. Chandra, T.D., Hadzilacos, V., Toueg, S.: The weakest failure detector for solving consensus. Journal of the ACM 43(4), 685–722 (1996)
4. Chandra, T.D., Toueg, S.: Unreliable failure detectors for reliable distributed systems. Journal of the ACM 43(2), 225–267 (1996)
5. Chaudhuri, S.: Agreement is harder than consensus: set consensus problems in totally asynchronous systems. In: PODC 1990: Proceedings of the ninth annual ACM symposium on Principles of Distributed Computing, pp. 311–324. ACM Press, New York (1990)
6. Delporte-Gallet, C., Fauconnier, H., Guerraoui, R., Hadzilacos, V., Kouznetsov, P., Toueg, S.: The weakest failure detectors to solve certain fundamental problems in distributed computing. In: PODC 2004: Proceedings of the twenty-third annual ACM symposium on Principles of Distributed Computing, pp. 338–346. ACM Press, New York (2004)
7. Delporte-Gallet, C., Fauconnier, H., Guerraoui, R., Kouznetsov, P.: Mutual exclusion in asynchronous systems with failure detectors. Journal of Parallel and Distributed Computing 65(4), 492–505 (2005)

8. Delporte-Gallet, C., Fauconnier, H., Guerraoui, R., Tielmann, A.: The weakest failure detector for message passing set-agreement. In: Taubenfeld, G. (ed.) DISC 2008. LNCS, vol. 5218, pp. 109–120. Springer, Heidelberg (2008)
9. Delporte-Gallet, C., Fauconnier, H., Toueg, S.: The minimum failure detector for non-local tasks in message-passing systems. Article id hal-00401844, Hyper Article en Ligne (April 2009), http://hal.archives-ouvertes.fr/hal-00401844
10. Fischer, M.J.: The consensus problem in unreliable distributed systems (a brief survey). In: Karpinski, M. (ed.) FCT 1983. LNCS, vol. 158, pp. 127–140. Springer, Heidelberg (1983)
11. Guerraoui, R., Herlihy, M., Kouznetsov, P., Lynch, N.A., Newport, C.C.: On the weakest failure detector ever. In: PODC 2007: Proceedings of the twenty-sixth Annual ACM Symposium on Principles of Distributed Computing, pp. 235–243. ACM Press, New York (2007)
12. Guerraoui, R., Kapalka, M., Kouznetsov, P.: The weakest failure detectors to boost obstruction-freedom. In: Dolev, S. (ed.) DISC 2006. LNCS, vol. 4167, pp. 399–412. Springer, Heidelberg (2006)
13. Hadzilacos, V.: On the relationship between the atomic commitment and consensus problems. In: Simons, B., Spector, A.Z. (eds.) Fault-Tolerant Distributed Computing. LNCS, vol. 448, pp. 201–208. Springer, Heidelberg (1990)
14. Halpern, J.Y., Ricciardi, A.: A knowledge-theoretic analysis of uniform distributed coordination and failure detectors. In: PODC 1999: Proceedings of the eighteenth annual ACM symposium on Principles of Distributed Computing, pp. 73–82. ACM Press, New York (1999)
15. Herlihy, M., Shavit, N.: The topological structure of asynchronous computability. Journal of the ACM 46(6), 858–923 (1999)
16. Jayanti, P., Toueg, S.: Every problem has a weakest failure detector. In: PODC 2008: Proceedings of the twenty-seventh annual ACM Symposium on Principles of Distributed Computing, pp. 75–84. ACM Press, New York (2008)
17. Saks, M.E., Zaharoglou, F.: Wait-free k-set agreement is impossible: The topology of public knowledge. SIAM J. Comput. 29(5), 1449–1483 (2000)
18. Zielinski, P.: Automatic classification of eventual failure detectors. In: Pelc, A. (ed.) DISC 2007. LNCS, vol. 4731, pp. 465–479. Springer, Heidelberg (2007)
19. Zielinski, P.: Anti-Omega: the weakest failure detector for set agreement. In: PODC 2008: Proceedings of the twenty-seventh annual ACM Symposium on Principles of Distributed Computing, pp. 55–64. ACM Press, New York (2008)

Enhanced Fault-Tolerance through Byzantine Failure Detection

Rida A. Bazzi[1] and Maurice Herlihy[2]

[1] Arizona State University, Tempe, AZ 85287-8809, USA
[2] Brown University, Providence RI 02912, USA

Abstract. We consider a variant of the Byzantine failure model in which Byzantine processes are eventually detected and silenced, and investigate the fault-tolerance of the classical broadcast and agreement problems. We show that if all Byzantine processes are eventually detected, then it is possible to solve the broadcast problem in the presence of any number of Byzantine processes. If only a fraction of the Byzantine processes can be detected, then we show that it is possible to solve consensus (and broadcast) if the total number of processes is $N \geq 2f + 3F + 1$, where f is the number of Byzantine processes that are eventually detected and F is the number of those that are never detected. We show that $2f + 3F + 1$ is a lower bound to solve the consensus and broadcast problems.

1 Introduction

In the standard synchronous model of computation, it is not possible to solve consensus or broadcast in the presence of Byzantine failures if N, the number of processes, is less than $3F$, where F is the upper bound on the number of Byzantine processes. In the asynchronous model, both broadcast and consensus are impossible even if one process can crash [1].

To understand the extent to which these limitations are fundamental, researchers have considered various ways of strengthening the models or weakening the problems. In the synchronous model, *message authentication* [2] circumvents the $N > 3F$ bound, allowing consensus to be solved in the presence of any number of Byzantine processes. *Randomization* [3,4] allows consensus to be solved in an *expected* constant number of rounds, circumventing the $(F + 1)$-round lower bound in the standard model [5]. In the asynchronous crash-failure model, the impossibility of consensus can be circumvented by extending the model to encompass *failure detectors* [6] or by relaxing the agreement requirement [7]. These variants yield insight into how powerfully the various assumptions built into specific models affect the kinds of computations possible in general.

Here, we consider the classical broadcast and agreement problems in the synchronous model and a variant of the Byzantine model in which some Byzantine processes are eventually detected and silenced. It turns out there is a substantial gap between the model where *all* Byzantine processes are eventually detected and silenced, and the model where some may never be silenced.

T. Abdelzaher, M. Raynal, and N. Santoro (Eds.): OPODIS 2009, LNCS 5923, pp. 129–143, 2009.
© Springer-Verlag Berlin Heidelberg 2009

If *all* Byzantine processes are eventually silenced, then *broadcast* is remarkably robust: we give a broadcast algorithm that tolerates *any number* of Byzantine processes. Consensus is less robust: it has no solution if the correct processes are in the minority [8]. If even one Byzantine process can evade detection, the situation is radically different. We can solve both consensus and broadcast if N, the total number of processes, is greater than or equal to $2f + 3F + 1$, where f is the number of transient (eventually detected) Byzantine processes, and F the number of permanent (never detected) Byzantine processes. Moreover, we show that neither broadcast nor consensus is possible if $N \leq 2f + 3F + 1$.

Our model is partly motivated by the *Sybil attack*, in which Byzantine processes can assume multiple identities, so the number of faulty processes appears to be larger than it is. These impostors, or perhaps just most of them, are eventually detected and eliminated. The Sybil attack was identified and introduced by Douceur [9]. There are several proposals for techniques to detect and eliminate forged identities ([10,11] for example).

The rest of the paper is organized as follows. Section 2 motivates and defines our model. Section 3 presents a broadcast protocol in the presence of an arbitrary number of eventually-detected Byzantine processes. This result is obviously optimal for this model. Section 4 presents a consensus protocol consensus when some Byzantine processes may pass undetected, and shows that this consensus protocol is optimal. Section 5 presents related work.

2   Model

We consider a synchronous, message-passing environment with N processes. Some processes may be *Byzantine* and misbehave in arbitrary ways, either by sending malicious messages or crashing. Some Byzantine processes can be eventually detected and silenced. There are at most f *transient* Byzantine processes that are eventually silenced (crash), and at most F *permanent* Byzantine processes that never crash. A discussion of how our model relates to other models in the literature is given in Sect. 5.

Faulty processes cannot impersonate correct processes, meaning that Byzantine processes cannot send messages that appear to have originated from non-Byzantine processes.[1]

The *broadcast* problem is similar to the celebrated *Byzantine Generals* problem [12]. One process, the *broadcaster*, sends a message to the others. If the broadcaster is correct, then all correct processes must *receive* that value. If the broadcaster is faulty, then all correct processes must either *receive* the same value, or all decide not to receive any value at all. More precisely, we require *agreement*: all processes receive the same value, *validity*: if the broadcaster is correct, all processes receive the value it sent, and *termination*: all processes receive or decide a value after a finite number of steps.

---

[1] In practice, unique non-forgeable identities for non-faulty processes can be implemented using public keys [10].

The *consensus* problem is the usual one: each process starts with a private input value, and all correct processes must halt after deciding the same value which is one of input values of correct processes.

3   Broadcast with Complete Eventual Detection

In this section, we consider solving the broadcast problem in a setting in which all Byzantine processes are eventually silenced (they appear to crash). We show that it is possible to solve the problem for any number of failures ($N > f$). Our solution is modular. We first introduce a weaker problem that we call *one-shot broadcast* and show it can be solved when $N > f$. We then show how to "pipeline" instances of the one-shot broadcast to solve the broadcast problem.

One way to understand this algorithm is to consider the interaction between the safety and liveness aspects of this problem. We know from the classical lower bounds that as long as the number of undetected Byzantine processes is a third or more of the total number of processes, both broadcast and consensus are impossible. During this period, the *safety* challenge is to prevent the undetected Byzantine processes from tricking the correct processes into making incorrect, premature decisions. When enough Byzantine processes are eventually detected, the *liveness* challenge is to ensure that the correct process eventually converge on correct decisions, even without the explicit ability to tell how many undetected Byzantine processes remain.

3.1   The One-Shot Broadcast Protocol

Protocol Requirements. We first describe a *one-shot* broadcast protocol (Fig. 1). In this protocol, processes attempt to receive a value sent by a designated broadcaster b. Each time this protocol is executed, either all correct processes receive the same value, or all correct processes explicitly fail to decide (receive $\star$). The one-shot protocol should satisfy four properties.

- *Weak Validity* If the broadcaster is correct and a correct process receives a value other than $\star$, then the received value is the broadcaster's value.
- *Strong Validity in the absence of failures.* If the one-shot broadcast is invoked by correct processes at a point in the execution before which all faulty processes have crashed and after which there are no new crashes, then no correct process receives $\star$.
- *Agreement* All correct processes *receive* the same value.
- *Termination* Every correct process that invokes one-shot broadcast will eventually *receive* a value or explicitly fail to receive a value.

The main difference between the one-shot broadcast and the broadcast problems is the validity requirement: in the one shot-broadcast, correct processes can fail to receive the broadcaster's value even if it is correct. Note that if we do not require strong validity in the absence of failures, it is trivial to implement the one-shot broadcast by having all processes receive $\star$ in every execution.

01: *faulty* is initialized to $\emptyset$ if the one-shot broadcast is invoked in round 0

02: $\forall q \in \mathcal{P}$: **send** $(v, faulty)$ to q
03: $\forall q \in \mathcal{P}$: **if** q silent **then** $faulty := faulty \cup \{q\}$
04: **if** $b \in faulty$ **then** $v := \perp$
                           else $v :=$ value received from b
05: // compare faulty set with received faulty sets, including own's old faulty set
06: $clean := \bigwedge_{q \notin faulty}(faulty = faulty_q)$; $lastClean := 0$
07: $\forall q \in \mathcal{P} - faulty$: **send** $(v, faulty, clean)$ **to** q
08: **for** $i := 1$ **to** $f + 2$ **do**
09:        $\forall q \in \mathcal{P}$: **if** q silent **then** $faulty := faulty \cup \{q\}$
10:        $clean = \bigwedge_{q \notin faulty}(clean_q \wedge (faulty = faulty_q) \wedge (v = v_q))$
11:        **if** $clean$ **then** $lastClean := i$
12:        $\forall q \in \mathcal{P} - faulty$: **send** $(v, faulty, clean)$ **to** q
13: $Chains := \emptyset$
14: **if** $lastClean = f + 2$ **then**
15:        $Chains := \{[]\}$
16: **for** $i := 1$ **to** $f + 1$
17:        $\forall q \notin faulty$: **send** $Chains$ **to** q
18:        **if** received $Chains_q$ from q and $lastClean > f + 1 - i$ **then**
19:              **forall** $c \in Chains_q$ and $len(c) = i$ **and** $well\text{-}formed(c)$ **do**
20:                   $c' := [q, c]$
30:                   $Chains := Chains \cup \{c'\}$
31: $decided := \emptyset$; $faultyChains = \emptyset$
32: $decision :=$ **false**
33: **repeat**
34:        $\forall q \notin faulty$: **send** $faultyChains$ to q
35:        $\forall q \in \mathcal{P}$: **if** q silent **then** $faulty := faulty \cup \{q\}$
36:        $\forall q \in \mathcal{P}$: **if** q decided **then** $decided := decided \cup \{q\}$
37:        **forall** $q \notin faulty$ **do**
38:              **forall** $c \in faultyChains_q$ **do**
39:                   **if** $[q, c] \in Chains$ **then**
40:                       $Chains := Chains - \{[q, c]\}$
41:        $faultyChains := \emptyset$
42:        **forall** $c \in Chains$ **do**
43:              **if** $head(c) \in faulty$ **then**
44:                   $faultyChains := faultyChains \cup \{c\}$
45:                   $Chains := Chains - \{c\}$
46:              **elseif** $(\forall q \in tail(c) : q \in faulty$ and $head(c) \in decided)$ **or** $c == []$ **then**
47:                   $decision :=$ **true**
48:                   $\forall q \notin faulty$: **send** $(p, \text{decided})$ to q
49: **until** $Chains = \emptyset$ **or** $decision = $ **true**
50: **if** $decision$ **then**
51:        **return** v
52: **else**
53:        **return** $\star$

Fig. 1. One-shot broadcast protocol executed by process p

Protocol Overview. We now outline the intuition behind the protocol. We say that a round is *clean* for p if p learns of no new failures during that round. It may learn of a failure either because a process fails to send p a message, or because p learns that another process has a different view of the execution The view we are interested in is the identity of the faulty processes and the broadcaster's value passed between processes. Consider an execution in which the broadcaster starts in a particular round, and the correct processes encounter an arbitrarily long sequence of clean rounds. At the beginning, all correct processes have the same *faulty* sets, and every round from that point on is clean. After enough clean rounds, the correct processes must decide (by strong validity) because it is possible that all Byzantine processes have crashed and all rounds will henceforth be clean. How many clean rounds are needed for a process to decide?

Consider a correct process p that decides after observing m clean rounds. It is possible that other correct processes observed only $m - 1$ clean rounds (but not fewer) because they became aware of a last-round failure that escaped p's notice. If p decides and is correct, then other correct processes must eventually go with that decision. These others cannot tell whether p is correct, in which case they must eventually agree, or whether p is a Byzantine process trying to trick them into deciding the wrong value.

If p is correct then after m clean rounds, in round $m + 1$, it sends the others an empty chain [] of witnesses indicating that it decided unilaterally after it saw m clean rounds. Suppose q has seen $m - 1$ clean rounds. When it receives p's decision and (empty) witness chain, q can also decide, but it must now use p as a witness to justify its decision. It sends the others the singleton witness chain $[p]$.

At this point, q cannot tell whether p is faulty. Suppose now that p is faulty, and it sent every other process a message indicating that it saw only $m - 1$ clean rounds and did not decide. Now suppose a correct r that has seen only $m - 2$ clean rounds receives q's decision and chain. While r has seen only only $m - 2$ clean rounds, q claims that p claims to have seen m clean rounds. The number of consecutive clean rounds seen by two correct processes can differ by one, but not two, because a failure observed in the next-to-the-last round will be reported to all correct processes in the last round. It follows that r can deduce that at least one of p or q is faulty, and r be in no hurry to decide. It can wait until one of the two (or both) processes crash. If p crashes, r goes along with q because q's claim is believable. If q crashes, then r can reject q's decision. If r goes along with q, r must provide a two-witness chain $[q, p]$ to justify its decision to the others. Informally the chain means that r decided because r has seen $m - 2$ clean rounds and heard from q that q heard from p that p decided, and r verified that p is indeed faulty, implying that q may be a correct process fooled into deciding by p. Since q may be correct, and may have decided, r should go along.

A correct process s that has seen $m - 3$ clean rounds and receiving the chain $[q, p]$ from r would either go along with r (after it verifies that both p and q are faulty), or it will ignore r's decision if it detects that r has crashed. If s goes along with r, it justifies its decision to the others by sending send the chain $[r, q, p]$, meaning that s verified that q and p are faulty and that it received the chain $[q, p]$ from r.

Extending this kind of reasoning, a process decides if it ends up with a witness chain that is either empty (meaning that process sending the chain decided by itself), or the chain consists of a non-faulty head followed by known faulty processes. Roughly speaking, a process decides if it can find an honest process that either decided on its own, or one that can prove it was the innocent victim of known Byzantine hoaxers. No chain of witnesses can be longer than $f + 1$ because it would then contain at least two correct processes. So, $m = f + 2$ clean rounds are enough for a process to decide.

The protocol we present here does not follow this scenario exactly. Instead, to simplify the protocol, the chains are processed with in two stages. First, chains are assembled without any commitments (no decisions). Second, decisions are made using received chains as outline above, but a chain whose head is faulty is discarded and any other chains based on it are recalled. This process continues until a process decides, or until all chains are discarded in which case $\star$ is received.

Detailed Description. The broadcaster b sends a value v to all the processes in the first round. This value is the input of b. The protocol proceeds in three phases. In the first phase (Lines 01–12), the processes exchange views for $f + 2$ rounds. We do not use explicit round numbers because an instance of the one-shot broadcast can be started in any round. The first time one-shot broadcast is invoked, the *faulty* set is initialized to $\emptyset$. Later on, *faulty* has whatever value it has in the round the protocol is invoked. Initially (Lines 02-04), b broadcasts its value. Each process then updates *faulty*, adding to the set all processes from which no messages were received. The *faulty* set is updated at each round messages are expected. In the first round (line 04), processes set their local value of v to the value they receive from b if $b \notin faulty$ or to $\bot$ otherwise. The initial value of v for processes other than b is therefore irrelevant and we do not explicitly initialize it. The first round is deemed *clean* if all correct processes have identical *faulty* sets. The *lastClean* counter is initialized to 0 before entering the main loop (Line 06). After b's initial broadcast (Line 02), each process broadcasts the value it received, its set of faulty processes, and its value of *clean* (indicating whether the last iteration was clean) The processes then exchange view for $f + 2$ rounds, updating *faulty* (Line 09), *clean* (Line 10), and a local *lastClean* variable (Line 11) tracking the known clean iteration in this phase. Finally, each process broadcasts the same information to the others (Line 12).

There are two more phases, one where chains are assembled, and another where faulty chains are discarded and decisions are made. At the start of the second phase, a process that has seen $f + 2$ clean rounds (Line 14) bases its decision on the empty chain [] (Line 15). Although some decisions in this phase are tentative (and may be discarded in the next phase), decisions based on the empty chain will not be discarded. Each process sends its chains to the others (Line 17). A chain is *well-formed* if it has unique process ids (no repetitions) and does not include either the sending or receiving process id. A process q that receives a chain in a given round tentatively decides based on that chain if the chain is not too short compared to the number of clean rounds that q saw (Lines 18-19), and the chain is valid (Line 19). Processes ignore invalid chains.

We use $[p, c]$ to denote a chain whose head is process p and whose tail is chain c. The *head* operator returns the first process in the chain: $head([p, c])$ is p, and *tail* returns the tail chain: $tail([p, c])$ is c. For every chain c that q receives from p, q appends p to c, recording the chain $[p, c]$ (Lines 19-20). These exchanges continue for $f + 1$ rounds (Lines 16-30). The code does not show explicitly tentative decisions. Tentative decisions are implicit with the acceptance of a chain.

In the final phase, processes try to make tentative decisions permanent. They repeatedly assemble a set of chains deemed to be *faulty* (the *faultyChains* set). Process p deems a chain to be faulty if the head of the chain has failed and removes such a faulty chain from the set of chains and adds it to *faultyChains* (Lines 43-45). Each process also removes a chain from *Chains* if the chain is recalled by its head. Specifically, if $c \in faultyChains_q$ and q is not known to be faulty, then p would remove $[q, c]$ from *Chains* if it is already there (Lines 37-40). At the end of the phase, a process decides if it has a chain c such that $head(c)$ has already decided, and is not known to be faulty, but all processes in $tail(c)$ are known to be faulty (Line 46-47). A process that decides informs other processes of the decision (Line 48) and processes update the set *decided* at the start of the next iteration after they receive notification of a decision (Line 36). A process p updates *decided* by adding any process q that has decided to its decided set. If no chains remain, the process does not decide a value.

Correctness. We show that the protocol satisfies weak and strong validity, termination, and agreement. For brevity in the proofs we say that p "decides" when it sets $decision_p$ to true.

Lemma 1. *No correct process is added to another correct process's* faulty *set.*

Proof. Process q is added to $faulty_p$ only if q omits to send a message to p, which will not happen if q is correct.   □

Lemma 2. *If p and q are both correct, then* lastClean$_p$ *and* lastClean$_q$ *differ by at most 1.*

Proof. The first time p fails to see a clean round, it broadcasts that information to q (line 12). If this is the last iteration of the loop, then $lastClean_q$ could have been incremented at most one more time than $lastClean_p$. If this is not the last iteration of the loop, then p will set $clean_q$ to **false** in the next iteration of the loop (line 10) and $lastClean_q$ will not be incremented for the remaining iterations of the loop (line 11).   □

This lemma implies:

Lemma 3. *If correct p accepts a chain at round i, then all correct q will accept chains at rounds $i + 1$ and higher.*

Lemma 4. *If p is correct, and* lastClean$_p = 0$, *then p does not decide.*

Proof. If $lastClean_p = 0$, p accepts no chains, and does not decide.   □

Lemma 5. *If p is correct, and* lastClean$_p$ = 0, *then no process decides.*

Proof. Suppose, instead, that q decides. By Lemma 4, $lastClean_q > 0$. Because $lastClean_p = 0$, Lemma 2 implies that $lastClean_q = 1$. It must have decided based on a chain c of length $f + 1$, which must consist of a single correct process, r, followed by f faulty processes. But r must have sent $tail(c)$ to q in the previous round, implying that $lastClean_r \geq 2$. We now have two correct processes, p and r, where $lastClean_p = 0$ and $lastClean_r \geq 2$, contradicting Lemma 2.   □

Lemma 6. *If a correct p decides, then every correct q does the same.*

Proof. There are two ways p might decide (Line 46). First, if $Chains_p$ contains the empty chain, then $lastClean_p = f + 2$, and, for any correct q, $lastClean_q \geq f + 1$ (Lemma 2). When p sent that empty chain to q (Line 17), q accepted the chain (Line 18) because $lastClean_q \geq f + 1$, and added the chain $[p]$ to $Chains_q$ (Line 20). It will not discard this chain, because q will never add p to *faulty* and p will never declare the empty chain to be invalid. Eventually, q will decide because chain $[p]$ consists of a decided head and a (vacuously) faulty tail.

Otherwise, suppose p found a non-empty chain c such that $r = head(c) \in decided_p$ and $tail(c) \subseteq faulty_p$. Suppose r is correct. It accepted $tail(c)$ in round i, and sent c to both p and q at round $i + 1$. By Lemma 3, p and q both accept c. When r announces that it has decided, r will be in both $decided_p$ and $decided_q$. Because c is in $Chains_p$ after r decided, r did not tell either p or q to discard c. Eventually, $faulty_p$ and $faulty_q$ will agree, so q will decide as soon as $tail(c) \subseteq faulty_q$.

Suppose r is faulty. Because p is correct, it sent c to q at some round i, and q accepted c (Lemma 3), so $[p, c] \in Chains_q$. Eventually p will announce it has decided, and the processes in c will be in $faulty_r$, so if q has not already decided, it will decide based on the chain $[p, c]$.   □

Lemma 7 (Agreement). *No two correct processes decide different values.*

Proof. If p decides, then $lastClean_p > 0$ (Lemma 5). This means that the correct processes must have seen one clean round (line 11) and therefore must have received the same value from the broadcaster (test for equal values in line 10). By Lemma 6, either all correct processes decide or none of them do. If they decide, they decide the unique value they received from the broadcaster in the first phase.   □

Lemma 8 (Weak Validity). *If the broadcaster is correct and correct p decides, then p decides the broadcaster value.*

Proof. Follows the same reasoning as in Lemma 7.   □

Lemma 9 (Termination). *Each one-shot broadcast attempt terminates.*

Proof. For each correct p, the one-shot broadcast terminates either when p decides, or when its set of valid chains $Chains_p$ becomes empty. If p's protocol does

```
a[] // unbounded array
for i = 1 to ∞
    a[i] = ⋆
    fork a[i] = oneShotProtocol()
    if ∃j, v such that a[j] == v ≠ ⋆ and a[k] == ⋆ for 1 ≤ k < j ≤ i
        receive v
```

Fig. 2. Pipelining One-Shot Protocols

not terminate, then $Chains_p$ never becomes empty. Let c be the shortest chain always in $Chains_p$, and let $head(c) = q$. If q is faulty, p will eventually discard that chain, so q must be correct. If every process in $tail(c)$ is faulty, p will eventually be able to decide based on c, so some correct r must appear in $tail(c)$. But because r is correct, it must have sent a prefix c' of c to p. By Lemma 3, p accepted c', and stored $[r, c']$ in $Chains_p$. Because r is correct, p never discards that chain, contradicting our assumption that c is p's minimal chain that is never discarded. □

Lemma 10 (Strong Validity in the absence of failures). *If the broadcaster is correct and all processes invoke the one-shot broadcast protocol in round i and if there are no new failures that occur at or after round i, then all processes receive the broadcaster value.*

Proof. If there are no new failure at or after round i then rounds i through $i + f + 1$ are all clean and all correct processes can decide at the end of the first phase (they would still have to run the second and third phase though to confirm the decision). The value they decide is the broadcaster's value if it is correct or $\perp$ if it is not correct. □

3.2   The Broadcast Protocol

The actual broadcast protocol is constructed by "pipelining" one-shot protocols as shown in Fig. 2. There is an array a that is used to store values received by various instances of the one-shot protocol. At each round, the protocol "forks" a new one-shot protocol instance (that is, it creates a new thread running the one-shot protocol executing in parallel both with its caller and with earlier instances). The protocol instance forked in round i stores its result (either a value or $\star$) in $a[i]$. The protocol *receives* the value received by the instance forked at round i if it (the i'th instance) receives a value other than $\star$ and every instance forked at an earlier round $j < i$ fails to receive a value (receives $\star$).

Agreement follows from the fact that for every invocation, $a[i]$ would eventually be identical for all correct processes. Validity follows from the weak validity of one-shot broadcast. Termination follows from the fact that once all the faulty processes have crashed (have been detected), by Lemma 10, an instance of the one-shot broadcast will successfully receive a value other than $\star$. We omit the detailed proofs.

3.3 Performance

It should be clear that any solution could be delayed indefinitely before faulty processes are detected; this follows from the fault-tolerance bounds for agreement [5].
Nevertheless, one can consider the performance in failure-free runs. Our protocol
requires $2f + 2$ rounds in that case. That can be optimized to $f + 4$ as a process
that decides after the first phase need not participate in all $f + 1$ rounds of the
second phase; they only need to participate in the first round of the second phase.

4   Consensus and Broadcast with Partial Eventual Detection

In this section we consider a mixed failure model in which up to f faulty processes
are eventually detected and up to F faulty processes are never detected. We first
show that if the total number of processes $N \leq 2f+3F$, then neither consensus nor
broadcast can be solved in this model. Then, we present a consensus protocol (that
can be used to solve broadcast) with optimal fault tolerance requiring $N > 2f+3F$.

4.1 Lower Bound

Lemma 11. *There is no solution to the broadcast problem if* $N \leq 2f+3F$ *and* $F > 0$.

Proof. The proof is a standard indistinguishability argument. Without loss of
generality, consider executions of a full information protocol. Divide the processes
into five groups: A_0, A_1, B_0, B_1, and B_{01}, where $|A_0| = |A_1| = f$ and $|B_0| = |B_1| = |B_{01}| = F$.

First, consider an execution e_{01} in which only the processes in B_{01} are faulty.
In the 0'th round, b sends 0 to processes in $A_0 \cup B_0$ and 1 to processes in $A_1 \cup B_1$.
All other processes send "no input" in the 0'th round. In subsequent rounds, each
process in B_{01} is "two-faced:" to A_0 and B_0 it acts as if it had received 0 from
b in the 0'th round, and to A_1 and B_1 as if it had received 1 from b in the 0'th
round. Otherwise, it acts correctly. Specifically, B_{01} behaves as follows. In round
$i \geq 1$, processes in B_{01} send to processes $A_0 \cup B_0$ messages that are identical to the
messages sent by processes in $A_0 \cup B_0$ in round i (since the protocol is deterministic
and $A_0 \cup B_0$ are correct in e_{01}, this completely defines the messages). Similarly, in
round i, processes in B_{01} send to processes in $A_1 \cup B_1$ messages that are identical to
messages that processes in $A_1 \cup B_1$ send in the i'th round. Since in this execution
only processes in B_{01} are faulty and permanently Byzantine, this execution can
go on arbitrarily long with no process crashing. By hypothesis, the processes must
agree on a value, without loss of generality 0, after some r rounds.

Now consider an execution e_1 of the protocol in which only the processes in A_0
and B_0 are transient or permanent Byzantine processes (possible because $|B_0 \cup A_0| = f+F$), b is correct and sends 1 to all processes in the 0'th round. In each sub-
sequent round, faulty processes in A_0 and B_0 send the same messages they sent in
e_{01}, thus behaving incorrectly. This execution is indistinguishable from e_{01} to processes in A_1 and B_1, so after r rounds they decide 0, which is incorrect. Because the

model does not provide any time guarantee on how long it takes transient Byzantine processes to fall silent, they can fall silent at the end of round $r + 1$. $\quad\square$

4.2 Consensus Protocol Description

We present a consensus protocol with optimal fault-tolerance in the mixed model. The protocol works correctly if the total number of processes N is greater than $2f + 3F$. In what follows, we assume $N = 2f + n$, where $n > 3F$. To simplify the exposition, the protocol we present requires continuous participation in the execution of its main loop even after agreement is reached. It is relatively straightforward to modify it to eliminate this requirement, but we omit the description for lack of space.

Each process has a current *preference*, v_d, initialized to its input value (Line 01). Each process keeps track of other processes known to be faulty (because they failed to send a message). The protocol proceeds in a series of iterations. In each iteration, each process p broadcasts its preference and collects the results (Lines 03-04). If all but F of the non-faulty processes agree on a value, p announces a *landslide* for that value, and adapts that value as its preference. If, instead, a majority of the non-faulty processes agree on a value, p announces a *majority* for that value, and adapts that value as its preference. Otherwise p leaves its preference unchanged. Next, p broadcasts the results of the first exchange. If all but F of the non-faulty processes agree that there was a landslide, p decides that value. If, instead, a majority agree that there was either a landslide or a majority, then p takes that value as its preference, but does not decide. So far, this protocol ensures validity and agreement in the presence of undetected Byzantine processes, but not termination. The pattern of message exchanges of the protocol is similar to those of other consensus protocols in which processes try to establish an overwhelming majority for a value with the knowledge that such a majority cannot be made to "flip" by faulty processes (phase-king protocol for example [13]). The difficulty in our case is that even if a process gets overwhelming support for one value, the correct processes are not numerous enough to force a decision and an approach like a phase king does not seem to work.

To guarantee termination, we use a *phase committee*; instead of taking a phase-king value, we take a majority value of a new set of processes in each round. This leaves the question of how to deal with faulty processes that can poison the majority value in any committee they belong to. The solution is to consider all but F processes for a committee as follows. At the end of each iteration (Lines 31-38), p constructs a set $S_{potential}$ of *potentially* correct processes by taking all but F of the processes it had not deemed faulty. We require that after enough rounds, p has considered every possible potential set, including the actual set of correct processes. Process p examines the preferences of this set of processes, and sets its preference to the majority value. We show that eventually, this majority value is stable and valid, and that the protocol ensures that when the potential set matches the actual set of correct processes, the preferences of the correct processes do not change. Termination is guaranteed once all the transient Byzantine processes fail.

01: $v_d = v_{in}$

02: **repeat**
03: $\quad \forall q \in \mathcal{P} - faulty$: send v_d to q
04: $\quad \forall r \in \mathcal{P} - faulty$: $v[r]$ = value received from r
05: $\quad \forall q \in \mathcal{P}$: **if** q silent **then** $faulty = faulty \cup \{q\}$

06: $\quad$ **if** $\exists v_0 : |\{r \notin faulty : v[r] == v_0\}| \geq 2f + n - F - |faulty|$ **then**
07: $\quad\quad\quad v_d = v_0$
08: $\quad\quad\quad \forall q \in \mathcal{P} - faulty$: send $(landslide, v_d)$ to q
09: $\quad$ **elseif** $\exists v_0 : |\{r \notin faulty : v[r] == v_0\}| \geq f + n - F - |faulty|$ **then**
10: $\quad\quad\quad v_d = v_0$
11: $\quad\quad\quad \forall q \in \mathcal{P} - faulty$: send $(majority, v_d)$ to q
12: $\quad$ **else**
13: $\quad\quad\quad \forall q \in \mathcal{P} - faulty$: send $(\star, v_d)$ to q

14: $\quad \forall r \in \mathcal{P} - faulty$: $v[r]$ = value received from r
15: $\quad \forall q \in \mathcal{P}$: **if** q silent **then** $faulty = faulty \cup \{q\}$
16: $\quad$ **if** $\exists v_0 : |\{r \notin faulty : v[r] == (landslide, v_0)\}| \geq 2f + n - F - |faulty|$ **then**
17: $\quad\quad\quad v_d = v_0$
18: $\quad\quad\quad \forall q \in \mathcal{P} - faulty$: send $(landslide, v_d)$ to q
19: $\quad$ **elseif** $\exists v_0 : |\{r \notin faulty : v[r] == (landslide, v_0) \vee v[r] == (majority, v_0)\}|$
$\quad\quad\quad\quad\quad \geq f + n - F - |faulty|$ **then**
20: $\quad\quad\quad v_d = v_0$
21: $\quad\quad\quad \forall q \in \mathcal{P} - faulty$: send $(majority, v_d)$ to q
22: $\quad$ **else**
23: $\quad\quad\quad \forall q \in \mathcal{P} - faulty$: send $(\star, v_d)$ to q

24: $\quad \forall r \in \mathcal{P} - faulty$: $v[r]$ = value received from r
25: $\quad \forall q \in \mathcal{P}$: **if** q silent **then** $faulty = faulty \cup \{q\}$
26: $\quad$ **if** $\exists v_0 : |\{r \notin faulty : v[r] == (landslide, v_0)\}| + | \geq 2f + n - F - |faulty|$ **then**
27: $\quad\quad\quad v_d = v_0$
28: $\quad\quad\quad decide = true$
29: $\quad$ **elseif** $\exists v_0 : |\{r \notin faulty : v[r] == (landslide, v_0) \vee v[r] = (majority, v_0)\}|$
$\quad\quad\quad\quad\quad \geq f + n - F - |faulty|$ **then**
30: $\quad\quad\quad v_d = v_0$

31: $\quad \forall q \in \mathcal{P} - faulty$: send v_d to q
32: $\quad \forall r \in \mathcal{P} - faulty$: $v[r]$ = value received from r
33: $\quad \forall q \in \mathcal{P}$: **if** q silent **then** $faulty = faulty \cup \{q\}$

34: $\quad$ **new** $S_{potential}$
35: $\quad$ **if** $|\{r \in S_{potential} - faulty : v[r] == v_d\}| \geq f + n - 2F - |faulty|$ **then**
36: $\quad\quad\quad v_d = v_d$
37: $\quad$ **else**
38: $\quad\quad\quad v_d$ = majority value of processes in $S_{potential}$

Fig. 3. Consensus protocol executed by process p in the mixed model

4.3   Correctness of Consensus with Partial Eventual Detection

Lemma 12. *If a correct process p decides v_0 in an iteration, then every correct process q will have $v_d = v_0$ at the end of the iteration.*

Proof. If p decides v_0, then it has received $2f + (n - F) - |faulty_p|$ values equal to $(\texttt{landslide}, v_0)$ from processes that are not in $faulty_p$ (Lines 24-25, 26-28). Of these processes, there are at least $2f + (n - F) - |faulty_p| - (f + F - |faulty_p|) = f + n - 2F$ processes that are correct and all of them send $(\texttt{landslide}, v_0)$ to q in line 18; let r be one such process. r must have received $2f + (n - F) - |faulty_r|$ messages of the form $(\texttt{landslide}, v_0)$ in line 14 (checked in line 16). Every other correct process must have received $2f + (n - F) - |faulty_r| - (f + F - |faulty_r|) = f + n - 2F$ messages of the form $(\texttt{landslide}, v_0)$ in line 14. This leaves $f + 2F$ messages that can be different from $(\texttt{landslide}, v_0)$. Given that $f + 2F < f + n - F$, it follows that every correct process will send a value of the form $(\texttt{majority}, v_0)$ or $(\texttt{landslide}, v_0)$ in line 21 or line 18. Every correct process will receive from every correct process a value of the form $(\texttt{majority}, v_0)$ or $(\texttt{landslide}, v_0)$ in line 24 and would set $v_d = v_0$ in line 27 or in line 30. The only remaining opportunity for a correct process to change its value is in line 38. We argue that is not possible. In line 31, all correct processes send v_0. At most F of them are excluded from $S_{potential}$ and it follows that at least $f + n - 2F$ correct processes in $S_{potential}$ send v_0. Since $|S_{potential}| = 2f + n - F$, and $n > 3F$, we have $f + n - 2F > |S_{potential}|/2$ so a majority of the values are equal to v_0 and at the end of the iteration all correct processes have $v_d = v_0$. □

Lemma 13 (Agreement). *If a correct process decides a value, then no correct process will decide a different value*

Proof. By the previous lemma, once a process decides v_0, all correct processes will have $v_d = v_0$ at the end of the iteration. Assume all processes start an iteration with $v_d = v_0$. Since there are $f + n - F$ correct processes, they will all send messages of the form $(\texttt{majority}, v_0)$, or $(\texttt{landslide}, v_0)$ in lines 8, 11, 18, or 21. At the end of line 31, all correct processes send v_0 and by an argument identical to that in the previous lemma, they all have $v_d = v_0$ at the end of the iteration. □

Lemma 14 (Termination). *Eventually all correct processes decide.*

Proof. We consider the execution from the time all transient Byzantine processes are detected to be faulty. From that point on the only faulty processes are the F permanent Byzantine processes. Of the remaining processes, up to f, but possibly less, are in the *faulty* set of every correct process. Consider the first iteration i in which $S_{potential}$ contains no Byzantine processes. Elements of $S_{potential}$ are then either correct or in the set *faulty* of every correct process. It follows that at the end of that iteration, all processes will calculate the same value for v_d either by setting it to the (same) majority or by not changing it. In iteration $i + 1$, all correct processes start with the same value from v_d. In line 06, the condition evaluates to true and in line 08 they all send $(\texttt{landslide}, v_d)$. Again, in line 16, they all received $(\texttt{landslide}, v_d)$ from all correct processes and send $(\texttt{landslide}, v_d)$ in line 18. Finally, in line 26 they all receive $(\texttt{landslide}, v_d)$ and decide if they have not decided earlier. □

4.4   Performance

In failure free runs, processes can decide in a constant number of rounds. In non failure-free runs, it is possible that the number of iterations is exponential in F even after all f processes are detected. That would be the number of iterations needed to ensure the choice of a set $S_{potential}$ consisting solely of correct processes. It is not clear how to improve this number.

5   Related Work

Failure detectors have been used to encapsulate synchrony assumptions to deal with crash failures [6]. Doudou et al. [14] argue that a failure detector for Byzantine failures should be intimately linked to the algorithm that uses it. While this argument seems convincing, it seems less applicable to Sybil attacks, where the fault of creating a bogus identity is essentially independent of the underlying algorithm.

Agreement problems have been studied in a variety of timing and failure models, with varying validity requirements. We restrict attention to work most closely related to ours. The model we consider is similar to Widder et al. [8], who consider *mortal-Byzantine* processes. This model is motivated by the prospect of transient faults (say, due to cosmic rays) that might be detected by a hardware monitor that forces a process to crash if it exhibits too many faults. They provide an algorithm for consensus for $n > 2f$, but they do not consider a model that mixes permanent with detected Byzantine failures. They present a lower bound of $n > 2f$ for consensus. This bound is subsumed by our more general lower bound for the mixed model. Also, unlike our work, and given the lower bound for consensus, the work only considers the case in which faulty processes are a minority. In our work, we consider the broadcast problem and allow the faulty processes to be a majority. The technique of waiting for one of two processes to crash if they give conflicting views was used in [8] and also in [15] in the context of failure detectors. Our *phase committee* technique and the construction of chains to implement broadcast are new.

Li and Mazieres [16] consider Byzantine storage systems when more than one-third of the processes can be faulty. Their system provides either (1) safety, but not liveness, or (2) they provide a property called "fork*" consistency, which allows correct process' states to diverge. Chun et al. [17] augment their storage system with new kinds of trusted subsystems that ensure either safety only, or both safety and liveness. Our work guarantees both safety and eventual liveness without introducing weaker correctness conditions or trusted subsystems.

A number of papers consider *hybrid* models that mix Byzantine failures with other kinds of failures ([18,19] for example). In these models, unlike ours, processes display a single failure mode: Byzantine processes remain Byzantine, fail-stop processes remain fail-stop, and so on. For example, in the original work of Thambidurai and Park [18], three types of failures are considered. They present an algorithm that require $N > 3F + 2s + b$, where s is the number of processes subject to symmetric failures and b is the number of processes subject to benign failures. While this seems similar to our requirement for the consensus protocol, our results are fundamentally different: for some unbounded period during the execution, and unlike any other work we are familiar with, we do not place any restrictions on the number of processes behaving arbitrarily in the system. In the *scattered Byzantine* model [20], processes alternate between periods of Byzantine and correct behavior. Except for some trivial limiting cases, the results for these models do not apply to ours.

References

1. Fischer, M., Lynch, N., Paterson, M.: Impossibility of distributed commit with one faulty process. Journal of the ACM 32(2) (April 1985)
2. Dolev, D., Strong, H.R.: Authenticated algorithms for byzantine agreement. SIAM J. Comput. 12(4), 656–666 (1983)
3. Ben-Or, M.: Another advantage of free choice (extended abstract): Completely asynchronous agreement protocols. In: PODC, pp. 27–30 (1983)
4. Feldman, P., Micali, S.: Optimal algorithms for byzantine agreement. In: STOC, pp. 148–161 (1988)
5. Lynch, N.A.: Distributed Algorithms. Morgan Kaufmann Publishers Inc., San Francisco (1996)
6. Chandra, T.D., Toueg, S.: Unreliable failure detectors for reliable distributed systems. JACM 43(2), 225–267 (1996)
7. Dolev, D., Lynch, N.A., Pinter, S.S., Stark, E.W., Weihl, W.E.: Reaching approximate agreement in the presence of faults. JACM 33(3), 499–516 (1986)
8. Widder, J., Gridling, G., Weiss, B., Blanquart, J.-P.: Synchronous consensus with mortal byzantines. DSN 0, 102–112 (2007)
9. Douceur, J.R.: The sybil attack. In: Druschel, P., Kaashoek, M.F., Rowstron, A. (eds.) IPTPS 2002. LNCS, vol. 2429, pp. 251–260. Springer, Heidelberg (2002)
10. Bazzi, R.A., Konjevod, G.: On the establishment of distinct identities in overlay networks. Distributed Computing 19(4), 267–287 (2007)
11. Yu, H., Gibbons, P.B., Kaminsky, M., Xiao, F.: Sybillimit: A near-optimal social network defense against sybil attacks. In: IEEE Symposium on Security and Privacy, pp. 3–17 (2008)
12. Pease, M.C., Shostak, R.E., Lamport, L.: Reaching agreement in the presence of faults. JACM 27(2), 228–234 (1980)
13. Berman, P., Garay, J.A.: Asymptotically optimal distributed consensus (extended abstract). In: Ronchi Della Rocca, S., Ausiello, G., Dezani-Ciancaglini, M. (eds.) ICALP 1989. LNCS, vol. 372, pp. 80–94. Springer, Heidelberg (1989)
14. Doudou, A., Garbinato, B., Guerraoui, R.: Encapsulating failure detection: From crash to byzantine failures. In: Blieberger, J., Strohmeier, A. (eds.) Ada-Europe 2002. LNCS, vol. 2361, pp. 24–50. Springer, Heidelberg (2002)
15. Guerraoui, R., Herlihy, M., Kouznetsov, P., Lynch, N.A., Newport, C.C.: On the weakest failure detector ever. In: PODC, pp. 235–243 (2007)
16. Li, J., Mazières, D.: Beyond one-third faulty replicas in byzantine fault tolerant systems. In: NSDI (2007)
17. Chun, B.G., Maniatis, P., Shenker, S., Kubiatowicz, J.: Attested append-only memory: making adversaries stick to their word. SIGOPS Oper. Syst. Rev. 41(6), 189–204 (2007)
18. Thambidurai, P.M., Park, Y.-K.: Interactive consistency with multiple failure modes. In: SRDS, pp. 93–100 (1988)
19. Siu, H.S., Chin, Y.H., Yang, W.P.: A note on consensus on dual failure modes. IEEE Transactions on Parallel and Distributed Systems 7(3), 225–230 (1996)
20. Anceaume, E., Delporte-Gallet, C., Fauconnier, H., Hurfin, M., Le Lann, G.: Designing modular services in the scattered byzantine failure model. In: ISPDC, pp. 262–269 (2004)

Decentralized Polling with Respectable Participants

Rachid Guerraoui[1], Kévin Huguenin[2],
Anne-Marie Kermarrec[3], and Maxime Monod[1,*]

[1] EPFL
[2] Université de Rennes 1 / IRISA
[3] INRIA Rennes - Bretagne Atlantique

Abstract. We consider the polling problem in a social network where participants care about their reputation: they do not want their vote to be disclosed nor their misbehaving, if any, to be publicly exposed. Assuming this reputation concern, we show that a simple secret sharing scheme, combined with verification procedures, can efficiently enable polling without the need for any central authority or heavyweight cryptography.

More specifically, we present DPol, a simple and scalable distributed polling protocol where misbehaving nodes are exposed with a non-zero probability and the probability of dishonest participants violating privacy is balanced with their impact on the accuracy of the polling result. The trade-off is captured by a generic parameter of the protocol, an integer k we call the *privacy parameter*, so that in a system of N nodes with $B < \sqrt{N}$ dishonest participants, the probability of disclosing a participant's vote is bounded by $(B/N)^{k+1}$, whereas the impact on the polling result is bounded by $(6k + 2)B$.

We report on the deployment of DPol over 400 PlanetLab nodes. The polling result suffers a relative error of less than 10% in the face of message losses, crashes and asynchrony inherent in PlanetLab. In the presence of dishonest nodes, our experiments show that the impact on the polling result is $(4k + 1)B$ on average, consistently lower that the theoretical bound of $(6k + 2)B$.

1 Introduction

Social networks are growing exponentially, and one of the most celebrated examples, Facebook, currently boasts more than 200 million active users. Many of these users regularly share images and videos as well as discuss various social and political matters. They do so both with close friends and people they hardly know. A particularly important task in such networks is *polling*, such as the recent one about the terms of service of Facebook – initiated by Facebook managers [9], or the organizers of a Saturday night party asking in a social group

---

* Maxime Monod has been partially funded by the Swiss National Science Foundation with grant 20021-113825.

T. Abdelzaher, M. Raynal, and N. Santoro (Eds.): OPODIS 2009, LNCS 5923, pp. 144–158, 2009.

whether partners should be invited too. In many cases, such a polling can be expressed in a *binary* form: each participant starts with +1 or −1, expressing the answer to a question, and the goal is to compute the sum of the initial values. To be meaningful, a polling protocol should tolerate dishonest participants trying to bias the polling or discover other participants' votes.

An easy way to conduct a poll is to use a central server (e.g., Facebook Poll [1]). Each participant sends its vote to a central entity, which subsequently aggregates all votes and computes the outcome. Beside the non-scalability of this solution however, privacy is not ensured as participants might generally not want their vote (and maybe even the subject of the poll or the result) to be seen by a central entity, be it trusted or not [12]. Distributed *aggregation* is a simple, yet naive, alternative to avoid a central server: participants aggregate votes so that once these are summed up, it is impossible to know the vote of a participant. However, since participants contribute to the outcome's computation, they may bias the result by corrupting intermediary results. To prevent the initial bootstrapping vote to be known, every vote could be split (homomorphic secret sharing). However, a dishonest participant can still create an invalid initial set of shares (e.g., voting for an arbitrary large value) and bias the result.

Not surprisingly, devising a distributed polling protocol that ensures privacy while tolerating dishonest participants that might want to bias the votes is very challenging. This is particularly true if the goal is to devise a practical, hence simple, peer-to-peer protocol that does not rely on any heavyweight cryptography (e.g., asymmetric cryptography). The motivation of this work is to address this challenge by exploiting the special nature of social networks. A defining characteristic of such networks is the one to one mapping between social network identities and real ones (as opposed to virtual world platforms such as SecondLife). Participants in such networks do care about their *reputation*: information related to a user is intimately considered to reflect the associated *real* person. We leverage this concern and propose an approach which, instead of masking (e.g., BFT [3]) or preventing (e.g., cryptography) dishonest behaviors, dissuades such behaviors. This is achieved by executing, in addition to the polling algorithm, a distributed verification protocol which tags the profiles of the participants. For instance, if the testimonies of Alice and Bob demonstrate that Mallory misbehaved, their profiles are tagged with "Alice and Bob jointly accused Mallory" and the profile of Mallory is tagged with "Mallory has been accused by Alice and Bob". No participant would like to be tagged as dishonest (by a protocol that does not wrongly accuse participants as we will describe below). Moreover, assuming a system with a large majority of honest participants, the risk for a participant to be caught wrongly accusing others is high. For instance, if a participant is accused only by users that are related in the social network (i.e., friends forming a coalition), the accusation would be suspect and thus not be taken into account and this would eventually backfire on the accuser. In a social network, this kind of attacks can indeed be easily detected by a human reader or by an automated graph analysis tool inspired from SybilLimit [13].

We consider a system of both honest and dishonest participants. The former follow the protocol assigned to them while the latter might not. Should they deviate from the protocol, they never do anything that will jeopardize their reputation with certainty (i.e., with probability 1). In this context, we present DPol, a simple decentralized polling protocol. In a nutshell, DPol works as follows. Participants, clustered in fully connected groups, known as *offices*, make use of a simple secret sharing scheme to encode their vote. Then they send the shares of their vote (*ballots*) to proxies, belonging to another group (an office). Each office computes a partial tally that is further broadcast to all other groups. Each participant eventually outputs the same tally. DPol is fully decentralized and does not assign specific roles to any participant. This results in a simple, scalable, and easy to deploy protocol. The spatial complexity of DPol is $\mathcal{O}(\sqrt{Nk})$ and the number of messages sent is $\mathcal{O}(\sqrt{Nk})$, k being the *privacy parameter* and N the number of participants.

We bound the impact of dishonest participants and balance this with the level of privacy ensured. More specifically, in a system of N participants with $B < \sqrt{N}$ dishonest participants (which is a reasonable assumption in a social network with a limited number of sybil identities [13]), we can choose any integer k such that the probability for a given participant to have its vote recovered by dishonest participants is bounded by $(B/N)^{k+1}$ and the impact on the result is bounded by $(6k + 2)B$. This is due to our underlying simple secret sharing scheme enabling to expose, with certainty, dishonest participants affecting the outcome more than $6k + 2$ with only public verifications, i.e., without requiring to reveal the participants' vote. As we show in the paper, private verifications expose, with a non-zero probability, dishonest participants further (i.e., even if their impact is less than $6k + 2$), but require to inspect the content of a subset of ballots.

Consider for illustration a system of 10,000 participants with 99 dishonest participants ($\lceil\sqrt{N}\rceil - 1$) and assume a proportion α of participants voting $+1$. For instance, setting $k = 1$ ensures privacy with probability 99.99% and for any $\alpha > 0.54$, 100% of the participants compute the right binary decision (i.e., the sign of the outcome). While e-voting requires stronger guarantees, this amply fits polling applications requirements.

DPol is indeed easy to deploy and we report on its deployment over 400 PlanetLab participants. The polling result suffers a relative error of less than 10% in the face of message losses, crashes and asynchrony inherent in PlanetLab. In the presence of dishonest participants, our experiments show that the impact on the polling result is $(4k + 1)B$ on average, consistently lower that the theoretical bound of $(6k + 2)B$.

The rest of the paper is organized as follows: Section 2 describes our system model. Section 3 gives a detailed description of DPol together with its formal analysis. The impact of dishonest participants is presented in Section 4. Experimental results from PlanetLab are reported in Section 5. Section 6 reviews related work and Section 7 concludes the paper and proposes perspectives on future work.

2   System Model

We consider a system of N uniquely identified nodes representing participants. Each node p votes for a binary value $v_p \in \{-1, +1\}$ and the expected output of the polling algorithm is $\sum_p v_p$. Each participant in the social network is assigned a profile that can be tagged by DPol.

Nodes can either be honest or dishonest. Honest nodes strictly follow the protocol and contribute to the verifications as long as their privacy is not compromised. More specifically, honest nodes always collaborate with verification procedures that do not require them to reveal their ballots (i.e., public verifications). However, they may refuse to reveal their ballots for a verification procedure (i.e., private verification). Dishonest nodes may misbehave either to promote their opinion or reveal the opinion of honest nodes. Yet, they are rational in the sense that they never behave in such a way that their reputation is tarnished with certainty, i.e., they do not perform attacks that can be detected with probability 1 by means of public verification procedures. Dishonest nodes do not wrongfully blame honest nodes as it is rather easy for a human reader, when looking at other users' profiles, to distinguish between legitimate and wrongful blames, e.g., a single node blaming at random a very large number of nodes or a group of nodes always blaming together. We consider colluding dishonest nodes as a single coalition $\mathcal{B}$ ($|\mathcal{B}| = B$). When dishonest nodes collaborate to bias the outcome of the poll, they are assumed to share the same opinion. Still, they act selfishly in the sense that they prefer protecting their own reputation rather than covering up their suspected accomplices. For the sake of readability, we consider that the coalition always promotes -1 in the rest of the paper. A single coalition represents the worst case scenario for both discovering a node's vote and biasing the result of the polling.

Theoretical analysis (Section 3.3) assumes reliable channels and non-faulty nodes. We revisit these assumptions by measuring the impact of message losses and crashes in the implementation (Section 5).

In order to make DPol scalable and to allow for efficient verifications we assume a structured overlay which could be provided by the social network infrastructure. Note that the overlay is independent from the social graph. The N nodes are clustered into r ordered groups, from g_0 to g_{r-1}. A node p in group g_i maintains two sets of nodes: a set $\mathcal{P}_o$ of *officemates* containing all nodes belonging to the same group ($\mathcal{P}_o = g_i \backslash \{p\}$) and a fixed-size set $\mathcal{P}_p$ of *proxies*, containing nodes in the next group ($\mathcal{P}_p \subseteq g_{i+1 \bmod r}$). Therefore, all groups virtually form a ring, g_1 being the successor of g_r. Each group g_i is a clique. We define a *client* of a node p, a node for which p acts as a proxy. Every node maintains a list of its clients in the previous group ($\mathcal{P}_c \subseteq g_{i-1}$). A node discards every message originating from a node that is not in $\mathcal{P}_c \cup \mathcal{P}_o$. We assume a random uniform distribution of nodes across the r groups and nodes in the successor groups are distributed uniformly at random as proxies in the predecessor groups.

3   The Polling Protocol

We first give an overview of DPol. Then we prove its correctness and provide a theoretical analysis of its complexity, considering only honest nodes. Finally, we analyze how the protocol resists a privacy attack, i.e., dishonest nodes recovering the vote of a node. Attacks on the outcome of the poll, i.e., dishonest nodes biasing the result, are discussed in Section 4.

3.1   Polling in a Nutshell

DPol is composed of three phases: *(i)* voting, *(ii)* counting and *(iii)* broadcasting. During the voting phase, a node generates a set of ballots reflecting its opinion and sends each ballot to one of its proxies. In the counting phase, each node in a group computes the sum of the votes of the nodes in the previous group (local tally). This is achieved by having each proxy summing up the ballots it has received and broadcasting the result to its officemates. Finally, the local tallies are forwarded along the ring so that all nodes eventually compute the final outcome.

Algorithm 1. DPol at node p in group g_i, $i \in \{1, \dots, r\}$

Input: a vote $v \in \{-1, +1\}$
Variables: an individual tally $t'' = 0$
a local tally $t' = 0$
an array of local tally sets $S[\{1, \dots, r\} \to \varnothing]$
a local tally array $T[\{1, \dots, r\} \to \bot]$
Output: the global tally $\hat{t}$

Polling Algorithm

1: vote(v, $\mathcal{P}_p$)
2: local_count(t'', $\mathcal{P}_p$)
3: $t' = t' + t''$
4: local_tally_broadcast(i, t'', $\mathcal{P}_p$)
5: $\hat{t} = \sum_i T[i]$

Voting phase

procedure vote(v,$\mathcal{P}_p$) **is**
6:     $b = v$
7:     **for each** *proxy* $\in \mathcal{P}_p$ **do**
8:         send [BALLOT, b] (*proxy*)
9:         $b = -b$
10:    **end for**
upon event $\langle$ receive | [BALLOT, b] $\rangle$ **do**
11:    $t'' = t'' + b$

Intermediate Counting phase

procedure local_count(t'',$\mathcal{P}_o$) **is**
12:    **for each** *officemate* $\in \mathcal{P}_o$ **do**
13:        send [INDIVIDUALTALLY, t''] (*officemate*)
14:        $b = -b$
15:    **end for**
upon event $\langle$ receive | [INDIVIDUALTALLY, t] $\rangle$ **do**
16:    $t' = t' + t$

Local Tally Broadcasting & Forwarding phase

procedure local_tally_broadcast(i, t'', $\mathcal{P}_p$) **is**
17:    **for each** *proxy* $\in \mathcal{P}_p$ **do**
18:        send [LOCALTALLY, i, t'] (*proxy*)
19:    **end for**
upon event $\langle$ receive | [LOCALTALLY, i_{group}, t] $\rangle$ **do**
20:    $S[i_{group}] = S[i_{group}] \cup \{t\}$
21:    **if** ($S[i_{group}] = |\mathcal{P}_c|$) **then**
22:        $T[i_{group}] = $ choose($S[i_{group}]$)
23:        local_tally_broadcast(i,$T[i_{group}]$)
24:    **end if**

function choose($\mathcal{A}$) **returns** local tally **is**
25:    **return** the most represented local tally in $\mathcal{A}$

3.2   Description

Voting. The ballot generation is inspired by the simple secret sharing scheme introduced in [4] and shares similarities with the Vote/Anti-Vote/Vote system [11]. In order to vote for a given value $v \in \{-1, +1\}$, a node generates $2k + 1$ *ballots* $b_1, \dots, b_{2k+1} \in \{-1, +1\}$ representing its vote, where k is an integer called privacy parameter. The intuition is to create $k + 1$ ballots of a given tendency (positive or negative) and k opposite ballots, resulting, when summed, in a single vote

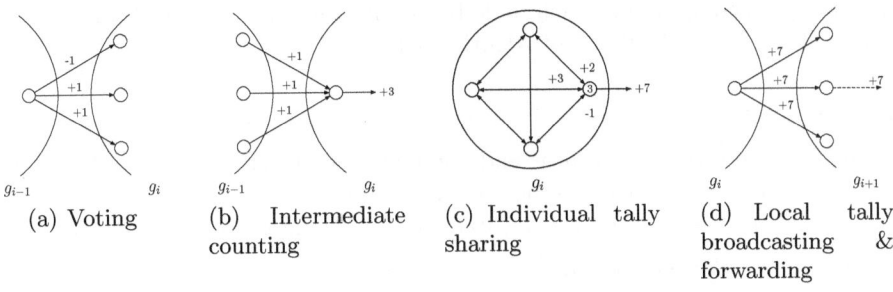

g_{i-1} g_i g_{i-1} g_i g_i g_i g_{i+1}

(a) Voting   (b) Intermediate   (c) Individual tally   (d) Local   tally
                    counting   sharing   broadcasting   &
                                                                    forwarding

Fig. 1. Key phases of DPol. (a) A node in g_{i-1} generates 3 ($k = 1$) ballots $\{-1, +1, +1\}$ and sends them to its proxies in g_i. (b) A node in g_i collects its received ballots $\{+1, +1, +1\}$ and sums them to $+3$ (individual tally) that it shares with its office-mates in g_i as depicted in (c). (c) A node receives every expected individual tallies $\{-1, +3, +2\}$, computes and sends the local tally ($+7$) to its proxies in the next group g_{i+1} as depicted in (d). (d) These proxies forward the local tally to theirs in g_{i+2}.

$v' = v$. Each ballot is defined as $b_j = v$ if j is odd and $b_j = -v$ if j is even, so that $v' = \sum_{j=1}^{2k+1} b_j = v$.

Once a node has generated its $2k+1$ ballots, it sends each of them to a different proxy. The number of proxies is to be chosen accordingly, $|\mathcal{P}_p| = 2k + 1$. Lines 6–10 in Algorithm 1 detail the voting phase. Figure 1(a) depicts a node sending its $2k + 1$ ballots (e.g., $\{-1, +1, +1\}$) to its assigned proxies. Once every node in the system has received one ballot from each of its clients, the voting round is over.

Intermediate Counting. A group acts as a voting office for the preceding group on the ring. The officemates collect ballots from their clients (Figure 1(b)) and share intermediate results (Figure 1(c)). To this end, a proxy sums the ballots it received into an *individual tally* t'', as described in Algorithm 1, line 11. Once a node has received the expected number of ballots from its clients, it broadcasts the computed individual tally to its officemates, as depicted in Figure 1(b) (lines 12–15 in Algorithm 1). The officemates aggregate the received data, i.e., they sum each others' individual tallies and store the result into a *local tally* t' as shown in Figure 1(c) (line 16 in Algorithm 1).

Local Tally Forwarding. Once the intermediate counting phase is over, i.e., all the officemates have computed a local tally, each node sends its local tally to its proxies (lines 17–19 in Algorithm 1). Upon reception of a message containing a local tally, a proxy adds it to the set $\mathcal{S}[i]$ of possible values for g_i. When a proxy has received the expected number $|\mathcal{P}_c|$ of local tallies for a given group g_i, it decides on a local tally by choosing the most represented value in $\mathcal{S}[i]$ and stores it in $\mathcal{T}[i]$. When a local tally $\mathcal{T}[i]$ is assigned, it is further forwarded (Figure 1(d)) to the next group using the proxies (lines 20–24 in Algorithm 1). Local tallies are then forwarded in the system along the ring. When a local tally reaches its source (the group that emitted it), it is no longer forwarded. The global tally is computed at each node by simply summing the local tallies of all groups: $\hat{t} = \sum_{i=1}^{r} T[i]$ (line 5 of Algorithm 1).

3.3   Analysis

We analyze here the correctness and complexity of DPol assuming only honest nodes. We then consider the impact of the dishonest nodes on privacy. The impact of dishonest attacks on the accuracy of the polling is presented in Section 4.

Theorem 1 (Correctness). *Assume a system where each node p starts with a binary value v_p. The polling algorithm terminates and each node eventually outputs $\sum_p v_p$.*

Proof. (Accuracy) We first prove that the local tally computed in every group g_i reflects the vote of all nodes in g_{i-1}. The local tally computed in a group is the sum of the ballots received by its members. Each node p in g_{i-1} sends each of its ballots $b_{1,p}, \ldots, b_{2k+1,p}$ to one distinct proxy in g_i. Similarly, each proxy p' in g_i receives a set of ballots $\mathcal{B}_{p'}$ from its clients. Since we assume only honest nodes, the set of ballots sent by the nodes in g_{i-1} is the set of ballots received in g_i. Therefore, the local tally computed by each member of g_i is $t' = \sum_{p' \in g_i} \sum_{b \in \mathcal{B}_{p'}} b = \sum_{p \in g_{i-1}} \sum_{j=1}^{2k+1} b_{j,p} = \sum_{p \in g_{i-1}} [(k+1) \cdot v_p + k \cdot (-v_p)] = \sum_{p \in g_{i-1}} v_p$. Note that this follows from the homomorphic property of the simple secret sharing scheme. Since nodes do honestly forward the local tallies along the ring and the messages are eventually received, each node ends up with the correct values for the local tallies of every group, thus the correct global tally.

(Termination) A node knows the number of messages it is supposed to receive in each phase. Since every node sends the required number of messages and every message eventually arrives, each phase completes. As the algorithm is a finite sequence of phases, it is guaranteed to eventually terminate.

In a realistic scenario, crashes and message losses do occur and may affect correctness and termination. Failures of nodes and message losses may *(i)* affect the accuracy of the global tally, and *(ii)* prevent nodes from detecting the end of a phase or deciding on a local tally.

Proposition 1 (Spatial complexity). *The asymptotic size S of the state maintained at each node in group g_i is $\mathcal{O}(r \cdot k + |g_i|)$.*

Proof. A node maintains a set of proxies $(2k+1)$, the set of its officemates $(|g_i|)$ and the list of its clients (at most $|g_{i-1}|$). Additionally, a node stores a set of $2k+1$ possible values for each of the r local tallies to perform global counting, that is $S = \mathcal{O}(k) + \mathcal{O}(|g_i|) + \mathcal{O}(|g_{i-1}|) + \mathcal{O}(r \cdot k) = \mathcal{O}(r \cdot k + |g_i|)$.

Proposition 2 (Message complexity). *The asymptotic average number of messages M sent by a node in group g_i is $\mathcal{O}(r \cdot k + |g_i|)$.*

Proof. A node sends messages during the voting phase $(2k + 1$ ballots), the intermediate counting phase $(|g_i| - 1$ individual tallies), and the global counting phase which involves the dissemination of r local tallies along the ring using its $2k+1$ proxies, that is $M = \mathcal{O}(k) + \mathcal{O}(|g_i|) + \mathcal{O}(r \cdot k) = \mathcal{O}(r \cdot k + |g_i|)$.

Note that the parameters are not independent: the sizes of the groups are related and bound to the number of groups by the relation $\sum_{i=1}^{r} |g_i| = N$. The two quantities M and S are minimized when $r = \sqrt{N/k}$ and $|g_i| = \sqrt{Nk}$, and thus $M = S = \mathcal{O}(\sqrt{Nk})$.

Theorem 2 (Privacy). *The probability, for a given node, to have its vote recovered by a coalition of B dishonest nodes is bounded by $(B/N)^{k+1}$.*

Proof. The vote of a node is recovered by the dishonest nodes if and only if the $k + 1$ proxies that received the $k + 1$ ballots containing the most represented value collude. This event occurs with probability $\binom{B}{k+1}/\binom{N}{k+1}$. For all k, B and N, this probability is bounded by $(B/N)^{k+1}$.

4   Confining the Impact of Dishonest Nodes

In this section, we analyze the impact of dishonest nodes on DPol, assuming companion verification schemes to detect attacks and identify dishonest nodes. Detection is performed by the nodes themselves relying on some of them being honest, and verifications are performed by an external entity (e.g., the social network infrastructure), polling nodes to identify the dishonest ones. We distinguish two types of verifications: *(i)* public verifications that leverage only information that does not compromise the nodes' privacy (i.e., the content of the ballots), such as the individual tallies received from their officemates, and *(ii)* private verifications that may leverage all information including the content of the ballots.

To dissuade nodes from misbehaving, verifications must affect the profiles of the involved nodes. When an attack is detected and reported, the neighbors of the accused nodes (i.e., the nodes it communicates with, typically clients and proxies) are polled for the messages they exchanged. If the testimonies of p_1 and p_2 demonstrate that p_0 misbehaved, their profile is tagged with "p_1 and p_2 jointly accused p_0" and the profile of p_0 is tagged with "p_0 has been accused by p_1 and p_2".

We consider an overlay of $\sqrt{N}$ groups of size $\sqrt{N}$ ($\sqrt{N} \in \mathbb{N}$) and a perfect client/proxy matching, i.e., each node has exactly the same number ($2k + 1$) of clients and proxies.

In a first step, we assume that honest nodes do not want to disclose any of the ballots they sent or received (i.e., public verifications). In this context, we study the impact of colluding dishonest nodes.

In a second step, we assume that honest nodes are willing to sacrifice privacy for the sake of accuracy by revealing some ballots (i.e., private verification) and we prove that colluding nodes compromising the global tally within the bound may be caught with a non-zero probability.

4.1   Impact of a Dishonest Coalition under Public Verifications

Theorem 3. *For $B < \sqrt{N}$, each member of a dishonest coalition may affect the global tally up to $6k + 2$.*

Proof (Proof (structure)). The proof relies on the facts that *(i)* honest nodes always tell the truth and strictly follow the protocol (including verifications), and *(ii)* dishonest nodes do not behave in such a way that their reputation is decreased with certainty. Effectively, showing that the attacks with unbounded impact are detected by the honest nodes with probability 1 proves the theorem. A dishonest node may bias the protocol at all three phases. Lemmas 1-4 encompass all possible attacks, propose a detection scheme relying on honest nodes, and bound the impact of those that cannot be detected with probability 1. In addition, if an attack is detected, we prove that the dishonest node is exposed by the public verification. Summing the impacts of all these attacks (Lemmas 1 and 2) for each dishonest node gives a maximum impact $(2k + 2(2k + 1)) = (6k + 2)$ on the global tally.

Note that the proof relies on the assumption $B < \sqrt{N}$ to ensure that the dishonest coalition can neither "control" (there is at least one honest node in each group) nor "fool" an entire group without being detected (there are not enough dishonest nodes to both perform and cover dishonest actions). In fact, the weakest assumption needed is that $\forall i, |g_i \cap \mathcal{B}| + |g_{i+1} \cap \mathcal{B}| < \sqrt{N}$.

Lemma 1 (Voting). *A dishonest node can affect the global tally up to $2k$, when voting.*

Proof. Due to the overlay structure, a node can only send ballots to the proxies it is assigned (otherwise the ballots are discarded), i.e., a maximum of $2k + 1$ ballots. Therefore a dishonest node may affect the global tally by either *(i)* sending less ballots than it is supposed to or by *(ii)* sending more than $k + 1$ -1-ballots. In the worst case, the dishonest node sends $2k + 1$ -1-ballots, i.e., $-2k - 1$. Since a node voting -1 is supposed to send $k + 1$ -1-ballots and k +1-ballots, its maximum impact is $2k$.

Lemma 2 (Computing individual tallies). *There exists a public verification scheme so that, if a dishonest node modifies its individual tally by more than $2(2k + 1)$, the attack is detected with probability 1 and the node is exposed.*

Proof. The considered overlay structure ensures that all nodes have exactly $2k+1$ clients and thus receives $2k+1$ ballots during the voting phase. A dishonest node can modify its individual tally by inverting the +1-ballots it received, i.e., it turns them in -1-ballots, decreasing its individual tally accordingly. In addition, a dishonest node can also forge ballots. The latter attack is identified by its honest officemates if the individual tally is out of the range $[-(2k + 1), 2k + 1]$. Therefore, not to be publicly detected, a node corrupting or forging ballots must output an individual tally in that range. Consequently, the worst case occurs when a dishonest node receives $2k + 1$ +1-ballots and inverts them all when summing them, leading to a maximum impact of $2(2k + 1)$.

Lemma 3 (Broadcasting individual tallies). *There exists a public verification scheme so that, a dishonest node broadcasting inconsistent copies of its individual tally to honest nodes, i.e., sending different values to its honest officemates, is detected with probability 1 and the node is exposed.*

Proof. Before deciding on a local tally, every node broadcasts to its officemates the set of individual tallies it received. This way, an honest officemate trivially detects the inconsistency. Dishonest nodes are exposed when their neighbors are asked for the individual tallies they received from these nodes.

Note that broadcasting different individual tallies can help a dishonest node to impose an arbitrary value for the local tally. For instance, assume a proxy has 5 clients, i.e., $k = 2$, only two of them being dishonest. In that case, there is a majority of honest nodes. Consequently, if the honest nodes send the same local tally, it will be the one chosen by the proxy. However, if the dishonest nodes send different values as their individual tallies then honest nodes will compute different local tallies. The proxy will then decide on the arbitrary local tally sent by the dishonest nodes.

Lemma 4 (Forwarding local tallies). *There exists a public verification scheme so that, a group forwarding inconsistent copies of a local tally, i.e., nodes sending different values to their proxies, is detected with probability 1 and the dishonest nodes are exposed.*

Proof. An inconsistent local tally forwarding is detected assuming the following: before deciding on a local tally, a node broadcasts the set of received local tallies to its officemates. An inconsistency is detected if at least one of the following conditions is satisfied: (C1) an honest node received different local tallies from its clients, (C2) an honest node received different local tallies than its officemates. Consider j dishonest nodes concentrated in a group g_i forwarding an incorrect local tally to their proxies. Because of (C1), the clients of an honest node in g_{i+1} must all be dishonest. Since the number of clients of all nodes equals their number of proxies $(2k + 1)$, a coalition of j dishonest nodes can corrupt a maximum of j proxies. Therefore, the $\sqrt{N} - j$ remaining proxies in g_{i+1} must collude with the coalition in g_i to circumvent (C2). To conclude, not to be detected, such an attack requires j dishonest nodes in g_i and $\sqrt{N} - j$ dishonest nodes in g_{i+1}, that is a minimum number of $\sqrt{N}$ dishonest nodes in $g_i \cup g_{i+1}$. Assuming $B < \sqrt{N}$, either a dishonest node in g_i is exposed by a public verification scheme (since it broadcast a local tally that does not correspond to the sum of individual tallies it received) or a dishonest node in g_{i+1} is exposed by a public verification scheme (since it has broadcast a different local tally from the one it received).

4.2   Private Verifications

So far we only considered public verifications, i.e., where the content of the ballots is never disclosed. Assume now that the nodes accept, with a non-zero probability, to relax privacy for the sake of verifications and reveal *a subset* of the ballots they sent and/or received. Then, this partial information can be leveraged to detect the dishonest behaviors described in Lemmas 1 and 2.

Theorem 4. *There is a non-zero probability to detect a dishonest node when misbehaving, even if its impact is less than $6k + 2$.*

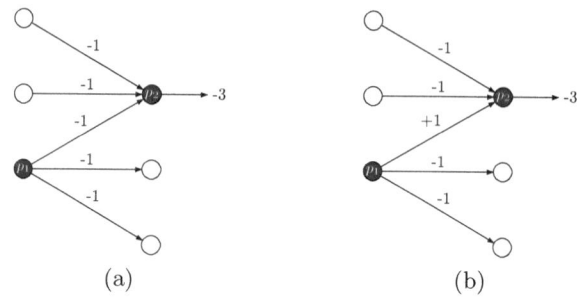

(a)   (b)

Fig. 2. Dishonest nodes have no gain in covering up each other

Proof. Regarding the voting phase, a dishonest node that sent $k+1+j$ -1-ballots and only $k-j+1$-ballots ($1 \leq j \leq k$) is unable to provide, for both kinds, the id of $k-j+1$ proxies to which it sent a +1-ballot. Therefore, a simple verification is to ask the suspected node to provide a list of proxies that can testify it sent at least j' ballots of each kind, for a random value j' ranging from 1 to k.

Note that an inspected node can disclose $j' = k$ without revealing its vote. Regarding the ballot corruption attack (Lemma 2), partial information about the ballots received by the inspected node can be leveraged to refine the bound on its individual tally: assume the inspected node received n_b ballots, if we further know that it received at least n_b^+ +1-ballots and n_b^- -1-ballots, then the range is refined from $[-n_b, n_b]$ to $[-n_b + 2n_b^+, n_b - 2n_b^-]$.

In both the aforementioned verifications, a dishonest node has no interest in covering another one up. Consider the examples depicted in Figure 2 where a dishonest node p_1 is the client of a dishonest node p_2. In Figure 2(a), if p_1's vote is verified and p_2 covers p_1 up, i.e., it testifies p_1 sent a +1-ballot, it exposes itself to a private verification on its individual tally (note that a node has to be consistent from one verification to another, thus, if the vote of p_2 is further verified, p_2 must stick to its first version about the ballots it received). The same situation occurs in Figure 2(b): if p_2's individual tally is verified and p_2 covers p_1 up, i.e., it testifies it sent a +1-ballot to p_2, it puts itself at risk, should it be subject to a private verification on its vote. Since dishonest nodes are selfish, they never cover each other up when privately verified. In conclusion, relaxing privacy ensures that every dishonest node has a non-zero probability to be exposed.

5   Implementation

The goal of the evaluation is to assess DPol with respect to the presented theoretical bound, and the impact of relaxing the assumptions made in the analysis. Our experiments show that, in a practical setting, DPol suffers as low as 10% in accuracy, and the average impact of dishonest nodes is around $(4k+1)B$.

5.1   Experimental Setup

In this section we report on the deployment of DPol on a 400 PlanetLab nodes testbed. This enables to stretch the algorithm in a real world setting, *(i)* in the presence of message losses, crashes and asynchrony inherent in PlanetLab, and *(ii)* when attacking the protocol by introducing dishonest nodes. We evaluate our algorithm with two different privacy parameter values $k = 1$ and $k = 2$.

Overlay. The cluster-ring-based overlay is built using a centralized bootstrapping entity keeping track of the whole set of nodes, assigning each node to a random group. Nodes have exactly $2k + 1$ proxies in the next group and the number of·clients of a node is $(2k + 1)\,|g_{i-1}|\,/\,|g_i|$ on average.

Communication and Asynchrony. Nodes communicate through UDP leading to message losses on the communication channels (with PlanetLab, we observed a loss rate ranging from 5% to 15%). In addition, PlanetLab nodes are unreliable, leading to expected messages to be lost due to senders crashes. Therefore, phase terminations cannot be detected by simply counting the number of received messages. In the local tally forwarding phase, when the number of possible values for a local tally grows beyond a given threshold $\gamma \cdot |\mathcal{P}_c|$, the node makes the decision for this particular local tally in Δt seconds. In our implementation, γ is set to 0.5 and Δt to 5 seconds. The two other phases are simply bounded in time.

5.2   Polling in Practice

Accuracy. Figure 3 depicts the accuracy of DPol among 400 PlanetLab nodes with $k = 2$. Figure 3(a) considers the value of the tally while Figure 3(b) considers the sign of the tally. Without loss of generality, we consider a proportion α of node voting +1 ranging from 0.5 to 1. In Figure 3(a), we plot the standard deviation on the computed tally for α in that range. For each run, we compute the average of the error when computing the tally (this is the difference between the tally on each node and the real one) over all nodes. Each point represents the average of this value over 20 independent runs. Note that the accuracy increases when α is close to 0.5. This is due to the fact that the closer the tally to 0.5, the fewer message losses impact the outcome: the closer the number of -1-ballots and +1-ballots, the closer to 0 the individual and local tallies.

Figure 3(b) displays the fraction of nodes deciding on the correct *sign* of the tally function of α. Effectively, even if the standard deviation is relatively small, some nodes may decide incorrectly on the sign of the outcome. Consider the organizers of a Saturday night party asking their friends in a social network whether partners should be excluded. As depicted in Figure 3(b), for $\alpha = 52.5\%$, some nodes would compute a different answer than the majority. This means that a minority of participants computing a negative result would come with their partners... Figure 3(b) (plain line) also shows the proportion of nodes that are unable to decide on a global tally (because their set of possible values never reach the threshold γ). We observe that this fraction remains very low (less than 4%) and is independent from α.

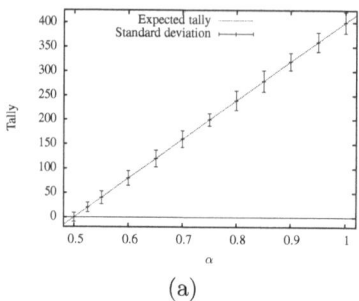
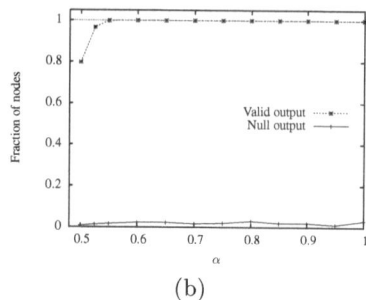

(a)   (b)

Fig. 3. Accuracy of the algorithm in presence of asynchrony, message losses and failures ($N = 400$ and $k = 2$)

Attacks. We consider the worst case: dishonest nodes do every possible attack that does not compromise their reputation with probability 1, i.e., every dishonest node *(i)* sends $2k + 1$ -1-ballots, and *(ii)* inverts every +1-ballot it receives. Figure 4 displays for $k = 1$ and $k = 2$, the resulting tally (sign on the upper part of the figure and value on the lower part), compared to the real one (dashed line), for $B = 19$ dishonest nodes ($B = \lceil \sqrt{N} \rceil - 1$) in a system of 400 nodes.

We observe that the dishonest coalition affects the outcome of the poll within the theoretical bound derived in the analysis (dotted lines in Figure 4). However, the average impact of the coalition is less than $6k + 2$ (considering the worst case where the dishonest proxy receives only +1-ballots and inverts them all). The theoretical bound is never reached as the average impact of a dishonest node depends on the actual number of ballots it can invert, this, in turn, depends on α. Effectively, a dishonest proxy receives $k + \alpha$ +1-ballots out of $2k + 1$ on average. Therefore, its impact is $2k + 2(k + \alpha) = 4k + 2\alpha$ on average. For $k = 2$, fitting our 55 data point cloud with a least-squares regression line (plain line in Figure 4) $a(\alpha - 0.5) + b$ gives $a = 791$ and $b = -163$. This is close to the expected parameter values $a = 2(N - B) = 760$ and $b = -B(4k + 1) = -180$. We use this

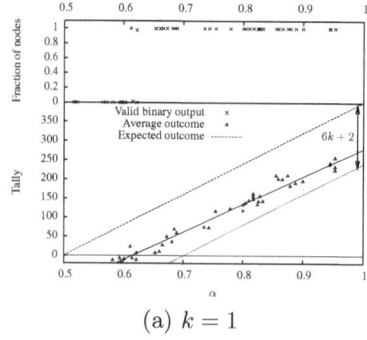
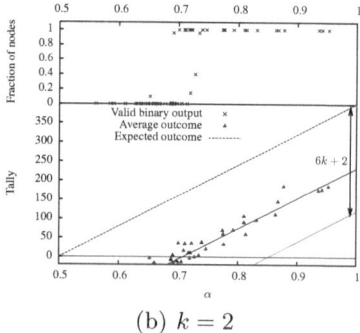

(a) $k = 1$ (b) $k = 2$

Fig. 4. Accuracy of the poll in the presence of dishonest nodes: with $N = 400$ and $B = 19$, dishonest nodes manage to confuse the majority of the nodes for *(a)* $\alpha < 0.62$ when $k = 1$, and *(b)* $\alpha < 0.73$ when $k = 2$

analysis to make a projection on larger scale systems. For $k = 1$ (Figure 4(a)), every node of the poll outputs a valid binary results when $\alpha > 0.62$, which is to be compared to $\alpha > 0.55$ observed in Figure 3(b) (without dishonest nodes). On average, we can analytically derive that with $N = 10,000$ and $B = 99$, the proportion α for which the nodes decide correctly is $\alpha > 0.52$.

6   Related Work

We discuss here related distributed voting protocols with a particular attention to those that are not based on the intractability of mathematical computations. Similarly to most protocols without cryptography, our work ensures privacy via secret sharing techniques. Also, our solution distances itself from related work in the sense that no participant has a special role (following the peer-to-peer paradigm), resulting in an increased scalability and robustness.

A large amount of work on secret sharing schemes (introduced by Rivest et al. in [10]) has been published in the late 80's. In [2], Benaloh proposed a scheme for sharing secrets privately based on polynomials. Since this scheme is an homorphism with respect to addition, it can be used for polling. However, a dishonest participant can easily corrupt the shares, thus potentially significantly impacting the final outcome.

Assuming a majority of honest participants, Rabin and Ben-Or extended Benaloh's secret sharing and proposed *verifiable secret sharing scheme* (VSS) [8]. Based on VSS, they proposed a multiparty protocol to compute privately the sum of the participants' inputs with an exponentially small error on the output. Beyond the fact that these techniques assume a fully connected network, synchronous links and broadcast channels, they involve higher mathematics. Moreover, since there is no control over the inputs themselves (contrarily to DPol where the ballot are in $\{-1, 1\}$ and therefore the vote is at max $\pm(2k + 1)$), a dishonest participant may still share an arbitrarily high value and can thus affect the outcome in a potentially unbounded way. The strength of this class of protocols is to ensure strong privacy to participants, including the dishonest ones but this makes such schemes hardly suitable for polling applications. Note that this also applies to complex secret sharing scheme and private multiparty computation such as AMPC [7].

In [6], Malkhi et al. proposed an e-voting protocol based on AMPC and enhanced check vectors. While powerful, this protocol differs from our work since participants have distinct and predefined roles (dealers, talliers, and receivers). This may result in decreased scalability and robustness if specific nodes fail.

7   Conclusion

We considered DPol, a simple decentralized polling protocol and proved that it can be made private and accurate in a social network, where participants are concerned over their reputation, by means of verification procedures, opening the way to a novel and promising way to perform secure distributed computations.

In addition we believe that our work can be extended to distributed applications that are not critical (i.e., that are not sensitive to small deviation on their outcome). A natural and interesting perspective is the extension of our polling protocol to n-ary inputs providing doodle-like services [5]. Also, designing an automated tool to help users of a social network to evaluate the reputation of a participant by cross-checking information such as tags and social graphs is definitely a very interesting and challenging problem.

References

1. Kremsa Design, Inc. Facebook Poll,
   http://www.facebook.com/apps/application.php?id=20678178440
2. Benaloh, J.C.: Secret sharing homomorphisms: Keeping shares of a secret secret. In: Odlyzko, A.M. (ed.) CRYPTO 1986. LNCS, vol. 263, pp. 251–260. Springer, Heidelberg (1987)
3. Castro, M., Liskov, B.: Practical Byzantine Fault Tolerance and Proactive Recovery. TOCS 20(4), 398–461 (2002)
4. Delporte-Gallet, C., Fauconnier, H., Guerraoui, R., Ruppert, E.: Secretive birds: Privacy in population protocols. In: Tovar, E., Tsigas, P., Fouchal, H. (eds.) OPODIS 2007. LNCS, vol. 4878, pp. 329–342. Springer, Heidelberg (2007)
5. Doodle: Easy Scheduling, http://www.doodle.com
6. Malkhi, D., Margo, O., Pavlov, E.: E-Voting without 'Cryptography'. In: Blaze, M. (ed.) FC 2002. LNCS, vol. 2357, pp. 1–15. Springer, Heidelberg (2003)
7. Malkhi, D., Pavlov, E.: Anonymity without 'Cryptography'. In: Syverson, P.F. (ed.) FC 2001. LNCS, vol. 2339, pp. 108–126. Springer, Heidelberg (2002)
8. Rabin, T., Ben-Or, M.: Verifiable Secret Sharing and Multiparty Protocols with Honest Majority. In: STOC, pp. 73–85 (1989)
9. Richmond, R.: Facebook Tests the Power of Democracy, April 23 (2009)
10. Rivest, R., Shamir, A., Tauman, Y.: How to Share a Secret. CACM 22, 612–613 (1979)
11. Rivest, R., Smith, W.: Three Vvoting Protocols: ThreeBallot, VAV, and twin. In: EVT, p. 16 (2007)
12. Stelter, B.: Facebook's Users Ask Who Owns Information, February, 17 (2009)
13. Yu, H., Gibbons, P., Kaminsky, M., Xiao, F.: SybilLimit: A Near-Optimal Social Network Defense against Sybil Attacks. In: SP, pp. 3–17 (2008)

Efficient Power Utilization in Multi-radio Wireless Ad Hoc Networks

Roy Friedman and Alex Kogan

Department of Computer Science, Technion
{roy,sakogan}@cs.technion.ac.il

Abstract. Short-range wireless communication capabilities enable the creation of ad hoc networks between devices such as smart-phones or sensors, spanning, e.g., an entire high-school or a small university campus. This paper is motivated by the proliferation of devices equipped with multiple such capabilities, e.g., Blue-Tooth (BT) and WiFi for smart-phones, or ZigBee and WiFi for sensors. Yet, each of these interfaces has significantly different, and, to a large extent complementing, characteristics in terms of energy efficiency, transmission range, and bandwidth. Consequently, a viable ad hoc network composed of such devices must be able to utilize the combination of these capabilities in a clever way. For example, BT is an order of magnitude more power efficient than WiFi, but its transmission range is also an order of magnitude shorter. Hence, one would want to shut down as many WiFi transmitters as possible, while still ensuring overall network connectivity. Moreover, for latency and network capacity reasons, in addition to pure connectivity, a desired property of such a solution is to keep the number of BT hops traversed by each transmission below a given threshold k.

This paper addresses this issue by introducing the novel *k-Weighted Connected Dominating Set (kWCDS)* problem and providing a formal definition for it. A distributed algorithm with a proven approximation ratio is presented, followed by a heuristic protocol. While the heuristic protocol has no formally proven approximation ratio, it behaves better than the first protocol in many practical network densities. Beyond that, a tradeoff between communication overhead and the quality of the resulting $kWCDS$ emerges. The paper includes simulation results that explore the performance of the two protocols.

1 Introduction

A wireless ad hoc network is composed of devices that are capable of communicating directly with their neighbors (roughly speaking, nodes that are nearby). Many such devices are battery-operated, e.g., laptops, smart-phones and wireless sensors. Thus, their operational life-time before the battery should be recharged or replaced is limited. Among all subsystems operating inside these devices, wireless communication is accounted for the major consumption of power [7, 18]. Additionally, platforms enabled with multiple wireless communication interfaces are becoming quite common. This turns the problem of efficient power usage by the wireless communication subsystem even more acute.

T. Abdelzaher, M. Raynal, and N. Santoro (Eds.): OPODIS 2009, LNCS 5923, pp. 159–173, 2009.

Known proximity wireless communication technologies include established standards, such as Blue-Tooth (BT) and WiFi, along with emerging standards, such as ZigBee and WiMax. These technologies differ dramatically from one another in their maximum transmission range, energy requirements and available bandwidth [8, 18]. For example, transmitting with a typical BT radio consumes 13.3 times less power than with a typical WiFi radio, but BT radio's transmission range is 10 times shorter [18]. Since the power consumed by radios in *idle* state is on the same order of magnitude as in *sending* and *receiving* states [1, 3, 7, 18], a systematic approach for creating power-efficient networks is required. Using such an approach, one should be able to shut down as many power-consuming radios as possible, while still maintain a connected topology. In addition, in order to keep latency and network capacity under some predetermined boundaries, a desired property of such a topology is to ensure that the number of low-bandwidth hops traversed by each message is limited by some threshold.

Most previous research on power utilization in wireless networks considers devices equipped with a single radio. The proposed solutions maintain energy-efficient topology by selecting overlays of active nodes [3, 21, 22] or by adjusting transmission ranges of the nodes [10, 14, 17]. The drawbacks in both approaches include lost connectivity and radios left idle, which still consume a significant portion of power. In addition, applying these solutions separately on each of the available interfaces will not benefit from the potential of an integrated approach.

Our contributions: Our first contribution is the introduction of a formal approach for reducing the energy consumption of wireless networks consisting of nodes owning two interfaces, one of which has a smaller transmission range and a lower power consumption than the other. The problem of energy consumption in multi-radio networks was considered by a few papers [1, 18]; all of them take heuristic approaches. We are not aware of any previous work that tries to capture the problem from a formal theoretic perspective. Thus, in addition to the novelty of the solutions proposed hereafter, the approach taken to model the problem is also new.

Specifically, we formulate a new optimization problem, which we call *k-Weighted Connected Dominating Set* ($kWCDS$). It is a generalization of the well-known graph theoretic problem of finding minimal *Connecting Dominating Set* (CDS). In the definition of $kWCDS$, we distinguish between *short* and *long* communication edges, corresponding to the interface with shorter and longer transmission ranges, respectively. A solution to the $kWCDS$ problem is a set of nodes, so that every node in the system is close enough (up to k short edges) to some node in the set, while all nodes in the set form a sub-network connected by long edges. An arbitrary parameter k controls the latency that applications running on devices may experience (e.g., instead of passing through one long edge, a message may pass through up to k short edges). Each node in the system is assigned a weight, which captures its remaining battery power, and we seek a solution having minimal total weight of nodes in the selected set. Consequently, an optimal solution to the $kWCDS$ problem provides a power-efficient topology where nodes in the selected set have high remaining power and stay with both interfaces turned on, while all other nodes turn off their power-hungry long range interface.

Second, we provide a centralized $kWCDS$ algorithm with a proven approximation factor. This protocol is based in part on ideas presented by Guha and Khuller for

CDS [11] and includes two phases: building a k-Weighted Dominating Set ($kWDS$) and then extending it to a $kWCDS$. For the second phase, we provide a deterministic construction through calculating a spanning tree. Yet, we also prove that whenever nodes are uniformly distributed, every $kWDS$ is w.h.p. also $kWCDS$. This is regardless of how the $kWDS$ was obtained.[1] The significance of this third contribution of our work is that in many practical settings, the second phase of the protocol can be skipped, and a $kWCDS$ is obtained very efficiently.

Our fourth contribution includes presenting two distributed asynchronous protocols for the $kWCDS$ problem. The first of these is a distributed version of the centralized algorithm with a proven approximation factor, which is directly derived from the centralized algorithm. The second protocol is heuristic. It does not have a proven approximation factor, but in practice behaves similarly in most settings, yet is much more message efficient. A formal time and message communication complexity analysis is provided for both.

Finally, we simulate the performance of our algorithms with typical parameters of WiFi and BT technologies and show that as the number of nodes in the system increases, a large portion of nodes may turn off their WiFi radios while remaining connected to the rest of the network at the BT level. In the discussion section, we explain how the $kWCDS$ problem can be extended to networks with an arbitrary number of interfaces and outline a solution for the extended problem.

2   Related Work

Optimizing energy consumption of wireless networks is a widely studied topic. The proposed solutions include maintaining energy-efficient topology by selecting overlays of active nodes (e.g., [3, 21, 22]) and by adjusting transmission range of the nodes (e.g., [10, 14, 17]). The first set of solutions builds upon the observation that, when the density of nodes is sufficient, only a small portion of nodes, forming the overlay, need to have their radios turned on to forward traffic of active connections, while other nodes may turn their radios off. The underlying assumption of this approach, supported by several works [1, 3, 7, 18], is that power consumed by radios in *idle* state is non-negligible compared to active communication (i.e., *sending* and *receiving* states). As mentioned before, the main drawback of these solutions is lost connectivity, which makes this approach inappropriate in systems with heavy communication patterns. The second set of solutions assumes nodes have radios with variable transmission range, which can be adjusted to decrease the power consumption significantly and decrease the interference. Such adjustments, however, also hurt the network connectivity and increase the diameter of the network (in terms of number of hops), while power consumption in idle state still remains a problem.

Several papers discuss the differences between selected types of wireless technologies in terms of the properties we are interested in, i.e., transmission range and power usage. For example, Bahl et al. [1] compare between TR1000 low-power radio and an $802.11b$ card and show tremendous differences in power consumption (e.g., the power

---

[1] Notice that this is in contrast to the weighted CDS problem, where most weighted dominating sets are not connected.

consumed during *sending* state has a ratio of 1:235). In another study [8], BT and 802.11*b* cards are compared, showing less dramatic, yet very significant differences.

Bahl et al. [1] indicate the advantages hidden in an efficient usage of multiple radios in the same device. They consider several problems of wireless computing, such as energy management and capacity enhancement, and provide interesting experimental data, showing significant benefits for multi-radio systems over traditional single radio ones. Their protocols explicitly assume, however, that all radios have the same transmission range or the neighboring devices are located closely enough to be able to communicate one with another through all available interfaces, and in case of a mismatch, the system reverts to a single radio mode. In addition, the results are presented as a set of heuristic approaches, without any theoretic framework.

Pering et al. [18] introduce CoolSpots, which reduces the power consumption of mobile devices with WiFi and BT interfaces by extending traditional WiFi hot-spots and controlling which interface to enable for which type of communication. The paper considers single-hop communication between a mobile phone and a hot-spot and provides empirical evaluation of several policies for managing multi-radio switching.

Our approach is based on the definition of a new optimization problem that generalizes the well-known CDS problem. Finding a CDS that has a minimal number of nodes is known to be NP-complete and, in fact, it is also hard for approximation [11]. Guha and Khuller in their seminal work [11] present a (centralized) approximation algorithm for a minimal CDS with an approximation factor of $\ln n + O(1)$, where n is the number of nodes. They also provide a $3 \ln n$-approximation algorithm for the version of CDS where vertices of a graph have weights. The ideas of this algorithm serve as a basis for the solution for our optimization problem.

Our decentralized, deterministic construction of the k-weighted connected dominating set incurs a linear (in number of nodes) running time. Several papers propose more efficient distributed, randomized construction of dominating sets. Jia et al. [13] showed such an algorithm that finds $O(\log n)$-approximated dominating set w.h.p. in $O(\log n \log \delta)$ time w.h.p., where δ is the maximal degree of any node. This result is used by Dughashi et al. [6] to construct a connected dominating set in polylogarithmic time. The above results are non-deterministic, and either do not ensure connectivity of the dominating set [13] or do not address the issue of weighted nodes [6]. In addition, their approximation factor is still $O(\log n)$. Other related results are due to Kuhn et al. [15, 16], who show an upper and lower bounds on the approximation factor of constant time algorithms. Yet, they also do not address the connectivity of the dominating sets and weighted nodes.

Due to the importance of CDS to networks without preconfigured infrastructure, such as wireless ad hoc networks, distributed approaches for building an approximated minimal CDS have been extensively studied (see, e.g., [2]). Without exception, these approaches consider single-radio networks. The main application of CDS in wireless ad hoc networks is to provide a virtual infrastructure, or overlay, in order to achieve scalability and efficiency. Such overlays are mainly used to improve routing schemes, where only nodes in the CDS are responsible for routing messages in the network (e.g., [19, 20, 21]). Other applications of CDS include already mentioned efficient power management [3, 21, 22] and clustering [4, 12].

3   System Model and Preliminaries

The system consists of a set of nodes, communicating by exchanging messages over a wireless network. Each node is equipped with two wireless network interfaces A and B, with transmission ranges R and r, respectively, so that $R \geq r$. We assume that, under same conditions, the power consumed by B is lower than the power consumed by A. In other words, it is preferred to use interface B over A for communication whenever possible. Note that we do not make any assumptions on the technology type of A and B. In particular, our protocols do not require the values of R and r to be known.

The communication network is modeled as an undirected graph $G = (V, E_l \cup E_s)$, where V represents the set of nodes and E_l (E_s) represents the set of edges between two nodes that can communicate directly using interface A (B). The communication network is connected at the level of the interface A, i.e., (V, E_l) is a connected graph. Each node is assigned a positive weight w, which is set to the reciprocal of its remaining battery power. Communication links of both types are bidirectional, reliable and FIFO. Each node has a unique identifier, *ID*, and executes asynchronously.

In the *k-Weighted Connected Dominating Set* ($kWCDS$) problem, the input is a graph $G = (V, E_l \cup E_s)$ and a positive weight function w defined on the nodes where:

- V is a set of nodes. Denote $n = |V|$.
- E_l (E_s) is a set of *long (short)* edges. Denote by δ_s the maximal degree of any node in G_s.
- Each short edge also appears in the set of long edges, i.e., $(v, u) \in E_s \Rightarrow (v, u) \in E_l$.
- The graph (V, E_l) is connected.

We refer to the graph $G_l = (V, E_l)$ ($G_s = (V, E_s)$) as a *long (short) instance* of G. For each node $v \in V$, we introduce the notation of *k-short-neighborhood*, $N_k(v)$, referring to the set of nodes at distance k or less (in the number of edges) from v in G_s, except for v itself.

The objective in the $kWCDS$ problem is to find a set S of nodes such that: (1) Every node $v \in V$ is either in S, or has a path of at most k short edges to some node in S, i.e., $\exists u \in S$ s.t. $v \in N_k(u)$. We say that u *k-covers* v, v is *k-covered* by u and S *k-covers* all nodes in G. (2) The subgraph induced by S on G_l is connected. (3) The total weight of nodes in S is minimal out of all sets standing in (1) and (2).

When S satisfies requirements (1) and (2), it is called a *k-Weighted Connected Dominating Set* ($kWCDS$) of G. If only requirement (1) is satisfied, S is called a *k-Weighted Dominating Set* ($kWDS$) of G.

For example, consider the graph depicted in Figure 1, where the weight of a node is equal to its ID. Both sets of nodes $\{1, 6, 8, 10\}$ and $\{1, 3, 4, 6, 8\}$ are $2WCDS$, but the latter has the minimal weight. Additionally, the set $\{1, 6, 8\}$ is not $2WCDS$, since node 8 is not connected by a long edge to the rest of the nodes in the set, although the nodes in $\{1, 6, 8\}$ 2-cover all other nodes in the graph. Note that for the case of $k = 1$ and $E_l = E_s$, the $kWCDS$ problem reduces to the CDS problem in vertex weighted graphs. Thus, finding the optimal solution for the $kWCDS$ problem is NP-hard.

Notice that for $k = 1$, a naïve approach for calculating the $1WCDS$ set exists. We could run any weighted CDS algorithm (e.g., [11]) and then define $1WCDS$ as a set

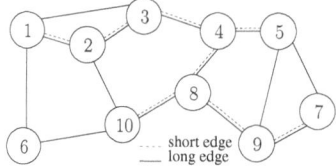

Fig. 1. Example graph

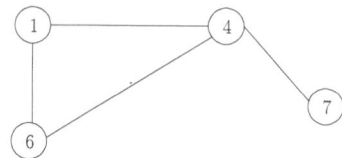

Fig. 2. Example super-graph

of all nodes in the system, except for any node v that is not in the calculated CDS set, but has a neighbor (from $N_1(v)$) in the CDS set. The following example, however, shows that such an approach may end up with a $1WCDS$ set that is $\Omega(n)$ from optimal: Consider a graph G consisting of $n-1$ nodes with a short (and thus, also a long) edge between any pair of nodes, and an additional node v that only has a long edge to every other node in G. Assume the weight of every node in G except for v is 2, and the weight of v is 1. The weighted CDS algorithm may choose node v as the only node in the weighted CDS (in fact, this is what the algorithm in [11] will do) and thus, the $1WCDS$ set will contain all nodes in the system, having the total weight of $2n-1$. At the same time, the weight of the optimal $1WCDS$ set is 3, which is the weight of v and some other node in G.

For our approximation algorithm, we define an auxiliary *super-graph* structure $SG(k)$ in the following way. Given the graph G and a subset of its nodes A, $SG(k) = (A, E)$ is a graph, where an edge exists between two nodes u and v if and only if there is a long edge between u or any node in its k-short-neighborhood and between v or any node in its k-short-neighborhood, accordingly. More precisely, $(u, v) \in E \Leftrightarrow \exists u' \in N_k(u) \cup \{u\} \wedge \exists v' \in N_k(v) \cup \{v\}$ s.t. $(u', v') \in E_l$. Note that each edge of the super-graph corresponds to at most $2k+2$ nodes and $2k+1$ long edges of the original graph. The super-graph $SG(2)$ for the graph in Figure 1 and a set $\{1, 4, 6, 7\}$ is shown in Figure 2. For example, there exists an edge between nodes 4 and 6, since $10 \in N_2(4)$ and $(6, 10) \in E_l$.

4   An Approximation Algorithm

We show first that the $kWDS$ set can be approximated by a factor of $k \ln \delta_s$ by a reduction to a weighted set cover problem out of G_s. Next, we argue that for practical systems, the calculated $kWDS$ set is already connected by long edges, thus, w.h.p., no further calculation is required. Finally, we discuss how to deterministically connect nodes in the $kWDS$ set by running an instance of a spanning tree algorithm.

4.1   Construction of $kWDS$

The following simple procedure constructs a $k \ln \delta_s$-approximation for the $kWDS$ set.

1. Create an instance of a weighted set cover problem by making each node an element, creating a set for each node v with all its neighbors in $N_k(v)$ and assigning the weight of the set to the weight of v.

2. Run a greedy algorithm that constructs a set cover by choosing sets based on the ratio of their weight to the number of new elements they cover. The chosen sets correspond to the $kWDS$ set in G.

Since every set that is created for each node in Step 1 contains at most δ_s^k elements, the weight of $kWDS$ found in Step 2 is at most $\ln \delta_s^k \cdot w(OPT)$, where $w(OPT)$ is the weight of the minimal $kWDS$ in G (see [5] for the detailed proof).

Lemma 1. *The algorithm presented above is a $k \ln \delta_s$-approximation for the $kWDS$ problem.*

4.2 From $kWDS$ to $kWCDS$

Probabilistic guarantees: We present a formal analysis of the probability for a $kWDS$ set to be unconnected. For simplicity, we assume that nodes are spread in two dimensional space; our analysis, however, can be easily extended to three dimensions. Interestingly, the analysis does not depend on the algorithm used to construct the $kWDS$ set, but only on the system parameters, i.e., k, r, R and n. Showing that for practical values for these parameters every $kWDS$ set is connected w.h.p., we claim that the simple algorithm presented above can also be used in practice to approximate w.h.p. the $kWCDS$ set by a factor of $k \ln \delta_s$.

Denote the sub-graph induced by the $kWDS$ set on G_l as G'. We note that if G' is unconnected, then there must be at least one edge $(u, v) \in G_l$ s.t. $(u, v) \notin G'$ *and* there is no path in G' between any node k-covering u and any node k-covering v. Denote a node k-covering u as u'; similarly, denote a node k-covering v as v'. It is possible that $u' = u$ and/or $v' = v$. The maximal physical distance between u' and v' is $R + 2kr$. If there is no path in G' between u' and v', then, in particular, there is no node in the $kWDS$ set that is located within the long transmission range of both u' and v'. In other words, there is no node in the $kWDS$ set that is located within distance R from both u' and v'. Consequently, there is no node in G_l that is located within distance $R - kr$ from both u' and v' (otherwise, it should be covered by some node in $kWDS$ which is within distance R from u' and v'). Denote this event as E.

Assuming uniformly distributed random and independent positioning of nodes on the field, we get that $\Pr(E) \leq (1 - \Pr(e))^{n-4}$, where e is the event of a node positioned within distance $R - kr$ from both u' and v' and $n - 4$ is the total number of nodes in the system, except for u, v, u' and v'. $\Pr(e)$ is given by the ratio between the area of the intersection of two circles with centers at distance $R + 2kr$ and radius $R - kr$, and between the area of the field. The area of the intersection of two circles is given by

$$A(R', d') = R'^2 cos^{-1}(\frac{d'}{R'}) - d'\sqrt{R'^2 - d'^2}$$

where R' is the radius of the circles and d' is a half of the distance between their centers (taken from mathematical books). Substituting $R' = R - kr$ and $d' = \frac{1}{2}R + kr$, and denoting $m = \frac{kr}{R}$, we get that

$$\Pr(e) = \frac{A(R - kr, \frac{1}{2}R + kr)}{A(field)} = \frac{R^2(1-m)^2 cos^{-1}(\frac{\frac{1}{2}+m}{1-m}) - \frac{\sqrt{3}}{2}(\frac{1}{2} + m)R^2\sqrt{1 - 4m}}{A(field)}$$

As long as $R > 4kr$, the area of the intersection of two circles is properly defined and $\Pr(e) > 0$. Given such R, r and k and given the area of the field, $\Pr(E)$ is bounded by c^{n-4}, where $c \in (0,1)$ is a constant. Recall that E_l denotes the set of edges in G_l. Using union bound, we get

$$\Pr(kWDS \text{ is not connected}) \leq |E_l| \cdot \Pr(E) \leq n^2 \cdot c^{n-4} \tag{1}$$

which approaches 0 when n grows. For example, taking $R = 150m$, $r = 10m$, field area of $500 \times 500 = 250,000m^2$ and 2000 nodes, we get that the probability for a $kWDS$ set to be unconnected is less than $2.88 \cdot 10^{-24}$ for $k = 1$ and less than $4.76 \cdot 10^{-9}$ for $k = 2$. Not surprisingly, this theoretical upper bound is echoed by the results of the simulations reported in Section 6.

Deterministic guarantees: Here, we provide a deterministic extension of the algorithm in Section 4.1 for constructing a $kWCDS$.

3. Create a super-graph $SG(k)$ from G and $kWDS$ and find a spanning tree (ST). The edges of the ST correspond to nodes (and long edges) in the original graph G, which along with the nodes in the $kWDS$ set form a $kWCDS$ set.

Referring back to the example graph in Figure 1, when calculating $2WCDS$, the greedy algorithm in Step 2 will choose first node 1, then node 4, 6 and, finally, node 7. The resulting $SG(2)$ super-graph is the one depicted in Figure 2. The spanning tree algorithm in step 3 will choose the edge $(4, 7)$ (adding node 5 or a pair of nodes 8 and 9 to $2WCDS$, depending on which nodes were chosen to represent the edge $(4, 7)$ in $SG(2)$) and two of the three remaining edges in $SG(2)$. For example, edges $(1, 6)$ and $(1, 4)$ will add node 3 or a pair of nodes 2 and 3 to $2WCDS$. Thus, the possible resulting $2WCDS$ set is $\{1, 2, 3, 4, 5, 6, 7\}$.

This example suggests that it is possible to slightly optimize Step 3 of the algorithm. We may assign a weight to each edge (v, u) in the super-graph $SG(k)$ as the weight of nodes in the lightest path between v and u in G_l (if both nodes are in the $kWDS$ set, the edge is assigned weight 0), and run a minimal spanning tree algorithm (MST) in Step 3. Such an approach, however, will not change the asymptotic approximation factor, and thus is not discussed further.

Denote by w_{max} and w_{min} the maximal and minimal weights of any node in the system, accordingly. The proof of the following theorem, omitted here due to lack of space, uses Lemma 1 and the fact that each edge in the calculated spanning tree corresponds to at most $2k + 2$ nodes in the graph G, $2k$ of which are not in $kWDS$.

Theorem 1. *The extended algorithm is a* $k \ln \delta_s (1 + 2k \frac{w_{max}}{w_{min}})$*-approximation for the* $kWCDS$ *problem.*

When $k = 1$ and the ratio $\frac{w_{max}}{w_{min}}$ is close to 1, our result matches asymptotically the approximation factor of $3 \ln n$ achieved by Guha and Khuller [11] for the related problem of CDS in vertex weighted graphs.

5 Distributed Construction of the $kWCDS$ Set

5.1 Algorithm 1

The lack of a centralized administration coupled with the potentially large number of nodes in ad hoc networks requires the $kWCDS$ set to be constructed in an effective distributed way. We present such an algorithm based on the centralized approximation algorithm given in the previous section.

The distributed algorithm runs in two phases. The first phase corresponds to steps 1 and 2 of the centralized algorithm, while the second phase corresponds to step 3. Thus, if the probabilistic guarantees of the first phase suffice, the algorithm may terminate right after it (without the second phase).

In the first phase, the dominating set $kWDS$ in the graph G_s is iteratively constructed. Initially, $kWDS$ is empty. For every node v, let $\delta^*(v)$ denote the number of nodes in $N_k(v)$ that are not k-covered by any node in $kWDS$ (initially, $\delta^*(v) = |N_k(v)|$). In each iteration, each node v calculates parameter $\alpha(v) = w(v)/\delta^*(v)$. Then, v sends its $\alpha(v)$ and gathers $\alpha(u)$ from all u at distance $2k$ or less from v in G_s. Node v joins $kWDS$ if its $\alpha(v)$ is smaller than any collected $\alpha(u)$ (using IDs to break ties).

In the second phase, all nodes in the $kWDS$ set are connected by running the distributed minimal spanning tree algorithm [9] on the super-graph $SG(k)$ created from G and $kWDS$. More specifically, only nodes in the $kWDS$ set run the distributed spanning tree algorithm. Every edge (v, u) in $SG(k)$ is emulated by nodes on the shortest path between v and u in G_l, so that every message sent by the algorithm on the edge, is actually transmitted along the corresponding path. As in the centralized counterpart, the resulting set of edges of the spanning tree defines the set of nodes that will serve, along with the nodes in the $kWDS$ set, as a $kWCDS$ set. Our choice of the MST algorithm of [9] is motivated by its simplicity and optimal asymptotical message complexity.

The pseudo-code for the distributed approximation algorithm described above is given in Algorithm 1. It uses the following local variables for each node i:

- α: array with values of α for node i and each node $j \in N_{2k}(i)$. Initially, all values are set to $\perp$.
- *state*: array that holds the state of each node $j \in N_k(i)$. The state can be *uncovered*, *covered* or *marked*. Initially, all values are set to *uncovered*.
- *done*: boolean array that specifies for each node $j \in N_1(i)$ whether j has finished the first phase of the algorithm. Initially, all values are set to *false*.

Notice that the first phase of the algorithm (i.e., all lines, except for Line 10) uses a barrier communication pattern, yet this does not imply any timing assumptions.

We assume that each node knows only its immediate neighbors in G_l and its k-short-neighborhood. The latter can be easily relaxed to knowing just the immediate neighbors in G_s (i.e., 1-short-neighborhood) by invoking the `distribute-and-collect` method, presented in Lines 11–16, before the algorithm is executed. All messages sent during the first phase of the algorithm are sent via short edges. All messages sent during the second phase (calculation of MST at Line 10) are sent via long edges.

Algorithm 1. code for node i

1: **do**
2:     $\alpha[i] := \texttt{calc-alpha}(state)$ $\triangleright \alpha(i) = w(i)/\delta^*(i)$
3:     $\texttt{distribute-and-collect}(\alpha, 2k)$
4:     **if** $\alpha[i] < \min\{\alpha[j] \mid j \in N_{2k}(i) \wedge \alpha[j] \neq \bot\}$ **then** $state[i] := marked$
5:     $\texttt{distribute-and-collect}(state, k)$
6:     **if** $state[j] = marked$ for any $j \in N_k(i)$ **then** $state[i] := covered$
7:     $\texttt{distribute-and-collect}(state, k)$
8: **while** $state[j] = uncovered$ for any $j \in N_k(i) \cup \{i\}$
9: broadcast $done$ to all neighbors

10: run the MST algorithm of [9]

$\texttt{distribute-and-collect}(array, \ radius):$
11: **foreach** q in $[1,2,...,radius]$ **do**
12:     broadcast $array$ to all neighbors
13:     receive $array_j$ from all $j \in N_1(i)$ s.t. $done[j] = false$
14:     **foreach** node l at distance q in G_s from i **do**
15:         **if** $\exists j \in N_1(i)$ s.t. $done[j] = false \wedge$ node l at distance $q - 1$ in G_s from j **then**
16:             $array_i[l] = array_j[l]$

when $done$ is received from j:
17: $done[j] = true$
18: $\alpha[j] = \bot$

The following lemma summarizes the properties of the distributed algorithm. It refers to $n_{ds} = |kWDS|$ as the number of nodes in the set found by the algorithm at the end of the first phase. The proof of the lemma is omitted due to lack of space.

Lemma 2. *Algorithm 1 approximates a solution to the $kWCDS$ problem with a performance ratio of $k \ln \delta_s (1 + 2k\frac{w_{max}}{w_{min}})$ in $O(kn_{ds})$ time, using $O(kn_{ds}(n_{ds} + n)))$ messages.*

5.2 Algorithm 2

The distributed algorithm presented in the previous section gathers information from nodes at distance $2k$ in each iteration, which causes it to send relatively many messages, especially in dense networks, and makes it very vulnerable to failures of nodes. In addition, we notice that, empirically, most of the $kWCDS$ set is constructed during the first iteration of the algorithm, while following iterations, although involving considerable portion of nodes, do not contribute significantly to the set.

As a result, we propose a simple modification for the algorithm, in which the $\alpha(v)$ parameter is calculated by each node v only once and distributed before the first iteration of the algorithm. This distribution is made at radius k, as opposed to $2k$ in the original version. Consequently, the decision whether a node should join the set considers only neighbors at distance k. Note that every node joining the set in the original algorithm at the first iteration, does so also in the modified algorithm at its first iteration. This

Table 1. Density vs. number of nodes

# of nodes	density (nodes/km^2)	# of WiFi neighbors per node (avg.)	# of BT neighbors per node (avg.)
200	800	21.11	0.22
1000	4000	105.26	1.22
2000	8000	209.48	2.46
3000	12000	314.99	3.71
4000	16000	419.23	4.92

is because if a node has the smallest α among all of its neighbors at distance $2k$, it obviously has the smallest α within all of its neighbors at distance k. Consequently, one can expect that the approximation ratio of the modified algorithm will be higher but close to that of the original algorithm. In addition, the number of messages distributed by the modified algorithm is expected to be lower compared to the original algorithm, especially when the number of iterations is high.

The complexity properties of Algorithm 2 are summarized in the following lemma. Its proof is similar to the proof of Lemma 2.

Lemma 3. *Algorithm 2 approximates a solution to the $kWCDS$ problem in $O(kn_{ds})$ time, using $O(kn_{ds}(n_{ds} + n)))$ messages.*

6   Simulation Results

We assume a simulation area of size $500\text{x}500m^2$. Nodes are assigned random locations in the simulation area. Their weights are chosen randomly from $(0, 1)$ range. The number of nodes varies from 200 to 4000 in steps of 200. The long transmission range (R) is set to $100m$, while the short transmission range (r) is set to $10m$. These numbers are taken according to the nominal transmission ranges of WiFi and BT technologies, as reported in [8]. The parameter of the $kWCDS$ problem (k) is set to one of the values 1, 3, 5, 7 and 9. Every reported result is achieved by taking an average over 10 experiments run with the same settings.

We compared the performance of the first phases of the two proposed distributed algorithms (these phases calculate a $kWDS$ set). To complete the picture and compare the performance of full solutions for the $kWCDS$ problem, we also implemented the MST algorithm by Gallager et al. [9]. In addition, we compared the performance of Algorithm 1 with the naïve $1WCDS$ approach presented in Section 3; the implementation of the latter is based on the weighted CDS algorithm presented in [11]. The performance metrics we considered were the total weight of the $kWCDS$ sets constructed by the two algorithms and the number of messages sent by the algorithms in the first phase only and in the full solution (including MST).

Table 1 presents some density properties of our experiments as a function of the number of nodes. As nodes are distributed uniformly, the rest of the data can be extrapolated using the linear ratio between the presented values and the number of nodes.

Figures 3(a) and 3(b) present the weight of the $kWCDS$ set obtained by the naïve $1WCDS$ algorithm and by Algorithm 1 for different values of k, as a total value and as a percentage of the total weight of nodes, respectively. The naïve approach heavily

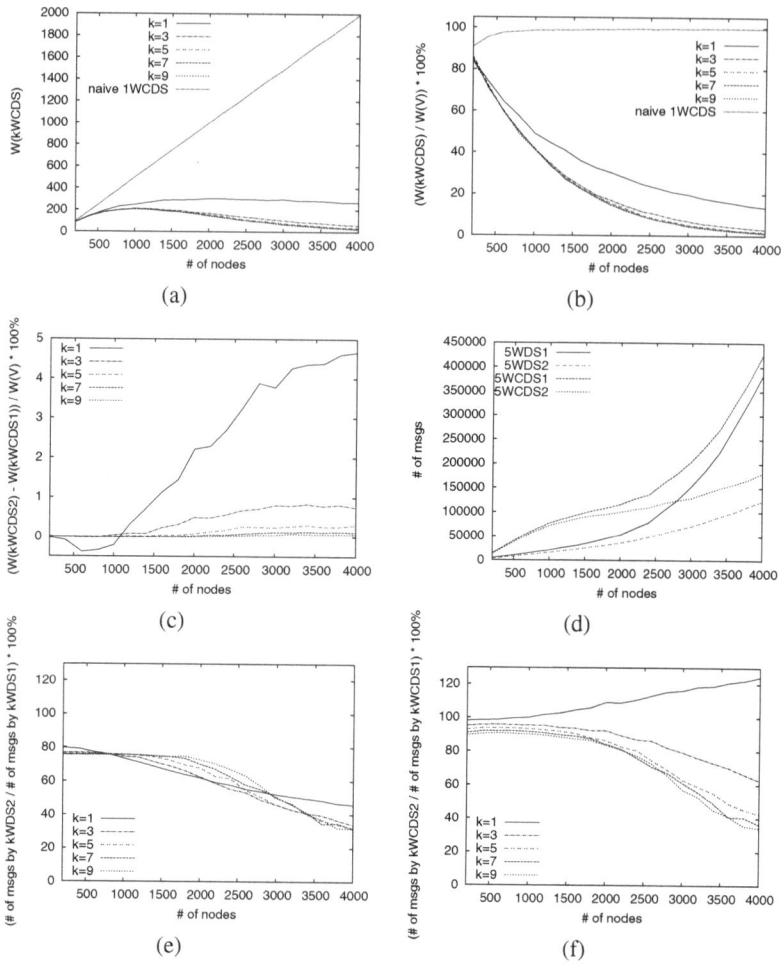

Fig. 3. (a), (b), (c): Approximation performance of Algorithm 1 with different k's compared to naïve $1WCDS$ algorithm ((a) and (b)) and to Algorithm 2 ((c)). W(X) stands for the total weight of nodes in the set X. (**d**): The number of messages sent by Algorithm 1 and Algorithm 2, when run with $k = 5$, in the first phase ($5WDS1$ for Algorithm 1 and $5WDS2$ for Algorithm 2) and in both phases ($5WCDS1$ and $5WCDS2$, respectively). (**e**), (**f**): Percentage of messages sent by the first phase (both phases, respectively) of Algorithm 2 from the number of messages sent by the first phase (both phases, respectively) of Algorithm 1.

overestimates the weight of the $1WCDS$ set. This happens since this approach selects an approximately constant number of nodes to CDS (this number can be estimated by the field area divided by the area covered by WiFi transmission). Thus, only a small and constant fraction of nodes located close to nodes in CDS are excluded from $1WCDS$. On the other hand, the percentage of the weight of the $kWCDS$ sets produced by Algorithm 1 drops as the number of nodes is increased. Additionally, for the large number of nodes and $k \geq 3$, the weight of the $kWCDS$ set gradually reduces. This means that adding more nodes to the system creates an even more power-efficient topology (to a large extent, Figure 3(b) predicts the energy that could be saved). This happens because dense networks are less partitioned at the BT level.

Another observation from Figure 3(b) is that when the number of nodes is below 2000 and $k \geq 5$, the weight of the $kWCDS$ set is insensitive to further increases in k. A possible explanation could be that when the network is sparse at the BT level, further increase in k does not result in larger $2k$-short-neighborhoods from which more optimal nodes could be selected. When the network becomes dense, however, the relative weight of the $kWCDS$ set does not justify further increase in k, as it will not change the weight of the set dramatically (e.g., for 4000 nodes, the weight of nodes in $5WCDS$ is only 1.98% of the total weight, while the weight of nodes in $9WCDS$ is 1.24%). This result is significant, as it indicates that there is no need to increase k (and as a side-effect, produce longer paths of short edges, increasing the communication latency) in order to create lighter $kWCDS$ sets and save more power. Additionally, as our analysis in Section 4.2 suggests, smaller values for k increase the probability that the $kWDS$ set found by the first phase of the algorithms will already be connected, and thus, the MST phase could be eliminated. This theoretical analysis is verified by our simulations: all $kWDS$ sets produced by both Algorithm 1 and 2 in all experiments were connected.

Figure 3(c) compares the approximation performance of Algorithm 1 and 2. For fewer than 1400 nodes, the performance of both algorithms is very similar: the ratio between the difference of weights of the $kWCDS$ sets found by Algorithm 2 and Algorithm 1 and between the total weight tends to 0 and does not depend on k. As the number of nodes grows, Algorithm 1 performs slightly better, with a clear correlation between k and the relative approximation performance.

Figure 3(d) presents the number of messages sent by both algorithms when run with $k = 5$, during the first phase and during both phases. For fewer than 2000 nodes, the number of messages sent by both algorithms is roughly linear in the number of nodes. This is because in sparse networks, both algorithms converge fast. For larger numbers of nodes, Algorithm 1 incurs a steeper increase in the number of messages, since it requires more iterations to converge in denser networks, as it considers larger neighborhoods.

Figures 3(e) and 3(f) present a comparison of the number of messages sent by both algorithms in their first phase only and in the full solution (including the MST phase), respectively. Along with Figure 3(c), they expose a trade-off existing between the two proposed algorithms in the weight of the produced $kWCDS$ set vs. the number of sent messages. When only the first phase is considered (Figure 3(e)), the number of messages sent by Algorithm 2 is below 80% of the number of messages sent by Algorithm 1, reducing to as low as 31.6% as the number of nodes grows. The reduction occurs due to larger k-short-neighborhoods resulting in a higher number of iterations required by both algorithms to complete their first phase. Consequently, the modification made in Algorithm 2 plays a more significant role.

When messages sent by the MST phase are also considered (Figure 3(f)), the savings produced by Algorithm 2 in the number of sent messages are still significant for $k \geq 3$, especially for large number of nodes. This is because in dense networks, as Figure 3(d) suggests, the number of messages sent in the first phase is much larger than the number of messages sent in the second phase. Thus, better performance in the first phase of

Algorithm 2 (in the number of sent messages, as shown in Figure 3(e)) is very significant. For $k = 1$ and large number of nodes, Algorithm 2 sends more messages than its
counterpart. This is because the $1WDS$ sets produced by the first phase of Algorithm 2
are considerably larger (and heavier, as shown in Figure 3(c)) than those produced by
Algorithm 1, requiring more messages to be sent by the MST phase.

7   Discussion

We proposed a new optimization problem for wireless ad hoc networks whose devices
are equipped with two wireless interfaces having different properties (e.g., transmission range and power consumption). A solution to this problem defines a topology
where some nodes turn off their power-hungry interface, while every node still remains connected to the rest of the network by at least one interface. We provided two
distributed algorithms that approximate an optimal solution for the problem; the first
has a proven approximation factor, while the second implements a simple heuristic
approach without a formally proven approximation bound. Empiric evaluation shows
that when the network is dense, both algorithms enable a large portion of nodes to
turn one of their radios off, leading to potentially significant power savings and longer
battery life.

Our simulations also reveal that for practical network densities, the heuristic protocol produces overlays comparable to ones produced by the first protocol, yet requiring
significantly less communication. In extremely dense networks, the overlays produced
by the first protocol are more effective at the price of excessive number of messages
when compared to the heuristic protocol. Additionally, we have also found that using small values for k (e.g., $k = 5$) is enough to create a power efficient topology,
and no further increase in k would help significantly. This result is encouraging, since
large values of k may increase the communication latency and decrease the network
capacity.

Although we considered devices with two interfaces only, the optimization problem
can be easily extended to an arbitrary number of interfaces in a recursive way. Suppose every device in a network has m interfaces. The $k_1 k_2 ... k_{m-1} WCDS$ problem is
to find a set $\{S_1 = V, S_2, S_3, ..., S_m\}$ of subsets of nodes, so that every node in S_i,
$1 \leq i \leq m - 1$, is in S_{i+1} or is at distance of at most k_i edges (of interface i)
from some node in S_{i+1}, and all nodes in S_m are connected by edges of interface m.
A solution for the $k_1 k_2 ... k_{m-1} WCDS$ problem can be developed from an iterative application of the proposed solution for the $kWCDS$ problem: Define S_1 to contain all
nodes in the network and run one of our algorithms considering only edges of interface
1 and m; the output of the algorithm is S_2. Next, apply the algorithm on nodes in S_2
and consider only edges of interface 2 and m. This will give S_3; and so on.

Recall that Jia et al. [13] have shown a randomized approximation algorithm for the
weighted dominating set problem with a fast running time. It might be interesting to
probabilistically improve the running time of our solution for $kWCDS$ by extending
their work to solve the $kWDS$ problem. Due to the analysis in Section 4.2, the resulting
approach would provide probabilistic guarantees on the connectivity of the resulting set
and would have a polylogarithmic running time, both w.h.p..

References

1. Bahl, P., Adya, A., Padhye, J., Walman, A.: Reconsidering wireless systems with multiple radios. ACM SIGCOMM Comput. Commun. Rev. 34(5), 39–46 (2004)
2. Blum, J., Ding, M., Thaeler, A., Cheng, X.: Connected dominating set in sensor networks and MANETs. In: Handbook of Combinatorial Optimization, pp. 329–369 (2005)
3. Chen, B., Jamieson, K., Balakrishnan, H., Morris, R.: Span: An energy-efficient coordination algorithm for topology maintenance in ad hoc wireless networks. ACM Wireless Networks Journal, 85–96 (2001)
4. Chen, Y.P., Liestman, A.L.: Approximating minimum size weakly-connected dominating sets for clustering mobile ad hoc networks. In: Proc. ACM MobiHoc, pp. 165–172 (2002)
5. Chvatal, V.: A greedy heuristic for the set-covering problem. Math. of Operations Research 4(3), 233–235 (1979)
6. Dubhashi, D., Mei, A., Panconesi, A., Radhakrishnan, J., Srinivasan, A.: Fast distributed algorithms for (weakly) connected dominating sets and linear-size skeletons. J. of Computer and System Sciences 71(4), 467–479 (2005)
7. Feeney, L.M., Nilsson, M.: Investigating the energy consumption of a wireless network interface in an ad hoc networking environment. In: INFOCOM, pp. 1548–1557 (2001)
8. Ferro, E., Potorti, F.: Bluetooth and Wi-Fi wireless protocols: a survey and a comparison. IEEE Wireless Communications 12(1), 12–26 (2005)
9. Gallager, R.G., Humblet, P.A., Spira, P.M.: A distributed algorithm for minimum-weight spanning trees. ACM Trans. Program. Lang. Syst. 5(1), 66–77 (1983)
10. Gomez, J., Campbell, A.: Variable-range transmission power control in wireless ad hoc networks. IEEE Transactions on Mobile Computing 6(1), 87–99 (2007)
11. Guha, S., Khuller, S.: Approximation algorithms for connected dominating sets. Algorithmica 20, 374–387 (1998)
12. Han, B., Jia, W.: Clustering wireless ad hoc networks with weakly connected dominating set. J. Parallel Distrib. Comput. 67(6), 727–737 (2007)
13. Jia, L., Rajaraman, R., Suel, T.: An efficient distributed algorithm for constructing small dominating sets. In: Proc. ACM PODC, pp. 33–42 (2001)
14. Kirousis, L.M., Kranakis, E., Krizanc, D., Pelc, A.: Power consumption in packet radio networks. Theoretical Computer Science 243(1-2), 289–305 (2000)
15. Kuhn, F., Moscibroda, T., Wattenhofer, R.: What cannot be computed locally? In: Proc. ACM PODC, pp. 300–309 (2004)
16. Kuhn, F., Wattenhofer, R.: Constant-time distributed dominating set approximation. In: Proc. ACM PODC, pp. 25–32 (2003)
17. Li, L., Halpern, J.Y., Bahl, P., Wang, Y.-M., Wattenhofer, R.: Analysis of a cone-based distributed topology control algorithm for wireless multi-hop networks. In: Proc. ACM PODC, pp. 264–273 (2001)
18. Pering, T., Agarwal, Y., Gupta, R., Power, C.: Coolspots: Reducing the power consumption of wireless mobile devices with multiple radio interfaces. In: Proc. ACM MOBISYS, pp. 220–232 (2006)
19. Sinha, P., Sivakumar, R., Bharghavan, V.: Enhancing ad hoc routing with dynamic virtual infrastructures. In: Proc. INFOCOM, pp. 1763–1772 (2001)
20. Sivakumar, R., Das, B., Bharghavan, V.: Spine routing in ad hoc networks. Cluster Computing 1(2), 237–248 (1998)
21. Wu, J., Dai, F., Gao, M., Stojmenovic, I.: On calculating power-aware connected dominating sets for efficient routing in ad hoc wireless networks. J. Communications and Networks, 59–70 (2002)
22. Xu, Y., Heidemann, J., Estrin, D.: Geography-informed energy conservation for ad hoc routing. In: Proc. MOBICOM, pp. 70–84 (2001)

Adversarial Multiple Access Channel with Individual Injection Rates

Lakshmi Anantharamu[1], Bogdan S. Chlebus[1], and Mariusz A. Rokicki[2,*]

[1] Department of Computer Science and Engineering, University of Colorado Denver, Denver, CO 80217, U.S.A.
[2] Department of Computer Science, University of Liverpool, Liverpool L69 3BX, U.K.

Abstract. We study deterministic distributed broadcasting on a synchronous multiple-access channel. Packets are injected into stations by a window-type adversary that is constrained by an individual injection rate of each station and a window w. We investigate what queue sizes and packet latency can be achieved with the maximum throughput of one packet per round. A protocol knows the number n of all the stations but does not know the window nor the individual rates of stations. We study the power of full sensing and acknowledgment based protocols as compared to general adaptive ones. We show that individual injection rates make it possible to achieve bounded packet latency by full sensing protocols, what is in contrast with the model of global injection rates for which stability and finite waiting times are not achievable together by general protocols. We show that packet latency is $\Omega\left(w \frac{\log n}{\log w}\right)$ when $w \leq n$ and it is $\Omega(w)$ when $w > n$. We give a full sensing protocol for channels with collision detection and an adaptive one for channels without collision detection that achieve $\mathcal{O}(\min(n + w, w \log n))$ packet latency. We develop a full sensing protocol for a channel without collision detection that achieves $\mathcal{O}(n + w)$ queues and $\mathcal{O}(nw)$ packet latency.

1 Introduction

We study performance of broadcast protocols on multiple access channels in the framework of adversarial queuing. Packets are injected into stations by a window-type adversary that is restricted by an injection rate and a window w. Adversarial queuing for multiple access channels, as introduced in [11,12], concerned adversaries determined by global injection rates for all the stations. We consider individual rates: the adversary's aggregate injection rate is partitioned into separate rates assigned to individual stations.

The performance of a broadcast protocol is normally measured in terms of packet delay and queue sizes. The weakest expectation about the time spent by packets in the system is that it is not infinite, so that every packet is eventually successfully transmitted: this is called fairness in [11,12]. Packet latency denotes

* This work was supported by the Engineering and Physical Sciences Research Council Grant EP/G023018/1.

T. Abdelzaher, M. Raynal, and N. Santoro (Eds.): OPODIS 2009, LNCS 5923, pp. 174–188, 2009.

the maximum time any packet spends in a queue. Stability means that the number of packets stored in local queues is bounded in all rounds. The throughput of a protocol is the maximum rate for which it is stable. General protocols may use control bits piggybacked on transmitted packets. We use the terminology introduced in [11,12]: protocols that do not use control bits are called full sensing while those that use control bits are called adaptive.

Our results. We study the worst-case performance of broadcasting when traffic demands are specified as adversarial environments modeled by window adversaries with individual injection rates associated with stations and when protocols are both distributed and deterministic. We allow the adversaries to be such that the associated aggregate injection rate (the sum of all the individual rates) is 1, which is the maximum that allows for stability. The goal is to explore what quality of service can be achieved for individual injection rates and compare the adversarial environments defined by individual rates with global ones, under maximum broadcast loads of 1 packet per round. The underlying motivation for this work was that individual injection rates are more realistic in moderate time spans and hopefully the limitations on quality of service with throughput 1 discovered in [12] would not hold when the rates are individual. Indeed, bounded packet latency turns out to be achievable with individual injection rates when the aggregate rate is 1. This is in contrast with global injection rates for which achieving finite waiting times is impossible for throughput 1, as was shown in [12].

We prove upper and lower bounds on queue size and packet latency, which depend on the classes of protocols and whether collision detection is available or not. The most restricted acknowledgment based protocols cannot achieve throughput 1, which strengthens the result for global injection rates [12]. We give a protocol of $\mathcal{O}(\min(n + w, w \log n))$ packet latency when collision detection is available. An adaptive protocol can achieve similar performance, as we show that control bits allow to simulate collision detection with a constant overhead per round. A bounded packet latency can be achieved by full sensing protocols in channels without collision detection: we develop a protocol with $\mathcal{O}(n + w)$ size queues and $\mathcal{O}(nw)$ packet latency. The optimality of our full sensing protocol for channels without collision detection in terms of packet latency is left open.

Related work. The previous work on dynamic broadcasting in multiple-access channels has been mostly carried out under the assumption that packets were injected subject to stochastic constraints. Such systems can be modeled as Markov chains with stability understood as ergodicity. Alternatively, stability may mean that throughput equals the injection rate. Popular early broadcast protocols like Aloha [1] and binary exponential backoff [22] have been extensively studied with stochastic injection rates; Gallager [15] gives an overview of early work in this direction. For recent papers, see the work by Goldberg, et al. [18,19], Håstad, et al. [21], and Raghavan and Upfal [23]. Stability of backoff protocols for multiple-access channels with packet injection controlled by a window adversary was studied by Bender, et al. [9] in the queue-free model: they showed that exponential backoff is stable for $\mathcal{O}(1/\log n)$ arrival rates and unstable for arrival rates of $\Omega(\log \log n/\log n)$. Awerbuch, et al. [8] developed a randomized protocol for multiple-access channels competing against an adaptive jamming adversary that achieves a constant throughput for the non-jammed rounds.

Adversarial queueing as a methodology to study the performance of deterministic distributed broadcast protocols for multiple-access channels in the model with queues was introduced by Chlebus, et al. [11]. They defined latency to be fair when it was $\mathcal{O}(\text{burstiness/rate})$ and stability to be strong when queues were $\mathcal{O}(\text{burstiness})$, with burstiness understood as the maximum number of packets that can be injected in a round. It was shown in [11] that no protocol could be strongly stable for $\omega(\frac{1}{\log n})$ rates and full sensing protocols achieving fair latency for $\mathcal{O}(1/\text{polylog } n)$ rates were given. In a subsequent work, Chlebus, et al.[12] investigated the quality of service for the maximum throughput, that is, the maximum rate for which stability is achievable. They developed a stable protocol with $\mathcal{O}(n^2 + \text{burstiness})$ queues against adversaries of injection rate 1, which means that throughput 1 is achievable. They also showed limitations of throughput 1: achieving fairness is impossible, queues need to be $\Omega(n^2 + \text{burstiness})$, and protocols need to be adaptive.

Adversarial queuing has been used as a methodology to capture the notion of stability of protocols without statistical assumptions about injection rates in store-and-forward routing. Borodin, et al. [10] proposed this first in the context of greedy contention-resolution routing protocols. The subsequent work by Andrews, et al. [4] concentrated on the notion of universal stability, which for a protocol denotes stability in any network, and for a network denotes stability of an arbitrary protocol executed by the network, both properties to hold under injection rates less than 1. Álvarez, et al. [2] applied adversarial models to capture phenomena related to routing with varying priorities of packets and to study their impact on universal stability. Andrews and Zhang [7] gave a universal protocol to control traffic when nodes operate as switches that need to reserve the suitable input and output ports to move a packet from the input port to the respective output one. Álvarez, et al. [3] addressed the stability of protocols in networks with links prone to failures with adversarial modeling of failures. Andrews and Zhang [5] studied adversarial traffic in networks where nodes represent switches connecting inputs with outputs so that routed packets encounter additional congestion constrains at nodes when they compete with other packets for input and output ports. Andrews and Zhang [6] studied routing in wireless networks when data arrivals and transmission rates are governed by an adversary.

Gilbert, et al. [17] proposed to model disruptive interference in multi-channel single-hop networks by a jamming adversary. This was further investigated by Dolev, et al. [14] who considered restricted gossiping in which a constant fraction of rumors needs to be disseminated when the adversary can disrupt one frequency per round, Gilbert, et al. [16] who studied gossiping in which the adversary can disrupt up to t frequencies per round and eventually all but t nodes learn all but t rumors, and by Dolev, et al. [13] who considered synchronization of a multi-channel under adversarial jamming.

2   Preliminaries

The letter n denotes the number of stations attached to a channel. Each station has a unique integer name in the range between 1 and n.

Properties of multiple-access channels. A channel operates synchronously: an execution of a protocol is structured as a sequence of rounds. It takes one round for a station to transmit a messages. A message successfully received by a station is said to be *heard* by the station. A broadcast system is a *multiple-access channel* if communication is governed on the logical level by the following two rules: (1) a message transmitted by a station is delivered to all the stations in the same round, and (2) a transmitted message is heard by all stations if and only if its transmission does not overlap in time with any other transmissions.

Multiplicity of transmissions determines three cases: When no stations transmit in a round, then such a round is *silent*, and *silence* is what the stations receive then from the channel as feedback. When exactly one station transmits in a round, then the message is heard by all the stations in the same round. Multiple transmission in the same round result in a *conflict for access* to the channel, which is called *collision*. When a collision occurs, then no station can hear any message. The channel is *with collision detection* when the feedback from the channel allows the stations to distinguish between silence and collision, otherwise the channel is *without collision detection*. If no collision detection mechanism is available, then stations perceive collision as silence.

Adversaries. An *adversary* generates a number of packets in each round and next, for each packet, assigns a station to inject the packet in this round. We define the *burstiness* of an adversary to be the number of packets that can be injected into the system in the same round. An adversary is defined by constraints on the patterns of injection expressed in terms of injection rates at stations and burstiness.

We consider constraints on adversaries formulated as restrictions on what can be injected separately at each station and also by what can be injected into all the stations combined. Constraints are *global* if they are determined only by the total numbers of packets injected in time intervals, without any concern about the stations the packets are injected into. Traffic constraints are *local* when the patterns of injection are considered separately and independently for each station. Constraints for the whole network implied by local ones are called *aggregate* in this paper, observe that this notion is weaker than global constraints. In particular, we may have local and global/aggregate burstiness, and local and global/aggregate injection rates. We refer to the adversaries defined only by global restrictions on injection rates as the model of *global injection rate*, these adversaries were used in [11,12]. In this paper we introduce adversaries of local injection rates.

We define *window adversaries with individual injection rates* as follows. Let there be given a positive integer number w called *window*. Each station i has its *share* s_i such that $\sum_{i=1}^{n} s_i \leq w$. The adversary may insert up to s_i packets into station i in every time interval of w contiguous rounds. The *local injection rate* of station i is defined to be $\rho_i = s_i/w$ and the *aggregate injection rate* denotes $\rho = (\sum_{i=1}^{n} s_i)/w$. We refer to such a window adversary as being of *local type* $(\langle s_i \rangle_{1 \le i \le n}, w)$ and of *aggregate type* (ρ, w). The notion of aggregate type is similar to that of global type as considered in [11,12]. For a window adversary of local type $(\langle s_i \rangle_{1 \le i \le n}, w)$ with aggregate rate ρ, the *local burstiness at station i* is its share s_i and the *aggregate* one is $\delta = \sum_{i=1}^{n} s_i$, so that $\rho = \delta/w$.

Broadcast protocols. Each station has its packets stored in a local queue. We use protocols with FIFO queuing.

When stations execute a protocol, then the *state of a station* is determined by the values of its private variables. A protocol knows the number n of all the stations, in the sense that is may be a part of code as a constant, but it does not know the window nor the individual rates of an adversary. The contents of packets do not affect execution of a broadcasting protocol, as packets are treated as abstract tokens. A *message* may include a packet and control bits. For instance, a protocol may attach an 'over' bit to a transmitted packet to indicate that the station will not transmit in the next round. A message of only control bits is legitimate.

A protocol is formally defined by what constitutes states and rules governing transitions between states. An *event* in a round consists of the following actions at each station in the order given: (1) the station either performs a transmission or pauses, as determined by its state, (2) the station receives a feedback from the channel, in the form of either hearing a message with contents or collision or silence, (3) new packets are injected into the station, (4) a state transition occurs.

A state transition is determined by the state at the end of the previous round, the packets injected in the round, and the feedback from the channel in the round. State transitions involve the following operations: Injected packets are immediately enqueued by a station. A transmitted packet is discarded and a new packet to transmit is obtained by dequeuing the queue. If a message is to be transmitted in the next round, then it is prepared as a part of state transition. An *execution* of a protocol is a sequence of events occurring in consecutive rounds.

Natural subclasses of deterministic protocols for adversarial settings in multiple access channel were defined in [11,12], we use the same classification. We call a protocol *full sensing* when additional control bits are never used in messages. A general protocol that is not full sensing is called *adaptive*; such protocols may send control bits in messages.

A protocol is *acknowledgment based* if the question whether the currently handled packet is to be transmitted in a given round is decided depending only on which consecutive round it is that the station is working on the packet to be broadcast, counting from the first round assigned to the packet. An acknowledgment based protocol can be interpreted as determined by an unbounded binary sequence assigned to each station and interpreted as follows: if the ith bit is a 1, then the station transmits the currently processed packet in the ith round, counting from the first round when the packet was started to be processed, while a 0 as the ith bit makes the station pause in the ith round. Such a sequence is called the *transmission sequence* of the station.

A protocol is *conflict free* if in any execution in any round at most one station transmits. A protocol that is not conflict free is called *conflict prone*.

Stability occurs when the total number of packets in queues at the stations is bounded in all rounds. *Packet latency* means the maximum length of time intervals spent by packets in queues waiting to be heard on the channel.

Design of protocols. For a given window adversary of local injection rates, station i is *active* when its share s_i is a positive number. Station i has been *discovered* in the course of an execution when a packet transmitted by i has been heard on the channel.

We describe two data structures used when stations work to discover their shares. In one approach, each station i has a private array C_i of n entries. The entry $C_i[j]$ stores an estimate of the share s_j of station j, for $1 \le j \le n$. Every station i will modify the entry $C_i[k]$ in a round in the same way as other stations do. Therefore we may drop the indices and refer to the entries of the arrays as $C[j]$ rather than as $C_i[j]$. The array C is initialized to $C[j] = 0$ for every $1 \le j \le n$. The sum $\gamma = \sum_{i=1}^{n} C[i]$ is an estimate of the aggregate burstiness $\delta = \sum_{i=1}^{n} s_i$. When station i enters a state implying $s_i > C[i]$ then i considers itself *underestimated*. Detecting underestimation is implemented by having every station keep track of the transmissions in the past γ rounds. When a station i detects that some $k > C[i]$ packets have been injected within some γ consecutive rounds, where k is maximum with this property so far, then i decides it is *underestimated by the amount* $k - C[i]$ in this round.

In another approach, each station i uses a list $D_i = \langle d_i(1), d_i(2), \ldots, d_i(\ell) \rangle$ of bits, where initially the lists are empty and the length ℓ is the same in all stations and it is $\ell \le w$ at all times. The lists are maintained so as to satisfy the following invariants: (1) for each station j, when $d_i(j)$ has been determined for all i, then for precisely one i it is a 1 and the others are 0's, (2) the number of occurrences of 1 at D_i has the same meaning as $C[i]$ and denotes the current estimate of the share of i. The number ℓ is an estimate on the burstiness of the adversary, similarly as γ for array C. We will use $C[i]$ to denote the number of occurrences of 1 in D_i, even when lists D are only used and arrays C are not explicitly maintained. If a protocol has the property that $C[i]$ is increased at most by the amount that station i considers to be underestimated by, then the inequality $C[i] \le s_i$ holds at all times, for every $1 \le i \le n$. Our protocols will have this property satisfied, and for them the inequality $\gamma \le \delta$ will hold.

We use arrays C when stations have global knowledge about the station for which an update of the current estimate of its share is to be performed. It may happen that such knowledge is lacking: an underestimated station transmits successfully but the other stations do not know which station transmitted: then we use lists D, as the transmitting stations can append 1 at the end of D while every other station appends 0. Our protocols have stations manipulate auxiliary lists. Whenever we use such lists, there is a *main pointer* associated with each list pointing at *current* entry. The main pointer either stays put in a round or it is advanced by one position in the round in a cyclic order of the list.

3   Impossibility and Lower Bounds

An acknowledgment based protocol is determined by having each station assigned its individual transmission sequence of 0's and 1's. The first bit in such a sequence needs to be 1, unless the protocol is unstable. To argue that this is the case, suppose otherwise that some station p has a transmission sequence starting with 0. When p starts to process a new packet, then p pauses for the first round, so an adversary that injects only into station p creates an infinite sequence of silent rounds. The resulting execution makes the protocol unstable if the injection rate of p is more than $1/2$.

Theorem 1. *No acknowledgement based protocol is stable even for two stations against window adversary of burstiness 2 and aggregate injection rate 1.*

Proof. Define a round to be *void* when no packet is heard in the round. Consider an acknowledgment protocol for two stations p and q and suppose it is stable. This implies that a station transmits a new packet immediately. We define an execution of the protocol with an infinite sequence $t_1, t_2, \ldots$ of rounds such that there are at least i void rounds by round t_i. The adversary will inject two packets in each odd-numbered round, a packet per station, and no packets in even-numbered rounds. This means that each station has its individual injection rate equal to $1/2$. There will be at least i packets in queues in round t_i.

Define t_1 to be the first round. This round is silent as stations did not have any packets prior to this round. A collision occurs in the second round: each station got a new packet in the first round, so it transmits immediately. Define t_2 to be the second round. We will have each round number t_i even for $i > 1$, which means in particular that the adversary does not inject packets in these rounds.

Suppose the execution has been determined through an even round t_i. If $t_i + 1$ is void then define $t_{i+1} = t_i + 2$. Otherwise some station, say p, transmits in round $t_i + 1$. Station p will continue transmitting for as long as it has packets, because it transmits a new packet immediately. If in one such a round t station q transmits concurrently with p, then this results in a collision and we define t_{i+1} to be t if t is even or $t + 1$ otherwise. Suppose this is not the case, so p keeps transmitting alone. At some round after $t_i + 1$ station p will not have a packet to transmit, since its injection rate is $1/2$: let $t' > t_i + 1$ be the first such a round. Observe that t' has to be odd as otherwise a new packet would have got injected into p in round $t' - 1$ so p would have a packet to transmit in round t'. If q does not transmit in round t', then this round t' is silent and we are done: define t_{i+1} to be $t' + 1$, as this round number is even. Otherwise q transmits in round t' successfully. Simultaneously both stations obtain new packets in round t', so each has at least one available packet at the end of this round. Each station transmits in round $t' + 1$, as for each of them it is a first round of processing a new packet. This is because p did not have a packet in round t' and q transmitted in round t'. Define t_{i+1} to be the void round $t' + 1$. This completes the inductive construction of the sequence t_i and by this produces a contradiction with the assumption that the protocol is stable.   □

Theorem 2. *For any protocol for a system of n stations for an adversary of window w, packet latency is $\Omega\left(w \frac{\log n}{\log w}\right)$ when $w \leq n$ and it is $\Omega(w)$ when $w > n$, in some execution of the protocol.*

Proof. For $w \leq n$ we consider adversaries for which each station has share equal to either 0 or 1. Greenberg and Winograd [20] considered a static version of the broadcast problem in which some k packets are located initially among $k \leq n$ stations, at most a packet per station, and the goal is to have all packets heard on the channel. They showed that for any protocol it takes $\Omega\left(k \frac{\log n}{\log k}\right)$ time to achieve this goal for some execution of the protocol. Protocols that we use handle dynamic broadcast, but can be applied to the static version. A translation to the static version of broadcast is straightforward: let the adversary inject w packets in the first round, at most one packet per station. When $w > n$, then the adversary may inject w packets in the first round and it takes $\Omega(w+n) = \Omega(w)$ rounds to hear them all. □

Theorem 3. *For any conflict free protocol for n stations there is an execution in which a packet is delayed by $\Omega(nw)$ rounds against a window adversary with $w = \Theta(n)$ and an aggregate injection rate less than 1.*

Proof. Let $n = k + 3$ for a positive integer k. Take an arbitrary conflict free protocol for n stations and an adversary with $w = k + 2 = n - 1$. Declare one station to be *heavy* and the remaining ones to be *mavericks*. The share of the heavy station is k, and one of the mavericks has 1 as its share, so the cumulative injection rate is $(k+1)/(k+2) < 1$. Partition an execution into disjoint segments of consecutive $(k + 1)(k + 2)$ rounds. Consider an execution $\mathcal{E}_1$ in which the adversary injects only into the heavy station: k packets per $k + 2$ consecutive rounds, for a total of $k(k + 2)$ packets during each segment. This leaves a room for $k + 2$ "exploratory" rounds during a segment of $\mathcal{E}_1$, available to locate the maverick with a positive share. The idea is that a protocol cannot locate such a maverick without incurring a $\Omega(n^2)$ delay. We specify an execution $\mathcal{E}_2$ which has the same prefix as $\mathcal{E}_1$ until the first injection into a maverick. Suppose there is a segment S of $\mathcal{E}_1$ in which less than $k + 2$ mavericks are scheduled to transmit. Take an execution $\mathcal{E}_2$ in which the adversary injects into a maverick that is not scheduled to transmit in S in the round just before S is to begin. This packet waits $(k + 1)(k + 2)$ rounds. Otherwise, suppose every maverick is scheduled to transmit at least once during every segment of $\mathcal{E}_1$. If some maverick is scheduled to transmit more than once, then the number of packets in the heavy station increases during this segment. If only such segments are in $\mathcal{E}_1$ then the protocol is unstable and packet delays are arbitrarily large. Otherwise there is a segment S during which each maverick is scheduled to transmit exactly once. Partition S into first and second halves, each of $(k+1)(k+2)/2$ rounds. If the last maverick is to transmit in the first half, then consider $\mathcal{E}_2$ in which the adversary injects into this last maverick just after its scheduled transmission in S. If the last maverick is to transmit in the second half, then consider $\mathcal{E}_2$ in which the adversary injects into this last maverick just before S is to begin. In both cases the packet injected into the last maverick will wait for at least $(k + 1)(k + 2)/2$ rounds. □

4   Two Protocols of Small Latency

In this section we show that if either collision detection is available or control bits can be sent in messages, then protocols with packet latency that is close to optimal can be developed.

Full sensing with collision detection. We develop full sensing protocol UPGRADE-COLLISION that uses collision detection to provide small latency. This protocol in turn uses two protocols BINARY-SEARCH-COLLISION and CYCLIC-UPDATE-COLLISION executed in sequence. A station i uses list D_i of bits to implement its estimate of shares. Initially the list D_i is empty. A station i that upgrades its share appends a 1 to the end of its list D_i while all the other stations appends a 0 to their lists. The lists D_i are used to structure transmissions as follows: the station whose current entry in D_i is a 1 transmits while the others pause.

UPGRADE-COLLISION begins by invoking BINARY-SEARCH-COLLISION. A count of the number of collisions heard is maintained throughout an execution. If the total count of collisions reaches n then protocol BINARY-SEARCH-COLLISION terminates and CYCLIC-UPDATE-COLLISION takes over.

Protocol BINARY-SEARCH-COLLISION works as follows. The protocol runs a main thread that uses the lists D_i with the pointers advanced cyclically. Any underestimated station becomes *persistent* in the sense that it keeps transmitting as long as it has packets with the only exception when being scheduled to transmit in the main thread. This continues as long as silence or a packet are heard. If a collision occurs then the main thread pauses for a duration of binary-search thread and resumes only after the binary-search thread terminates; in particular, the main pointers associated with lists D_i are not advanced while the main thread pauses. Binary-search thread is performed over all the stations using intervals of names of stations, starting with the interval of $[1, n]$ comprising all the names. At each step only stations in the current interval that want to upgrade their shares transmit. If a collision is heard then the interval is partitioned and processed recursively using a stack. The left interval is pursued first while the right interval is pushed on the stack. If a silence is heard for the current interval then such an interval is abandoned and the next interval is popped from the stack. If a packet is heard then a station that transmitted the packet withholds the channel and transmits a number of packets up to its share's upgrade followed by silence. Such a station appends a 1 to its list D_i for each such a transmission of a packet while the other stations append a 0 each. Binary-search thread terminates after the stack becomes empty. The main thread resumes after this.

Lemma 1. *Packet latency of* BINARY-SEARCH-COLLISION *is at most* $\mathcal{O}(w \log n)$ *when it is executed against an adversary of window w in a system of n stations.*

Proof. Packet delay may be caused by either the burstiness or the time spent to upgrade the shares. The former contributes at most w. The latter contributes at most $1 + \lg n$ per each upgrade, where $\lg n$ is the binary logarithm of n, and these void rounds for each share upgrade occur only once. As there are at most w upgrades, the total packet delay is at most $w(2 + \lg n)$.   □

Protocol CYCLIC-UPDATE-COLLISION operates as follows. There are two threads: main one and update one. Both the threads work concurrently unless paused for share upgrade. The main thread uses lists D: a station i that has a 1 as a current entry in its list D_i in a round transmits if it has a packet. The update thread works by using a cyclic list of the names of all the stations. A station that is current on this list is referred to as current in the thread. Such a station transmits only if it finds itself underestimated and has a packet to do so. If such a packet in update thread is heard then the station turns *persistent* in the sense that it keeps transmitting a packet in every round. A station that is persistent turns back to non-persistent if its queue becomes empty or if there is a collision or if it becomes current again in the update thread. There is only one persistent station at any time. If a collision is heard then both the main and update threads pause for share upgrade. Now the current station in update thread is given a chance to transmit. If it wants to upgrade its share then it transmits a number of times up to its share upgrade followed by silence. This is performed together with appending 1's to the list D_i of the transmitting station and 0's to such lists of the other stations, an entry for each transmission of a packet. After a silent round any persistent station is given a chance to upgrade its share. If such a station exists then it upgrades up to its share followed by a silent round, again with appending binary digits to lists D. After two silent rounds both the main thread and update one resume.

Lemma 2. *Packet latency of* CYCLIC-UPDATE-COLLISION *is at most* $q + 4w$ *when it is executed against an adversary of window* w *in a system of* n *stations with an initial queue of size* q.

Proof. Packet delay may be caused by either the original number of packets inherited in the queue or the burstiness or the time spent to upgrade shares. The queue contributes q and burstiness at most w. An update costs at most 3 void rounds: one collision and two silences. These void rounds for share upgrades happen only once. As there are at most w upgrades, the total packet delay is as claimed. □

Theorem 4. *Protocol* UPGRADE-COLLISION *provides* $\mathcal{O}(\min(n + w, w \log n))$ *packet latency for a channel with collision detection against an adversary of window* w *in a system of* n *stations.*

Proof. If protocol CYCLIC-UPDATE-COLLISION is not invoked, then packet latency is given by Lemma 1. When CYCLIC-UPDATE-COLLISION is invoked, then there are $\mathcal{O}(n)$ packets in queues in the round of invocation. Then $\mathcal{O}(n + w)$ becomes a bound given by Lemma 2, which now is an upper bound on packet latency. □

Adaptive without collision detection. Next we show how to simulate protocol UPGRADE-COLLISION to obtain an adaptive protocol when collision detection is not available. We call the simulating protocol UPGRADE-SILENCE as silences trigger upgrades of shares. This protocol simulates the two protocols in UPGRADE-COLLISION by running two simulating protocols BINARY-SEARCH-SILENCE and CYCLIC-UPDATE-SILENCE, respectively. The simulation proceeds as follows.

Regarding the main thread, a station without packets scheduled to transmit transmits a control bit to indicate this, rather than pause and make the round silent. So a silence occurs only when the modified protocol causes collision. The binary-search thread in BINARY-SEARCH-COLLISION relies on collision detection but now collision is heard as silence. We resolve in the next round $t+1$ if silence in round t during the binary-search thread is actually a silence or collision as follows: all the stations that transmitted in round t transmit together with station 1. Station 1 simply transmits a control bit in round $t + 1$. There are two possible events occurring in round $t + 1$: either silence or a message is heard. Silence indicates that more than one station transmitted, as station 1 transmitted: this means that there was collision in round t. If a message is heard in round $t+1$ then this means that round t was silent, as station 1 managed to have its transmission in round $t + 1$ heard. The simulation of CYCLIC-UPDATE-SILENCE proceeds similarly as of the main thread in BINARY-SEARCH-COLLISION.

Theorem 5. *Protocol* UPGRADE-SILENCE *gives* $\mathcal{O}(\min(n + w, w \log n))$ *packet latency for a channel without collision detection against an adversary of window w in a system of n stations.*

Proof. The simulation we employ results in a constant overhead per each round that contributes to packet latency of the simulated protocol. Therefore packet latency is of the order of a bound for the simulated protocol, which is as in Theorem 4.   □

5   Full Sensing without Collision Detection

We call COLORFUL-STATIONS a full sensing protocol for a channel without collision detection developed next. The protocol uses a list of discovered stations: a newly discovered active station is appended to the list, and there is a pointer associated with the list that is advanced in a cyclic manner. An execution of the protocol is structured to begin with a stage we call preparation, which is followed by iterated phases. A *phase* consists of three stages: a pure stage occurs first, it is followed by an update, and finally a makeup concludes the phase.

The *preparation* stage is organized such that every station has one round to transmit at a time, assigned in a round robin manner. A station with a packet available transmits one when the station's turn comes up, otherwise the station pauses during its time slot. The preparation terminates when the station that transmitted first is scheduled to transmit again. All stations i whose packets have been heard during the preparation become discovered and $C[i] \leftarrow 1$ is set.

During a *pure* stage, the discovered stations proceed through a sequence of transmissions, starting from the current station. Station i has a segment of consecutive $C[i] > 0$ rounds allotted for exclusive transmissions: it keeps transmitting as long as it has packets, otherwise station i pauses. The pointer is advanced, and the next station takes over, when either the current station i has used up the whole segment of $C[i]$ assigned rounds or just after station i did not transmit while scheduled to. Tokens are created and assigned to discovered stations during a pure stage. Every station keeps a list of the tokens and their assignments in its private memory and performs operations on tokens in exactly the same way as other stations. All operations on tokens are triggered by silences. When a station i holds a token, then the color *green* of the token indicates that the token was generated when i was silent during a round in a segment of $C[i]$ rounds allotted for i to transmit. The *red* color of a token held by station i indicates that it was some other station j, for $i \neq j$, that was silent during a round in a segment of $C[j]$ rounds allotted to j to transmit and which generated the token. A discovered station may hold either no token or a green one or a red one in a round. In the beginning of a pure stage no station holds a token. Let a station i be silent in a round assigned to i to transmit, which generates a token. If i does not hold a token yet, then the new token is colored green and it is assigned to i. If i already holds a green token, then the new token is colored red and it is assigned to the first available discovered station that does not hold a token yet, in the order of their names. If i holds a red token, then the new token is colored green, it is assigned to i, while the original red token held by i is reassigned to a discovered station that does not hold a token. A discovered station is *colored* by the color of the token it holds when an update begins. After every discovered station has gained a color, a pure stage terminates.

An *update* stage gives every station one opportunity to transmit exclusively for a contiguous segment of rounds. A station i that is underestimated by the amount x transmits x times which is followed by silence. This results in an immediate increment $C[i] \leftarrow C[i] + x$ at all stations. When a station simply pauses in the first round assigned to it, then the corresponding entry in the array C is not modified.

A *makeup* stage follows next. The red stations spend this stage working to unload their packets while the green stations pause. Red stations transmit in the cyclic order inherited from the list, starting from the current station if it is red or otherwise the next red one following the current station on the list. A red station i has a segment of consecutive $C[i]$ rounds allotted for exclusive transmissions. A silent round by a red station results in changing the color of the station to green and advancing the pointer to the next red station. A makeup stage concludes as soon as there are no red stations. Consider the beginning of a makeup stage, with all the discovered stations colored. Let G and R denote the sets of green and red stations, respectively. Let g be the sum $\sum_{i \in G} C[i] = g$ of the entries of the array C over the green stations, and r a similar sum $\sum_{i \in R} C[i] = r$ of the entries of the array C over the red stations, so that $g + r = \gamma$. We additionally require that makeup stage terminates after $3nr/g$ rounds.

When a packet is heard in a round, then the packet is dequeued while simultaneously at most one packet on the average could be inserted. It follows that such rounds contribute only to fluctuations of the queues by $\mathcal{O}(w)$ packets, as w is an upper bound on the burstiness, so we may restrict our attention to packets injected during silent rounds only when evaluating the size of queues. At most n silent rounds occur during the last n rounds of the preparation stage and during every following stage. For accounting purposes, we partition silent rounds into *blocks* defined as follows. The first block comprises the silences incurred during the last n rounds of the preparation, of the first pure stage and the first update stage. The next block consists of at most $3n$ silences incurred during the immediately following makeup, pure and update stages. This continues throughout the execution, a block comprising silences in consecutive makeup, pure and update stages. The idea is to show that a makeup stage takes care of the preceding block of silent rounds, in terms of compensating some stations for the time lost by not being allowed to transmit.

Lemma 3. *A makeup stage takes $\mathcal{O}(nw)$ rounds.*

Proof. We need to estimate the time by which all red stations go green. By the inequality $\gamma \leq \delta$, the sets G of green stations and R of red stations have had packets injected into them with the cumulative rates of at most g/γ and r/γ, respectively, during the current phase. Let us call *old* the packets injected into red stations during all silent update rounds of the preceding block. There are less than $3n \cdot \frac{r}{\gamma}$ old packets in the red stations when a makeup stage begins. Let us call *new* the packets injected into red stations during makeup rounds. The makeup rounds when the red stations transmit can be partitioned into disjoint segments of γ rounds each. During such a segment of γ rounds, the first r rounds may be considered as devoted to unloading new packets injected into red stations during this segment, while the remaining g rounds could be treated as unloading the old packets injected into red stations during the preceding block of silent rounds. There are less than $3n \cdot \frac{r}{\gamma}$ old packets. Handling them requires $3n \cdot \frac{r}{\gamma} \cdot \frac{1}{g}$ segments of length g each. Every such a segment is taken from a contiguous interval of γ makeup rounds. This is possible when at least

$$3n \cdot \frac{r}{\gamma} \cdot \frac{1}{g} \cdot \gamma = 3n \cdot \frac{r}{g} \tag{1}$$

makeup rounds are partitioned into such segments of length γ each. This bound is a part of code of the makeup stage. We have that bound (1) is at most $3nw$, as $r \leq \gamma \leq w$ and $g \geq 1$, so it is $\mathcal{O}(nw)$. $\qquad\square$

Theorem 6. *Queues are $\mathcal{O}(n + w)$ and packet latency is $\mathcal{O}(nw)$ when protocol* Colorful-Stations *is executed against adversaries of window w in systems of n stations.*

Proof. A packet injected at a phase is heard by the end of the next phase. For each station, its queue becomes empty at some point during each phase. This is because contributing a silence converts the station green. When all stations become such then a phase is over. There are less than $3n$ silent rounds during a phase. The fluctuation of the size of the queues due to these rounds is $\mathcal{O}(n + w)$. This means that queues are $\mathcal{O}(n + w)$. To estimate latency, let us examine each kind of stages. Take pure stages first. The inequality $\gamma \leq w$ holds by the inequality $\gamma \leq \delta$. We consider two cases. When $\gamma < w$, then a pure stage takes $\mathcal{O}(n + w)$ rounds. Otherwise, when $\gamma = w$, then there is no general upper bound on the duration of a pure stage. Observe however that a packet is delayed by $\mathcal{O}(n + w)$ rounds during such a stage, as $\mathcal{O}(n + w)$ is an upper bound on the number of packets parked while the throughput is equal to the input rate. An update stage takes $\mathcal{O}(n + w)$ rounds by its design. A delay due to the makeup stage is $\mathcal{O}(nw)$ by Lemma 3. The latter bound determines the latency by being the biggest among the contributions to packet delays by all kinds of stages.   □

Protocol COLORFUL-STATIONS is conflict free, so it follows from Theorem 3 that packet latency has to be $\Omega(nw)$ for suitable adversaries.

6   Conclusion

We introduced a model of adversarial queuing on multiple access channels in which individual injection rates are associated with stations. This paper attempts to compare window adversaries of individual injection rates with adversaries of global injection rates in terms of quality of service for the maximal throughput of 1. The main discovered difference is that bounded packet latency is achievable when a separate injection rate is associated with each station by an adversary, even by full sensing protocols that do not know anything about the adversary. The partitioning of aggregate rate among the stations constrains the adversary but is unknown to the stations. The bounds on queue size and packet latency of our protocols are not expressed in terms of the distribution of the aggregate injection rate among the stations: they are given only in terms of the number n of stations and the burstiness, which equals the window w for the aggregate rate 1. We developed protocols with packet latency close to asymptotically optimal in two cases: when protocols are adaptive and channels are without collision detection and when protocols are full sensing but channels are with collision detection. Packet latency of full sensing protocols for channels without collision detection turned out to be more challenging to control: the protocol we developed achieves $\mathcal{O}(nw)$ bound on packet latency. This protocol avoids conflicts for access to the channel: we showed that packet latency has to be $\Omega(nw)$ for such protocols. The question if a full sensing protocol can achieve packet latency that is asymptotically less than nw for channels without collision detection for window-type adversaries of individual injection rates remains open.

References

1. Abramson, N.: Development of the Alohanet. IEEE Transactions on Information Theory 31, 119–123 (1985)
2. Álvarez, C., Blesa, M.J., Díaz, J., Serna, M.J., Fernández, A.: Adversarial models for priority-based networks. Networks 45, 23–35 (2005)
3. Álvarez, C., Blesa, M.J., Serna, M.J.: The impact of failure management on the stability of communication networks. In: Proceeding of the 10th International Conference on Parallel and Distributed Systems (ICPADS), pp. 153–160 (2004)
4. Andrews, M., Awerbuch, B., Fernández, A., Leighton, T., Liu, Z., Kleinberg, J.: Universal-stability results and performance bounds for greedy contention-resolution protocols. Journal of the ACM 48, 39–69 (2001)

5. Andrews, M., Zhang, L.: Achieving stability in networks of input-queued switches. IEEE/ACM Transactions on Networking 11, 848–857 (2003)
6. Andrews, M., Zhang, L.: Routing and scheduling in multihop wireless networks with time-varying channels. ACM Transactions on Algorithms 3(3), article 33 (2007)
7. Andrews, M., Zhang, L.: Stability results for networks with input and output blocking. In: Proceedings of the 30th ACM Symposium on the Theory of Computing (STOC), pp. 369–377 (1998)
8. Awerbuch, B., Richa, A., Scheideler, C.: A jamming-resistant MAC protocol for single-hop wireless networks. In: Proceedings of the 27th Symposium on Principles of Distributed Computing (PODC), pp. 45–54 (2008)
9. Bender, M.A., Farach-Colton, M., He, S., Kuszmaul, B.C., Leiserson, C.E.: Adversarial contention resolution for simple channels. In: Proceedings of the 17th ACM Symposium on Parallel Algorithms (SPAA), pp. 325–332 (2005)
10. Borodin, A., Kleinberg, J.M., Raghavan, P., Sudan, M., Williamson, D.P.: Adversarial queuing theory. Journal of the ACM 48, 13–38 (2001)
11. Chlebus, B.S., Kowalski, D.R., Rokicki, M.A.: Adversarial queuing on the multiple-access channel. In: Proceedings of the 25th ACM Symposium on Principles of Distributed Computing (PODC), pp. 92–101 (2006)
12. Chlebus, B.S., Kowalski, D.R., Rokicki, M.A.: Maximum throughput of multiple access channels in adversarial environments. Distributed Computing 22, 93–116 (2009)
13. Dolev, S., Gilbert, S., Guerraoui, R., Kuhn, F., Newport, C.C.: The wireless synchronization problem. In: Proceedings of the 28th ACM Symposium on Principles of Distributed Computing (PODC), pp. 190–199 (2009)
14. Dolev, S., Gilbert, S., Guerraoui, R., Newport, C.C.: Gossiping in a multi-channel radio network. In: Pelc, A. (ed.) DISC 2007. LNCS, vol. 4731, pp. 208–222. Springer, Heidelberg (2007)
15. Gallager, R.G.: A perspective on multiaccess channels. IEEE Transactions on Information Theory 31, 124–142 (1985)
16. Gilbert, S., Guerraoui, R., Kowalski, D.R., Newport, C.: Interference-resilient information exchange. In: Proceedings of the 28th IEEE International Conference on Computer Communications (INFOCOM), pp. 2249–2257 (2009)
17. Gilbert, S., Guerraoui, R., Newport, C.C.: Of malicious motes and suspicious sensors: On the efficiency of malicious interference in wireless networks. Theoretical Computer Science 410, 546–569 (2009)
18. Goldberg, L.A., Jerrum, M., Kannan, S., Paterson, M.: A bound on the capacity of backoff and acknowledgement-based protocols. SIAM Journal on Computing 33, 313–331 (2004)
19. Goldberg, L.A., MacKenzie, P., Paterson, M., Srinivasan, A.: Contention resolution with constant expected delay. Journal of the ACM 47, 1048–1096 (2000)
20. Greenberg, A.G., Winograd, S.: A lower bound on the time needed in the worst case to resolve conflicts deterministically in multiple access channels. Journal of the ACM 32, 589–596 (1985)
21. Håstad, J., Leighton, T., Rogoff, B.: Analysis of backoff protocols for multiple access channels. SIAM Journal on Computing 25, 740–774 (1996)
22. Metcalfe, R.M., Boggs, D.R.: Ethernet: distributed packet switching for local computer networks. Communications of the ACM 19, 395–404 (1976)
23. Raghavan, P., Upfal, E.: Stochastic contention resolution with short delays. SIAM Journal on Computing 28, 709–719 (1998)

NB-FEB: A Universal Scalable Easy-to-Use Synchronization Primitive for Manycore Architectures

Phuong Hoai Ha[1], Philippas Tsigas[2], and Otto J. Anshus[1]

[1] University of Tromsø, Department of Computer Science, Faculty of Science,
NO-9037 Tromsø, Norway
{phuong,otto}@cs.uit.no
[2] Chalmers University of Technology, Department of Computer Science and
Engineering, SE-412 96 Göteborg, Sweden
tsigas@chalmers.se

Abstract. This paper addresses the problem of universal synchronization primitives that can support *scalable* thread synchronization for large-scale manycore architectures. The universal synchronization primitives that have been deployed widely in conventional architectures, are the *compare-and-swap* (CAS) and *load-linked/store-conditional* (LL/SC) primitives. However, such synchronization primitives are expected to reach their scalability limits in the evolution to manycore architectures with thousands of cores.

We introduce a *non-blocking* full/empty bit primitive, or NB-FEB for short, as a promising synchronization primitive for parallel programming on manycore architectures. We show that the NB-FEB primitive is *universal, scalable, feasible* and *easy to use*. NB-FEB, together with registers, can solve the consensus problem for an arbitrary number of processes (*universality*). NB-FEB is *combinable*, namely its memory requests to the same memory location can be combined into only one memory request, which consequently makes NB-FEB scalable (*scalability*). Since NB-FEB is a variant of the original full/empty bit that always returns a value instead of waiting for a conditional flag, it is as feasible as the original full/empty bit, which has been implemented in many computer systems (*feasibility*). We construct, on top of NB-FEB, a non-blocking software transactional memory system called NBFEB-STM, which can be used as an abstraction to handle concurrent threads *easily*. NBFEB-STM is space efficient: the space complexity of each object updated by N concurrent threads/transactions is $\Theta(N)$, which is optimal.

1 Introduction

Universal synchronization primitives [9] are essential for constructing non-blocking synchronization mechanisms for parallel programming, such as non-blocking software transactional memory [8,10,12,17]. Non-blocking synchronization eliminates the concurrency control problems of mutual exclusion locks,

T. Abdelzaher, M. Raynal, and N. Santoro (Eds.): OPODIS 2009, LNCS 5923, pp. 189–203, 2009.

such as priority inversion, deadlock and convoying. As manycore architectures with thousands of cores are expected to be our future chip architectures [2], universal synchronization primitives that can support scalable thread synchronization for such large-scale architectures are desired.

However, the conventional universal primitives such as *compare-and-swap* (CAS) and *load-linked/ store-conditional* (LL/SC) are expected to reach their scalability limits in the evolution to manycore architectures with thousands of cores. The universal primitives are usually built on top of conventional cache-coherent protocols. Experimental studies have recently shown that the universal primitives, which lock the entire memory bank to ensure atomicity (i.e. coarse-grained synchronization), are not scalable for multicore architectures [19]. The authors of [19] also experimentally show that the original (blocking) *full/empty bit* (FEB), which lock only the memory location under consideration (i.e. fine-grained synchronization), scales much better. Moreover, the conventional cache-coherent protocols are considered inefficient for large-scale manycore architectures [2]. As a result, several emerging multicore architectures, such as the NVIDIA CUDA, the ClearSpeed CSX, the IBM Cell BE and the Cyclops-64, utilize a fast local memory for each processing core rather than a coherent data cache.

For the emerging manycore architectures without a coherent data cache, the CAS and LL/SC primitives are not scalable either since they are not *combinable* [3,11]. Primitives are combinable if their memory requests to the same memory location (arriving at a switch of the processor-to-memory interconnection network) can be combined into *only one* memory request. Separate replies to the original requests are later created from the reply to the combined request (at the switch). The combining technique has been implemented in the NYU Ultracomputer [4] and the IBM RP3 machine [14], and has been shown to be a promising technique for large-scale multiprocessors to alleviate the performance degradation due to a synchronization "hot spot". The CAS primitives are not combinable since the success of a $CAS(x, a, b)$ primitive depends on the current value of the memory location x. For m-bit locations (e.g. 64-bit words), there are 2^m possible values and therefore, a combined request that represents k $CAS(x, a, b)$ requests, $k < 2^m$, must carry as many as k different checking-values a and k new values b. Although the *single-valued* $CAS_a(x, b)$ [3], which will atomically swap b to x if x equals a is combinable, the number of instructions CAS_a must be as many as the number of integers a that can be stored in one memory word (e.g. 2^{64} CAS_a instructions for 64-bit words, where $a = 0, 1 \cdots, 2^{64} - 1$). Note that the value domains of x, a and b must be the same. This fact makes the *single-valued* CAS_a unfeasible for hardware implementation. Note that the LL/SC primitives are not combinable since the success of a SC primitive depends on the state of its reservation bit at the memory location that has been set previously by the corresponding LL primitive. Therefore, a combined request that represents k SC requests (from different processes/processors) must carry as many as k store values.

Another universal primitive called *sticky bit* has been suggested in [15], but it has not been deployed so far due to its usage complexity. A sticky bit is a data object that holds 0, 1 or $\perp$ and supports the following operations: $Jam(v)$, which sets the value to v and returns *Success* atomically if the value was $\perp$ or v; *Flush()*, which sets the value to $\perp$; and *Read()*, which returns the current value of the object. To the best of our knowledge, the universal construction using the sticky bit in [15] does not prevent a delayed thread, even after being helped, from jamming the sticky bits of a cell that has been re-initialized and reused. Since the universal construction is built on a doubly-linked list of cells, it is not obvious how an external garbage collector (supported by the underlying system) can help solve the problem. Moreover, the space complexity of the universal construction for an object is as high as $O(N^3)$ [15] [1] , where N is the number of processes.

This paper suggests a novel synchronization primitive, called NB-FEB, as a promising synchronization primitive for parallel programming on manycore architectures. What makes NB-FEB a promising primitive is its following four main properties. NB-FEB is:

Feasible: NB-FEB is a *non-blocking* variant of the conventional full/empty bit that *always returns* the old value of the variable instead of waiting for its conditional flag to be set (or cleared) (cf. Section 3). This simple modification makes NB-FEB as *feasible* as the original (blocking) full/empty bit, which has been implemented in many computer systems such as HEP, Tera (or Cray MTA-2), MDP, Sparcle, M-Machine, and Eldorado. The original full/empty bit is also used to design a *synchronization array* – a dedicated hardware structure for pipelined inter-thread communication [16].

Universal: This simple modification, however, significantly increases the synchronization power of full/empty bits, making NB-FEB as powerful as *CAS* or *LL/SC*. NB-FEB, together with registers, can solve wait-free[2] consensus [9] for an arbitrary number of processes, the essential property for constructing non-blocking synchronization mechanisms (cf. Section 3.1). Note that due to *blocking*, the original full/empty bit is as weak as read/write registers with respect to synchronization power: it, together with registers, cannot solve *wait-free* consensus for even two processes.

Scalable: NB-FEB is *combinable*, namely its memory requests to the same memory location can be combined into only one memory request (cf. Section 3.2). This empowers NB-FEB with the ability to provide *scalable* thread synchronization for large-scale manycore architectures [4,14].

Easy-to-use: The original full/empty bit is well-known as a *special-purpose* primitive for fast producer-consumer synchronization and has been used extensively in specific domains of applications (e.g. parallel graph algorithms). In this paper, by providing an abstraction on top of NB-FEB, we show that NB-FEB can be deployed easily as a *general-purpose* primitive. We construct, on

---

[1] Each object needs $O(N^2)$ cells of size $O(N)$.

[2] An implementation is *wait-free* if it guarantees that any process can complete any operation on the implemented object in a finite number of steps, regardless of the execution speeds on the other processes.

top of NB-FEB, a non-blocking software transactional memory system called NBFEB-STM, which can be used as an abstraction to handle concurrent threads *easily*. NBFEB-STM is space efficient: the space complexity of each object updated by N concurrent threads/transactions is $\Theta(N)$, the optimal (cf. Section 4).

The rest of this paper is organized as follows. Section 2 presents the shared memory and interconnection network models assumed in this paper. Sections 3 describes the NB-FEB primitive in detail and proves its universality and combinability properties. Section 4 introduces and analyzes NBFEB-STM, the obstruction-free multi-versioning STM constructed on top of the NB-FEB primitive. Section 5 concludes this paper. Because of space limitations, most proofs are omitted from this version of the paper and can be found in [7].

2   Models

Similarly to previous research on the synchronization power of synchronization primitives [9], this paper assumes the linearizable shared memory model. Due to NB-FEB combinability, as in [11] we assume that the processor-to-memory interconnection network is *nonovertaking* and that a reply message is sent back on the same path followed by the request message. The intermediate nodes on the communication path from a processor to a global shared memory module can be either switches of a multistage interconnection network [11] or memory modules of a multilevel memory hierarchy [3]. The intermediate nodes can detect requests destined for the same destination and maintain the queues of requests. In this paper, we assume that such a combining network is provided and we mainly focus on the combining logic of the new primitive. For the design details of the combining network, the reader is referred to [4]. No memory coherent schemes are assumed.

3   NB-FEB Primitives

NB-FEB is a set of four primitives: *test-flag-and-set TFAS* (cf. Algorithm 1), *Load* (Algorithm 2), *store-and-clear SAC* (Algorithm 3) and *store-and-set SAS* (Algorithm 4). Each variable x has an associated full-empty bit $flag_x$. Primitive *TFAS* will atomically write value v to variable x (and set $flag_x$ to *true*) if $flag_x$ is *false*. The primitive always returns the (previous) value of pair $(x, flag_x)$ regardless of the value of $flag_x$. Primitive *SAC* atomically writes v to x, sets $flag_x$ to *false* and returns the previous value of $(x, flag_x)$. Primitive *SAS* is similar to *SAC* except that *SAS* sets $flag_x$ to *true*. Regarding conditional load primitives such as *load-if-set* and *load-if-clear* in the original FEB, a processor can check the flag value, $flag_x$, returned by the unconditional load primitive *Load* to determine if it was successful.

When the value of $flag_x$ returned is not needed, we just write $r \leftarrow \text{TFAS}(x, v)$ instead of $(r, flag_r) \leftarrow \text{TFAS}(x, v)$, where r is x's old value. The same applies to

SAC and SAS. For *Load*, we just write $r \leftarrow x$ instead of $r \leftarrow \text{LOAD}(x)$. In this paper, the flag value returned is needed only for combining NB-FEB primitives.

Algorithm 1 . TFAS(x: variable, v: value): Test-Flag-And-Set, a non-blocking variant of the original Store-if-Clear-and-Set primitive, which *always* returns the old value of x.

$(o, flag_o) \leftarrow (x, flag_x)$;
if $flag_x = $ **false** then
    $(x, flag_x) \leftarrow (v, \textbf{true})$;
end if
return $(o, flag_o)$;

Algorithm 2. LOAD(x: variable)

return $(x, flag_x)$;

Algorithm 3 . SAC(x: variable, v: value): Store-And-Clear

$(o, flag_o) \leftarrow (x, flag_x)$;
$(x, flag_x) \leftarrow (v, \textbf{false})$;
return $(o, flag_o)$;

Algorithm 4 . SAS(x: variable, v: value): Store-And-Set

$(o, flag_o) \leftarrow (x, flag_x)$;
$(x, flag_x) \leftarrow (v, \textbf{true})$;
return $(o, flag_o)$;

Algorithm 5. SICAS(x: variable, v: value): Store-If-Clear-And-Set, one of the original FEB primitives, which waits for $flag_x$ to be clear (or $false$).

Wait for $flag_x$ to be **false**;
$(x, flag_x) \leftarrow (v, \textbf{true})$;

Algorithm 6 . LISAC(x: variable): Load-If-Set-And-Clear, one of the original FEB primitives, which waits for $flag_x$ to be set (or $true$).

Wait for $flag_x$ to be **true**;
$flag_x \leftarrow \textbf{false}$;
return x;

Algorithm 7 . TFAS_CONSENSUS (*proposal*: value)

Decision: shared variable. The shared variable is initialized to $\bot$ with a clear flag (i.e. $flag_{Decision} = \textbf{false}$).

Output: a value agreed by all processes.
1T: $(first, flag_{first})$ $\leftarrow$
        TFAS($Decision, proposal$);
2T: if $first = \bot$ then
3T: return $proposal$;
4T: else
5T: return $first$;
6T: end if

3.1   *TFAS*: A Universal Primitive

In this section, we will show that *TFAS* is a universal primitive like CAS. Note that due to blocking, the original full/empty bit primitives such as *store-if-clear-and-set* (cf. Algorithm 5) and *load-if-set-and-clear* (cf. Algorithm 6) are as weak as read/write registers with respect to synchronization power: they, together with registers, cannot solve *wait-free* consensus [9] for even two processes.

Lemma 1. *(Universality) The* test-flag-and-set *primitive (or TFAS for short) is universal.*

The wait-free consensus algorithm is shown in Algorithm 7. Processes share a variable called *Decision*, which is initialized to $\bot$ with a *false* flag. Each process p proposes its value ($\neq \bot$) called *proposal* by calling TFAS_CONSENSUS (*proposal*).

    The TFAS_CONSENSUS procedure is clearly wait-free since it contains no loops. It is not difficult to see that the procedure will return the proposal of the first process executing *TFAS* on the *Decision* variable to all processes.

3.2 Combinability

Lemma 2. *(Combinability) NB-FEB primitives are combinable.*

Proof. Figure 1 summarizes the combining logic of NB-FEB primitives on a memory location x. The first column is the name of the first primitive request and the first row is the name of the successive primitive request. For instance, the cell $[SAS, TFAS]$ is the combining logic of SAS and $TFAS$ in which SAS is followed by $TFAS$. Let v_1, v_2, r and f_r be the value of the first primitive request, the value of the second primitive request, the value returned and the flag returned, respectively. In each cell, the first line is the combined request, the second is the reply to the first primitive request and the third (and forth) is the reply to the successive primitive request. The values 0 and 1 of f_r in the reply represent *false* and *true*, respectively.

Consider cell $[TFAS, TFAS]$ as an example. The cell describes the case where request $TFAS(x, v_1)$ is followed by request $TFAS(x, v_2)$, at an intermediate node (e.g. a switch) of the processor-to-memory interconnection network. At the node, the two input requests are combined into only one output request $TFAS(x, v_1)$ (line 1), which will be forwarded further to the corresponding memory controller. When receiving a reply (r, f_r) to the combined request, the intermediate node at which the requests were combined, creates separate replies to the two original requests. The reply to the first original request, $TFAS(x, v_1)$, is (r, f_r) (line 2) as if the request was executed by the memory controller. The reply to the successive request, $TFAS(x, v_2)$, depends on whether the combined request $TFAS(x, v_1)$ has successfully updated the memory location x. If $f_r = 0$, $TFAS(x, v_1)$ has successfully updated x with its value v_1. Therefore, the reply to the successive request $TFAS(x, v_2)$ is $(v_1, 1)$ as if the request was executed right after the first request $TFAS(x, v_1)$. If $f_r = 1$, $TFAS(x, v_1)$ has failed to update the x variable. Therefore, the reply to the successive request $TFAS(x, v_2)$ is $(r, 1)$.   □

Due to the combining logic in Figure 1, the set of primitives $TFAS$ (universal primitive), *Load* (read-primitive), SAC and SAS (write-primitives) are closed under the combining operation: the combination of any two primitives of the set belongs to the set (e.g. cell $[SAC, TFAS]$ is SAS). Namely, all concurrent requests to the same memory location can be combined into *only one* request. Based on previous experimental results of combinable primitives in the literature such as *fetch-and-add* [4,14], NB-FEB would be scalable in practice.

4 NBFEB-STM: Obstruction-Free Multi-versioning STM

Like previous obstruction-free[3] multi-versioning STM called LSA-STM [17], the new software transactional memory called NBFEB-STM assumes that objects are only accessed and modified within transactions. NBFEB-STM assumes that

---

[3] A synchronization mechanism is *obstruction-free* if any thread that runs solo (i.e. without encountering a synchronization conflict from a concurrent thread) for long enough, makes progress.

there are no nested transactions, namely each thread executes only one transaction at a time. NBFEB-STM, like other obstruction-free STMs [10,12,17], is designed for garbage-collected programming languages (e.g. Java). A variable reclaimed by the garbage collector is assumed to have all bits 0 when it is reused. Note that there are non-blocking garbage collection algorithms that do not require synchronization primitives other than reads and writes while they still guarantee the non-blocking property for application-threads. Such a garbage collection algorithm is presented in [7].

$(x,[v_1])$	The successive primitive with parameters $(x,[v_2])$			
	Load	SAC	SAS	TFAS
Load	Load	SAC(v_2)	SAS(v_2)	TFAS(v_2)
	(r,f_r)	(r,f_r)	(r,f_r)	(r,f_r)
	(r,f_r)	(r,f_r)	(r,f_r)	(r,f_r)
SAC	SAC(v_1)	SAC(v_2)	SAS(v_2)	SAS(v_2)
	(r,f_r)	(r,f_r)	(r,f_r)	(r,f_r)
	$(v_1,0)$	$(v_1,0)$	$(v_1,0)$	$(v_1,0)$
SAS	SAS(v_1)	SAC(v_2)	SAS(v_2)	SAS(v_1)
	(r,f_r)	(r,f_r)	(r,f_r)	(r,f_r)
	$(v_1,1)$	$(v_1,1)$	$(v_1,1)$	$(v_1,1)$
TFAS	TFAS(v_1)	SAC(v_2)	SAS(v_2)	TFAS(v_1)
	(r,f_r)	(r,f_r)	(r,f_r)	(r,f_r)
	Like 5th	Like 5th	Like 5th	if f_r=0: $(v_1,1)$
	column	column	column	else: $(r,1)$

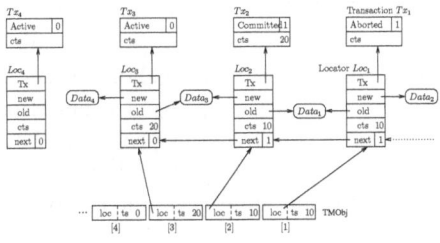

Fig. 1. The combining logic of NB-FEB primitives on a memory location x

Fig. 2. The data structure of a transactional memory object $TMObj$ in NBFEB-STM

Primitives *TFAS*, *SAC* and *Load* are used to implement NBFEB-STM. Note that primitive *SAS* is included in NB-FEB to make the set of NB-FEB primitives closed under the combining operation (cf. cell [*SAC*, *TFAS*] in Figure 2). Since NB-FEB primitives are combinable, NBFEB-STM eliminates all conventional synchronization hot spots in STMs (cf. Lemma 10).

4.1 Challenges and Key Ideas

Unlike the STMs using CAS [10,12,17], NBFEB-STM using *TFAS* and *SAC* must handle the problem that *SAC*'s interference with concurrent *TFAS* will violate the atomicity semantics expected on variable x. Overlapping $TFAS_1$ and $TFAS_2$ both may successfully write their new values to x if *SAC* interference occurs.

The key idea is not to use the transactional memory object $TMObj$ [4] [10,12,17] that needs to switch its pointer frequently to a new locator (when a transaction commits). Such a $TMObj$ would need *SAC* in order to clear the pointer's flag, allowing the next transaction to switch the pointer. Instead, NBFEB-STM keeps a linked-list of locators for each object and integrates a write-once pointer *next* into each locator (cf. Figure2). When opening an object O for write, a transaction T tries to append its locator to O's locator-list by changing the *next* pointer of the head-locator[5] of the list using *TFAS*. Due to the semantics of *TFAS*, only one of

---

[4] The reader is assumed to be familiar with the basic concepts of STMs, which are nicely presented in the seminal paper [10].

[5] The head-locator is the last element of O's singly-linked list whose next pointer is *null* (e.g. Loc_3 in Figure 2)

the concurrent transactions trying to append their locators succeeds. The other transactions must retry in order to find the new head and then append their locators to the new head. Using the locator-list, each *next* pointer is changed only once and thus its flag does not need to be cleared during the lifetime of the corresponding locator. This prevents SAC from interleaving with concurrent $TFAS$. The *next* pointer, together with its locator, will be reclaimed by the garbage collector when the lifetime of the locator is over. The garbage collector ensures that a locator will not be recycled until no thread/transaction has a reference to it.

Linking locators together creates another challenge on the space complexity of NBFEB-STM. Unlike the STMs using CAS, a delayed/halted transaction T in NBFEB-STM may prevent all locators appended after its locator in a locator-list from being reclaimed. As a result, T may make the system run out of memory and thus prevent other transactions from making progress, violating the obstruction-freedom property. The key idea to solve the space challenge is to break the list of obsolete locators into pieces so that a delayed transaction T prevents from being reclaimed only the locator that T has a direct reference as in the STMs using CAS. The idea is based on the fact that only the head of O's locator-list is needed for further accesses to the O object.

However, breaking the list of an obsolete object O also creates another challenge on finding the head of O's locator-list. Obviously, we cannot use a head pointer as in non-blocking linked-lists since modifying such a pointer requires CAS. The key idea is to utilize the fact that there are no nested transactions and thus each thread has at most one *active* locator[6] in each locator list. Therefore, by recording the latest locator of each thread appended to O's locator-list, a transaction can find the head of O's locator list. The solution is elaborated further in Section 4.3 and Section 4.4.

Based on the key ideas, we come up with the data structure for a transactional memory object that is illustrated in Figure 2 and presented in Algorithm 8.

4.2   Data Structures

A transactional memory object $TMObj$ in NBFEB-STM is an array of N pairs (pointer, timestamp), where N is the number of concurrent threads/transactions, as shown in Figure 2. Item $TMObj[i]$ is modified only by thread t_i and can be read by all threads. Pointer $TMObj[i].loc$ points to the locator called Loc_i corresponding to the latest transaction committed/aborted by thread t_i. Timestamp $TMObj[i].ts$ is the commit timestamp of the object referenced by $Loc_i.old$. After successfully appending its locator Loc_i to the list by executing $TFAS(head.next, Loc_i)$, t_i will update its own item $TMObj[i]$ with its new locator Loc_i. The $TMObj$ array is used to find the head of the list of locators $Loc_1, \cdots, Loc_N$. Note that since contemporary large-scale multicore architectures (e.g. NVIDIA CUDA with up to 30 cores [13]) deploy high memory bandwidth to deal with the high latency of shared memory accesses, reading/writing to an array with several elements such as $TMObj$ will not be problematic on manycore architectures. For

---

[6] An *active* locator is a locator that is still in use, opposite to an *obsolete* locator.

instance, the NVIDIA CUDA currently allows each core to read/write to a large segment of shared memory (e.g. 128 bytes) in a single memory transaction.

For each locator Loc_i, in addition to fields Tx, old and new that reference the corresponding transaction object, the old data object and the new data object, respectively, as in DSTM[10], there are two other fields cts and $next$. The cts field records the commit timestamp of the object referenced by old. The $next$ field is the pointer to the next locator in the locator list. The $next$ pointer is modified by NB-FEB primitives.

In Figure 2, values $\{0, 1\}$ in the $next$ pointer denote the values $\{false, true\}$ of its flag, respectively. The $next$ pointer of the head of the locator list, $Loc_3.next$, has its flag clear (i.e. 0) while the $next$ pointers of previous locators (e.g. $Loc_1.next$, $Loc_2.next$) have their flags set (i.e. 1) since their $next$ pointers were changed. The $next$ pointer of a new locator (e.g. $Loc_4.next$) is initialized to $(\bot, 0)$. Due to the garbage collector semantics, all locators Loc_j reachable from the $TMObj$ shared object by following their $Loc_j.next$ pointers, will not be reclaimed.

For each transaction object Tx_i, in addition to fields $status$, $readSet$ and $writeSet$ corresponding to the status, the set of objects opened for read, and the set of objects opened for write, respectively, there is a field cts recording Tx_i's commit timestamp (if Tx_i committed) as in LSA-STM [17].

4.3   Algorithm

A thread t_i starts a transaction T by calling the STARTSTM(T) procedure (Algorithm 8). The procedure sets $T.status$ to $Active$ and clears its flag using SAC (cf. Algorithm 3). The procedure then initializes the lazy snapshot algorithm (LSA) [17] by calling LSA_START. NBFEB-STM utilizes LSA to preclude inconsistent views by $live$ transactions, an essential aspect of transactional memory semantics [6]. The LSA has been shown to be an efficient mechanism to construct consistent snapshots for transactions [17]. Moreover, the LSA can utilize up to $(N + 1)$ versions of a transactional memory object $TMObj$ recorded in N locators of $TMObj$'s locator list. Note that the global counter CT in LSA can be implemented by the $fetch\text{-}and\text{-}increment$ primitive [4], a combinable (and thus scalable) primitive [11]. Except for the global counter CT, the LSA in NBFEB-STM does not need any strong synchronization primitives other than $TFAS$. The ABORT(T) operation in LSA, which is used to abort a transaction T, is replaced by $TFAS(T.status, Aborted)$. Note that the $status$ field is the only field of a transaction object T that can be modified by other transactions.

Read-accesses. When a transaction T opens an object O for read, it invokes the OPENR procedure (Algorithm 11). The procedure simply calls the LSA_OPEN procedure of LSA [17] in the $Read$ mode to get the version of O that maintains a consistent snapshot with the versions of other objects being accessed by T. If no such a version of O exists, LSA_OPEN will abort T and consequently OPENR will return $\bot$ (line 3R). That means there is a conflicting transaction that makes T unable to maintain a consistent view of all the object being accessed by T. Otherwise, OPENR returns the version of O that is selected by LSA. This version is guaranteed by LSA to belong to a consistent view of all the objects being accessed by T. Up to $(N + 1)$ versions are available for each object O in NBFEB-STM (cf. Lemma 7). Since NBFEB-STM utilizes LSA, read-accesses to an object O are invisible to other transactions and thus do not change O's locator list.

Write-accesses. When a transaction T opens an object O for write, it invokes the OPENW procedure (cf. Algorithm 13). The task of the procedure is to append to the head of O's locator list a new locator L whose Tx and *old* fields reference to T and O's latest version, respectively. In order to find O's latest version, the procedure invokes FINDHEAD (cf. Algorithm 10) to find the current head of O's locator list (line 3W). When the head called H is found, the procedure determines O's latest version based on the status of the corresponding transaction $H.Tx$ as in DSTM [10], by invoking INITLOC (line 4W). If the $H.Tx$ transaction committed, O's latest version is $H.new$ with commit timestamp $H.Tx.cts$ (lines 2I-4I, Algorithm 12). A copy of O's latest version is created and referenced by $L.new$ (line 5I) (cf. locators Loc_2 and Loc_3 in Figure 2 as H and L, respectively, for an illustration). If the $H.Tx$ transaction aborted, O's latest version is $H.old$ with commit timestamp $H.cts$ (lines 7I-9I) (cf. locators Loc_1 and Loc_2 in Figure 2 as H and L, respectively, for an illustration). If the $H.Tx$ transaction is active, OPENW consults the contention manager [5,18] (line 13I, Algorithm 12) to solve the conflict between the T and $H.Tx$ transactions. If T must abort, OPENW tries to change $T.status$ to *Aborted* using *TFAS* (lines 15I-16I, Algorithm 12) and returns $\perp$ (line 5W, Algorithm 13). Note that other transactions change $T.status$ only to *Aborted*, and thus if *TFAS* at line 15I fails, $T.status$ has been changed to *Aborted* by another transaction. If $H.Tx$ must abort, OPENW changes $H.Tx.status$ to *Aborted* using *TFAS* (line 18I, Algorithm 12) and checks $H.Tx.status$ again.

The latest version of O is then checked to ensure that it, together with the versions of other objects being accessed by T, belongs to a consistent view using LSA_OPEN with "Write" mode (line 7W). If it does, OPENW tries to append the new locator L to O's locator list by changing the $H.next$ pointer to L (line 11W). Note that the $H.next$ pointer was initialized to $\perp$ with a clear flag, before H was successfully appended to O's locator list (line 24I, Algorithm 12). If OPENW does not succeed, another locator has been appended as a new head and thus OPENW must retry to find the new head (line 12W). Otherwise, it successfully appends the new locator L as the new head of O's locator list. OPENW, which is being executed by a thread t_i, then makes $O[i].ptr$ reference to L and records $L.cts$ in $O[i].ts$ (line 15W). This removes O's reference to the previous locator $oldLoc$ appended by t_i, allowing $oldLoc$ to be reclaimed by the garbage collector. Since $oldLoc$ now becomes an obsolete locator, its *next* pointer is reset (line 16W) to break possible chains of obsolete locators reachable by a delayed/halted thread, helping $oldLoc$'s descendant locators in the chains be reclaimed. For each item j in the O array such that timestamp $O[j].ts < O[i].ts$, the $O[j].ptr$ locator now becomes obsolete in a sense that it no longer keeps O's latest version although it is still referenced by $O[j]$ (since only thread t_j can modify $O[j]$). In order to break the chains of obsolete locators, OPENW resets the *next* pointer of the $O[j].ptr$ locator so that $O[j].ptr$'s descendant locators can be reclaimed by the garbage collector (lines 17W-18W). This chain-breaking mechanism makes the space complexity of an object updated by N concurrent transactions/threads in NBFEB-STM be $\Theta(N)$, the optimal (cf. Theorem 1).

In order to find the head of O's locator list as in OPENW, a transaction invokes the FINDHEAD(O) procedure (cf. Algorithm 10). The procedure atomically reads O into a local array *start* (line 2F). Such a multi-word read operation is supported by emerging multicore architectures (e.g. CUDA [13]) which deploy high memory bandwidth to deal with the high latency of shared memory accesses. In the contemporary chips of these architectures, a read operation can atomically read 128 bytes. In general, such a multi-word read operation can be implemented as an atomic snapshot using only single-word read and single-word write primitives[7] [1]. FINDHEAD finds the item $start_{latest}$ with the highest timestamp in *start* and searches for the head from locator $start_{latest}.ptr$ by following the *next* pointers until it finds a locator H whose *next* pointer is $\perp$ (lines 3F-6F). Since some locators may become obsolete and their *next* pointers were reset to $\perp$ by concurrent transactions (lines 16W and 18W in Algorithm 13), FINDHEAD needs to check H's commit timestamp against the highest timestamp of O at a moment after H is found (lines 8F-10F). If H's commit timestamp is greater than or equal to the highest timestamp of O, H is the head of O's locator list (cf. Lemma 4). Otherwise, H is an obsolete locator and FINDHEAD must retry (line 10F). The FINDHEAD procedure is lock-free, namely it will certainly return the head of O's locator list after at most N iterations unless a concurrent thread has completed a transaction and subsequently has started a new one, where N is the number of concurrent (updating) threads (cf. Lemma 5). Note that as soon as a thread obtains *head* from FINDHEAD (line 3W of OPENW, Algorithm 13), the locator referenced by *head* will not be reclaimed by the garbage collector until the thread returns from the OPENW procedure.

Commitments. When committing, read-only transactions in NBFEB-STM do nothing and always succeed in their commit phase as in LSA-STM [17]. They can abort only when trying to open an object for read (cf. Algorithm 11). Other transactions T, which have opened at least one object for write, invoke the COMMITW procedure (Algorithm 9). The procedure calls the LSA_COMMIT procedure to ensure that T still maintains a consistent view of objects being accessed by T (line 1C). T's commit timestamp is updated with the timestamp returned from LSA_COMMIT (line 2C). Finally, COMMITW tries to change $T.status$ to *Committed* (line 3C). $T.status$ will be changed to *Committed* at this step if it has not been changed to *Aborted* due to the semantics of *TFAS*.

---

[7] Note that single-word read/write primitives are combinable [11].

Algorithm 8. STARTSTM(T: transaction)

$TMObj$: array[N] of $\{ptr, ts\}$. Pointer $TMObj[i].ptr$ points to the locator called Loc_i corresponding to the latest transaction committed/aborted by thread t_i. Timestamp $TMObj[i].ts$ is the commit timestamp of the object referenced by $Loc_i.old$. N is the number of concurrent threads/transactions. $TMObj[i]$ is written only by thread t_i.

$Locator$: **record** tx, new, old: pointer; cts: timestamp; **end**. The cts timestamp is the commit timestamp of the old version.

$Transaction$: **record** $status$: $\{Active, Committed, Aborted\}$; cts: timestamp; **end**. NBFEB-STM also keeps read/write sets as in LSA-STM, but the sets are omitted from the pseudocode since managing the sets in NBFEB-STM is similar to LSA-STM.

1S: SAC($T.status, Active$); // Store-and-clear
2S: LSA_START(T) // Lazy snapshot algorithm

Algorithm 9. COMMITW(T: Transaction): Try to commit an update transaction T by thread p_i

1C: $CT_T \leftarrow$ LSA_COMMIT(T); // Check consistent snapshot. CT_T is T's unique commit timestamp from LSA.
2C: $T.cts \leftarrow CT_T$; // Commit timestamp of T if T manages to commit.
3C: TFAS($T.status, Committed$);

Algorithm 10. FINDHEAD(O: TMObj): Find the head of the locator list

Output: reference to the head of the locator list

1F: **repeat**
2F: $start \leftarrow O$; // Read O to a local array atomically.
3F: Let $start_{latest}$ be the item with highest timestamp;
4F: $tmp \leftarrow start_{latest}.ptr$; // Find a (possible) head, starting from $start_{latest}.ptr$.
5F: **while** $tmp.next \neq \perp$ **do**
6F: $tmp \leftarrow tmp.next$;
7F: **end while**
8F: $start' \leftarrow O$; // Check if current tmp is the actual head.
9F: Let $start'_{latest}$ be the item with highest timestamp;
10F: **until** $tmp.cts \geq start'_{latest}.ts$;
11F: **return** tmp;

Algorithm 11. OPENR(T: Transaction; O_i: TMObj): Open a transactional object for read

Output: reference to a *data* object if succeeds, or $\perp$.

1R: LSA_OPEN($T, 0_i,$ "Read"); // LSA's OPEN procedure
2R: **if** $T.status = Aborted$ **then**
3R: **return** $\perp$;
4R: **else**
5R: **return** the version chosen by LSA_OPEN;
6R: **end if**

4.4   Analysis

In this section, we prove that NBFEB-STM fulfills the three essential aspects of transactional memory semantics [6]:

Instantaneous commit: Committed transactions must appear as if they executed instantaneously at some unique point in time, and aborted transactions, as if they did not execute at all.

Preluding inconsistent views: The state (of shared objects) accessed by *live* transactions must be consistent.

Preserving real-time order: If a transaction T_i commits before a transaction T_j starts, then T_i must appear as if it executed before T_j. Particularly, if a transaction T_1 modifies an object O and commits, and then another transaction T_2 starts and reads O, then T_2 must read the value written by T_1 and not an older value.

We present some key properties of NBFEB-STM that make NBFEB-STM fulfill the three aspects. Because of space limitations, proofs are in the full version of this paper [7].

Algorithm 12 . INITLOC($newLoc$, $head$: Locator; T: Transaction): Initialize a new locator

Output: $\perp$ if $T.status = Aborted$
1I: **for** $i = 0$ to 1 **do**
2I: **if** $head.tx.status = Committed$ **then**
3I: $newLoc.old \leftarrow head.new$;
4I: $newLoc.cts \leftarrow head.tx.cts$;
5I: $newLoc.new \leftarrow$ COPY($head.new$); // Create a duplicate
6I: **break**;
7I: **else if** $head.tx.status = Aborted$ **then**
8I: $newLoc.old \leftarrow head.old$;
9I: $newLoc.cts \leftarrow head.cts$;
10I: $newLoc.new \leftarrow$ COPY($head.old$);
11I: **break**;
12I: **else**
13I: $myProgession \leftarrow$ CM(O_i,"$Write$"); // $head.tx$ is active $\Rightarrow$ Consult the contention manager
14I: **if** $myProgression =$ **false then**
15I: TFAS($T.status$, $Aborted$); // If fails, another has executed this TFAS.
16I: **return** $\perp$;
17I: **else**
18I: TFAS($head.tx.status$, $Aborted$);
19I: **continue**; // Transaction $head.tx$ has committed/aborted $\Rightarrow$ Check $head.tx.status$ one more time (line 2I).
20I: **end if**
21I: **end if**
22I: **end for**
23I: $newLoc.tx \leftarrow T$;
24I: SAC($newLoc.next$, $\perp$); // Store-and-clear

Algorithm 13. OPENW(T: Transaction; O: TMObj): Open a transactional memory object for write by a thread p_i

Output: reference to a *data* object if succeeds, or $\perp$.
1W: $newLoc \leftarrow$ new Locator;
2W: **while** true **do**
3W: $head \leftarrow$ FINDHEAD(O); // Find the head of O's list.
4W: **if** INITLOC($newLoc$, $head$, T) $= \perp$ **then**
5W: **return** $\perp$;
6W: **end if**
7W: LSA_OPEN(T, O, "$Write$"); // LSA's OPEN procedure.
8W: **if** $T.status = Aborted$ **then**
9W: **return** $\perp$; // Performance (not correctness): Don't add $newLoc$ to O if T has aborted due to, for instance, LSA_OPEN.
10W: **end if**
11W: **if** TFAS($head.next$, $newLoc$) $\neq \perp$ **then**
12W: **continue**; // Another locator has been appended $\Rightarrow$ Find the head again
13W: **else**
14W: $oldLoc = O[i]$;
15W: $O[i] \leftarrow (newLoc, newLoc.cts)$; // Atomic assignment; p_i's old locator is unlinked from O.
16W: SAC($oldLoc.next$, $\perp$); // $oldLoc$ may be in the chain of a sleeping thread $\Rightarrow$ Stop the chain here
17W: **for** each item L_j in O such that $L_j.ts < O[i].ts$ **do**
18W: SAC($L_j.ptr.next$, $\perp$) // Reset the $next$ pointer of the obsolete locator
19W: **end for**
20W: **return** $newLoc.new$;
21W: **end if**
22W: **end while**

Lemma 3. *A locator L_i with timestamp cts_i does not have any links/references to another locator L_j with a lower timestamp $cts_j < cts_i$.*

Lemma 4. *The locator returned by* FINDHEAD(O) *(Algorithm 10) is the head H of O's locator list at the time-point* FINDHEAD *found $H.next = \perp$ (line 5F).*

Lemma 5. *(Lock-freedom)* FINDHEAD(O) *will certainly return the head of O's locator list after at most N repeat-until iterations unless a concurrent thread has completed a transaction and subsequently has started a new one, where N is the number of concurrent threads updating O.*

Since NBFEB-STM uses the lazy snapshot algorithm LSA [17], the second correctness criterion *Precluding inconsistent views* will follow if we can prove that the LSA algorithm is correctly integrated into NBFEB-STM.

Lemma 6. *The versions kept in N locators $O[j].ptr, 1 \leq j \leq N$, for each object O are enough for checking the validity of a transaction T using the LSA algorithm [17].*

Lemma 7. *The number of versions available for each object in NBFEB-STM is up to $(N + 1)$, where N is the number of threads.*

Definition 1. *The value of a locator L is either $L.new$ if $L.tx.status = Committed$, or $L.old$ otherwise.*

Lemma 8. *In each O's locator list, the old value $L'.old$ of a locator L' is not older than the value of its previous locator [8] L.*

Lemma 9. *For each object O, there are at most $4N$ locators that cannot be reclaimed by the garbage collector at any time-point, where N is the number of update threads.*

Theorem 1. (Space complexity) *The space complexity of an object updated by N threads in NBFEB-STM is $\Theta(N)$, the optimal.*

Lemma 10. (Contention reduction) *NBFEB-STM has a lower contention level than CAS-based STMs.*

5   Conclusions and Future Work

We have introduced a new non-blocking full/empty bit primitive called NB-FEB, as a promising synchronization primitive for parallel programming on manycore architectures. We have provided a theoretical treatment of the primitive to support our claim that it is a promising primitive to consider for further research. Particularly, we have proven that i) it is universal, ii) it is combinable and thus, based on previous experimental results, it would be scalable in practice. In order to prove that it can be deployed easily as a general-purpose synchronization primitive, we have shown how to construct a non-blocking software transactional memory system NBFEB-STM with optimal space complexity using this primitive. NBFEB-STM can be used as a building block to implement concurrent algorithms conveniently.

Although the combinability makes NB-FEB promising for manycore architectures where high-contention executions are expected more frequent, experimental work is needed for future research to clearly identify the applications and system settings where NB-FEB is faster/slower than CAS or LL/SC.

Acknowledgments. The authors wish to thank the anonymous reviewers for their helpful and thorough comments on the earlier version of this paper. Phuong Ha's and Otto Anshus's work was supported by the Norwegian Research Council (grant numbers 159936/V30 and 155550/420). Philippas Tsigas's work was supported by the Swedish Research Council (VR) (grant number 37252706).

---

[8] A locator L is a *previous* locator of a locator L' if starting from L we can reach L' by following *next* pointers.

References

1. Afek, Y., Attiya, H., Dolev, D., Gafni, E., Merritt, M., Shavit, N.: Atomic snapshots of shared memory. J. ACM 40(4), 873–890 (1993)
2. Asanovic, K., et al.: The landscape of parallel computing research: A view from Berkeley. TR No. UCB/EECS-2006-183, Univ. of California, Berkeley (2006)
3. Blelloch, G.E., Gibbons, P.B., Vardhan, S.H.: Combinable memory-block transactions. In: Proc. of the ACM Symp. on Parallel Algorithms and Architectures (SPAA), pp. 23–34 (2008)
4. Gottlieb, A., et al.: The NYU Ultracomputer—designing a MIMD, shared-memory parallel machine (extended abstract). In: Proc. of the Intl. Symp. on Computer Architecture (ISCA), pp. 27–42 (1982)
5. Guerraoui, R., Herlihy, M.P., Pochon, B.: Polymorphic contention management. In: Fraigniaud, P. (ed.) DISC 2005. LNCS, vol. 3724, pp. 303–323. Springer, Heidelberg (2005)
6. Guerraoui, R., Kapalka, M.: On the correctness of transactional memory. In: Proc. of the ACM Symp. on Principles and Practice of Parallel Programming (PPoPP), pp. 175–184 (2008)
7. Ha, P.H., Tsigas, P., Anshus, O.J.: Nb-feb: An easy-to-use and scalable universal synchronization primitive for parallel programming. TR No. CS-2008-69, Univ. of Tromsø, Norway (2008), http://www.cs.uit.no/~phuong/nbfeb_tr.pdf
8. Harris, T., Fraser, K.: Language support for lightweight transactions. In: Proc. of the ACM Conf. on Object-oriented Programing, Systems, Languages, and Applications (OOPSLA), pp. 388–402 (2003)
9. Herlihy, M.: Wait-free synchronization. ACM Transaction on Programming and Systems 11(1), 124–149 (1991)
10. Herlihy, M., Luchangco, V., Moir, M., Scherer III, W.N.: Software transactional memory for dynamic-sized data structures. In: Proc. of Symp. on Principles of Distributed Computing (PODC), pp. 92–101 (2003)
11. Kruskal, C.P., et al.: Efficient synchronization of multiprocessors with shared memory. ACM Trans. Program. Lang. Syst. 10(4), 579–601 (1988)
12. Marathe, V.J., Scherer III, W.N., Scott, M.L.: Adaptive software transactional memory. In: Fraigniaud, P. (ed.) DISC 2005. LNCS, vol. 3724, pp. 354–368. Springer, Heidelberg (2005)
13. NVIDIA. NVIDIA CUDA Compute Unified Device Architecture, Programming Guide, version 1.1. NVIDIA Corporation (2007)
14. Pfister, G.F., et al.: The IBM research parallel processor prototype (RP3): Introduction and architecture. In: ICPP, pp. 764–771 (1985)
15. Plotkin, S.A.: Sticky bits and universality of consensus. In: Proc. of Symp. on Principles of Distributed Computing (PODC), pp. 159–175 (1989)
16. Rangan, R., Vachharajani, N., Vachharajani, M., August, D.: Decoupled software pipelining with the synchronization array. In: Proc. of the Intl. Conf. on Parallel Architecture and Compilation Techniques (PACT), pp. 177–188 (2004)
17. Riegel, T., Felber, P., Fetzer, C.: A lazy snapshot algorithm with eager validation. In: Dolev, S. (ed.) DISC 2006. LNCS, vol. 4167, pp. 284–298. Springer, Heidelberg (2006)
18. Scherer III, W.N., Scott, M.L.: Advanced contention management for dynamic software transactional memory. In: Proc. of Symp. on Principles of Distributed Computing (PODC), pp. 240–248 (2005)
19. Sridharan, S., Rodrigues, A., Kogge, P.: Evaluating synchronization techniques for light-weight multithreaded/multicore architectures. In: Proc. of the ACM Symp. on Parallel Algorithms and Architectures (SPAA), pp. 57–58 (2007)

Gradient Clock Synchronization Using Reference Broadcasts

Fabian Kuhn[1] and Rotem Oshman[2]

[1] Faculty of Informatics, University of Lugano, Switzerland
[2] Computer Science and Artificial Intelligence Laboratory, MIT, USA

Abstract. Reference-Broadcast Synchronization (RBS) is a technique that allows a set of receivers in a broadcast network to accurately estimate each others' clock values. RBS provides a relative time-frame for conversion between the local clocks of different nodes, and can be used to synchronize nodes to an external time-source such as GPS. However, RBS by itself does not output a logical clock at every node, and so it does not solve internal clock synchronization.

In this work we study the theoretical properties of RBS in the worst-case model, in which the performance of a clock synchronization algorithm is measured by the worst-case skew it can incur. We suggest a method by which RBS can be incorporated in standard internal clock synchronization algorithms. This is achieved by separating the task of estimating the clock values of other nodes in the network from the task of using these estimates to output a logical clock value.

The separation is modelled using a virtual *estimate graph*, overlaid on top of the real network graph, which represents the information various nodes can obtain about each other. RBS estimates are represented in the estimate graph as edges between nodes at distance 2 from each other in the original network graph. A clock synchronization algorithm then operates on the estimate graph as though it were the original network.

To illustrate the merits of this approach, we modify a recent optimal gradient clock synchronization algorithm to work in this setting. The modified algorithm transparently takes advantage of RBS estimates. Its quality of synchronization depends on the diameter of the estimate graph, which is typically much smaller than the diameter of the original network graph.

Keywords: Gradient Clock Synchronization, Wireless Networks.

1 Introduction

The evolving field of wireless networks poses new and interesting challenges to time synchronization, leading to renewed attention to this venerable problem in recent years. Sensor networks in particular are subject to constraints on computation power and energy consumption, and often require a greater degree of synchronization than traditional distributed applications.

In a multi-hop sensor network it is frequently the case that neighboring nodes must be closely synchronized, while far-apart nodes can tolerate greater clock

T. Abdelzaher, M. Raynal, and N. Santoro (Eds.): OPODIS 2009, LNCS 5923, pp. 204–218, 2009.

skew: neighboring nodes interfere with each other when they try to transmit, and are also more likely to cooperate for the purpose of some local computation. This gives rise to the problem of *gradient clock synchronization*, in which the synchronization between two nodes improves the closer they are to each other. The problem was first formulated in [6], where it is shown that in a network of diameter D, no algorithm can guarantee a skew that is better than $\Omega(\log D / \log \log D)$ even between adjacent nodes. Subsequent work has improved the lower bound to $\Omega(\log D)$, and come up with algorithms that match it [9,10].

The wireless broadcast medium also offers opportunities for better synchronization. Although contention may cause unpredictable delays before a message is broadcast, once a message is transmitted, it is received by all nodes in the sender's neighborhood almost instantaneously. Reference broadcast synchronization (RBS) [4] takes advantage of this to let the *neighbors* of the sender estimate each other's clock values with great accuracy. RBS can be extended to multi-hop networks, to allow any node in the network to estimate the clock value of any other node. However, by itself, RBS does not output a *logical clock* at every node, and so it is not a clock synchronization algorithm in the traditional sense.

In this paper we suggest an approach by which RBS, or any other estimation method (including external time sources), can be seamlessly incorporated in many clock synchronization algorithms, in order to reduce the effective diameter of the network and achieve better synchronization. We suggest a separation between the *estimate layer*, which is responsible for estimating other nodes' clock values, and the algorithm that uses these estimates to compute a local logical clock. The estimate layer runs underneath the algorithm and provides it with an *estimate graph* G^{est}. Each edge $\{u, v\}$ of G^{est} represents an estimate that node u can get for node v's clock value (and vice-versa), along with an associated *uncertainty*. RBS estimates are represented in G^{est} as edges between nodes at distance 2 from each other in the original network graph.

Almost any clock synchronization algorithm can be used on top of the estimate layer, as long as the algorithm can handle networks with non-uniform uncertainty on the links. The resulting synchronization between nodes u, v depends on their *effective distance* $\mathrm{dist}(u, v)$, and on the *effective diameter* of the network graph. These are defined by the corresponding distances in the estimate graph G^{est}. Using RBS it is possible to reduce the effective diameter to $O((\rho \cdot \mathcal{T} + u_{\mathrm{rcv}}) \cdot D + \mathcal{T})$, where D is the diameter of the original network, $\mathcal{T}$ is a bound on the message delay, ρ is a bound on clock drift (typically very small), and u_{rcv} is a bound on the receiver uncertainty (also very small [4]), which bounds the time it takes a node to process a message it receives.

Our main contributions are as follows. In Section 4 we define the estimate layer, and show how to incorporate point-to-point messages and RBS. In Section 5, we illustrate the applicability of our approach by modifying the algorithm of [10] to work on top of the estimate layer. Significantly, this involves extending it to a heterogeneous network; in [10] it is assumed that all links are subject to the same bounds on message delay. Finally, in Section 6 we prove that the algorithm achieves gradient clock synchronization, with the skew between nodes

u and v bounded by $O(\text{dist}(u,v) \cdot \log_{1/\rho} \mathcal{D})$ in networks with effective diameter $\mathcal{D}$ and drift bounded by ρ. This is asymptotically optimal. The proof is based on the proof in [10], but in our view it is cleaner and somewhat simpler.

2   Related Work

The problem of establishing a common notion of time is at the core of many distributed systems and applications and has been widely studied, from both theoretical and a practical points of view. In most of the existing work on clock synchronization, the nodes of a network compute estimates about each others' clock values by exchanging messages. Based on the information obtained, each node computes a local logical clock. Typically, the accuracy of clock estimates is determined by the uncertainty about the propagation delay of messages. In [12], it is shown that even if hardware clocks experience no drift, no clock synchronization algorithm can prevent a clock skew of $\Omega(D)$ in a network of diameter D. This lower bound on the maximum clock skew between any two nodes is matched by an algorithm described in [20] and by many subsequent algorithms (e.g. [2,14,5,10,9,15,16]). Clock synchronization algorithms and lower bounds that accommodate non-uniform uncertainties are described, for example, in [1,3,7].

In [6], Fan and Lynch introduced the gradient clock synchronization problem. It is shown that even on a path of length D, no algorithm can guarantee a clock skew smaller than $\Omega(\log D/\log \log D)$ between adjacent nodes. This bound has been improved to $\Omega(\log D)$ in [10] and it is shown in [9,10] that the new bound in indeed tight.

The special properties, constraints, and requirements of wireless ad hoc and sensor networks make clock synchronization especially challenging. There is a considerable amount of work on the problem (e.g. [5,18,19,21,13,17]). Particularly interesting is the work on reference broadcast synchronization [4,8], which exploits the property of sharing a single communication channel to obtain high accuracy clock estimates of nearby nodes.

3   Preliminaries

In the sequel we use $\mathbb{R}^{\geq 0}$ to denote the set of non-negative reals and $\mathbb{N}^{>0}$ to denote the positive integers.

We model a wireless network as an undirected graph $G = (V, E)$, where V is the set of nodes, and $\{u, v\} \in E$ iff u is in reception range of v and vice-versa. We abstract away low-level details of contention management, message loss and so on, by assuming reliable message delivery with message delays bounded by a parameter $\mathcal{T}$.

Each node v in the network has access to a local hardware clock H_v, which is subject to drift bounded by $\rho < 1$. We assume that for all $t_1 \leq t_2$,

$$(1 - \rho)(t_2 - t_1) \leq H_v(t_2) - H_v(t_1) \leq (1 + \rho)(t_2 - t_1).$$

The hardware clock increases continuously, and for the analysis we assume it is differentiable.

The goal of gradient clock synchronization is to output a local logical clock L_v at every node v, which is closely-synchronized with all the other logical clocks. Formally, an algorithm is said to achieve f-gradient clock synchronization, for a function $f : \mathbb{R}^{\geq 0} \to \mathbb{R}^{\geq 0}$, if it satisfies the following requirement.

Requirement 31. *For all $u, v \in V$ and times t we have*

$$L_v(t) - L_u(t) \leq f\left(\text{dist}(u, v)\right).$$

Here $\text{dist}(u, v)$ stands for the distance between u and v, which informally corresponds to the accuracy of information u and v can acquire about each other. Traditionally, $\text{dist}(u, v)$ is defined as the minimal sum of the uncertainties regarding message delay on any path between u and v (see, e.g., [2]). In the next section we redefine $\text{dist}(u, v)$ to incorporate reference broadcast synchronization.

In addition to f-gradient synchronization, we require the logical clocks to behave like "real" clocks. Specifically, the logical clocks should be strictly increasing, and they should always be within a linear envelope of real time. In particular, the logical clocks are continuous. This is captured by the following requirement.

Requirement 32. *There exist $\alpha \in (0, 1)$ and $\beta \geq 0$ such that for all $t_1 \leq t_2$,*

$$(1 - \alpha)(t_2 - t_1) \leq L_u(t_2) - L_u(t_1) \leq (1 + \beta)(t_2 - t_1).$$

4 The Estimate Layer

The estimate layer encapsulates point-to-point messages, reference broadcast synchronization, and any other means the nodes in the network have of obtaining information about the logical clock values of other nodes. The estimate layer provides an undirected *estimate graph* $G^{\text{est}} = (V, E^{\text{est}})$, where each edge $u, v \in E^{\text{est}}$ represents some method by which nodes u and v can estimate each others' logical clock values. Note that G^{est} can be different from the underlying network graph G; for example, RBS is represented in G^{est} as edges connecting nodes at distance 2 from each other in G. We use $N(u) := \{v \in V \mid u, v \in E^{\text{est}}\}$ to denote u's neighborhood in G^{est}.

The estimate layer provides each node $u \in V$ with a set of local variables $\left\{ \tilde{L}_u^v : v \in N(u) \right\}$, which represent u's current estimates for the logical clock values of its neighbors in G^{est}. Since the estimates are typically inaccurate, we associate with every edge $e \in E^{\text{est}}$ an *uncertainty* ϵ_e. The estimate layer guarantees the following property.

Property 1 (Estimate quality). For any edge $(u, v) \in E^{\text{est}}$ and time t, we have

$$L_v(t) - \epsilon_{\{u,v\}} \leq \tilde{L}_u^v(t) \leq L_v(t) + \epsilon_{\{u,v\}}.$$

Two methods of obtaining logical clock estimates are described below. We describe each method and bound the error associated with it, and then show how to combine multiple methods.

Direct estimates. Following the style of algorithms suggested in [11,9,10], we assume that every node broadcasts its logical clock value to all its neighbors once every subjective ΔH time units (that is, after its hardware clock has increased by ΔH), where ΔH is a parameter. These messages provide a direct estimate of the node's logical clock value. When node u receives a message from v at time t, it sets $\tilde{L}_u^{v,\text{direct}} \leftarrow L$. Between messages from v, node u increases $\tilde{L}_u^{v,\text{direct}}$ at the rate of its own hardware clock.

The error of a direct estimate can be shown to be bounded by

$$-(\alpha+\rho)\left(\frac{\Delta H}{1-\rho}+\mathcal{T}\right) \leq L_v(t) - \tilde{L}_u^{v,\text{direct}}(t) \leq (\beta+\rho)\left(\frac{\Delta H}{1-\rho}+\mathcal{T}\right) + (1-\rho)\mathcal{T}.$$

Note that at this point, our error bound is asymmetric. It is straightforward to obtain a symmetric guarantee in the style of Prop. 1. Specifically, if $\beta = O(1)$, we have $\left|L_v(t) - \tilde{L}_u^{v,\text{direct}}(t)\right| = O(\Delta H + \mathcal{T})$.

RBS estimates. An RBS estimate is obtained by comparing the logical clock values that various nodes record when some common event occurs; in our case, a broadcast by a shared neighbor. We give a simple way to obtain RBS estimates, which is optimal as regards worst-case analysis, but differs from the more practical treatment in [4].

We use $\mathcal{H}_u$ to denote node u's *history*, a set of triplets (x, L, H) where x is a unique event identifier and L, H record node u's logical and hardware clock values when it observed the event. After recording event x, node u sends a report(u, x, L) message, which is propagated until it reaches all other nodes that observed the same event. In our case, report$(\cdot)$ messages need to be re-broadcast only once, so that they reach the 2-neighborhood of the node that originated the report.

The accuracy of RBS depends on two factors.

1. *Receiver uncertainty* is the time required for nodes to process the common event and record their logical clock value. The receiver uncertainty is bounded by u_{rcv} if whenever an event x occurs at real time t, there is some $t_x \in [t, t+u_{\text{rcv}}]$ such that for all $t' \geq t_x$ we have $(x, L_u(t_x), H_u(t_x)) \in \mathcal{H}_u(t')$.
2. *Propagation delay* is the time it takes for nodes that observe an event to receive report$(\cdot)$ messages from other nodes that observed it. This delay contributes to the inaccuracy of the estimate, because while the report is propagated the clocks continue to drift apart. We say that the propagation delay is bounded by $\mathcal{P}$ if whenever a node u experiences an event x at real time t, every node $v \in N^2(u)$ receives a report(u, x, L) message no later than time $t + \mathcal{P}$.
   In our case, because report$(\cdot)$ messages need to be re-broadcast only once, the propagation delay is bounded by $\mathcal{P} \leq u_{\text{rcv}} + 2\left(\frac{\Delta H}{1-\rho} + \mathcal{T}\right)$: after observing the event, node u waits at most $\frac{\Delta H}{1-\rho}$ time units and then broadcasts the message, which takes at most $\mathcal{T}$ time units to arrive; its neighbors do the same.

When node u receives a report(v, x, L) message at time t, it looks up the corresponding triplet (x, H', L') recorded in its own history. It uses $H_u - H'$ to estimate the time that has passed since x occurred, and sets

$$\tilde{L}_u^{v,\mathrm{rbs}} \leftarrow L + H_u - H'.$$

Every broadcast by a node is an event that its neighbors use to get estimates of each others' logical clock values. RBS estimates are accurate up to the following bound.

$$-(\alpha + \rho)\left(\frac{\Delta H}{1 - \rho} + \mathcal{P}\right) - (1 - \alpha)u_{\mathrm{rcv}} \leq L_v(t) - \tilde{L}_u^{v,\mathrm{rbs}}(t) \leq$$

$$\leq (\beta + \rho)\left(\frac{\Delta H}{1 - \rho} + \mathcal{P}\right) + (1 - \rho)u_{\mathrm{rcv}}.$$

Assuming $u_{\mathrm{rcv}} \ll \Delta H + T$, the RBS estimates are a significant improvement over direct estimates between nodes at distance 2 as long as the clock synchronization algorithm guarantees that $\alpha, \beta \ll 1$. In particular, if $\alpha, \beta = O(\rho)$, we obtain $\left|L_v(t) - \tilde{L}_u^{v,\mathrm{rbs}}(t)\right| = O(u_{\mathrm{rcv}} + \rho(\Delta H + T))$.

Combining multiple estimates. As we have seen, each node may have multiple ways of estimating the clock values of its neighbors in G^{est}. Let $\tilde{L}_u^{v,1}, \ldots, \tilde{L}_u^{v,m}$ be the various estimates that u has for v's logical clock value, and let $\epsilon_{\mathrm{low}}^1, \ldots, \epsilon_{\mathrm{low}}^m$ and $\epsilon_{\mathrm{high}}^1, \ldots, \epsilon_{\mathrm{high}}^m$ be error bounds such that for all $i \in \{1, \ldots, m\}$ and time t we have $-\epsilon_{\mathrm{low}}^i \leq L_v(t) - \tilde{L}_u^{v,i}(t) \leq \epsilon_{\mathrm{high}}^i$. Node u computes a combined estimate with symmetric error, given by

$$\tilde{L}_u^v(t) := \frac{\min_i\left(\tilde{L}_u^{v,i}(t) + \epsilon_{\mathrm{high}}^i\right) - \max_i\left(\tilde{L}_u^{v,i}(t) - \epsilon_{\mathrm{low}}^i\right)}{2}. \tag{1}$$

The uncertainty of the combined estimate is bounded by

$$\epsilon_{\{u,v\}} := \min_i\left\{\frac{\epsilon_{\mathrm{low}}^i + \epsilon_{\mathrm{high}}^i}{2}\right\}.$$

Effective distance and diameter. Let $\mathcal{P}$ denote the set of all paths in the graph G^{est} (including non-simple paths), and let $\mathcal{P}(v) \subseteq \mathcal{P}$ denote the set of paths that start at node v. Given a path $P = v_0, \ldots, v_k \in \mathcal{P}$, we denote $\epsilon_P := \sum_{i=0}^{k-1} \epsilon_{\{v_i, v_{i+1}\}}$. Given two nodes $u, v \in V$, the distance between u and v is defined by

$$\mathrm{dist}(u, v) := \min_{P = u, \ldots, v} \epsilon_P, \tag{2}$$

and the diameter of the graph G^{est} is defined by

$$\mathcal{D} := \max_{u,v} \mathrm{dist}(u, v). \tag{3}$$

In the following assume that we have a clock synchronization algorithm that guarantees $\alpha, \beta = O(\rho)$. Let $d_e(u, v)$ be the length of the shortest even-length path and let $d(u, v)$ be the length of the shortest path between two nodes u and v in G. When using RBS estimates, we have $\mathrm{dist}(u, v) = O\big(d_e(u, v) \cdot (\rho(\Delta H + T) + $

u_{rcv})). Further, when using both direct and RBS estimates, we have $\text{dist}(u, v) = O\big(d(u, v) \cdot (\rho(\Delta H + \mathcal{T}) + u_{\text{rcv}}) + \Delta H + \mathcal{T}\big)$. Consequently, we obtain

$$\mathcal{D} = O\big((1 + \rho D)(\Delta H + \mathcal{T}) + u_{\text{rcv}} D\big),$$

where D is the diameter of the underlying network G. As the receiver uncertainty u_{rcv} is typically small, this is a significant improvement over the "true" diameter of G.

5   An Optimal Gradient Clock-Synchronization Algorithm

In this section we modify the algorithm of [10] to work on top of the estimation layer presented in the previous section.

To satisfy Requirement 32, the algorithm increases the logical clock in a continuous manner, with no discrete jumps. At each point during the execution a node is either in *fast mode* or in *slow mode*. In slow mode, u increases its logical clock at a rate of $\frac{d}{dt} H_u(t)$; in fast mode, the logical clock rate is $(1 + \mu)\frac{d}{dt} H_u(t)$, where μ is a parameter.

Each node continually examines its estimates for the logical clock values of its neighbors in G^{est}. To compensate for the uncertainty on edge e we use a parameter κ_e, which is defined as

$$\kappa_e := \frac{2}{\lambda} \cdot \epsilon_e \qquad (4)$$

for some constant $0 < \lambda < 1/4$ [1]. For a path $P \in \mathcal{P}$, we define $\kappa_P := \frac{2}{\lambda} \cdot \epsilon_P$.

If a node u finds that it is too far behind, it goes into fast mode and uses the fast rate of $(1 + \mu)\frac{d}{dt} H_u(t)$. The following rule is used to determine when to go into fast mode; informally, it states that some neighbor is far ahead, and no neighbor is too far behind.

Definition 1 (Fast condition FC). *At time t, a node $u \in V$ satisfies the fast condition, denoted FC, if there is some integer $s \in \mathbb{N}$ for which following conditions are satisfied:*

(FC1) $\exists v \in N(u) : \tilde{L}_u^v(t) - L_u(t) \geq (s - 1 - \lambda)\,\kappa_{\{u,v\}}$, *and*
(FC2) $\forall v \in N(u) : L_u(t) - \tilde{L}_u^v(t) \geq (s - 1 + \lambda)\,\kappa_{\{u,v\}}$.

Conversely, if a node is far behind some neighbor, and no other neighbor is too far ahead of it, it enters slow mode and uses the slow rate. The rule for entering slow mode is as follows.

Definition 2 (Slow condition SC). *At time t, a node $u \in V$ satisfies the* slow *condition, denoted SC, if there is an integer $s \in \mathbb{N}^{>0}$ for which the following conditions are satisfied:*

(SC1) $\exists v \in N(u) : L_u(t) - \tilde{L}_u^v(t) \geq \left(s - \frac{1}{2} - \lambda\right) \cdot \kappa_{\{u,v\}}$, *and*
(SC2) $\forall v \in N(u) : \tilde{L}_u^v(t) - L_u(t) \leq \left(s - \frac{1}{2} + \lambda\right) \cdot \kappa_{\{u,v\}}$.

---

[1]The choice of 2 in the definition of κ_e is arbitrary; it is sufficient to have $\kappa_e > \frac{1}{\lambda} \cdot \epsilon_e$.

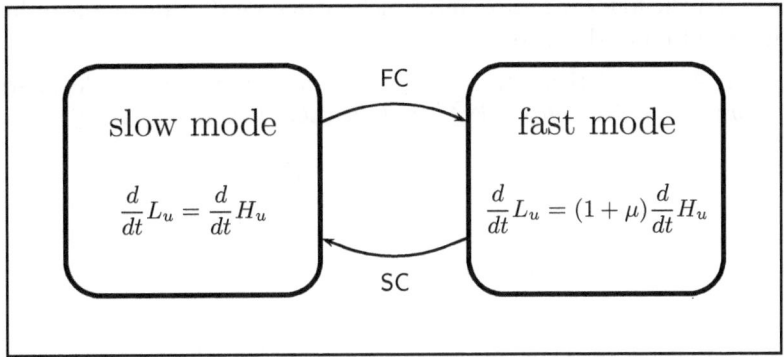

Fig. 1. A possible concrete implementation of the algorithm

The specification of the algorithm is nondeterministic. Whenever SC or FC are satisfied for some node, that node must be in slow or fast mode, respectively; this part of the specification is deterministic. However, when neither SC nor FC are satisfied, the node's behavior is nondeterministic, and the node can be in either slow or fast mode.

To show that the algorithm is realizable, we show that the two conditions are disjoint, which ensures that no node is required to be in both fast mode and slow mode at the same time. The proof is technical and we omit it here.

Lemma 1. *No node can satisfy* SC *and* FC *at the same time.* □

One possible implementation of the algorithm is shown in Fig. 1. In this implementation, the nondeterminism in the specification is resolved by having a node stay in its current state until SC or FC are satisfied, and then transition to the appropriate state. When neither SC nor FC are satisfied the node simply stays in its current state. We stress that this is only one possible choice; the algorithm performs correctly regardless of what nodes do when SC and FC are not satisfied.

6   Analysis

In this section we show that the algorithm achieves $O\left(\text{dist}(u, v) \cdot \log \mathcal{D}\right)$-gradient synchronization. The proofs of some lemmas are omitted; they appear in the full version of this paper.

We define a parameter $\sigma \geq 2$, which serves as the base for the logarithm in the gradient skew bound. The correctness of the algorithm relies on the following assumption, which (informally) states that μ is large enough to allow nodes that are behind to catch up.

Property 2 (Requirement on μ). We require

$$\mu > 4\sigma \frac{\rho}{1 - \rho}. \tag{5}$$

We show that the following invariant, which we denote $\mathcal{L}$, is maintained throughout any execution of the algorithm.

Definition 3 (Legal State). *We say that the network is in a* legal state *at time t if and only if for all $s \in \mathbb{N}^{>0}$ and all paths $P = v_0, \ldots, v_k$, if*

$$\kappa_P(t) \geq C_s := \frac{4}{\lambda} \cdot \frac{\mathcal{D}}{\sigma^s},$$

then

$$L_{v_k}(t) - L_{v_0}(t) \leq s \cdot \kappa_P.$$

In particular, if the network is legal at time t, then for every two nodes u, v and integer $s \geq 1$ such that $\text{dist}(u, v) \geq C_s$, we have $L_u(t) - L_v(t) \leq s \cdot \frac{2}{\lambda} \cdot \text{dist}(u, v)$. The gradient synchronization property follows (see Corollaries 1, 2).

To show that the network is always in the safety region defined by the legal state condition, we show that whenever some path comes close to having illegal skew, the algorithm acts to decrease the skew, pulling the system back into the safety region.

Unfortunately, the proof is not straightforward. We cannot guarantee that a node will always "realize" when it is on a path that has too much skew: each node only has knowledge of its local neighborhood, and this local image may not reflect a large skew further down the path. We can, however, show that when the skew is close to being illegal, the nodes that are "the most behind" or "the most ahead", in a sense defined formally below, *will* realize that they must act to correct the skew. We will show that such nodes enter fast or slow mode as appropriate.

Since we can only argue about the clock rate of nodes that roughly speaking maximize some notion of weighted skew (defined below), we will use the following technical lemma.

Lemma 2. *Let $g_1, \ldots, g_n : \mathbb{R}^{\geq 0} \to \mathbb{R}^{\geq 0}$ be differentiable functions, and let $[a, b]$ be an interval such that for all $i \in \{1, \ldots, n\}$ and $x \in (a, b)$, if $g_i(x) = \max_j g_j(x)$ then $\frac{d}{dx} g_i(x) \leq r$. Then for all $x \in [a, b]$, $\max_i g_i(x) \leq \max_i g_i(a) + r \cdot (x - a)$.*

Next we define two different notions of "weighted skew": one captures how much a node v_0 is ahead of any other node, and the other captures how far behind it is. The weights in both cases are proportional to the uncertainty on the path, but use different constants. These notions correspond exactly to the the fast and slow conditions, respectively.

Definition 4. *Given an integer $s \in \mathbb{N}$, a time t, and a path $P = v_0, \ldots, v_k \in \mathcal{P}$, we define*

$$\Xi_P^s(t) := L_{v_0}(t) - L_{v_k}(t) - (s - 1) \cdot \kappa_P, \quad and \quad \Xi_{v_0}^s(t) := \max_{P \in \mathcal{P}(v_0)} \Xi_P^s(t).$$

Definition 5. *Given an integer $s \in \mathbb{N}$, a time t, and a path $P = v_0, \ldots, v_k \in \mathcal{P}$, we define*

$$\Psi_P^s(t) := L_{v_k}(t) - L_{v_0}(t) - \left(s - \frac{1}{2} \right) \cdot \kappa_P, \quad and \quad \Psi_{v_0}^s(t) := \max_{P \in \mathcal{P}(v_0)} \Psi_P^s(t).$$

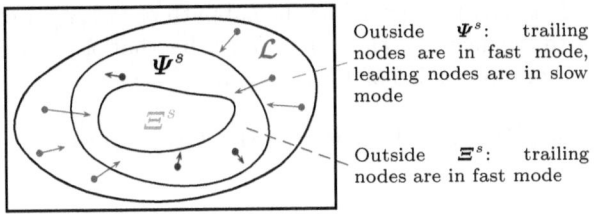

Outside $\boldsymbol{\Psi}^s$: trailing nodes are in fast mode, leading nodes are in slow mode

Outside $\boldsymbol{\Xi}^s$: trailing nodes are in fast mode

Fig. 2. Regions $\boldsymbol{\Xi}^s$, $\boldsymbol{\Psi}^s$ and $\mathcal{L}$. Arrows illustrate the possible dynamics acting on the weighted skew in each region.

These definitions induce "inner safety regions" $\boldsymbol{\Xi}^s := [\max_v \Xi_v^s \le 0]$ and $\boldsymbol{\Psi}^s := [\max_v \Psi_v^s \le 0]$ for any $s \in \mathbb{N}^{>0}$, with $\boldsymbol{\Xi}^s \subseteq \boldsymbol{\Psi}^s \subseteq \mathcal{L}$ (see Fig. 2).

The next lemma can be thought of as bounding how far the system can stray outside the boundary of $\boldsymbol{\Xi}^s$ and $\boldsymbol{\Psi}^s$ while still being in a legal state.

Lemma 3. *If the network is in a legal state at time t, then for all nodes $u \in V$ and integers $s \ge 1$ we have $\Xi_u^s(t) < C_{s-1}$ and $\Psi_u^s(t) < C_{s-1}$.* $\qquad \square$

Next we show that when the system is outside the region $\boldsymbol{\Xi}^s$, nodes that are "the most behind" (maximize Ξ with respect to some other node) will be acting to catch up, and when the system is outside the region $\boldsymbol{\Psi}^s$, nodes that are "the most ahead" will be held back from moving too quickly.

Lemma 4. *Let $P = v_0, \ldots, v_k \in \mathcal{P}(v_0)$ be a path starting at v_0 for which $\Xi_P^s(t) = \Xi_{v_0}^s(t)$ at some time t. If $\Xi_{v_0}^s(t) > 0$, then v_k is in fast mode at time t.*

Lemma 5. *Let $P = v_0, \ldots, v_k \in \mathcal{P}(v_0)(t)$ be a path starting at v_0 for which $\Psi_P^s(t) = \Psi_{v_0}^s(t)$ at some time t. If $\Psi_{v_0}^s(t) > 0$, then v_k is in slow mode at time t.*

The proofs of the two lemmas are similar. We give the proof of Lemma 4 here.

Proof (Lemma 4). We set out to show that v_k satisfies FC.

Consider any path $P' = v_0, \ldots, v \in \mathcal{P}(v_0)$ that ends at a neighbor v of v_k. Since $\Xi_P^s(t) = \Xi_{v_0}^s(t) = \max_{Q \in \mathcal{P}(v_0)} \Xi_Q^s(t)$, we have $\Xi_{P'}^s(t) \le \Xi_P^s(t)$; that is,

$$L_{v_0}(t) - L_v(t) - (s-1) \cdot \kappa_{P'} \le L_{v_0}(t) - L_{v_k}(t) - (s-1) \cdot \kappa_P.$$

Re-arranging yields

$$L_v(t) - L_{v_k}(t) \ge (s-1) \cdot (\kappa_P - \kappa_{P'}),$$

and applying Property 1 we obtain

$$\tilde{L}_{v_k}^v(t) - L_{v_k}(t) \ge L_v(t) - \epsilon_{\{v,v_k\}} - L_{v_k}(t) \ge$$
$$\ge (s-1) \cdot (\kappa_P - \kappa_{P'}) - \epsilon_{\{v,v_k\}}. \qquad (6)$$

To show (FC1) is satisfied, let P' be the subpath $v_0, \ldots, v_{k-1}$ of P, where $v_{k-1} \in N(v)$. Note that since $\Xi_P(t) > 0$ it must be that $k > 0$, and thus v_{k-1} is well-defined. For this choice of P', (6) yields

$$\tilde{L}_{v_k}^{v_{k-1}}(t) - L_{v_k}(t) \geq (s-1) \cdot (\kappa_P - \kappa_{P'}) - \epsilon_{\{v_{k-1}, v_k\}} =$$

$$= (s-1) \cdot \kappa_{\{v_{k-1}, v_k\}} - \epsilon_{\{v_{k-1}, v_k\}} \overset{(4)}{>} (s-1-\lambda) \kappa_{\{v_{k-1}, v_k\}}.$$

This shows that (FC1) is satisfied. To show that (FC2) holds, let $v \in N(v_k)$ be any neighbor of v_k, and let $P' = v_0, \ldots, v_k, v$ be the path obtained by appending v to the path P. In this case (6) yields

$$L_{v_k}(t) - \tilde{L}_{v_k}^{v}(t) \leq (s-1) \cdot (\kappa_{P'} - \kappa_P) + \epsilon_{\{v, v_k\}} =$$

$$= (s-1) \cdot \kappa_{\{v, v_k\}} + \epsilon_{\{v, v_k\}} \overset{(4)}{<} (s-1+\lambda) \cdot \kappa_{\{v, v_k\}}.$$

Hence, the second condition is satisfied as well, and node v_k is in fast mode. □

Suppose that at time t, node v has $\Xi_v^s(t) > 0$. From Lemma 4, all the nodes that maximize Ξ_v^s are in fast mode, trying to catch up to v, and their logical clock rate is at least $(1-\rho)(1+\mu)$. Thus, whenever it is positive, Ξ_v^s decreases at an average rate of at least $(1-\rho)(1+\mu)$, *minus* the rate by which v increases its own logical clock. To formalize this observation, define

$$\mathcal{I}_v(t_1, t_2) := L_v(t_2) - L_v(t_1) \tag{7}$$

to be the amount by which v increases its logical clock over the time interval $[t_1, t_2]$. Since $\frac{d}{dt} L_v(t) \geq \frac{d}{dt} H_v(t) \geq 1 - \rho$ we have the following property.

Property 3. For all nodes v and times t_1, t_2 we have $\mathcal{I}_v(t_1, t_2) \geq (1-\rho)(t_2 - t_1)$.

Now we can state the following lemma.

Lemma 6 (Catch-Up Lemma). *Let v_0 be a node and let $[t_0, t_1]$ be a time interval such that for all $t \in (t_0, t_1)$ we have $\Xi_{v_0}^s(t) > 0$. Then for all $t \in [t_0, t_1]$,*

$$\Xi_{v_0}^s(t) \leq \Xi_{v_0}^s(t_0) + \mathcal{I}_{v_0}(t_0, t) - (1-\rho)(1+\mu)(t - t_0).$$

Similarly, whenever $\Psi_v^s(t) > 0$, the nodes that maximize Ψ_v^s are in slow mode, and their logical clocks increase at a rate of at most $1 + \rho$. Thus, whenever it is positive, $\Psi_v^s(t)$ increases at an average rate of at most $1 + \rho$, again minus v's increase to its own logical clock. This is captured by the following lemma.

Lemma 7 (Waiting Lemma). *Let v_0 be a node and let $[t_0, t_1]$ be a time interval such that for all $t \in (t_0, t_1)$ we have $\Psi_{v_0}^s(t) > 0$. Then for all $t \in [t_0, t_1]$,*

$$\Psi_{v_0}^s(t) \leq \Psi_{v_0}^s(t_0) - \mathcal{I}_{v_0}(t_0, t) + (1+\rho)(t - t_0).$$

The proofs of Lemmas 6 and 7 involve a straightforward application of Lemma 2.

We have so far argued that if v_0 is too far ahead of other nodes then those nodes will be in fast mode, and if v_0 is too far behind other nodes then those nodes will be in slow mode. What does v_0 *itself* do when it is too far behind? Observe that if there is some path $P = v_0, \ldots, v_k$ such that $\Psi_P^s(t) > 0$, then for the inverted path $P' = v_k, \ldots, v_0$ we have $\Xi_{P'}^s(t) > \Psi_P^s(t) > 0$. Thus, informally speaking, whenever v_0 is too far behind some other node it will be "pulled forward" at the fast rate. The next lemma quantifies how much ground v_0 makes up during an interval in which it is far behind: it states that given sufficient time, the node makes up all the initial weighted skew Ψ_v^s, *in addition* to its minimal rate of progress $(1 - \rho)$.

Lemma 8. *For any node v_0, integer $s \in \mathbb{N}^{>0}$ and time interval $[t_0, t_1]$ where $t_1 \geq t_0 + \frac{C_{s-1}}{(1-\rho)\mu}$, if the network is in a legal state at time t_0, then*

$$\mathcal{I}_{v_0}(t_0, t_1) \geq \Psi_{v_0}^s(t_0) + (1 - \rho)(t_1 - t_0).$$

Proof (Lemma 8). If $\Psi_{v_0}^s(t_0) \leq 0$, the claim follows immediately from Property 3. Thus, assume that $\Psi_{v_0}^s(t_0) > 0$, and let $P = v_0, \ldots, v_k$ be a path such that $\Psi_P^s(t_0) = \Psi_{v_0}^s(t_0)$. From the definitions of Ψ and Ξ, for the inverted path $P' = v_k, \ldots, v_0$ we have $\Xi_{P'}^s(t_0) > \Psi_P^s(t_0)$, and therefore, $\Xi_{v_k}^s(t_0) > \Psi_{v_0}^s(t) > 0$. If there is a time $t \in [t_0, t_1]$ such that $\Xi_{v_k}^s(t) \leq 0$, let $\bar{t}$ be the infimum of such times. Otherwise, let $\bar{t} = t_1$. Observe that

$$\mathcal{I}_{v_0}(t_0, \bar{t}) = L_{v_0}(\bar{t}) - L_{v_0}(t_0) = \Xi_{P'}^s(t_0) - \Xi_{P'}^s(\bar{t}) + \mathcal{I}_{v_k}(t_0, \bar{t})$$
$$> \Psi_P^s(t_0) - \Xi_{v_k}^s(\bar{t}) + \mathcal{I}_{v_k}(t_0, \bar{t}) = \Psi_{v_0}^s(t_0) - \Xi_{v_k}^s(\bar{t}) + \mathcal{I}_{v_k}(t_0, \bar{t}).$$

Since $\bar{t} \leq t_1$ and $\mathcal{I}_{v_0}(t_0, \cdot)$ is increasing and interval-additive, to prove the claim it is sufficient to show that $\mathcal{I}_{v_k}(t_0, \bar{t}) \geq \Xi_{v_k}^s(\bar{t}) + (1 - \rho)(\bar{t} - t_0)$.

Consider first the case where $\bar{t} < t_1$. In this case $\bar{t}$ is the infimum of times t where $\Xi_{v_k}^s(t) \leq 0$. Since $\Xi_{v_k}^s(\cdot)$ is continuous, it follows that $\Xi_{v_k}^s(\bar{t}) = 0$, and using Property 3 we obtain $\mathcal{I}_{v_k}(t_0, \bar{t}) \geq \Xi_{v_k}^s(\bar{t}) + (1 - \rho)(\bar{t} - t_0)$.

Otherwise, if $\bar{t} = t_1$, then for all $t \in [t_0, t_1)$ we have $\Xi_{v_k}^s(t) > 0$. Applying Lemma 6 to the interval $[t_0, t_1]$ we obtain

$$\Xi_{v_k}^s(t_1) \leq \Xi_{v_k}^s(t_0) + \mathcal{I}_{v_k}(t_0, t_1) - (1 - \rho)(1 + \mu)(t_1 - t_0) \leq$$
$$\overset{\text{Lemma 3}}{\leq} C_{s-1} + \mathcal{I}_{v_k}(t_0, t_1) - (1 - \rho)\mu \cdot \frac{C_{s-1}}{(1-\rho)\mu} - (1 - \rho)(t_1 - t_0) =$$
$$= \mathcal{I}_{v_k}(t_0, t_1) - (1 - \rho)(t_1 - t_0),$$

which yields the desired result. $\square$

Now we are ready to put all the pieces together and prove the main theorem:

Theorem 1. *The network is always in a legal state.*

Proof. Suppose for the sake of contradiction that this is not the case, and let $\bar{t}$ be the infimum of times when the legal state condition is violated. Then there is some path $P = v_0, \ldots, v_k$ and some $s \geq 1$ such that $\kappa_P \geq C_s$ but

$$L_{v_0}(\bar{t}) - L_{v_k}(\bar{t}) \geq s \cdot \kappa_P. \tag{8}$$

For the legal state condition to be violated, the system must be far outside the boundary of Ψ^s:

$$\Psi_{v_k}^s(\bar{t}) \geq L_{v_0}(\bar{t}) - L_{v_k}(\bar{t}) - \left(s - \frac{1}{2}\right) \cdot \kappa_P \overset{(8)}{\geq} \frac{1}{2}\kappa_P \geq \frac{1}{2}C_s = \frac{1}{2\sigma}C_{s-1}. \quad (9)$$

However, Lemma 7 tells us that whenever $\Psi_{v_k}^s$ is large it cannot increase quickly, which gives v_k time to catch up. Specifically, if t_0 is the supremum of times $t \leq \bar{t}$ such that $\Psi_{v_k}^s(t) \leq 0$, then Lemma 7 shows that

$$\Psi_{v_k}^s(\bar{t}) \leq \Psi_{v_k}^s(t_0) - \mathcal{I}_{v_k}(t_0, \bar{t}) + (1 + \rho)(\bar{t} - t_0) \overset{\text{(Prop. 3)}}{\leq} 2\rho(\bar{t} - t_0). \quad (10)$$

Let $t_1 := \bar{t} - \frac{C_{s-1}}{(1-\rho)\mu}$. Combining (9) and (10), we see that $t_0 \leq \bar{t} - \frac{C_{s-1}}{4\sigma\rho} \overset{(5)}{\leq} \bar{t} - \frac{C_{s-1}}{(1-\rho)\mu} = t_1$. Thus, by Lemma 8, the interval $[t_1, \bar{t}]$ is sufficient for v_k to increase its clock by

$$\mathcal{I}_{v_k}(t_1, \bar{t}) \geq \Psi_{v_k}^s(t_1) + (1 - \rho)(\bar{t} - t_1). \quad (11)$$

Applying Lemma 7 again, we obtain

$$\Psi_{v_k}^s(\bar{t}) \overset{\text{(Lemma 7)}}{\leq} \Psi_{v_k}^s(t_1) - \mathcal{I}_{v_k}(t_1, \bar{t}) + (1 + \rho)(\bar{t} - t_1) \overset{(11)}{\leq} 2\rho\frac{C_{s-1}}{(1 - \rho)\mu} \overset{(5)}{<} \frac{1}{2\sigma}C_{s-1},$$

in contradiction to (9).

As an easy corollary we obtain the following.

Theorem 2. *The global skew of the algorithm is bounded by $\frac{4}{\lambda} \cdot \mathcal{D}$.* □

There is some flexibility in setting the parameter μ, which governs the maximal speed of the logical clocks. We illustrate two possible choices.

By (5), the choice of μ limits the choice of σ, the parameter introduced in Definition 3. The value of σ serves as the base of the logarithm in the gradient function. If we set $\mu \approx 1$, we can set $\sigma = \Theta(1/\rho)$, achieving optimal gradient clock-synchronization and matching the lower bound of [10]. However, for this choice of μ we get $\beta \approx 1$, meaning that in fast mode logical clocks progress at almost twice the rate of real time. An alternative is to choose μ as $\Theta(\rho/(1-\rho))$, which yields $\beta = O(\rho)$. The cost is choosing σ as a constant, which is no longer optimal. This is formalized below.

Corollary 1. *If $\mu = \Theta(1/(1-\rho))$, the algorithm achieves $O\left(\text{dist}(u, v) \cdot \log_{1/\rho} \mathcal{D}\right)$-gradient synchronization, with a global skew of $O(\mathcal{D})$.* □

Corollary 2. *If $\mu = \Theta(\rho/(1 - \rho))$, the algorithm achieves $O\left(\text{dist}(u, v) \cdot \log \mathcal{D}\right)$-gradient synchronization, with a global skew of $O(\mathcal{D})$. When using direct and RBS estimates, we get $\mathcal{D} = O\left((1 + \rho D)(\Delta H + \mathcal{T}) + u_{\text{rcv}} \cdot D\right)$ in this case, where D is the diameter of G.* □

7   Conclusion

In this work we introduced a method of seamlessly incorporating reference broadcast synchronization (RBS) into the theoretical study of internal clock synchronization. We argue that by separating the task of estimating other nodes' clock values from the task of combining these estimates to come up with a logical clock, one obtains a cleaner and more general framework.

The approach taken here is reminiscent of, e.g., [2], [14] and [15]; in these works, various assumptions on message delay are represented as bounds on the difference between times at which a pair of events occur (e.g., the sending and receipt of a message). Using this abstract representation, general algorithms are presented which can handle many forms of delay assumptions. We take one step further by decoupling the physical network graph from the estimate graph, which is used to represent all information that nodes can acquire about each other. The approach extends to handle not only RBS but any means of acquiring clock estimates. For example, if certain nodes in the network have access to an external time source such as GPS, the estimate graph would contain edges between such nodes, since they can use the external time source to estimate each others' clock values (similar to RBS).

The estimate graph serves as a base layer on which classical clock synchronization algorithms can run, including, with minor modifications, those of [2] and [15] (which provide only global clock synchronization). In this work we further modified a recent gradient clock synchronization algorithm [10], to obtain an algorithm that provides gradient synchronization in broadcast networks.

References

1. Attiya, H., Hay, D.C., Welch, J.L.: Optimal clock synchronization under energy constraints in wireless ad-hoc networks. In: Anderson, J.H., Prencipe, G., Wattenhofer, R. (eds.) OPODIS 2005. LNCS, vol. 3974, pp. 221–234. Springer, Heidelberg (2006)
2. Attiya, H., Herzberg, A., Rajsbaum, S.: Optimal clock synchronization under different delay assumptions. SIAM Journal on Computing 25(2), 369–389 (1996)
3. Cristian, F.: Probabilistic clock synchronization. Distributed Computing 3, 146–158 (1989)
4. Elson, J., Girod, L., Estrin, D.: Fine-grained network time synchronization using reference broadcasts. ACM SIGOPS Operating Systems Review 36(SI), 147–163 (2002)
5. Fan, R., Chakraborty, I., Lynch, N.: Clock synchronization for wireless networks. In: Higashino, T. (ed.) OPODIS 2004. LNCS, vol. 3544, pp. 400–414. Springer, Heidelberg (2005)
6. Fan, R., Lynch, N.: Gradient clock synchronization. Distributed Computing 18(4), 255–266 (2006)
7. Halpern, J., Megiddo, N., Munshi, A.: Optimal precision in the presence of uncertainty. In: Proc. of 17th Symp. on Theory of Computing (STOC), pp. 346–355 (1985)

8. Karp, R., Elson, J., Papadimitriou, C., Shenker, S.: Global synchronization in sensornets. In: Farach-Colton, M. (ed.) LATIN 2004. LNCS, vol. 2976, pp. 609–624. Springer, Heidelberg (2004)
9. Lenzen, C., Locher, T., Wattenhofer, R.: Clock synchronization with bounded global and local skew. In: Prof. of 49th IEEE Symp. on Foundations of Computer Science (FOCS), pp. 500–510 (2008)
10. Lenzen, C., Locher, T., Wattenhofer, R.: Tight bounds for clock synchronization. In: Proc. of the 28th ACM Symp. on Principles of Distributed Computing (PODC) (to appear, 2009)
11. Locher, T., Wattenhofer, R.: Oblivious gradient clock synchronization. In: Dolev, S. (ed.) DISC 2006. LNCS, vol. 4167, pp. 520–533. Springer, Heidelberg (2006)
12. Lundelius, J., Lynch, N.: An upper and lower bound for clock synchronization. Information and Control 62(2/3), 190–204 (1984)
13. Meier, L., Thiele, L.: Brief announcement: gradient clock synchronization in sensor networks. In: Proc. of 24th ACM Symp. on Principles of Distributed Computing (PODC), p. 238 (2005)
14. Moses, Y., Bloom, B.: Knowledge, timed precedence and clocks (preliminary report). In: Proc. of the 13th ACM Symp. on Principles of Distributed Computing (PODC), pp. 294–303 (1994)
15. Ostrovsky, R., Patt-Shamir, B.: Optimal and efficient clock synchronization under drifting clocks. In: Proc. of 18th ACM Symp. on Principles of Distributed Computing (PODC), pp. 400–414 (1999)
16. Patt-Shamir, B., Rajsbaum, S.: A theory of clock synchronization. In: Proc. of 26th ACM Symp. on Theory of Computing (STOC), pp. 810–819 (1994)
17. Pussente, R.M., Barbosa, V.C.: An algorithm for clock synchronization with the gradient property in sensor networks. J. Parallel Distrib. Comput. 69(3), 261–265 (2009)
18. Römer, K.: Time synchronization in ad hoc networks. In: Proc. of 2nd Symp. on Mobile Ad Hoc Networking and Computing (MOBIHOC), pp. 173–182 (2001)
19. Sivrikaya, F., Yener, B.: Time synchronization in sensor networks: A survey. IEEE Network 18(4), 45–50 (2004)
20. Srikanth, T.K., Toueg, S.: Optimal clock synchronization. Journal of the ACM 34(3), 626–645 (1987)
21. Sundararaman, B., Buy, U., Kshemkalyani, A.: Clock synchronization for wireless sensor networks: A survey. Ad Hoc Networks 3(3), 281–323 (2005)

Brief Announcement: Communication-Efficient Self-stabilizing Protocols for Spanning-Tree Construction*

Toshimitsu Masuzawa[1], Taisuke Izumi[2],
Yoshiaki Katayama[2], and Koichi Wada[2]

[1] Osaka University, Suita 565-0871, Japan
[2] Nagoya Institute of Technology, Nagoya 466-8555, Japan

Abstract. Most of self-stabilizing protocols require every pair of neighboring processes to communicate with each other repeatedly and forever even after converging to legitimate configurations. Such permanent communication impairs efficiency, but is necessary in nature of self-stabilization. So it is challenging to minimize the number of process pairs communicating after convergence. In this paper, we investigate possibility of *communication-efficient* self-stabilization for spanning-tree construction, which allows only $O(n)$ pairs of neighboring processes to communicate repeatedly after convergence.

1 Introduction

A self-stabilizing protocol can eventually recover its intended behavior regardless of the initial configuration. Its high adaptability is usually acquired at the cost of efficiency. A crucial difference in cost between self-stabilizing and non-self-stabilizing protocols lies in the cost of communication *after convergence*. It is quite evident for static problems, e.g., spanning-tree construction. Self-stabilizing protocols cannot allow any process to terminate its communication after convergence, while non-self-stabilizing ones can allow every process to terminate all the activity. Actually, most of self-stabilizing protocols require every pair of neighbors to communicate repeatedly after convergence. This leads high communication load and make the protocols unacceptable in some real situations. Only a few papers [5,6] are dedicated to *communication-efficient* self-stabilization that allows only a small number of process pairs to communicate forever.

Contribution of this work: We introduce $\diamond$-*k-communication-efficiency* as an efficiency measure of self-stabilization after convergence. We investigate its possibility for *spanning-tree construction* and show the following results.

(a) When a unique root is designated, there exists a self-stabilizing protocol that allows each process, after convergence, to read the state only from its parent (i.e., $\diamond$-$(n-1)$-communication-efficient where n is the number of processes).

---

* This work is supported in part by MEXT: Global COE Program and JSPS: Grant-in-Aid for Scientific Research ((B)19300017, (C)21500012, (C)21500013).

T. Abdelzaher, M. Raynal, and N. Santoro (Eds.): OPODIS 2009, LNCS 5923, pp. 219–224, 2009.

(b) When each process has a unique identifier but a unique root is not designated, no protocol can allow even a single pair of processes to eventually
stop communication between them (i.e., $\Diamond$-$o(m)$-communication-efficiency
is unattainable where m is the number of links).
(c) When each process has a unique identifier and knows an upper bound N ($n \leq$
$N < 2n$) of n a priori (but a unique root is not designated), there exists a
protocol that allows each process, after convergence, to read the states only
from its parent and children (i.e., $\Diamond$-$2(n-1)$-communication-efficient). The
restriction $N < 2n$ on the upper bound N is the weakest because $\Diamond$-$o(m)$-
communication-efficiency becomes unattainable when $N = 2n$.

The results (a) and (b) bring out the contrast between self-stabilization and
communication-efficient self-stabilization: existence of a unique root is sufficient
for attaining communication-efficiency but existence of unique process identifiers
is not, however, self-stabilizing (but not communication-efficient) spanning-tree
construction is possible with either assumption.

Related works: Aguilera *et al.*[1] introduced the concept of *communication-
efficiency* in implementation of failure detector Ω. Following the work, some papers [2,3,4,7] investigated communication-efficient implementations of Ω.
Delporte-Gallet *et al.*[5] considered communication-efficient self-stabilizing leader
election in the fully-synchronous system with process crashes. These consider
global communication and aim to reduce the *total* number of communicating
process pairs. Devismes *et al.*[6] introduced $\Diamond$-k-*stability* as communication-
efficiency with a *local* criterion, which allows each process to repeatedly read
the states only from k neighbors after convergence. They investigated its possibility for the maximal independent set and the maximal matching.
    Spanning-tree construction is one of the most investigated subjects in self-
stabilization, but most of the protocols require every pair of neighbors to communicate repeatedly after convergence. To the best of our knowledge, no previous
paper has shed light on communication-efficiency of spanning-tree construction.

2   Preliminaries

A *distributed system* $\mathcal{S} = (P, L)$ consists of set $P = \{v_1, v_2, \ldots, v_n\}$ of n processes
and set L of bidirectional (communication) links. Action of each process v is
defined by *guarded commands* of the form $\langle guard_v \rangle \longrightarrow \langle statement_v \rangle$. The guard
$\langle guard_v \rangle$ is a Boolean expression on the states of v and its neighbors. When the
guard evaluates true, $\langle statement_v \rangle$ is executed to change the state of v.
    A *configuration* (i.e., a global state) of a distributed system is specified by
an n-tuple $\sigma = (s_1, s_2, \ldots, s_n)$ where s_i stands for the state of process v_i. For
configurations σ and σ', $\sigma \mapsto \sigma'$ denotes the transition from σ to σ', i.e., σ
changes to σ' by actions of some processes. An *execution* is an infinite sequence
of configurations $E = \sigma_0, \sigma_1, \sigma_2, \ldots$ satisfying $\sigma_j \mapsto \sigma_{j+1}$ ($j \geq 0$). We consider
an *asynchronous* distributed system where we make no assumption on the speed

of processes. To evaluate the time complexity of protocols, we introduce (asynchronous) *rounds* for an execution $E = \sigma_0, \sigma_1, \sigma_2, \ldots$. The first round of E is defined to be the minimal partial execution $\sigma_0, \sigma_1, \ldots, \sigma_k$ where each of the enabled processes in σ_o makes an action or becomes disabled. The second and later rounds of E are defined recursively for the execution $\sigma_k, \sigma_{k+1}, \sigma_{k+2}, \ldots$.

A (static) problem is defined by a *specification predicate* over the *output variables* of all the processes. A configuration is said to be *legitimate* if the output variables of all the processes satisfy the specification predicate.

Definition 1. *The* spanning-tree construction *problem is defined as follows. Each process v has an output variable* $prnt_v$ *to designate one of its neighbors as a parent. For the root process r,* $prnt_r = \bot$ *holds to denote that it has no parent. The specification predicate is satisfied if and only if variables* $prnt_v$ *of all the processes form a spanning-tree of the distributed system.*

A *self-stabilizing protocol* for a static problem is defined by two requirements, *convergence* and *closure*. The convergence requires a protocol to eventually reach a legitimate configuration. The closure requires that every process never changes its output variables at a legitimate configuration. A protocol is said to be *silent* if the states (including all variables) of all processes eventually remain unchanged.

Let $E = \sigma_0, \sigma_1, \ldots$ be an execution. For each process v, let $R_v^i(E)$ be the set of v's neighbors from which v reads some variables in the step from σ_{i-1} to σ_i (if v is activated). Let $R_v(E) = R_v^1(E) \cup R_v^2(E) \cup \cdots$.

Definition 2. *A protocol is $\Diamond$-k-communication-efficient if in every execution E, there is a suffix E' such that $\sum_{i=1}^{n} |R_{v_i}(E')| \leq k$.* □

While the $\Diamond$-k-communication-efficiency focuses on the total number of communicating process pairs, Devismes *et al.*[6] introduced the concept of $\Diamond$-k-*stability* with a local criterion of communication-efficiency.

Definition 3. *A protocol is $\Diamond$-k-stable if in every execution E, there is a suffix E' such that every process v satisfies $|R_v(E')| \leq k$.* □

3   Communication-Efficient Spanning-Tree Construction

3.1   Protocol *Tree-R* on Rooted Networks

Protocol 3.1 presents a $\Diamond$-$(n-1)$-communication-efficient and $\Diamond$-1-stable self-stabilizing protocol *Tree-R* for constructing a spanning-tree on arbitrary networks. The protocol assumes existence of a *unique root* process, say r. The main idea for attaining the communication-efficiency is that every process v has a variable d_v to store the distance from the root r on the constructed tree and checks its consistency only by comparing d_v with that of its parent.

Theorem 1. *Protocol Tree-R is a self-stabilizing silent protocol for spanning-tree construction in an arbitrary network with a unique root. It is $\Diamond$-$(n-1)$-communication-efficient and $\Diamond$-1-stable, and its stabilization time is $O(n)$ rounds.*

Protocol 3.1. A communication-efficient self-stabilizing protocol *Tree-R*

---

actions of root process $v(=r)$
  true $\longrightarrow$ $prnt_v = \bot$; $d_v = 0$; $cons_v :=$ true;
    /* $cons_v$ is a local variable s.t. $cons_v =$ true iff v is locally consistent
actions of non-root process $v(\neq r)$
  switch $(cons_v)$
    case true: /* executed in legitimate configurations
      $d_v \neq d_{prnt_v} + 1$ $\longrightarrow$ $cons_v :=$ false; /* v reads *only* d_{prnt_v} from $prnt_v$
    case false:
      true $\longrightarrow$
        $prnt_v := w$ $(\in N_v)$ s.t. $d_w = \dot{min}\{d_u \mid u \in N_v\}$;
        $d_v := d_{prnt_v} + 1$; $cons_v :=$ true; /* N_v is the set of neighbors of v

---

Remark: The spanning-tree constructed by protocol *Tree-R* is not a breadth-first or depth-first one, while most of self-stabilizing (but not communication-efficient) protocols construct breadth-first or depth-first trees. Actually, we can show that $\diamond$-$O(n)$-communication-efficiency is unattainable for constructing these restricted spanning-trees in some networks.

3.2   Impossibility on Networks with Process IDs

Protocol *Tree-R* assumes existence of a unique root process. Instead of the assumption, we sometimes assume that processes have distinct identifiers. Self-stabilizing spanning-tree construction is possible with the assumption of distinct identifiers (but without a predetermined unique root). However, the following theorem shows that $\diamond$-$o(m)$-communication-efficiency is impossible to attain under the assumption, where m is the number of links in the distributed system.

Theorem 2. *Any self-stabilizing protocol for constructing a spanning-tree in any non-rooted network with distinct process identifiers requires repeated communication between every pair of neighbors even after convergence to a legitimate configuration.*

3.3   Protocol *Tree-ID* on Networks with Process IDs

Protocol 3.2 presents a $\diamond$-$2(n-1)$-communication-efficient self-stabilizing protocol *Tree-ID* for constructing a spanning-tree on arbitrary networks. The protocol assumes that each process v has a unique identifier id_v and knows the number n of processes in the network. Each process v has variables $root_v$, $size_v$ and $CHLD_v$ in addition to the variables used in protocol *Tree-R*. Variable $root_v$ stores the root identifier of the tree v belongs to, $CHLD_v$ stores the children of v, and $size_v$ stores the number of processes in the subtree rooted at v.

  The strategy for attaining the communication-efficiency is the same as *Tree-R*: every non-root process v checks its consistency only by comparing variable d_v with that of its parent. However, this strategy alone is not sufficient. Consider

Protocol 3.2. A communication-efficient self-stabilizing protocol *Tree-ID*

```
actions of process v
  switch(cons_v)
    case true /* executed in legitimate configurations
        ((prnt_v = ⊥ and (root_v ≠ id_v or d_v ≠ 0 or size_v ≠ n)) or
        (prnt_v ≠ ⊥ and (root_v < id_v or root_v ≠ root_prnt_v or d_v ≠ d_prnt_v + 1 ))or
        ∃u ∈ CHLD_v[prnt_u ≠ id_v] or size_v ≠ ∑_{u∈CHLD_v} size_u + 1 or
        cons_prnt_v = false)
        ⟶ cons_v := false;
    case false
        true ⟶
            root_v := max({root_u | u ∈ N_v, d_u ≤ n − 2} ∪ {id_v});
            if root_v = id_v then
                prnt_v := ⊥; d_v := 0;
            else if (prnt_v ≠ ⊥ and root_prnt_v = root_v and d_prnt_v ≤ n − 2) then
                d_v := d_prnt_v + 1;
            else
                prnt_v := id_u s.t. d_u = min{d_w | w ∈ N_v, root_w = root_v};
                d_v := d_prnt_v + 1;
            CHLD_v := {u ∈ N_v | prnt_u = id_v};
            size_v := ∑_{u∈CHLD_v} size_u + 1;
            if ((prnt_v = ⊥) and (size_v = n)) or
                ((prnt_v ≠ ⊥) and (cons_prnt_v = true))) then
                cons_v := true;
```

the initial configuration where multiple trees exist, and variables $prnt_v$ and d_v of every process are consistent. If a process pair never communicates with each other, the processes may fail to detect existence of other trees.

To circumvent the difficulty, we make use of the number n of processes: the root finds the number of processes in its tree and allows each process in the tree to communicate with all of its neighbors until the tree covers the whole network. When a process finds another tree rooted at a process with a larger identifier than its current root, the process changes its parent to join the newly found tree. Consequently, the tree rooted at the process r with the maximum identifier eventually covers the whole network, which is detected when $size_r = n$ holds. When the root r detects the completion of spanning-tree construction, it transfers each process to the communication-saving mode. Variable $cons_v$ is used to relay the information whether the tree covers the whole network or not.

Theorem 3. *Protocol Tree-ID is a self-stabilizing silent protocol for constructing a spanning-tree in arbitrary networks where each process has a distinct identifier and knows the number n of processes a priori. It is $\Diamond$-2(n − 1)-communication-efficient and its stabilization time is $O(n)$ rounds.*

Protocol using neighbors' identifiers: When each process initially knows, instead of n, the identifiers of its neighbors, $\Diamond$-2(n−1)-communication-efficiency is attainable: by broadcasting the process identifiers in the tree, each process need not communicate with neighbors connected by non-tree links. Thus, at a legitimate configuration, each process communicates only with its parent and children.

Protocol using an upper bound of the network size: Protocol *Tree-ID* uses the *exact* number n of processes, however, it can be modified to work with an *upper bound* N of n satisfying $n \le N < 2n$. The key observation for the modification is that only a single tree can contain the majority of processes. This leads us to the following strategy: to reduce communication after convergence, a process reads the states only from its parent and (a subset of) its children when it belongs to a *major tree* consisting of $N/2$ processes or more. On the other hand, to detect another tree (if exists), a process reads the states from all the neighbors when the tree it belongs to is not a major tree. When the process finds a major tree in its neighbors, the process changes its parent to join the major tree. If such a neighbor does not exist, a larger identifier has higher priority as in protocol *Tree-ID*. By the strategy, we can design a $\diamond$-$2(n-1)$-communication-efficient self-stabilizing protocol for the spanning-tree construction.

Remark: We make restriction on N such that $N < 2n$. This restriction is necessary to attain the communication-efficiency. Actually we can show that $\diamond$-$o(m)$-communication-efficiency is unattainable when $N = 2n$: every pair of processes have to communicate repeatedly and forever. In this sense, the restriction of $N < 2n$ is the weakest for attaining communication-efficiency.

Acknowledgements. We are grateful to Sébastien Tixeuil and Stéphane Devismes for their helpful discussions.

References

1. Aguilera, M.K., Delporte-Gallet, C., Fauconnier, H., Toueg, S.: Stable leader election. In: Welch, J.L. (ed.) DISC 2001. LNCS, vol. 2180, pp. 108–122. Springer, Heidelberg (2001)
2. Aguilera, M.K., Delporte-Gallet, C., Fauconnier, H., Toueg, S.: On implementing omega with weak reliability and synchrony assumptions. In: Proc. of the 22nd PODC, pp. 306–314 (2003)
3. Aguilera, M.K., Delporte-Gallet, C., Fauconnier, H., Toueg, S.: Communication-efficient leader election and consensus with limited link synchrony. In: Proc. of the 23rd PODC, pp. 328–337 (2004)
4. Biely, M., Widder, J.: Optimal message-driven implementations of omega with mute processes. ACM TAAS 4, 4:1–4:22 (2009)
5. Delporte-Gallet, C., Devismes, S., Fauconnier, H.: Robust stabilizing leader election. In: Masuzawa, T., Tixeuil, S. (eds.) SSS 2007. LNCS, vol. 4838, pp. 219–233. Springer, Heidelberg (2007)
6. Devismes, S., Masuzawa, T., Tixeuil, S.: Communication efficiency in self-stabilizing silent protocols. In: Proc. of the 29th ICDCS, pp. 474–481 (2009)
7. Larrea, M., Fernandez, A., Arevalo, S.: Optimal implementation of the weakest failure detector for solving consensus. In: Proc. of the 19th SRDS, pp. 52–59 (2000)

On the Impact of Serializing Contention Management on STM Performance

Tomer Heber*, Danny Hendler, and Adi Suissa**

Department of Computer Science
Ben-Gurion University of the Negev
Be'er Sheva, Israel

Abstract. Transactional memory (TM) is an emerging concurrent programming abstraction. Numerous software-based transactional memory (STM)
implementations have been developed in recent years. STM implementations
must guarantee transaction atomicity and isolation. In order to ensure progress,
an STM implementation must resolve transaction collisions by consulting a
contention manager (CM).

Recent work established that *serializing contention management* - a
technique in which the execution of colliding transactions is serialized for
eliminating repeat-collisions - can dramatically improve STM performance in
high-contention workloads. In low-contention and highly-parallel workloads,
however, excessive serialization of memory transactions may limit concurrency
too much and hurt performance. It is therefore important to better understand
how the impact of serialization on STM performance varies as a function of
workload characteristics.

We investigate how serializing CM influences the performance of STM
systems. Specifically, we study serialization's influence on STM *throughput*
(number of committed transactions per time unit) and *efficiency* (ratio between
the extent of "useful" work done by the STM and work "wasted" by aborts) as the
workload's level of contention varies. Towards this goal, we implement CBench
- a synthetic benchmark that generates workloads in which transactions have
(parameter) pre-determined length and probability of being aborted in the lack of
contention reduction mechanisms. CBench facilitates evaluating the efficiency of
contention management algorithms across the full spectrum of contention levels.

The characteristics of TM workloads generated by real applications may vary
over time. To achieve good performance, CM algorithms need to monitor these
characteristics and change their behavior accordingly. We implement adaptive
algorithms that control the activation of serialization CM according to measured
contention level, based on a novel low-overhead serialization algorithm. We then
evaluate our new algorithms on CBench-generated workloads and on additional
well-known STM benchmark applications. We believe our results shed light on
the manner in which serializing CM should be used by STM systems.

1 Introduction

The advent of multi-core architectures is accelerating the shift from single-threaded
applications to concurrent, multi-threaded applications. Efficiently synchronizing ac-

* Supported by grants from Intel Corporation and the Lynne and William Frankel Center for
Computer Sciences.
** Supported by the *Israel Science Foundation* (grant number 1344/06).

T. Abdelzaher, M. Raynal, and N. Santoro (Eds.): OPODIS 2009, LNCS 5923, pp. 225–239, 2009.

cesses to shared memory is a key challenge posed by concurrent programming. Conventional techniques for inter-thread synchronization use lock-based mechanisms, such as mutex locks, condition variables, and semaphores. An implementation that uses coarse-grained locks will not scale. On the other hand, implementations that use fine-grained locks are susceptible to problems such as deadlock, priority inversion, and convoying. This makes the task of developing scalable lock-based concurrent code difficult and error-prone.

Transactional memory (TM) [14,20] is a concurrent programming abstraction that is viewed by many as having the potential of becoming a viable alternative to lock-based programming. Memory transactions allow a thread to execute a sequence of shared memory accesses whose effect is atomic: similarly to database transactions [22], a TM transaction either has no effect (if it fails) or appears to take effect instantaneously (if it succeeds).

Unlike lock-based programming, transactional memory is an optimistic synchronization mechanism: rather than serializing the execution of critical regions, multiple memory transactions are allowed to run concurrently and can commit successfully if they access disjoint data. Transactional memory implementations provide hardware and/or software support for dynamically detecting conflicting accesses by concurrent transactions and for resolving these conflicts (a.k.a. collisions) so that atomicity and progress are ensured. *Software transactional memory* (STM), introduced by Shavit and Touitou [20], ensures transactional semantics through software mechanisms; many STM implementations have been proposed in recent years [6,7,11,12,13,15,16,18].

TM implementations typically delegate the task of conflict resolution to a separate *contention manager* (CM) module [13]. The CM tries to resolve transaction conflicts once they are detected. When a transaction detects a conflict with another transaction, it consults the CM in order to determine how to proceed. The CM can then decide which of the two conflicting transactions should continue, and when and how the other transaction should be resumed.

Up until recently, TM implementations had no control of transaction threads, which remained under the supervision of the system's transaction-ignorant scheduler. Consequently, the contention managers of these "conventional" (i.e., non-scheduling) implementation [2,8,9,19] have only a few alternatives for dealing with transaction conflicts. A conventional CM can only decide which of the conflicting transactions can continue (this is the *winner transaction*) and whether the other transaction (the *loser transaction*) will be aborted or delayed. A conventional CM can also determine how long a loser transaction must wait before it can restart or resume execution.

1.1 Transaction Scheduling and Serializing Contention Management

A few recent works introduced transaction scheduling for increasing the efficiency of contention management. Yoo and Lee [23] introduced *ATS* – a simple user-level transaction scheduler, and incorporated it into RSTM [16] – a TM implementation from the University of Rochester – and into LogTM [17], a simulation of a hardware-based TM system. To the best of our knowledge, ATS is the first adaptive scheduling-based CM algorithm. ATS uses a *local* (per thread) adaptive mechanism to monitor the level of contention (which they call *contention intensity*). When the level of contention exceeds a parameter threshold, transactions are being serializied to a single scheduling queue. As they show, this approach can improve performance when workloads lack parallelism. Ansari et al. [1] proposed *steal-on-abort*, a transaction scheduler that avoids wasted work by allowing transactions to "steal" conflicting transactions so that they execute serially.

Dolev et al. [3] introduced CAR-STM, a user-level scheduler for collision avoidance and resolution in STM implementations. CAR-STM maintains per-core transaction queues. Whenever a thread starts a transaction (we say that the thread becomes *transactional*), CAR-STM assumes control of the transactional thread instead of the system scheduler. Upon detecting a collision between two concurrently executing transactions, CAR-STM aborts one transaction and moves it to the transactions queue of the other; this effectively serializes their execution and ensures they will not collide again.

We emphasize that serializing contention management cannot be supported by conventional contention managers, since, with these implementations, transactional threads are under the control of a transaction-ignorant system scheduler. Conventional contention managers only have control over the length of the waiting period imposed on the losing transaction before it is allowed to resume execution. In general, waiting-based contention management is less efficient than serializing contention management. To exemplify this point, consider a collision between transactions T_1 and T_2. Assume that the CM decides that T_1 is the winner and so T_2 must wait.

- If T_2 is allowed to resume execution too soon, it is likely to collide with T_1 again. In this case, either T_2 has to resume waiting (typically for a longer period of time), or, alternatively, the CM may now decide that T_2 wins and so T_1 must wait. In the latter case, T_1 and T_2 may end up repeatedly failing each other in a livelock manner without making any progress.
- On the other hand, if the waiting period of T_2 is too long, then T_2 may be unnecessarily delayed beyond the point when T_1 terminates.

Contrary to waiting-based contention management, with serializing contention management the system is capable of resuming the execution of T_2 immediately after T_1 terminates, resulting in better performance.

Dolev et al. incorporated CAR-STM into RSTM [16] and compared the performance of the new implementation with that of the original RSTM implementation, by using STMBench7 [10], a benchmark that generates realistic workloads for STM implementations. Their results show that serializing contention management can provide orders-of-magnitude speedup of execution times for high-contention workloads. However, excessive serialization of memory transactions may limit concurrency too much and hurt the performance of low-contention, highly-parallel workloads. It is therefore important to better understand how the impact of serialization on STM performance varies as a function of workload characteristics and how CM algorithms can adapt to these variations.

1.2 Our Contributions

The performance of an STM system can be characterized in terms of both its *throughput* (number of committed transactions per time unit) and *efficiency* (ratio between the extent of "useful" work done by the STM and work "wasted" by aborts) as the workload's level of contention changes. We approximate the efficiency of an STM execution by using the formula $commits/(aborts + commits)$, where *commits* and *aborts* respectively denote the numbers of committed and aborted transactions in the course of the execution.

We investigate how serializing CM influences STM throughput and efficiency. Our contributions towards obtaining this goal are the following.

- The characteristics of TM workloads generated by real applications may vary over time. To achieve good performance, CM algorithms need to monitor these characteristics and change their behavior accordingly. We implement and evaluate several novel adaptive algorithms that control the activation of serialization CM according to measured contention level. Both local-adaptive (in which each thread adapts its behavior independently of other threads) and global-adaptive policies are considered. Our adaptive algorithms are based on a novel low-overhead serialization mechanism. We evaluate these algorithms on workloads generated by CBench (described shortly), by an RSTM micro-benchmark application, and by Swarm - a more realistic application that is also provided by RSTM's benchmark suite.
- We introduce *CBench* - a synthetic benchmark that generates workloads in which transactions have pre-determined length and probability of being aborted (both provided as CBench parameters) when no contention reduction mechanisms are employed. CBench facilitates evaluating the effectiveness of both conventional and serializing CM algorithms across the full spectrum of contention levels.

Our results establish that applying serializing CM adaptively can improve STM performance considerably for high-contention workloads, while incurring no visible overhead for low-contention, highly-parallel workloads. Our empirical evaluation also highlights the importance of *stabilized* adaptive mechanisms, used to prevent frequent oscillations between serializing and conventional modes of operation that hurt performance.

The rest of the paper is organized as follows. We describe our new algorithms in Section 2. The CBench benchmark is presented in Section 3, followed by a description of our experimental evaluation in Section 4. Section 5 concludes with a short discussion of our results.

2 Algorithms

Table 1 summarizes the novel adaptive algorithms that we introduce and evaluate. These algorithms can be partitioned to the following two categories.

- *Partially-adaptive*: these are algorithms in which the contention-manager uses a conventional CM algorithm (we use the well-known Polka algorithm [19]) until a transaction collides for the k'th time, for some predetermined parameter k. Starting from the k'th collision (if the transaction fails to commit before that), a partially-adaptive CM starts using a serialization-based CM algorithm (which we describe shortly) until the transaction commits. We call k the *degree* of the algorithm and let PA_k denote the partially adaptive algorithm of degree k.
- *Fully-adaptive*: these algorithms (henceforth simply referred to as *adaptive* algorithms) collect and maintain simple statistics about past commit and abort events. Unlike partially-adaptive algorithms, adaptive algorithms collect these statistics

Table 1. Adaptive and partially-adaptive algorithms

PA_k	Partially adaptive algorithm of degree k: serialize starting from the k'th collision
A_L	Fully adaptive algorithm, local (per-thread) mode control
A_G	Fully adaptive algorithm, global (system-wide) mode control
A_{LS}	Fully adaptive algorithm, local (per-thread) stabilized mode control
A_{GS}	Fully adaptive algorithm, global (system-wide) stabilized mode control

across transaction boundaries. With adaptive algorithms, threads may oscillate an arbitrary number of times between serializing and conventional modes of operation, even in the course of performing a single transaction. An adaptive algorithm can be either local or global. With *local* adaptive algorithms, each thread maintains its own statistics and may change its modus operandi independently of other threads. In *global* adaptive algorithms, centralized statistics is maintained and the modus operandi is system-wide rather than thread-specific. As we describe later in this section, under certain circumstance, adaptive algorithms may be susceptible to a phenomenon of *mode oscillation* in which they frequently oscillate between serializing and conventional modes of operation. We have therefore also evaluated adaptive algorithms enhanced with a simple *stabilizing mechanism*. We henceforth denote the local and global non-stabilized adaptive algorithms by A_L and A_G, respectively, and the respective stabilized versions by A_{LS} and A_{GS}.

All our adaptive algorithms maintain an estimate cl of the contention level, that is updated whenever a commit or abort event occurs. Similarly to [23], cl is updated by performing exponential averaging. That is, upon a commit/abort event e, cl is updated according to the formula $cl_{new} \leftarrow \alpha \cdot cl_{old} + (1 - \alpha)C$, for some $\alpha \in (0,1)$, where C is 1 if e is an abort event and 0 otherwise. With A_L and A_{LS}, each thread updates its own cl variable; with A_G and A_{GS}, all threads share a single global cl variable. Under algorithm A_L (A_G), a thread employs serializing CM if the value of its local (the global) cl variable exceeds a parameter threshold value t, and employs a conventional CM algorithm otherwise. Algorithms A_{LS} and A_{GS} use both a low threshold value tl and a high threshold value $th > tl$. They both switch to a serializing modus operandi when the value of the corresponding cl variable exceeds th, and revert to a conventional modus operandi when cl's value decreases beyond tl. As our results establish, this simple stabilizing mechanism improves the performance of our adaptive algorithms considerably.

2.1 The Underlying Serialization Algorithm

The serialization mechanism used by both our partially-adaptive and adaptive algorithms (when they operate in serialization mode) is a low-overhead serializing algorithm, henceforth referred to as LO-SER. The pseudo-code of algorithm LO-SER appears in Figure 1. The basic idea is that every transactional thread has a condition variable associated with it. Upon being aborted, a *loser* transaction is serialized by sleeping on the condition variable of the winner transaction. When a winner transaction commits, it wakes up all threads blocked on its condition variable, if any. In our implementation, we use Pthreads conditional variables and mutexes.

The implementation of LO-SER is complicated somewhat because of the need to deal with the following issues: (1) operations on condition-variables and locks are expensive; we would like such operations to be performed only by threads that are actually involved in collisions. Specifically, requiring every commit operation to broadcast on its condition variable would incur high overhead in low-contention workloads; (2) deadlocks caused by cycles of threads blocked on each other's condition variables must be avoided, and (3) race conditions such as having a loser transaction wait on a winner's condition variable after the winner already completed its transaction must not occur.

Fedorova et al. [5] (see Section 5) implement a serializing mechanism that is very similar to LO-SER. Unlike LO-SER, however, that mechanism requires *every* commit operation to broadcast on a condition variable. We now describe algorithm LO-SER in more detail, explaining how it copes with the above issues.

We have implemented LO-SER on top of RSTM [16]. The (per-thread) variables required by LO-SER were added as new fields of RSTM's transaction descriptors (lines **4-7**). (To simplify presentation, field names are not prefixed with a descriptor name in the pseudo-code of Figure 1. Variables of a thread different than the one executing the code are subscripted with that thread's index.) With LO-SER, each thread has a condition variable c, and a mutex m that ensures the atomicity of operations on c and prevents race conditions, as described below (the rest of the new variables are explained when they are used.)

Upon a collision between the transactions of threads t and t' (line **25**), the current thread's contention manager function is called (line **26**) and, according to its return code, a CAS operation is called to abort either the current thread's transaction (line **33**) or the other thread's transaction(line **30**).[1] The CAS operation of line line 30 atomically writes 3 values: a code indicating that the transaction is aborted, the index of the winning thread[2], and the timestamp of the winning transaction. To facilitate atomic update of these 3 values, they are packed within a single 64-bit word (line **1**). Each thread t maintains a timestamp, initialized to 0 and incremented whenever a transaction of t commits or aborts. As we soon describe, timestamps are used for preventing race condition that may cause a transaction to serialize behind a wrong transaction.

A transaction that aborts itself in (line **33**) proceeds immediately to execute the code of lines (lines **10-24**). A transaction aborted by another thread will execute this code when it identifies it was aborted. Upon abort, a thread first rolls back its transaction (line **11**) by initializing its descriptor and releasing objects captured by it (not shown in Figure 1). It then increments its timestamp (line **12**). If the thread, w, causing the abort, is in the midst of an active transaction (lines **13-14**), it may still be performing the respective winning transaction. Thread t now prepares for serialization. It first sets its *waiting* flag (line **15**) to prevent other transactions from serializing behind it and avoid waiting cycles. It then tries to acquire w's lock (line **16**). After acquiring w's lock,

---

[1] An RSTM CM may also return a WAIT code in line **26**, indicating that the calling transaction should retry its conflicting operation. Our implementation does not change RSTM's behavior in this case. Similarly, failures of CAS operations are dealt with by RSTM as usual. Both scenarios are therefore not described by the high-level pseudo-code provided by Figure 1.

[2] Upon starting, a transactional thread registers and receives an index to the transaction descriptors table. When it exits, the corresponding descriptor becomes available.

```
1  struct extendedStatus                        25  upon Collision(t, t')
2  |  status: 2, winner: 12, winnerTs: 50:      26  |  int res = t.CM(t')
   |  int                                       27  |  if res == ABORT_OTHER then
3  end                                          28  |  |  int v = t'.eStat
4  struct TransDesc                             29  |  |  if v.status == ACTIVE then
5  |  m: mutex, c: cond, ts initially 0: int,   30  |  |  |  t'.eStat.CAS
6  |  release = F, waiting = F: boolean,                  |  |  |     (v,<ABORT,t,t.ts>)
7  |  eStat: extendedStatus,                    31  |  |  end
   |  // RSTM descriptor fields                 32  |  else if res == ABORT_SELF then
8  |  CM: CMFunction, ...                       33  |  |  t.eStat = <ABORT,t',t'.ts>
9  end                                          34  |  end
10 upon ABORT of thread t's transaction         35 end
11 |  Roll back t's transaction                 36 upon COMMIT by thread t
12 |  ts++                                       37 |  ts++
13 |  w=eStat.winner                             38 |  if eStat.CAS(<ACTIVE,0,0>,
14 |  if eStat_w.status == ACTIVE then                    <COMMITTED,0,0>)
15 |  |  waiting=true                                  then
16 |  |  m_w.lock()                              39 |  |  if release then
17 |  |  release_w=true                          40 |  |  |  m.lock()
18 |  |  if ts_w==eStat.winnerTs                 41 |  |  |  c.broadcast()
   |  |     ∧(¬waiting_w) then                   42 |  |  |  release=false
19 |  |  |  c_w.wait(m_w)                        43 |  |  |  m.unlock()
20 |  |  end                                     44 |  |  end
21 |  |  m_w.unlock()                            45 |  end
22 |  |  waiting=false                           46 end
23 |  end
24 end
```

Fig. 1. Low-Overhead Serialization Algorithm (LO-SER) Pseudo-code for thread t

t sets w's *release* flag (line **17**) to indicate to w that there may be waiting threads it has to release when it commits. If w did not yet change its timestamp since it collided with t's transaction, and if w is currently not serialized behind another thread itself (line **18**), then t goes to sleep on w's condition variable by calling $c_w.wait(m_w)$ (line **19**). A reference to m_w is passed as a parameter so that the call releases m_w once t blocks on c_w; this is guaranteed by the Pthreads implementation. The Pthreads implementation guarantees also that when t is released from the waiting of (line **19**) (after being signalled by w) it holds m_w. Thread t therefore releases m_w in (line **21**) and resets its *waiting* flag (line **22**).

Upon committing, thread t first increments its timestamp (line **37**) to prevent past losers from serializing behind its future transactions. Then t commits by performing a CAS on its status word (line **38**) (see Footnote 1). If it succeeds and its *release* flag is set (line **39**), then t acquires its lock, wakes up any threads that may be serialized behind it, resets its *release* flag and finally releases its lock (lines **40–43**).

We prove the following properties of the LO-SER algorithm in the full paper.

Lemma 1. *The LO-SER algorithm satisfies the following properties:*

1. *At all times, threads waiting on condition variables (at line **19**) do not form a cycle.*
2. *If a thread waits (at line **19**) on the condition variable of some thread w, then w is in the midst of performing a transaction. That is, its status is either ACTIVE or ABORTED.*
3. *Assume thread p performs a broadcast (at line **41**) at time t, and let t' < t denote the previous time when p performed a broadcast, or the time when the algorithm starts if no broadcast by p was performed before t. Then p won some collision during the interval (t',t).*

3   CBench

Several benchmarks have been introduced in recent years for evaluating the performance of TM systems. Some of these benchmarks (e.g., RSTM's micro-benchmarks) implement simple TM-based concurrent data-structures such as linked list and red-black tree, while others use more realistic applications (e.g. STMBench7 [10] and Swarm [21]). However, to the best of our knowledge, none of these benchmarks allow generating workloads with an accurate pre-determined contention level.

We introduce *CBench* - a novel benchmark that generates workloads of pre-determined length where each transaction has a pre-determined probability of being aborted when no contention reduction mechanism is employed. Both transaction length and abort-probability are provided as CBench parameters. CBench facilitates evaluating the performance of both serializing and conventional CM algorithms as contention varies, which, in turn, makes it easier to study the impact of these algorithms, in terms of their effect on throughput and efficiency, across the contention range.

Using CBench is composed of two stages: *calibration* and *testing*. In the calibration stage, CBench is called with a *TLength* parameter, specified in units of accesses to transactional objects. E.g, when called with *TLength=1000*, the total number of transactional object accesses made by each transaction is 1000. A CBench transaction accesses two types of transactional objects: *un-contended* objects and *contended* objects. Un-contended objects are private to each thread, and accesses to them are used to extend transaction length. Contended objects, on the other hand, may be accessed by all transactions and are used to control contention level.

The calibration stage of CBench proceeds in iterations. At the beginning of each iteration, CBench fixes the numbers of reads and writes of contended objects (respectively called *contended-reads* and *contended writes*) to be performed by each transaction; which objects are to be accessed by each transaction is determined randomly and uniformly before the iteration starts. CBench then creates a single thread per system core and lets these threads repeatedly execute transactions for a pre-determined period of time, during which it counts the total number of commits and aborts incurred. During this execution, the contention manager used is the *RANDOM* algorithm.[3] Let *commits* and *aborts* respectively denote the total number of commits and aborts that occur during

---

[3] Upon a collision, *RANDOM* randomly determines which transaction should abort and the aborted transaction immediately restarts. Since *RANDOM* does not apply any contention-reduction technique, it is a good baseline for assessing the impact of contention reduction algorithms.

the execution of the iteration's workload, then its respective abort probability is given by *aborts/(commits+aborts)*. This value is recorded by CBench (in a CBench data file) and is associated with the respective numbers of contended reads and writes. The calibration process continues performing iterations, varying the numbers of contended reads and writes, until a fine-resolution "coverage" of all contention levels has been generated. That is, for every abort probability p, the CBench data file contains an entry specifying the numbers of contended reads and writes required to create a workload with abort probability p' such that $|p - p'| < 1\%$.

In the testing stage, CBench is called with an abort-probability parameter. The entry with the closest abort-probability is read from CBench's data file (created for the required transaction length) and is used to generate workloads with the input contention level. CBench then creates one thread per core and starts generating its test workload.

4   Experimental Evaluation

All our experiments were performed on a 2.60 GHz 8 core 4xXEON-7110M server, with 16GB RAM and 4MB L2 cache and with HyperThreading disabled, running the 64-bit Gentoo Linux operating system, and using RSTM. Our experiments evaluate two partially-adaptive algorithms (PA_1 and PA_{100}), all our fully-adaptive algorithms (A_L, A_{LS}, A_G and A_{GS}), a few conventional CM algorithms (Random, Polka and Greedy, configured with the invisible-readers and lazy abort settings), and CAR-STM.

4.1   CBench

Figure 2-(a) shows the throughput of some of the algorithms we evaluated, across the full contention spectrum of workloads generated by CBench with *TLength=1500*. We observe that the throughput of PA_{100} and Polka is practically identical (and we therefore only show a single bar representing both). The reason for that is that PA_{100} employs Polka until a transaction collides for the 100'th time, thus it rarely performs serialization. Since all fully-adaptive algorithms behave similarly for low and medium contention levels, we only show A_{LS} in Figure 2-(a).

CAR-STM has high overhead, causing its throughput to be less than 60% that of all other algorithms in the lack of contention. The key reason for that is that, with CAR-STM, a transaction is executed by a dedicated transaction-queue thread and not by the thread that created it (see [3]). Our serialization algorithms, on the other hand, do not seem to incur any overhead in the lack of contention and perform as well as the conventional CM algorithms when contention is low. When contention increases, the throughput of the conventional CM algorithms quickly deteriorates, and, for very high contention levels, they are significantly outperformed by the serializing algorithms.

Comparing PA_1 and PA_{100} reveals that they provide more-or-less the same throughput for low contention levels. For medium contention levels (0.3-0.8), PA_{100}'s throughput is higher by up to 8%, but for very high contention-levels PA_1 is the clear winner and exceeds PA_{100}'s throughput by up to 60%. This behavior can be explained as follows. In low contention-levels there are hardly any collisions so both algorithms behave in the same manner. In medium contention-levels there are a few collisions, but the probability that two colliding transactions will collide again is low; under these circumstances, it is better to use Polka rather than to serialize, and serialization incurs the cost of waiting until the winner transaction terminates. Finally, under high-contention, serialization is the better strategy and using a conventional CM such as Polka is inefficient. A_{LS} obtains the "the best of all worlds" performance: it is as good as PA_{100} when contention is low, and as good as PA_1 when contention is high.

Zooming into high-contention workloads (Figure 2-(b)) highlights the impact of the stabilization mechanism. Whereas A_L and A_{LS} provide the same throughput up to contention-level 0.8, under high-contention A_{LS} outperforms A_L by up to 16%. This is because, under high-contention, A_L oscillates between serialization and non-serializing modi operandi: when contention exceeds A_L's threshold, it starts serializing. When serializing decreases the level of contention, A_L reverts to non-serialization mode, which hurts its performance. A_{LS} eliminates this oscillation and therefore obtains higher throughput. The behavior of A_L and A_G is almost identical on CBench workloads, therefore A_G's curve is not shown in Figure 2-(b). Similarly to the local adaptive algorithm, A_{GS} provides higher throughput than A_G under high contention but by a smaller margin (up to 6%).

Figure 2-(c) shows the efficiency of the evaluated algorithms. Efficiency deteriorates as contention-level increases. CAR-STM's efficiency is best, since it limits parallelism more than all other algorithms. When contention is maximal, CAR-STM obtains the highest efficiency (0.41) among all algorithms, and PA_1 together with A_{LS} are second best (but far behind with 0.13 efficiency). All other low-overhead serialization algorithms have efficiency levels between 0.09-0.12, whereas Polka, Greedy and Random obtain the lowest efficiency figures (0.05, 0.03 and less than 0.01, respectively).

4.2   RandomGraph

RandomGraph [15] operates on a graph data-structure consisting of a linked-list of vertices and of linked-lists (one per vertex) for representing edges. Supported operations are: (1) insertion of a node and a set of random edges to existing vertices, and (2) the removal of a node and its edges. The number of vertices is restricted to 256, which generates workloads characterized by high-contention and relatively long transactions. The impact of all serialization algorithms on RandomGraph's throughput is considerable, as can be seen in Figure 3-(a). (Since the throughputs of A_L and A_G are very similar on RandomGraph, the curves of A_G and A_{GS} are not shown.)

Under high contention, all serializing CM algorithms provide throughput which is orders of magnitude higher than that of the conventional algorithms. A_{LS} and A_{GS} significantly outperform A_L and A_G, respectively, for all concurrency levels higher than 1. The stabilizing mechanism improves the throughput of the local adaptive algorithm by approximately 30% for 2 threads, and by almost 50% for 4 threads. The gap decreases for 8, 16 and 32 threads (18%, 13% and 8%, respectively) but remains significant. The contribution of stabilization to the global adaptive algorithm is somewhat smaller but is also significant, and reaches its maximum for 2 threads (19%).

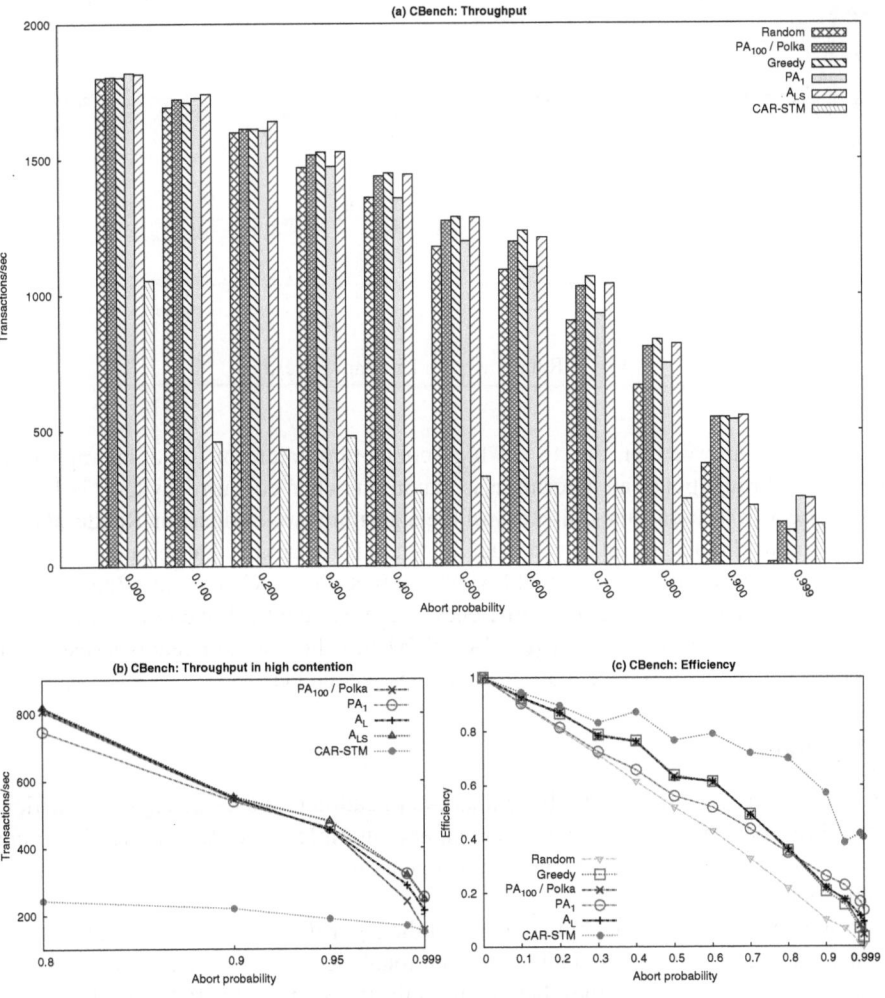

Fig. 2. CBench Evaluation Results

When analyzing this behavior, we find that both the local and the global adaptive algorithms suffer from frequent oscillations between serializing and conventional modes of operation. The stabilization mechanism greatly reduces these oscillations. The local algorithm suffers from this phenomenon more than the global one, since the probability that a single thread will win a few collisions in a row is non-negligible; this thread will then shift to a conventional modus operandi. When *all threads* update history statistics, such fluctuations are more rare. CAR-STM's performance is much better than the conventional algorithms, but much worse than the low-overhead serializing

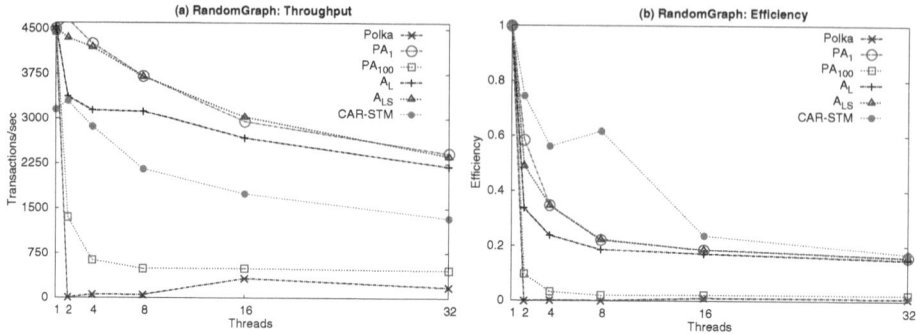

Fig. 3. RandomGraph Evaluation Results

algorithms. Observe that, due to the high-contention nature of RandomGraph work-loads, the throughput of all algorithms is maximum when concurrency level is 1.

Figure 3-(b) presents the efficiency of the algorithms we evaluate on RandomGraph-generated workloads. It can be seen that, in general, algorithms that serialize more have higher efficiency. The conventional CM algorithms (Polka, Greedy and Random) have the lowest efficiency (since their efficiency is almost identical, we only show Polka's curve), followed closely by PA_{100}. CAR-STM has the best efficiency across all the concurrency range by a wide margin and PA_1 is second best.

4.3   Swarm

Swarm [21] is a more realistic benchmark-application that uses a single transactional thread for rendering objects on the screen, and multiple transactional threads for con-currently updating object positions. Swarm generates workloads characterized by very high contention.

Figure 4 shows the throughput of some of the algorithms we evaluated on the Swarm benchmark. The throughput of all the conventional algorithms (Polka, Greedy and Ran-dom) is the lowest; since they behave roughly the same, only Polka is shown. The throughput of PA_{100} also deteriorate very quickly and, with the exception of 2 threads, its performance is very similar to that of Polka. The best algorithm on Swarm in al-most all concurrency levels is CAR-STM. It seems that its strong serialization works best for Swarm's workloads. The stabilized algorithms A_{LS} and A_{GS} are slightly better than their non-stabilized counterpart algorithms in almost all concurrency levels, but the gap is very small. The reason for that is that Swarm's contention levels are so high, that A_L and A_G operate almost constantly in serialization mode. Also here, the through-put of A_L and A_G is almost identical, hence we only show the graphs of the global adaptive algorithm. The relation between the efficiency levels of evaluated algorithms on Swarm is similar to that seen on RandomGraph, hence an efficiency graph is not shown.

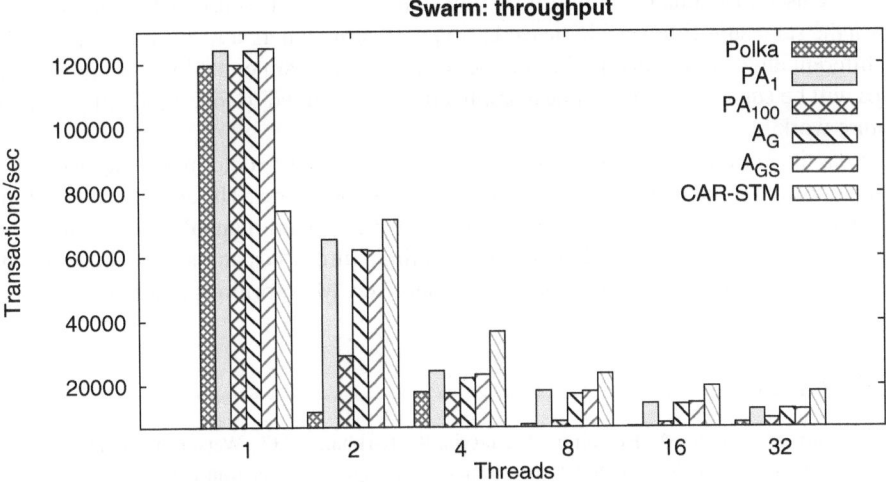

Fig. 4. Throughput on Swarm-generated workload

5 Discussion

In this paper we investigated the influence of serializing contention management algorithms on the throughput and efficiency of STM systems. We implemented CBench, a synthetic benchmark that generates workloads possessing pre-determined (parameter) length and contention-level. We also implemented LO-SER - a novel low-overhead serialization algorithm and, based on it, several adaptive and partially-adaptive CM algorithms. We then evaluated these algorithms on workloads generated by CBench, by an RSTM micro-benchmark application, and by the Swarm application.

Several significant conclusions can be drawn from our work. First, we observe that CM algorithms that apply a low-overhead serializing mechanism adaptively can significantly improve both STM throughput and efficiency in high-contention workloads while, at the same time, incurring no visible overheads for low-contention workloads. Second, we have demonstrated the importance of incorporating a stabilizing mechanism to (both local and global) adaptive algorithms, for preventing mode oscillations that hurt performance under high contention.

Recent work addresses serializing CM algorithms from various perspectives. Dragojevic et al. [4] presented *Shrink*, a user-level transaction scheduler that bases its scheduling decisions on the access patterns of past transactions. *Shrink* can therefore prevent collisions before they occur. *Shrink* uses a serialization mechanism similar to that of Yoo and Lee [23]. Fedorova et al. [5] propose and evaluate several kernel-level scheduling-based mechanisms for TM contention management. They also implement a serializing mechanism that is very similar to LO-SER. Unlike LO-SER, however, that mechanism requires *every* commit operation to broadcast on a condition variable; with LO-SER, broadcast system calls are avoided in the absence of collisions.

Our evaluation did not discover significant performance/efficiency differences between global and local adaptive serializing CM algorithms. However, all the applications we have used to evaluate our algorithms are symmetric, in the sense that all threads perform the same algorithm (with the exception of Swarm, where a *single* thread performs a different algorithm than all other threads). It seems plausible that local adaptive policies will be superior for asymmetric applications. We intend to investigate this issue in future work.

Adaptive serializing CM algorithms use threshold values to determine when to switch from a conventional mode to a serializing mode and vice versa. The adaptive algorithms presented in this paper use fixed thresholds that were tuned manually per application. A mechanism for automatically finding the optimal thresholds and for dynamically adjusting them will increase the usability of adaptive CM algorithms and is also left for future work.

References

1. Ansari, M., Luján, M., Kotselidis, C., Jarvis, K., Kirkham, C.C., Watson, I.: Steal-on-abort: Improving transactional memory performance through dynamic transaction reordering. In: HiPEAC, pp. 4–18 (2009)
2. Attiya, H., Epstein, L., Shachnai, H., Tamir, T.: Transactional contention management as a non-clairvoyant scheduling problem. In: PODC, pp. 308–315 (2006)
3. Dolev, S., Hendler, D., Suissa, A.: CAR-STM: scheduling-based collision avoidance and resolution for software transactional memory. In: PODC, pp. 125–134 (2008)
4. Dragojevic, A., Guerraoui, R., Singh, A.V., Singh, V.: Preventing versus curing: avoiding conflicts in transactional memories. In: PODC, pp. 7–16 (2009)
5. Fedorova, A., Felber, P., Hendler, D., Lawall, J., Maldonado, W., Marlier, P., Muller, G., Suissa, A.: Scheduling support for transactional memory contention management. In: PPoPP (to appear, 2010)
6. Felber, P., Riegel, T., Fetzer, C.: Dynamic performance tuning of word-based software transactional memory. In: PPOPP, pp. 237–246 (February 2008)
7. Fraser, K.: Practical lock-freedom. Ph. D. dissertation, UCAM-CL-TR-579, Computer Laboratory, University of Cambridge (2004)
8. Guerraoui, R., Herlihy, M., Pochon, B.: Polymorphic contention management. In: Fraigniaud, P. (ed.) DISC 2005. LNCS, vol. 3724, pp. 303–323. Springer, Heidelberg (2005)
9. Guerraoui, R., Herlihy, M., Pochon, B.: Towards a theory of transactional contention managers. In: PODC, pp. 316–317 (2006)
10. Guerraoui, R., Kapalka, M., Vitek, J.: Stmbench7: a benchmark for software transactional memory. SIGOPS Oper. Syst. Rev. 41(3), 315–324 (2007)
11. Harris, T., Fraser, K.: Language support for lightweight transactions. In: OOPSLA, pp. 388–402 (2003)
12. Herlihy, M.: SXM software transactional memory package for C#, http://www.cs.brown.edu/~mph
13. Herlihy, M., Luchangco, V., Moir, M., Scherer III, W.N.: Software transactional memory for dynamic-sized data structures. In: PODC, pp. 92–101 (2003)
14. Herlihy, M., Moss, J.E.B.: Transactional memory: Architectural support for lock-free data structures. In: ISCA, pp. 289–300 (1993)
15. Marathe, V.J., Scherer III, W.N., Scott, M.L.: Adaptive software transactional memory. In: Fraigniaud, P. (ed.) DISC 2005. LNCS, vol. 3724, pp. 354–368. Springer, Heidelberg (2005)
16. Marathe, V.J., Spear, M.F., Heriot, C., Acharya, A., Eisenstat, D., Scherer, I.W.N., Scott, M.L.: Lowering the overhead of nonblocking software transactional memory. In: Workshop on Languages, Compilers, and Hardware Support for Transactional Computing (TRANSACT 2006) (2006)

17. Moore, K.E., Bobba, J., Moravan, M.J., Hill, M.D., Wood, D.A.: Logtm: Log-based transactional memory. In: Proceedings of the 12th International Conference on High Performance Computer Architecture, pp. 254–265 (2006)
18. Saha, B., Adl-Tabatabai, A.-R., Hudson, R.L., Minh, C.C., Hertzberg, B.: Mcrt-stm: a high performance software transactional memory system for a multi-core runtime. In: PPOPP, pp. 187–197 (2006)
19. Scott, M.L., Scherer III, W.N.: Advanced contention management for dynamic software transactional memory. In: PODC, pp. 240–248 (2005)
20. Shavit, N., Touitou, D.: Software transactional memory. Distributed Computing 10(2), 99–116 (1997)
21. Spear, M.F., Silverman, M., Dalessandro, L., Michael, M.M., Scott, M.L.: Implementing and exploiting inevitability in software transactional memory. In: ICPP, pp. 59–66 (2008)
22. Vossen, G., Weikum, G.: Transactional information systems. Morgan Kaufmann, San Francisco (2001)
23. Yoo, R.M., Lee, H.-H.S.: Adaptive transaction scheduling for transactional memory systems. In: SPAA, pp. 169–178 (2008)

On the Efficiency of Atomic Multi-reader, Multi-writer Distributed Memory

Burkhard Englert[1], Chryssis Georgiou[2], Peter M. Musial[3,*], Nicolas Nicolaou[4], and Alexander A. Shvartsman[4,**]

[1] Comp. Engineering and Comp. Science, California State University Long Beach
[2] Department of Computer Science, University of Cyprus
[3] Department of Computer Science, University of Puerto Rico
[4] Computer Science and Engineering, University of Connecticut

Abstract. This paper considers quorum-replicated, multi-writer, multi-reader (MWMR) implementations of survivable atomic registers in a distributed message-passing system with processors prone to failures. Previous implementations in such settings invariably required two rounds of communication between readers/writers and replica owners. Hence the question arises whether it is possible to have single round read and/or write operations in this setting.

We thus devise an algorithm, called SFW, that exploits a new technique called *server side ordering* (SSO), which –unlike previous approaches– places partial responsibility for the ordering of write operations on the replica owners (the servers). With SSO, *fast* write operations are introduced for the very first time in the MWMR setting. We prove that our algorithm preserves atomicity in all permissible executions. While algorithm SFW shows that in principle fast writes are possible, we also show that under certain conditions the MWMR model imposes inherent limitations on any quorum-based fast write implementation of a *safe read/write register* and potentially even restricts the number of writer participants in the system. In this case our algorithm achieves near optimal efficiency.

1 Introduction

Data survivability is essential in distributed systems. Replication is broadly used to sustain critical data in networked settings prone to failures, and a variety of distributed storage systems have been designed to replicate and maintain data residing at distinct network locations or servers. Together with replication come the problems of maintaining consistency among the replicas and of efficiency of access to data, all in the presence of failures.

A long string of research has been addressing the consistency challenge by devising efficient, wait-free, atomic (linearizable [22]) read/write sharable objects in message-passing systems (e.g., [1,2,3,6,8,15,16,21,24,27]). An atomic read/write

---

* Part of this work was performed while the author was affiliated with: Comp. Sci. Dept., Naval Postgraduate School, USA.
** Work supported in part by the NSF awards 0702670, 0121277, and 0311368.

T. Abdelzaher, M. Raynal, and N. Santoro (Eds.): OPODIS 2009, LNCS 5923, pp. 240–254, 2009.

object, or register [23], provides the semantics of a sequentially accessed single object. The underlying implementations replicate the object at several failure-prone servers and allow concurrent reading and writing by failure-prone clients. The *efficiency* of read or write operations is measured in terms of the number of communication rounds between clients and servers.

Prior Work. In the SWMR model, Attiya et al. [3] achieve consistency by exploiting the intersecting sets of majorities in combination with $\langle timestamp, value \rangle$ pairs, comprised of a logical clock and the associated replica value. A write operation increments the writer's local timestamp and delivers the new timestamp-value pair to a majority of servers, taking one round. A read operation obtains timestamp-value pairs from some majority, then propagates the pair corresponding to the highest timestamp to some majority of servers, thus taking two rounds. Avoiding the second communication round may lead to violations of atomicity when reads are concurrent with a write.

The majority-based approach in [3] is readily generalized to quorum-based approaches (e.g., [27,9,24,10,19]). In this context, a *quorum system* [17,30,12,29,28] is a collection of subsets of server identifiers with pairwise non-empty intersections. The work of [10] shows that the read operations must write to as many replica servers as the maximum number of failures allowed. A dynamic atomic memory implementation using reconfigurable quorums is given in [24] (with several practical refinements in [18,13,14,5]), where the sets of servers can arbitrarily change over time as processes join and leave the system. When the set of servers is not being reconfigured, the read and write protocols involve two communication rounds. Retargeting this work to ad-hoc mobile networks, Dolev *et al.* [7] formulated the GeoQuorums approach. There (and in [5]), some reads involve a single communication round when it is confirmed that the corresponding write operation has completed.

Starting from [3] a common folklore belief developed that "atomic reads must write". Dutta et al. [8] present the first *fast* atomic SWMR implementation where all operations take a *single* communication round. They show that fast behavior is achievable only when the number of reader processes R is inferior to $\frac{S}{t} - 2$, where S is the number of servers, t of whom may crash. They also showed that fast implementations in the MWMR model are impossible in the presence of a single server failure. Georgiou et al. [16] introduced the notion of *virtual nodes* that enables an unbounded number of readers. They define the notion of *semifast* implementations were only a single read operation per write needs to be "slow" (take two rounds). Their algorithm requires that the number of virtual nodes V is inferior to $\frac{S}{t} - 2$; this does not prevent multiple readers as long as at least one virtual node exists. They also show that semifast MWMR implementations are impossible.

Other works, e.g., [1,20,21,15], pursue bounds on the efficiency of distributed storage in a variety of organizational and failure models. For example, [20,1], explore conditions under which two round operations are required by safe and regular SWMR registers.

Recently quorum-based approaches were further explored in the context of efficient atomic registers [21,15]. Guerraoui and Vukolić [21] defined the notion of *Refined Quorum Systems* (RQS), where quorums are classified in three categories, according to their intersection size with other quorums. The authors characterize these properties and develop an efficient Byzantine-resilient SWMR atomic object implementation and a solution to the consensus problem. In synchronous failure-free runs their implementation is fast. Georgiou et al. [15] specified the properties that a general quorum system must possess in order to achieve single round operations in the presence of crashes and asynchrony. They showed that fast and semifast quorum-based SWMR implementations are possible iff a common intersection exists among all quorums, hence a single point of failure exists in such solutions (i.e., any server in the common intersection), making such implementations not robust. To trade efficiency for improved fault-tolerance, *weak-semifast* implementations are introduced in [15] that require at least one single slow read per write operation, and where all writes are fast. In addition, they present a client-side prediction tool called *Quorum Views* that enables fast read operations in general quorum-based implementations even under read/write concurrency. Simulation results demonstrated the effectiveness of this approach, showing that a small fraction of read operations need to be slow under realistic scenarios. A question that naturally follows is whether it is possible to have weak-semifast atomic MWMR register implementations.

Contributions. Intrigued by the above developments this work aims to answer the following question: *Under what conditions may one obtain efficient atomic read/write register implementations in the MWMR model?* To this end, we incorporate a new technique that enables single communication round, i.e., fast, write and read operations in that model. Our contributions are as follows.

1. To enable *fast write* operations we introduce a new technique called *Server Side Ordering (SSO)* that assigns to the server processes the responsibility of maintaining and incrementing logical timestamps, that are used by both readers and writers and helps to ensure atomicity. Previous algorithms, placed this responsibility on the writer's side. (In the presence of asynchrony and failures, SSO alone does not suffice to guarantee atomicity: using SSO by itself may result in the generation of non unique timestamps for each write operation.)

2. We developed a quorum-based implementation for atomic MWMR registers, called SFW, that (a) employs the SSO technique by having the servers assign logical timestamps to writes. and (b) ensures uniqueness of timestamps by combining them with each writer's local write ordering. This hybrid approach guarantees uniqueness of tags among the read and write participants for every written value and allows the writers and readers to reason about the state of the system. To the best of our knowledge, this is the *first* MWMR atomic register implementation that provides the possibility of fast reads *and* writes.

3. Lastly, we develop a framework for reasoning about impossibility and lower bounds for MWMR implementations. In an *n-wise* quorum system any n

quorums have a common non-empty intersection. We call two operations
consecutive if they are complete, not concurrent, and originate at two distinct processes. Two operations are *quorum shifting* if they are consecutive
and the two originating processes receive replies from two distinct quorums
during these operations. We prove lower bounds on the number of consecutive, quorum shifting fast write operations that an execution of a safe register
implementation may contain. We show that a safe register implementation
is impossible in an n-wise quorum system, where not all quorums have a
common intersection, if any execution contains more than $n-1$ consecutive,
quorum shifting single round write operations. This ultimately implies that
in an implementation with only fast writes there cannot be more than $n-1$
writers. Algorithm SFW is nearly optimal since it approaches this bound as
it yields executions with up to $n/2$ consecutive fast write operations, while
maintaining atomicity.

Document Structure. In Section 2 we present our model and definitions. The
algorithm, SFW, is presented in Section 3. The inherent limitations of MWMR
model and the conditions under which it is possible to obtain fast write operations, are presented in Section 4. Because of space limitations, omitted proofs
can be found in the full version of the manuscript [4].

2   Model and Definitions

We consider the asynchronous message-passing model. There are three distinct
finite sets of processors: a set of readers $\mathcal{R}$, a set of writers $\mathcal{W}$, and a set of $\mathcal{S}$
servers. The identifiers of all processors are unique and comparable. Communica-
tion among the processors is accomplished via reliable communication channels.
Servers are arranged into intersecting sets, or *quorums*, that together form a
quorum system $\mathbb{Q}$. For a set of quorums $\mathcal{A} \subseteq \mathbb{Q}$ we denote the intersection of the
quorums in $\mathcal{A}$ by $I_\mathcal{A} = \bigcap_{Q \in \mathcal{A}} Q$. We define specializations of quorum systems
based on the number of quorums that together have a non-empty intersection.

Definition 1. *A quorum system $\mathbb{Q}$ is called an **n-wise quorum system** if for
any $\mathcal{A} \subseteq \mathbb{Q}$, s.t. $|\mathcal{A}| = n$ we have $I_\mathcal{A} \neq \emptyset$ holds. We call n the **intersection
degree** of $\mathbb{Q}$.*

In a common quorum system any two quorums intersect, and so any quorum
system is a *2-wise* (pairwise) quorum system. At the other extreme, a $|\mathbb{Q}|$-*wise*
quorum system has a common intersection among all quorums. From the definition it follows that an n-*wise* quorum system is also a k-*wise* quorum system,
for $2 \leq k \leq n$. We will organize the servers into n-*wise* quorum systems known
to all the participants as needed.

   Algorithms presented in this work are specified in terms of *I/O automata* [26,25],
where an algorithm A is a composition of automata A_i, each assigned to some process i. Each A_i is defined in terms of a set of states $states(A_i)$ that includes the

initial state σ_0, a signature $sig(A_i)$ that specifies input, output, and internal actions (external signature consists of only input and output actions), and *transitions*, that for each action ν gives the triple $\langle \sigma, \nu, \sigma' \rangle$ defining the transition of A_i from state σ to state σ'. Such a triple is also called a *step*. An *execution fragment* ϕ of A_i is a finite or an infinite sequence $\sigma_0, \nu_1, \sigma_1, \nu_2, \ldots, \nu_r, \sigma_r, \ldots$ of alternating states and actions, such that every $\sigma_k, \nu_{k+1}, \sigma_{k+1}$ is a step of A_i. If an execution fragment begins with an initial state of A_i then it is called an *execution*. We say that an execution fragment ϕ' of A_i, *extends* a finite execution fragment ϕ of A_i if the first state of ϕ' is the last state of ϕ. The concatenation of ϕ and ϕ' is the result of the extension of ϕ by ϕ' where the duplicate occurrence of the last state of ϕ is eliminated, yielding an execution fragment of A_i.

A process i *crashes* in an execution ϕ if it contains a step $\langle \sigma_k, fail_i, \sigma_{k+1} \rangle$ as the last step of A_i. A process i is *faulty* in an execution ϕ if i crashes in ϕ; otherwise i is *correct*. A quorum $Q \in \mathbb{Q}$ is non-faulty if $\forall i \in Q$, i is correct; otherwise Q is faulty. We assume that at least one quorum in $\mathbb{Q}$ is non-faulty in any execution.

Atomicity. We aim to implement atomic read/write memory, where each object is replicated at servers. Each object has a unique name, x from some set X, and object values v come from some set V_x; initially each x is set to a distinguished value v_0 ($\in V_x$). Reader p requests a read operation ρ on an object x using action $read_{x,p}$. Similarly a write operation is requested using action $write(*)_{x,p}$ at writer p. The steps corresponding to such actions are called *invocation* steps. An operation terminates with the corresponding $read$-$ack(*)_{x,p}$ or $write$-$ack_{x,p}$ action; these steps are called *response* steps. An operation π is *incomplete* in an execution when the invocation step of π does not have the associated response step; otherwise we say that π is *complete*. We assume that requests made by read and write processes are *well-formed*: a process does not request a new operation until it receives the response for a previously invoked operation.

In an execution, we say that an operation (read or write) π_1 *precedes* another operation π_2, or π_2 *succeeds* π_1, if the response step for π_1 precedes in real time the invocation step of π_2; this is denoted by $\pi_1 \rightarrow \pi_2$. Two operations are *concurrent* if neither precedes the other.

Correctness of an implementation of an atomic read/write object is defined in terms of the *atomicity* and *termination* properties. Assuming the failure model discussed earlier, the termination property requires that any operation invoked by a correct process eventually completes. Atomicity is defined as follows [25]. For any execution of a memory service, if all the read and the write operations that are invoked complete, then the read and write operations can be partially ordered by an ordering $\prec$, so that the following properties are satisfied:

P1. The partial order is consistent with the external order of invocation and responses, that is, there do not exist operations π_1 and π_2, such that π_1 completes before π_2 starts, yet $\pi_2 \prec \pi_1$.

P2. All write operations are totally ordered and every read operation is ordered with respect to all the writes.

P3. Every read operation ordered after any writes returns the value of the last write preceding it in the partial order, and any read operation ordered before all writes returns the initial value of the object.

For the rest of the paper we assume a single register memory system. By composing multiple single register implementations, one may obtain a complete atomic memory [25]. Thus, we omit further mention of object names.

Efficiency and Fastness. We measure the efficiency of an atomic register implementation in terms of *communication round-trips* (or simply rounds). A round is defined as follows [8,16,15]:

Definition 2. *Process p performs a communication round during operation π if all of the following hold:*

1. p sends request messages that are a part of π to a set of processes,

2. any process q that receives a request message from p for operation π, replies without delay.

3. when process p receives enough replies it terminates the round (either completing π or starting new round).

Operation π is *fast* [8] if it completes after its first communication round; an implementation is fast if in each execution all operations are fast. *Semifast* implementations as defined in [16] allow some read operations to perform two communication rounds. Briefly, an implementation is semifast if the following properties are satisfied: (a) writes are fast, (b) reads complete in one or two rounds, (c) only a single complete read operation is slow (two round) per write operation, and (d) there exists an execution that contains at least one write and one read operation and all operations are fast. Finally, *weak-semifast* implementations [15] satisfy properties (a), (b), and (d), but eliminate the property (c), allowing multiple slow read operations per write. As shown in [8,16] no MWMR implementation of atomic memory can be fast or semifast. So we focus our attention on implementations where both reads and writes maybe slow. We use quorum systems and tags to maintain, and impose an ordering on, the values written to the register replicas. We say that a quorum $Q \in \mathbb{Q}$, *replies* to a process p for an operation π during a round, if $\forall s \in Q$, s receives messages during the round and replies to these messages, and p receives all of the replies.

Given that any subset of readers or writers may crash, the termination of an operation cannot depend on the progress of any other operation. Furthermore we guarantee termination only if servers' replies within a round of some operation do not depend on receipt of any message sent by other processes. Thus we can construct executions where only the messages from the invoking processes to the servers, and from the servers to the invoking processes are delivered. Lastly, to guarantee termination under the assumed failure model, no operation can wait for more than a singe quorum to reply within the processing of a single round.

3   SSO-Based Algorithm

In this section we present algorithm SFW that utilizes a technique, called SSO, to introduce fast read *and* write operations. In traditional MWMR atomic register implementations, the writer is solely responsible for incrementing the tag that imposes the ordering on the values of the register. With the new technique, and our hybrid approach, this task is now also assigned to the servers, hence the name *Server Side Ordering* (SSO).

At a first glance, SSO appears to be an intuitive and straightforward approach: servers are responsible to increment the timestamp associated with their local replica whenever they receive a write request. Yet, this technique proved to be extremely challenging. Traditionally, two phase write operations were querying the register replicas for the latest timestamp, then they were incrementing that timestamp and finally they were assigning the new timestamp to the value to be written. Such methodology established that each individual writer was responsible to decide a *single* and *unique* timestamp to be assigned to a written value. In contrary, the new technique promises to redeem the writer for the query phase by moving the association of the written value to a timestamp (and thus its ordering) to the replica owners (servers). This however introduces new complexity to the problem since *multiple* and *different* timestamps may now be assigned to the same write request (and thus the same written value). Since timestamps are used to order the write operations, then multiple timestamps for a single write imply the appearance of the same operation in different points in the execution timeline. Hence the great challenge is to provide clients with enough information so that they decide a unique ordering for each written value to avoid violation of atomicity. For this purpose we combine the server generated timestamps with writer generated operation counters.

Algorithm SFW involves two predicates. One for the write protocol and one for the read protocol. Both protocols evaluate the distribution of a tag within the quorum that replies to a write/read operation respectively.

The algorithm, depicted in Figures 1,2 and 3, uses $\langle tag, value \rangle$ pairs to impose ordering on the values written to the register. In contrast with the traditional approach where the tag is a two field tuple, this algorithm requires the tag to be a triple. In particular the *tag* is of the form $\langle ts, wid, wc \rangle \in \mathbb{N} \times \mathcal{W} \times \mathbb{N}$, where the fields ts and wid are used as in common tags and represent the timestamp and writer identifier respectively. Field wc represents the write operation counter and facilitates the ability to distinguish between write operations. Initially the tag is set to $\langle 0, \min(\mathcal{W}), 0 \rangle$ in every process. In contrast to ts, wc is incremented by the writer before invokes a write operation and it denotes the sequence number of that write. Recall that by our key technique, the tags (and particularly the timestamps in the tags) are incremented by the server processes. Thus if a tag was a tuple of the form $\langle ts, wid \rangle$, then two server processes s_i and s_j may associate two different tags $\langle ts_i, w \rangle$ and $\langle ts_j, w \rangle$ to a single write operation. Any operation however that witness such tags cannot distinguish whether the tags refer to a single or different write operations from w. By introducing the new term the tags will become $\langle ts_i, w, wc \rangle$ and $\langle ts_j, w, wc \rangle$, and thus any

```
 1: at each writer w
 2: procedure initialization:
 3: tag ← ⟨0, wid, 0⟩,  wc ← 0,  wid ← writer id,  rCounter ← 0
 4: procedure write(v)
 5: wc ← wc + 1
 6: send (W, tag, wc, rCounter) to all servers
 7: wait until receive (WACK, inprogress, confirmed, rCounter) from some quorum Q ∈ ℚ
 8: rcvM ← {⟨s, m⟩ : m = (WACK, inprogress, confirmed, rCounter) ∧ s sent m ∧ s ∈ Q}
 9: T = {⟨ts, wid, wc⟩ : ⟨ts, wid, wc⟩ ∈ m.inprogress ∧ ⟨s, m⟩ ∈ rcvM}        /* find unique tags */
10: if ∃τ, MS, A : τ ∈ T ∧ MS = {s : ⟨s, m⟩ ∈ rcvM ∧ τ ∈ m.inprogress} ∧
        A ⊆ Q s.t. 0 ≤ |A| ≤ n/2 − 1 ∧ I_{A∪{Q}} ⊆ MS then
11:     tag = τ
12:     if |A| =≥ max(0, n/2 − 2) then
13:         rCounter ← rCounter + 1
14:         send (RP, tag, tag.wc, rCounter) to all servers
15:         wait until receive (RPACK, inprogress, confirmed, rCounter) from some quorum Q ∈ ℚ
16:     end if
17: else
18:     tag = max_{⟨ts,wid,wc⟩}(T); rCounter ← rCounter + 1
19:     send (RP, tag, tag.wc, rCounter) to all servers
20:     wait until receive (RPACK, inprogress, confirmed, rCounter) from some quorum Q ∈ ℚ
21: end if
22: return(OK)
23:
```

Fig. 1. Pseudocode for Writer protocol

```
 1: at each server s
 2: procedure initialization:
 3: tag ← ⟨0, 0, 0⟩, inprogress ← {}, confirmed ← ⟨0, 0, 0⟩, counter[0...|ℛ| + |𝒲|] ← 0
 4: procedure serve()
 5: upon rcv(msgT, tag', wc', rCounter') from q ∈ 𝒲 ∪ ℛ and rCounter' ≥ counter[pid(q)] do
 6: if tag < tag' then
 7:     ⟨tag.ts, tag.wid, tag.wc⟩ = ⟨tag'.ts, tag'.wid, tag'.wc⟩
 8: end if
 9: if msgT = W then
10:     ⟨tag.ts, tag.wid, tag.wc⟩ = ⟨tag.ts + 1, tag'.wid, wc'⟩            /* tag'.wid = pid(q) */
11:     inprogress = (inprogress − {τ : τ ∈ inprogress ∧ τ.wid = pid(q)}) ∪ ⟨tag.ts, pid(q), tag.wc⟩
12: end if
13: if confirmed < tag' then
14:     confirmed ← tag'
15: end if
16: counter[pid(q)] ← rCounter'
17: send (ack, inprogress, confirmed, counter[pid(q)])
18:
```

Fig. 2. Pseudocode for Server protocol

operation establishes that the same write operation was assigned two different timestamps. The triples can be compared alphanumerically. In particular we say that $tag_1 > tag_2$ if $tag_1.ts > tag_2.ts$, or $tag_1.ts = tag_2.ts \wedge tag_1.wid > tag_2.wid$, or $tag_1.ts = tag_2.ts \wedge tag_1.wid = tag_2.wid \wedge tag_1.wc > tag_2.wc$.

Server. The server maintains the register replica and acts depending on the message it receives. The local state of a server process s, is defined by three local variables: (1) the tag_s variable which is the local tag stored in the server, (2) the

```
1: at each reader r
2: procedure initialization:
3:   tag ← ⟨0, 0, 0⟩, rCounter ← 0
4: procedure read()
5:   rCounter ← rCounter + 1
6:   send (R, tag, tag.wc, rCounter) to all servers
7:   wait until receive (RACK, inprogress, confirmed, rCounter) from some quorum Q ∈ ℚ
8:   rcvM ← {⟨s, m⟩ : m = (RACK, inprogress, confirmed, rCounter) ∧ s sent m ∧ s ∈ Q}
9:   maxC = maxₘ∈rcvM (m.confirmed)                    /* find the maximum confirmed tag */
10:  inP = {⟨ts, wid, wc⟩ : ⟨ts, wid, wc⟩ ∈ ⋃⟨s,m⟩∈rcvM m.inprogress}
11:  if ∃τ, MS, B : (τ ∈ inP ∧ τ > maxC) ∧ MS = {s : ⟨s, m⟩ ∈ rcvM ∧ τ ∈ m.inprogress} ∧
       B ⊆ ℚ s.t. 0 ≤ |B| ≤ n/2 − 2 ∧ I_{B∪{Q}} ⊆ MS then
12:      tag ← τ
13:      if |B| =≥ max(0, n/2 − 2) then
14:          rCounter ← rCounter + 1
15:          send (RP, tag, tag.wc, rCounter) to all servers
16:          wait until receive (RPACK, inprogress, confirmed, rCounter) from some quorum Q ∈ ℚ
17:      end if
18:  else
19:      tag ← maxC; MC ← {s : (⟨s, m⟩ ∈ rcvM) ∧ (m.confirmed = maxC)}
20:      if ∄C : C ⊆ ℚ ∧ |C| ≤ m − 2 ∧ I_{C∪Q} ⊆ MC then
21:          rCounter ← rCounter + 1
22:          send (RP, tag, tag.wc, rCounter) to all servers
23:          wait until receive (RPACK, inprogress, confirmed, rCounter) from some quorum Q ∈ ℚ
24:      end if
25:  end if
26:  return(tag)
```

Fig. 3. Pseudocode for Reader protocol

$confirmed_s$ variable which stores the largest tag known by s that has been returned by some reader or writer process and, (3) the $inprogress_s$ set which includes all the latest tags assigned by s to write requests. Each server s waits to receive a read or write message from operation initiated at some process p. Where this message contains: (a) the type of the message $msgType$, (b) the last tag returned by p ($msgtag$), (c) the value to be written if p invokes a write operation or the latest value returned by p if p invokes a read operation, (d) a counter $msgwc$ that specifies the sequence number of this operation if p invokes a write or is equal to $msgtag.wc$ if p invokes a read, and (e) a counter to help the server distinguish between new and stale messages from p. Upon receipt of any type of message, s updates its local and confirmed tags if they are smaller than the tag enclosed in the received message. In particular if $msgtag > tag_s$ (resp. $msgtag > confirmed_s$) then s assigns $tag_s = msgtag$ (resp. $confirmed_s = msgtag$). In addition to the above updates, if s receives a WRITE message from p, then s generates a new tag $newt = ⟨tag_s.ts + 1, p, msgwc⟩$, by incrementing the timestamp included in its local timestamp by 1 and assigning the new timestamp to the write operation from p. Note that the new tag generated is greater than both tag_s and $msgtag$. The server then pairs the new tag to the value included in the write message and changes its local tag to $tag_s = newt$. Then s adds $newt$ in the $inprogress$ set ,and removes any tag maintained previously in that set for any write operation from p. Once it completes its local update, s acknowledges every message received by sending its $inprogress_s$ set and $confirmed_s$ variable to the requesting process.

Writer. To uniquely identify all write operations, a writer w maintains a local variable wc that is incremented each time w invokes a write operation. Essentially that variable counts the number of write operations performed by w and every such write can be identified by the tuple $\langle w, wc \rangle$, by any process in the system. To perform a write operation $\omega = \langle w, wc \rangle$, w sends messages to all of the servers and waits for a quorum of these, Q, to reply. Once enough replies arrive (each server's *inprogress* set and *confirmed* variable), w collects all of the tags assigned to ω by each server in Q. Then it applies a predicate on the collected tags. In few words the predicate is used to checks if any of the collected tags appear in some intersection of Q with at most $\frac{n}{2} - 1$ (see proof sketch below why this is sufficient) other quorums, where n the intersection degree of the deployed quorum system. If there exists such a tag τ then the writer adopts τ as the tag of the value it tried to write; otherwise the writer adopts the maximum among the collected tags in the replied quorum. The writer proceeds in a second communication round to propagate the tag assigned to the written values if: (a) the predicate holds but the tag is only propagated in an intersection of Q with more than $\frac{n}{2} - 2$ other quorums, or (b) the predicate does not hold. In any other case the write operation is fast and completes in a single communication round. More formally the writer predicate is the following, where $|A|$ is rounded down to the nearest integer:

Writer predicate for a write ω (PW): $\exists \ \tau, A, MS$ where: $\tau \in \{\langle ., \omega \rangle :$ $\langle ., \omega \rangle \in inprogress_s(\omega) \ \wedge \ s \in Q\}$, $A \subseteq \mathbb{Q}, 0 \leq |A| \leq \frac{n}{2} - 1$, and $MS = \{s : s \in Q \ \wedge \ \tau \in inprogress_s(\omega)\}$, s.t. either $|A| \neq 0$ and $I_A \cap Q \subseteq MS$ or $|A| = 0$ and $Q = MS$.

Reader. The main difference between reader and writer protocols is that the reader has to examine each tag assigned to *all* of the write operations contained in *inprogress* sets of the servers that replied. (In contrast, writer examines only the tags assigned only to its own write operation.)

The reader proceeds by sending messages to all the servers and waits for some quorum of these to reply. Soon as enough replies arrive, it computes the maximum confirmed tag $maxConf$, and populates the set inP with all tags from *inprgoress* set reported by each of the replying servers. Then the reader chooses the largest tag $maxT$ found in inP and checks if: (a) $maxConf \geq maxT$, or (b) whether $maxT$ satisfies a reader predicate (defined below). If neither condition is valid, then $maxT$ tag is removed from inP and $maxT$ is assigned the next largest tag in inP, then the two checks are repeated. If inP becomes empty, then $maxConf$ is returned along with its associated value. If (a) holds, then some tag that has already been returned by some process is higher than any remaining tag in inP. In this case reader returns $maxConf$ and its assigned value. If (b) holds, then reader returns the tag and the associated value that satisfies its predicate. The reader is requires to ensure that the tag is propagated in an intersection between the replied quorum and at most $\frac{n}{2} - 2$ other quorums, where n the intersection degree of the quorum system. A read operation is slow and performs a second communication round if: (1) the predicate holds but the tag is propagated in an intersection between Q and exactly $\frac{n}{2} - 2$ other quorums, or (2) the reader decides to return $maxConf$, but this was received from no complete intersection or an intersection between Q and $n - 1$ other quorums. The tag and the associated value that will be returned by the read operation are propagated to some quorum of servers during the second communication round. More formally the reader predicate is, where $|B|$ is rounded down to the nearest integer:

Reader predicate for a read ρ (**PR**): $\exists \, \tau, B, MS$, where: $\max(\tau) \in \bigcup_{s \in Q_i} inprogress_s(\rho)$, $B \subseteq \mathbb{Q}, 0 \leq |B| \leq \frac{n}{2} - 2$, and $MS = \{s : s \in Q_i \wedge \tau \in inprogress_s(\rho)\}$, s.t. either $|B| \neq 0$ and $I_B \cap Q_i \subseteq MS$ or $|B| = 0$ and $Q_i = MS$.

Theorem 1. *Algorithm* SFW *implements a MWMR atomic read/write register.*

Proof (Sketch). The key challenge is to show that every reader and writer process decide on a single unique tag for each write operation, despite the fact that servers may assign different tags to that same write operation. To this end, we first show that in an n-wise quorum system, if some process p obtains replies from the servers of some quorum, then p may witness only a single tag per write operation to be distributed in a k-wise intersection, for $k < \frac{n+1}{2}$.

Writer's perspective: Based on the above observation, we show that only a single (unique) tag may satisfy the write predicate (**PW**). Observe that if there is a tag τ that satisfies **PW**, then it follows that τ is distributed in an intersection of at most $\frac{n}{2}$ quorums (i.e. $\frac{n}{2}$-wise intersection, including the replying quorum); otherwise, if no tag satisfies **PW** then the write operation is associated with the unique maximum tag received by the writer.

Reader's perspective: The goal is to show that if a read ρ returns a tag τ for a write ω, then τ was also the tag assigned to ω by the writer that invoked ω. Observe that a read operation returns a tag τ for a write ω in two cases: (a) τ satisfied the reader predicate **PR**, or (b) τ was equal to the max confirmed tag. In the first case the predicate ensures that τ was distributed in an intersection of at most $\frac{n}{2} - 1$ quorums (including the replying quorum). Thus the writer should have observed the tag in at least an $\frac{n}{2}$-wise intersection, and hence τ would satisfy the writer's predicate as well. Furthermore, τ should be the only tag that satisfies the two predicates since it is distributed in an intersection that consists of less than $\frac{n+1}{2}$ quorums. If the reader returns τ because of case (b) then it follows that τ was confirmed by either a reader that was about to return τ because it satisfied its predicate, or by the writer that decided to associate τ with its write operation ω. Either way this was a unique tag and thus returning the confirmed tag maintains its uniqueness.

Using the proof of uniqueness of a tag assigned to a write operation, we proceed to show that the atomic properties are satisfied. In particular we show the following: (1) the monotonicity of the tag in all participants, (2) that if a write operation proceeds a read operation then the read returns a tag greatest or equal to the one associated to the write operation, (3) If a write $\omega_1 \rightarrow \omega_2$ then ω_2 is associated with a higher tag than the tag associated to ω_1, and (4)

If there are two read operation s.t. $\rho_1 \to \rho_2$ then ρ_2 decides and returns a value associated with a higher or equal tag than the one returned by ρ_1.

4 Write Optimality

We now investigate the conditions under which it is possible for an execution of a MWMR register implementation to contain only fast write operations. In particular we show that by exploiting an n-$wise$ quorum system, it is possible to have executions with only fast write operations iff a certain number of "consecutive" write operations are contained in the execution. In extend, we show that this result imposes bounds on the number of writer participants in the system. We conclude this section by exploring the relation of our findings to fast implementations like [8]. We argue that our results generalize the characteristics of such implementations. In that respect, direct application of our results on the model of [8] yield the same bounds presented in that paper. For space limitations proofs appear in the full version of the paper [4].

We consider all operations that alter the tag value at some set of servers to be write operations. In an execution, an operation π invoked by process p is said to *contact* a subset of servers $\mathcal{G} \subseteq \mathcal{S}$, denoted by $cont_p(\mathcal{G}, \pi)$, if for every server $s \in \mathcal{G}$: (a) s receives the messages sent by p within π, (b) s replies to p, and (c) p receives the reply from s. If $cont_p(\mathcal{G}, \pi)$ occurs and additionally no other server (i.e., $s \notin \mathcal{G}$) receives any message from p within π then we say that π *strictly contacts* $\mathcal{G}$, and is denoted by $scnt_p(\mathcal{G}, \pi)$. Next we give two important definitions.

Definition 3. *Two operations π_1, π_2 are **consecutive** in an execution if: (i) they are invoked from processes p_1 and p_2, s.t. $p_1 \neq p_2$, (ii) they are complete, and (iii) $\pi_1 \to \pi_2$ or $\pi_2 \to \pi_1$ (they are not concurrent).*

In lieu to the above definition, a *safe register* constitutes the weakest consistency guarantee in the chain, and is defined [23] as property **S1**: *Any read operation that is not concurrent to any write operation returns the value written by the last preceding write operation.*

Definition 4. *A set of operations Π in an execution is called **quorum shifting** if $\forall \pi_1, \pi_2 \in \Pi$ strictly contact quorums $Q', Q'' \in \mathbb{Q}$ respectively, then π_1 and π_2 are consecutive and $Q' \neq Q''$.*

Given the two definitions above, we now show the ensuing lemma.

Lemma 1. *A read operation that succeeds a set of fast write operations Π, may retrieve the latest written value only from the servers that received messages from all the write operations in Π.*

Given an n-$wise$ quorum system we show that if there are $n - 1$ consecutive, quorum shifting fast write operations in an execution then safe register implementations are possible.

Lemma 2. *Any execution fragment ϕ of a safe register implementation that uses an n-$wise$ quorum system $\mathbb{Q}$ s.t. $2 \leq n < |\mathbb{Q}|$, contains at most $n - 1$ consecutive, quorum shifting, fast write operations for any number of writers $W \geq 2$.*

We now show that safe register implementations are not possible if we extend any execution that contains $n - 1$ consecutive writes, with one more consecutive, quorum shifting write operation. It suffices to assume a very basic system consisting of two writers w_1 and w_2, and one reader r. Thus our results hold for at least two writers.

Theorem 2. *No execution fragment ϕ of a safe register implementation that exploits an n-wise quorum system $\mathbb{Q}$ s.t. $2 \leq n < |\mathbb{Q}|$, can contain more than $n-1$ consecutive, quorum shifting, fast write operations for any number of writers $W \geq 2$.*

Remark 1. By close investigation of the predicates of Algorithm SFW, one can see that SFW approaches the bound of Theorem 2, as it produces executions that contain up to $n/2$ fast consecutive write operations, while maintaining atomic consistency. Obtaining a tighter upper bound is subject of future work.

Note that Theorem 2 is not valid in the following two cases: (i) Only a single writer exists in the system, (ii) There is a common intersection among all the quorums in the quorum system. In the first case the sole writer imposes the ordering on the tags introduced in the system and in the second case that ordering is imposed by the common servers that need to be contacted by every operation. It follows by the same theorem that it is impossible to have more than $n - 1$ *consecutive* fast write operations then it is also prohibited to have more than $n - 1$ *concurrent* fast write operations. Since no communication between the writers is assumed and achieving agreement in an asynchronous distributed system with a single failure (on the set of concurrent writes) is impossible, by [11], then we can obtain the following corollary:

Corollary 1. *No MWMR implementation of a safe register, that exploits an n-wise quorum system $\mathbb{Q}$ s.t. $2 \leq n < |\mathbb{Q}|$ and contains only fast writes is possible, if $|\mathcal{W}| > n - 1$.*

Moreover assuming that readers also may alter the value of the register, and thus write, then the following theorem holds:

Theorem 3. *No MWMR implementation of a safe register, that exploits an n-wise quorum system $\mathbb{Q}$ s.t. $2 \leq n < |\mathbb{Q}|$ and contains only fast operations is possible, if $|\mathcal{W} \cup \mathcal{R}| > n - 1$.*

Recall that [8] proved the impossibility of implementations where both writes and reads are fast in the MWMR model, while Theorem 3 complements that result by presenting the exact participation conditions under which such implementations could have been possible. They also showed that in the case of a single writer (i.e. $|\mathcal{W}| = 1$), a bound $|\mathcal{R}| < \frac{|\mathcal{S}|}{f} - 2$ is imposed on the number of readers, where f is the total number of allowed server failures. The authors assumed that $f \leq |\mathcal{S}|/2$, and they adopted the technique of communicating with $|\mathcal{S}| - f$ servers for each operation. This technique however depicts a quorum system where every member has a size of $|\mathcal{S}| - f$. The following lemma presents the intersection degree of such a system.

Lemma 3. *The intersection degree of a quorum system $\mathbb{Q}$ where $\forall Q_i \in \mathbb{Q}$, $|Q_i| = |\mathcal{S}| - f$ is equal to $\frac{|\mathcal{S}|}{f} - 1$.*

Note that by Lemma 3 and Theorem 3, the system in [8] could only accommodate:

$$|\mathcal{W} \cup \mathcal{R}| \leq (\frac{|\mathcal{S}|}{f} - 1) - 1 \Rightarrow 1 + |\mathcal{R}| \leq \frac{|\mathcal{S}|}{f} - 2 \Rightarrow |\mathcal{R}| \leq \frac{|\mathcal{S}|}{f} - 3$$

and thus their bound follows. This leads us to the following remark.

Remark 2. Fast implementations, such as the one presented in [8], follow our proved restrictions on the number of participants in the service.

References

1. Abraham, I., Chockler, G., Keidar, I., Malkhi, D.: Byzantine disk paxos: Optimal resilience with Byzantine shared memory. Distributed Computing 18(5), 387–408 (2006); Preliminary version appeared in PODC 2004
2. Aguilera, M., Keidar, I., Malkhi, D., Shraer, A.: Dynamic atomic storage without consensus. In: Proceedings of the twenty-eight annual ACM symposium on Principles of distributed computing (PODC 2009), pp. 17–25 (2009)
3. Attiya, H., Bar-Noy, A., Dolev, D.: Sharing memory robustly in message passing systems. Journal of the ACM 42(1), 124–142 (1996)
4. Burkhard, E., Georgiou, C., Musial, P., Nicolaou, N., Shvartsman, A.A.: On the efficiency of atomic multi-reader, multi-writer distributed memory (2009), http://www.cse.uconn.edu/ncn03001/pubs/TRs/EGMNS09TR.pdf
5. Chockler, G., Gilbert, S., Gramoli, V., Musial, P.M., Shvartsman, A.A.: Reconfigurable distributed storage for dynamic networks. J. Parallel Distrib. Comput. 69(1), 100–116 (2009)
6. Chockler, G., Keidar, I., Guerraoui, R., Vukolic, M.: Reliable distributed storage. IEEE Computer (2008)
7. Dolev, S., Gilbert, S., Lynch, N., Shvartsman, A., Welch, J.: GeoQuorums: Implementing atomic memory in mobile ad hoc networks. Distributed Computing 18(2), 125–155 (2005)
8. Dutta, P., Guerraoui, R., Levy, R.R., Chakraborty, A.: How fast can a distributed atomic read be? In: Proceedings of the 23rd ACM symposium on Principles of Distributed Computing (PODC), pp. 236–245 (2004)
9. Englert, B., Shvartsman, A.A.: Graceful quorum reconfiguration in a robust emulation of shared memory. In: Proceedings of International Conference on Distributed Computing Systems (ICDCS), pp. 454–463 (2000)
10. Fan, R., Lynch, N.A.: Efficient replication of large data objects. In: Fich, F.E. (ed.) DISC 2003. LNCS, vol. 2848, pp. 75–91. Springer, Heidelberg (2003)
11. Fischer, M.J., Lynch, N.A., Paterson, M.S.: Impossibility of distributed consensus with one faulty process. J. ACM 32(2), 374–382 (1985)
12. Garcia-Molina, H., Barbara, D.: How to assign votes in a distributed system. Journal of the ACM 32(4), 841–860 (1985)
13. Georgiou, C., Musial, P.M., Shvartsman, A.A.: Long-lived RAMBO: Trading knowledge for communication. Theoretical Computer Science 383(1), 59–85 (2007)

14. Georgiou, C., Musial, P.M., Shvartsman, A.A.: Developing a consistent domain-oriented distributed object service. IEEE Transactions of Parallel and Distributed Systems (2009); Preliminary version appeared in NCA 2005
15. Georgiou, C., Nicolaou, N., Shvartsman, A.A.: On the robustness of (Semi) fast quorum-based implementations of atomic shared memory. In: Taubenfeld, G. (ed.) DISC 2008. LNCS, vol. 5218, pp. 289–304. Springer, Heidelberg (2008)
16. Georgiou, C., Nicolaou, N., Shvartsman, A.A.: Fault-tolerant semifast implementations for atomic read/write registers. Journal of Parallel and Distributed Computing 69(1), 62–79 (2009); Preliminary version appeared in SPAA 2006
17. Gifford, D.K.: Weighted voting for replicated data. In: Proceedings of the 7th ACM Symposium on Operating Systems Principles (SOSP), pp. 150–162 (1979)
18. Gilbert, S., Lynch, N., Shvartsman, A.A.: RAMBO II: Rapidly reconfigurable atomic memory for dynamic networks. In: Proceedings of International Conference on Dependable Systems and Networks (DSN), pp. 259–268 (2003)
19. Gramoli, V., Anceaume, E., Virgillito, A.: SQUARE: scalable quorum-based atomic memory with local reconfiguration. In: Adams, C., Miri, A., Wiener, M. (eds.) SAC 2007. LNCS, vol. 4876, pp. 574–579. Springer, Heidelberg (2007)
20. Guerraoui, R., Vukolić, M.: How fast can a very robust read be? In: Proceedings of the 25th ACM symposium on Principles of Distributed Computing (PODC), pp. 248–257 (2006)
21. Guerraoui, R., Vukolić, M.: Refined quorum systems. In: Proceedings of the 26th ACM Symposium on Principles of Distributed Computing (PODC), pp. 119–128 (2007)
22. Herlihy, M., Wing, J.: Linearizability: A correctness condition for concurrent objects. ACM Transactions on Programming Languages and Systems 12(3), 463–492 (1990)
23. Lamport, L.: On interprocess communication, parts I and II. Distributed Computing 1(2), 77–101 (1986)
24. Lynch, N., Shvartsman, A.A.: RAMBO: A reconfigurable atomic memory service for dynamic networks. In: Malkhi, D. (ed.) DISC 2002. LNCS, vol. 2508, pp. 173–190. Springer, Heidelberg (2002)
25. Lynch, N.A.: Distributed Algorithms. Morgan Kaufmann, San Francisco (1996)
26. Lynch, N., Tuttle, M.: An introduction to input/output automata. CWI-Quarterly, 219–246 (1989)
27. Lynch, N.A., Shvartsman, A.A.: Robust emulation of shared memory using dynamic quorum-acknowledged broadcasts. In: Proceedings of Symposium on Fault-Tolerant Computing, pp. 272–281 (1997)
28. Malkhi, D., Reiter, M.: Byzantine quorum systems. Distributed Computing 11, 203–213 (1998)
29. Peleg, D., Wool, A.: Crumbling walls: A class of high availability quorum systems. In: Proceedings of 14th ACM Symposium on Principles of Distributed Computing (PODC), pp. 120–129 (1995)
30. Thomas, R.H.: A majority consensus approach to concurrency control for multiple copy databases. ACM Trans. Database Syst. 4(2), 180–209 (1979)

Abortable Fork-Linearizable Storage*

Matthias Majuntke, Dan Dobre, Marco Serafini, and Neeraj Suri

TU Darmstadt, DEEDS Group,
Hochschulstraße 10, 64289 Darmstadt, Germany
{majuntke,dan,marco,suri}@cs.tu-darmstadt.de

Abstract. We address the problem of emulating a shared read/write memory in a message passing system using a storage server prone to Byzantine failures. Although cryptography can be used to ensure confidentiality and integrity of the data, nothing can prevent a malicious server from returning obsolete data. Fork-linearizability [1] guarantees that if a malicious server hides an update of some client from another client, then these two clients will never see each others' updates again. Fork-linearizability is arguably the strongest consistency property attainable in the presence of a malicious server. Recent work [2] has shown that there is no fork-linearizable shared memory emulation that supports *wait-free* operations. On the positive side, it has been shown that *lock-based* emulations exist [1,2]. Lock-based protocols are fragile because they are blocking if clients may crash. In this paper we present for the first time *lock-free* emulations of fork-linearizable shared memory. We have developed two protocols, LINEAR and CONCUR. With a correct server, both protocols guarantee linearizability and that every operation successfully completes in the absence of step contention, while interfering operations terminate by aborting. The CONCUR algorithm additionally ensures that concurrent operations invoked on different registers complete successfully.

Keywords: Fork-linearizability, abortable objects, lock-freedom, shared memory, online collaboration.

1   Introduction

Fast broadband access to the Internet allows users to benefit from online services such as storing their data remotely and sharing it with other users. Examples for such services, also known as storage or computing "clouds" are Amazon S3, Nirvanix CloudNAS, and Microsoft SkyDrive [3]. These services offer full data administration such that a user does not need to care for backups or server maintenance and the data is available on demand. Such an infrastructure makes online collaboration (multiple users working on the same logical data) based on shared storage very attractive. Examples of existing solutions for online collaboration are the well-known revision control systems like CVS [4] and SVN [5],

---

* Research funded in part by IBM Faculty Award, Microsoft Research, and DFG GRK 1362 (TUD GKmM).

T. Abdelzaher, M. Raynal, and N. Santoro (Eds.): OPODIS 2009, LNCS 5923, pp. 255–269, 2009.

the storage management system WebDAV [6], upcoming Web 2.0 applications [7] like Google docs [8], and a large number of distributed file systems [9].

Online collaboration usually assumes that the participating clients trust each other — otherwise there exists no basis for reasonable communication. However, when the shared storage is provided by a third party, clients may not fully trust the service, e.g. it can corrupt or leak sensitive data. Cryptographic techniques such as hash functions, message authentication codes (MACs) and signatures can be used to prevent unauthorized access to data (confidentiality) and un-detectable corruption of the data (integrity). Progress and consistency cannot always be guaranteed when the storage service[1] is untrusted. A malicious server may simply refuse to process client requests and it can violate linearizability by omitting a recent update of one client and presenting an outdated value to another client. This split brain attack is called *forking* and cannot be prevented. However, once a forking attack is mounted, it can be easily detected using a *fork-linearizable* storage protocol. *Fork-linearizability* [1] ensures that once two clients are forked, they never see each others' updates after that without reveal-ing the server as faulty. Without fork-consistency, a malicious server is able to present data updates to clients in such a way that no client can say whether the set of updates of other clients it sees is complete or not, nor can such malicious behavior be easily detected, making reliable collaboration impossible. Once such a partitioning occurs, the clients stop hearing from each other. A client that has not seen updates from another client for a while can use out-of-band communi-cation (as e.g. phone or e-mail) to find out if the server is misbehaving.

Recent work [2] has shown that even if the server behaves correctly, clients cannot complete their operations independently from each other because this introduces a vulnerability that can be exploited by a Byzantine server to violate fork-linearizability. This means that in an asynchronous system there is no *wait-free* [10] emulation of fork-linearizable storage on a Byzantine server. On the positive side, the SUNDR [1] protocol and the concurrent protocol by Cachin *et al.* [2] show the existence of fork-linearizable Byzantine emulations using locks. However, lock-based protocols are problematic as they can block in the presence of faulty clients that crash while holding the lock.

Paper Contributions. In this paper we present two *lock-free* emulations of fork-linearizable shared memory on an untrusted server. In runs in which the server behaves correctly, our proposed protocols LINEAR and CONCUR ensure lineariz-ability [11], and that each operation executed in the absence of concurrency suc-cessfully completes. Under concurrency, operations may complete by aborting. Both protocols emulate a shared memory consisting of n single-writer multiple-reader (SWMR) registers, one for each of the n clients, where register i is up-dated only by client C_i and may be read by all clients. While both protocols address lock-free fork-linearizability, they solve two distinct issues. The LIN-EAR protocol, which is the first *lock-free* fork-linearizable implementation at all, offers a communication complexity of $\mathcal{O}(n)$. The CONCUR protocol improves

---

[1] We will use the terms storage service, storage server, and server interchangeably.

on the handling of concurrent operations such that overlapping operations accessing *different* registers are not perceived as concurrent, and therefore they are not aborted. However, it has a communication complexity of $\mathcal{O}(n^2)$. Both protocols allow concurrent operations to abort in order to circumvent the impossibility result by Cachin *et al.* [2]. The necessary condition for aborting is step contention [12], and thus, pending operations of crashed clients never cause other operations to abort. As a final contribution, note that the existence of abortable fork-linearizable storage implies the existence of obstruction-free [13] fork-linearizable storage.

We now give a rough intuition of why aborting helps to circumvent the given impossibility of wait-free fork-linearizability. With both our protocols, if multiple operations compete for the same register, then there is only one winner and all other operations are aborted. On a correct server, this strategy ensures that all successful operations applied to the same register access the register sequentially. Operations have timestamps attached to them and the sequential execution establishes a total order on operations and the corresponding timestamps. The algorithm ensures that a forking attack breaks the total order on timestamps. If a malicious server does not present the most recent update to a read operation, then the timestamps of the omitted write operation and that of the read operation become incomparable and the two clients are forked. The algorithm guarantees that also future operations of those two clients cannot be ordered and thus they remain forked forever.

2   Related Work

Mazières and Shasha [1] have introduced the notion of fork-linearizability and they have implemented the first fork-linearizable multi-user network file system SUNDR. The SUNDR protocol may block in case a client crashes even when the storage server is correct. Cachin *et al.* [2] implements a more efficient fork-linearizable storage protocol based on SUNDR which reduces communication complexity from $\mathcal{O}(n^2)$ to $\mathcal{O}(n)$. The presented protocols are blocking and thus they have the same fundamental drawback as SUNDR. The authors [2] also prove that there is no wait-free emulation of fork-linearizable storage. They do so by exhibiting a run with concurrent operations where some client has to wait for another client to complete. Oprea and Reiter [14] define the weaker notion of fork-sequential consistency. Intuitively the difference to fork-linearizability is that fork-sequential consistency does not necessarily preserve the real-time order of operations from different clients. In a recent work, Cachin *et al.* [15] show that there is no wait-free emulation of fork-sequential consistent storage on a Byzantine server. It is important to note that these impossibility results do not rule out the existence of emulations of fork-linearizable storage with abortable operations [16] or weaker liveness guarantees such as obstruction-freedom [13]. Cachin *et al.* [17] presents the storage service FAUST which wait-free emulates a shared memory with a new consistency semantics called *weak fork-linearizability*. The notion of weak fork-linearizability weakens fork-linearizability in two fundamental ways. After being forked, two clients may see each others' updates once (at-most-on-join property) and secondly, the real-time order among the operations which are the last of each client is not ensured.

Li and Mazières [18] study systems where storage is implemented from $3f + 1$ server replicas and more than f replicas are Byzantine faulty. They present a storage protocol which ensures *fork* consistency*. Similar to weak fork-linearizability, fork* consistency allows that two forked clients may be joined at most once (at-most-one-join property).

The notion of abortable objects has been introduced by Aguilera *et al.* [16]. The paper shows the existence of a universal abortable object construction from abortable registers. It is the first construction of an obstruction-free universal type from base objects weaker than registers. In a follow-up paper [19] it has been shown that in a partially synchronous system, abortable objects can be boosted to wait-free objects. This makes abortable objects, including our abortable fork-linearizable read/write emulation very attractive.

Summing up, to date there is no lock-free emulation of fork-linearizable storage even though lock-free solutions can be made practically wait-free using boosting techniques as described by Aguilera *et al.* [19].

3   System Model and Definitions

Similar to the models used in recent work on fork-linearizability [2],[1], we consider a distributed system consisting of a single server S and n clients $C_1, \ldots, C_n$. The clients may fail by crashing but they never deviate from the protocol. The server may be faulty and deviate arbitrarily from its protocol exhibiting non-responsive-arbitrary faults [20] (Byzantine [21]). The clients communicate with the server by sending messages over reliable channels directly to the server, forming an asynchronous network. The *shared functionality* provided by the server is a *read/write register*. A read/write register provides *operations* by which the clients can access the register. An operation is defined by two *events*, an *invocation* event and a *response* event. To represent an abort of execution, there are two types of response events: ABORT and OK events respectively. An additional event type constitute *crash* events representing the act of a client failing. We call operation *op complete*, if there exists a matching response event to the invocation event of *op*, else *op* is denoted as *incomplete*. An operation is *successful*, iff it is complete and the response event is an OK event. An operation is *aborted*, if it is complete and the response event is an ABORT event. Operation *op precedes* operation *op'* iff *op* is complete before the invocation event of *op'*. If *op* precedes *op'* we denote *op* and *op'* as *sequential* operations. Else, if neither operation precedes the other, then *op* and *op'* are said to be are *concurrent*. An *execution* of the system is defined as the sequence of events occurring at the clients.

A read/write register $X[i]$ provides a *Read* and a *Write* operation to the clients. The response event to a client's operation is either OK or ABORT. Client C_i may use the *Write* operation to store a value v from domain *Value* in register $X[i]$, denoted as $Write(i, v)$. If the response to a *Read* of register $X[i]$ is OK, then a value v is returned, denoted as $Read(i) \to v$. The server implements n single-writer multiple-reader (SWMR) registers $X[1 \ldots n]$ where each client C_i writes only to $X[i]$ and may read from all other registers. The *sequential specification* of a register requires that if a *Read* operation returns a value, it returns the value written by the last preceding *Write* operation.

We assume that each client interacts *sequentially* with the read/write register, i.e. a client invokes a new operation only after the previous operation has completed.

Further we assume that clients have access to a digital signature scheme used by each client to *sign* its messages such that any other client can determine the authenticity of a message by *verifying* the corresponding signature. Further, the Byzantine server is not able to forge the signatures.

The consistency condition for the read/write register is defined in terms of the sequence σ of events the shared register exhibits in an execution as observed by the clients. Such a sequence, also called *history*, contains invocation, response, and crash events. To ease the definition of consistency conditions and the reasoning about correctness, we define two transformations to derive simpler histories from more complicated ones, while maintaining plausibility of execution. Intuitively, the transformations remove all operations from a history that do not take effect.

Definition 1. An operation *op* of client *takes effect* if and only if

1. *op* is *successful* OR
2. *op* is a *Write* operation *and*
   there exists a *Read* operation that returns the value written by *op*.

We now define the two transformations CRASHCOMPLETE and ABORTCOMPLETE.

Definition 2. The transformations CRASHCOMPLETE and ABORTCOMPLETE take a sequence of events σ as input and return a sequence of events σ' as output.

- CRASHCOMPLETE: We define σ' returned by CRASHCOMPLETE by construction: At first we add all events from σ to σ'. Then, we remove the invocation events of *incomplete* operations that did not take effect and the corresponding crash event if one exists[2] from σ'. Next, we add a matching OK event to each remaining *incomplete* operation and remove all remaining crash events in σ'.
- ABORTCOMPLETE: We define σ' returned by ABORTCOMPLETE by construction: At first we add all events from σ to σ'. Then, we remove all events of aborted operations in σ' that did not take effect. Next, we replace all remaining ABORT events in σ with matching OK events.

---

[2] Note, that the last operation of each client in σ might be incomplete even if the client did not crash.

Variables used by Algorithm 2 and 3:

sig signature   /* signature /*
abort boolean   /* flags if operation is aborted /*
value_suc value   /* written value of last successful write /*
retval value   /* return value of the read operation /*

Variables used by Algorithm 2:

op_cnt integer   /*   operation counter /*
op, x_op, lso operation with fields $id = (client\_id, op\_cnt, type, reg)$, *value, tsv, sig*
                                            /* operation structure /*
$tsv_{comp}[1..n]$ vector of integers   /* ts vector of last completed operation /*
ts_{suc} integer   /* timestamp of last successful operation /*

Variables used by Algorithm 3:

op_cnt[1..n] array of integer   /* operation counter /*
op, x_op, lso operation with fields $id = (client\_id, op\_cnt, type, reg)$, *value, tsm, sig*
                                            /* operation structure /*
$tsm_{comp}^{1..n}[1..n]$ timestamp matrix of integers   /* ts matrix of last completed
                                                        operation /*
$ts_{suc}[1..n]$ vector of integers   /* timestamps of last successful operations /*

Fig. 1. Variables for Algorithms 2 and 3

Transformation CRASHCOMPLETE removes incomplete operations that did not take effect from σ. This is reasonable as such events do not influence the execution. Instead of removing them, such events could also be moved to the end of sequence σ. The same argument applies to aborted operations that do not take effect which are removed by transformation ABORTCOMPLETE. By first applying transformation CRASHCOMPLETE and then transformation ABORTCOMPLETE to sequence σ, we have transformed σ into a sequence of events containing only *successful* operations. On the transformed sequence we give two equivalent definitions of *fork-linearizability* taken from recent work of Cachin *et al.* [2].

Definition 3 (Fork-Linearizability). A sequence of events σ observed by the clients is called *fork-linearizable* with respect to a functionality F if and only if for each client C_i, there exists a subsequence σ_i of σ consisting only of completed operations and a sequential permutation π_i of σ_i such that:

1. All completed operations in σ occurring[3] at client C_i are contained in σ_i; and
2. π_i preserves the real-time order of σ_i; and
3. the operations of π_i satisfy the sequential specification of F; and
4. for every $op \in \pi_i \cap \pi_j$, the sequence of events that precede op in π_i is the same as the sequence of events that precede op in π_j.

---

[3] All successful operations of client C_i occur at client C_i; together with condition 3. this further includes all operations on which an operation of client C_i causally depends, i.e. operations that have written a value client C_i reads.

Definition 4 (Global Fork-Linearizability). A sequence of events σ observed by the clients is called *fork linearizable* with respect to a functionality F if and only if there exists a sequential permutation π of σ such that:

1. π preserves the real-time order of σ; and
2. for each client C_i there exists a subsequence π_i of π such that:
   (a) events in π occurring at client C_i are contained in π_i; and
   (b) the operations of π_i satisfy the sequential specification of F; and
   (c) for every $op \in \pi_i \cap \pi_j$, the sequence of events that precede op in π_i is the same as the sequence of events that precede op in π_j.

Using two distinct but equivalent definitions of fork-linearizability simplifies the correctness proof of protocol LINEAR (by using Definition 3) and of protocol CONCUR (by using Definition 4). The notion of fork-linearizability and global fork-linearizability has shown to be equivalent [2].

4   The Protocols

In this section we present two lock-free protocols LINEAR and CONCUR that emulate a fork-linearizable shared memory on a Byzantine server. The LINEAR protocol is based on *vectors* of timestamps (described later in section 4.2) resulting in a communication complexity of $\mathcal{O}(n)$. The LINEAR protocol serializes all operations, and therefore it aborts concurrent operations even if they are applied to distinct registers. The CONCUR protocol (introduced later in section 4.3) allows for concurrent operations if they are applied to distinct registers and only operations on the same register are serialized. To achieve this, timestamp *matrices* are used leading to a communication complexity of $\mathcal{O}(n^2)$.

4.1   Protocol Properties

As mentioned above, LINEAR and CONCUR introduced emulate the shared functionality of a read/write register among a collection of clients and a (possibly) Byzantine server S. The LINEAR (CONCUR) protocol consists of two algorithms, run by the clients and the server respectively. If the server is faulty, it may refuse to respond to client requests or return (detectably) corrupted data such that liveness of the emulated functionality is violated. A malicious server may also mount a forking attack and partition clients. However, if the server behaves correctly, we require that the emulation does not block and clients are not forked.

   To formalize the desired properties of the LINEAR and CONCUR protocol, we redefine the notion of *sequential* and *concurrent* operations under step contention [22] when the server is correct. We say that two operations op and op' are *sequential under step contention* if op' does not perform steps at the server S after op performed its first step and before op performed its last step at server S. Otherwise, op and op' are *concurrent under step contention*. The LINEAR and CONCUR protocol satisfy *Fork-consistency* and two liveness properties *Nontriviality* and *Termination*:

Algorithm 1. Read / Write Operation of Client i

$Read(j)$ **do**	$Write(v)$ **do**
$\quad rw\_operation(\text{READ}, \perp, j)$	$\quad rw\_operation(\text{WRITE}, v, i)$
$\quad$ **if** *abort* **then** return ABORT	$\quad$ **if** *abort* **then** return ABORT
$\quad$ return *retval*	$\quad$ return OK

Fork-consistency: Every execution of the LINEAR and CONCUR protocols satisfies fork-linearizability with respect to a shared read/write register emulated on a Byzantine server S. If S is correct, then every execution is complete and has a linearizable history.

Nontriviality: When the server is correct, in an execution of the LINEAR (resp. CONCUR) protocol every operation that returns *abort* is concurrent under step contention with another operation (resp. with another operation on the same register).

Termination: When the server is correct and σ is the sequence of events exhibited by an execution of the LINEAR or CONCUR protocol, then after applying transformation CRASHCOMPLETE to σ, every operation in σ is complete.

4.2 The LINEAR Protocol

The LINEAR protocol is based on two main ideas. The first idea is that when two or more operations access the registers concurrently, all but one are aborted. In the protocol, operations need two rounds of communication with the server, and an operation op is aborted if a first round message of another operation arrives at the server between the points in time when the first round message and the second round message of op is received by the server. Hence, among the concurrent operations, the LINEAR protocol does not abort the "newest" operation. This scheme ensures that a pending operation of a crashed client does not interfere with other operations. Observe that using this strategy of aborting, successful operations execute in isolation and therefore accesses to the shared memory are serialized.

As a second idea, the LINEAR protocol assigns vector timestamps to operations such that a partial order $\leq$ on operations can be defined based on these timestamp vectors. The basic principle is that a client reads the most recent timestamp vector from the server during the first round, increments its own entry and writes the updated timestamp vector back to the server. Since successful operations run in isolation, the corresponding timestamp vectors are totally ordered, as no two successful operations read the same timestamp vector during the first round. Clearly, a Byzantine server may fork two clients, but then there are operations of these two clients op and op' with incomparable timestamp vectors. By the requirement of fork-linearizability, these two clients must not see any later updates of each other. For this purpose, the protocol ensures that the two clients remain forked by preventing any client from committing an operation op'' which is both greater than op and op'.

Algorithm 2. LINEAR Protocol, Algorithm of Client i	**Algorithm 3.** CONCUR Protocol, Algorithm of Client i
2.1 $rw\_operation(\text{TYPE}, value, r)$ **do**	3.1 $rw\_operation(\text{TYPE}, value, r)$ **do**
2.2 $abort \leftarrow false$	3.2 $abort \leftarrow false$
2.3 $op\_cnt \leftarrow op\_cnt + 1$	3.3 $op\_cnt[r] \leftarrow op\_cnt[r] + 1$
2.4 $op.id \leftarrow (i, op\_cnt, \text{TYPE}, r)$	3.4 $op.id \leftarrow (i, op\_cnt[r], \text{TYPE}, r)$
2.5 send $\langle \text{SUBMIT}, op.id \rangle$ to server	3.5 send $\langle \text{SUBMIT}, op.id \rangle$ to server
2.6 **wait for** message $\langle \text{SUBMIT\_R}, x\_op, lso \rangle$	3.6 **wait for** message $\langle \text{SUBMIT\_R}, x\_op, lso \rangle$
2.7 **if not** $\text{verify}(lso.sig) \wedge \text{verify}(x\_op.sig)$ **then halt**	3.7 **if not** $\text{verify}(lso.sig) \wedge \text{verify}(x\_op.sig)$ **then halt**
2.8 **if not** $\forall k \neq i : tsv_{comp}[k] \leq lso.tsv[k] \wedge ts_{suc} = lso.tsv[i]$ **then halt**	3.8 **if not** $\forall k \neq i : tsm^r_{comp}[k] \leq lso.tsm^r[k] \wedge ts_{suc}[r] = lso.tsm^r[i]$ **then halt**
2.9 **if not** $x\_op.id.client\_id = r$ **then halt**	3.9 **if not** $x\_op.id.client\_id = r$ **then halt**
2.10 **if not** $x\_op \leq lso \wedge lso.tsv[r] = x\_op.tsv[r]$ **then halt**	3.10 **if not** $x\_op \leq lso \wedge lso.tsm^r[r] = x\_op.tsm^r[r]$ **then halt**
	3.11 **forall** $k = 1..n, k \neq r$ **do**
	3.12 **if not** $tsm^k_{comp}, lso.tsm^k$ are comparable **then halt**
	3.13 $op.tsm^k \leftarrow \max\{tsm^k_{comp}, lso.tsm^k\}$
	3.14 $op.tsm^r \leftarrow lso.tsm^r$
2.11 $op.tsv \leftarrow lso.tsv$	3.15 $op.tsm^r[i] \leftarrow op\_cnt[r]$
2.12 $op.tsv[i] \leftarrow op\_cnt$	
2.13 **if** $\text{TYPE} = \text{WRITE}$ **then** $op.value \leftarrow value$	3.16 **if** $\text{TYPE} = \text{WRITE}$ **then** $op.value \leftarrow value$
2.14 $sig \leftarrow \text{sign}(op.id||op.value||op.tsv)$	3.17 $sig \leftarrow \text{sign}(op.id||op.value||op.tsm)$
2.15 $op.sig \leftarrow sig$	3.18 $op.sig \leftarrow sig$
2.16 send $\langle \text{COMMIT}, op \rangle$ to server	3.19 send $\langle \text{COMMIT}, op \rangle$ to server
2.17 **wait for** message $\langle \text{COMMIT\_R}, ret\_type \rangle$	3.20 **wait for** message $\langle \text{COMMIT\_R}, ret\_type \rangle$
2.18 $tsv_{comp} \leftarrow op.tsv$	3.21 $tsm_{comp} \leftarrow op.tsm$
2.19 **if** $ret\_type = \text{ABORT}$ **then**	3.22 **if** $ret\_type = \text{ABORT}$ **then**
2.20 $op.value \leftarrow value_{suc}$	3.23 $op.value \leftarrow value_{suc}$
2.21 $abort \leftarrow true$	3.24 $abort \leftarrow true$
2.22 **else**	3.25 **else**
2.23 $ts_{suc} \leftarrow op\_cnt$	3.26 $ts_{suc}[r] \leftarrow op\_cnt[r]$
2.24 $value_{suc} \leftarrow op.value$	3.27 $value_{suc} \leftarrow op.value$
2.25 **if** $\text{TYPE} = \text{READ}$ **then** $retval \leftarrow x\_op.value$	3.28 **if** $\text{TYPE} = \text{READ}$ **then** $retval \leftarrow x\_op.value$

Description of the LINEAR Protocol. The shared memory emulated by the LINEAR protocol consists of n SWMR registers $X[1], \ldots, X[n]$ such that client C_i may write a value from set *Value* only to register $X[i]$ and may read from any register. The detailed pseudo-code of the LINEAR protocol appears in Algorithm 1, 2 and 4 and the variables used are described in Figure 1.

A client performs two rounds of communication with the server S for both *Read* and *Write* operations (see Algorithm 1). This is implemented by calling procedure *rw_operation* (Algorithm 2) with type READ or WRITE respectively. When executing *rw_operation*, the client sends a SUBMIT message to the server S announcing a read or write operation and waits for a matching response. The server S responds with a SUBMIT_R message containing information on the current state of the server and the value to be read. In the second communication round, the client sends a COMMIT message to the server and waits for a COMMIT_R message to complete the operation. The COMMIT_R message is either of type OK or ABORT indicating to the client the outcome of the operation.

Algorithm 4. LINEAR Protocol, Algorithm of Server S	Algorithm 5. CONCUR Protocol, Algorithm of Server S
Variables:	**Variables:**
4.1 Pnd set of operation ids /* pend. ops */	5.1 $Pnd[1..n]$ array of set of operation ids
4.2 $Abrt$ set of operation ids /* pending ops to be aborted */	5.2 $Abrt[1..n]$ array of set of operation ids /* pending ops to be aborted */
4.3 **upon** receiving message ⟨SUBMIT, id⟩ from client i **do**	5.3 **upon** receiving message ⟨SUBMIT, id⟩ from client i **do**
4.4 $Abrt \leftarrow Pnd$	5.4 $Abrt[id.reg] \leftarrow Pnd[id.reg]$
4.5 $Pnd \leftarrow Pnd \cup \{id\}$	5.5 $Pnd[id.reg] \leftarrow Pnd[id.reg] \cup \{id\}$
4.6 send ⟨SUBMIT_R, $X[id.reg], lso$⟩ to client i	5.6 send ⟨SUBMIT_R, $X[id.reg], lso[id.reg]$⟩ to client i
4.7 **upon** receiving message ⟨COMMIT, op⟩ from client i **do**	5.7 **upon** receiving message ⟨COMMIT, op⟩ from client i **do**
4.8 $Pnd \leftarrow Pnd \setminus \{op.id\}$	5.8 $Pnd[op.id.reg] \leftarrow Pnd[op.id.reg] \setminus \{op.id\}$
4.9 **if** $op.id \in Abrt$ **then**	5.9 **if** $op.id \in Abrt[op.id.reg]$ **then**
4.10 send ⟨COMMIT_R, ABORT⟩ to client i	5.10 send ⟨COMMIT_R, ABORT⟩ to client i
4.11 **else**	5.11 **else**
4.12 $X[i] \leftarrow op$	5.12 $X[i] \leftarrow op$
4.13 $lso \leftarrow op$	5.13 $lso[op.id.reg] \leftarrow op$
4.14 send ⟨COMMIT_R, OK⟩ to client i	5.14 send ⟨COMMIT_R, OK⟩ to client i

Each operation op has a timestamp vector of size n assigned to it during the protocol. The timestamp vector is part of the operation data structure and is denoted as $op.tsv$. The timestamp vector is used to define a partial order $\leq$ on operations. For two operations op and op' we say that $op \leq op'$ iff $op.tsv[i] \leq op'.tsv[i]$ for all $i = 1 \ldots n$. Operations of the LINEAR protocol have the data structure of a 4-tuple with entries id, $value$, tsv and sig, where sig is a signature on the operation by the client, tsv is the timestamp vector, $value$ is the value to be written by the operation. Note that for simplicity of presentation, a *Read* operation rewrites the value of the client's last successful *Write*. The entry id is a 4-tuple $(client\_id, op\_cnt, type, reg)$ itself, where $client\_id$ equals i for C_i, op_cnt is a local timestamp of the client which is incremented during every operation, $type$ indicates whether the operation is a READ or a WRITE, and reg determines the index of the register the client intends to read from. For *Write* operations of client C_i, reg is always i. The server S maintains the n registers in a vector $X[1..n]$, where each $X[i]$ stores the last successful operation of C_i. Further, the server maintains an copy of the latest successful operation in variable lso.

When client C_i invokes a new operation op on register $X[r]$, it increments its local timestamp op_cnt, sets the entries of $op.id$ to the operation type and register r, and sends $op.id$ in a SUBMIT message to the server (lines 2.2–2.5). The server labels the received operation op as *pending*. If the server receives the SUBMIT message of another operation before the COMMIT message of op, then op is aborted. The server then responds with a SUBMIT_R message containing the last successful operation lso, and the last successful operation x_op applied to register $X[r]$ (lines 4.4–4.6).

After receiving operations lso and x_op from the server, client C_i performs a number of consistency checks (lines 2.7–2.10). If any of the checks fails, which implies that the server is misbehaving, then the client halts. In the first check, C_i verifies the signatures of lso and x_op. The next check is needed to determine a consistent timestamp vector for operation op. The goal is to obtain a timestamp vector for *op* which is greater than both *lso*'s timestamp vector and that of C_i's last *completed* operation. The timestamp vector of the latter is stored in tsv_{comp} at C_i. The client checks that all but the ith entry in *lso.tsv* are greater or equal than the corresponding entries in tsv_{comp}. C_i's entry *lso.tsv*[i] must equal the timestamp of the last *successful* operation stored in ts_{suc}. Checks three and four are needed only by *Read*: C_i checks that x_op is indeed the content of register $X[r]$. The last check verifies that *lso* is at least as large as x_op and that *lso.tsv*[r] equals $x\_op.tsv[r]$.

If all checks are passed, C_i increments its own entry *lso.tsv*[i] and *lso.tsv* becomes the timestamp vector of *op*. Then, C_i signs *op.id*, the write value and the timestamp vector *op.tsv*, and sends *op* in a COMMIT message to the server (lines 2.11–2.16). The server, removes *op.id* from the set of pending operations and checks if it has to be aborted. As mentioned earlier, if this is case, a SUBMIT message of another operation was received before the COMMIT of *op* and the server replies with ABORT (lines 4.8–4.10). Else, *op* is stored in $X[i]$ and also stored in *lso* as the last successful operation and the server replies with OK (lines 4.12–4.14).

When client C_i receives the COMMIT_R message for operation *op*, *op* is completed and thus tsv_{comp} is updated with *op.tsv*. If *op* is successful, then additionally ts_{suc} becomes the ith entry of *op.tsv*. If *op* is a READ, then the value of x_op is returned (lines 2.18–2.25).

Correctness Arguments. Instead of returning the most recent value written to register $X[j]$ by a write operation op_w, a Byzantine server may return an old value written by op'_w. Let C_i be the client whose read operation op_r reads the stale value written by op'_w. Observe that the Byzantine server returns a stale version of *lso* to C_i. Let us assume that all checks in Algorithm 2 are passed, thus C_i is unaware of the malicious behavior of the server. Note, that the jth entry in the timestamp vector of op'_w is smaller than the corresponding entry of op_w, as both are operations of client C_j whose jth entry increases with every operation. As the check in line 2.10 is passed, the jth entry in op_r's timestamp vector is also smaller than the one of op_w. As C_i increments the ith entry in the timestamp vector during op_r but not the jth entry, op_r and op_w are incomparable. We argue that in this situation, no client commits an operation which is greater than both op_w and op_r. As no client other than C_i increments the ith entry in a timestamp vector, all operation of other clients that "see" op_w have a timestamp vector whose ith entry is smaller than $op_r.tsv[i]$ and whose jth entry is larger than $op_r.tsv[j]$. Thus, such operations are also incomparable with op_r and do not join op_w and op_r. When client C_i "sees" such an operation incomparable to op_r as the latest successful operation *lso*, the check in line 2.8 is not passed because the ith entry of *lso* is smaller than the timestamp of C_i's last successful operation. Hence, C_i stops the execution. Analogously, the same arguments can be applied for client C_j and operation op_w.

As all checks are passed when the server behaves correctly, it is not difficult to see that with a correct server, all operations invoked by correct clients complete. Also with a correct server, operations are only aborted in the specified situations. For a detailed correctness proof we refer to our technical report [23].

4.3   The CONCUR Protocol

The CONCUR protocol differs from the LINEAR protocol in the way how concurrent access to the server is handled. In contrast to the LINEAR protocol, in the CONCUR protocol concurrent operations that access different registers at the server are not aborted. However, the same aborting scheme as in the LINEAR protocol is used in the CONCUR protocol on a register basis in order to serialize all accesses to the same register. This means, that a correct server aborts operation op accessing register i if and only if a SUBMIT message of another operation accessing register i is received while op is pending.

To deal with concurrent operations, in the CONCUR protocol, instead of one timestamp vector, each operation is assigned n timestamp vectors, each corresponding to one register. Such n timestamp vectors form the *timestamp matrix* of an operation. The basic idea is that when a client accesses register j then the client updates its own entry in the jth timestamp vector of the timestamp matrix. It is important to note that even with a correct server, the CONCUR protocol allows that two clients with concurrent operations may read the same timestamp matrix from the server and update different timestamp vectors such that the corresponding operations become incomparable. However, the CONCUR protocol ensures that (1) operations of the same client are totally ordered by $\leq$ and (2) operations accessing the same register at the server are totally ordered by $\leq$. This is sufficient to show that for any operation op, all operations op causally depends on, are ordered before op by $\leq$. Further, the CONCUR protocol ensures that two forked operations — i.e. for some i, the ith timestamp vectors in the timestamp matrices of the two operations are incomparable — will never be rejoined by another operation.

Description of the CONCUR Protocol. The CONCUR protocol has the same message pattern as the LINEAR protocol and provides the same interface to the clients (Algorithm 1). The CONCUR protocol uses a different implementation of procedure *rw_operation* as described in Algorithm 3, Figure 1, and Algorithm 5. As the CONCUR protocol follows the structure of the implementation of the LINEAR protocol, in the following we highlight only the differences between the two protocols. The *operation* data structure differs from the LINEAR protocol only to the fact that the timestamp vector tsv is replaced by a timestamp matrix tsm (Figure 1).

When client C_i invokes a new operation op on register r, it generates a new operation id which it sends to the server in a SUBMIT message (lines 3.2–3.5). One difference is that C_i maintains a *separate* operation counter for each register $op\_cnt[1..n]$. The server replies with operations lso and x_op contained in a SUBMIT_R message. Here, x_op is the last successful operation stored in register

r, and lso is the last successful operation that accessed register r. Note, that lso may not be stored in register r. The server maintains information on pending operations for each register separately (lines 5.4–5.6).

The first and the third check are identical to the LINEAR protocol. The second check on operations lso and x_op performed by the client corresponds to the second check in the LINEAR protocol. As CONCUR operations hold a timestamp matrix, the check is performed on the rth timestamp vectors of the timestamp matrices of lso and x_op. The goal is to obtain a timestamp matrix that makes op greater than the last completed operation of C_i and the last successful operation accessing register r, stored in lso. Like in the LINEAR protocol, the last check ensures that lso is greater than x_op and, unlike LINEAR, that the rth entries in the rth timestamp vector of the timestamp matrices of lso and x_op are equal. This particular entry is the one which has been updated during x_op (lines 3.7–3.10).

To determine the timestamp matrix for op, client C_i selects the rth timestamp vector from lso as rth timestamp vector of op and for all other indices it takes the maximum timestamp vector from lso and C_i's last completed operation. Finally, client C_i increments its own entry in the rth timestamp vector using $op\_cnt[r]$ (lines 3.12–3.15). The remainder of the protocol is analogous to the LINEAR protocol.

Correctness Arguments. First, we show that all completed operations of client C_i are totally ordered by $\leq$. This is reasonable as C_i cannot know if an aborted operation was actually aborted by the malicious server. To achieve this, as the timestamp matrix of a new operation op of C_i depends on operation lso received in the SUBMIT_R message, the check in line 3.8 is needed: It guarantees together with lines 3.14–3.15 that the rth timestamp vector of lso is greater than the one of C_i's last completed operation stored in tsm_{comp}. For the remaining timestamp vectors it holds by line 3.12–3.13, as in each case the maximal timestamp vector among lso and tsm_{comp} is picked, that they are greater than the respective one of C_i's last completed operation. Hence, operation op is greater than the last completed operation of C_i.

Second, we show that when C_i reads value $op_w.value$ from register j during op then op is greater than the corresponding operation op_w under $\leq$. Analogously, by the check in line 3.12 and lines 3.13–3.15, it also holds that op is greater than operation lso. As the check in line 3.10 ensures that op_w is smaller or equal than lso, by transitivity, op is greater than op_w.

These two proof sketches give an intuition how the CONCUR protocol ensures that all operations, op causally depends on, are ordered by $\leq$ before op. For a detailed proof of the safety and liveness properties of the CONCUR protocol, we refer to our technical report [23].

4.4   Complexity

In the LINEAR and CONCUR protocol all operations need two communication rounds to complete. We argue why two rounds are necessary for *Write* operations:

The reasoning is based on the fact that the information possibly written by some *one*-round *Write* is independent from some operations of other clients. Consider the following sequential run with a correct server and clients C_1 and C_2: $Write_1(1, x)$, $Read_2(1) \rightarrow x$, $Write_1(1, y)$, $Read_2(1) \rightarrow y$. Note, that by the one-round assumption, $Write_1(1, y)$ does not depend on the preceding $Read_2(1) \rightarrow x$. Thus, a Byzantine server may "swap" the order of these two operations unnoticeably. Hence, we can construct a run with a Byzantine server, which is indistinguishable for C_2: $Write_1(1, x)$, $Write_1(1, y)$, $Read_2(1) \rightarrow x$, $Read_2(1) \rightarrow y$. As C_2's second *Read* returns y, the run violates the sequential specification and thereby also fork-linearizability. Thus, two rounds are needed for *Write* operations and the *Write* operations emulated by the LINEAR and CONCUR protocol are optimal in this sense. We conjecture, that *Read* operations can be optimized in the the LINEAR and CONCUR protocol to complete after a single round. This would also imply that *Read* operations can be made *wait-free*.

The messages exchanged during the LINEAR protocol have size $\mathcal{O}(2(n + \iota + |v| + \varsigma))$, where ι is the length of an operation id, $|v|$ denotes the maximal length of a value from *Value* and ς is the length of a signature. The message complexity of the CONCUR protocol is in $\mathcal{O}(2(n^2 + \iota + |v| + \varsigma))$.

5   Conclusion

We have presented lock-free emulations of fork-linearizable shared memory on a Byzantine server, LINEAR and CONCUR. The LINEAR protocol is based on timestamp vectors and it has a communication complexity of $\mathcal{O}(n)$. It is the first lock-free protocol that emulates fork-linearizable storage at all. The impossibility result by Cachin *et al.* [2] is circumvented by aborting concurrent operations. The CONCUR protocol improves on the LINEAR protocol in the way how concurrent operations are handled. In the CONCUR protocol only concurrent operations accessing the same register need to be aborted. To achieve this, the CONCUR protocol relies on timestamp matrices and has a communication complexity of $\mathcal{O}(n^2)$.

References

1. Mazières, D., Shasha, D.: Building Secure File Systems out of Byzantine Storage. In: PODC, pp. 108–117. ACM, New York (2002)
2. Cachin, C., Shelat, A., Shraer, A.: Efficient Fork-Linearizable Access to Untrusted Shared Memory. In: PODC, pp. 129–138. ACM, New York (2007)
3. Cachin, C., Keidar, I., Shraer, A.: Trusting the Cloud. ACM SIGACT News, Distributed Computing in the Clouds 40(2), 81–86 (2009)
4. CVS: Concurrent Versions System (visited) (June 2009), http://www.nongnu.org/cvs/
5. SVN: Subversion (visited) (June 2009), http://subversion.tigris.org/
6. Whitehead Jr., E.J.: World Wide Web Distributed Authoring and Versioning (WebDAV): An Introduction. Standard View 5(1), 3–8 (1997)

7. Yang, J., Wang, H., Gu, N., Liu, Y., Wang, C., Zhang, Q.: Lock-free Consistency Control for Web 2.0 Applications. In: WWW, pp. 725–734. ACM, New York (2008)
8. Google Inc.: Google docs (visited) (June 2009), at http://docs.google.com
9. Wikipedia: List of file systems, distributed file systems (visited) (June 2009), at http://en.wikipedia.org/wiki/List_of_file_systems
10. Herlihy, M.: Wait-Free Synchronization. ACM Trans. Program. Lang. Syst. 13(1), 124–149 (1991)
11. Herlihy, M.P., Wing, J.M.: Linearizability: A Correctness Condition for Concurrent Objects. ACM Trans. Program. Lang. Syst. 12(3), 463–492 (1990)
12. Attiya, H., Guerraoui, R., Hendler, D., Kuznetsov, P.: The Complexity of Obstruction-Free Implementations. J. ACM 56(4), 1–33 (2009)
13. Herlihy, M., Luchangco, V., Moir, M.: Obstruction-Free Synchronization: Double-Ended Queues as an Example. In: ICDCS, Washington, DC, USA, p. 522. IEEE Computer Society Press, Los Alamitos (2003)
14. Oprea, A., Reiter, M.K.: On consistency of encrypted files. In: Dolev, S. (ed.) DISC 2006. LNCS, vol. 4167, pp. 254–268. Springer, Heidelberg (2006)
15. Cachin, C., Keidar, I., Shraer, A.: Fork Sequential Consistency is Blocking. Inf. Process. Lett. 109(7), 360–364 (2009)
16. Aguilera, M.K., Frolund, S., Hadzilacos, V., Horn, S.L., Toueg, S.: Abortable and Query-Abortable Objects and Their Efficient Implementation. In: PODC: Principles of distributed computing, pp. 23–32. ACM, New York (2007)
17. Cachin, C., Keidar, I., Shraer, A.: Fail-Aware Untrusted Storage. In: DSN (2009)
18. Li, J., Mazières, D.: Beyond One-Third Faulty Replicas in Byzantine Fault Tolerant Systems. In: NSDI (2007)
19. Aguilera, M.K., Toueg, S.: Timeliness-Based Wait-Freedom: A Gracefully Degrading Progress Condition. In: PODC 2008: Proceedings of the twenty-seventh ACM symposium on Principles of distributed computing, pp. 305–314. ACM, New York (2008)
20. Jayanti, P., Chandra, T.D., Toueg, S.: Fault-tolerant Wait-free Shared Objects. J. ACM 45(3), 451–500 (1998)
21. Pease, M., Shostak, R., Lamport, L.: Reaching Agreement in the Presence of Faults. J. ACM 27(2), 228–234 (1980)
22. Attiya, H., Guerraoui, R., Kouznetsov, P.: Computing with Reads and Writes in the Absence of Step Contention. In: Fraigniaud, P. (ed.) DISC 2005. LNCS, vol. 3724, pp. 122–136. Springer, Heidelberg (2005)
23. Dobre, D., Majuntke, M., Serafini, M., Suri, N.: Abortable Fork-Linearizable Storage. Technical Report TR-TUD-DEEDS-07-03-2009 (July 2009), http://www.deeds.informatik.tu-darmstadt.de/matze/afcs.pdf

On the Computational Power of Shared Objects

Gadi Taubenfeld

The Interdisciplinary Center, P.O.Box 167, Herzliya 46150, Israel
tgadi@idc.ac.il
http://www.faculty.idc.ac.il/gadi/

Abstract. We propose a new classification for evaluating the strength of shared objects. The classification is based on finding, for each object of type o, the strongest progress condition for which it is possible to solve consensus for *any* number of processes, using any number of objects of type o and atomic registers. We use the strongest progress condition to associate with each object a number call the *power number* of that object. Objects with higher power numbers are considered stronger. Then, we define the *power hierarchy* which is an infinite hierarchy of objects such that the objects at level i of the hierarchy are exactly those objects with power number i. Comparing our classification with the traditional one which is based on fixing the progress condition (namely, wait-freedom) and finding the largest number of processes for which consensus is solvable, reveals interesting results. Our equivalence and extended universality results, provide a deeper understanding of the nature of the relative computational power of shared objects.

Keywords: Shared objects, consensus numbers, power numbers, wait-freedom, k-obstruction-freedom, wait-free hierarchy, power hierarchy, universality.

1 Introduction

Motivation

Alice, the CTO of MultiBrain Inc., was excited when she told her spouse Bob about the new multi-core computer that her company has just bought. "It has 128 cores and it is extremely powerful" she said, "we are already writing concurrent applications that will take advantage of its high level of parallelism".

Bob, a theoretician, has asked her if they intend to use locks in their concurrent applications. "No" said Alice, "we have decided to avoid using locks". "And what are the type of atomic operations the machine supports?" asked Bob. "Swap, and reads and writes" answered Alice.[1] "What about compare-and-swap, and load-link/store-conditional?" asked Bob. "No" answered Alice, "only atomic swap, and reads and writes are supported". "Well" said Bob, "for many interesting applications you will not be able to use more than two of these 128 cores simultaneously, so do not expect to get too much speedup". "Why?" asked Alice, "we have paid so much for that machine, it must be able to do better".

---

[1] A swap operation takes a shared register and a local register, and atomically exchange their values.

T. Abdelzaher, M. Raynal, and N. Santoro (Eds.): OPODIS 2009, LNCS 5923, pp. 270–284, 2009.

"There is a fundamental result" explained Bob, "that using the type of atomic operations that your machine supports, it is possible to solve consensus and many other important problems for two processes only, assuming that the required progress condition is wait-freedom". "You got me worried for a minute" said Alice, "for all our practical purposes, we can do with a much weaker progress condition than wait-freedom". "Such as?" asked Bob. "You tell me" answered Alice, "what is the *strongest* progress condition for which it is possible to solve consensus and all the other important problems for *any* number of processes using only atomic swap, and reads and writes?". "Interesting question",said Bob .

We propose a new classification for evaluating the strength of shared objects, which is based on finding the strongest progress condition for which it is possible to solve consensus for *any* number of processes. Such a classification enables to answer Alice's question for any type of object. Comparing our classification with the traditional one reveals interesting results.

Consensus Numbers and the Wait-Free Hierarchy

The traditional approach for understanding the relative computational power of shared objects is to classify them according to their consensus numbers. Objects with higher numbers are considered stronger. In order to define the notion of a consensus number, we first define the consensus problem and two known progress conditions.

The (binary) consensus problem is to design an algorithm in which all correct processes reach a common decision based on their initial opinions. We assume that a process may fail only by crashing (i.e., fail-stop). The problem is defined as follows. There are n processes $p_1, p_2, \ldots, p_n$. Each process p_i has an input value $x_i \in \{0, 1\}$. The requirements of the consensus problem are that there exists a *decision value* v such that: (1) each non-faulty process eventually decides on v, and (2) $v \in \{x_1, x_2, \ldots, x_n\}$. In particular, if all input values are the same, then that value must be the decision value.

Two of the most extensively studied progress conditions, in order of decreasing strength, are wait-freedom [5] and obstruction-freedom [6]. *Wait-freedom* guarantees that every process will always be able to complete its pending operations in a finite number of its own steps, regardless of the behavior of the other processes. *Obstruction-freedom* guarantees that a process will be able to complete its pending operations in a finite number of its own steps, if all the other processes "hold still" (i.e., do not take any steps) long enough. That is, obstruction-freedom guarantees progress for any process that eventually executes in isolation long enough, however, it do not guarantee progress under contention.

The *consensus number* of an object of type o, denoted $CN(o)$, is the largest n for which it is possible to solve consensus for n processes, using any number of objects of type o and atomic registers, assuming that the required progress condition is *wait-freedom*. If no largest n exists, the consensus number of o is infinite (denoted ∞). The *wait-free hierarchy* is an infinite hierarchy of objects such that the objects at level i of the hierarchy are exactly those objects with consensus number i.

It is known that, in the wait-free hierarchy, for any positive i, in a system with i processes: (1) no object at level less than i together with atomic registers can implement any object at level i; and (2) each object at level i together with atomic registers can implement any object at level i or at a lower level [5]. If instead of wait-freedom, only obstruction-freedom is required, the hierarchy collapses.

An object o is *universal* for n processes if any object which has sequential specification has a wait-free linearizable implementation using atomic registers and objects of type o in a system with at most n processes.[2] In [5], it is proven that consensus for n processes is universal in a system with n processes, for any positive n. An immediate implication of this result is that, an object o is universal in a system with n processes if and only if the consensus number of o is at least n.

Power Numbers and the Power Hierarchy

Instead of the traditional classification of fixing a single progress condition (namely, wait-freedom) and finding the largest number of processes for which consensus is solvable, we propose a classification which is based on finding the strongest progress condition for which it is possible to solve consensus for *any* number of processes. For a set of processes P, let $|P|$ denotes the size of P. Consider the following generalization of the notion of obstruction-freedom:

> For any $k \geq 1$, the progress condition k-*obstruction-freedom* guarantees that for every set of processes P where $|P| \leq k$, every process in P will be able to complete its pending operations in a finite number of its own steps, if all the processes not in P do not take steps for long enough.

The progress condition k-obstruction-free does not guarantee progress under contention of more than k processes. These infinitely many progress conditions cover the spectrum between obstruction-freedom and wait-freedom. The progress condition 1-obstruction-freedom is the same as obstruction-freedom. When the maximum number of processes is a fixed number, say n, k-obstruction-freedom is the same as wait-freedom, for all $k \geq n$.

> The *power number* of an object of type o, denoted $PN(o)$, is the largest k for which it is possible to solve consensus for any number processes, using any number of objects of type o and atomic registers, assuming that the required progress condition is k-*obstruction-freedom*. If no largest k exists, the power number of o is infinite (denoted ∞). The *power hierarchy* is an infinite hierarchy of objects such that the objects at level i of the hierarchy are exactly those objects with power number i.

In the above definitions, the objects of type o and the atomic registers are all assumed to be wait-free. That is, each operation that is invoked by a process on these basic objects always terminates, regardless of the behavior of the other processes. Next we generalize the notion of universality which was defined earlier in the context of the wait-free hierarchy.

---

[2] Sequential specification specifies how the object behaves when operations are applied sequentially. Linearizability implies that each operation should appear to take place instantaneously at some point in time, and that the relative order of non-concurrent operations is preserved.

An object o is *k-universal* if any object which has sequential specification has a *k-obstruction-free* linearizable implementation using atomic registers and objects of type o for any number of processes.

Clearly, if an object is k-universal its is also universal for k processes. An interesting question, that we resolve later, is whether an object that is universal for k processes is also k-universal in a system with *more than* k processes.

Summary of Contributions

A new approach. We propose a new classification for evaluating the strength of shared objects, which is based on the new notions of *power numbers* and the *power hierarchy*. The new classification together with the technical results mentioned below, provide a deeper understanding into the nature of the relative computational power of shared objects.

An equivalence result. We show that the traditional approach which is based on determining the consensus number of an object and our approach, are two sides of the same coin. We prove that the wait-free hierarchy and power hierarchy are equivalent. That is, the consensus number of an object equals to its power number. The new classification together with the equivalence result, does not yet fully enables to answer Alice's question.

An extended universality result. We extend the known universality result for the wait-free hierarchy in the following non-trivial way. If the consensus number (or the power number) of an object o is k, then not only o is universal for k processes, o is also k-universal in a system with *any* number of processes. Put another way, an object is universal for k processes if and only if it is k-universal for any number of processes. Now, we can fully answer Alice's question. The consensus number of a swap object is 2. Thus, using the type of atomic operations that Alice's machine supports, any object or problem which has sequential specification has a 2-obstruction-free linearizable implementation for any number of processes; and this claim does not hold for 3-obstruction-freedom.

Related Work

The consensus problem was formally defined in [14]. The impossibility result that there is no consensus algorithm that can tolerate even a single crash failure in an asynchronous model was first proved for the message-passing model in [3], and later has been extended for the shared memory model in which only atomic read/write registers are supported, in [12]. A recent survey which covers many related impossibility results can be found in [2].

The power of various shared objects has been studied extensively in shared memory environments where processes may fail benignly, and where every operation is wait-free. In [5], Herlihy classified shared objects by their consensus number and defined the wait-free hierarchy. He found the consensus number of many objects and, in particular, proved that the consensus number of an atomic swap object is 2. Additional results regarding the wait-free hierarchy can be found in [8,10].

Objects that can be used, together with atomic registers, to build wait-free implementations of any other object are called *universal objects*. Previous work provided methods, called universal constructions, to transform sequential specifications of arbitrary shared objects into wait-free concurrent implementations that use universal objects [5,15]. In [15] it is proved that sticky bits are universal, and independently, in [5] it is proved that wait-free consensus objects are universal. A bounded space version of the universal construction from [5] appears in [9]. The universal construction that we use to prove Theorem 3 conceptually mimics the original construction from [5].

As already mentioned, two extensively studied conditions are wait-freedom [5], and obstruction-freedom [6]. It is shown in [6] that obstruction-free consensus is solvable using atomic registers. Wait-free consensus algorithms that use read and write operations in the absence of (process) contention, or even in the absence of step contention, and revert to using strong synchronization operations when contention occurs, are presented in [1,11,13]. Linearizability is defined in [7].

The notion of k-obstruction-freedom is presented in [17], as part of a transformation that is used to fuse objects which avoid locking and locks together in order to create new types of shared objects. A weaker set of progress conditions, called k-obstacle-freedom, which cover the spectrum between obstruction-freedom and non-blocking (sometimes called lock-freedom) is defined in [17]. Results similar to those presented in this paper for k-obstruction-freedom, can also be proved w.r.t. k-obstacle-freedom.

2 An Equivalence Result

We show below that the traditional approach which is based on determining the consensus number of an object and our approach, are two sides of the same coin. Our first technical result is that the wait-free hierarchy and power hierarchy are equivalent. Put another way, we show that the consensus number of an object equals to its power number.

To simplify the presentation, it is sometimes convenient to use the notion of a consensus object instead of consensus algorithm (the two notions are essentially the same). A consensus object o supports one operation: $o.propose(v)$ satisfying: (1) *Agreement*: In any run, the $o.propose()$ operation returns the same value, called the *consensus value*, to every process that invokes it. (2) *Validity*: In any run, if the consensus value is v, then some process invoked $o.propose(v)$. When the value $v \in \{0, 1\}$ the object is called a binary consensus object. Throughout the paper, unless otherwise stated, by a consensus object we mean a binary consensus object; and by n-*consensus* we mean a multi-valued consensus object where $v \in \{0, 1, ..., n - 1\}$.

Theorem 1 (Equivalence). *For any object of type o, $PN(o) = CN(o)$.*

Proof. In the sequel, the term k-obstruction-free consensus algorithm, means a consensus algorithm which, for *any* number of processes, is correct assuming that the required progress condition is k-obstruction-freedom. It follows immediately from the definitions that, for any $k \geq 1$, a k-obstruction-free consensus algorithm is also a wait-free consensus algorithm for k processes. This simple observation implies that, for any object type o, $PN(o) \leq CN(o)$. The difficult part of the proof is to show that, for any $k \geq 1$, it is possible to implement a k-obstruction-free consensus algorithm using only wait-free consensus objects for k processes and atomic read/write registers. Such an implementation together with the above observation implies the theorem. Below we present such an implementation of a k-obstruction-free consensus algorithm and prove its correctness.

In the implementation we use a function, called $set_k()$, from the positive integers into sets of size k of process ids. We do not care how exactly the function is implemented, we only care that, for every positive integer k, there exists a function $set_k()$ which satisfies the following property: For every set of k process ids P and every positive integer s there exists $t \geq s$ such that $P = set_k(t)$. That is, every set of k process ids appears infinitely often.

The algorithm proceeds in rounds. The notion of a *round* is used only for the sake of describing the algorithm. We do *not* assume a synchronous model of execution in which all the processes are always executing the same round, and where no process can move to the next round before all others have finished the previous round. Each process has a preference for the decision value in each round; initially this preference is the input value of the process. If no decision is made in a round then the processes advance to the next round, and try again to reach agreement.

Algorithm 1. k-OBSTRUCTION-FREE CONSENSUS FOR ANY NUMBER OF PROCESSES USING ATOMIC REGISTERS AND WAIT-FREE CONSENSUS OBJECTS FOR k PROCESSES:
program for process p_i with input in_i (where $in_i \in \{0,1\}$).

shared registers
$x[0..\infty, 0..1]$ infinite array of bits, initially $x[0,0] = x[0,1] = 1$ and all other entries are 0
$con[1..\infty]$ infinite array of wait-free consensus objects for k processes
$decide$ ranges over $\{\perp, 0, 1\}$, initially $\perp$

local registers
r_i integer, initially 1
v_i bit, initially in_i

```
1  while decide =⊥ do
2      if x[rᵢ, vᵢ] = 0 then if x[rᵢ, 1 − vᵢ] = 1 then vᵢ := 1 − vᵢ else x[rᵢ, vᵢ] := 1 fi fi
3      if x[rᵢ − 1, 1 − vᵢ] = 0 then decide := vᵢ  /*no conflict in prev round */
4          else if pᵢ ∈ setₖ(rᵢ) then vᵢ := con[rᵢ].propose(vᵢ) fi    /*update pref */
5      fi
6      rᵢ := rᵢ + 1
7  od
8  decide(decide)
```

In round $r \geq 1$, process p_i first checks if the flag of its preference v_i is already set. If it is not set and the flag of $1 - v_i$ is set, p_i changes its preference to $1 - v_i$. If both flags are not set, p_i flags its preference v_i by writing 1 to $x[r, v_i]$ (line 2). Then, p_i reads the flag $x[r-1, 1-v_i]$. If the flag $x[r-1, 1-v_i]$ is not set, then every process that reaches round r with the conflicting preference $1 - v_i$ will find that only $x[r, v_i]$ is set to 1, and will change its preference to v_i. Consequently, process p_i can safely decide on v_i, and it writes v_i to *decide* (line 3). Otherwise, p_i checks if it belongs to the set $set_k(r)$. If it does, p_i proposes its current preference v_i to $con[r]$ and updates its preference to be the value agreed upon in $con[r]$. Then, p_i proceeds to round $r + 1$ (line 4).

If only up to k processes with conflicting preferences participate in round r, and all them are in $set_k(r)$, then all of them will reach round $r + 1$ with the same preference which is the value agreed upon in $con[r]$. When all processes reach a round with the same preference, a decision is reached either in that round or the next round.

Theorem 2. *Algorithm 1 is a correct k-obstruction-free consensus algorithm for any number of processes, using atomic registers and wait-free consensus objects for k processes.*

Before we prove the theorem, we make the following observations:

- Let Algorithm 2 be a modified version of Algorithm 1, where line 4 is omitted. Then, Algorithm 2 is a correct 1-obstruction-free consensus algorithm for any number of processes using atomic registers only.
- Let $y[1..\infty]$ be an infinite array of swap objects, which range over $\{\bot, 0, 1\}$, initially all set to $\bot$, and let $temp_i$ be a local register of process p_i. Let Algorithm 3 be a modified version of Algorithm 1, where line 4 is replace with:
  "**else** $temp_i := v_i$; $swap(y[i], temp_i)$; **if** $temp_i \neq \bot$ **then** $v_i := temp_i$ **fi**"
  Then, Algorithm 3 is a correct 2-obstruction-free consensus algorithm for any number of processes using atomic registers and swap objects.
- Let $y[1..\infty]$ be an infinite array of test&set bits, initially all set to 0, and let Algorithm 4 be a modified version of Algorithm 1, where line 4 is replace with:
  "**else if** $test\&set(y[r_i]) = 1$ **then if** $x[r_i, 1 - v_i] = 1$ **then** $v_i := 1 - v_i$ **fi fi**"
  Then, Algorithm 4 is a correct 2-obstruction-free consensus algorithm for any number of processes using atomic registers and test&set bits[3].

Below we present a correctness proof of the algorithm. Let $r \geq 1$ and $v \in \{0, 1\}$. Process p_i *reaches* round r, if it executes Statement 2 with $r_i = r$. Process p_i *prefers* the value v in round r, if $v_i = v$ when p_i reaches round r. Process p_i *commits* to the value v in round r, if it executes the assignment *decide* $:= v$ with $r_i = r$.

Lemma 1. *If all processes reaching round r have the same preference v for round r, then all nonfaulty processes reaching round r commit to v either in round r or in round $r + 1$.*

Proof. Suppose all processes reaching round r have the same preference v for round r. Then, whenever some process p_i sets the bit $x[r, v_i]$ to 1, v_i equals v. Consequently, no process ever sets $x[r, 1 - v]$ to 1, and hence $x[r, 1 - v]$ always equals 0. Now consider a process p reaching round r. Assuming that p continues to take steps in round r, p will either (1) finds $x[r - 1, 1 - v] = 0$ at Statement 3, and commits to the value v in round r, or (2) will continue to round $r + 1$ with preference v. In the second case, all

---

[3] A test&set bit, say r, is a shared bit that supports two operations: (1) *test&set*, which writes 1 to r, and returns the old value (which is either 0 or 1); and (2) *reset*, which writes 0 into r (and does not return a value).

processes reaching round $r + 1$ have the same preference v for round $r + 1$, thus, p will find $x[r, 1 - v] = 0$ at round $r + 1$, and will commit to the value v in round $r + 1$.   □

Lemma 2 (validity). *If p_i decides on a value v then $in_j = v$ for some p_j.*

Proof. If there are two processes that have different inputs then the lemma holds trivially. Suppose all processes start with the same input in. Then, by Lemma 1, all non-faulty processes will commit to in in the first round or the second round (actually the second round in this case), will execute the statement **decide**($decide$), at the end of one of these two rounds, and will decide on in.   □

Lemma 3. *If some process commits to v in round r then all processes reaching round $r + 1$ prefer v and commit to v in round $r + 1$.*

Proof. Suppose some process p commits to v in round r. Since p finds $x[r-1, 1-v] = 0$ at Statement 3, it follows that every process with preference $1 - v$ for round r, will find in Statement 2 that $x[r, 1 - v] = 0$ and $x[r, v] = 1$, and will change its preference to v. This implies that for a committed value v, no process ever sets $x[r, 1 - v]$ to 1 in round r. It follows that all processes reaching round $r + 1$ prefer v in round $r + 1$, and since they will find in round $r + 1$ that $x[r, 1 - v] = 0$, they will all commits to v in round $r + 1$.   □

Lemma 4 (agreement). *No two processes decide on conflicting values.*

Proof. We show that no two processes commit to conflicting values. This implies that no two processes decide on conflicting values. Assume to the contrary that two processes commit to conflicting values. This means that there exist nonfaulty processes p_0 and p_1 such that p_0 commits to 0 in round r and p_1 commits to 1 in round r'. First suppose that $r \neq r'$. Without loss of generality, let $r < r'$. Since p_0 commits to 0 in round r, from Lemma 3 all processes reaching round $r + 1$, and in particular p_1, commit to 0 in round $r + 1$; a contradiction. Now suppose that $r = r'$. In round r, process p_0 commits to 0, and process p_1 commits to 1. Since process p_0 finds $x[r - 1, 1] = 0$ at Statement 3, process p_1 must find $x[r, 1] = 0$ and $x[r, 0] = 1$ at Statement 2 and change it preference to 0 in round r. Consequently, it is not possible that both commit in round r.   □

Lemma 5. *Let P be an arbitrary non empty set of at most k processes, and let r be a positive integer such that $P \subseteq set_k(r)$. If the processes in P complete the execution of round r and round $r + 1$, before any of the other processes reach round r, then all nonfaulty processes reaching round $r + 1$ (1) have the same preference, say v, for round $r + 1$, and (2) commit to v either in round $r + 1$ or in round $r + 2$.*

Proof. Assume first the processes in P all have the *same* preference v, and complete the execution of round r and round $r + 1$ before any of the other process reaches round r. Since it is assumed that they execute round r without interference from the other processes, they will reach also round $r + 1$ with the same preference v, and with $x[r, 1 - v] = 0$. No process that will arrive later will be able to change the value of $x[r, 1 - v]$. Thus, in round $r + 1$ they will commit to v. Every other process that will reach round r

later, will find in Statement 2 that $x[r, 1 - v] = 0$ and $x[r, v] = 1$, and will change its preference to v in case it was $1 - v$. This implies that no process ever sets $x[r, 1 - v]$ to 1 in round r. It follows that all processes reaching round $r + 1$ prefer v in round $r + 1$, and since they will find in round $r + 1$ that $x[r, 1 - v] = 0$, they will all commit to v in round $r + 1$.

Now, assume that the processes in P reach round r with *different* preferences (i.e., some prefer 0 and some 1), and complete the execution of round r and round $r + 1$ before any of the other process reaches round r. Clearly, it is not possible that each one of the processes in P changes its preferences while executing Statement 2 in round r. If only the processes with input 0 (resp. input 1) change their preference while executing Statement 2 in round r, then we are in a case, similar to a one already covered, where all the processes in P reach round r with the same preference.

Thus, let us assume that not all the processes change their preference while executing Statement 2, in round r, and thus both $x[r, v]$ and $x[r, 1 - v]$ will be set to 1. In such a case, Statement 4 ensures that all the processes in P will reach round $r + 1$ with the same preference with the same preference v, which is the value agreed upon in $con[r]$. Since it is assumed that they execute round $r + 1$ without interference from the other processes, they will reach also round $r + 2$ with the same preference v, and with $x[r + 1, 1 - v] = 0$. No process that will arrive later will be able to change the value of $x[r + 1, 1 - v]$. Thus, in round $r + 2$ they will commit to v. Every other process that will reach round $r + 1$ later, will find in Statement 2 that $x[r + 1, 1 - v] = 0$ and $x[r + 1, v] = 1$, and will change its preference to v in case it was $1 - v$, and will later reach round $r + 2$ with preference v. This implies that no process ever sets $x[r + 1, 1 - v]$ to 1 in round $r + 1$. It follows that all processes reaching round $r + 2$ prefer v, and since they will find in round $r + 2$ that $x[r + 1, 1 - v] = 0$, they will all commit to v in round $r + 2$.   □

Lemma 6 (liveness with k-obstruction-freedom). *Let P be an arbitrary non-empty set of at most k processes. Each nonfaulty process eventually decides and terminates, regardless whether the other processes are faulty or not, in every run in which from some point on all the processes, except those in P, do not take any steps until the nonfaulty processes in P decide.*

Proof. Assume that from some point on, say from time t, all the processes, except those in P, "hold still" (i.e., do not take any steps) until the nonfaulty processes in P decide. Let $r_i(t)$ be the value of the local register r_i at time t. Define the maximum round reached at time t, denoted $r(t)$, as: $r(t) = \text{maximum}(\{r_j(t) \mid j \in \text{set of all process'}$ identifiers$\})$. Let r' be the smallest integer such that $r(t) \leq r'$ and $P \subseteq set_k(r')$. Then, it follows from Lemma 5 that each nonfaulty process commits before or during round $r' + 2$, and later executes the statement **decide**(*decide*) and decides.   □
This completes the proof of Theorem 1.   □

3   An Extended Universality Result

An object o is *universal* for k processes if any object which has sequential specification has a wait-free linearizable implementation using atomic registers and objects of type o

in a system with at most k processes [5]. Lets assume that we know that o is universal in a system with k processes, what can we say about the computational power of o in a system with more than k processes? As we prove below, in such a case it follows from our extended universality result that o is also k-universal in a system with *any* number of processes. That is, any object which has sequential specification has a *k-obstruction-free* linearizable implementation using atomic registers and objects of type o for any number of processes.

Theorem 3 (Extended Universality). *For any object o and positive integer $k \geq 1$,*

1. *A k-obstruction-free consensus object is k-universal.*
2. *o is k-universal if and only if $PN(o) \geq k$.*
3. *o is k-universal if and only if $CN(o) \geq k$.*
4. *o is k-universal if and only if o is universal for k processes.*

Proof. Proving Part 1 of the theorem is difficult. So, before proving it, we first explain why all the other three statements are simple consequences of Theorem 1 and Part 1 of Theorem 3. **Part 2:** If o is k-universal then, by definition, k-obstruction-free consensus can be implemented using atomic registers and objects of type o, and hence $PN(o) \geq k$. If $PN(o) \geq k$, then by Theorem 2, k-obstruction-free consensus can be implemented using atomic registers and objects of type o, and thus, by Part 1 of Theorem 3, o is k-universal. **Part 3:** This item follows immediately from Part 2 and the fact that $PN(o) = CN(o)$ (i.e., Theorem 1). **Part 4:** In a system with at most k processes, k-obstruction-free is the same as wait-freedom, thus, if an object is k-universal its is clearly also universal for k processes. If an object, say o, is universal for k processes, by definition, o can implement consensus objects for k processes. Thus, by Theorem 2, k-obstruction-free consensus algorithm can be implemented using atomic registers and objects of type o. Thus, by Part 1 of Theorem 3, o is k-universal.

To prove Part 1 of Theorem 3, we present below a universal construction that implements any k-obstruction-free object o from k-obstruction-free consensus objects and atomic registers. The construction conceptually mimics the original construction for the wait-free model from [5]. The basic idea behind the construction is as follows: an object o is implemented as a linked list which is represented as an unbounded array. The entries of the array represent a sequence of invocations applied to the object. A process invokes an operation by threading a new invocation onto the end of the list. The current state of the objects corresponds to applying the sequence of invocations to the object.

First we need to generalize Algorithm 1. Recall that by *n-consensus* we mean a multivalued consensus object where the input value taken from the set $\{0, 1, ..., n-1\}$.

Theorem 4. *For any positive integers k and n, it is possible to implement a k-obstruction-free n-consensus object for any number of processes, using atomic registers and k-obstruction-free binary consensus objects for any number of processes.*

Proof. Starting from k-obstruction-free binary consensus objects for any number of processes, we can trivially get wait-free binary consensus objects for k processes. It is well know that using atomic registers and wait-free binary consensus objects for k processes, it is simple to implement wait-free n-consensus objects for k processes ([16], page 329). Below we show that using atomic registers and wait-free n-consensus objects for k processes, it is possible to implement a k-obstruction-free n-consensus object for any number of processes. To do that, we present below Algorithm 2 which is a simple modification of Algorithm 1.

Algorithm 2. k-OBSTRUCTION-FREE n-CONSENSUS FOR ANY NUMBER OF PROCESSES USING ATOMIC REGISTERS AND WAIT-FREE n-CONSENSUS OBJECTS FOR k PROCESSES:
program for process p_i with input in_i (where $in_i \in \{0, 1, ..., n-1\}$) .

shared registers
$x[0..\infty, 0..n-1]$ infinite array of bits, initially entries of $x[0..n-1]$ are 1, all other entries are 0
$con[1..\infty]$ infinite array of wait-free n-consensus objects for k processes
$decide$ ranges over $\{\bot, 0, 1, ..., n-1\}$, initially $\bot$

local registers
r_i integer, initially 1 ; v_i integer, initially in_i ; j integer

```
1   while decide =⊥ do
2       if x[rᵢ, vᵢ] = 0 then
3           j := 0; while j < n and x[rᵢ, j] = 0 do j := j + 1 od
4               if j < n then vᵢ := j else x[rᵢ, vᵢ] := 1 fi fi
5           j := 0; while(vᵢ = j) or (j < n and x[rᵢ − 1, j] = 0) do j := j + 1 od
6           if j = n then decide := vᵢ        /* no conflict in previous round */
7               else if pᵢ ∈ setₖ(rᵢ) then vᵢ := con[rᵢ].propose(vᵢ) fi /* update pref */
8       fi
9       rᵢ := rᵢ + 1
10  od
11  decide(decide)
```

In round $r \geq 1$, process p_i first checks if the flag of its preference v_i is already set (line 2). If it is not set and a flag for some other value is set, p_i changes its preference to the smallest such value. If non of the flags are set, p_i flags its preference v_i by writing 1 to $x[r, v_i]$ (line 4). Then, p_i reads all the flags from round $r-1$ (line 5). If non of the flags from round $r-1$ (excluding its own) is set, then every process that reaches round r with a conflicting preference, will find that only $x[r, v_i]$ is set to 1, and will change its preference to v_i. Consequently, process p_i can safely decide on v_i, and it writes v_i to $decide$ (line 6).

Otherwise, p_i checks if it belongs to the set $set_k(r)$. If it does, p_i proposes its current preference v_i to $con[r]$ and updates its preference to be the value agreed upon in $con[r]$ (line 7). Then, p_i proceeds to round $r+1$. If only up to k processes with conflicting preferences participate in round r, and all of them are in $set_k(r)$, then all of them will reach round $r+1$ with the same preference which is the value agreed upon in $con[r]$. When all processes reach a round with the same preference, a decision is reached either in that round or the next round.

The assumption that n is finite and a priori known, can be removed by replacing the while loops in lines 3 and 5, with a known snapshot algorithm for unbounded number of processes. from [4]. □

We assume any shared object, o, is specified by two relations:

$$apply \subset \text{INVOKE} \times \text{STATE} \times \text{STATE},$$

$$\text{and } reply \subset \text{INVOKE} \times \text{STATE} \times \text{RESPONSE},$$

where INVOKE is the object's domain of invocations, STATE is its domain of states (with a designated set of start states), and RESPONSE is its domain of responses.

1. The *apply* relation denotes a state change based on the pending invocation and the current state. Invocations do not block: it is required that for every invocation and current state there is a target state.
2. The *reply* relation determines the calculated response, based on the pending invocation and the updated state. It is required that for any pair INVOKE × STATE there is a target state and a response.

Let o be an an arbitrary k-obstruction-free object which can be specified as described above. We present a universal construction that implements o from k-obstruction-free consensus objects and atomic registers. Since, by Theorem 4, k-obstruction-free n-consensus objects can be implemented from k-obstruction-free binary consensus objects and atomic registers, we will use in the construction below only k-obstruction-free n-consensus objects. The construction is similar to the one for the wait-free model from [16], where the wait-free n-consensus objects are replaced with k-obstruction-free n-consensus objects.

In the actual implementation there are two principal data structures:

1. For each process i there is an unbounded array, $Announce[i][1..\infty]$, each element of which is a *cell* which can hold a single invocation. The $Announce[i][j]$ entry describes the j-th invocation (operation name and arguments) by process i on o.
2. The object is represented as an unbounded array $Sequence[1..\infty]$ of process-id's, where for each positive integer g, $Sequence[g]$ is a k-obstruction-free n-consensus object. Intuitively, if $Sequence[k] = i$ and $Sequence[1], \ldots, Sequence[k-1]$ contains the value i in exactly $j-1$ positions, then the k-th invocation on o is described by $Announce[i][j]$. In this case, we say that $Announce[i][j]$ has been *threaded*.

The universal construction of any k-obstruction-free object o is described below as the code process i executes to implement an operation on o with invocation *invoke*. For simplicity, we will assume that the input values for an *n-consensus* object are taken from the set $\{1, ..., n\}$ (instead of $\{0, 1, ..., n-1\}$).

In outline, the construction works as follows: process i first announces its next invocation, and then threads unthreaded, announced invocations onto the end of $Sequence$. It continues until it sees that its own operation has been threaded, computes a response, and returns. To ensure that each announced invocation is eventually threaded, the correct processes first try to thread any announced, unthreaded cell of process ℓ into entry $Sequence[k]$, where $\ell = k \pmod{n} + 1$. This "helping" technique guarantees that once process ℓ announces an operation, at most n other operations can be threaded before the operation of process ℓ is threaded.

ALGORITHM 3. A UNIVERSAL CONSTRUCTION:
program for process $i \in \{1, \ldots, n\}$ with invocation *invoke*

shared
  Announce$[1..n][1..\infty]$ array of cells which range over INVOKE $\cup \{\bot\}$,
    initially all cells are set to $\bot$
  Sequence$[1..\infty]$ array of k-obstruction-free n-consensus objects
local to process i
  MyNextAnnounce integer, initially 1   /* next vacant cell */
  NextAnnounce$[1..n]$ array of integers, initially 1

                                                            /* next operation */
  CurrentState $\in$ STATE, initially the initial state of o /* i's view */
  NextSeq integer, initially 1   /* next entry in *Sequence* */
  Winner range over $\{1, \ldots, n\}$ /* last process threaded */
  ℓ range over $\{1, \ldots, n\}$ /* process to help */
                      /* write *invoke* to a vacant cell in *Announce*[i] */
1   *Announce*$[i][MyNextAnnounce]$:= the invocation *invoke*
2   *MyNextAnnounce* := *MyNextAnnounce* + 1
3   **while** ((*NextAnnounce*$[i]$ < *MyNextAnnounce*) **do**
                              /* continue until *invoke* is threaded */
                              /* each iteration threads one operation */
4   ℓ := *NextSeq* (mod n) + 1   /* select process to help */
5   **while** *Announce*$[\ell][NextAnnounce[\ell]] = \bot$ /* valid? */
7   **do**
6   ℓ := $\ell + 1$ /* not valid; help next process */
7   **od**
9   *Winner* := *Sequence*$[NextSeq].propose(\ell)$ /* propose ℓ */
                              /* a new cell has been threaded by *Winner* */
                              /* update *CurrentState* */
10   *CurrentState* := $apply(Announce[Winner][NextAnnounce[Winner]], CurrentState)$
11   *NextAnnounce*$[Winner]$:= *NextAnnounce*$[Winner]$ + 1
12   *NextSeq* := *NextSeq* + 1
13   **od**
14   *return(reply(invoke, CurrentState))*

Process i keeps track of the first index of *Announce*$[i]$ that is vacant in a variable denoted *MyNextAnnounce*, and first writes the invocation into *Announce*$[i][MyNextAnnounce]$, and (line 2) increments *MyNextAnnounce* by 1. To keep track of which cells it has seen threaded (including its own), process i keeps n counters in an array *NextAnnounce*$[1..n]$, where each *NextAnnounce*$[j]$ is one plus the number of times i has read cells of j in *Sequence*. Hence *NextAnnounce*$[j]$ is the index of *Announce*$[j]$ where i looks to find the next operation announced by j. We notice that, having incremented *MyNextAnnounce*:

  NextAnnounce$[i] = MyNextAnnounce - 1$ until the current operation of process
  i has been threaded.

This inequality is thus the condition (line 3) in the while loop (lines 3 – 13) in which process i threads cells. Once process i's invocation is threaded (and $NextAnnounce[i]$ = $MyNextAnnounce$), it exits the loop and returns the associated response value (line 14). Process i keeps an index $NextSeq$ which points to the next entry in $Sequence[1..\infty]$ whose element it has not yet accessed.

To thread cells, process i proposes (line 9) the id of process ℓ to the k-obstruction-free consensus object $Sequence[NextSeq]$, and after a decision is made, records the consensus value for $Sequence[NextSeq]$ in the local variable $Winner$ (line 9). The value in $Sequence[NextSeq]$ is the identity of the process whose cell has just been threaded. After choosing to help process ℓ (line 4), process i checks that $Announce[\ell][NextAnnounce[\ell]]$ contains a valid operation invocation. As discussed above, process i gives preference (line 4) to a different process for each cell in $Sequence$. Thus, all active processes will eventually agree to give preference to any pending invocation, ensuring it will eventually be threaded.

Once process i knows the id of the process whose cell has just been threaded, as recorded in $Winner$, it can update (line 10) its view of the object's state with the winner invocation, and increment its records of process $Winner$'s successfully threaded cells (line 11) and the next unread cell in $Sequence$ (line 12). Having successfully threaded a cell, process i returns to the top of the while loop (line 3). Eventually, the invocation of process i will be threaded and the condition at the while loop (line 3) will be *false*. At this point, the value of the variable $CurrentState$ is the state of the object after process i's invocation has been applied to the object. Based on this state, process i can return the appropriate response. This completes the proof of Theorem 3.   □

4   Discussion

"Please explain me" requested Bob once he understood the new results, "when you write a concurrent application for your new machine, and contention goes above two, what do you do?". "In such cases, contention resolution schemes such as exponential backoff, are used" explained Alice, "and since with a machine which supports an atomic swap, we can easily deal with contention of two threads, the contention resolution scheme can kick-in only once three threads are contending, and not before. Furthermore, once the contention resolution scheme kicks-in, it is enough to use it until two, and not just one, contending threads stay alive. From a practical point a view, this is a big performance gain". "I see" said Bob, "so there is a tradeoff between how strong the progress condition should be, and how often the contention resolution scheme will kick-in". "Exactly" said Alice, "this is one of the reasons why the new classification and results are so helpful".

References

1. Attiya, H., Guerraoui, R., Kouznetsov, P.: Computing with reads and writes in the absence of step contention. In: Fraigniaud, P. (ed.) DISC 2005. LNCS, vol. 3724, pp. 122–136. Springer, Heidelberg (2005)
2. Fich, F.E., Ruppert, E.: Hundreds of impossibility results for distributed computing. Distributed Computing 16(2-3), 121–163 (2003)

3. Fischer, M.J., Lynch, N.A., Paterson, M.S.: Impossibility of distributed consensus with one faulty process. Journal of the ACM 32(2), 374–382 (1985)
4. Gafni, E., Merritt, M., Taubenfeld, G.: The concurrency hierarchy, and algorithms for unbounded concurrency. In: Proc. 20th ACM Symp. on Principles of Distributed Computing, pp. 161–169 (August 2001)
5. Herlihy, M.P.: Wait-free synchronization. ACM Trans. on Programming Languages and Systems 13(1), 124–149 (1991)
6. Herlihy, M.P., Luchangco, V., Moir, M.: Obstruction-free synchronization: Double-ended queues as an example. In: Proc. of the 23rd Int. Conf. on Dist. Computing Systems (2003)
7. Herlihy, M.P., Wing, J.M.: Linearizability: a correctness condition for concurrent objects. Toplas 12(3), 463–492 (1990)
8. Jayanti, P.: Robust wait-free hierarchies. Journal of the ACM 44(4), 592–614 (1997)
9. Jayanti, P., Toueg, S.: Some results on the impossibility, universality, and decidability of consensus. In: Proc. of the 6th Int. Workshop on Distributed Algorithms. LNCS, vol. 674, pp. 69–84. Springer, Heidelberg (1992)
10. Lo, W.-K., Hadzilacos, V.: All of us are smarter than any of us: Nondeterministic wait-free hierarchies are not robust. SIAM Journal on Computing 30(3), 689–728 (2000)
11. Luchangco, V., Moir, M., Shavit, N.: On the uncontended complexity of consensus. In: Fich, F.E. (ed.) DISC 2003. LNCS, vol. 2848, pp. 45–59. Springer, Heidelberg (2003)
12. Loui, M.C., Abu-Amara, H.: Memory requirements for agreement among unreliable asynchronous processes. Advances in Computing Research 4, 163–183 (1987)
13. Merritt, M., Taubenfeld, G.: Resilient consensus for infinitely many processes. In: Fich, F.E. (ed.) DISC 2003. LNCS, vol. 2848, pp. 1–15. Springer, Heidelberg (2003)
14. Pease, M., Shostak, R., Lamport, L.: Reaching agreement in the presence of faults. Journal of the ACM 27(2), 228–234 (1980)
15. Plotkin, S.A.: Sticky bits and universality of consensus. In: Proc. 8th ACM Symp. on Principles of Distributed Computing, pp. 159–175 (1989)
16. Taubenfeld, G.: Synchronization Algorithms and Concurrent Programming, p. 423. Pearson / Prentice-Hall (2006)
17. Taubenfeld, G.: Contention-sensitive data structures and algorithms. In: Keidar, I. (ed.) DISC 2009. LNCS, vol. 5805, pp. 157–171. Springer, Heidelberg (2009)

Weak Synchrony Models and Failure Detectors for Message Passing (k-)Set Agreement[*]

Martin Biely[1,2], Peter Robinson[1], and Ulrich Schmid[1]

[1] Embedded Computing Systems Group, Technische Universität Wien, Austria
{biely,robinson,s}@ecs.tuwien.ac.at
[2] LIX, Ecole polytechnique, France

Abstract. The recent discovery of the weakest failure detector $\mathcal{L}$ for message passing set agreement has renewed the interest in exploring the border between solvable and unsolvable problems in message passing systems. This paper contributes to this research by introducing two novel system models $\mathcal{M}^{\mathrm{anti}}$ and $\mathcal{M}^{\mathrm{sink}}$ with very weak synchrony requirements, where $\mathcal{L}$ can be implemented. To the best of our knowledge, they are the first message passing models where set agreement is solvable but consensus is not. We also generalize $\mathcal{L}$ by a novel "$(n-k)$-loneliness" failure detector $\mathcal{L}(k)$, which allows to solve k-set agreement but not $(k-1)$-set agreement. We also present an algorithm that solves k-set agreement with $\mathcal{L}(k)$, which is anonymous in that it does not require unique process identifiers. This reveals that $\mathcal{L}$ is also the weakest failure detector for anonymous set agreement. Finally, we analyze the relationship between $\mathcal{L}(k)$ and other failure detectors, namely the limited scope failure detector $\mathcal{S}_{n-k+1}$ and the quorum failure detector Σ.

1 Introduction

In recent years, the quest for weak system models resp. failure detectors [11], which add just enough synchrony resp. failure information to purely asynchronous systems to circumvent impossibility results [19], has been an active research topic in distributed computing. Most work in this area falls into one of the following two categories: (1) Identifying weak failure detectors, and (2) strengthening the synchrony assumptions of the asynchronous model just enough to implement these weak failure detectors. Due to the FLP impossibility result [19], which established that consensus among n processes with just $f = 1$ crash failures is impossible to solve in asynchronous systems, the focus of (1) was primarily the *consensus* problem. After the eventual leader oracle Ω [10], which eventually outputs the identifier of one correct process everywhere, was proved to be the weakest failure detector

---

[*] A brief announcement of this paper was accepted at DISC'09. Martin Biely and Peter Robinson have been supported by the Austrian BM:vit FIT-IT project *TRAFT* (proj. no. 812205) and the Austrian Science Foundation (FWF) project P20529, respectively. Correspondence to: Embedded Computing Systems Group (E182/2), Technische Universität Wien, Treitlstrasse 3, A-1040 Vienna (Austria). Fax: +43(1)58801-18297.

T. Abdelzaher, M. Raynal, and N. Santoro (Eds.): OPODIS 2009, LNCS 5923, pp. 285–299, 2009.

for solving consensus when a majority of the processes is correct, the research primarily shifted towards (2). The first implementation of Ω was provided by [26] and was based on rather strong synchrony assumptions (i.e., a variant of the partially synchronous model of [18]). The subsequent quest for the weakest synchrony assumptions for implementing Ω was started by [1], and resulted in a series of papers [1,2,27,25] in which the number of required timely links has been reduced considerably. In the most recent paper [25], it is shown that a single eventual moving f-source, i.e., a correct process that eventually has f (possibly changing) timely outgoing links in every broadcast, is sufficient for implementing Ω, and thus for solving consensus. Conversely, [5] revealed that Ω is sufficient for implementing an eventual $(n-1)$-source.

More recently, *set agreement* has been identified as a promising target for further exploring the solvability border in asynchronous systems. In [38], a failure detector called *anti-Ω* was shown to be the weakest for shared memory systems [37]. Like Ω, anti-Ω also returns the identifier of some process. The crucial difference to Ω is that anti-Ω eventually never outputs the identifier of some *correct* process and does not need to stabilize on a single process identifier. A variant of anti-Ω, called anti-Ω_k [38], returns $n - k$ processes and was first conjectured to be the weakest failure detector [32] and later shown to be the weakest failure detector for k-set agreement [21] in shared memory systems.

In [15], it has been shown that the quorum failure detector Σ is the weakest to implement shared memory in a message passing system when a majority of the processes may fail. Moreover, the combination of Σ and Ω was proved to be the weakest failure detector for solving consensus for any number of failures. For k-set agreement (with $k > 1$), however, an analogous combination (i.e., $\langle \Sigma, \text{anti-}\Omega_k \rangle$) is not the weakest failure detector, as k-set agreement is too weak for implementing atomic registers, whereas the proof of $\langle \Sigma, \Omega \rangle$ being the weakest failure detector for consensus critically depends upon the ability to implement atomic registers using consensus [35]. Indeed, besides providing the weakest failure detector $\mathcal{L}$ for $(n-1)$-set agreement in message passing systems, [16] proved that this "loneliness" failure detector $\mathcal{L}$ is strictly weaker than Σ. Recently, [8] introduced the quorum family Σ_k, showed that Σ_k is necessary for solving k-set agreement and that the failure detector family $\Pi_k \simeq \langle \Sigma_k, \Omega_k \rangle$ coincides with the weakest failure detectors $\langle \Sigma, \Omega \rangle$ for $k = 1$, and $\mathcal{L}(n-1)$ for $k = n-1$. However, no algorithm that solves general message passing k-set agreement with Π_k is known. Thus, the quest for message passing k-set agreement is still open.

This paper is devoted to k-set agreement in message passing systems, and provides the following contributions: (1) We introduce two novel system models $\mathcal{M}^{\text{anti}}$ and $\mathcal{M}^{\text{sink}}$, which provide just enough synchrony to implement $\mathcal{L}$ but are not strong enough to solve consensus. To the best of our knowledge, these models are the first message passing models where set agreement is solvable but consensus is not. (2) We define a novel failure detector $\mathcal{L}(k)$ that generalizes $\mathcal{L}$ to k-set agreement, and show that it is sufficient to solve k-set agreement. Since our $\mathcal{L}(k)$-based k-set agreement algorithm does not use process identifiers, it also works in anonymous systems. This implies that $\mathcal{L}$ is also the weakest failure detector for set agreement in anonymous systems. (3) We show that there is no algorithm that solves $(k-1)$-set agreement with $\mathcal{L}(k)$. (4) Finally, we compare $\mathcal{L}(k)$ to the limited scope failure detector $\mathcal{S}_{n-k+1}$ [29], which has also been employed for k-set agreement. For the "canonical" cases ($k = 1$ and $k = n - 1$), we show that one of the two failure detectors is strictly stronger than the other; for any other choice of k, however, they are incomparable. As a consequence, neither $\mathcal{L}(k)$ nor $\mathcal{S}_{n-k+1}$ can be the weakest failure detector for general k-set agreement.

2   System Models and Problem Definition

The models we consider in this paper are based on the standard asynchronous model of [19], which we denote by $\mathcal{M}^{\mathrm{async}}$ and introduce informally below. We consider a set Π of n distributed processes, which communicate via message passing over a fully-connected point-to-point network made-up of unidirectional links with finite but unbounded message delays. Links need not be FIFO but are assumed to be reliable[1] for simplicity. Every process executes an instance of a distributed algorithm and is modeled as a deterministic state machine. Its execution consists of a sequence of zero-time *steps*, where a single process performs a state transition according to its transition function, in addition to either receiving a (possibly empty) set of previously sent messages, or sending messages to an arbitrary set of processes (including itself). A *run* α of a distributed algorithm consists of a sequence of local steps of all the processes. For analysis purposes, we assume the existence of a discrete global clock T, which ticks whenever a process takes a step. Note that processes do not have access to T.

Among the n processes, at most f can fail at any time by *crashing*. A process may crash within a step and does not take further steps afterwards. A *correct* process is one that never crashes. We call a process *alive at time t* if it does not crash before or at time t. Moreover, a process is alive in a time interval I when it is alive at every tick of T in I. The *failure pattern* of α is a function $F : T \to 2^{\Pi}$ that outputs the set of crashed processes for a given time t. Clearly, $\forall t \geqslant 0 : F(t) \subseteq F(t + 1)$. Moreover, let $F = \bigcup_{t \geqslant 0} F(t)$ be the set of faulty processes. The set of possible failure patterns is called *environment*. In this paper we admit any environment that allows up to $n - 1$ crashes.

A run α is *admissible in* $\mathcal{M}^{async}$ (1) if every correct process takes infinitely many steps, (2) a message is only received at time t by process p if it was sent by some process q to it at some time $t' \leqslant t$, and (3) every message sent to p is eventually received if p is correct. We say that an algorithms *halts* when it reaches a terminal state, where it remains for infinitely many steps.

2.1   k-Set Agreement

We now state the properties of the k-set agreement problem [13]. When $k = n - 1$, the problem is also referred to simply as set agreement. When $k = 1$, the

---

[1] In Section 3.2, we discuss relaxations of this assumption.

definition used here is equivalent to uniform consensus [12]. Note that it is well
known that k-set agreement is impossible in purely asynchronous systems when
$f \geqslant k$ processes might crash [9,24,34]. Every process starts with a proposal value
v and must eventually irrevocably decide on some value as follows:

k-Agreement: Processes must decide on at most k different values.
Validity: If a correct process decides on v, then v was proposed by some process.
Termination: Every correct process must eventually decide.

2.2   Failure Detectors

A failure detector [11] $\mathcal{D}$ is an oracle that can be queried by processes in any step,
before making a state transition. The behaviour of $\mathcal{D}$ in a run α depends on the
failure pattern F, which defines the set of admissible *failure detector histories*.
The value of a query of a process p in a step at time t is defined by the history
function $H(p,t)$, which maps process identifiers and time to the *range* of output
symbols of $\mathcal{D}$. Let A be an algorithm that uses $\mathcal{D}$ and let α be a run of A with
failure pattern $F(t)$.

We denote the model where runs are admissible in $\mathcal{M}^{\mathrm{async}}$ and processes can
query failure detector $\mathcal{D}$ in any step as $(\mathcal{M}^{\mathrm{async}}, \mathcal{D})$. If an algorithm A solves
problem P in $(\mathcal{M}^{\mathrm{async}}, \mathcal{D})$, we say that $\mathcal{D}$ *solves* P. We say that algorithm
$A_{\mathcal{D} \to \mathcal{D}'}$ transforms $\mathcal{D}$ to $\mathcal{D}'$, if processes maintain output variables $output_{\mathcal{D}'}$
that emulate failure detector histories of $\mathcal{D}'$ that are admissible for F. We say
that $\mathcal{D}'$ is *weaker* than $\mathcal{D}$ and call $\mathcal{D}$ *stronger* than $\mathcal{D}'$, if such an algorithm
$A_{\mathcal{D} \to \mathcal{D}'}$ exist. If there is also an algorithm $A_{\mathcal{D}' \to \mathcal{D}}$, we say that $\mathcal{D}$ and $\mathcal{D}'$ are
equivalent. If no such algorithm $A_{\mathcal{D}' \to \mathcal{D}}$ exists, we say that $\mathcal{D}$ is *strictly stronger*
than $\mathcal{D}'$; *strictly weaker* is defined analogously. If neither $A_{\mathcal{D} \to \mathcal{D}'}$ nor $A_{\mathcal{D}' \to \mathcal{D}}$
exists then we say that $\mathcal{D}$ and $\mathcal{D}'$ are *incomparable*. A failure detector $\mathcal{D}'$ is the
weakest for problem P if $\mathcal{D}$ is weaker than any failure detector $\mathcal{D}$ that solves P.

Recently, it was shown in [16] that the "loneliness"-detector $\mathcal{L}$ is the weakest
failure detector for message passing set agreement. Intuitively speaking, there
is one (possibly crashed) process where $\mathcal{L}$ perpetually outputs FALSE, and, if all
except one process p have crashed, $\mathcal{L}$ eventually outputs TRUE at p forever.

We now present our generalization of $\mathcal{L}$ for k-set agreement, which we denote
by $\mathcal{L}(k)$ (with $\mathcal{L} = \mathcal{L}(n-1)$). Instead of loneliness it detects "$(n-k)$-loneliness",
i.e., it detects the case where at most $n-k$ processes are still alive.

Definition 1. *The $(n-k)$-loneliness detector $\mathcal{L}(k)$ outputs* TRUE *or* FALSE, *such
that for all environments $\mathcal{E}$ and $\forall F \in \mathcal{E}$ it holds that there is a set of processes
$\Pi_0 \subseteq \Pi$, $|\Pi_0| = n - k$ and a correct process q such that:*

$$\forall p \in \Pi_0 \ \forall t \colon H(p,t) = \text{FALSE} \tag{1}$$
$$|F| \geqslant k \implies \exists t \ \forall t' \geqslant t \colon H(q,t') = \text{TRUE} \tag{2}$$

Another class of failure detectors for k-set agreement are the limited scope failure
detectors introduced in [29,23]. Such failure detectors have the strong completeness property (Eq. (4)) of the *strong* failure detector $\mathcal{S}$ [11], but their accuracy

is limited to a set of processes called the scope (Eq. (3)). In the special case where the scope comprises all processes, $\mathcal{S}_n$ coincides with $\mathcal{S}$.[2] It was shown in [30] that $\mathcal{S}_{n-k+1}$ is sufficient for k-set agreement.

Definition 2. *The* strong failure detector with *x*-limited scope *is denoted as* $\mathcal{S}_x$ *and is defined such that for all environments* $\mathcal{E}$ *and* $\forall F \in \mathcal{E}$, *there is a set* $Q \subseteq \Pi : |Q| = x$ *such that:*

$$\exists p \in (Q \setminus F) \ \forall t \ \forall q \in Q: \ p \notin H(q,t) \tag{3}$$

$$\forall p \in F \ \exists t \ \forall q \in \Pi: \ p \in H(q,t) \tag{4}$$

3   Weak System Models for Set Agreement

In this section, we introduce two system models $\mathcal{M}^{\mathrm{anti}}$ and $\mathcal{M}^{\mathrm{sink}}$ with very weak synchrony conditions. By implementing $\mathcal{L}$ in both of these models, we show that they are strong enough to solve set agreement. In order to allow this, we need to restrict the set of admissible runs of $\mathcal{M}^{\mathrm{async}}$ by adding some—albeit very weak—synchrony conditions. While set agreement is solvable in either one of these models, the partial synchrony-like assumptions of $\mathcal{M}^{\mathrm{sink}}$ are fundamentally different from the time-free message-ordering properties of model $\mathcal{M}^{\mathrm{anti}}$.

3.1   The Model $\mathcal{M}^{\mathrm{anti}}$

In some applications, like VLSI Systems-on-Chip [20], a message-driven execution model [36,7,33], where computing steps are triggered by the arrival of messages instead of the passage of time, is advantageous over the usual time-driven execution model. The model $\mathcal{M}^{\mathrm{anti}}$ presented in this section belongs to this category. Inspired by the round-trip-based model introduced in [28,31], we specify our synchrony requirements as conditions on the order of round-trip message arrivals. In this model computations proceed in asynchronous rounds: At the start of a round, every process p sends a $(query)$-message to all processes, including itself. If a process receives a $(query)$-message from some process q, it sends a $(resp)$-message to q. When p has received at least $n - f$ $(resp)$-messages, it *starts a new round*, by sending out another $(query)$-message to all processes. Since we aim at $(n-1)$-set agreement with $f = n - 1$ here, processes hence start their new round after receiving just 1 response. In the case where all other processes crash, the remaining process will end up receiving only messages sent by itself.

Definition 3 (Anti-Source). *Let p be a correct or faulty process. Process p is an* anti-source, *if, whenever p sends a query to all processes, then the response from some other (possibly changing) process arrives at p before process p starts a new round.*

---

[2] For the case $k > f$ (which is not relevant here as $f = n - 1$) [29] also provides a transformation $T_{\mathcal{S}_k \to \mathcal{S}}$.

Algorithm 1. $\mathcal{L}$ in Model $\mathcal{M}^{\mathrm{anti}}$	**Algorithm 2.** $\mathcal{L}$ in Model $\mathcal{M}^{\mathrm{sink}}$
1: **Vars:**	1: **Vars:**
2: $counter \in \mathbb{N}$	2: $output_{\mathcal{L}} \in \{\text{TRUE, FALSE}\}$
3: $output_{\mathcal{L}}, alone \in \{\text{TRUE, FALSE}\}$	3: $phase, maxSeen \in \mathbb{Z}$
4: **Initially:**	4: **Initially:**
5: $output_{\mathcal{L}} \leftarrow \text{FALSE};$	5: $output_{\mathcal{L}} \leftarrow \text{FALSE}$
6: $startRound()$	6: $phase \leftarrow -1$
	7: $maxSeen \leftarrow -1$
7: **upon** rcv $(resp)$ from procs Q **do**	8: $startPhase()$
8: $counter \leftarrow |Q|$	
9: **if** $\{p\} \neq Q$ **then**	9: **every** η steps **do:**
10: $alone \leftarrow \text{FALSE}$	10: $startPhase()$
11: **if** $counter \geqslant n - f$ **then**	
12: **if** $alone = \text{FALSE}$ **then**	11: **upon** receive $(alive, ph')$ **do**
13: $startRound()$	12: $maxSeen \leftarrow \max(maxSeen, ph')$
14: **else**	13: **upon** expiration of $timer$ **do**
15: $output_{\mathcal{L}} \leftarrow \text{TRUE}$	14: **if** $maxSeen \geqslant phase$ **then**
	15: $timer \leftarrow \Phi\eta + \Delta$
16: **upon** receive $(query)$ from q **do**	16: start $timer$
17: send $(resp)$ do q	17: **else**
	18: $output_{\mathcal{L}} \leftarrow \text{TRUE}$
18: **procedure** $startRound()$	
19: $alone \leftarrow \text{TRUE}$	19: **procedure** $startPhase()$
20: $counter \leftarrow 0$	20: $phase \leftarrow phase + 1$
21: send $(query)$ to all	21: send $(alive, phase)$ to all remote

Intuitively speaking, an anti-source is an (unknown) process whose round-trips with itself are never the fastest. Note that this definition also implies that the anti-source can never be the last remaining correct process.

Definition 4. *Let α be a run of a distributed algorithm. Then, α is* admissible *in $\mathcal{M}^{\mathrm{anti}}$ if the following holds:*
1. *Run α is admissible in $\mathcal{M}^{async}$.*
2. *At least one process is an anti-source in α.*

Algorithm 1 provides an implementation of the loneliness failure detector $\mathcal{L}$ in $\mathcal{M}^{\mathrm{anti}}$: A process sets its $output_{\mathcal{L}}$ to TRUE if and only if it receives its own reply to its round-trip first. In every run, the anti-source p will always receive the reply message from some other process first and therefore never changes its variable $output_{\mathcal{L}}$ to TRUE.

Theorem 1. $\mathcal{L}$ *is implementable in $\mathcal{M}^{\mathrm{anti}}$.*

Proof. Let p be an anti-source in a run of Algorithm 1. At the start of every round, process p sends a $(query)$-message to all other processes. By the definition of an anti-source, p always receives a $(resp)$-message to its query from some process $q \neq p$ as its first reply. Process p will therefore pass the test in Line 9 and set *alone* ← FALSE. It follows that p will always pass the test in Line 12 and therefore *output$_\mathcal{L}$* remains on FALSE forever, which entails Property (1).

To show Property (2), we suppose that q is the only correct process in α. Then there is a time after which q does not receive any more messages from other processes. That is, there is a time t such that whenever q sends out a (*query*)-message, it only receives its own response, hence, it never sets *alone* ← FALSE at any time $t' \geqslant t$. The one (*resp*) message that q receives, however, is sufficient to subsequently cause q to set *output$_\mathcal{L}$* to TRUE in Line 15.   □

3.2   The Model $\mathcal{M}^{\mathrm{sink}}$

The model $\mathcal{M}^{\mathrm{sink}}$ is similar to the weak-timely link (WTL) models [2,1,27,25], which are derived from the classic partially synchronous models [18,17]. Essentially, the WTL models assume that processes are partially synchronous [18] while trying to minimize the synchrony requirements on communication delays.

In the model $\mathcal{M}^{\mathrm{anti}}$, there is no time bound on the duration of a round-trip as only the arrival order matters. Our second model $\mathcal{M}^{\mathrm{sink}}$ enforces a similar order by means of explicit communication delay bounds and message timeouts, like the WTL models. A naïve approach would be to simply assume a bound on the round trip time, which is essentially equivalent to requiring a moving bi-directional link from one process. Note that this assumption would make one process permanently 1-*accessible* (in the notation of [27]), which turned out to be unnecessarily strong for our purposes.

As in [18], we assume two bounds Φ and Δ, where Φ bounds the relative speed of processes, whereas Δ bounds the transmission delay of a timely message m, i.e., the number of steps of processes take during the transmission of m. We also assume that processes can only either send messages or receive a possibly empty set of messages in a step. We say that a message m is delivered *timely* over the link (p,q) iff it is sent by p at time t and received by q not after the first reception step q takes at or after $t + \Delta$. Note that this definition implies that all messages sent to a crashed process (or a process that crashes before taking the decisive reception step) are considered to be delivered timely.

As in the WTL models (and in contrast to [18]), we do not assume Δ to hold for all messages. Rather, we base our synchrony conditions on a "sink", i.e., a process q that can always receive some messages timely.

Definition 5 (Sink). *A process q is a* sink *in a run α if there is a correct process p such any message sent to q (before it may possibly crash) is delivered timely to q.*

Note that we only consider p to be correct here to keep the definition simple. Indeed, when the sink q crashes, then p may crash as well, as long as it does so only after q. Note that this is actually the decisive difference between q being a sink and p being a perpetual 1-source (in the notation of [1]). This is not the end of the road, however, as this synchrony requirement can be further weakened when one considers algorithms with a "round like" structure — that is, algorithms where each process repeatedly sends messages to all other processes, as it is often the case for heartbeat-based failure detector implementations. For such algorithms, one could also use the following Definition 6, where the timely process p may change. Note, however, that in contrast to the timely f-source model with moving timely links [25], we cannot rely on single (send-)event as a common reference point.

Definition 6 (Sink'). *A process q is a* sink *in a run α if, for every $i \geqslant 1$, there is a (possibly changing) process p such that the i-th message sent by p to q is delivered timely to q.*

Note carefully that, since all messages sent to crashed processes are by definition delivered timely, a sink can also be a faulty process.

Definition 7 (Model $\mathcal{M}^{\text{sink}}$). *Let α be a run of a distributed algorithm. Then, α is admissible in $\mathcal{M}^{\text{sink}}$ if the following holds:*

1. *Run α is admissible in $\mathcal{M}^{async}$.*
2. *There is a bound Φ, such that in every interval of Φ ticks on T every process that is alive throughout the interval takes at least one step.*
3. *At least one process is a sink in α.*

At a first glance, it might be surprising that model $\mathcal{M}^{\text{sink}}$ is a non-eventual model, i.e., a model where all model properties must hold at all times. This is necessary in order to implement $\mathcal{L}$ (see Definition 1), which is a non-eventual failure detector. In fact, this is no peculiarity of set agreement: The weakest failure detector for $n-1$ resilient consensus is $\langle \Sigma, \Omega \rangle$, which is also non-eventual (see [14]). Moreover, the definition of $\mathcal{L}$ makes it necessary that at least one process never falsely suspects "loneliness", i.e., the model parameters Φ and Δ must be known (and hold right from the start). While it would be sufficient if only the sink knew the real model parameters Φ and Δ, we do not assume that the sink is known in advance, so all processes must in fact know Φ and Δ. However, if the messages sent by some fixed process p to the sink q were always timely, it would be sufficient if just p and q respected Φ and Δ.

Algorithm 2 shows a simple protocol that implements $\mathcal{L}$ in model $\mathcal{M}^{\text{sink}}$: Variable $output_{\mathcal{L}}$ contains the simulated failure detector output. Every process p periodically sends out $(alive, phase)$-messages that carry the current phase-counter $phase$. In addition, it sets a timer that is implemented using simple step counting. If p does not receive a timely $(alive, ph')$-message that was sent by some other process in the current (or a future) phase, it sets $output_{\mathcal{L}} \leftarrow$ TRUE in Line 18. Note that the timer is not re-armed in this case; the algorithm continues to send $(alive, phase)$-messages to the other processes, however. It is important to observe that Algorithm 2 also works in *anonymous* systems, where processes do not have unique identifiers but can only distinguish their neighbors via local port numbers, cp. [4,3]. In Section 4, we will also provide an anonymous algorithm that solves set agreement with $\mathcal{L}$.

Lemma 1. *If process q is a sink, then q never executes Line 18 of Algorithm 2.*

Proof. We must show that q receives the $(alive, k)$-message from some process before its timer runs out the $(k + 1)$-st time, for any $k \geqslant 0$. Since q is a sink, the $(alive, k)$ is delivered timely to q from some process p. Let $T(\psi)$ denote the time on our global clock T when event ψ takes place somewhere in the system. Suppose that p sends the $(alive, k)$-message in some step ψ_p. By the code of the algorithm, process p must have executed $k\eta$ steps.[3] Since processes are partially synchronous, we have $T(\psi_p) \leqslant \Phi k\eta$. Now suppose that q's timer expires in step ψ_q for the $(k + 1)$-st time. That is, q has made $(k + 1)(\Phi\eta + \Delta)$ steps by ψ_q. Obviously, we have $T(\psi_q) \geqslant (k+1)(\Phi\eta+\Delta)$. Considering that the message from p to q is delivered timely, we are done if we can show $T(\psi_p) + \Delta \leqslant T(\psi_q)$. We find $\forall k \geqslant 0:\ T(\psi_p)+\Delta \leqslant k\Phi\eta+\Delta < (k+1)\Phi\eta+\Delta \leqslant (k+1)(\Phi\eta+\Delta) \leqslant T(\psi_q)$, which completes the proof. $\qquad\square$

Theorem 2. *Algorithm 2 implements failure detector $\mathcal{L}$ in model $\mathcal{M}^{sink}$ for $f = n - 1$.*

Proof. Let α be a run of Algorithm 2 in $\mathcal{M}^{\text{sink}}$, and p be any sink. Lemma 1 implies that p perpetually outputs FALSE in α (until it crashes), so (1) holds.

For proving (2), suppose that $n - 1$ processes crash in α. Since there must be some process from which p receives timely messages, p cannot be the only correct process in α. Let $q \neq p$ be the only correct process in α. Since q only sends its *alive*-messages to remote processes and no other process is alive, q's timer will eventually expire without receiving any message, i.e., q will set $output_{\mathcal{L}} \leftarrow$ TRUE in Line 18. $\qquad\square$

Comparing $\mathcal{M}^{sink}$ to an f-Source Model. It is interesting to compare $\mathcal{M}^{\text{sink}}$ to the f-source model $\mathcal{S}_{f*}^{\rightarrow}$ of [25], which is strong enough to solve consensus by implementing Ω for $f < n/2$. Just like $\mathcal{M}^{\text{sink}}$, model $\mathcal{S}_{f*}^{\rightarrow}$ assumes that processes are partially synchronous and that processes can send a message to multiple receivers in a single step. Moreover, in every run that is admissible in $\mathcal{S}_{f*}^{\rightarrow}$, there is some correct process p that is an eventual moving-f-source, i.e., p has at least f outgoing timely links, i.e., messages are delivered timely, to a (possibly changing) set of f processes. Since we consider a perpetual model $\mathcal{M}^{\text{sink}}$, with failure patterns where up to $n - 1$ processes can crash, we will compare it to a perpetual model $\mathcal{S}_{n-1*}^{\rightarrow}$ that contains at least one *perpetual* moving-$(n-1)$-source p. Clearly, since $n - 1$ are all remote processes, there is no point in assuming that these links are moving here. Since every process $q \neq p$ receives all messages from p timely, every such q is a sink. Hence, it is not difficult to show that $\mathcal{M}^{\text{sink}}$ has weaker synchrony requirements than $\mathcal{S}_{n-1*}^{\rightarrow}$; see [6] for the proof.

Theorem 3. *Any run α that is admissible in the (perpetual) model $\mathcal{S}_{n-1*}^{\rightarrow}$ is admissible in $\mathcal{M}^{sink}$, but there are runs admissible in $\mathcal{M}^{sink}$ that are not admissible in $\mathcal{S}_{n-1*}^{\rightarrow}$.*

---

[3] For simplicity, we assume that all processes initially start up at the same time.

3.3 Consensus Impossibility

Given these similarities with a model where consensus is solvable, the question of whether our models are also strong enough to solve consensus arises naturally. We now show that this question can be answered in the negative. Due to the fact that our models are very close to the asynchronous model, the proof is surprisingly simple.

Theorem 4. *Consider a message passing system of size $n \geqslant 3$, where up to $n - 1$ processes may crash. There is no algorithm that solves consensus in model $\mathcal{M}^{anti}$ or in model $\mathcal{M}^{sink}$.*

Proof. Suppose, for a contradiction, that there is an algorithm A^{sink} (resp. A^{anti}) that solves consensus in model $\mathcal{M}^{sink}$ (resp. $\mathcal{M}^{anti}$).
$\mathcal{M}^{sink}$: Consider a run α of A^{sink} where some process p is initially dead. Since p satisfies the definition of a sink, there are no other synchrony requirements on the links connecting the remaining correct processes. Hence the set of the runs where p is initially dead is indistinguishable from the set of runs generated by A^{sink} in a system $\mathcal{M}^{async}$ with just $n - 1 \geqslant 2$ processes, where processes are partially synchronous, all links are asynchronous, and $f = n - 2 \geqslant 1$ processes can still crash. This contradicts the impossibility results in [17, Table 1].
$\mathcal{M}^{anti}$: Consider a run α of A^{anti}, where some process p is initially dead. Since p satisfies the definition of an anti-source, there are no other synchrony requirements at all in $\mathcal{M}^{anti}$. Therefore, the set of these runs where p is initially dead is indistinguishable from the set of runs generated by A^{anti} in a system $\mathcal{M}^{async}$ with $n - 1 \geqslant 2$ processes, where still $f = n - 2 \geqslant 1$ processes can crash. This, however, contradicts the FLP impossibility [19].   □

4   Solving k-Set Agreement with $\mathcal{L}(k)$

In this section, we present an algorithm that solves k-set agreement in the asynchronous model augmented with a failure detector [11,10] where each step a process takes, comprises receiving a message, querying the failure detector ($\mathcal{L}(k)$ in our case), and finally sending messages to other processes. The original algorithm for solving $(n-1)$-set agreement with $\mathcal{L}$ [16] requires a total order on process identifiers. Algorithm 3, in contrast, also works in anonymous systems.

We denote by X^r the possibly empty array containing all x-values after the assignment in line 17 while the round variable rnd was set to r. We assume that X^r is ordered by decreasing values, i.e., $X^r[1]$ is the maximal value, if it exists. Furthermore, we denote the number of nonempty entries in X^r by $|X^r|$.

Lemma 2. *For any round $r \geqslant 0$, the number of unique values in X^r is $u_r \leqslant k - a_r$, where a_r is the number of processes which never sent $(round, r, x)$.*

Proof. First, we observe that x is updated by a process p only after receiving $n - k$ $(round, r, y)$ messages from other processes.

Algorithm 3. Solving k-set agreement with $\mathcal{L}(k)$

1: **in the first step:**
2: $x \leftarrow v$
3: $rnd \leftarrow 0$
4: send $(round, 0, x)$ to remote processes

5: **in any later step:**
6: receive messages
7: **if** $\mathcal{L}(k) = \text{TRUE}$ **then**
8:     send (dec, x) to all
9:     decide x
10:     halt
11: **else if** received (dec, y) **then**
12:     send (dec, y) to all
13:     decide y
14:     halt
15: **else if** received $n - k$ remote $(round, rnd, y)$ msgs **then**
16:     $S \leftarrow \{y_1, \ldots, y_{n-k}\} \cup \{x\}$
17:     $x \leftarrow \min(S)$
18:     **if** $rnd = k + 1$ **then**
19:         send (dec, x) to all
20:         decide x
21:         halt
22:     $rnd \leftarrow rnd + 1$
23:     send $(round, r, x)$ to all remote processes

Let p be the process which assigns the largest value in line 17. Since any process p sets x to the minimum of the $n - k$ round r values received, there must be $n - k - 1$ messages containing values $y \geqslant x$ among those received by p.

Considering that $|X^r| \leqslant n - a_r$, it follows that only $n - a_r - (n - k + 1) \leqslant k - a_r - 1$ values in X^r can be smaller than p's minimum. Thus, processes assign at most $k - a_r$ different values to x and subsequently send them as $(round, r+1, x)$-messages. □

Lemma 3. *Processes do not decide on more than k different values.*

Proof. Regarding the number of different decision values, processes deciding due to receiving a (dec, y) message (line 13) make no difference, since some other process must have decided on y using another method before. Thus we can ignore this case here.

What remains are decisions due to $\mathcal{L}(k)$ being TRUE (line 9) and due to having received $n - k$ messages in round $k + 1$ (line 20). For each $r \geqslant 0$, we denote by ℓ_r the number of processes which have decided due to their failure detector output being TRUE while their $rnd = r$. Thus the number of processes that have decided in line 9 with $rnd \leqslant r$ for some $r \geqslant 0$ is $\Sigma_{s=0}^{r} \ell_s$. In the following we use Σ^r as an abbreviation for this sum. Since processes halt after deciding, we can deduce that the number of processes which do not send round r messages a_r, is at least Σ^{r-1}. Thus, Lemma 2 tells us that $u_r \leqslant k - \Sigma^{r-1}$.

Now we assume by contradiction, that there are actually $D > k$ decisions, with $D = u_{k+1} + \Sigma^{k+1}$, that is the number of different values decided on in line 20 plus those that decided based on $\mathcal{L}(k)$. Thus we get $u_{k+1} > k - \Sigma^{k+1}$, and by using the above property of u_r, we deduce that $\Sigma^{k+1} > \Sigma^k$, and thus $\ell_{k+1} \geqslant 1$. These processes must have decided on some values in X^k, however, which leads to the realisation that $D = u_k + \Sigma^k$. We can repeat this argument until we reach $D = u_1 + \Sigma^0 = u_1 + \ell_0$. Here, Lemma 2 gives us the trivial upper bound $u_1 \leqslant k$, which entails the requirement $\ell_0 \geqslant 1$ as $D > k$.

By now, we have shown that, assuming $D > k$ decisions $\ell_r \geqslant 1$ is required for $r \in \{0, \dots, k+1\}$. In other words we have deduced that $\Sigma^{k+1} \geqslant k+1$ processes have decided due to their $\mathcal{L}(k)$ output being TRUE. This contradicts property (2) of $\mathcal{L}(k)$, thus proving the Lemma.

Theorem 5. *Algorithm 3 solves k-set agreement in the asynchronous system augmented with $\mathcal{L}(k)$, even when there are no unique identifiers.*

Proof. *Validity* is evident, since no value other than the initial values v of processes are ever assigned directly or indirectly to x. k-*Agreement* follows from Lemma 3, and since either $n - k$ processes send messages in each round or some process has $\mathcal{L}(k) =$ TRUE, every correct process *terminates*.   □

From [16], we know that $\mathcal{L}$ can be extracted anonymously from any failure detector D which solves set-agreement using some algorithm A: Every process executes an independent instance of A using D as failure detector. The simulated $\mathcal{L}$ outputs TRUE at p only after A has terminated at p. In conjunction with Theorem 5, this implies the following fact:

Corollary 1. *$\mathcal{L}$ is the weakest failure detector for set agreement in anonymous message passing systems.*

Theorem 5 showed that $\mathcal{L}(k)$ is sufficient for k-set agreement. We now prove that it is not (much) stronger than necessary, as $\mathcal{L}(k)$ is too weak to solve $(k-1)$-set agreement.

Theorem 6. *No algorithm can solve $(k-1)$-set agreement with $\mathcal{L}(k)$, for any $2 \leqslant k \leqslant n-1$.*

Proof. We assume by contradiction that such an algorithm A exists. Now consider the failure detector history where processes $p_1, \dots, p_k$ output TRUE perpetually, while the other processes output FALSE. Clearly, this defines a legal history for $\mathcal{L}(k)$ in a run where the $n - k$ processes $p_{k+1}, \dots, p_n$ crash initially. For the remaining k processes, the failure detector provides no (further) information about failures, as it outputs TRUE perpetually. Since A is able to solve $(k-1)$-set agreement in any such run by assumption, it can also be used to solve $(k-1)$-set agreement in an asynchronous system of k processes, equipped with a *dummy* failure detector [22] that always outputs TRUE. This contradicts the $(n-1)$-set agreement impossibility in a system of n processes [34,9,24].   □

5   Relation of $\mathcal{L}(k)$ to $\mathcal{S}_{n-k+1}$ and Σ

In this section, we discuss how the $\mathcal{L}(k)$ failure detector relates to the limited accuracy failure detector $\mathcal{S}_{n-k+1}$ (see Definition 2). Theorem 7 shows that, except in the canonical cases $k = 1$ and $k = n - 1$, these failure detectors are incomparable. The proofs of this section can be found in the technical report [6].

Theorem 7. *Failure detector $\mathcal{S}_n$ is strictly weaker than $\mathcal{L}(1)$, and $\mathcal{S}_2$ is strictly stronger than failure detector $\mathcal{L}(n-1)$. For $1 < k < n - 1$, $\mathcal{L}(1)$ and $\mathcal{S}_{n-k+1}$ are incomparable. Neither $\mathcal{L}(k)$ nor $\mathcal{S}_{n-k+1}$ is the weakest failure detector for general message passing k-set agreement.*

Despite this, $\mathcal{L}(k)$ appears to be a promising candidate for the weakest failure detector for message passing k-set agreement in anonymous systems, i.e., without unique process ids.

As a final relation, we now explore the relation between $\mathcal{L}(k)$ and Σ. The general case for $\mathcal{L}(k)$ can be deduced from the more specific result of [16, Lemma 4] by finding a suitable partitioning; see [6] for the proof.

Lemma 4. *$\mathcal{L}(k)$ is not stronger than Σ, if $n > 2$ and $k \geqslant 2$.*

Moreover, Theorem 4 implies that either $\mathcal{L}(k)$ is strictly weaker than Σ or the two are not comparable. In either case, when adding another failure detector to Σ, say anti-Ω_k, the combined failure detector is stronger than Σ, therefore, any such combined failure detector cannot be the weakest for k-set agreement in message passing systems, when $k > 1$.

6   Conclusions

We introduced two novel message passing models that provide just enough synchrony for set agreement but not enough for consensus. We also showed how to implement the weakest loneliness failure detector $\mathcal{L}$ for set agreement in these models, and proved that $\mathcal{L}$ is also the weakest failure detector for set agreement in anonymous systems. Finally, we generalized $\mathcal{L}$ to the $(n-k)$-loneliness failure detector $\mathcal{L}(k)$, which allows to solve k-set agreement but not $(k-1)$-set agreement. Part of our future research will be devoted to the relationship between (anonymous and non-anonymous) failure detectors and the synchrony conditions necessary for implementing them. One direction is the question of whether our models can be generalized for k-set agreement. Tightly connected to this question is the still ongoing search for the weakest failure detector for message passing k-set agreement.

References

1. Aguilera, M.K., Delporte-Gallet, C., Fauconnier, H., Toueg, S.: On implementing Omega with weak reliability and synchrony assumptions. In: Proceedings of the 22nd ACM Symposium on Principles of Distributed Computing, pp. 306–314 (July 2003)

2. Aguilera, M.K., Delporte-Gallet, C., Fauconnier, H., Toueg, S.: Communication-efficient leader election and consensus with limited link synchrony. In: Proceedings of the 23rd ACM Symposium on Principles of Distributed Computing (PODC 2004), St. John's, Newfoundland, Canada, pp. 328–337. ACM Press, New York (2004)

3. Angluin, D.: Local and global properties in networks of processors (extended abstract). In: Proceedings of the Twelfth Annual ACM Symposium on Theory of Computing, pp. 82–93. ACM, New York (1980)

4. Attiya, H., Snir, M., Warmuth, M.K.: Computing on an anonymous ring. J. ACM 35(4), 845–875 (1988)

5. Biely, M., Hutle, M., Penso, L.D., Widder, J.: Relating stabilizing timing assumptions to stabilizing failure detectors regarding solvability and efficiency. In: Masuzawa, T., Tixeuil, S. (eds.) SSS 2007. LNCS, vol. 4838, pp. 4–20. Springer, Heidelberg (2007)

6. Biely, M., Robinson, P., Schmid, U.: Weak synchrony models and failure detectors for message passing k-set agreement. Research Report 51/2009, Technische Universität Wien, Inst. Technische Informatik, 182-2, 1040 Vienna, Austria (2009)

7. Biely, M., Widder, J.: Optimal message-driven implementation of Omega with mute processes. In: Datta, A.K., Gradinariu, M. (eds.) SSS 2006. LNCS, vol. 4280, pp. 110–121. Springer, Heidelberg (2006)

8. Bonnet, F., Raynal, M.: Looking for the weakest failure detector for k-set agreement in message-passing systems: Is Π_k the end of the road? In: Guerraoui, R., Petit, F. (eds.) SSS 2009. LNCS, vol. 5873, pp. 129–164. Springer, Heidelberg (2009)

9. Borowsky, E., Gafni, E.: Generalized FLP impossibility result for t-resilient asynchronous computations. In: STOC 1993: Proceedings of the twenty-fifth annual ACM symposium on Theory of computing, pp. 91–100. ACM, New York (1993)

10. Chandra, T.D., Hadzilacos, V., Toueg, S.: The weakest failure detector for solving consensus. Journal of the ACM 43(4), 685–722 (1996)

11. Chandra, T.D., Toueg, S.: Unreliable failure detectors for reliable distributed systems. Journal of the ACM 43(2), 225–267 (1996)

12. Charron-Bost, B., Schiper, A.: Uniform consensus is harder than consensus. J. Algorithms 51(1), 15–37 (2004); Also published as Tech. Rep. DSC/2000/028, Ecole Polytechnique Fédérale de Lausanne

13. Chaudhuri, S.: More choices allow more faults: set consensus problems in totally asynchronous systems. Inf. Comput. 105(1), 132–158 (1993)

14. Delporte-Gallet, C., Fauconnier, H., Guerraoui, R.: Shared Memory vs Message Passing. LPD-REPORT 001, Ecole Polytechnique Federale de Lausanne (2003)

15. Delporte-Gallet, C., Fauconnier, H., Guerraoui, R., Hadzilacos, V., Kouznetsov, P., Toueg, S.: The weakest failure detectors to solve certain fundamental problems in distributed computing. In: Proceedings of the 23rd ACM Symposium on Principles of Distributed Computing (PODC 2004), pp. 338–346. ACM Press, New York (2004)

16. Delporte-Gallet, C., Fauconnier, H., Guerraoui, R., Tielmann, A.: The weakest failure detector for message passing set-agreement. In: Taubenfeld, G. (ed.) DISC 2008. LNCS, vol. 5218, pp. 109–120. Springer, Heidelberg (2008)

17. Dolev, D., Dwork, C., Stockmeyer, L.: On the minimal synchronism needed for distributed consensus. Journal of the ACM 34(1), 77–97 (1987)

18. Dwork, C., Lynch, N., Stockmeyer, L.: Consensus in the presence of partial synchrony. Journal of the ACM 35(2), 288–323 (1988)

19. Fischer, M.J., Lynch, N.A., Paterson, M.S.: Impossibility of distributed consensus with one faulty process. Journal of the ACM 32(2), 374–382 (1985)

20. Fuegger, M., Schmid, U., Fuchs, G., Kempf, G.: Fault-Tolerant Distributed Clock Generation in VLSI Systems-on-Chip. In: Proceedings of the Sixth European Dependable Computing Conference (EDCC-6), pp. 87–96. IEEE Computer Society, Los Alamitos (2006)
21. Gafni, E., Kuznetsov, P.: The weakest failure detector for solving k-set agreement. In: 28th ACM Symposium on Principles of Distributed Computing (PODC) (2009)
22. Guerraoui, R., Herlihy, M., Kouznetsov, P., Lynch, N., Newport, C.: On the weakest failure detector ever. In: Proceedings of the twenty-sixth annual ACM Symposium on Principles of Distributed Computing (PODC 2007), pp. 235–243. ACM, New York (2007)
23. Guerraoui, R., Schiper, A.: "gamma-accurate" failure detectors. In: Babaoğlu, Ö., Marzullo, K. (eds.) WDAG 1996. LNCS, vol. 1151, pp. 269–286. Springer, Heidelberg (1996)
24. Herlihy, M., Shavit, N.: The asynchronous computability theorem for t-resilient tasks. In: STOC 1993: Proceedings of the twenty-fifth annual ACM symposium on Theory of computing, pp. 111–120. ACM, New York (1993)
25. Hutle, M., Malkhi, D., Schmid, U., Zhou, L.: Chasing the weakest system model for implementing omega and consensus. IEEE Transactions on Dependable and Secure Computing (to appear, 2009)
26. Larrea, M., Fernández, A., Arévalo, S.: Optimal implementation of the weakest failure detector for solving consensus. In: Proceedings of the 19th IEEE Symposium on Reliable Distributed Systems (SRDS), Nürnberg, Germany, pp. 52–59 (October 2000)
27. Malkhi, D., Oprea, F., Zhou, L.: Ω meets paxos: Leader election and stability without eventual timely links. In: Fraigniaud, P. (ed.) DISC 2005. LNCS, vol. 3724, pp. 199–213. Springer, Heidelberg (2005)
28. Mostefaoui, A., Mourgaya, E., Raynal, M.: Asynchronous implementation of failure detectors. In: Proceedings of the International Conference on Dependable Systems and Networks (DSN 2003), San Francisco, CA, June 22–25 (2003)
29. Mostéfaoui, A., Raynal, M.: Unreliable failure detectors with limited scope accuracy and an application to consensus. In: Pandu Rangan, C., Raman, V., Sarukkai, S. (eds.) FST TCS 1999. LNCS, vol. 1738, pp. 329–340. Springer, Heidelberg (1999)
30. Mostéfaoui, A., Raynal, M.: k-set agreement with limited accuracy failure detectors. In: PODC 2000: Proceedings of the 19th annual ACM symposium on Principles of distributed computing, pp. 143–152. ACM, New York (2000)
31. Mostefaoui, A., Raynal, M., Travers, C.: Crash-resilient time-free eventual leadership. In: Proceedings of the 23rd IEEE Symposium on Reliable Distributed Systems (SRDS 2004), pp. 208–217. IEEE Computer Society, Los Alamitos (2004)
32. Raynal, M.: k-anti-Ω. Rump session at PODC 2007 (August 2007)
33. Robinson, P., Schmid, U.: The Asynchronous Bounded-Cycle Model. In: Kulkarni, S., Schiper, A. (eds.) SSS 2008. LNCS, vol. 5340, pp. 246–262. Springer, Heidelberg (2008)
34. Saks, M., Zaharoglou, F.: Wait-free k-set agreement is impossible: The topology of public knowledge. SIAM J. Comput. 29(5), 1449–1483 (2000)
35. Schneider, F.B.: Implementing fault-tolerant services using the state machine approach: a tutorial. ACM Comput. Surv. 22(4), 299–319 (1990)
36. Widder, J., Schmid, U.: The Theta-Model: Achieving synchrony without clocks. Distributed Computing 22(1), 29–47 (2009)
37. Zielinski, P.: Automatic classification of eventual failure detectors. In: Pelc, A. (ed.) DISC 2007. LNCS, vol. 4731, pp. 465–479. Springer, Heidelberg (2007)
38. Zielinski, P.: Anti-Ω: the weakest failure detector for set agreement. In: PODC 2008: Proceedings of the twenty-seventh ACM symposium on Principles of distributed computing, pp. 55–64. ACM, New York (2008)

Unifying Byzantine Consensus Algorithms with Weak Interactive Consistency

Zarko Milosevic, Martin Hutle, and André Schiper

Ecole Polytechnique Fédérale de Lausanne (EPFL)
1015 Lausanne, Switzerland
{zarko.milosevic,martin.hutle,andre.schiper}@epfl.ch

Abstract. The paper considers the consensus problem in a partially synchronous system with Byzantine processes. In this context, the literature distinguishes *authenticated Byzantine* faults, where messages can be signed by the sending process (with the assumption that the signature cannot be forged by any other process), and *Byzantine* faults, where there is no mechanism for signatures (but the receiver of a message knows the identity of the sender). The paper proposes an abstraction called *weak interactive consistency* (*WIC*) that unifies consensus algorithms with and without signed messages. WIC can be implemented with and without signatures.

The power of WIC is illustrated on two seminal Byzantine consensus algorithms: the Castro-Liskov PBFT algorithm (no signatures) and the Martin-Alvisi FaB Paxos algorithms (signatures). WIC allows a very concise expression of these two algorithms.

1 Introduction

Consensus is probably the most fundamental problem in fault tolerant distributed computing. Consensus is related to the implementation of state machine replication, atomic broadcast, group membership, etc. The problem is defined over a set of processes Π, where each process $p_i \in \Pi$ has an initial value v_i, and requires that all processes agree on a common value.

With respect to process faults, consensus can be considered with different fault assumptions. On the one end of the spectrum, processes fail only by crashing (so called *benign* faults); on the other end, faulty processes can exhibit an arbitrary (and even malicious) behavior. Among the latter, two fault models are considered in literature [1]: *authenticated Byzantine* faults, where messages can be signed by the sending process (with the assumption that the signature cannot be forged by any other process), and *Byzantine* faults, where there is no mechanism for signatures (but the receiver of a message knows the identity of the sender).[1] Consensus protocols that assume *Byzantine* faults (without authentication) are harder to develop and prove correct [3]. As a consequence, they tend to be more complicated and harder to understand than the protocols that assume

---

[1] In [2], the latter is called Byzantine faults with *oral messages*.

T. Abdelzaher, M. Raynal, and N. Santoro (Eds.): OPODIS 2009, LNCS 5923, pp. 300–314, 2009.
© Springer-Verlag Berlin Heidelberg 2009

authenticated Byzantine faults, even when they are based on the same idea. The existence of these two fault models raises the following question: is there a way to transform an algorithm for authenticated Byzantine faults into an algorithm for Byzantine faults, or vice versa?

This question has been addressed by Srikanth and Toueg in [3] for the Byzantine agreement problem,[2] by defining the *authenticated broadcast* primitive. Authenticated broadcast is a communication primitive that provides additional guarantees compared to, *e.g.*, a normal (unreliable) broadcast. Srikanth and Toueg solve Byzantine agreement using authenticated broadcast, and show that authenticated broadcast can be implemented with and without signatures.

However, authenticated broadcast does not encapsulate all the possible uses of signed messages when solving consensus. One typical example is the Fast Byzantine Paxos algorithm [4], which relies on signed messages whenever the coordinator changes.

Complementing the approach of [3], we define an abstraction different from authenticated broadcast that we call *weak interactive consistency*.[3] Interactive consistency is defined in [7] as a problem where correct processes must agree on a vector such that the ith element of this vector is the initial value of the ith process if this process is correct. Our abstraction is a weaker variant of interactive consistency, hence the name "weak" interactive consistency. Similarly to authenticated broadcast, weak interactive consistency can be implemented with and without signatures. We illustrate the power of weak interactive consistency by reexamining two seminal Byzantine consensus algorithms: the Castro-Liskov PBFT algorithm, which does not use signatures [8], and the Martin-Alvisi FaB Paxos algorithm, which relies on signatures [4]. We show how to express these two algorithms using the weak interactive consistency abstraction, and call these two algorithms CL (for Castro-Liskov), resp. MA (for Martin-Alvisi).

Both CL and MA are very concise algorithms. Moreover, replacing in CL weak interactive consistency with a signature-free implementation basically leads to the original signature-free PBFT algorithm, while replacing in MA weak interactive consistency with a signature-based implementation basically leads to the original signature-based FaB Paxos algorithm. In the latter case, the algorithm obtained is almost identical to the original algorithm; in the former case, the differences are slightly more important (the differences are explained in [9]). In addition, using MA with a signature-free implementation of WIC allows us to derive a signature-free variant of FaB Paxos.

---

[2] In this problem, a transmitter sends a message to a set of processes, all processes eventually deliver a single message, and (i) all correct processes agree on the same message, (ii) if the transmitter is correct, then all correct processes agree on the message of the transmitter.

[3] In [5], Lamport defines "Weak Interactive Consistency Problem", as a general problem of reaching agreement. In [6], Doudou et al. define an abstraction called "Weak Interactive Consistency", with a different definition than ours. They use this abstraction to derive a state machine replication protocol resilient to authenticated Byzantine faults.

The rest of the paper is structured as follows. Weak interactive consistency is informally introduced in Section 2. Section 3 defines our model, and formally defines weak interactive consistency. In Section 4 we show that weak interactive consistency can be implemented with and without signatures. Section 5 describes the MA consensus algorithm (FaB Paxos expressed using weak interactive consistency) and the CL consensus algorithm (PBFT expressed using weak interactive consistency). Section 6 discusses related work, and Section 7 concludes the paper. For space reason, some proofs are omitted. They can be found in [9].

2 Weak Interactive Consistency: An Informal Introduction

2.1 On the Use of Signatures

We start by addressing the following question: where are signatures used in coordinator based consensus algorithms? Signatures are typically used each time the coordinator changes, as done for example in the FaB Paxos algorithm [4]. The corresponding communication pattern is illustrated in Fig. 1(a), and addresses the following issue. Assume that the previous coordinator has brought the system into a configuration where a process already decided v; in this case, in order to ensure safety (*i.e.*, agreement) the new coordinator can only propose v. This is done as follows. First every process sends its current estimate to the new coordinator (v_i sent by p_i to p_1 in Fig. 1(a)). Second, if the coordinator p_1 receives a quorum of messages, then p_1 applies a function f that returns some value x. The quorum ensures that if a process has already decided v, then f returns v. Finally, the value returned by f is then sent to all (x sent by p_1 in Fig. 1(a)).

This solution does not work with a Byzantine coordinator: the value sent by the coordinator p_1 might not be the value returned by f. Safety can here be ensured using signatures: Processes p_i sign the estimates v_i sent to the coordinator p_1, and p_1 sends x together with the quorum of signed estimates it received. This allows a correct process p_i, receiving x from p_1, to verify whether x is consistent with the function f. If not, then p_i ignores x.

Are signatures mandatory here? We investigate this question, first addressing safety and then liveness.

2.2 Safe Updates Requires Neither Signatures Nor a Coordinator

As said, safety means that if a process has decided v, and thus a quorum of processes had v as their estimate at the beginning of the two rounds of Fig. 1(a), then each process can only update its estimate to v. This property can be ensured without signatures and without coordinator: each process p_i simply sends v_i to all, and each process p_i behaves like the coordinator: if p_i receives a quorum of messages, it updates its estimate with the value returned by f.

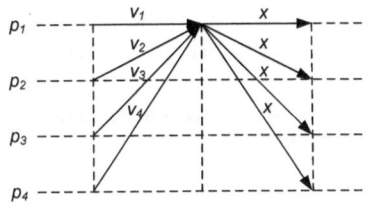
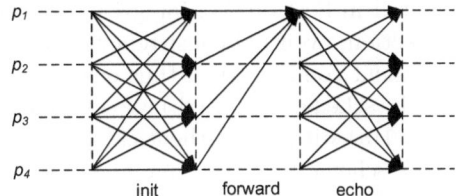

(a) Coordinator change: p_1 is the new coordinator.

(b) Three rounds to get rid of signatures when changing coordinator to p_1

Fig. 1.

This shows that updating the estimate maintaining safety does not require a coordinator. However, as we show in the next section, a coordinator is reintroduced for liveness.

2.3 Coordinator for Liveness

The coordinator in Fig. 1(a) has two roles: (i) it ensures safety (using signatures), and (ii) it tries to bring the system into a univalent configuration (if not yet so), in order to ensure liveness (*i.e.*, termination) of the consensus algorithm. A configuration typically becomes v-valent as soon as a quorum of correct processes update their estimate to v. This is ensured by a correct coordinator, if its message is received by a quorum of correct processes. Ensuring that a quorum of correct processes update their estimate to the same value v can also be implemented without signatures with an all-to-all communication schema, *if all correct processes receive the same set (of quorum size) of values*. Indeed, if two correct processes apply f to the same set of values, they update their estimate to the same value.

However, ensuring that all correct processes receive the same set of messages is problematic in the presence of Byzantine processes: (i) a Byzantine process can send v to some correct process p_i and v' to some other correct process p_j, and (ii) a Byzantine process can send v to some correct process p_i and nothing to some other correct process p_j.

These problems can be addressed using two all-to-all rounds and one all-to-coordinator rounds, as shown in Fig. 1(b) (to be compared with the "init" round followed by the "echo" round of authenticated broadcast, see [3]).

These three rounds can be seen as one all-to-all super-round that "always" satisfies integrity and "eventually" satisfies consistency:

Integrity. If a correct process p receives v from a correct process q in super-round r, then v was sent by q in super-round r.

Consistency. (i) If a correct process p_i sends v in super-round r, then every correct process receives v from p_i in super-round r, and (ii) all correct processes receive the same set of messages in super-round r.

As noted in Section 2.2, integrity ensures safety. As noted at the beginning of this section, eventual consistency allows us to eventually bring the system into a univalent configuration, thus ensuring liveness.

In the scheme of Fig. 1(b) we combine the concept of a coordinator as depicted in Fig. 1(a) with the authentication scheme of [3].

This scheme provides that in synchronous rounds (which eventually exist in a partially synchronous model, see Section 3), messages received by a correct coordinator in the "forward" round (see Fig. 1(b)), are received by all correct processes in the "echo" round (see Fig. 1(b)).[4] Note that without having the coordinator, the authentication scheme of [3] is not able to provide a super-round such that all processes receive the same set of messages at the end of this super-round, since a Byzantine process can always prevent this from happening.

We call the problem of always ensuring integrity and eventually consistency the *weak interactive consistency* problem, or simply *WIC*.[5] We show below that WIC is a unifying concept for Byzantine consensus algorithms. WIC can be implemented with signatures in two rounds (Fig. 1(a)), or without signatures in three rounds (Fig. 1(b)), as shown in Section 4.

3   Model and Definition of WIC

Assuming synchronous rounds is a strong assumption that we do not want to consider here. On the other side, an asynchronous system is not strong enough: WIC is not implementable in such a system. We consider a third option, *i.e.*, a partially synchronous system [1], or rather a slightly weaker variant of this model: we assume that the system alternates between good periods (during which the system is synchronous) and bad periods (during which the system is asynchronous). As in [1], we consider an abstraction on top of the system model, namely a round model, defined next. Using this abstraction rather than the raw system model improves the clarity of the algorithms and simplifies the proofs.

Among the n processes in our system, we assume that at most t are Byzantine. We do not make any assumption about behavior of Byzantine processes. The set of correct processes is denoted by $\mathcal{C}$.

3.1   Basic Round Model

In each round r, a process p sends a message according to a sending function S_p^r to a subset of processes, and, at the end of this round, computes a new state according to a transition function T_p^r, based on the vector of messages it received and its current state. Note that this implies that a message sent in round r can only be received in round r (rounds are *closed*). The state of process p in round

---

[4] The relay property of authenticated broadcast ensures that if a messages is received by a correct process in some round r', then it is received by all correct processes the latest in round $r' + 1$ in the synchronous case.

[5] The relation with "interactive consistency" [7], is explained in Section 1.

r is denoted by s_p^r; the message sent by a correct[6] process is denoted by $S_p^r(s_p^r)$; messages received by process p in round r are denoted by μ_p^r.

In every round of the basic round model, if a correct process sends v, then every correct process receives v or nothing. This can formally be expressed by the following predicate ($\bot$ represents no message reception):

$$\mathcal{P}_{int}(r) \equiv \forall p, q \in \mathcal{C} : (\mu_p^r[q] = S_q^r(s_q^r)) \vee (\mu_p^r[q] = \bot)$$

3.2   Characterizing a Good Period

During a bad period, except $\mathcal{P}_{int}$, no guarantees on the messages a process receives can be provided: it can even happen that no messages at all are received. During a good period it is possible to ensure, for all rounds r in the good period, that all messages sent in round r by a correct process are received in round r by all correct processes. This is formally expressed by the following predicate:

$$\mathcal{P}_{good}(r) \equiv \forall p, q \in \mathcal{C} : \ \mu_p^r[q] = S_q^r(s_q^r)$$

The reader can find in [1] the implementation of rounds that satisfy $\mathcal{P}_{good}$ during a good period in the presence of Byzantine processes.

3.3   WIC Predicate

We have informally defined WIC by an integrity property and by a consistency property that must hold "eventually". The integrity property is expressed by the predicate $\mathcal{P}_{int}$. "Eventual" consistency formally means that there exists a round r in which consistency holds:

$$\mathcal{P}_{cons}(r) \equiv \forall p, q \in \mathcal{C} : \ (\mu_p^r[q] = S_q^r(s_q^r)) \ \wedge \ (\mu_p^r = \mu_q^r)$$

Therefore, WIC is formally expressed by the following predicate:

$$\boxed{\forall r : \mathcal{P}_{int}(r) \wedge \exists r : \mathcal{P}_{cons}(r)}$$

Note that $\mathcal{P}_{cons}(r)$ is stronger than $\mathcal{P}_{good}(r)$. Consider two correct processes p and q, and a Byzantine process sending message m to all processes in round r: $\mathcal{P}_{good}(r)$ allows m to be received by p and not by q; $\mathcal{P}_{cons}(r)$ does not allow this.

4   Implementing WIC

For implementing WIC, we show in this section that rounds that satisfy $\mathcal{P}_{good}$ can be transformed into a round that satisfies $\mathcal{P}_{cons}$. This transformation can be formally expressed thanks to the notion of *predicate translation*. Given some round r, we say that an algorithm A is a k-round translation of predicate $\mathcal{P}$ (*e.g.*, $\mathcal{P}_{good}$) into predicate $\mathcal{P}'$ (*e.g.*, $\mathcal{P}_{cons}$), if round r consists of k micro-rounds $\langle r, 1 \rangle$

---

[6] Note that referring to the state of a faulty process does not make sense.

Algorithm 1. Translation with signatures

```
1: Initialization:                              9: Round ρ = ⟨r, 2⟩ :
2:    ∀q ∈ Π : received_p[q] ← ⊥               10:    S_p^ρ:
                                                11:       if p = coord(r) then
3: Round ρ = ⟨r, 1⟩ :                           12:          send received_p to all
4:    S_p^ρ:                                     13:    T_p^ρ:
5:       send σ_p(m_p, r) to coord(r)           14:       for all q ∈ Π do
6:    T_p^ρ:                                     15:          M_p[q] ← ⊥
7:       if p = coord(r) then                   16:          if signature of μ_p^ρ[coord(r)][q] is valid then
8:          received_p ← μ_p^ρ                  17:             (msg, round) ← σ^{-1}(μ_p^ρ[coord(r)][q])
                                                18:             if round = r then
                                                19:                M_p[q] ← msg
```

to $\langle r, k \rangle$ such that: (i) $\mathcal{P}$ holds for each micro-round $\langle r, i \rangle$, $i \in [1, k]$; (ii) each process p execute A in each round $\langle r, i \rangle$, $i \in [1, k]$; (iii) for each process p, the message m_p sent by p in micro-round $\langle r, 1 \rangle$ is the message sent by p in round r; (iv) for each process p, the messages received by p in round r are computed by p at the end of micro-round $\langle r, k \rangle$; and (v) $\mathcal{P}'$ holds for round r. We also say that round r is *simulated* by the k micro-rounds $\langle r, 1 \rangle$ to $\langle r, k \rangle$.

We give two translations, one with and one without digital signatures. Both translations rely on a coordinator. The translation with signatures requires two micro-rounds with the communication pattern of Fig. 1(a) whereas the translation without signatures requires three micro-rounds with the communication pattern of Fig. 1(b)[7]. The coordinator of round r is denoted by $coord(r)$.

We will analyze the two translations in the following cases: (i) $coord(r)$ is correct and the micro-rounds satisfy $\mathcal{P}_{good}$, and (ii) $coord(r)$ may be faulty and only $\mathcal{P}_{int}$ holds for the micro-rounds. In case (i), we have a translation of $\mathcal{P}_{good}$ into $\mathcal{P}_{cons}$. Case (ii) ensures that the translation is harmless during bad periods, or if the coordinator is faulty.

Therefore, the big picture is the following. If we assume a sufficient long good period, then [1] shows how to implement rounds for which $\mathcal{P}_{good}$ eventually holds. Moreover, the rotating coordinator paradigm eventually ensures rounds with a correct coordinator. Together, this eventually ensures case (i).

4.1   Translation with Signatures

Algorithm 1 is a 2-round translation with signatures that preserves $\mathcal{P}_{int}$ (*i.e.*, if $\mathcal{P}_{int}$ holds for every micro-round, then $\mathcal{P}_{int}$ holds for the round). Moreover, when $coord(r)$ is correct, it translates $\mathcal{P}_{good}$ into $\mathcal{P}_{cons}$. At the beginning of Algorithm 1 every process p has a message m_p (line 5); at the end every process p has a vector $\boldsymbol{M}_p$ of received messages (lines 15, 19)[8]. Vector $received_p$ (line 8) represents the messages that p received (one element per process). Message m signed by p is denoted by $\sigma_p(m)$. The function σ^{-1} allows us to get back the original message out of a signed message.

---

[7] In Section 2 we used terms super-round and round. From here on, we use term *round* for what we called *super-round* and *micro-round* for what we called *round*.

[8] When round r is simulated using Algorithm 1, m_p is initially set to the $S_p^r(s_p^r)$ and in the end $\boldsymbol{\mu}_p^r$ is set to $\boldsymbol{M}_p$.

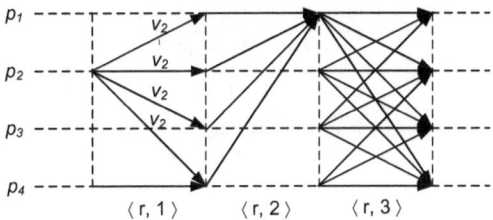

Fig. 2. Translation without signatures from the point of view of v_2 sent by p_2 (p_1 is the coordinator)

Algorithm 1 is straightforward: each process p sends its signed message m_p to the coordinator (line 5) in micro-round $\langle r, 1 \rangle$. In micro-round $\langle r, 2 \rangle$, the coordinator forwards all messages received (line 12).

Proposition 1. *Algorithm 1 preserves $\mathcal{P}_{int}(r)$.*

Proposition 2. *If $coord(r)$ is correct, then Algorithm 1 translates $\mathcal{P}_{good}$ into $\mathcal{P}_{cons}$.*

4.2   Translation without Signatures

Algorithm 2 is a 3-round translation with signatures, inspired by [8], that preserves $\mathcal{P}_{int}$ (*i.e.*, if $\mathcal{P}_{int}$ holds for every micro-round, then $\mathcal{P}_{int}$ holds for the round). Moreover, when $coord(r)$ is correct, it translates $\mathcal{P}_{good}$ into $\mathcal{P}_{cons}$. It requires $n \geq 3t + 1$. At the beginning of Algorithm 2 every process p has a message m_p (line 7); at the end every process p has a vector M_p of received messages (lines 22, 24)[9].

We informally explain Algorithm 2 using Fig. 2 Compared to Fig. 1(b), Fig. 2 shows only the messages relevant to v_2 sent by p_2. Process p_1 is the coordinator. In micro-round $\langle r, 1 \rangle$, process p_2 sends v_2 to all. In micro-round $\langle r, 2 \rangle$, all processes send the value received from p_2 to the coordinator. The coordinator then compares the value received from p_2 in micro-round $\langle r, 1 \rangle$, say v_2, with the value indirectly received from the other processes. If at least $2t + 1$ values v_2 have been received by the coordinator p_1, then p_1 keeps v_2 as the value received from p_2. Otherwise p_1 sets the value received from p_2 to $\bot$. This guarantees that, if p_1 keeps v_2, then at least $t + 1$ correct processes have received v_2 from p_2 in micro-round $\langle r, 1 \rangle$.

Finally, in micro-round $\langle r, 3 \rangle$ every process sends the value received from p_2 in micro-round $\langle r, 1 \rangle$ to all. The final value received from p_2 at the end of micro-round $\langle r, 3 \rangle$ is computed as follows at each process p_i. Let val_i be the value received by p_i from coordinator p_1 in micro-round $\langle r, 3 \rangle$. If val_i is $\bot$ then p_i receives $\bot$ from p_2. Process p_i receives $\bot$ from p_2 in another case: if p_i did not

---

[9] When round r is simulated using Algorithm 2, m_p is initially set to the $S_p^r(s_p^r)$ and in the end μ_p^r is set to M_p.

Algorithm 2. Translation without signatures ($n \geq 3t + 1$)

1: **Initialization:**
2:     $\forall q \in \Pi : received_p[q] \leftarrow \perp$

3: **Round** $\rho = \langle r, 1 \rangle :$
4:     $S_p^\rho:$
5:         send m_p to all
6:     $T_p^\rho:$
7:         $received_p \leftarrow \boldsymbol{\mu}_p^\rho$

8: **Round** $\rho = \langle r, 2 \rangle :$
9:     $S_p^\rho:$
10:        send $received_p$ to $coord(r)$
11:    $T_p^\rho:$
12:        **if** $p = coord(r)$ **then**
13:            **for all** $q \in \Pi$ **do**
14:
$$\textbf{if } \left| \left\{ q' \in \Pi : \boldsymbol{\mu}_p^\rho[q'][q] = received_p[q] \right\} \right| < 2t + 1 \textbf{ then}$$

15:                $received_p[q] \leftarrow \perp$

16: **Round** $\rho = \langle r, 3 \rangle :$
17:    $S_p^\rho:$
18:        send $\langle received_p \rangle$ to all
19:    $T_p^\rho:$
20:        **for all** $q \in \Pi$ **do**
21:            **if** $(\boldsymbol{\mu}_p^\rho[coord(r)][q] \neq \perp) \wedge$
$$\left| \left\{ i \in \Pi : \boldsymbol{\mu}_p^\rho[i][q] = \boldsymbol{\mu}_p^\rho[coord(r)][q] \right\} \right| \geq t + 1$$
            then
22:                $\boldsymbol{M}_p[q] \leftarrow \boldsymbol{\mu}_p^\rho[coord(r)][q]$
23:            **else**
24:                $\boldsymbol{M}_p[q] \leftarrow \perp$

---

receive $t + 1$ values equal to val_i in micro-round $\langle r, 3 \rangle$. Otherwise, at least $t + 1$ values received by p_i in micro-round $\langle r, 3 \rangle$ are equal to val_i, and p_i receives val_i from p_2.

Proposition 3. *Algorithm 2 preserves* $\mathcal{P}_{int}(r)$.

Proof. Let p, q be two correct processes. Assume for the sake of contradiction that $S_p^r(s_p^r) = v$, $\boldsymbol{M}_q[p] = v'$, where $v' \neq v$, $v' \neq \perp$. Therefore, by line 21, we have $\left| \{ i : \boldsymbol{\mu}_q^\rho[i][p] = v' \} \right| \geq t + 1$. Consequently, for at least one correct process c we have $\boldsymbol{\mu}_q^\rho[c][p] = v'$. Element $\boldsymbol{\mu}_q^\rho[c][p]$ is the message received by c from p in round $\langle r, 1 \rangle$, which is $received_c[p]$. However, $received_c[p] = v'$ is in contradiction with the assumption that p and c are correct. $\qquad \square$

Proposition 4. *If* $coord(r)$ *is correct, then Algorithm 2 translates* $\mathcal{P}_{good}$ *into* $\mathcal{P}_{cons}$.

Proof. Let p, q be two correct processes, and s some other process (not necessarily correct). Let c be the correct coordinator. Let $\mathcal{P}_{good}(\langle r, 1 \rangle)$, $\mathcal{P}_{good}(\langle r, 2 \rangle)$ and $\mathcal{P}_{good}(\langle r, 3 \rangle)$ hold. We first show (i) $\boldsymbol{M}_p[q] = S_q^r(s_q^r)$, and then (ii) $(\boldsymbol{M}_p[s] = v \neq \perp) \Rightarrow (\boldsymbol{M}_q[s] = v)$. Note that from (ii) it follows directly that $(\boldsymbol{M}_p[s] = \perp) \Rightarrow (\boldsymbol{M}_q[s] = \perp)$.

(i): In micro-round $\langle r, 1 \rangle$, process q sends $v = S_q^r(s_q^r)$ to all, and because of $\mathcal{P}_{good}(\langle r, 1 \rangle)$, v is received by all correct processes. For all those correct processes i, we have $received_i[q] = v$ (*). In micro-round $\langle r, 2 \rangle$, every correct process forwards v to the coordinator c, and c receives all these messages. Since $n \geq 3t + 1$ there are at least $2t + 1$ correct processes. Therefore the condition of line 14 is false for q because $|\{ q' \in \Pi : \boldsymbol{\mu}_c^\rho[q'][q] = received_c[q] \}| \geq 2t + 1$, i.e., $received_c[q]$ is not set to $\perp$. By (*) above, we have $received_c[q] = v$. Because of $\mathcal{P}_{good}(\langle r, 3 \rangle)$ all messages sent by correct processes in micro-round $\langle r, 3 \rangle$ are received by all correct processes. Thus, for p at line 21, we have $\boldsymbol{\mu}_p^\rho[coord(r)][q] \neq \perp$. Moreover, by (*), condition $\left|\left\{i \in \Pi : \boldsymbol{\mu}_p^\rho[i][q] = \boldsymbol{\mu}_p^\rho[coord(r)][q]\right\}\right| \geq t+1$ is true. This leads p to execute line 22, *i.e.*, assign v to $\boldsymbol{M}_p[q]$.

(ii): Let us assume $\boldsymbol{M}_p[s] = v \neq \bot$, and consider Algorithm 2 from the point of view of p. Consider the loop at line 20 for process s. By line 22, we have $\boldsymbol{\mu}_p^\rho[coord(r)][s] = v$. Since the coordinator is correct, in order to have $\boldsymbol{\mu}_p^\rho[coord(r)][s] = v$, the condition of line 14 is true at c for process s, *i.e.*, $\left|\left\{q' \in \Pi : \boldsymbol{\mu}_c^\rho[q'][s] = received_c[s]\right\}\right| \geq 2t+1$. This means that at least $2t+1$ processes, including at least $t+1$ correct processes, have received from s in micro-round $\langle r, 1 \rangle$ the same message that c received from s, namely v $(\star)$. In micro-round $\langle r, 3 \rangle$, these $t+1$ correct processes send *received* to all. Because $\mathcal{P}_{good}(\langle r, 3 \rangle)$ holds, all these messages are received by q in round $\langle r, 3 \rangle$ $(\star\star)$. Consider now Algorithm 2 from the point of view of q, and again the loop at line 20 for process s. Since the coordinator is correct, it sends at line 18 the same message to p and to q, *i.e.*, at q we also have $\boldsymbol{\mu}_q^\rho[coord(r)][s] = v$. By $(\star)$ and $(\star\star)$, the condition $\left|\left\{i \in \Pi : \boldsymbol{\mu}_q^\rho[i][s] = \boldsymbol{\mu}_q^\rho[coord(r)][s]\right\}\right| \geq t+1$ is true. Therefore q executes line 22 with $\boldsymbol{\mu}_p^\rho[coord(r)][s] = v$. $\qquad\square$

5 Achieving Consensus with WIC

In this section we show how to express the consensus algorithms of Castro-Liskov [8] and Martin-Alivisi [4] using WIC. The algorithm of Castro and Lisko solves a sequence of instances of consensus (state machine replication). For simplicity, we consider only one instance of consensus.

Consensus is defined by agreement, termination and a validity property. We consider two validity properties, weak and strong validity [1]:

Agreement. No two correct processes decide differently.
Termination. All correct processes eventually decide.
Weak Validity. If all processes are correct and if a correct process decides v, then v is the initial value of some process.
Strong Validity. If all correct processes have the same initial value v and a correct process decides, then it decides v.

Both, [8] and [4] achieve only weak validity. Weak validity allows correct processes to decide on the initial value of a Byzantine process. With strong validity, however, this is only possible if not all correct processes have the same initial value. We give algorithms for both, weak and strong validity, and show that strong validity is in fact easy to ensure.

5.1 On the Use of WIC

We express the algorithms of this section in the round model defined in Section 3. All rounds of MA and CL require $\mathcal{P}_{int}$ to hold. Some of the rounds require $\mathcal{P}_{cons}$ to eventually hold. These rounds can be simulated using, *e.g.*, Algorithm 1 or Algorithm 2. We explicitly mention those rounds of MA and CL as rounds "in which $\mathcal{P}_{cons}$ must eventually hold". The other rounds of MA and CL are ordinary rounds.

Algorithm 3. MA (weak validity)

1: **Initialization:**	10: **Round** $r = 2$:
2: $x_p \leftarrow v_p \in V$	11: S_p^r:
	12: send x_p to all
3: **Round** $r = 1$:	13: T_p^r:
4: S_p^r:	14: **if** $\exists \bar{v} \neq \bot : \#(\bar{v}) \geq \lceil (n + 3t + 1)/2 \rceil$ **then**
5: **if** $p = coord$ **then**	15: DECIDE $\bar{v}$
6: send x_p to all	
7: T_p^r:	16: **Round** $r \geq 3$:
8: **if** $\mu_p^r[coord] \neq \bot$ **then**	17: Same as Algorithm 4 without **Initialization**
9: $x_p \leftarrow \mu_p^r[coord]$	

Algorithm 4. MA (strong validity)

1: **Initialization:**	10: **Round** $r = 2\phi$:
2: $x_p \leftarrow v_p \in V$	11: S_p^r:
	12: send x_p to all
3: **Round** $r = 2\phi - 1$:	13: T_p^r:
4: /* in which $\mathcal{P}_{cons}$ must eventually hold */	14: **if** $\exists \bar{v} \neq \bot : \#(\bar{v}) \geq \lceil (n + 3t + 1)/2 \rceil$
5: S_p^r:	**then**
6: send x_p to all	15: DECIDE $\bar{v}$
7: T_p^r:	
8: **if** $\#(\bot) \leq t$ **then**	
9: $x_p \leftarrow \min \{ v : \not\exists v' \in V \ s.t. \ \#(v') > \#(v) \}$	

5.2 MA Algorithm

The algorithm of Martin and Alvisi [4] is expressed in the context of "proposers", "acceptors" and "learners". For simplicity, we express here consensus without considering these roles.

We give two algorithms. The first solves consensus with weak validity and is given as Algorithm 3. In the first phase it corresponds to the "common case" protocol of [4]. All later phases correspond to the "recovery protocol" of [4] (cf. Algorithm 4). The second algorithm solves consensus with strong validity, and is even simpler: all phases are identical, see Algorithm 4. In both algorithms, the notation $\#(v)$ is used to denote the number of messages received with value v, i.e., $\#(v) \equiv \left| \{ q \in \Pi \ : \ \mu_p^r[q] = v \} \right|$.

For MA with weak validity, the first phase needs an initial coordinator, which is denoted by $coord$. Note that WIC is relevant only to rounds $2\phi - 1$, $\phi > 1$, of Algorithm 4. If rounds $2\phi - 1$ are simulated using Algorithm 1, we get the original algorithm of [4]. If rounds $2\phi - 1$ are simulated using Algorithm 2, we get a new algorithm. In this new algorithm, similarly to the algorithm in [4], fast decision is possible in two rounds; however, signatures are not used in the recovery protocol.

Both algorithms require $n \geq 5t+1$. Agreement, weak validity and strong validity hold without synchrony assumptions. Termination requires (i) one phase ϕ such that $\mathcal{P}_{cons}(2\phi - 1)$ holds, and (ii) one phase $\phi' \geq \phi$ such that $\mathcal{P}_{good}(2\phi')$ holds.

Theorem 1. *If $n \geq 5t + 1$ then Algorithm 3 (resp. Algorithm 4) ensures weak (resp. strong) validity and agreement. Termination holds if in addition the following condition holds:*

$$\exists \phi : \ \mathcal{P}_{cons}(2\phi - 1) \wedge \exists \phi' \geq \phi : \ \mathcal{P}_{good}(2\phi')$$

Algorithm 5. CL (weak validity)

1: **Initialization:**	13: **Round** $r = 3\phi - 1 = 2$:
2: $x_p \leftarrow v_p \in V$	14: S_p^r:
3: $pre\text{-}vote_p \leftarrow \emptyset$ /* see Algorithm 6 */	15: **if** $\exists (v, \phi) \in pre\text{-}vote_p$ **then**
4: $vote_p \leftarrow \bot$ /* see Algorithm 6 */	16: send $\langle v \rangle$ to all
5: $tVote_p \leftarrow 0$ /* see Algorithm 6 */	17: T_p^r:
	18: **if** $\#(v) \geq \lceil (n + t + 1)/2 \rceil$ **then**
6: **Round** $r = 3\phi - 2 = 1$:	19: $vote_p \leftarrow v$
7: S_p^r:	20: $tVote_p \leftarrow \phi$
8: **if** $p = coord$ **then**	
9: send $\langle x_p \rangle$ to all	21: **Round** $r = 3\phi = 3$:
10: T_p^r:	22: S_p^r:
11: **if** $\mu_p^r[coord] \neq \bot$ **then**	23: **if** $tVote_p = \phi$ **then**
12: add $(\mu_p^r[coord], \phi)$ to $pre\text{-}vote_p$	24: send $\langle vote_p \rangle$ to all
	25: T_p^r:
	26: **if** $\exists \bar{v} \neq \bot : \#(\bar{v}) \geq \lceil (n+t+1)/2 \rceil$ **then**
	27: DECIDE $\bar{v}$
	28: **Round** $r \geq 4$:
	29: Same as Algorithm 6 without **Initialization**

Note that $n \geq 5t + 1$ is only needed for terrmination, while only $n \geq 3t + 1$ is needed for agreement and strong validity.

5.3   CL Algorithm

The algorithm of Castro and Liskov [8] solves a sequence of instances of consensus (state machine replication). For simplicity, we consider only one instance of consensus. As for MA, we give two algorithms.

The first solves consensus with weak validity and is given as Algorithm 5. In the first phase it corresponds to the "common case" protocol of [8]. All later phases correspond to the "view change protocol" of [8] (cf. Algorithm 6). The second algorithm solves consensus with strong validity, and is even simpler: all phases are identical, see Algorithm 6. In both algorithms, the notation $\#(v)$ is used to denote the number of messages received with value v, i.e., $\#(v) \equiv \left| \{ q \in \Pi \ : \ \mu_p^r[q] = v \} \right|$.

For CL with weak validity, the first phase needs an initial coordinator, which is denoted by $coord$. In round 1 of this phase the coordinator sends its initial value to all. In round 2 every process that has received the initial value from the coordinator in round 1 resends this value to all. Every process p, upon receiving this value from at least $\lceil (n + t + 1)/2 \rceil$ processes, updates $vote_p$ and $tVote_p$ (lines 19 and 20), and then sends $vote_p$ to all in round 3. A process receiving in round at least $\lceil (n + t + 1)/2 \rceil$ messages with the same value v, decides v. For CL with weak validity, WIC is relevant only to rounds $3\phi - 2$, $\phi > 1$ (cf. Algorithm 6). If rounds $3\phi - 2$, $\phi > 1$ are simulated using Algorithm 2, we get an algorithm close to the original algorithm of [8] (the differences are explained in [9]). If rounds $3\phi - 2$, $\phi > 1$ are simulated using Algorithm 1, we get a variant of PBFT with signatures.

CL with strong validity (see Algorithm 6) consists of a sequence of phases ϕ, where each phase ϕ has three rounds $3\phi - 2$, $3\phi - 1$ and 3ϕ. The role of the variables is explained in comments, see lines 2–5. WIC is needed only in round $3\phi - 2$. Rounds $3\phi - 1$ and 3ϕ are the same as rounds 2 and 3 of Algorithm 5.

Algorithm 6. CL (strong validity)

```
1: Initialization:
2:    x_p ← v_p ∈ V                                          /* v_p is the initial value of p */
3:    pre-vote_p ← ∅      /* set of (v, φ), where φ is the phase in which v is added to pre-vote_p */
4:    vote_p ← ⊥                                                    /* the most recent vote */
5:    tVote_p ← 0                                    /* phase in which vote_p was last updated */

6: Procedure pre-vote_p.add(v, φ) :
7:    if ∃(v, φ') ∈ pre-vote_p then
8:        remove (v, φ') from pre-vote_p
9:    add (v, φ) to pre-vote_p

10: Round r = 3φ − 2 :                           /* round in which P_cons must eventually hold */
11:    S_p^r :
12:        send ⟨vote_p, tVote_p, pre-vote_p, x_p⟩ to all
13:    T_p^r :
14:        proposals_p ← ∅ ; I_p ← ∅                           /* temporary variables */
15:        if μ_p^r contains at least ⌈(n + t + 1)/2⌉ messages ⟨vote, tVote, pre-vote, x⟩ then
16:            for all m ∈ μ_p^r do
17:                if
                    |{m' ∈ μ_p^r : (m'.tVote < m.tVote) ∨ (m'.tVote = m.tVote ∧ m'.vote = m.vote)}| ≥
                    ⌈(n + t + 1)/2⌉ and
                    |{m' ∈ μ_p^r : ∃(v, φ') ∈ m'.pre-vote s.t. φ' ≥ m.tVote ∧ v = m.vote}| ≥ t + 1 then
18:                    proposals_p ← proposals_p ∪ m.vote
19:            if |proposals_p| > 0 then
20:                pre-vote_p.add(min(proposals_p), φ)
21:            else if exist at least ⌈(n + t + 1)/2⌉ messages m' ∈ μ_p^r : m'.vote = ⊥ then
22:                I_p ← {m.x s.t. m ∈ μ_p^r}
23:                x̄ ← min {v : ∄v' ∈ I_p s.t. #(v') > #(v)}
24:                pre-vote_p.add(x̄, φ)

25: Round r = 3φ − 1 :
26:    S_p^r :
27:        if ∃(v, φ) ∈ pre-vote_p then
28:            send ⟨v⟩ to all
29:    T_p^r :
30:        if #(v) ≥ ⌈(n + t + 1)/2⌉ then
31:            vote_p ← v
32:            tVote_p ← φ

33: Round r = 3φ :
34:    S_p^r :
35:        if tVote_p = φ then
36:            send ⟨vote_p⟩ to all
37:    T_p^r :
38:        if ∃v̄ ≠ ⊥ : #(v̄) ≥ ⌈(n + t + 1)/2⌉ then
39:            DECIDE v̄
```

Both algorithms (CL with weak validity and CL with strong validity) require $n \geq 3t+1$. Agreement, weak validity and strong validity hold without synchrony assumptions. Termination requires (i) one phase ϕ such that $\mathcal{P}_{cons}(3\phi - 2)$, $\mathcal{P}_{good}(3\phi - 1)$ and $\mathcal{P}_{good}(3\phi)$ hold.

Theorem 2. *If $n \geq 3t + 1$ then Algorithm 5 (resp. Algorithm 6) ensures weak (resp. strong) validity and agreement. Termination holds if in addition the following condition holds:*

$$\exists\phi : \ \mathcal{P}_{cons}(3\phi - 2) \wedge \mathcal{P}_{good}(3\phi - 1) \wedge \mathcal{P}_{good}(3\phi).$$

6   Related Work

Unification. To the best of our knowledge, there is little work that has tried to unify algorithms for Byzantine faults that use signatures and algorithms that do not use signatures. We are only aware of the work of Skrikanth and Toueg [3] related to *authenticated broadcast* (as already mentioned in Section 1). Further there is the work of Neiger and Toueg [10] who have developed methods to automatically translate protocols tolerant of benign faults to ones tolerant of more severe faults, including Byzantine faults, in the context of synchronous systems. Abstractions introduced by Lampson in [11] are relevant only to PBFT [8], and its hard to see how these abstractions can be extended to other Byzantine consensus protocols. Orthogonal to our approach, [12] proposes a solution for implementing digital signatures using MACs (message authentication codes).

Byzantine consensus algorithms. Several models with Byzantine faults have been considered for solving consensus or closely related problems, such as Byzantine agreement or state machine replication. The early work of Lamport, Shostak and Pease [7,2] considers a synchronous system and proposes algorithms for Interactive Consistency and Byzantine agreement with and without signatures. A weaker system model, namely partial synchrony, has been considered by Dwork, Lynch and Stockmeyer [1]. This is also the model we consider in this paper. In [1], the authors propose two consensus algorithms for Byzantine faults: one that uses signatures, and one without signatures. In [13], the authors consider a system with less synchrony than provided by partially synchrony, and describe a consensus algorithm that does not use signatures. Randomized consensus can be solved in an asynchronous system with Byzantine faults, as shown first in [14]. In [15], the authors solve consensus with Byzantine faults assuming a system equipped with a *Trusted Timely Computing Base* (TTCB).

Our CL algorithm is a simplified version of PBFT. Other authors have tried to increase the efficiency of PBFT, *e.g.* [16]. Recently, [17] has proposed a consensus algorithm for Byzantine faults that ensures strong validity, in which the decision is possible in the first round.

7   Conclusion

The paper has introduced the *weak interactive consistency* (or *WIC*) abstraction, and has shown that WIC allows to unify Byzantine consensus algorithms with and without signatures. This has been illustrated on two seminal Byzantine consensus algorithm, namely on the FaB Paxos algorithm [4] and on the PBFT algorithm [8]. In both cases this leads to a very concise algorithm. Apart from these two algorithms, we also managed to express two other algorithms for Byzantine faults using WIC: the algorithms for Byzantine faults of [1] and a deterministic version of the algorithm for Byzantine faults of [14], which is the basis for the algorithm in [13]. Therefore, we conjecture that WIC is the abstraction that underlines all Byzantine consensus algorithms for partial synchronous systems.

Acknowledgements. We would like to thank Nuno Santos for his comments on an earlier version of the paper.

References

1. Dwork, C., Lynch, N., Stockmeyer, L.: Consensus in the presence of partial synchrony. Journal of the ACM 35(2), 288–323 (1988)
2. Lamport, L., Shostak, R., Pease, M.: The byzantine generals problem. ACM Trans. Program. Lang. Syst. 4(3), 382–401 (1982)
3. Srikanth, T.K., Toueg, S.: Simulating authenticated broadcasts to derive simple fault-tolerant algorithms. Distributed Computing 2(2), 80–94 (1987)
4. Martin, J.P., Alvisi, L.: Fast byzantine consensus. Transactions on Dependable and Secure Computing 3(3), 202–214 (2006)
5. Lamport, L.: The weak byzantine generals problem. J. ACM 30(3), 668–676 (1983)
6. Doudou, A., Guerraoui, R., Garbinato, B.: Abstractions for devising byzantine-resilient state machine replication. In: SRDS (2000)
7. Pease, M., Shostak, R., Lamport, L.: Reaching agreement in the presence of faults. Journal of the ACM 27(2), 228–234 (1980)
8. Castro, M., Liskov, B.: Practical byzantine fault tolerance and proactive recovery. ACM Transactions on Computer Systems 20(4), 398–461 (2002)
9. Milosevic, Z., Hutle, M., Schiper, A.: Unifying byzantine consensus algorithms with weak interactive consistency (LSR-REPORT-2009-003)
10. Neiger, G., Toueg, S.: Automatically increasing the fault-tolerance of distributed algorithms. J. Algorithms 11(3), 374–419 (1990)
11. Lampson, B.: The abcd's of paxos. In: PODC, p. 13. ACM Press, New York (2001)
12. Aiyer, A.S., Alvisi, L., Bazzi, R.A., Clement, A.: Matrix signatures: From mACs to digital signatures in distributed systems. In: Taubenfeld, G. (ed.) DISC 2008. LNCS, vol. 5218, pp. 16–31. Springer, Heidelberg (2008)
13. Aguilera, M.K., Delporte-Gallet, C., Fauconnier, H., Toueg, S.: Consensus with byzantine failures and little system synchrony. In: DSN, pp. 147–155 (2006)
14. Ben-Or, M.: Another advantage of free choice: Completely asynchronous agreement protocols. In: PODC, pp. 27–29. ACM, New York (1983)
15. Correia, M., Neves, N.F., Lung, L.C., Veríssimo, P.: Low complexity byzantine-resilient consensus. Distributed Computing 17(3) (2005)
16. Kotla, R., Alvisi, L., Dahlin, M., Clement, A., Wong, E.L.: Zyzzyva: speculative byzantine fault tolerance. In: SOSP, pp. 45–58 (2007)
17. Song, Y.J., van Renesse, R.: Bosco: One-step byzantine asynchronous consensus. In: Taubenfeld, G. (ed.) DISC 2008. LNCS, vol. 5218, pp. 438–450. Springer, Heidelberg (2008)

Safe AND Eventually Safe: Comparing Self-stabilizing and Non-stabilizing Algorithms on a Common Ground

(Extended Abstract)

Sylvie Delaët[1], Shlomi Dolev[2,*], and Olivier Peres[2,**]

[1] Univ Paris Sud; LRI; CNRS; Orsay F-91405
sylvie.delaet@lri.fr
[2] Department of Computer Science, Ben-Gurion University of the Negev
dolev@cs.bgu.ac.il, olivier@bgu.ac.il

Abstract. Self-stabilizing systems can be started in any arbitrary state and converge to exhibit the desired behavior. However, self-stabilizing systems can be started in predefined initial states, in the same way as non-stabilizing systems. In this case, a self-stabilizing system can mask faults just like any other distributed system. Moreover, whenever faults overwhelm the systems beyond their capabilities to mask faults, the stabilizing system recovers to exhibit eventual safety and liveness, while the behavior of non-stabilizing systems is undefined and may well remain totally and permanently undesired. We demonstrate the importance of defining the initial state of a self-stabilizing system in a specific case of distributed reset over a system composed of several layers of self-stabilizing algorithms. A self-stabilizing stabilization detector ensures that, at first, only the very first layer(s) takes action, and that then higher levels are activated, ensuring smooth restarts, while preserving the stabilization property. The safety of initialized self-stabilizing systems, combined with their better ability to regain safety and liveness following severe conditions, is then demonstrated over the classical fault masking modular redundancy architecture.

Keywords: self-stabilization, safety.

1 Introduction

A distributed algorithm operates in a system consisting of several processes in order to perform a given task. For example, the mutual exclusion task is defined by a set of infinite executions in which at most one process executes the critical section in any configuration, and every process executes the critical section

---

* Partially supported by the ICT Programme of the European Union under contract number ICT-2008-215270, US Air Force, and Rita Altura chair in computer science.
** Partially supported by the ICT Programme of the European Union under contract number ICT-2008-215270.

T. Abdelzaher, M. Raynal, and N. Santoro (Eds.): OPODIS 2009, LNCS 5923, pp. 315–329, 2009.

infinitely often. A *self-stabilizing* algorithm [10,11] has an additional property: it guarantees to eventually execute its task, by reaching a *legitimate configuration*, regardless of the state in which the processes and communication links are started. Self-stabilization can thus be used to overcome any set of transient failures, e.g. arbitrary memory corruptions due to single upset events [21] caused by cosmic rays, or hardware malfunction in abnormal conditions, e.g. excessive heat. Some algorithms are supposed to remain safe at all times while they carry out their task. For example, the part of the mutual exclusion task definition stating that no two processes may access the critical section simultaneously is a safety property. Safety, however, is impossible when very high levels of failures overwhelm the system, e.g., when more than a third of the processes are Byzantine, or in extreme cases, when, say, all the processes disappear.

The fact that self-stabilizing systems have the added ability to regain consistency when started in an arbitrary configuration indicates that the designers of self-stabilizing algorithms consider all configurations, including those where safety does not hold. Clearly, all configurations are not safe. However, a self-stabilizing algorithm can be initialized, just like any distributed algorithm, in an initial configuration. In this case, it can provide safety during its execution. If the system is initialized in any other configuration, it converges, without safety, to a legitimate configuration, which is already an improvement over non-stabilizing sytems.

It is clear that in a self-stabilizing system, all starting configurations are not equally desirable. Likewise, not all illegitimate configurations are equally bad: some of them are close to a legitimate configuration, i.e. they only require a few steps of the algorithm to reach legitimacy, while others are much farther away. Therefore, each self-stabilizing algorithm should have a set of initial configurations. These configurations must be safe, which adds the requirement of proving *initial safety*.

This ensures that when the system is started in an initial configuration, there is no need to overcome any problem stemming from the starting configuration. Thus, safety is guaranteed throughout the execution, and eventually a legitimate configuration is attained.

However, initial configurations are not intended to provide a direct solution to the task. Rather than encoding a complete solution like a legitimate configuration, an initial configuration should not contain any wrong information. For example, an initial configuration for an algorithm that builds a breadth-first-search (BFS) tree should not itself describe a BFS tree. A good initial configuration would be one where every process has no parent and no child.

It is typically possible to reset the system into an initial configuration by having all the processes write predefined default values into their local variables, without requiring remote information. In conjunction with a self-stabilizing reset algorithm that resets layered algorithms, e.g. mutual exclusion algorithms using the output of a spanning tree algorithm [13], the use of initialized stabilization detectors allows fast and safe convergence.

In a nutshell, we suggest that each self-stabilizing algorithm should have a set of initial configurations from which it converges smoothly and safely. Being self-stabilizing, the system will however converge from any configuration at all. Initializing the system is thus good, but not mandatory.

Related Works

Reset. The goal of a *distributed reset algorithm* [2] is to place the whole system in a predefined configuration. Combined with the ability to detect that some unwanted property holds [1,5,17,18], this enables resetting the system to a configuration that begins a recovery operation. Some self-stabilizing reset algorithms have been proposed [2,3,8]. They optimize the time complexity [8] and/or the space complexity [3].

Safety and liveness. The classical tool for reasoning about a distributed system is temporal logic, which considers separately two types of properties: safety and liveness. A safety property states that some bad event never happens. For example, in the *mutual exclusion* problem specification, it is guaranteed that no two processes access a critical section at the same time. A liveness property states that some good event will happen, no matter how the execution proceeds, e.g. all the processes access the critical section infinitely often.

Self-stabilizing algorithms are designed to be able to reach a legitimate configuration when started in any configuration. Thus, liveness properties, being eventual properties, hold. Safety properties, on the other hand, need a closer examination.

Safety of self-stabilizing systems. The design of safe self-stabilizing systems was studied by Ghosh and Bejean [15]. They presented a framework that not only captures the fact that a self-stabilizing system has safety properties, but also expresses how safe it is, in terms of a discrete metric and a *safety margin*. The framework was later extended by Bejean, Ghosh and Rao [6] to allow for more realistic continuous metrics. This framework is related to the safety of legitimate configurations, rather than on the definition of initial configurations and the initial safety of self-stabilizing algorithms.

Gouda, Cobb and Huang introduced tri-redundant systems [16], in which variables are replicated and whenever a process requests to read the value of a variable, the majority value among the replicas is returned. This helps building safe systems assuming faults occur during the execution, rather than before its beginning, as we assume.

In the context of snap-stabilization, Cournier, Datta, Petit and Villain introduced, in [7], a notion similar to that of initial configurations. Even then, initial configurations can improve the system, especially if another algorithm uses its output. Also, not all algorithms can be made snap-stabilizing, and we show in this paper that some existing self-stabilizing algorithms can exhibit safety properties without any modification; e.g. we show in this paper a routing table algorithm that, started in a configuration where all the tables are empty, is safe.

System Settings

We define an algorithm as a set of variables and a set of actions. A *process* is a state machine resulting from a given algorithm. A *system* is a set of processes linked by a communication medium. A *configuration* is the collection of the states of all the processes of a system and the state of the communication medium.

A *step* is a state transition of one of the processes, including communication actions through the communication medium attached to the process. It takes a process in some state and leaves it in a new state according to the state transition of the automaton representing the process, executing the relevant communication operations with neighboring processes.

An *execution* $(c_0, a_0, c_1, \ldots, c_i, a_i, c_{i+1}, \ldots)$ is an infinite alternate sequence of configurations and actions in a system such that for all $i \in \mathbb{N}$, c_i is a configuration and a_i is a step that takes the system in configuration c_i and leaves it in configuration c_{i+1}. We only consider *fair* execution, in which any step which can be taken an infinite number of times is taken at some point.

A *prefix* of an execution $(c_0, a_0, c_1, \ldots, c_k, a_k)$ for some $k \in \mathbb{N}$ is the first k configurations and atomic steps of the execution. A *suffix* of an execution for some $k \in \mathbb{N}$ is the infinite alternate sequence of configurations and atomic steps $(c_k, a_k, c_{k+1}, a_{k+1}, \ldots)$ that follows a prefix of the execution for k. A suffix of an execution is thus itself an execution.

Let P be a predicate on the configurations of a system S and $\mathcal{E}$ be an execution of S. We say that P is *eventually* true in $\mathcal{E}$ if and only if there exists a suffix $\mathcal{E}'$ of $\mathcal{E}$ such that P holds in all configurations of $\mathcal{E}'$.

Basic properties. In this paper, we focus on the safety of self-stabilizing systems, defined as follows.

Safety property. A *safety* property for a given system is a predicate on executions that holds on all the executions of that system.

The other kind of property generally used in proving the correction of distributed algorithms is *liveness*.

Liveness property. A *liveness* property on a given system is a predicate on executions verified over any suffix of an execution of that system.

In the context of self-stabilization, since the starting configuration is generally arbitrary, safety can typically only be guaranteed in a suffix of the execution.

Eventual safety property. An *eventual safety* property for a given system is a safety property for some suffix of any execution of that system.

Since, in this paper, the set of initial configurations of every algorithm is known, we can be more specific.

Initial safety property. An *initial safety* property for a given system is a safety property for all the executions starting from an initial configuration of the system.

Self-stabilization. Given a set $\mathcal{I}$ of initial configurations and an initial safety property P, an algorithm is self-stabilizing to a set $\mathcal{L}$ of *legitimate configurations* if and only if it satisfies the following requirements:

- *initial safety*: for every execution $\mathcal{E}$ that starts in $c \in \mathcal{I}$, $P(\mathcal{E})$ is true,
- *convergence*: the execution of the algorithm, started in any configuration, eventually leads to a configuration in $\mathcal{L}$,
- *closure*: the execution of any step of the algorithm from any $c \in \mathcal{L}$ yields a configuration $c' \in \mathcal{L}$.

In the rest of this paper, several kinds of failures can take place during executions.

Stopping failure. A *stopping failure*, or a *crash*, happens when a process stops taking steps. Depending on the context, the process can be allowed to *restart*, i.e. resume taking steps, or not.

Transient failure. A *transient failure* is an arbitrary modification of a configuration. It can affect either one or several processes, or the communication medium, causing them to be set to an arbitrary state from their state space.

As a convention, we do not allow an execution to contain transient failures, but consider that the starting configuration of any execution occurs after the last transient failure. Self-stabilizing algorithms are expected to converge to a legitimate configuration regardless of their starting configuration, which effectively captures all possible transient failures or sequences thereof.

The rest of this extended abstract is organized as follows. In Section 2, we give a formal framework for analyzing self-stabilizing algorithms with reference to their starting configurations, using the Update protocol as an example. This framework helps understanding the self-stabilizing stabilization detectors which we introduce in Section 3. Composed with self-stabilizing algorithms started in initial configurations, they assist in obtaining smooth restarts. Section 4 is devoted to the modular redundancy case study: how a self-stabilizing algorithm designed with initial safety in mind provides more safety than an ordinary redundant system, especially in the presence of unexpectedly severe failures. We conclude our paper in Section 5. Some details are omitted from this extended abstract[1].

2   Initial, Reacheable, Legitimate, Corrupted Configurations

We introduce a framework that assigns a *weight* to each process and each configuration of an *information gathering algorithm*. Typical routing and census algorithms are in this category. We extend the definition given by Delaët and Tixeuil for their census algorithm [9] as follows.

The weight of a process is *zero* if the process has gathered all the information it can obtain, *one* if the information it has is *reacheable*, i.e. partial but correct, *two*

---

[1] See BGU Technical Report #0905 2009.

otherwise. Roughly speaking, since, in the algorithms that we consider, processes do not delete complete correct information or accept any wrong information, the weight of each process can only decrease monotonically toward *zero*.

The weight of a configuration is a string of all the weights of the processes in decreasing order (first *twos*, then *zeros*, then *ones*). A string of *zeros* denotes a legitimate configuration. A string of *ones* and *zeros* denotes a configuration that does not contain any wrong information. Any weight containing a *two* denotes a configuration reached by a transient failure and therefore may violate the *initial safety* requirement.

The fact that the weight of a process can never increase in these algorithms, combined with the convergence property of self-stabilizing processes which forces that weight to eventually decrease, assists in proving the correctness of the algorithm. The weight also helps in characterizing convergence by comparing the strings. For two strings on a given number of processes, the string that has the greatest number of *twos* is heavier. If both strings have the same number of *twos*, then the string that has the greater number of *ones* is heavier. Thus, a higher weight directly denotes a configuration that is farther from a legitimate configuration.

We now discuss how this definition applies to fixed output self-stabilizing algorithms. Non-fixed output algorithms essentially benefit from initial configurations when they are *composed* with fixed output algorithms, as shown in Section 3.

A fixed output algorithm carries out a calculation and produces one result. For example, a self-stabilizing spanning tree algorithm eventually leaves the system in a configuration where the variables that encode the topology describe a spanning tree. Then, this topology does not change anymore in the rest of the execution.

Some fixed output algorithms work by accumulating information. For example, in a census algorithm, each process gradually learns new process identifiers until it knows them all. On the other hand, the algorithm has to make sure that if a process knows an identifier that does not exist, then this identifier is eventually removed.

In this context, an initial configuration should be a minimum-information configuration. In a census algorithm, an initial configuration is one where each process knows no other process, except itself. Similarly, in an initial configuration, no process has chosen a new name in a renaming algorithm or a color in a coloring algorithm, no process is part of the topology or the particular set being built in a graph algorithm.

The fact that initial configurations put a fixed output algorithm $\mathcal{A}$ in the beginning of an execution where it will not acquire false information means that an algorithm using the output of $\mathcal{A}$ will not make wrong moves. It thus brings additional safety to the system. Resetting a system to an initial configuration may thus be appropriate in situations where the system as a whole should behave conservatively, i.e. when mistakes have a high cost.

C1	$A, B := \emptyset, \emptyset$
C2	**forall** $q \in N_p$ **do** read(q); $A := A \cup e_q$ **od**
C3	$A := A \setminus\setminus \langle p, *, * \rangle$; $A := A{++}\langle *, *, 1 \rangle$
C4	**forall** $q \in$ processors(A) **do** $B := B \cup \{\text{mindist}(q, A)\}$ **od**
C5	$B := B \cup \{\langle p, x_p, 0 \rangle\}$; $e_p := \text{initseq}(B)$
C6	write

Fig. 1. Update Protocol for Process p

The Update Protocol Example

To show in details how initial configurations facilitate convergence, we now consider Dolev and Herman's *update protocol* [12], a minimum distance vector algorithm for asynchronous shared register systems, given in Figure 1. In this algorithm, each process p maintains a routing table e_p that contains, at most, one entry per process in the system. An entry consists of a process identifier, an originator process identifier and an integer distance. Each process periodically scans its neighbors' routing tables, merges them all in a set A, and extracts from A the shortest path to each process in A, which yields p's new routing table.

We define the set $\mathcal{I}$ of initial configurations for this algorithm as the configurations where all the processes have an empty routing table. This is consistent with the definition of an initial configuration: a process can easily delete its routing table when a reset occurs. It is also clear that an empty routing table does not contain any wrong information.

Throughout any execution started in a configuration of $\mathcal{I}$, entries are added to the routing tables in a way that preserves the following invariants:
($i1$) Only valid information is obtained: if the routing table of process p contains $\langle q, x_q, d \rangle$ then there is at least one path from p to q, and there is a path from p to q whose first component is x_q and whose length is d.
($i2$) The information remains transitively distributed: if the routing table of process p contains $\langle q, x_q, d \rangle$ with $d > 1$, then there exists a neighbor r of p such that the routing table of r contains $\langle q, x_q, d' \rangle, d' > d$.

Closure and convergence of the Update algorithm have already been proven [12]. In Theorem 1, we prove its initial safety, i.e. that the system never acquires wrong information. The proof is omitted from this extended abstract (and can be found in BGU Technical Report #0905 2009).

Theorem 1. *Let Σ be a system started in an initial configuration. In any failure-free execution, all the routing table entries preserve invariants (i1) and (i2).*

3   Detecting Stabilization

Initial configurations can also be used to design *self-stabilizing stabilization detectors*. Such a detector provides a boolean output over an algorithm $\mathcal{A}$ to estimate whether $\mathcal{A}$ is in a legitimate configuration. When the system is started in an arbitrary configuration, this detector typically can output wrong answers for an unknown number of steps before eventually giving the right answer forever. We show in this section that starting the system in an initial configuration allows to overcome this drawback and obtain a stabilization detector that outputs *false* as long as the system has not converged and eventually outputs *true* forever when the system has converged. In other words, if the system is started in an initial configuration, the detector is reliable, thereby increasing the safety of the system.

In many self-stabilizing algorithms, the state of each process progresses until it becomes *canonical*, as described by Delaët and Tixeuil [9], such that the system is in a safe configuration when all the processes are in a canonical state. This property was used, for example, by Dolev and Tzachar [14] to design a method that, with certain assumptions, transforms probabilistic self-stabilizing algorithms that use an infinite number of random bits so that they use a bounded number of random bits. Our stabilization detector is built on the same grounds.

Fair Composition

Let A be a self-stabilizing algorithm, let B be an algorithm that has a read-only access to the variables of A such that if A is self-stabilizing, then B is self-stabilizing. Then, as shown by Dolev, Israeli and Moran [13], the *fair composition* $A \oplus B$ obtained by the concatenation of the code and variables of A and B is a self-stabilizing algorithm. This property is useful for writing modular algorithms and reusing previously written code.

Recall that a configuration has weight 0 if it is legitimate, 1 if it only contains correct information, 2 otherwise. This definition can be extended to composed self-stabilizing algorithms. Intuitively, it is easy to see that a global legitimate configuration requires all the composed systems to be in a legitimate configuration. Similarly, the global system contains only correct information if and only if each individual system only contains correct information.

Formally, let $P = \oplus_{i \in [\![1,m]\!]} P_i$. A configuration c of P is an initial configuration if and only if in c, for all i, P_i is in an initial configuration. The weight of a configuration c of P is a vector of w_j such that for each j, $w_j(P) = \max_{i \in [\![1,m]\!]} w_j(P_i)$.

Self-stabilizing Stabilization Detector

We assume that processes acquire the neighbor list of any process along with its identifier. This means that knowing a process implies also knowing the identifiers of all its neighbors. This also means that as soon as all the identifiers of reachable process are in the routing table, the legitimate configuration is known.

The stabilization detector is specified to work as follows:

- when the system is started in an arbitrary configuration, the SD eventually outputs *true* forever after the update algorithm has reached a legitimate configuration;
- when the system is started in an initial configuration, the output of the SD is always false until a legitimate configuration is reached, then eventually true.

$$
\begin{array}{l}
\text{stabilized} = \forall q \in \text{processors}(e_p),\ \forall n \in \text{neighbors}(q),\ \langle n, x_n, d \rangle \in e_p \text{ s.t.} \\
\qquad d = \text{mindist}_{\text{id}}(n, e_p) \wedge x_p = \text{minproc}_{\text{id}}(n, e_p) \\[2mm]
\text{legitimate} = \text{stabilized}_p \bigwedge_{q \in \text{processors}(e_p)} \text{stabilized}_q
\end{array}
$$

Fig. 2. Stabilization Detector Algorithm

The stabilization detector for the update algorithm is implemented as shown in Figure 2. The minproc function returns the process to contact in order to reach a given process, taking the implementation of the set functions into account. Each process has a *stabilized* register that indicates whether the local state of the process is the one that belongs in a legitimate configuration.

Then, the *legitimate* predicate returns whether the process estimates that the global configuration is legitimate. It does so by checking that all the local *stabilized* predicates are true.

It is trivial to see that *legitimate* eventually returns true if the system is in a legitimate configuration. It also returns true in some configurations where the routing tables contain nonexistent processes. Since such processes are eliminated during convergence, the output can only be wrong for a limited number of steps. Also, since such processes cannot be added to the routing tables if the system is started in an initial configuration, the output can never be wrong in that case.

Fair Composition with a Stabilization Detector. In the general case of two composed algorithms, A and B, both started in an initial configuration, the system as a whole benefits from the added safety. The point is that B can trust the values of the variables of A. For example, if A provides a broadcast service using a topology that it builds, B can use it knowing that messages may not reach all the processes, but will not be duplicated, as could happen if the topology were, at first, arbitrary. If A if a graph coloring algorithm, then B knows that the color provided by A is different from that of the neighbors, even though there is no optimality guarantee at that point, and thus the color might change later.

4   Safer Than Safe: The Modular Redundancy Case Study

In this section, we present a classical masking fault-tolerant algorithm that is not self-stabilizing and we demonstrate its lack of safety in the presence of an unexpected number of stopping failures or transient failures. We then present our self-stabilizing version of this algorithm and show that, while still masking the same classes of faults, it comes with added safety in the presence of more serious failures.

The n-MR principle was identified very early as a fundamental tool for fault tolerance [20]. Nowadays, it is used both in hardware and in software. In hardware, it is used to compensate for very harsh, high-noise working conditions, e.g. in satellites [4]. In software, it can be used in setups where one or several machines can experience temporary failures, including large scale systems [19].

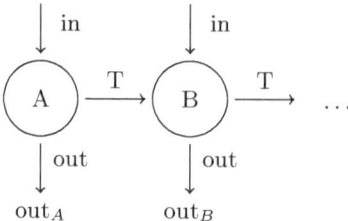

Fig. 3. Principle of a State Machine

A typical value for n is 3, hence the common name *Triple Modular Redundancy* (TMR). In the rest of the section, we use n in definitions and algorithms and assume that $n = 3$ in examples.

As opposed to tri-redundancy [16], modular redundancy considers the system as a whole. As such, each process makes no attempt at correcting itself, but the system is permanently engaged in global stabilization. Both approaches have advantages of their own: tri-redundant systems, as a fine-grained approach, works well on parallel systems, while the coarser-grained modular redundancy is better suited for distributed systems.

The n-MR algorithm transforms a regular state machine into a replicated state machine. As shown in Figure 3, a state machine can receive input data and change state accordingly (e.g. from A to B in Figure 3). The *transition function* T of a state machine maps each state and input to a new state (possibly the same). An output function, called *out*, maps states to output data.

The n-MR system, shown in Figure 4, is synchronous. It consists of an *input*, common to all the processes, an odd number n of computing processes, a *voter* that outputs the majority value among the n processes, and a shared memory consisting of n cells. Any process can read and modify the contents of any cell of the shared memory, but if two concurrent write operations occur simultaneously, the result is undefined.

Classically, this system works as follows. Consider a state machine with transition function T and a function *out* that maps states to outputs. The n-MR system replicates this state machine n times and allows to tolerate a wide range of failures described below.

Each transition of the original state machine becomes a *cycle* of the n-MR system. During each cycle, an input value I is received. Each of the processes changes its internal state according to T and calculates a new output value. The voter then outputs the majority value. If one of the computing processes fails in any way, providing a majority of the others do not fail, their correct output provides a sufficient majority. Thus, n-MR is a *masking* fault tolerance technique, in that under the minimal functionality assumption that a majority of processes never fails, the user connected to the output of the voter is in no way aware of the failures. The input and the voter are very simple and robust circuits, and thus are assumed not to fail.

This setup is clearly meant to add safety to the original state machine. The property that should be enforced throughout the execution is that the voter

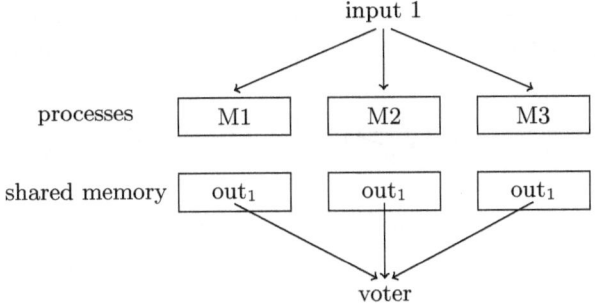

Fig. 4. n-modular Redundancy System

Variables
    state: process state
    r: $[\![0, m]\!]$ (* $m > n$ *)

Code
```
r ← maj(r) + 1
if (r mod n = 0) then begin
    state ← maj(states)
    state ← T(state,I)
end
mem[p + (r mod n)] ← out(state)
```

Fig. 5. n-modular redundancy algorithm

produces the output that would be given by the original state machine in the absence of failure.

Let us now consider a self-stabilizing version of this algorithm, as shown in Figure 5. Every execution is organized in cycles of n rounds. Each round consists of loading the most common clock value (an arbitrary rule breaks ties) and incrementing it modulo m, an integer greater than n. Then, if the round is the first of a new cycle, each process p loads a state consistent with the other processes. Again, the most common state is chosen. In case more than one value is most common, a deterministic rule is used to choose one of them. Then, p reads its input and changes its state accordingly, thus calculating its new output, **out(state)**.

During each round, p updates its round counter r by first loading the majority value for round counters among the processes (a deterministic rule break ties), then incrementing the result modulo an arbitrary value greater than n. Then, p writes in one memory cell determined uniquely by the identifier of p and the round number, thereby ensuring, in the absence of failures, that exactly one process attempts to write in each memory cell.

As an immediate consequence, it is enough that one process remains alive for at least $\lceil \frac{n}{2} \rceil$ rounds for the voter to output the right answer. It is also possible for a collection of processes to write the right outputs in the shared memory

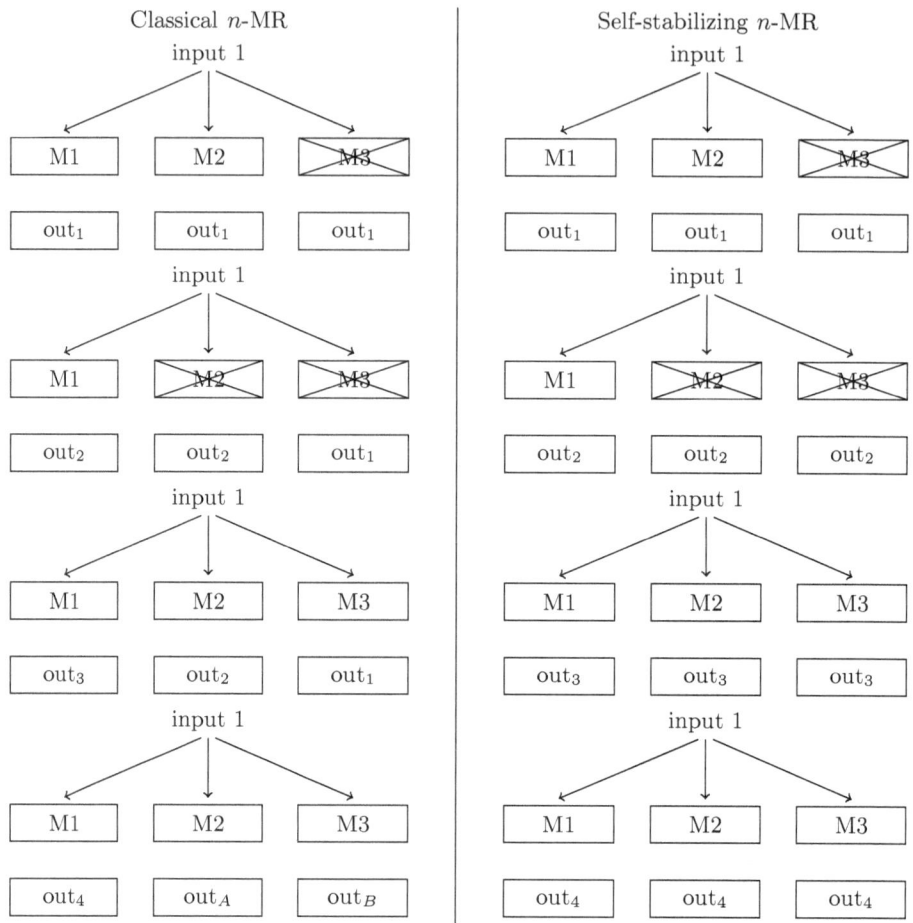

Fig. 6. Classical n-MR versus self-stabilizing n-MR

in different rounds, if some processes crash and others recover: since all the processes choose the same state from which to resume, they cannot erase a correct value. This is an improvement over the classical modular redundancy, which does not consider recoveries after crashes. Moreover, even if consistency is violated, leading to a wrong majority vote, the transition function is eventually respected so that the sequence of states forms an execution.

An execution is given in Figure 6. The left column shows the self-stabilizing algorithm, while the right column shows the classical algorithm. In both cases, M3 stops in the first step, M2 stops in the second step, and both recover in the third step. In the case of the self-stabilizing algorithm, since all the processes load the same stored state in the beginning of each round, this results in a configuration in which all the processes are in the same state. In other words, the system has fully recovered from these failures. The classical algorithm, on the other hand, enters an inconsistent configuration in which no two processes have the same state. Since, in the absence of failures, all the processes will now apply their transition function to identical inputs, the system has no way of recovering.

Proof sketch for self-stabilization. For initial safety, it is easy to see that if the system is started with all the processes in the same state, as in the non-stabilizing case, then it behaves like a regular modular redundancy system. Convergence is achieved as follows: at latest, the next time that the value of the round counter ($r \bmod n$) is 0, all the live processes load the same state at the same time. This yields a configuration where all the processes are in the same state, i.e. a legitimate configuration. Closure is an immediate consequence of the specification of the state machines: since all the processes have the same transition function and the system is synchronous, in all subsequent configurations, all the processes are in the same state.

Benefits of this approach. Suppose that this algorithm, assuming crash/recovery failures, is started in an initial configuration. It then provides the same service as the non-stabilizing algorithm, tolerating $n1$ stopping failures. If transient failures change the state of any minority of the processes, then there remains a majority of correct outputs. In addition, since the system is self-stabilizing, it provides a protection against any combination of transient failures, even transient failures that corrupt the state of all the processes. All the processes eventually load the same arbitrary state simultaneously, thus recovering from these failures in the sense that they start to implement an execution of the simulated machine from an arbitrary state. In case all the processes fail, at least they eventually become synchronized again, which is better than behaving erratically, as does a non-stabilizing system.

5   Conclusion

We devoted this paper to a study of the safety of self-stabilizing systems. Our main contribution is the definition of initial configurations, i.e. preferred starting configurations, from which a self-stabilizing algorithm can safely converge toward a legitimate configuration. Evidently, being self-stabilizing, the algorithm converges if initialized in any other configuration too.

This allows to compare self-stabilizing and non-stabilizing algorithms on an equal grounds. Non-stabilizing algorithms take advantage of their initial state to provide safety, so can self-stabilizing algorithms.

We gave a generic framework for analyzing self-stabilizing information gathering algorithms with reference to their initial configurations and we applied this framework to composed algorithms and stabilization detection.

As an example, we introduce self-stabilizing modular redundancy. This system is safer than usual NMR, since our system not only masks failures just like a normal NMR, it also adds eventual safety if faults that no algorithm could mask overwhelm the system.

We believe that specifying initial configurations with self-stabilizing algorithms should be standard. It provides the user who wants to run the algorithm with instructions on how to start the system in order to obtain the best possible conditions, combining safety, in normal conditions, and eventual safety, in the presence of a very high number of failures.

To sum up, we argue that self-stabilizing systems should no longer be regarded as only eventually safe, but as safe **and** eventually safe.

References

1. Afek, Y., Dolev, S.: Local stabilizer. Journal of Parallel and Distributed Computing 62(5), 745–765 (2002)
2. Arora, A., Gouda, M.: Distributed reset. IEEE Transactions on Computers 43, 316–331 (1990)
3. Awerbuch, B., Ostrovsky, R.: Memory-efficient and self-stabilizing network RESET (extended abstract). In: PODC, pp. 254–263 (1994)
4. Banu, R., Vladimirova, T.: On-board encryption in earth observation small satellites. In: 40th Annual IEEE International Carnahan Conference on Security Technology, pp. 203–208 (2006)
5. Beauquier, J., Delaët, S., Dolev, S., Tixeuil, S.: Transient fault detectors. Distributed Computing 20(1), 39–51 (2007)
6. Bejan, A., Ghosh, S., Rao, S.: An extended framework of safe stabilization. In: Jackson, D.J. (ed.) Computers and Their Applications, ISCA, pp. 276–282 (2006)
7. Cournier, A., Datta, A.K., Petit, F., Villain, V.: Enabling snap-stabilizatio. In: ICDCS, pp. 12–19. IEEE Computer Society, Los Alamitos (2003)
8. Cournier, A., Devismes, S., Villain, V.: From self- to snap- stabilization. In: SSS, pp. 199–213 (2006)
9. Delaët, S., Tixeuil, S.: Tolerating transient and intermittent failures. Journal of Parallel and Distributed Computing 62(5), 961–981 (2002)
10. Dijkstra, E.: Self stabilizing systems in spite of distributed control. Communications of the Association of the Computing Machinery 17(11), 643–644 (1974)
11. Dolev, S.: Self-Stabilization. MIT Press, Cambridge (2000)
12. Dolev, S., Herman, T.: Superstabilizing protocols for dynamic distributed systems. Chicago Journal of Theoretical Computer Science 3(4) (1997)
13. Dolev, S., Israeli, A., Moran, S.: Self stabilization of dynamic systems. In: Proceedings of the MCC Workshop on Self-Stabilizing Systems, MCC Technical Report No. STP-379-89 (1989)
14. Dolev, S., Tzachar, N.: Randomization adaptive self-stabilization. CoRR, abs/0810.4440 (2008)
15. Ghosh, S., Bejan, A.: A framework of safe stabilization. In: Huang, S.-T., Herman, T. (eds.) SSS 2003. LNCS, vol. 2704, pp. 129–140. Springer, Heidelberg (2003)
16. Gouda, M.G., Cobb, J.A., Huang, C.-T.: Fault masking in tri-redundant systems. In: Datta, A.K., Gradinariu, M. (eds.) SSS 2006. LNCS, vol. 4280, pp. 304–313. Springer, Heidelberg (2006)

17. Herman, T., Pemmaraju, S.V.: Error-detecting codes and fault-containing self-stabilization. Inf. Process. Lett. 73(1-2), 41–46 (2000)
18. Huang, C.-T., Gouda, M.G.: State checksum and its role in system stabilization. In: ICDCS Workshops, pp. 29–34. IEEE Computer Society, Los Alamitos (2005)
19. Yen, I.l.: Specialized n-modular redundant processors in large-scale distributed systems. In: Proceedings of the 1996 15 th Symposium on Reliable Distributed Systems, pp. 12–21 (1996)
20. Lyons, R.E., Vandervulk, W.: The use of triple-modular redundancy to improve computer reliability. IBM Journal of Research and Development, 200–209 (1962)
21. Normand, E.: Single event upset at ground level. IEEE Trans. Nuclear Science 43, 2742–2751 (1996)

Proactive Fortification of Fault-Tolerant Services

Paul Ezhilchelvan, Dylan Clarke, Isi Mitrani, and Santosh Shrivastava

School of Computing Science, Newcastle University, UK

Abstract. We present an approach for incorporating intrusion resilience to replicated services, irrespective of the service replication used and of the fault types tolerated. The approach, termed as FORTRESS, involves fortifying a fault-tolerant service using proxies that block clients from accessing the servers directly, and periodically refreshing proxies and servers with diverse executables generated using code randomization. These two features make it hard for an attacker to compromise a server when no proxy has been compromised. An analytical evaluation establishes that if attackers cannot intrude servers without first having compromised a proxy, fortifying even a passively replicated service can offer greater resilience than building that service as a deterministic state machine and actively replicating it over diverse platforms. Finally, the FORTRESS architecture is presented where proactive code randomization is achieved by proactive replacement of server and proxy nodes. Examining the state transfer protocol executed during node replacement shows that the processing overhead per replacement is no more than the overhead for changing the leader or the primary replica in replication management.

Keywords: Intrusion tolerance, Replication, State machines, Primary-Backup, Agreement, Code randomization, Analytical evaluations.

1 Introduction

An intrusion is a possible outcome of attacks and an attack involves attempts at exploiting vulnerabilities present in nodes. All known intrusion-resilient schemes work with state machine replication, SMR for short, of services. They require that the service be built as a deterministic state machine, DSM for short, and be replicated on $n, n > 3$, diverse nodes so that intrusions in up to f, $f < n/3$, nodes can be tolerated. However, it is difficult, often practically impossible, to build a large class of both emerging and existing applications as DSMs.

Complying with the DSM requirement means that *all* sources of nondeterminism are identified and compensated [19]. Such sources can be present at all levels of the node system: use of timeouts, coin-toss and OS calls (e.g., timeofday) at the application level, use of inheritance and polymorphism at the programming level, multi-threading at the middleware level and task scheduling at the OS level. Catering for non-determinism emanating from several levels is enormously complex and can be error prone if the service to be provided is computation-intensive. To the best of our knowledge, no computationally intensive application

T. Abdelzaher, M. Raynal, and N. Santoro (Eds.): OPODIS 2009, LNCS 5923, pp. 330–344, 2009.
© Springer-Verlag Berlin Heidelberg 2009

(e.g., a stateful web-service) has been developed using COTS technology (e.g., EJB) as a DSM for the purposes of replication; moreover, SMR approach in practice has so far been primarily limited to achieving serialisable and dependable read and write operations involving public keys [13] and files [8].

Thus, for a large class of applications, SMR-based intrusion resilience poses a circular problem: compensating for non-determinism is complex and can lead to presence of bugs that in turn make SMR pointless. In this paper, we present, motivate and analyze the effectiveness of an approach for incorporating intrusion resilience for any replicated fault-tolerant system. Specifically, the type of replication can be SMR or Primary-Backup (PB for short) where the DSM requirement is not enforced; the type of faults tolerated may be crash or arbitrary (e.g., soft errors [3]) so long as failure-independence prevails.

1.1 The Approach, Assumptions and Contributions

The main ideas behind the proposed approach are 2-fold: make server vulnerabilities harder to uncover and exploit, and also make the attendant mechanisms impose minimal disruption to service provisioning. Achieving the former involves having the replicated server system or the *server tier* 'fortified' by a *proxy tier* that consists of two or more proxy nodes. Proxies forward client requests to servers and return signed responses of the replicated server to clients. They thus block direct access to, and thereby hide the vulnerabilities of, server nodes from the adversary. The latter therefore has to guess server vulnerabilities or exploit a proxy to gain direct server access or do both. To thwart these attempts from succeeding, proxies are periodically refreshed with *diverse executables* [14] and servers are also refreshed but with identical executables that are different at each refresh. Server executables being identical at any moment facilitates efficient state update of backups in PB replication and output voting in SMR.

A recent work on *proactive obfuscation* [14], which very much inspired this paper, implements a mechanism for online generation of diverse executables of the service code and installs each node with a freshly generated diverse executable once in a given period. Thus, in each period, the adversary is faced with a fresh set of diverse executables. Note that this is different to *proactive recovery* [8,23,20] in which the same code is re-installed at each refresh and the diversity therefore remains *fixed*. Here, the adversary can familiarize himself with the fixed diversity over time; he could progressively customize his attacks effectively and gain intrusions. Periodic installation of *varying* diversity limits the time available for an adversary to get familiar with the executable being used.

Throughout this paper, we assume the obfuscation mechanism of [14] for generating online diverse executables for both servers and proxies. We note that these executables can be created during compilation, loading or at run-time. The capacity for automatic generation of diverse executables for any given code is facilitated by randomization techniques - such as instruction set randomization (e.g., [2], [10]), heap randomization [4] and address re-ordering (e.g., [25,5]). An executable generated using any of these techniques has a high probability of success in preventing an attacker from gaining control over the host node, i.e., preventing a node *compromise*. An attack on it can sometimes lead to crashing of the host node. Thus, having more proxies helps in maintaining service availability. It cannot however help in server fortification. Even if one proxy is compromised, the adversary will have direct access to servers (that have the same executable).

Fortification protects the server tier from intrusions if servers are refreshed before a vulnerability of the server executable is discovered using a compromised proxy or is correctly guessed without direct access to servers; i.e., if, within the server refresh period, an adversary is prevented from achieving the following: (1) compromising a proxy and (2) correctly guessing a server vulnerability when no proxy is compromised.

Proxies perform limited functionality (compared to servers) and their code is likely to contain fewer or no exploitable bugs. Hence, an adversary achieving (1) is hard and can be made even harder by refreshing proxies more often than servers. Note that proxies do not maintain service state and can be refreshed with minimum service disruption.

Several researchers have examined the effectiveness of randomization techniques: [18] on address re-ordering and [24] on instruction set randomization. These studies indicate that an adversary can uncover a vulnerability in executables produced by these techniques, by launching a multi-phased attack and by observing the target node behavior between phases. This observation is not possible unless a proxy is compromised. Thus, when no proxy is compromised, an adversary cannot deterministically deduce the exact nature of any vulnerability in a server executable; since the server code can be randomized in a large number of ways to generate an executable, we will assume that the probability that an adversary correctly guesses an exploitable vulnerability in a server executable within some finite duration, is zero. That is, achieving (2) above is assumed not possible for an adversary.

Proactive recovery/obfuscation systems periodically refresh the nodes *in situ*: a node logically exits the SMR system for being refreshed and joins the system after state restoration. So, a replica cannot perform any useful work for some time during *each* period and, in the remaining duration, it is burdened with assisting others in their state restoration. Both slow down the SMR management and the system performance, and we seek an alternative.

In our approach, nodes of a given tier are replaced *en masse* using spare nodes that are installed with necessary executables just before replacement. We term this method of periodic node refresh as *proactive replacement*. It allows off-line generation and installation of executables. State transfer needs to be done during server tier replacement and the overhead, we argue, is similar to changing leader/coordinator/primary during replication management. Admittedly, replacement requires spare nodes. This cost is affordable with ever-falling hardware price and is justified given the alternative.

Our approach thus has three features: (i) a 2-tier structure for a generic replicated server system; (ii) use of diverse executables to minimize the possibilities of proxy compromise and of server compromise without a compromised proxy;

(iii) proactive replacement for applying diverse executables. Henceforth, our approach will be referred to as FORTRESS.

The paper makes two principal contributions. We analytically establish that, given 4-fold *fixed* diversity, the 2-tier system constructed is more resilient than a 1-tier SMR system of 4 nodes, provided that the adversary cannot identify an exploitable server vulnerability without having compromised a proxy first. This result holds irrespective of the server replication and of the periodic refresh strategy used. It establishes FORTRESS features (i) and (ii) above as the effective way of incorporating intrusion-tolerance for an arbitrary fault-tolerant system. The second contribution concerns feature (iii), the proactive replacement. We qualitatively argue its benefits and that its cost, excluding spare nodes, is smaller than that of proactive, *in situ* schemes.

The paper is structured as follows. Next section briefly surveys the vast body of recent related work. Section 3 presents the 2-tier arrangement in detail and the FORTRESS architecture. This is followed by the analytical study on resilience comparison in Section 4. Concluding remarks are in Section 5.

2   Related Work

Known intrusion tolerance strategies require that the service be replicated in SMR style [17,16]. The replicas have fixed diversity and protection measures (e.g.,[9]) against known vulnerabilities. These provisions were once considered to be sufficient (see [7]). In a subsequent paper, Castro and Liskov [8] revisited this consideration and proposed proactive recovery for avoiding intrusions exceeding more than the threshold f in an f–tolerant SMR system. As per this scheme, all server nodes are periodically recovered without stopping the SMR system: at most f nodes at a time (logically) exit the system to be re-started so that the effects of any intrusion that occurred are annulled; re-started nodes re-join the system after restoring the service state *and* before the next batch is to exit. State restoration succeeds because $n > 3f$ and batched recoveries do not overlap leaving at least $(f + 1)$ correct nodes to obtain the recent service state from.

Proactive recovery requires strict synchrony assumptions and secure, intrusion-resistant components within each (even compromised) node. Notably, these requirements, stated below, are quite different to the weakest environments in which SMR can be managed, namely partial synchrony and malicious behavior by exploited nodes (see also [22]): (i) a trusted re-boot system that initiates, and ensures completion of, node re-start; (ii) synchrony assumptions for timely exchange and processing of state transfer messages so that the batched recoveries never overlap; and, (iii) a read-only memory securely holding correct copies of OS and service code.

With at most f nodes in recovery for some duration in each period, the service can be unavailable for brief periods if $n = 3f + 1$. This potential unavailability is addressed in [23,26] using distinct approaches. In [23], the total number of replicas (n) is increased so that SMR is managed by considering the recovering nodes as crashed ones; moreover, the three requirements above are realized through architecture hybridization [21] where each intrusion-prone, asynchronous server node has an intrusion-resistant, synchronous co-processor securely embedded within it, and these co-processors are connected by synchronous channels. Thus, the complementary provisions for proactive recovery and SMR are made to co-exist in elegant separation.

In [26], at most f nodes are periodically replaced by an equal number of re-covered spare nodes using an agreement-based membership-change algorithm. Using a quorum of $(n - f)$ nodes, the following are agreed on: the sets of leavers and joiners, the point of change with respect to the ordered stream of client requests. Membership change involves state transfer to joiners. How-ever, [26] assumes partial synchrony for reaching agreement. So, if quorums leading to agreements on two successive membership changes contain f com-promised nodes and leave out f slow but correct nodes, the time for next (partial) replacement cannot be within any assumed bound. Also, without a trusted name server, returning clients in [26] may find all the old servers to have been replaced.

Proactive recovery, *per se*, cannot cater for repairing an exploited vulnera-bility and hence for adversaries who swiftly re-exploit the same vulnerability. Repair requires detection. For detecting a compromised node, at least $(f + 1)$ *correct* nodes [1] are needed. With only at most f nodes being recovered or replaced at a time, detection of exploited nodes cannot be facilitated dur-ing recovery or after partial replacement. Alternatively, repair can be effected in the form of installing a different executable. [20] considers a *fixed* set of pre-configured executables to choose from during recovery. A more robust ap-proach, as noted earlier, is proactive obfuscation [14]. A trusted server system and a synchronous delivery system are employed in [14] to dynamically gener-ate and to securely deliver a distinctly diverse code to every recovering node, respectively.

All proactive schemes surveyed above impose a constant overhead of at least $\lceil \frac{n}{f} \rceil$ state restorations per period and also require SMR as a pre-condition. As noted before, catering for non-determinism can be error-prone. The authors of [19] who made a limited attempt on a CORBA application advocate that non-determinism cannot be guaranteed to be eliminated until all levels of the system have been inspected for it. Though PB replication has some non-determinism related issues (e.g., primary making an external invocation prior to crashing), they can be systemically identified and effectively dealt with. The engineering details for an enterprise application can be found in [11].

One of the main design features of [15] is to use proxies as intermediaries between clients and servers in order to minimize the possibility of server com-promises by clients - a design rationale shared by FORTRESS. In [15], proxies are also used to enhance the intrusion-resilience of an SMR system of web servers that read and update a reliable database server; for example, proxies monitor server behaviors through a challenge-response arrangement to detect a com-promised server and trigger a (reactive) recovery. Proxies in FORTRESS are lightweight so that their replacement is swift and can be more frequent.

3   The 2-Tier Approach and System Architecture

The proxy tier is made up of $f+1$, $f > 0$, nodes installed with diverse executables of the proxy code. The server tier is replicated for tolerance of ϕ faults and consists of nodes installed with an identical executable of the service code. When not intruded, nodes in server tier fail independent of each other. Faults can be crash or arbitrary. The latter causes a node to fail in an arbitrary manner that does not introduce faults in another node. We assume partial synchrony for managing server replication using established techniques (e.g., [12,8]).

   The total number of nodes in the server tier is: $(2\phi + 1)$, $(2\phi + 1)$ or $(3\phi + 1)$ if replication is PB, SMR for crash-tolerance (SMR-C, for short) or SMR for arbitrary faults (SMR-A), respectively. Server nodes are uniquely indexed and the indices are known to servers and proxies. Figure 1 depicts the 2-tier system for $f = 2$ and $\phi = 1$ and the three options for arranging server tier.

Client Interaction. Proxies interface between clients and servers, blocking direct access to the latter. Clients know proxies' addresses and public keys, servers' indices (not addresses) and public-keys, the type of replication, and the value of ϕ if replication is SMR-A. This is done using a trusted and replicated *name-server* (NS) that is read-only for clients. (Details in section 3.1.) Clients submit their requests to proxies which forward them to the server nodes; the latter do not accept any communication except from the proxies and the name server.

   In a PB server, the primary sends its response to backups which then sign the received response and return the signed response to every proxy. The primary, after having sent its response to backups, also signs and sends its response to proxies. In an SMR-C server tier, each server signs its own response and forwards it to each proxy. Proxies over-sign any one of the received responses and forward it to the client. A client accepts a response as valid if it has two authentic signatures - one from the proxy that sent the response and the other from one of the servers' signatures (identified by server index).

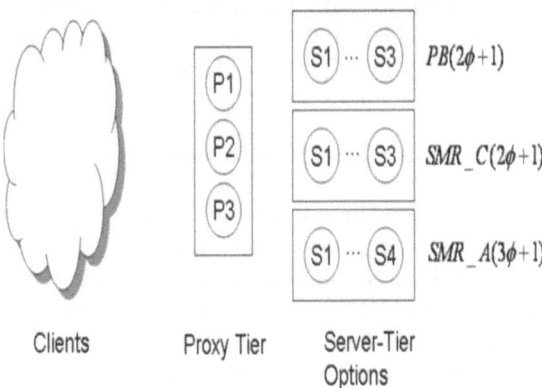

Fig. 1. The 2-Tier Arrangement

An SMR-A server tier sends a voted response with $(\phi + 1)$ distinct signatures to each proxy which, after authentication, signs and forwards the response to the client. A client accepts a response to be valid if it has $(\phi + 2)$ authentic signatures - the last one being from the proxy that forwarded the response and the rest from $(\phi + 1)$ distinct servers.

Node Replacement. FORTRESS replaces proxies at periodic instances and the duration of the period is specified. New proxies have freshly generated diverse executables installed in them. Installation and replacement is done by a trusted and replicated *controller unit* (CU) in cooperation with the name server. (Details in section 3.1.) The controller marks the outgoing nodes as 'replaced' which (logically) reside in the *recovery unit* (RU). After a specified number of proxy replacements, the controller replaces the proxies together with the server nodes. (Details of state transfer during server replacement are given in section 3.1.) The outgoing server nodes, like their proxy counterparts, are marked as 'replaced'.

Trusted Reboot Server (RS). It is responsible for re-booting the replaced nodes in the recovery unit. After re-boot completes, it informs the controller about the nodes which have completed their re-boot. The controller re-classifies these nodes as spares and may select them for future replacements.

Fatal intrusion. It occurs as soon as the adversary intrudes either all proxies or any one server node. When no proxy is compromised, an adversary will not have direct access to server nodes. He can only guess server vulnerabilities and cannot observe the effect of his attacks on servers. Moreover, in multi-phased attacks, the attacker needs to observe the target node's behavior between the phases. For example, the de-randomization attack [18] is done in two phases and observing the 'sleeping' of the target node is essential for eventual exploitation. With the proxy hiding the target server's behavior from the adversary, this essential observation is denied. All of these make the adversary's task of exploiting directly-inaccessible, unobservable servers immensely difficult. Compared to servers, proxies perform simpler computational tasks and can be harder to compromise due to their code containing fewer vulnerabilities. Moreover, proxies do not interact with each other, denying the adversary the advantages of attacking a second proxy from within the proxy tier. So, an adversary's action plan is likely to be: compromise a proxy and then the servers.

3.1   Fortress Architecture and Realisation

FORTRESS Architecture uses three trusted components: the name server (NS), the controller unit (CU), and reboot server (RS) - see Fig 2. The first two are SMR units replicated for fault-tolerance using fail-independent nodes and synchronous channels. FORTRESS also employs a server farm (SF) which is logically partitioned into the spare pool (SP), the recovery unit (RU) and the 2-tier system. (Table 1 lists and expands all these abbreviations.)

The following isolation measures are in force to protect trusted components and spare nodes from intrusions. Spare nodes in SP receive instructions only from

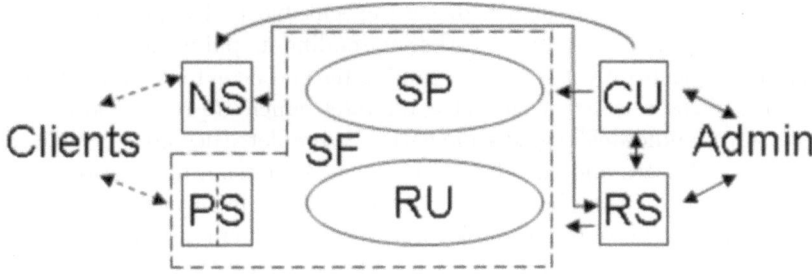

Fig. 2. FORTRESS Architecture

Table 1. Abbreviations

Abbreviation	Name
NS	Name Server
S	Server Tier
P	Proxy Tier
SP	Spare Pool
RU	Recovery Unit
CU	Controller Unit
RS	Reboot Server
SF	Server Farm {SP,RU,P,S}

CU until they are instructed to act as a proxy or server. CU receives no communication from any component other than RS and the trusted administrator. RS interacts with CU, NS and the administrator; it receives no communication from a replaced node until restart is complete. Communication among CU, NS, RS and spare nodes are done over separate, authenticated and synchronous channels which are indicated by solid lines in Fig 2, with arrows showing the permitted directions for information flows. The administrator ensures that SF has enough number of nodes in it.

Replacement Details. For brevity, let the server tier be SMR-A and be replaced together with the proxy tier. Before a replacement is due, CU randomly selects $2f+1$ candidate nodes for proxy tier and $4\phi+1$ candidate nodes for server tier out of the spare pool whose membership list it maintains. It then generates: a unique randomization key for all server candidates, a unique randomization key for each proxy candidate, a unique number (index) for each candidate. A randomization key is a procedure for randomizing the native service or proxy codes which the spare nodes freshly install during their re-start. Each node in SF has a secure read-only memory holding the re-start software.

Replicas of CU agree on their individual random selections and use a lottery agreement protocol (e.g., [6]) for the agreed selection also to be random. CU disseminates to each candidate an information triplet {candidate role, index, randomization key}; it also sends NS the addresses of candidate nodes and the information triplets.

A candidate node generates a diverse executable and a private-public key pair; it then requests NS for registration by sending its public key and index. NS accepts the requests only $f+1$ proxy candidates and $3\phi+1$ server candidates. It informs RS of the rejected or absent candidates which are re-booted to become spares again. Candidates' registration with NS completes despite a possible crash of $(f+\phi)$ candidates and the elapsed time since selection has a known bound. At the elapse of this time bound, CU instructs NS to initiate replacement.

NS deregisters the outgoing nodes and instructs them to hand-over; it separately instructs the incoming nodes to take-over, together with each other's addresses, public keys and indices. The incoming proxies request the outgoing proxies for any client requests that were received but not forwarded to the server tier. The incoming servers similarly request the outgoing ones for state transfer. Clients that find the cached address of the service invalid, will contact NS and obtain proxy addresses and server indices (as shown by dotted lines in Fig 2).

State Transfer. Each incoming server node awaits state information from at least $(2\phi+1)$ outgoing servers. Based on $(2\phi+1)$ pieces of state information received, incoming servers agree on: a checkpoint CP, a sequence of ordered requests O and a set UO of unordered client requests, subject to: (i) any request processed by at least one correct out-going server is present either in the agreed O and has the same order or is reflected in the agreed CP; (ii) any request received by at least $(\phi+1)$ correct out-going nodes is present in the agreed UO.

These two conditions are to be met despite the possibilities that at least ϕ out of $(2\phi+1)$ servers that supplied state information to an incoming server may not be correct, and that incoming nodes may not receive state information from the same set of $(2\phi+1)$ out-going ones. This is exactly being solved during a 'view-change' in a coordinator based, partially-synchronous, Byzantine tolerant order protocol, such as [8].

A view change is triggered in [8] when enough nodes in a replicated system suspect that the current coordinator is faulty. Here, the instruction from NS triggers state transfer. The other major difference is that, in a view-change, suppliers of state information and the actors who act on the supplied information are the same (which are the nodes of the same replicated system); in state transfer, suppliers are outgoing nodes and the actors the incoming ones. However, in both cases, actors as well as suppliers are $3\phi+1$ in total (with at most ϕ of them being faulty) and the restrictions imposed on the state information that the actors have to work on, are identical. Hence, it can be asserted that a view-change algorithm, as in [8], enables incoming nodes to build correct service state to start SMR processing. Similarly, a coordinator-change algorithm in [12] enables incoming nodes to build correct service state for PB or SMR-C tier. Transfer of CP is time consuming and can be amortized over time, if NS first instructs the old and new servers to 'prepare transfer' ahead of issuing them with 'hand-/take-over' instructions.

4   A Comparative Evaluation

We now analytically compare the intrusion-resilience of a 1-tier SMR system and a 2-tier system, given that a total of 4-fold diversity is available for building both systems and that an attacker cannot intrude a server without first compromising a proxy in the 2-tier system. Note that 4-fold diversity is the minimum requirement for building 1-tier SMR system for (the common case of) $f = 1$. During recovery/replacement, the existing diversity is assumed to be simply refreshed; that is, the diversity considered is of *fixed* nature and the effects of using diverse executables and code randomization are not considered. The metric for comparison is the expected time to fatal intrusion or system *lifetime* for short.

The 1-tier SMR system, S_1 for short, is made up of four nodes, each being distinctly diverse and recovered once periodically. The 2-tier system, denoted as S_2, divides the available 4-fold diversity into 3 for the proxy tier and 1 for the server tier. Note that any SMR management software can be used, in a limited form, for proxy functionality and hence the above division can be arbitrary. S_2 thus employs 3 proxies of distinct types, 3 identical server nodes for PB and SMR-C (figure 3(c)) and 4 for SMR-A. Thus, $f = 2$ and $\phi = 1$ as in figure 1. Only proxies are replaced periodically, with each incoming proxy being the same type as the one it replaces.

The replacement and recovery periods are of the same duration and nodes are assumed to be replaced/recovered instantly. This assumption makes the analysis independent of the proactive strategy pursued: recovery or replacement. Moreover, for *both* systems, repairing of exploited vulnerabilities is not considered. This is realistic for proactive recovery systems working with fixed diversity. Since re-exploitation of the same vulnerability can be swift, it is considered to be instantaneous. This means that once a node of type X is exploited, it remains compromised subsequently despite the fact that it is being recovered or replaced by another node of the same type. Finally, once an adversary identifies an exploitable vulnerability, he is assumed to exploit it instantaneously.

Both systems start at time T_0 when the adversary is assumed to know nothing of the vulnerabilities that might be present in nodes. Of interest are two instances (see figure 3(a)): T_1 and T_2 when the adversary compromises the first node and identifies an exploitable vulnerability in a second node, respectively. For S_1,

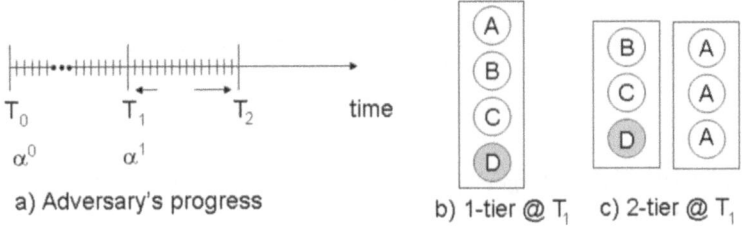

a) Adversary's progress   b) 1-tier @ T_1 c) 2-tier @ T_1

Fig. 3. Lifetime comparison

$T_2 - T_0$ is the time to fatal intrusion. For simplicity, we focus on time left for fatal intrusion after T_1 and the mean lifetime after T_1 will be denoted as ℓ.

We model the adversary by defining α_X as the probability that he uncovers an exploitable vulnerability in type X nodes during a replacement/recovery period, given that a type X node *has been accessible* to him during that period. Let replacement/recovery period denote a unit of time (shown as short regular intervals in 3(a)). Thus, α_X is the adversary's success rate for nodes of type X if he has direct access. Values of α_X for later periods cannot be smaller than those for earlier ones. When node type X is accessible from T_0, we denote the values of α_X at T_0 and T_1 as α_X^0 and α_X^1 respectively. Note that $\alpha_X^0 \leq \alpha_X^1$, and when nodes have no obvious deterministic bugs, $(T_1 - T_0)$ is large and $\alpha_X^0 < \alpha_X^1$. The four node types available are denoted as $\{A, B, C, D\} \ni X$.

4.1   1-Tier System

With no loss of generality, let node type D be the most vulnerable of all and is compromised at T_1 (figure 3(b)). The adversary can now do the following from T_1 onwards: attack the server nodes both as a client (as he was doing before T_1) *and* also as a controller of the compromised server replica of type D. This is modeled as the adversary *replicating* himself at the compromised server and two adversaries, the original and the replica, operating in parallel.

The *adversary replica* has access to service code and engages in interactions with target nodes for replica management - a privilege not available to the single adversary before T_1 and also now to the original adversary. We will however assume, optimistically from S_1's perspective, that the adversary replica's success rate is the same as the original. Note that this optimistic assumption can only lead to an over-estimation of ℓ_1 - the metric measuring the intrusion-resilience of S_1.

For analytical simplicity, we will assume for both the systems that the adversary's success rate is constant at α_X^1 for all periods in $[T_1, T_2]$ and for all $X \in \{A, B, C\}$. In reality, however, his success rate will increase over time, and the effect of this simplification can be ignored as we are only comparing the system lifetimes.

The probability that the adversary and his replica compromise at least one correct node in S_1 during any given period after T_1 is:

$$\gamma_1 = 1 - [(1 - \alpha_A^1)(1 - \alpha_B^1)(1 - \alpha_C^1)]^2. \tag{1}$$

The probability that $(T_2 - T_1)$ has i, $i \geq 0$, periods is $\gamma_1 \times (1 - \gamma_1)^i$. Thus,

$$\ell_1 = E(T_2 - T_1) = \frac{1 - \gamma_1}{\gamma_1}. \tag{2}$$

The smaller the γ_1, the larger ℓ_1 becomes and the more resilient S_1 is. Let α_{mx}^1 and α_{mn}^1 be defined as:

$$\alpha_{mx}^1 = \max\{\alpha_X^1 \mid X \in \{A, B, C\}\}, \tag{3}$$

$$\alpha_{mn}^1 = \min\{\alpha_X^1 \mid X \in \{A, B, C\}\}. \tag{4}$$

From (1) and (4):

$$\gamma_1 \geq 1 - (1 - \alpha_{mn}^1)^6 = 1 - (1 - 6\alpha_{mn}^1 + o(\alpha_{mn}^1)) \approx 6\alpha_{mn}^1. \tag{5}$$

4.2   2-Tier System

With no direct access to server nodes, the adversary attacks the proxies until T_1. Consider the case where the most vulnerable D type is *not* selected to be used in the proxy tier which therefore will comprise A, B and C type nodes. By the time the adversary compromises one of these less vulnerable proxies as a client, he could have compromised in S_1 the most vulnerable D-type (server) node and, by replicating himself, one of these three types. That is, T_1 for S_2 is earlier than T_2 for S_1. So we will only analyze the alternative case as shown in figure 3(c).

Let T_1 be identical for both systems even though a D-type node is acting only as a proxy in S_2. At T_1, the adversary's use of compromised proxy is modeled as follows. He replicates himself in the compromised proxy with no reduction in his computational power; the original and the replica attack in parallel. The original adversary, as before, attacks the proxies and has no direct access to servers; the adversary replica attacks server nodes but not the proxies that do not interact with each other.

As in S_1, we will retain the same simplification that the success rate for A-type server nodes remain constant for all periods in $[T_1, T_2]$ at, say, α_A. As the adversary replica gains direct access to server nodes for the first time at T_1, it is reasonable to suppose that $\alpha_A^0 < \alpha_A \leq \alpha_A^1$, where α_A^0 and α_A^1 are as defined for S_1.

Fatal intrusion occurs at the earliest occurrence of either (i) adversary uncovering exploitable vulnerabilities in all non-compromised proxies or (ii) adversary replica doing the same with any one of the server nodes. If (i) were to occur earlier, S_2 is obviously more resilient than S_1: between the compromise of second and third proxies, S_2 works correctly while S_1 would be fatally intruded. So, we will let (ii) be the earlier event. The probability that the adversary replica compromises at least one server during any given period after T_1 is:

$$\gamma_2 = 1 - [(1 - \alpha_A)]^k, \tag{6}$$

where $k = 3$ for PB and SMR-C, and $k = 4$ for SMR-A (fig. 1). As in (2),

$$\ell_2 = E(T_2 - T_1) = \frac{1 - \gamma_2}{\gamma_2}. \tag{7}$$

Note that since $\alpha_A \leq \alpha_A^1 \leq \alpha_{mx}^1$, it follows from (6) and (3):

$$\gamma_2 \leq 1 - (1 - \alpha_{mx}^1)^k = 1 - (1 - k\alpha_{mx}^1 + o(\alpha_{mx}^1)) \approx k\alpha_{mx}^1. \tag{8}$$

Claim. Given 4-fold fixed diversity, the 2-Tier system is more resilient than the 1-Tier, provided that (i) $\alpha_{mx}^1 < 1.5\alpha_{mn}^1$ and (ii) an adversary cannot intrude a server without having compromised at least one proxy.

Proof. In (6), $k \le 4$; by given, (5) and (8), $\gamma_2 < \gamma_1$; by (7) and (2), $\ell_2 > \ell_1$.

Proactive recovery systems for $f = 1$ assume that even if an adversary intrudes the most vulnerable one of 4 diverse nodes, he cannot intrude the remaining three at any time. If this assumption holds then $\alpha_{mn} = \alpha_{mx}$ at *all* time for that adversary. That is, $\alpha_{mx}^1 < 1.5\alpha_{mn}^1$.

Corollary. If the 1-Tier SMR system is resilient for a set of adversaries, then the 2-Tier system is always more intrusion-resilient against those adversaries, provided that (ii) of the claim above holds.

Remark. *Advantage in numbers.* For a class of adversaries, fortification makes even crash-tolerant replicated systems more resilient than intrusion-resilient SMR systems. Recall that the analysis is orthogonal to whether proactive recovery or replacement is used, and so the gains are solely due to 2-Tier structure and the fixed diversity being refreshed. The cost, of course, is in the number of nodes required: 7 nodes with proactive recovery (applied in parallel to both tiers) or $7 \times \rho$ $+2$ nodes for proactive replacement given that replaced nodes become ready for selection by CU in less than $(\rho - 1)$ periods.

5   Conclusions

We have presented and motivated an approach for enhancing a fault-tolerant replicated system into an intrusion-tolerant one as well, without requiring any changes to the nature of the existing replication management. The approach is ideally suited to a class of adversaries who cannot guess and exploit vulnerabilities in servers when the latter are not directly accessible. Even a crash-tolerant, primary-backup system can be made more resilient than an equivalent state machine replicated system. Thus, removed is the 'glass ceiling' that the known, intrusion-tolerant schemes impose on the range of fault-tolerant services that can be made intrusion resilient. In the extreme, the service may not even have to be replicated, yet intrusion resilience can be guaranteed but not fault-tolerance. Identifying the presence of this separation between two forms of tolerance is also a significant contribution.

FORTRESS can also be effective against those adversaries who can guess and exploit vulnerabilities in servers that are not directly accessible, but do so less accurately or take a longer time than if they were attacking a directly accessible server. We are currently evaluating gains in intrusion tolerance attained through fortification by considering adversaries who have different, non-zero probabilities of success in attacking servers when no proxy is compromised.

FORTRESS caters for several issues: replication for fault- and intrusion-tolerance and replica refresh through proactive replacement. Each one of these imposes an overhead, demands resources and adds complexity. Consequently, a variety of components, some trusted, are used and structured as per functionality. Proactive replacement is a new idea, an alternative to the proactive *in situ* schemes. Its benefits in reducing overhead to a small constant have been highlighted and also its cost which are a server farm and clients having to re-bind with the service which occurs commonly in enterprise distributed applications.

Acknowledgements. We thank the UK EPSRC for the two forms of financial support: the EPSRC Project *Networked Computing in Inter-organisation Settings* (EP/D037743/1) and Mr Clarke's PhD scholarship.

References

1. Agbaria, A., Friedman, R.: A replication- and checkpoint-based approach for anomaly-based intrusion detection and recovery. In: ICDCS Workshop on Security in Distributed Computing Systems, pp. 137–143 (2005)
2. Barrantes, E.G., Ackley, D.H., Forrest, S., Stefanovic, D.: Randomized instruction set emulation. ACM Trans. Information System Security 8(1), 3–40 (2005)
3. Baumann, R.: Soft errors in advanced computer systems. IEEE Design and Test 22(3), 258–266 (2005)
4. Berger, E.D., Zorn, B.: Diehard: Probabilistic memory safety for unsafe languages. In: Proceedings of the ACM SIGPLAN 2006 Conference on Programming Language Design and Implementation, pp. 158–168. ACM Press, New York (2006)
5. Bhatkar, S., DuVarney, D.C., Sekar, R.: Address obfuscation: an efficient approach to combat a board range of memory error exploits. In: SSYM 2003: Proceedings of the 12th conference on USENIX Security Symposium, pp. 105–120. USENIX Association, Berkeley (2003)
6. Broder, A.Z., Dolev, D.: Flipping coins in many pockets (byzantine agreement on uniformly random values). In: SFCS 1984: Proceedings of the 25th Annual Symposium on Foundations of Computer Science, pp. 157–170. IEEE Computer Society, Washington (1984)
7. Castro, M., Liskov, B.: Practical byzantine fault tolerance. In: OSDI 1999: Proceedings of the third symposium on Operating systems design and implementation, pp. 173–186. USENIX Association, Berkeley (1999)
8. Castro, M., Liskov, B.: Practical byzantine fault tolerance and proactive recovery. ACM TOCS 20(4), 398–461 (2002)
9. Fetzer, C., Xiao, Z.: Detecting heap smashing attacks through fault containment wrappers. In: Proc. SRDS 2001, pp. 80–89 (2001)
10. Kc, G.S., Keromytis, A.D., Prevelakis, V.: Countering code-injection attacks with instruction-set randomization. In: Proceedings of the 10th ACM Conference on Computer and Communications Security (CCS), Washingtion, DC, USA, pp. 272–280 (2003)
11. Kistijantoro, A.I., Morgan, G., Shrivastava, S.K., Little, M.C.: Enhancing an application server to support available components. IEEE Transactions on Software Engineering 34(4), 531–545 (2008)
12. Lamport, L.: Paxos made simple. SIGACT News 32(4), 51–58 (2001)
13. Marsh, M., Schneider, F.B.: Codex: A robust and secure secret distribution system. IEEE Transctions in Dependable and Secure Computing 1(1), 34–47 (2004)
14. Roeder, T., Schneider, F.B.: Proactive obfuscation. Technical report. Cornell University (March 2009)

15. Saidane, A., Nicomette, V., Deswarte, Y.: The design of a generic intrusion-tolerant architecture for web servers. IEEE Transactions on Dependable and Secure Computing 6(1), 45–58 (2009)
16. Schneider, F.B.: Implementing fault-tolerant services using the state machine approach: a tutorial. ACM Comput. Surv. 22(4), 299–319 (1990)
17. Schneider, F.B., Zhou, L.: Implementing trustworthy services using replicated state machines. IEEE Security and Privacy 3(5), 34–43 (2005)
18. Shacham, H., Page, M., Pfaff, B., Goh, E., Modadugu, N., Boneh, D.: On the effectiveness of address-space randomization. In: CCS 2004: Proc. of the 11th ACM conference on Computer and Communications Security, pp. 298–307. ACM, New York (2004)
19. Slember, J.G., Narasimhan, P.: Using program analysis to identify and compensate for nondeterminism in fault-tolerant, replicated systems. In: Proceedings of SRDS, pp. 251–263 (2004)
20. Sousa, P., Bessani, A.N., Correia, M., Neves, N.F., Verissimo, P.: Resilient intrusion tolerance through proactive and reactive recovery. In: Proc. 13th Pacific Rim International Symposium on Dependable Computing PRDC 2007 (To appear also in IEEE TPDS), December 17-19, pp. 373–380 (2007)
21. Sousa, P., Neves, N.F., Veríssimo, P.: Proactive resilience through architectural hybridization. In: SAC 2006: Proceedings of the 2006 ACM symposium on Applied computing, pp. 686–690. ACM, New York (2006)
22. Sousa, P., Neves, N.F., Verissimo, P.: Hidden problems of asynchronous proactive recovery. In: Workshop on Hot Topics in System Dependability (June 2007)
23. Sousa, P., Neves, N.F., Verissimo, P., Sanders, W.H.: Proactive resilience revisited: The delicate balance between resisting intrusions and remaining available. In: Proc. 25th IEEE Symposium on Reliable Distributed Systems SRDS 2006, October 2-4, pp. 71–82 (2006)
24. Sovarel, A.N., Evans, D., Paul, N.: Where's the feeb?: The effectiveness of instruction set randomization. In: Proceedings of the 14th USENIX security symposium, pp. 145–160. Usenix Association (2005)
25. Xu, J., Kalbarczyk, Z., Iyer, R.K.: Transparent runtime randomization for security. In: Proceedings of SRDS, October 2003, pp. 260–269 (2003)
26. Zhao, W., Zhang, H.: Proactive service migration for long-running byzantine fault-tolerant systems. IET Software 3(2), 154–164 (2009)

Robustness of the Rotor-router Mechanism

Evangelos Bampas[1,3], Leszek Gąsieniec[2,*], Ralf Klasing[3,**],
Adrian Kosowski[4,3], and Tomasz Radzik[5]

[1] School of Elec. & Comp. Eng., National Technical University of Athens, Greece
ebamp@cs.ntua.gr
[2] Dept of Computer Science, Univ. of Liverpool, UK
L.A.Gasieniec@liverpool.ac.uk
[3] LaBRI, CNRS / INRIA / Univ. of Bordeaux, France
ralf.klasing@labri.fr
[4] Dept of Algorithms and System Modeling, Gdańsk Univ. of Technology, Poland
adrian@kaims.pl
[5] Dept of Computer Science, King's College London, UK
tomasz.radzik@kcl.ac.uk

Abstract. We consider the model of exploration of an undirected graph G by a single *agent* which is called the *rotor-router mechanism* or the *Propp machine* (among other names). Let π_v indicate the edge adjacent to a node v which the agent took on its last exit from v. The next time when the agent enters node v, first a "rotor" at node v advances pointer π_v to the edge $next(\pi_v)$ which is next after the edge π_v in a fixed cyclic order of the edges adjacent to v. Then the agent is directed onto edge π_v to move to the next node. It was shown before that after initial $O(mD)$ steps, the agent periodically follows one established Eulerian cycle, that is, in each period of $2m$ consecutive steps the agent traverses each edge exactly twice, once in each direction. The parameters m and D are the number of edges in G and the diameter of G. We investigate robustness of such exploration in presence of faults in the pointers π_v or dynamic changes in the graph. We show that after the exploration establishes an Eulerian cycle,

(*i*) if at some step the values of k pointers π_v are arbitrarily changed, then a new Eulerian cycle is established within $O(km)$ steps;

(*ii*) if at some step k edges are added to the graph, then a new Eulerian cycle is established within $O(km)$ steps;

(*iii*) if at some step an edge is deleted from the graph, then a new Eulerian cycle is established within $O(\gamma m)$ steps, where γ is the smallest number of edges in a cycle in graph G containing the deleted edge.

Our proofs are based on the relation between Eulerian cycles and spanning trees known as the "BEST" Theorem (after de **B**ruijn, van Aardenne-**E**hrenfest, **S**mith and **T**utte).

Keywords: Graph exploration, Rotor-router mechanism, Propp machine, Network faults, Dynamic graphs.

* Partially funded by the Royal Society International Joint Project, IJP - 2007/R1.
** Additional support by the ANR projects ALADDIN and IDEA and the INRIA project CEPAGE.

T. Abdelzaher, M. Raynal, and N. Santoro (Eds.): OPODIS 2009, LNCS 5923, pp. 345–358, 2009.

1   Introduction

We investigate robustness of the single-agent exploration of an undirected connected graph G based on the *rotor-router mechanism*. In this model of graph exploration the agent has no operational memory and the whole routing mechanism is provided within the environment. The edges adjacent to each node v are arranged in a fixed cyclic order, which does not change during the exploration. Each node v maintains a *port pointer* π_v which indicates the edge traversed by the agents on its *last* exit from v. If the agent has not visited node v yet, then π_v points to the initial arbitrary edge adjacent to v. The next time when the agent enters node v, first the port pointer π_v is advanced to the edge $next(\pi_v)$ which is next after the edge π_v in the cyclic order of the edges adjacent to v, and then the agent is directed onto edge π_v to move to the next node. This is *one step* of the exploration. We can think about the process of advancing the port pointer π_v as if there was a "rotor" at node v moving pointer π_v around the cyclic order of the edges adjacent to v, hence the name the *rotor-router mechanism*. This model was introduced by Priezzhev *et al.* [11], was further studied and popularised by James Propp, and now is also referred to as the *Propp machine*.

Wagner *et al.* [14,15] showed that in this model, starting from an arbitrary configuration (arbitrary cyclic orders of edges, arbitrary initial values of the port pointers and an arbitrary starting node) the agent covers all edges of the graph within $O(nm)$ steps, where n and m are the number of nodes and the number of edges in the graph. Bhatt *et al.* [2] showed later that within $O(nm)$ steps the agent not only covers all edges but actually *enters (establishes) an Eulerian cycle*. More precisely, after the initial *stabilisation period* of $O(nm)$ steps, the agent keeps repeating the same Eulerian cycle of the directed graph $\mathbf{G}$ which is the directed symmetric version of graph G. Graph $\mathbf{G}$ contains two opposite arcs (v, u) and (u, v) for each edge $\{v, u\}$ in G. Subsequently Yanovski *et al.* [16] showed that the agent enters an Eulerian cycle within $2mD$ steps, where D is the diameter of the graph.

It has been frequently mentioned in the previous work that a useful property of graph exploration based on the rotor-router mechanism is its robustness. In case of link failures or other dynamic changes in the graph, after some additional stabilisation period the agent goes back into the regime of repeatedly traversing the graph along a (new) Eulerian cycle. We know that whatever the changes in the graph are, the length of that additional stabilisation period is $O(mD)$ (as shown in [16], that much time is sufficient for establishing an Eulerian cycle from *any* initial configuration) but no better bounds have been shown before.

Our results. In this paper we develop bounds on the length of that additional stabilisation period. These bounds depend on the extent of the failures or changes in the graph. Thus we assume that an Eulerian cycle has been already established and show the following.

(*i*) **Faults in port pointers.** If at some step the values of k pointers π_v are changed to arbitrary edges (that is, the value of π_v is changed to an arbitrary edge adjacent to node v), then a new Eulerian cycle is established within $O(m \min\{k, D\})$ steps.

(ii) **Addition of new edges.** If at some step k edges are added to the graph, then a new Eulerian cycle is established within $O(m \min\{k, D\})$ steps.

(iii) **Deletion of an edge.** If at some step an edge is deleted from the graph but the graph remains connected, then a new Eulerian cycle is established within $O(\gamma m)$ steps, where γ is the smallest number of edges in a cycle in graph G containing the deleted edge.

A faulty change of the value of the port pointer π_v at a node v might occur when something unexpected makes the node believe that π_v should be re-set to some default value. We assume that when a new edge $\{u, v\}$ is added, it is inserted in arbitrary places in the existing cyclic orders of edges adjacent to nodes u and v, but otherwise those cyclic orders remain as they were before. Similarly, when an edge $\{u, v\}$ is deleted, the cyclic orders of the remaining edges adjacent to nodes u and v remain as they were. On both addition and deletion of an edge $\{v, u\}$, we allow arbitrary changes of the values of the port pointers at nodes v and u. A concrete system would specify some default updates for the port pointers on insertion or deletion of an edge, but for our results we do not need to make any assumptions about those defaults.

Regarding our $O(\gamma m)$ bound for the case of deleting an edge, we note that there are non-trivial classes of graphs (e.g., random graphs) in which each edge belongs to a short cycle. For such graphs parameter γ is small and our bound implies that the additional stabilisation period is short.

Previous work. The previous work which is most directly relevant to our paper are Bhatt *et al.* [2] and Yanovski *et al.* [16], both already mentioned above. Bhatt *et al.* [2] considers also mechanisms enabling the agent to stop after exploring the whole graph. Yanovski *et al.* [16], in addition to proving the $2mD$ bound on the length of the stabilisation period, show also that this bound is asymptotically optimal in the worst-case, and study the case when there are $k \geq 2$ agents. Regarding the terminology, we note that the graph exploration model based on the rotor-router mechanism which we consider in this paper is called the *Edge Ant Walk algorithm* in [14,15,16], while the same model is described in [2] in terms of traversing a maze and marking edges with pebbles.

The rotor-router mechanism is the strategy of leaving a node v along the edge for which the most time has elapsed since its last traversal *in the direction from v*. Cooper *et al.* [4] consider an *undirected* variant of this *oldest-first* strategy which chooses the edge for which the most time has elapsed since its last traversal *in any direction*. They show that this undirected oldest-first strategy leads in the worst case to exponential cover time.

The rotor-router mechanism has been often studied as a deterministic analogue of the *random walk* on a graph, with the main objective of discovering similarities and differences between these two processes. In the context of balancing the workload in a network, the single agent is replaced with a number of agents, referred to as *tokens*. Cooper and Spencer [5] study d-dimensional grid graphs and show a constant bound on the difference between the number of tokens at a given node v in the rotor-router model and the expected number of tokens at v in the random-walk model. Subsequently Doerr and Friedrich [7] analyse in more detail the distribution of tokens in the rotor-router mechanism on the 2-dimensional grid.

The research area of graph exploration with simple agents (robots) is rich in models and approaches. Exploration with robots with bounded memory has been considered for example in [8,9,12]. Models which allow placement of some identifiers or markers on nodes or edges of the graph have been considered for example in [1,6]. Some graph exploration techniques are surveyed in [10].

Our analysis of the rotor-router mechanism is based on the relationship between the Eulerian cycles in the directed graph G and the spanning trees in the undirected graph G which underlies the following theorem. This theorem, sometimes referred to as the "BEST" theorem, was discovered by de **B**ruijn and van Aardenne-**E**hrenfest [3] on the basis of earlier work by **S**mith and **T**utte [13].

Theorem 1 (Bruijn, van Aardenne-Ehrenfest, Smith, Tutte)
The number of Eulerian cycles in the directed, symmetric version of an undirected connected graph $G = (V, E)$ is equal to $\prod_{v \in V} (d(v) - 1)!$ times the number of spanning trees of G, where $d(v)$ is the degree of node v in G.

In Section 2 we establish the terminology and notation used in this paper and give the basic properties of exploration based on the rotor-router mechanism. In Section 3 we describe the connection between the Eulerian cycles and spanning trees in the context of the rotor-router mechanism. In passing we show how Theorem 1 follows from our analysis of the rotor-router mechanism. In Section 4 we investigate in more detail the stabilisation period of exploration with the rotor-router mechanism. The analysis developed in Sections 3 and 4 culminates in Theorem 3, which can be viewed as a quantitative description of the progress of stabilising the exploration, that is, the progress towards establishing an Eulerian cycle. In Section 5 we give our bounds on the length of the additional stabilisation period after some failures or changes in the graph have occurred. All these results are simple consequences of Theorem 3. We point out that all of the obtained bounds are asymptotically tight in the worst case.

2   The Rotor-router Model

Let $G = (V, E)$ be an undirected connected graph with n nodes, m edges and diameter D. The directed graph $G = (V, E)$ is the directed symmetric version of G, where the set of arcs $E = \{(v, u), (u, v) : \{v, u\} \in E\}$. We will refer to the undirected links in graph G as *edges* and to the directed links in graph G as *arcs*. We will also keep using boldface symbols, as G and E, to stress that we refer to directed graphs and arcs. For a node $v \in V$, $d(v)$ denotes the degree of v in G.

We consider the rotor-router model (on graph G) with a single agent. The agent moves in discrete steps from node to node along the arcs of graph $\mathbf{G}$. A *configuration* at the current step is a triple

$$((\rho_v)_{v \in V}, (\pi_v)_{v \in V}, r),$$

where ρ_v is a cyclic order of the arcs (in graph $\mathbf{G}$) outgoing from node v, π_v is an arc outgoing from node v, which is referred to as *the (current) port pointer at node v*, and r is *the current node* – the node where the agent is at the current step. For each node $v \in V$, the cyclic order ρ_v of the arcs outgoing from v is fixed at the beginning of exploration and does not change in any way from step to step (unless an edge is dynamically added or deleted as discussed in the previous section). For an arc (v, u), let $next(v, u)$ denote the arc next after arc (v, u) in the cyclic order ρ_v.

During the current step, first the port pointer π_r at the current node r is advanced to the next arc outgoing from r (that is, π_r becomes $next(\pi_r)$), and then the agent moves from node r traversing the arc π_r. The exploration starts from some initial configuration and then keeps running without ever terminating. We consider in this paper the rotor-router model as a mechanism for exploration of a graph, so the most interesting questions for us are how quickly the agent explores the whole graph, and how evenly it keeps traversing the edges of the graph. The following two simple lemmas will be used in later analysis.

Lemma 1. *The agent visits each node infinitely many times (thus traverses each arc infinitely many times).*

Proof. If a node v is visited only finitely many times, then each node in the neighbourhood of v is visited only finitely many times. Thus, by induction, each node in the graph is visited only finitely many times, contradicting the assumption that the agent does not terminate. □

Lemma 2. *If in the current step i the agent leaves the current node r along an arc (r, y), then the first arc traversed for the second time during the period $i, i + 1, \ldots,$ is this arc (r, y).*

Proof. Let v be the first node which the agent exits $d(v) + 1$ times during the period $i, i + 1, \ldots$. That is, the agent exits node v for the first time at some step $j' \geq i$ along an arc (v, u), then it exits v once along all remaining arcs outgoing from v, and then it exits v again along arc (v, u) at some step $j'' > j'$. During the period $i, i + 1, \ldots j'' - 1$, for every node $z \in V$, the agent exits z at most $d(z)$ times. Thus the arcs traversed during the period $i, i + 1, \ldots, j'' - 1$ are all distinct, and arc (v, u) is the first arc traversed for the second time. If $j' \geq i + 1$, then during the period $i, i + 1, \ldots j'' - 1$ the agent must enter node v $d(v) + 1$ times, because during the period $i + 1, i + 2, \ldots j''$ the agent leaves node v $d(v) + 1$ times. Hence if $j' \geq i + 1$, then there is an arc incoming to node v which is traversed twice during the period $i, i + 1, \ldots j'' - 1$. This contradiction implies that $j' = i$, so $(v, u) = (r, y)$. □

3 Trees and Eulerian Cycles

If T is a tree in graph G (not necessarily spanning all nodes of G), then T obtained from T by directing all edges towards a selected node v in T is called an *in-bound tree* in G, and node v is the root of T. A subset of arcs H in G is an *in-bound tree with a root cycle*, if it is an in-bound tree with one additional arc outgoing from the root. That additional arc creates a (directed) cycle, which we call a root cycle. We can view H as consisting of one cycle (the root cycle) and a number of in-bound node-disjoint trees rooted at nodes of this cycle (only the roots of these trees belong to the root cycle).

Let $F = \{\pi_v : v \in V\}$ be the set of the current port pointers. For the current node r, we are interested in the structure of $F_r = F \setminus \{\pi_r\}$, since, as we show later, the structure of F_r is a good indicator of how far the agent is from entering an Eulerian cycle. The component of F_r containing the current node r is an *in-bound tree* rooted at r, which we call *the leading tree*. Each component H of F_r other than the leading tree is an *in-bound tree with a root cycle*.

The following Lemmas 3 and 4 show that the condition that the agent follows an Eulerian cycle and the condition that the leading tree spans all nodes of the graph are equivalent.

Lemma 3. *Assume that the current leading tree T spans all nodes of the graph. Then during the next $2m$ steps the agent traverses an Eulerian cycle in G. Moreover, the leading tree after these $2m$ steps is again the same tree T.*

Proof. Let r be the current node (and the root of the current leading tree T) and let (r, y) be the arc which the agent traverses in the current step. Let Γ be the cycle (the sequence of arcs) which the agent follows starting from this traversal of arc (r, y) and ending right before the second traversal of this arc. We show that Γ is an Eulerian cycle in G. For $u \neq r$, let $p(u)$ be the parent of u in tree T, that is, $(u, p(u)) = \pi_u$. From Lemma 2, all arcs on Γ are distinct, so it remains to show that Γ contains all arcs.

Cycle Γ contains all $d(r)$ arcs outgoing from node r: after following cycle Γ, the agent is about to traverse arc (r, y) again, so it must have already traversed all arcs outgoing from r. This means that Γ must also contain all $d(r)$ arcs incoming to r (no arc occurs twice on Γ), including all arcs $\pi_u = (u, p(u))$ with $p(u) = r$. When cycle Γ passes through such an arc $(u, p(u))$, then it must have already passed through all arcs outgoing from node u, since arc $(u, p(u)) = \pi_u$ is the last arc outgoing from node u to be taken by the agent. This further implies that Γ contains all arcs incoming to u, including all arcs $(w, p(w))$ with $p(w) = u$. By induction on the distance to node r in tree T, for each node v, cycle Γ contains all arcs outgoing from v.

Since the agent has traversed an Eulerian cycle, all port pointers are back to what they were before traversing Γ. Thus the leading tree after traversing Γ is the same as it was before traversing Γ.   □

Fig. 1 illustrates Lemma 3. The diagram on the left shows a graph and the current leading tree (arcs in bold) which spans all nodes. The current node r is the root of this tree. The diagram on the right shows the Eulerian cycle followed by the agent. We assume in this figure that the cyclic order of the arcs outgoing from a node is the anti-clockwise order, and that arc (r, x) is the current value of the port pointer π_r. Thus the first arc followed by the agent is arc $(r, y) = next(r, x)$.

Lemma 4. *Assume that at the current step i the leading tree T does not span all nodes of the graph. Then the route Γ traversed by the agent during the next $2m$ steps is not an Eulerian cycle.*

Proof. Consider the (non-empty) set A of the arcs incoming to tree T, that is, the arcs with the start nodes outside T and the end nodes in T. If after the next $2m$ steps the agent is not back in the starting node r, then Γ is not a cycle. Therefore assume that the agent comes back to node r after $2m$ steps. If during these $2m$ steps the agent traverses an arc in A more than once or does not traverse it at all, then obviously Γ is not an Eulerian cycle. Therefore assume now that each arc in A is traversed exactly once, and let (v, u) be the arc in A traversed last. Consider the order of the arcs outgoing from node v ending with the arc which is the value of the port pointer π_v at node v at step i: $(v, x_1), (v, x_2), \ldots, (v, x_{d(v)}) = \pi_v$. Arc (v, u) is the last arc in this order which belongs to Γ, but (v, u) is not the arc π_v: node u is in T but arc π_v does not lead to T (or otherwise node v would belong to the leading tree T). Thus Γ does not contain arc π_v, so it is not an Eulerian cycle. □

For the initial configuration $((\rho_v)_{v \in V}, (\pi_v^{init})_{v \in V}, r_{init})$, let

$$\tau = \tau((\rho_v)_{v \in V}, (\pi_v^{init})_{v \in V}, r_{init}) \leq \infty,$$

denote the first step when the leading tree spans all nodes of G. We use this parameter τ as our formal definition of the *stabilisation time*, and call these initial τ steps the *stabilisation period*. Lemma 3 implies immediately the following corollary.

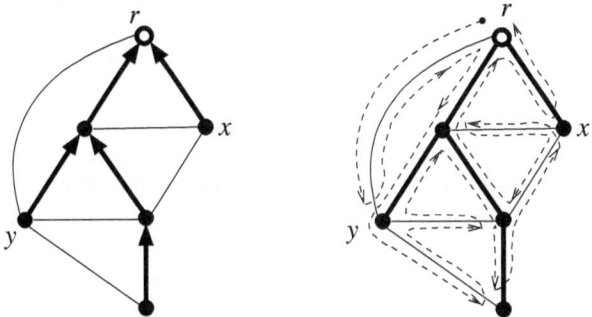

Fig. 1. Left: the leading tree spanning all nodes of the graph (arcs in bold). Right: the corresponding Eulerian cycle, assuming the anti-clockwise order of arcs outgoing from a node (other cycles are obtained for other cyclic orders of arcs).

Corollary 1. *After the stabilisation period, the agent keeps traversing the same Eulerian cycle.*

We refer to the Eulerian cycle which the agent keeps repeating after the stabilisation period as the *established Eulerian cycle*. Yanovski *et al.* [16] defined t_0 as the first step when all arcs of the graph are traversed and showed the following result.

Theorem 2. [16] *For any graph G, any cyclic order ρ_v of the arcs outgoing from each node $v \in V$, and any initial values of the port pointers π_v, $v \in V$, we have $t_0 \leq 2mD$, and from step $t_0 + 1$ the agent keeps repeating the same Eulerian cycle of graph G.*

The definitions of steps τ and t_0 are somewhat different, but these two steps cannot be far apart. Lemma 3 implies that $t_0 \leq \tau + 2m$. On the other hand, since from step t_0 the agent follows an Eulerian cycle (Theorem 2), then Lemma 4 implies that $\tau \leq t_0$.

We conclude this section by showing the connection between the rotor-router mechanism and Theorem 1. We fix a node r as the current node and an arc (r, x) as the current value of the port pointer π_r (the agent will follow in the current step arc $next(r, x)$). Let T denote an in-bound spanning tree of G rooted at node r, and let ρ_v denote a cyclic order of the arcs in G outgoing from v. Consider the assignment of Eulerian cycles of G to pairs $(T, (\rho_v)_{v \in V})$ given by Lemma 3. More precisely, assigns to a pair $(T, (\rho_v)_{v \in V})$ the Eulerian cycle of G which is followed by the agent starting from the configuration $((\rho_v)_{v \in V}, T \cup \{\pi_r\}, r)$, that is, starting with T as the leading tree. It is easy to verify that the cycles Γ' and Γ'' assigned to two distinct pairs $(T', (\rho'_v)_{v \in V})$ and $(T'', (\rho''_v)_{v \in V})$ are distinct.

We now show that each Eulerian cycle of graph G corresponds to some pair $(T, (\rho_v)_{v \in V})$. For an arbitrary Eulerian cycle Γ of G, for each $v \in V$, let ρ_v be the cyclic order of the arcs outgoing from a node v defined by the order of these arcs along Γ. Pick the beginning of cycle Γ such that edge (r, x) is the last edge on Γ. For each node $v \neq r$, let π_v be the last arc on Γ outgoing from v. The set of arcs $T = \{\pi_v : v \in V \setminus \{r\}\}$ does not contain a cycle, so it is an in-bound spanning tree of G rooted at node r. The agent starting from the configuration $((\rho_v)_{v \in V}, T \cup \{\pi_r\}, r)$ follows cycle Γ, so cycle Γ is assigned to the pair $(T, (\rho_v)_{v \in V})$.

The above one-to-one correspondence between the Eulerian cycles in G and the pairs $(T, (\rho_v)_{v \in V})$, where T is an in-bound spanning tree of G rooted at node r and ρ_v is a cyclic order of the arcs in G outgoing from v, gives a one-to-one correspondence between the Eulerian cycles in G and the pairs $(T, (\rho_v)_{v \in V})$, where T is a spanning tree in G: identify an in-bound spanning tree of G rooted at node r with the spanning tree of G obtained from T by disregarding the directions of arcs. The existence of a one-to-one correspondence between the Eulerian cycles in G and the pairs $(T, (\rho_v)_{v \in V})$ implies Theorem 1. Indeed, for a node $v \in V$, there are $(d(v) - 1)!$ distinct cyclic orders ρ_v. Thus the number of Eulerian cycles in G is equal to $\prod_{v \in V}(d(v) - 1)!$ times the number of spanning trees of G, as Theorem 1 states.

4   Evolution of the Leading Tree

With respect to the set of port pointers $F_r = F \setminus \{\pi_r\}$, where r is the current node, a node v is an *ancestor* of a node u if, and only if, the path in F_r starting from v passes through u. Each node is its own ancestor. If a node v belongs to the leading tree T, then the ancestors of v are all nodes on the path in T from v to the root r, including both v and r. If a node v does not belong to the leading tree T, then it belongs to a component H of F_r which is an in-bound tree with a root cycle. In this case, the ancestors of v are all nodes on the path in H from v to the cycle and all nodes on the cycle.

The following Lemmas 5 and 6, which describe changes of the leading tree, can be easily verified.

Lemma 5. *If a node belongs to the current leading tree, then it remains in the leading tree in all subsequent steps.*

Lemma 6. *Let v be a node which is not in the current leading tree. Node v enters the leading tree at the first step when the agent visits an ancestor of v.*

Fig. 2 shows an example how the leading tree changes when the agent does not go outside of the tree. Note that this figure shows only the leading tree, not the whole graph. Fig. 3 illustrates Lemma 6.

Lemma 7 below can be viewed as a generalisation of Lemma 3 to the case when the leading tree does not span all nodes. The neighbourhood of the leading tree T consists of the nodes which are not in T but are adjacent to the nodes in T.

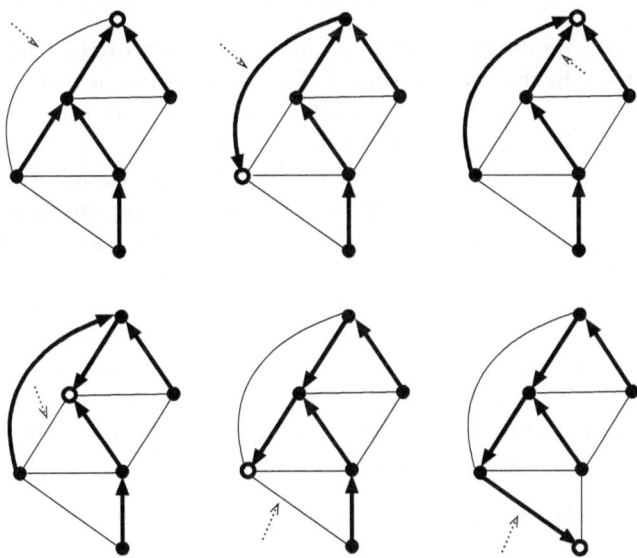

Fig. 2. The changing leading tree when the agent does not go outside the tree. The white node is the current node (and the root of the tree). The dotted arrow indicates the edge to be taken from the current node.

the current leading tree   the next leading tree

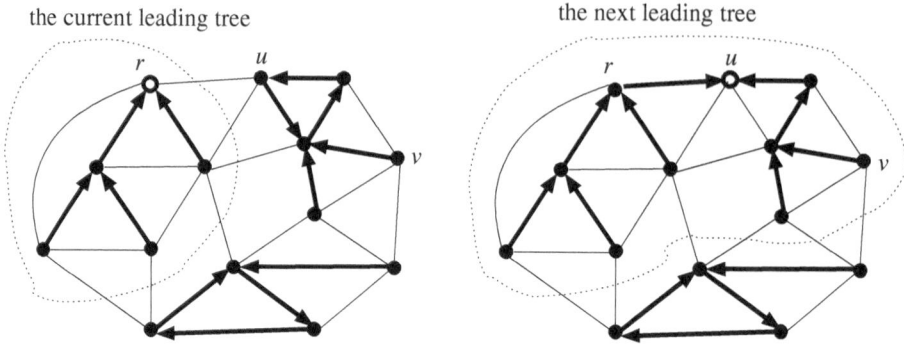

Fig. 3. The port pointers π_x, $x \neq r$, are shown as boldface arrows. Left: the current step, when node v is outside the leading tree. Right: the next step, when the agent visits an ancestor u of v and v enters the leading tree.

Lemma 7. *Each node which is in the current step in the neighbourhood of the leading tree T is visited within the next $2m$ steps.*

Proof. Let (r, s) be the arc traversed in the current step i, and then traversed again for the second time in a future step $j > i$. Lemma 2 implies that the arcs traversed in steps $i, i+1, \ldots, j-1$ are all distinct, so $j \leq i+2m$. We can show, similarly as in the proof of Lemma 3, that each arc outgoing from each node in tree T is traversed during the period $i, i+1, \ldots, j-1$. Thus each node v in the neighbourhood of tree T is visited at least once during this period.   □

Lemmas 6 and 7 imply that a node v which is outside of the leading tree but has an ancestor u in the neighbourhood of the leading tree will enter the leading tree within $2m$ steps. If a node v which is outside of the leading tree has an ancestor u in the neighbourhood of a node w which has an ancestor y in the neighbourhood of the leading tree, then v will enter the leading tree within $4m$ steps (node w will enter the leading tree within $2m$ steps and then node v will enter the leading tree within additional $2m$ steps), and so on. To formalise this, we define the *length of an arc* (v, u) as equal to 0, if $(v, u) \in F_r$, and equal to 1 otherwise. The *distance* from a node v to a node x is the minimum total length of a path from v to x in G. Note that the length of an arc and the distance from a node to another node are relative to the current step (and the current values of the port pointers). The distance from a node v to a node x is 0 if, and only if, x is an ancestor of v. Observe also that the distance from one node to any other node is never greater than the diameter D of the graph.

Theorem 3. *If the distance from a node v to the current node r is equal to k, then node v enters the leading tree within $2km$ steps.*

Proof. The proof is by induction on k. If the distance from a node v to the current node r is 0, then there is a path from v to r consisting of port pointers (arcs with length 0), so node v is in the leading tree already in the current step.

If the distance from a node v to the current node r is $k \geq 1$, then a shortest path from v to r (with respect to the current lengths of the arcs) follows first port pointers from v to an ancestor u of v (zero or more arcs of length 0), and then follows an arc (u, w) to a neighbour w of u which is not an ancestor of v (an arc of length 1). The distance from node w to the current node r is $k - 1$, so by the inductive hypothesis, node w enters the leading tree within $2(k - 1)m$ steps. Thus node u is in the neighbourhood of the leading tree within $2(k - 1)m$ steps, so Lemma 7 implies that node u is visited within $2km$ steps. This and Lemma 6 imply that node v enters the leading tree within $2km$ steps.   □

We note that Theorem 3 gives an alternative proof of the $O(mD)$ bound shown in [16] on the number of steps required in the rotor-router model to enter an Eulerian cycle. Recall that for any configuration of the rotor-router mechanism and any node v, the distance from v to the current node (w.r.t. the lengths of the arcs) is at most D. Using Theorem 3 we conclude that all nodes enter the leading tree within $2mD$ steps.

5   Faulty Port Pointers and Dynamic Changes of the Graph

In this section we give bounds on the number of steps needed to establish a new Eulerian cycle when some changes in the graph have occurred. All these bounds follow from Theorem 3. A spontaneous (faulty) change of the value of the port pointer π_v is a change to an arbitrary arc outgoing from node v.

After the stabilisation period, inserting or deleting an edge $\{v, u\}$ may be harmless if this operation does not change the port pointers at nodes v and u. If these port pointers remain as they were, then the leading tree does not change, so it continues spanning all nodes and a new Eulerian cycle is established immediately. However, recall from Section 1 that we assume that insertion or deletion of an edge $\{v, u\}$ may cause arbitrary changes of the values of the port pointers at nodes v and u. Recall also that we assume that the cyclic orders of the edges adjacent to nodes v and u excluding edge $\{v, u\}$ are the same after the insertion/deletion as they were before.

Theorem 4. *In the rotor-router model, after the stabilisation period, if k port pointers spontaneously change their values at some step, then a new Eulerian cycle is established within $2m \min\{k, D\}$ steps.*

Proof. Consider the leading tree right before those k changes of the port pointers. The stabilisation period has passed, so the leading tree spans all nodes. For each node $x \in V$, the length of the path P in the leading tree from x to the current node is equal to 0. When k port pointers change their values, then at most k arcs on path P change length from 0 to 1. This means that the new length of P is at most k, so the distance from x to the current node is at most k, and this distance is never greater than D. Thus Theorem 3 implies that all nodes in the graph will be back in the leading tree within $2m \min\{k, D\}$ steps.   □

Theorem 5. *In the rotor-router model, after the stabilisation period, if k new edges are added to the graph at some step, then an Eulerian cycle in the expanded graph is established within $2m \min\{2k, D\}$ steps.*

Proof. Adding k edges may result in changes of the values of up to $2k$ port pointers, so Theorem 4 implies that an Eulerian cycle is established in the expanded graph within $2m \min\{2k, D\}$ steps.   □

Theorem 6. *In the rotor-router model, after the stabilisation period, if at some step an edge $\{v, u\}$ is removed from the graph but without disconnecting it, then an Eulerian cycle in the new graph is established within $2\gamma m$ steps, where γ is the smallest number of edges on a cycle in G containing edge $\{v, u\}$.*

Proof. The removal of an edge $\{v, u\}$ from the graph may change the port pointers at nodes v and u. Similarly as in the proof of Theorem 4, consider the leading tree right before this edge removal. For each node $x \in V$, the length of the path P in the leading tree from x to the current node is equal to 0. When edge $\{v, u\}$ is removed, then two arcs on path P may change their length from 0 to 1, and

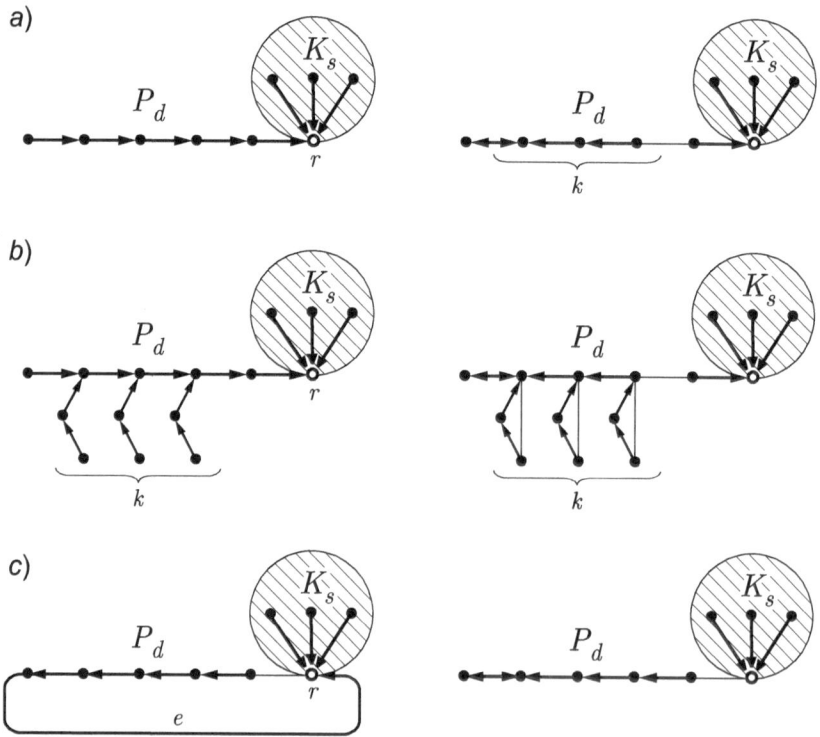

Fig. 4. Worst-case examples for the stabilization period of the rotor-router after changes to the graph: (a) modification of k port pointers, (b) addition of k edges, (c) removal of a single edge e

if arc (v, u) or arc (u, v) belongs to P, then we replace this arc with the $\gamma - 1$ arcs from a shortest cycle in G containing this arc. The length of the new path from x to the current node is at most γ (at most γ arcs have length 1), so the distance from x to the current node is at most γ. Thus Theorem 3 implies that all nodes in the graph are back in the leading tree within $2\gamma m$ steps.   □

The bounds which appear in Theorems 4, 5, and 6 are all asymptotically tight in the worst case. Indeed, for some values of parameters s and d, consider the lollipop graph $G_{s,d}$ obtained by merging a vertex r of the clique K_s with an end-vertex of the path P_d (cf. Fig. 4a). Let the agent be located at vertex r after the stabilization of the rotor-router. When k port pointers are altered at internal nodes of path P_d ($k < d$), the rotor-router will only stabilize to a new Eulerian cycle after visiting each of the edges of the clique at least k times. Hence, for any feasible set of parameters n, m, k, D there exists a graph with $\Theta(n)$ nodes, $\Theta(m)$ edges and diameter $\Theta(D)$, such that restoring the stable state of the rotor-router after modification of k port pointers requires $\Omega(m \min\{k, D\})$ steps. Thus, the bound in Theorem 4 is asymptotically tight in the worst case.

Likewise, by the construction shown in Fig. 4b, we obtain a worst-case lower bound of $\Omega(m \min\{k, D\})$ steps for the stabilization period after adding k new edges to the graph, asymptotically matching the bound in Theorem 5. Note that the addition of edges to the graph may by assumption result in modifications to pointer arrangements at the endpoints of added edges. Finally, Fig. 4c provides an example of a scenario in which removing a single edge leads to a stabilization period of $\Omega(\gamma m)$, asymptotically matching the bound in Theorem 6.

6   Conclusions

In this paper we have presented a quantitative evaluation of the robustness of the graph exploration based on the rotor-router mechanism. Our bounds on the length of the additional stabilisation period, required after some faults or changes have occurred in the graph, are asymptotically tight in the worst-case.

Our analysis can be applied to other possible models of faults and dynamic changes in the graph. For example, one may observe that our analysis implies that the rotor-router mechanism tolerates spontaneous changes of the cyclic orders of the edges. More precisely, if at some step after the stabilisation period the cyclic orders of edges change in any way but the port pointers remain the same (that is, they point to the same edges as before), then the agent immediately enters a new Eulerian cycle (no need for any additional stabilisation period).

Challenging questions arise with introduction of multiple agents to the rotor-router model. If we have many agents, then there are still interesting open questions left regarding the stabilisation and periodicity of exploration even in the static case (no faults, no dynamic changes of the graph).

References

1. Bender, M.A., Fernández, A., Ron, D., Sahai, A., Vadhan, S.P.: The power of a pebble: Exploring and mapping directed graphs. Inf. Comput. 176(1), 1–21 (2002)
2. Bhatt, S.N., Even, S., Greenberg, D.S., Tayar, R.: Traversing directed Eulerian mazes. J. Graph Algorithms Appl. 6(2), 157–173 (2002)
3. de Bruijn, N.G., Aardenne-Ehrenfest, T.: Circuits and trees in oriented linear graphs. Simon Stevin (Bull. Belgian Math. Soc.) 28, 203–217 (1951)
4. Cooper, C., Ilcinkas, D., Klasing, R., Kosowski, A.: Derandomizing random walks in undirected graphs using locally fair exploration strategies. In: Albers, S., et al. (eds.) ICALP 2009. LNCS, vol. 5556, pp. 411–422. Springer, Heidelberg (2009)
5. Cooper, J.N., Spencer, J.: Simulating a random walk with constant error. Combinatorics, Probability & Computing 15(6), 815–822 (2006)
6. Deng, X., Papadimitriou, C.H.: Exploring an unknown graph. Journal of Graph Theory 32(3), 265–297 (1999)
7. Doerr, B., Friedrich, T.: Deterministic random walks on the two-dimensional grid. Combinatorics, Probability & Computing 18(1-2), 123–144 (2009)
8. Fraigniaud, P., Ilcinkas, D., Peer, G., Pelc, A., Peleg, D.: Graph exploration by a finite automaton. Theoretical Computer Science 345(2-3), 331–344 (2005)
9. Gąsieniec, L., Pelc, A., Radzik, T., Zhang, X.: Tree exploration with logarithmic memory. In: Proceedings 19th ACM-SIAM Symposium on Discrete Algorithms, SODA 2007, pp. 585–594 (2007)
10. Gąsieniec, L., Radzik, T.: Memory efficient anonymous graph exploration. In: Broersma, H., Erlebach, T., Friedetzky, T., Paulusma, D. (eds.) WG 2008. LNCS, vol. 5344, pp. 14–29. Springer, Heidelberg (2008)
11. Priezzhev, V., Dhar, D., Dhar, A., Krishnamurthy, S.: Eulerian walkers as a model of self-organized criticality. Phys. Rev. Lett. 77(25), 5079–5082 (1996)
12. Reingold, O.: Undirected connectivity in log-space. J. ACM 55(4) (2008)
13. Tutte, W.T., Smith, C.A.B.: On unicursal paths in a network of degree 4. The American Mathematical Monthly 48(4), 233–237 (1941)
14. Wagner, I.A., Lindenbaum, M., Bruckstein, A.M.: Smell as a computational resource - a lesson we can learn from the ant. In: Proc. 4th Israel Symposium on Theory of Computing and Systems, ISTCS 1996, pp. 219–230 (1996)
15. Wagner, I.A., Lindenbaum, M., Bruckstein, A.M.: Distributed covering by ant-robots using evaporating traces. IEEE Transactions on Robotics and Automation 15, 918–933 (1999)
16. Yanovski, V., Wagner, I.A., Bruckstein, A.M.: A distributed ant algorithm for efficiently patrolling a network. Algorithmica 37(3), 165–186 (2003)

Brief Annoucement: Analysis of an Optimal Bit Complexity Randomised Distributed Vertex Colouring Algorithm*

(Extended Abstract)

Y. Métivier, J.M. Robson, N. Saheb-Djahromi, and A. Zemmari

Université de Bordeaux - LaBRI
351 cours de la Libération, 33405 Talence, France
{metivier,robson,saheb,zemmari}@labri.fr

1 Introduction

1.1 The Problem

Let $G = (V, E)$ be a simple undirected graph. A vertex *colouring* of G assigns colours to each vertex in such a way that neighbours have different colours.

In this paper we discuss how efficient (time and bits) vertex colouring may be accomplished by exchange of bits between neighbouring vertices. The distributed complexity of vertex colouring is of fundamental interest for the study and analysis of distributed computing. Usually, the topology of a distributed system is modelled by a graph and paradigms of distributed systems are encoded by classical problems in graph theory; among these classical problems one may cite the problems of vertex colouring, computing a maximal independent set, finding a vertex cover or finding a maximal matching. Each solution to one of these problems is a building block for many distributed algorithms: symmetry breaking, topology control, routing, resource allocation.

1.2 The Model

The Network. We consider the standard message passing model for distributed computing. The communication model consists of a point-to-point communication network described by a simple undirected graph $G = (V, E)$ where the vertices of V represent network processors and the edges represent bidirectional communication channels. Processes communicate by message passing: a process sends a message to another by depositing the message in the corresponding channel. We assume the system synchronous and synchronous wake up of processors: processors have access to a global clock and all processors start the algorithm at the same time.

Time Complexity. A round (cycle) of each processor is composed of the following three steps: 1. Send messages to (some of) the neighbours, 2. Receive

---

* This work was supported by grant No ANR-06-SETI-015-03 awarded by Agence Nationale de la Recherche

T. Abdelzaher, M. Raynal, and N. Santoro (Eds.): OPODIS 2009, LNCS 5923, pp. 359–364, 2009.

messages from (some of) the neighbours, 3. Perform some local computation. As usual (see for example Peleg [Pel00]) the time complexity is the maximum possible number of rounds needed until every node has completed its computation.

Bit Complexity. As is explained by Santoro in [San07] (Chapter 6) (see also [Gho06], Chapter 3) the cost of a synchronous distributed algorithm is both time and bits (whether a message contains 1 bit or it contains the Encyclopedia Britannica does not have the same cost). By definition, the bit complexity of a distributed algorithm (per channel) is the total number of bits exchanged (per channel) during its execution. Thus it is considered as a finer measure of communication complexity and it has been studied for breaking and achieving symmetry or for colouring in [BMW94, KOSS06, DMR08]. Dinitz et al. explain in [DMR08] that it may be viewed as a natural extension of communication complexity (introduced by Yao [Yao79]) to the analysis of tasks in a distributed setting. An introduction to this area can be found in Kushilevitz and Nisan [KN99].

Network and Processes Knowledge. The network is anonymous: unique identities are not available to distinguish the processes. We do not assume any global knowledge of the network, not even its size or an upper bound on its size. The processors do not require any position or distance information. Each processor knows from which channel it receives a message. An important fact due to the initial symmetry is: *there is no deterministic distributed algorithm for arbitrary anonymous graphs for vertex colouring assuming all vertices wake up simultaneously.*

1.3   Our Contribution

We present and analyse a randomised distributed vertex colouring algorithm. In this paper, we prove Theorem 1:

There exists a randomised distributed colouring algorithm for arbitrary graphs of size n that halts in time $O(\log n)$ with probability $1 - o(n^{-1})$ each message containing 1 bit.

Kothapalli et al. show in [KOSS06] that if only one bit can be sent along each edge in a round, then every distributed vertex colouring algorithm (in which every node has the same initial state and initially only knows its own edges) needs at least $\Omega(\log n)$ rounds with high probability[1] (w.h.p. for short) to colour the cycle of size n with any finite number of colours. From this result we deduce that our algorithm is optimal (bits and time) modulo multiplicative constants.

1.4   Related Work: Comparisons and Comments

Vertex colouring is a fundamental problem in distributed systems. It is mainly studied under two assumptions: (1) vertices have unique identifiers, and more generally, they have an initial colouring, (2) every vertex has the same initial state and initially only knows its own edges.

---

[1] With high probability means with probability $1 - o(n^{-1})$.

Vertex colouring is a classical technique to break symmetry. If vertices have unique identifiers (or if there is an initial colouring) then the initial local symmetry is naturally broken; otherwise, as usual, it is broken by using randomisation.

Vertices Have an Initial Colouring. In this case, as we said before, the local symmetry is broken and, generally, vertex colouring algorithms try to decrease the number of colours (for example, to $\Delta+1$ or to $O(\Delta)$ where Δ is the maximum vertex degree in the graph). Classical examples are given in [Pel00] (Chapter 7). The model assumes that each node has a unique $O(\log n)$ bit identifier. More recently, Kuhn and Wattenhofer [KW06] have obtained efficient time complexity algorithms to obtain $O(\Delta)$ colours in the case where every vertex can only send its own current colour to all its neighbours. Cole and Vishkin [CV86] show that there is a distributed algorithm which colours a cycle on n vertices with 3 colours and runs in $O(\log^* n)$. Lower bounds for colouring particular families of graphs are given in [Lin92]. This paper presents also an algorithm which colours a graph of size n with $O(\Delta^2)$ colours and runs in $O(\log^* n)$.

Vertices Have the Same Initial State and no Knowledge. In this case we have no choice: we use randomised algorithms. In [Joh99], Johansson analyses a simple randomised distributed vertex colouring algorithm. Each vertex u keeps a palette of colours initialised to $\{0, ..., d\}$ if the degree of u is d. The algorithm then proceeds in rounds. In a round each uncoloured vertex u randomly chooses a colour c from its palette. It sends c to its neighbours and receives a colour from each neighbour. If the colour c chosen by u is different from colours chosen by its neighbours then c becomes the final colour of u, u informs its neighbours and becomes passive. At the beginning of the next round each active vertex removes from its palette final colours of its neighbours.

Johanson proves that this algorithm runs in $O(\log n)$ rounds with high probability on graphs of size n. The size of each message is $\log n$ thus the bit complexity per channel of this algorithm is $O(\log^2 n)$.

In fact this algorithm may be viewed as a particular case of a general family of randomised algorithms in which vertices wake up with a certain probability to participate in a round (see [Lub93, FPS04]).

The table below summarises the comparison between Johanson's Algorithm and the algorithm presented in this paper: Algorithm $\mathcal{B}$.

	Time	Order of the colour of a vertex of degree d	Message size (number of bits)	Bit complexity (per channel)
Johansson's algorithm	$O(\log n)$	$d+1$ (guaranteed)	$\log n$	$O(\log^2 n)$
Algorithm $\mathcal{B}$	$O(\log n)$	$O(d)$ (on average)	1	$O(\log n)$

2   Algorithm $\mathcal{B}$

We describe the algorithm executed by each node. Our algorithm operates in synchronous rounds. At each round, some vertices are permanently coloured, and stop executing the algorithm, some edges are removed from the graph (symmetry is broken) and the other vertices continue the execution of the algorithm in the residual graph. Let $G = (V, E)$ be the initial graph, we denote by $(G_i)_{i \geq 0}$ the sequence of graphs induced by active vertices, where $G_0 = G$ and G_i is the residual graph obtained after the ith round.

Formally, each vertex v maintains a list $active_v$ of active vertices, i.e., neighbours which are not yet coloured and with which symmetry is not yet broken; initially $active_v$ is equal to $N(v)$ (the set of neighbours of v). We denote by $colour_v$ the colour of the vertex v which is the word formed by bits generated by the vertex v (we denote by $\oplus$ the concatenation operation on words); initially $colour_v$ is the empty word. The vertex v generates a random bit b_v; it concatenates b_v to $colour_v$, i.e., the new colour of v is $b_v \oplus colour_v$; it sends b_v to all its active neighbours, receives the bits sent by these vertices and then updates its list. This action is repeated until the symmetry is broken with all its neighbours and hence the vertex has obtained its final colour.

Remark 1. The colour of a node v is the concatenation of all the bits generated since from the start of execution of the algorithm to the time where v has no active neighbours. In a natural way, it may be interpreted as an integer.

3   Analysis of the Algorithm

The Expected Time Complexity. Each vertex v which is not already coloured generates a bit b_v, sends b_v to all its still active neighbours and receives b_u from each active neighbour u. If $b_v \neq b_u$ then v updates its list of active neighbours by dropping u from this list. In terms of the graph structure, this means that the edge $\{u, v\}$ is removed from the graph. Since the event $b_v \neq b_u$ occurs with probability $1/2$, it is easy to prove that:

Lemma 1. *Let $(G_i)_{i \geq 0}$ be the sequence of residual graphs obtained with Algorithm $\mathcal{B}$. The expected number of edges removed from the residual graph G_i after the $(i + 1)^{th}$ round is half the number of its edges.*

Then, we have:

Corollary 1. *There is a constant k_1 such that for any graph G of n vertices, the number of rounds to remove all edges from G is less than $k_1 \log n$ on average.*

Now we prove a more precise result:

Lemma 2. *There is a constant K_1 such that for any graph G of n vertices, the number of rounds to remove all edges from G is less than $K_1 \log n$ w.h.p.*

Proof. Initially the number of edges is less than $n^2/2$. Therefore after r rounds the expected number of edges remaining is less than $n^2/2^{r+1}$. In particular after $4 \log n - 1$ rounds it is less than $n^{-2}/2$ so that the probability that any edges remain is less than $n^{-2}/2$.   □

Finally:

Theorem 1. *Algorithm $\mathcal{B}$ computes a colouring for any arbitrary graph of size n in time $O(\log n)$ w.h.p., each message containing 1 bit.*

Local Complexity. In this section, we study the expected number of bits generated for a given vertex v with degree $d(v) = d$. Let L_d denote the number of bits generated on the vertex v and let $l_d = \mathbb{E}(L_d)$ its expected value. Let $I(v)$ denote the set of edges incident to v. At each round, any $e \in I(v)$ is removed with probability $1/2$, then the same arguments as in the previous section can be used to prove that $\mathbb{E}(L_d)$ is $O(\log d)$. However, id $d \to \infty$, using the Mellin transform, we prove a more precise result:

Proposition 1. *Let $G = (V, E)$ be a connected graph and $v \in V$ with $d(v) = d \to \infty$. Let l_d denote the expected number of bits generated by v before it obtains its final colour. Then $l_d = \log_2 d + \frac{1}{2} + \frac{\gamma}{\log 2} + Q(\log_2 d) + O(d^{-2})$, where $Q(u) = -\frac{1}{\log 2}\sum_{k\in\mathbb{Z}\backslash\{0\}} \Gamma\left(\frac{2ik\pi}{\log 2}\right) e^{-2ik\pi u}$ is a Fourier series with period 1 and with an amplitude which does not exceed 10^{-6}.*

Corollary 2. *Let v be a vertex; let $c(v)$ be the colour of v interpreted as an integer; then $\mathbb{E}(c(v)) = O(d)$.*

More exactly, we have the following result on the distribution of the r.v. L_d :

Lemma 3. *Let $d \geq 1$. We have: $\Pr(L_d=0)=0$, and $\Pr(L_d=k) = \left(1-\frac{1}{2^k}\right)^d - \left(1-\frac{1}{2^{k-1}}\right)^d$, if $k \geq 1$.*

Lemma 3 gives the probability distribution of the r.v. L_d. Thus, we can derive its variance:

Lemma 4. *Let $\mathbb{Var}$ denote the variance, if $d \to \infty$, then we have $\mathbb{Var}(L_d) = (\frac{1}{\log 2} - 1)\log_2 d + \frac{1}{12} + \frac{1}{6}\frac{\pi^2}{(\log 2)^2} - P(\log_2 d) + O(d^{-2})$, where $P(u) = Q(u)^2 + (2u + \frac{2\gamma}{\log 2} - \frac{2}{\log 2})Q(u)$ and Q is the Fourier series defined in Proposition 1.*

We then have:

Proposition 2. *The ratio R_d between L_d and $\log_2 d$ tends in probability to 1 as d tends to ∞.*

Now we can state a result more precise than Corollary 2:

Corollary 3. *Let v be a vertex; let $c(v)$ be the colour of v interpreted as an integer. Then for any $\varepsilon > 0$, $\lim_{d\to\infty} \Pr(c(v) \leq d^{1+\varepsilon}) = 1$.*

4   Conclusion and Further Developments

Algorithm $\mathcal{B}$ is a very simple and natural vertex colouring. In this paper we analyse its time and bit complexity (on an edge, on a vertex and over all the graph). To our knowledge this kind of analysis has never been done before. This analysis is non trivial and to obtain precise results we use some tools like the Mellin transform. It needs no initial knowledge and from the work of Kothapalli et al. [KOSS06] we deduce that it is optimal (modulo a multiplicative constant). Johansson's algorithm ensures a $d+1$ colouring for a vertex of degree d, while our algorithm needs a priori $O(d)$ colours (on average) for the same vertex. There are two natural questions, with the same initial knowledge: *(1) Is it possible to estimate the number of different colours Algorithm $\mathcal{B}$ needs? (2) Is it possible to improve the number of colours, using an optimal algorithm (for the bit complexity)?*

Acknowledgement

The authors are grateful to Christian Lavault for the corrections he suggested in the proofs using the Mellin transform.

References

[BMW94]   Bodlaender, H.L., Moran, S., Warmuth, M.K.: The distributed bit complexity of the ring: from the anonymous case to the non-anonymous case. Information and computation 114(2), 34–50 (1994)

[CV86]   Cole, R., Vishkin, U.: Deterministic coin tossing and accelerating cascades: micro and macro techniques for designing parallel algorithms. In: STOC, pp. 206–219 (1986)

[DMR08]   Dinitz, Y., Moran, S., Rajsbaum, S.: Bit complexity of breaking and achieving symmetry in chains and rings. Journal of the ACM 55(1) (2008)

[FPS04]   Finocchi, I., Panconesi, A., Silvestri, R.: An experimental analysis of simple, distributed vertex coloring algorithms. Algorithmica 41(1), 1–23 (2004)

[Gho06]   Ghosh, S.: Distributed systems - An algorithmic approach. CRC Press, Boca Raton (2006)

[Joh99]   Johansson, Ö.: Simple distributed $(\Delta + 1)$-coloring of graphs. Information Processing Letters 70(5), 229–232 (1999)

[KN99]   Kushilevitz, E., Nisan, N.: Communication complexity. Cambridge University Press, Cambridge (1999)

[KOSS06] Kothapalli, K., Onus, M., Scheideler, C., Schindelhauer, C.: Distributed coloring in $O(\sqrt{\log n})$ bit rounds. In: Proceedings of 20th International Parallel and Distributed Processing Symposium (IPDPS 2006), Rhodes Island, Greece, April 25-29. IEEE, Los Alamitos (2006)

[KW06]   Kuhn, F., Wattenhofer, R.: On the complexity of distributed graph coloring. In: Proceedings of the 25 Annual ACM Symposium on Principles of Distributed Computing (PODC), pp. 7–15. ACM Press, New York (2006)

[Lin92]   Linial, N.: Locality in distributed graph algorithms. SIAM J. Comput. 21, 193–201 (1992)

[Lub93]   Luby, M.: Removing randomness in parallel computation without a processor penalty. J. Comput. Syst. Sci. 47(2), 250–286 (1993)

[Pel00]   Peleg, D.: Distributed computing - A Locality-sensitive approach. In: SIAM Monographs on discrete mathematics and applications (2000)

[San07]   Santoro, N.: Design and analysis of distributed algorithms. Wiley, Chichester (2007)

[Yao79]   Yao, A.C.: Some complexity questions related to distributed computing. In: Proceedings of the 11th ACM Symposium on Theory of computing (STOC), pp. 209–213. ACM Press, New York (1979)

Brief Annoucement: Distributed Swap Edges Computation for Minimum Routing Cost Spanning Trees

Linda Pagli and Giuseppe Prencipe

Dipartimento di Informatica, Università di Pisa
{pagli,prencipe}@di.unipi.it

1 Introduction

Given a weighted graph $G(V_G, E_G)$ representing a communication network, with n nodes and m edges where the weights are positive integers, its *Spanning Tree* is typically used to route messages. In [1] the *routing cost* of a spanning tree is defined as the sum of the distances over all pairs of vertices of this tree. Hence, the most suitable spanning tree for the routing problem is the one minimizing the routing cost: the *Minimum Routing Cost Spanning Tree* (MRCST).

Since trees have the minimal possible number of edges, a single edge failure is enough to interrupt the communication. For this reason, it is very important that it is fault-tolerant at least for the failure of one edge. Two approaches can be followed after the failure of an edge e: one can compute from scratch a new *optimal* spanning tree for $G - e$; or re-connect the two disconnected component of the spanning tree with *the best possible edge*. For temporary network failures, this second approach is clearly preferable to the first one: in fact, it is more efficient to use a swap edge for the duration of the failure, and to quickly revert to the original tree after the failure has been fixed; in this way, the original routing tables do not need major changes. In addition, we also note that finding the spanning tree with minimum routing cost is known to be *NP-hard* [3].

For these reasons, the "swap-edge" approach has been followed to solve similar problems in sequential and distributed fashion; see for instance [2,4,6]. In our case, the *best possible edge* to select is the one that re-connects the two components disconnected by the fault of edge e, and leading to the new spanning tree for $G - e$ having the minimum routing cost. This edge can be pre-computed for any possible edge fault and stored to recover the routing process in case of fault.

The same problem has been solved for the sequential model in [6] in $O(nm)$ time complexity. To compute the cost of the spanning tree, the authors make use of the concept of the "routing load" of one edge, expressing the load of the different routes passing through this edge. The total cost is then computed by multiplying the routing load by the edge weight. We use here a different technique that computes the cost of a tree from the cost of its subtrees. Different is also the information we keep at each tree node in order to rebuild, in a distributed fashion, the tree after an edge fault. Our approach appears more suitable for the distributed solution, because allows us to treat contemporarely any possible edge fault.

T. Abdelzaher, M. Raynal, and N. Santoro (Eds.): OPODIS 2009, LNCS 5923, pp. 365–371, 2009.

In this paper, we will present the first, to our knowledge, distributed algorithm to compute the best swap edge for a minimum routing cost spanning tree, that works with message complexity $O(m \cdot n)$. Our algorithms works for any spanning tree of a 2-connected graph; hence, for its MRCST.

2   Definitions, Basic Properties, and Algorithm

Notation. Let $G = (V_G, E_G)$ be a simple undirected graph, with $n = |V|$ vertices and $m = |E|$ edges. A *subgraph* $G' = (V', E')$ of G is any graph where $V' \subseteq V_G$ and $E' \subseteq E_G$. If $V' \equiv V_G$, G' is a *spanning* subgraph. A *path* $P = (V_p, E_p)$ is a subgraph of G, such that $V_p = \{v_1, \ldots, v_s\} | v_i \neq v_j$, for $i \neq j$, and $(v_i, v_{i+1}) \in E_p$, for $1 \leq i \leq s - 1$. A spanning tree T of a given graph G is a *spanning* subgraph of G that is also a tree. Given a non-rooted tree T, we define its degree-1 nodes as the *leaves* of T; the non-leaves nodes in T will be referred to as the *internal* nodes of T.

A non negative real value called *weight* (or *length*) is associated to each edge e in G. Given a path P, the length of the path is the sum of the lengths of its edges. The *distance* $d_{G'}(x, y)$ (or simply $d(x, y)$) between two vertices x and y in a connected subgraph G' of G, is the length of the shortest path from x to y in G'.

Given a tree T, let u be a node in T; we will denote by T_u the version of T rooted in u. Furthermore, let $e = (u, v)$ be an edge in T; we will denote by $T_{u \backslash v}$ and $T_{v \backslash u}$ the two trees, rooted in u and v respectively, obtained by removing the edge (u, v) in T.

We will call the *weight* of T the sum of the distances of all paths between all pairs of nodes in a tree T, and denote it by $\mathcal{W}(T)$. That is,

$$\mathcal{W}(T) = \Sigma_{(i,j) \in V_T \times V_T} d_T(i, j).^1 \tag{1}$$

Furthermore, we define by $\mathcal{D}(u, T)$ the sum of the distances between u and all other nodes in T, and by $n(T)$ the number of nodes in T. Finally, let u' be a node in $T_{u \backslash v}$. We will denote by $\mathcal{D}_v(u', T)$ the sum of the distances between u' and each of the nodes in $T_{v \backslash u}$.

The Problem and the Model. Let T be any spanning tree of a given 2-connected graph $G(V_G, E_G)$. The fault (i.e., removal) of any edge e of T disconnects the tree into two subtrees; since G is 2-connected, there will exist at least one edge $f \in E_G \backslash E_T$, called the *swap edge for e*, able to re-connect T. Let us denote by $T'_{e|f}$ the spanning tree of G obtained by removing e and inserting f in T. We have:

Definition 1. *The* best swap edge *for a failing edge* $e \in T$ *is any swap edge* f *for* e *such that* $\mathcal{W}(T'_{e|f})$ *is mimimum.*

---

[1] Note that the weight of an edge (i, j) is considered only once in the sum.

By extending to non-rooted trees the definition of swap edge in [2], we have:

Property 1 (Swap Edge Property). An edge $f = (u, v) \in E_G \setminus E_T$ is a swap for $e = (x, y) \in E_T$ if and only if only one of u and v are in $T_{x \setminus y}$.

This test is easily made by having the tree labeled with a pre-order and inverse pre-order labeling (details on this can be found in [2]).

The problem addressed in this paper consists in computing, in a distributed way, the *best swap edge* for any possible fault of one of the edges of T, and will be denoted as the BSRT problem. In particular, the algorithm we will present works also for the *Minimum Routing Cost Spanning Tree* of G; that is, the spanning tree T of G such that $\mathcal{W}(T)$ is minimum.

We consider a *distributed computing system* with communication topology G. Each computational entity x is located at a node of G, has local processing and storage capabilities, has a distinct label $\lambda_x(e)$ from a totally ordered set associated to each of its incident edges e, knows the weight of its incident edges, and can communicate with its neighboring entities by transmission of bounded sequence of bits called messages[2]. The communication time includes processing, queueing, and transmission delays, and it is finite but otherwise unpredictable. In other words, the system is *asynchronous*. All the entities execute the same set of rules, called distributed algorithm.

Lemma 1. *Let T be a weighted tree, $e = (u, v)$ be an edge of T, and u' be a node in $T_{u \setminus v}$. Then, we have*

$$\mathcal{D}_v(u', T) = d(u', v) \cdot n(T_{v \setminus u}) + \mathcal{D}(v, T_{v \setminus u}), \tag{2}$$

$$\mathcal{D}(u', T) = \mathcal{D}(u', T_{u \setminus v}) + (d(u', u) + d(u, v)) \cdot n(T_{v \setminus u}) + \mathcal{D}(v, T_{v \setminus u}), \tag{3}$$

$$\mathcal{W}(T) = \mathcal{W}(T_{u \setminus v}) + \mathcal{W}(T_{v \setminus u}) + n(T_{v \setminus u}) \cdot \mathcal{D}(u, T_{u \setminus v}) + n(T_{u \setminus v}) \cdot \mathcal{D}_v(u, T). \tag{4}$$

Furthermore, it is easy to see that $\mathcal{W}(T) = \mathcal{W}(T_u)$, for all $u \in T$.

3   The Algorithm

Our distributed algorithm to solve the BSRT problem is articulated in 3 main phases. Let T be any spanning tree of a 2-connected weighted graph G.

Saturation phase. In this phase, using the well-known *saturation technique* [5], each node u in T will compute locally the following values: $\mathcal{W}(T)$, $\mathcal{D}(u, T)$, $n(T)$, and $\mathcal{W}(T_{u \setminus u_j})$, $\mathcal{D}(u, T_{u \setminus u_j})$, and $n(T_{u \setminus u_j})$ for each neighbor u_j of u in T. In this phase, also, a node r in T is elected as the root of the tree; we will denote by T_r the rooted version of T.

---

[2] Since our algorithm transmits sum of weights in a single message, the messages have length bounded by $O(W + \log n)$ bits, where W is the number of bits necessary to describe the maximum value of $\mathcal{W}(T)$, among all possible spanning trees T of G.

Swap phase. This phase starts the core of the algorithm: each node $u \in T_r$ computes the set of all candidate swap edges for the failure of edge $(u, parent(u))$, with $parent(u)$ the parent of u in T_r. We will denote this set for u by $\mathcal{S}(u)$.

Best Swap phase. Finally, each node u will locally determine which one, among the candidate swap edges in $\mathcal{S}(u)$, is the best one, as defined in Definition 1.

3.1   Saturation Phase

Step I: Collecting The computation starts from degree-1 nodes in T. Let u be a leaf in T, and u_1 its only neighbor: u sends to u_1 the following values: $\mathcal{D}(u, T_{u \setminus u_1}) = 0$, $\mathcal{W}(T_{u \setminus u_1}) = 0$, and $n(T_{u \setminus u_1}) = 1$.

Let u be an internal node of T, with neighbors $u_1, u_2, \ldots, u_i$: it waits until it receives the values $\mathcal{D}(u_j, T_{u_j \setminus u})$, $\mathcal{W}(T_{u_j \setminus u})$, and $n(T_{u_j \setminus u})$ from $i - 1$ neighbors. Then, it computes $\mathcal{D}(u, T_{u \setminus u_i})$, $\mathcal{W}(T_{u \setminus u_i})$, and $n(T_{u \setminus u_i})$, as follows.

First, $n(T_{u \setminus u_i}) = \Sigma_{j=1}^{i-1} n(T_{u_j \setminus u}) + 1$. Then, by definition, $\mathcal{D}(u, T_{u \setminus u_i}) = \Sigma_{j=1}^{i-1} \mathcal{D}_{u_j}(u, T)$; therefore, by Equation (2), it follows that $\mathcal{D}(u, T_{u \setminus u_i}) = \Sigma_{j=1}^{i-1} (d(u, u_j) \cdot n(T_{u_j \setminus u}) + \mathcal{D}(u_j, T_{u_j \setminus u}))$. Finally, we have

$$\mathcal{W}(T_{u \setminus u_i}) = \Sigma_{j=1}^{i-1} \mathcal{W}(T_{u_j \setminus u}) + \mathcal{D}(u, T_{u \setminus u_i}) +$$
$$+ \Sigma_{j=1}^{i-2} \Sigma_{k=j+1}^{i-1} (n(T_{u_k \setminus u}) \cdot \mathcal{D}_{u_j}(u, T) + n(T_{u_j \setminus u}) \cdot \mathcal{D}_{u_k}(u, T)).$$

We note that, node u has locally all the necessary information to compute $\mathcal{D}(u, T_{u \setminus u_i})$ and $\mathcal{W}(T_{u \setminus u_i})$. As its final action, node u sends to node u_i, referred to as the *recipient* of u, the values of $n(T_{u \setminus u_i})$, $\mathcal{D}(u, T_{u \setminus u_i})$, and $\mathcal{W}(T_{u \setminus u_i})$ just computed.

Step II: Exchanging After finite time, due to the saturation process, there will be two nodes, x and y, that will exchange on edge $s = (x, y)$ their $\mathcal{D}()$, $\mathcal{W}()$, and $n()$ values. In particular, at this time, both x and y have (locally) the following information: $\mathcal{D}(x, T_{x \setminus y})$, $\mathcal{W}(T_{x \setminus y})$, and $n(T_{x \setminus y})$; and $\mathcal{D}(y, T_{y \setminus x})$, $\mathcal{W}(T_{y \setminus x})$, and $n(T_{y \setminus x})$: s is called the *saturated edge*.

Lemma 2. *The total weight of T is*

$$\mathcal{W}(T) = \mathcal{W}(T_{x \setminus y}) + \mathcal{W}(T_{y \setminus x}) + n(T_{y \setminus x}) \cdot \mathcal{D}(x, T_{x \setminus y}) + n(T_{x \setminus y}) \cdot \mathcal{D}_y(x, T). \quad (5)$$

Furthermore, after the second step of the Saturation process, node x has locally all the information necessary to compute $\mathcal{W}(T)$, $n(T)$, and $\mathcal{D}(x, T)$.

Step III: Broadcasting In the third step of the Saturation phase, the values computed by the *saturated* nodes x and y are opportunely broadcast to all other nodes in T; also, during this phase, all nodes compute other values that will be used in the evaluation of the candidate swap edges.

In particular, the Broadcasting step starts in x and in y towards the nodes in $T_{x \setminus y}$ and $T_{y \setminus x}$, respectively. In the following we will describe the broadcast in $T_{x \setminus y}$; the argument is symmetric for $T_{y \setminus x}$.

Node x sends to all its neighbors but y the following values: $\mathcal{W}(T)$, $n(T)$, $\mathcal{D}(x,T)$, all available to x after previous step, by Lemma 2; we will refer to these values as the *broadcast set of x*. An internal node v in $T_{x \setminus y}$ waits until it receives the broadcast set from node k, with k the father of v in $T_{x \setminus y}$; note also that k is the recipient of v as defined in the Collecting step. At this time, it will compute $\mathcal{D}(v,T)$, and will forward its broadcast set to all of its neighbors but k: these nodes are the children of v in $T_{x \setminus y}$. We have:

Theorem 1. *After the saturation process, each node $u \in T$ has locally the following values: $\mathcal{W}(T)$, $\mathcal{D}(u,T)$, $n(T)$, and $\mathcal{W}(T_{u \setminus u_j})$, $\mathcal{D}(u, T_{u \setminus u_j})$, and $n(T_{u \setminus u_j})$ for each neighbor u_j of u in T. All these values are computed within the complexity of the saturation algorithm, that is in linear message complexity.*

Property 2. Let T be any spanning tree over a 2-connected graph G. If f is a swap edge for $e = (u,v) \in T$ in the rooted tree T_r, for any $r \in T$, then f is also a swap edge for e in T_q, for any other node q in T.

Hence, since the presence of a root node does not affect the property of an edge to be a swap edge, in the Exchanging phase one of the two saturated nodes is also elected as leader (e.g., the one with the smallest ID): this node is selected as the root of T. This info is clearly broadcasted to all other nodes in the tree during the Broadcasting phase. In the following, we will refer to the rooted version of T as T_r, with r the root of the tree. Also, we assume that a node u knows the weight of all its incident links, and can distinguish those that are part of T_r from those that are not; of those that are part of T_r, u can distinguish the one that leads to its parent from those leading to its children. Furthermore, we assume that each node u knows its distance from r and the distances of its neighbors from r. Finally, we assume that each node knows its pre-order and inverse pre-order labeling in T_r, as described in [2], as well as the labels of its neighbors: this labeling is necessary to verify the swap edge property introduced in Property 1. If not available, this information can be easily and efficiently acquired after the Saturation phase with a search of the tree.

3.2   Swap Phase

At the end of this phase, each node u will know the set of candidate swap edges for the possible failure of edge $(u, parent(u))$, that we will refer to as the *swap set* of u, and denote by $\mathcal{S}(u)$. The swap set of u is a set of 6-tuples $\langle (u',v'), d(u',v'), \mathcal{D}(u',T), \mathcal{D}(v',T), d(u',r), d(v',r) \rangle$, where: $f = (u',v')$ is a swap edge for $e = (u, parent(u))$; $\mathcal{D}(u',T)$ and $\mathcal{D}(v',T)$ are as computed in the Saturation phase; and $d(u',v')$, $d(u',r)$ and $d(v',r)$ are the weights of edge (u',v'), and the distance of u' and v' from r in T_r, respectively. Note that, by Property 1, exactly one node between u' and v' must be descendant of u in T_r; here, without loss of generality, we assume that u' is such a node.

This phase proceeds in a leaves-to-root fashion. The computation starts in the leaves of T_r: given a leaf u, any edge in G that is incident to u, with the obvious exception of $(u, parent(u))$, is clearly a candidate swap edge for u; hence, it is in $\mathcal{S}(u)$. This set is sent to $parent(u)$. An internal node $u \in T_r$ waits until it receives the candidate swap edges computed by *all* of its children. For each tuple $t = \langle (u', v'), \cdot, \cdot, \cdot, \cdot, \cdot \rangle$ received from the children, it check whether (u', v') is a swap edge for $e = (u, parent(u))$: in this case, this tuple is inserted in $\mathcal{S}(u)$. Then, u checks whether some of its incident edges in $G - e$ are swap edges for $e = (u, parent(u))$: in this case, these edges are placed in $\mathcal{S}(u)$ as well. The check is again made by testing Property 1. Therefore, we can state the following:

Lemma 3. *After the Swap phase, each node u in T_r correctly computes $\mathcal{S}(u)$, containing information on all the candidate swap edges for $(u, parent(u))$.*

Since in the worst case a node u can have $O(m)$ swap edges for $(u, parent(u))$, we can state that

Lemma 4. *The Swap phase takes $O(nm)$ message complexity in the worst case.*

3.3   Best Swap Phase

In the Best Swap Phase, the algorithm selects, for each node u, the best swap edge for $e = (u, parent(u))$ among those in $\mathcal{S}(u)$. In other words, it selects the candidate swap edge $f = (u_i, v_i)$, with $\langle f, \cdot, \cdot, \cdot, \cdot, \cdot \rangle \in \mathcal{S}(u)$, such that $\mathcal{W}(T'_{e|f})$ is minimum, where $T'_{e|f}$ is the tree obtained from T by deleting e and adding f.

Lemma 5. *For the failing edge $e = (u, parent(u)) \in T_r$, the value of $\mathcal{W}(T'_{e|f})$ for the swap edge $f = (u_i, v_i)$ for e, with $u_i \in T_{u \setminus v}$ and $v_i \in T_{v \setminus u}$, is given by:*

$$\mathcal{W}(T'_{e|f}) = \mathcal{W}(T_{u \setminus v}) + \mathcal{W}(T_{v \setminus u}) + n(T_{v \setminus u}) \cdot \mathcal{D}(u_i, T_{u \setminus v}) + \qquad (6)$$
$$+ \; n(T_{u \setminus v}) \cdot (d(u_i, v_i) \cdot n(T_{v \setminus u}) + \mathcal{D}(v_i, T_{v \setminus u})).$$

Also, after the Swap phase, node u can locally select the best swap edge for e.

Hence, after the Best Swap Edge phase, for each edge $e = (u, v) \in T_r$, with $v = parent(u)$, the best swap edge f^* for e is computed.

Theorem 2. *Given a 2-connected graph $G = (V_G, E_G)$ and any spanning tree T for G, the BSRT problem can be solved in $O(m \cdot n)$ message complexity in the worst case.*

Corollary 1. *Given a 2-connected graph $G = (V_G, E_G)$ and its Minimum Routing Cost Spanning Tree, the BSRT problem can be solved in $O(m \cdot n)$ message complexity in the worst case.*

References

1. Liebchen, C., Wunsch, G.: The zoo of the tree spanner problems. Discrete Applied Mathematics 156, 569–587 (2008)
2. Flocchini, P., Mesa Enriques, A., Pagli, L., Prencipe, G., Santoro, N.: Point-of-failure shortest-path rerouting: computing the optimal swap edges distributively. IEICE Transactions on Information and Systems 2(E89-D), 700–708 (2006)

3. Johnson, D.S., Lenstra, J.K., Kan, A.R.: The complexity of the network design problem. Networks 8, 279–285 (1978)
4. Nardelli, E., Proietti, G., Widmayer, P.: Swapping a failing edge of a single source shortest-paths tree is good and fast. Algoritmica 35, 56–74 (2003)
5. Santoro, N.: Design and Analysis of Distributed Algorithms. Wiley, Chichester (2007)
6. Wu, B.Y., Hsiao, C.Y., Chao, K.M.: The swap edges of a multiple-sources routing tree. Algorithmica 50(3), 299–311 (2008)

Author Index